PHILIP'S

ROAD ATLAS
Britain
and Ireland

www.philips-maps.co.uk

First published in 2009 by Philip's
a division of Octopus Publishing Group Ltd
www.octopusbooks.co.uk
Endeavour House, 189 Shaftesbury Avenue
London WC2H 8JY
An Hachette UK Company
www.hachette.co.uk
Fourth edition 2012
First impression 2012

ISBN 978-1-84907-216-8

Cartography by Philip's
Copyright © 2012 Philip's

Ordnance Survey® This product includes mapping data
licensed from Ordnance Survey®,
with the permission of the Controller
of Her Majesty's Stationery Office. © Crown copyright 2012.
All rights reserved. Licence number 100011710

The map of Ireland on pages XVIII–XIX is based on Ordnance Survey
Ireland by permission of the Government Permit Number 8798
© Ordnance Survey Ireland and Government of Ireland and

Ordnance Survey Northern Ireland on behalf of the
Controller of Her Majesty's Stationery Office
© Crown copyright 2012 Permit Number 110010.

Data for the speed cameras provided by **PocketGPSWorld.com Ltd**.

Information for National Parks, Areas of Outstanding Natural
Beauty, National Trails and Country Parks in Wales supplied by the
Countryside Council for Wales.

Information for National Parks, Areas of Outstanding Natural Beauty,
National Trails and Country Parks in England supplied by Natural
England. Data for Regional Parks, Long Distance Footpaths and
Country Parks in Scotland provided by Scottish Natural Heritage.

Gaelic name forms used in the Western Isles provided by
Comhairle nan Eilean.

Data for the National Nature Reserves in England provided by
Natural England. Data for the National Nature Reserves in Wales
provided by Countryside Council for Wales. Darparwyd data'n
ymwneud â Gwarchodfeydd Natur Cenedlaethol Cymru gan Gyngor
Cefn Gwlad Cymru.

Information on the location of National Nature Reserves in Scotland
was provided by Scottish Natural Heritage.

Data for National Scenic Areas in Scotland provided by the Scottish
Executive Office. Crown copyright material is reproduced with the
permission of the Controller of HMSO and the Queen's Printer for
Scotland. Licence number C02W0003960.

Photographic acknowledgements: page VI, Mark Sykes / Alamy;
page VII, bottom, George Clerk / iStockphoto.com.

Printed in China.

*Independent research survey, from research carried out by
Outlook Research Limited, 2005/06.
**Estimated sales of all Philip's UK road atlases since launch.

GW00724450

Road map symbols

Motorway, toll motorway
Motorway junction – full, restricted access
Motorway service area – full, restricted access
Motorway under construction

Primary route – dual, single carriageway
Service area, roundabout, multi-level junction
Numbered junction – full, restricted access
Primary route under construction
Narrow primary route
Primary destination

Derby

A34

A road – dual, single carriageway
A road under construction, narrow A road

B2135

B road – dual, single carriageway
B road under construction, narrow B road

Minor road – over 4 metres, under 4 metres wide
Minor road with restricted access

Distance in miles
Scenic route
Speed camera – single, multiple
Toll, steep gradient – arrow points downhill
Tunnel

National trail – England and Wales
Long distance footpath – Scotland

Railway with station
Level crossing, tunnel
Preserved railway with station

National boundary
County / unitary authority boundary

Car ferry, catamaran
Passenger ferry, catamaran
Hovercraft
Ferry destination, journey time – hrs : mins
Car ferry – river crossing
Principal airport, other airport

CALAIS 1:30
Ferry

National park
Area of Outstanding Natural Beauty – England and Wales National Scenic Area – Scotland
forest park / regional park / national forest
Woodland

Beach

Linear antiquity

Roman road

1066
795

Hillfort, battlefield – with date
Viewpoint, nature reserve, spot height – in metres
Golf course, youth hostel, sporting venue
Camp site, caravan site, camping and caravan site
Shopping village, park and ride

P&R

29
Adjoining page number – road maps

Road map scale 1: 200 000 or 3·15 miles to 1 inch

0 1 2 3 4 5 6 miles

0 1 2 3 4 5 6 7 8 9 10 km

Approach map symbols

Motorway
Toll motorway
Motorway junction – full, restricted access
Service area
Under construction
Primary route – dual, single carriageway
Service area
Multi-level junction
roundabout
Under construction
A195 A road – dual, single carriageway

B1288 B road – dual, single carriageway
Minor road – dual, single carriageway
Ring road
3 Distance in miles
Congestion charge area
COSELEY Railway with station
LOXDALE Tramway with station
M Underground or metro station

Town plan symbols

Motorway
Primary route – dual, single carriageway
A road – dual, single carriageway
B road – dual, single carriageway
Minor through road
One-way street
Pedestrian roads
Shopping streets
Railway with station
City Hall Tramway with station

Bus or railway station building
Shopping precinct or retail park
Park
Building of public interest
Theatre, cinema
Parking, shopmobility
Bank Underground station
West St Metro station
H Hospital, Police station
PO Post office

Tourist information

✝ Abbey, cathedral or priory
Ⅲ Ancient monument
Aquarium
Art gallery
Bird collection or aviary
Castle
Church
Country park
England and Wales
Scotland

Farm park
Garden
Historic ship
House
House and garden
Motor racing circuit
Museum
Picnic area
Preserved railway
Race course

Roman antiquity
Safari park
Theme park
Tourist information centre
i open all year
i open seasonally
Zoo
Other place of interest

Relief

Feet	metres
3000	914
2600	792
2200	671
1800	549
1400	427
1000	305
0	0

Speed Cameras

Fixed camera locations are shown using the 40 symbol.

In congested areas the 40 symbol is used to show that there are two or more cameras on the road indicated.

Due to the restrictions of scale the camera locations are only approximate and cannot indicate the operating direction of the camera. Mobile camera sites, and cameras located on roads not included on the mapping are not shown. Where two or more cameras are shown on the same road, drivers are warned that this may indicate that a SPEC system is in operation. These cameras use the time taken to drive between the two camera positions to calculate the speed of the vehicle.

England

A1(M) Baldock — Extra MSA

♿ ⚡ 🚻 👫 ((•))

A1(M) J10 · Northbound and southbound **54 F3** TL23443661
M&S Simply Food • WH Smith • KFC • Le Petit Four • McDonald's • Pizza Hut Express • Starbucks ⛽ Shell
🛏 Days Inn 🅿 2hrs
✉ A1(M), Junction 10, Baldock, Hertfordshire SG7 5TR
🖥 www.extraservices.co.uk
🕐 McDonald's open 24 hrs

A1(M) Peterborough
Extra MSA

⚡ 🚻 👫 ((•))

A1(M) J17 · Northbound and southbound **65 E8** TL13939395
M&S Simply Food • McColls • Namco • KFC • Le Petit Four • McDonald's • Pizza Hut Express ⛽ Shell, LPG
🛏 Days Inn 🅿 2 hrs
✉ Great North Road, Haddon, Peterborough PE7 8UQ
🖥 www.extraservices.co.uk
🕐 Shop in forecourt is open 24 hrs

A1(M) Blyth   Moto

♿ 🚻 👫 🚻 ((•))

A1(M) Junction 34 · Northbound and southbound
89 F7 SK62568827
Costa • Burger King • EDC • WH Smith • Coffee Nation ⛽ Esso
🛏 Travelodge ✉ Hill Top Roundabout, Blyth
S81 8HG 📞 01909 591841

A1(M) Wetherby   Moto

♿ ⚡ 🚻 👫 🚻 ((•))

A1(M): J46 · Northbound and southbound **95 D7** SE41525025
M&S Simply Food • Upper Crust • WH Smith • Burger King • Costa Coffee • EDC ⛽ BP 🛏 Days Inn
🅿 2 hrs ✉ Kirk Deighton, North Yorkshire LS22 5GT 📞 01937 545080 🖥 www.moto-way.co.uk
🕐 Forecourt outlets open 24 hrs

A1(M) Durham   RoadChef

⚡ 👫 ((•))

A1(M) J61 · Northbound and southbound **111 F6** NZ30843718
WH Smith • The Burger Company • Costa Coffee • Restbite ⛽ Total
🛏 Premier Inn 🅿 2 hrs
✉ Tursdale Road, Bowburn, County Durham DH6 5NP 📞 0191 377 9222 🖥 www.roadchef.co.uk
🕐 Fast food outlet and shop in forecourt open 24 hrs

A1(M) Washington   Moto

♿ ⚡ 🚻 👫 🚻 ((•))

A1(M) just north of J64 · Northbound and southbound
111 D5 NZ28375506
WH Smith • Burger King • Coffee Nation • Costa Coffee • EDC ⛽ BP
🛏 Travelodge 🅿 2 hrs
✉ Portobello, Birtley, County Durham DH3 2SJ 📞 0191 410 3436 🖥 www.moto-way.co.uk
🕐 WH Smith and outlets on forecourt open 24 hrs

M1 London Gateway
Welcome Break

⚡ 👫 ((•))

M1 between J2 and J4 · Northbound and southbound
41 E5 TQ20269369
WH Smith • Burger King • Eat In • Starbucks ⛽ Shell 🛏 Days Inn
🅿 2 hrs ✉ M1 J2/4, Mill Hill,

London NW7 3HB 📞 0208 906 0611 @ lgw.enquiry@ welcomebreak.co.uk
🖥 www.welcomebreak.co.uk
🕐 WH Smith open 24 hrs

M1 Toddington   Moto

♿ ⚡ 🚉 👫 🚻 ((•))

M1, 1 mile south of J12 · Northbound and southbound
40 B3 TL03092878
M&S Simply Food • WH Smith • Burger King • Coffee Nation • Costa Coffee • EDC • Krispy Kreme Doughnuts ⛽ BP, LPG available
🛏 Travelodge 🅿 2 hrs
✉ Toddington, Bedfordshire LU5 6HR 📞 01525 878400
🖥 www.moto-way.co.uk
🕐 Outlets on forecourts open 24 hrs

M1 Newport Pagnell
Welcome Break

⚡ 🚉 👫 ((•))

M1, north of J14 · Northbound and southbound
53 E6 SP85834351
WH Smith • Eat In • KFC • Starbucks ⛽ Shell 🛏 Days Inn 🅿 2 hrs
✉ M1 Motorway, J14/15, Newport Pagnell, Buckinghamshire MK16 8DS 📞 01908 217722
@ newport.enquiry@ welcomebreak.co.uk
🖥 www.welcomebreak.co.uk
🕐 WH Smith and shop in forecourt open 24 hrs

M1 Northampton   RoadChef

🚉 👫 ((•))

M1 J15A · Northbound and southbound **52 D5** SP72285732
Fonebitz • WH Smith • The Burger Company • Costa Coffee • Hot Food Co (southbound) • Restbite (northbound) • Wild Bean Cafe ⛽ BP 🅿 2 hrs
✉ M1 Junction 15A, Northampton, Northamptonshire NN4 9QY 📞 01604 831888
🖥 www.roadchef.co.uk
🕐 WH Smith and shop in forecourt open 24 hrs

M1 Watford Gap   RoadChef

⚡ 🚉 👫 ((•))

M1 between J16 and J17 · Northbound and southbound
52 C4 SP59956802
Fonebitz • WH Smith • Costa Coffee • Hot Food Co • Wimpy (northbound); The Burger Company • Costa Coffee • Restbite (southbound) ⛽ BP
🛏 Premier Inn (southbound)
🅿 2 hrs ✉ M1 Motorway, Northamptonshire NN6 7UZ 📞 01327 879001
🖥 www.roadchef.co.uk

M1 Leicester Forest East
Welcome Break

⚡ 🚉 🍽 👫 ((•))

M1 between J21 and J21A · Northbound and southbound
64 D2 SK53860267
Waitrose • WH Smith • Burger King • Eat In • KFC • Starbucks ⛽ BP, LPG available (northbound)
🛏 Days Inn ✉ Leicester Forest East, M1, Leicester, Leicestershire LE3 3GB 📞 0116 238 6801 @ lfe. enquiry@welcomebreak.co.uk
🖥 www.welcomebreak.co.uk
🕐 Eat In and WH Smith are open 24 hrs

Motorway service a[rea]

M1 Leicester   Moto

♿ ⚡ 🚻 👫 ((•))

M1 just off J22 · Northbound and southbound **64 C1** SK47651111
Costa • Burger King] • Coffee Nation ⛽ BP, LPG available
✉ Littleshaw Lane, Markfield LE67 9PP 📞 01530 244777
🖥 www.moto-way.co.uk

M1 Donington Park   Moto

♿ ⚡ 🚉 🚿 👫 🚻 🚚 ((•))

M1 J23A · Northbound and southbound **64 B1** SK46712513
Fone Bitz • M&S Simply Food • WH Smith • Burger King • Coffee Nation • Costa Coffee ⛽ BP, LPG available 🛏 Travelodge
🅿 2 hrs ✉ Castle Donington, Derby, East Midlands DE74 2TN 📞 01509 672220
🖥 www.moto-way.co.uk
🕐 Shop in forecourt and WH Smith open 24 hrs

M1 Trowell   Moto

♿ ⚡ 🚉 👶 🚻 👫 ((•))

M1 between J25 and J26 · Northbound and southbound
76 E4 SK49354073
M&S Simply Food • WH Smith • Burger King • Coffee Nation • Costa Coffee • EDC ⛽ BP 🛏 Travelodge
🅿 2 hrs ✉ Ilkeston, Trowell, Nottinghamshire NG9 3PL

📞 01159 320291
🖥 www.moto-way.co.uk
🕐 WH Smith and forecourt outlets are open 24 hrs

M1 Tibshelf   RoadChef

⚡ 🚹 👫 ((•))

M1, 2 miles north of J28 · Northbound and southbound
76 C4 SK44856031
Fone Bitz • WH Smith • The Burger Company • Costa Coffee • Restbite ⛽ Shell 🛏 Premier Inn (northbound only) 🅿 2 hrs
✉ Newton Wood Lane, Newton, Alfreton DE55 5TZ 📞 01773 760607 🖥 www.roadchef.co.uk
🕐 WH Smith and forecourt shop open 24 hrs

M1 Woodall   Welcome Break

👫 ((•))

M1, 2.5 miles north of J30 · Northbound and southbound
89 F5 SK47928006
WH Smith • Burger King • Eat In • KFC • Starbucks ⛽ Shell, LPG available (southbound) 🛏 Days Inn 🅿 2 hrs
✉ M2, Rainham, Gillingham, Kent ME8 8PQ 📞 01634 236900 🖥 www.moto-way. co.uk 🕐 WH Smith and shop in forecourt are open 24 hrs
✉ M1 Motorway, Sheffield, South Yorkshire S26 7XR
📞 0114 248 7992 @ woodall. enquiry@welcomebreak.co.uk
🖥 www.welcomebreak.co.uk
🕐 Eat In, WH Smith and outlets on forecourt open 24 hrs

M3 Fleet   Welcome Break

⚡ 🚉 🍽 👫 ((•))

M3 between J4A/J5 · Eastbound and westbound
27 D5 SU79885583

M1 Woolley Edge   Moto

♿ ⚡ 🚉 🚻 👫 ((•))

M1, just north of J38 · Northbound and southbound
88 C4 SE29841400
M&S Simply Food • WH Smith • Burger King • Coffee Nation • Costa Coffee • EDC ⛽ Esso 🛏 Travelodge
🅿 2 hrs ✉ West Bretton, Wakefield, West Yorkshire WF4 4LQ 📞 01924 830371
🖥 www.moto-way.co.uk
🕐 WH Smith and outlets on forecourt are open 24 hrs

M2 Medway   Moto

♿ ⚡ 🚉 🚿 👫 🚻 ((•))

M2 between J4 and J5 · Eastbound and westbound
30 C2 TQ81756344
WH Smith • Burger King • Coffee Nation • Costa Coffee ⛽ BP, LPG available (eastbound)
🛏 Travelodge 🅿 2 hrs

M3 Winchester   Moto

♿ ⚡ 🚉 🚿 🚻 👫 ((•))

M3, 4 miles north of J9 · Northbound and southbound
26 F3 SU52303550
WH Smith • Burger King • Coffee Nation • Costa Coffee • EDC ⛽ Shell, LPG available 🛏 Premier Inn
🅿 2 hrs ✉ Shroner Wood, Winchester, Hampshire SO21 1PP
📞 01962 791140
🖥 www.moto-way.co.uk
🕐 Outlets on forecourt open 24 hrs

M4 Heston   Moto

♿ ⚡ 🚉 🚿 🚻 👫 ((•))

M4 1 mile east of J3 · Eastbound and westbound
28 B2 TQ11777778
WH Smith • Burger King • Coffee Nation • Costa Coffee • EDC • Krispy Kreme Doughnuts ⛽ BP, LPG (westbound) 🛏 Travelodge

---

Waitrose • WH Smith • Burger King • Eat In • KFC • Starbucks ⛽ Shell (southbound, LPG available); BP (northbound) 🛏 Days Inn 🅿 2 hrs ✉ Fleet, Hampshire GU51 1AA
📞 01252 788 500 @ fleet. enquiry@welcomebreak.co.uk
🖥 www.welcomebreak.co.uk
🕐 Eat In and WH Smith open 24 hrs

2 hrs ✉ Phoenix Way, Heston, Hounslow, London TW5 9NB
☎ 0208 590 2101
🖥 www.moto-way.co.uk
☾ Coffee Nation and WH Smith are open 24 hrs

M4 Reading – eastbound
Moto

♿ 🚿 🛁 ♿ ♟ 👫 WC (())

M4 Junctions 11-12 · Eastbound
26 C4 SU67177012

M&S · Costa · Burger King · EDC · WH Smith · Krispy Kreme · Coffee Nation ⛽ BP 🛏 Travelodge
P 2 hrs ✉ Burghfield, Reading RG30 3UQ ☎ 01189 566966
🖥 www.moto-way.co.uk
☾ WH Smith and outlets in the forecourt are open 24 hrs

M4 Reading – westbound
Moto

♿ 🚿 🛁 👫 WC (())

M4 Junctions 11-12 · Westbound
26 C4 SU67046985

M&S · Costa · Burger King · EDC · WH Smith · Upper Crust · Krispy Kreme · Coffee Nation ⛽ BP
🛏 Travelodge P 2 hrs ✉ Burghfield, Reading RG30 3UQ
☎ 01189 566966
🖥 www.moto-way.co.uk
☾ WH Smith and outlets in the forecourt are open 24 hrs

M4 Chieveley
Moto

♿ 🚿 🛁 ♿ WC 👫 (())

M4 J13 · Eastbound and westbound 26 B2 SU48157268

M&S Simply Food · WH Smith · Burger King · Coffee Nation · Costa Coffee · EDC ⛽ BP, LPG available
🛏 Travelodge P 2 hrs ✉ Oxford Road, Hermitage, Thatcham, Berkshire, RG18 9XX
☎ 01635 248024
🖥 www.moto-way.co.uk
☾ WH Smith open 24 hrs

M4 Membury
Welcome Break

♿ 👫 (())

M4, 4 miles west of J14 · Eastbound and westbound
25 B8 SU30847601

Waitrose · WH Smith · Burger King · Eat In · KFC · Starbucks ⛽ BP LPG available (eastbound)
🛏 Days Inn P 2 hrs ✉ Woodlands Road, Membury, near Lambourn, Berkshire RG17 7TZ ☎ 01488 674360
@ membury.enquiry@welcomebreak.co.uk
🖥 www.welcomebreak.co.uk
☾ Eat In, WH Smith and forecourt shop open 24 hrs

M4 Leigh Delamere
Moto

♿ 🛢 🛁 🚿 🛁 ♿ WC 👫 (()) 🐾

M4 just west of J17 · Eastbound and westbound
24 B3 ST89077899

Fonebitz · M&S Simply Food · WH Smith · Burger King · Coffee Nation · Costa Coffee · EDC ⛽ BP, LPG available 🛏 Travelodge
P 2 hrs ✉ Chippenham, Wiltshire SN14 6LB ☎ 01666 837691 (eastbound); 01666 842015 (westbound) 🖥 www.moto.co.uk ☾ WH Smith and shop and coffee shops in the forecourt are open 24 hrs

M5 Frankley
Moto

♿ 👫 (())

M5 J3 · Northbound and southbound 62 F3 SO98938120

M&S Simply Food · WH Smith · Burger King · Coffee Nation · Costa Coffee · EDC ⛽ Esso 🛏 Travelodge (southbound only) P 2 hrs ✉ Illey Lane, Birmingham, West Midlands B32 4AR ☎ 0121 550 3131 🖥 www.moto-way.co.uk
☾ Coffee Nation and WH Smith open 24 hrs

M5 Strensham – southbound
RoadChef

M5 southbound, just before J8 · Southbound only
50 F4 SO90413993

Cotton Traders · Fonebitz · WH Smith · Costa Coffee · Hot Food Company · McDonalds · Soho Coffee Company ⛽ BP P 2 hrs ✉ M5 Motorway, Lower Strensham, Worcestershire WR8 9LJ ☎ 01684 290577 🖥 www.roadchef.co.uk
☾ The outlets on the forecourt are open 24 hrs

M5 Strensham – northbound
RoadChef

£ 👫 (())

M5, 1 mile north of J8 · Northbound only
50 E3 SO89344072

Cotton Traders · Fonebitz · Subway · WH Smith · Costa Coffee · Pizza Hut Express · Restbite · Wimpy ⛽ Texaco, LPG available 🛏 Premier Inn P 2 hrs ✉ M5 Motorway, Lower Strensham, Worcestershire WR8 9LJ ☎ 01684 293004 🖥 www.roadchef.co.uk
☾ The outlets on the forecourt are open 24 hrs

M5 Michaelwood
Welcome Break

£ 👫 (())

M5, just north of J14 · Northbound and southbound
36 E4 ST70409541

WH Smith · Burger King · Eat In · KFC · Starbucks ⛽ BP 🛏 Days Inn P 2 hrs ✉ Lower Wick, Dursley, Gloucestershire GL11 6DD ☎ 01454 260631 @ michaelwood.enquiry@welcomebreak.co.uk
🖥 www.welcomebreak.co.uk ☾ WH Smith and shop in forecourt open 24 hrs

M5 Gordano
Welcome Break

£ ✖ 🛁 👫 (())

M5 J19 · Northbound and southbound 23 B7 ST50977563

Waitrose · WH Smith · Burger King · Eat In · KFC · Starbucks ⛽ Shell 🛏 Days Inn P 2 hrs ✉ Portbury, Bristol BS20 7XG ☎ 01275 373624 @ gordano.enquiry@welcomebreak.co.uk
🖥 www.welcomebreak.co.uk
☾ WH Smith open 24 hrs

M5 Sedgemoor Southbound
RoadChef

£ 🛢 👫 (())

M5, 7 miles south of J21
23 D5 ST35815259

WH Smith · The Burger Company · Costa Coffee · Restbite ⛽ Total 🛏 Days Inn P 2 hrs ✉ M5 Southbound Rooksbridge, Axbridge, Somerset SA24 0JL
☎ 01934 750888

www.roadchef.co.uk
☾ Shop on forecourt is open 24 hrs

M5 Sedgemoor Northbound
Welcome Break

M5, 3 miles north of J22
23 D5 ST35815259

WH Smith · Burger King · Coffee Primo · Eat in ⛽ Shell 🛏 Days Inn P 2 hrs ✉ M5 Motorway Northbound, Bridgwater, Somerset BS24 0JL ☎ 01934 750730 @ sedgemoor.enquiry@welcomebreak.co.uk
🖥 www.welcomebreak.co.uk
☾ WH Smith and shop on forecourt are open 24 hrs

M5 Bridgwater
Moto

♿ 🛢 🚿 🛁 ♿ WC 👫 (())

M5, J24 · Northbound and southbound 22 F5 ST30403441

WH Smith · Burger King · Coffee Nation · Costa Coffee · EDC ⛽ BP 🛏 Travelodge P 2 hrs ✉ Huntsworth Business Park, Bridgwater, Somerset TA6 6TS
☎ 01278 456800
🖥 www.moto-way.co.uk
☾ WH Smith and shop in forecourt are open 24 hrs

M5 Taunton Deane
RoadChef

£ 👫 (())

M5 between J25 and J26 · Northbound and southbound
11 B7 ST19592035

Fonebitz (southbound only) · WH Smith · The Burger Company · Costa Coffee · Restbite ⛽ Shell 🛏 Premier Inn (southbound only) P 2 hrs ✉ Trull, Taunton, Somerset TA3 7PF ☎ 01823 271111 🖥 www.roadchef.co.uk
☾ Outlets on forecourt are open 24 hrs

A38 / M5 Tiverton
Moto

♿ 👫 WC

M5 Junction 27. · Northbound and southbound
11 C5 ST04901386

Costa · Burger King 🛏 Travelodge P 2 hrs. No HGVs
✉ Tiverton EX16 7HD
☎ 01884 829423

M5 Cullompton
Extra MSA

£ 👫

M5, J28 · Northbound and southbound 10 D5 ST02660798

WH Smith · Le Petit Four · McDonald's ⛽ Shell P 2 hrs ✉ Old Station Yard, Station Road, Cullompton, Devon EX15 1NS
☎ 01522 523737
🖥 http://extraservices.co.uk
☾ WH Smith and shop in forecourt open 24 hrs

M5 Exeter
Moto

🛁 🛢 ♿ WC ♿ (())

M5 J30 · Northbound and southbound 10 E4 SX96779180

M&S Simply Food · WH Smith · Burger King · Coffee Nation · Costa Coffee · EDS · Harry Ramsden ⛽ BP 🛏 Travelodge P 2 hrs ✉ Sandygate, Exeter, Devon EX2 7HF ☎ 01392 436266
🖥 www.moto-way.co.uk
☾ WH Smith open 24 hrs

M6 Corley
Welcome Break

£ 👫 (())

M6, 2.5 miles west of J3 · Eastbound and westbound
63 F7 SP30898604

Waitrose · WH Smith · Burger King · Eat In · KFC · Starbucks ⛽ Shell 🛏 Days Inn P 2 hrs ✉ Highfield Lane, Corley, Staffordshire CV7 8NR ☎ 01676 540111 @ corleyenquiry@welcomebreak.co.uk
🖥 www.welcomebreak.co.uk
☾ The outlets in the forecourt are open 24 hrs

M6 Norton Canes
Road Chef

£ 👫 (())

M6 Toll between JT6 and JT7 · Eastbound and westbound
62 D4 SK02290745

WH Smith · The Burger Company · Costa Coffee · Restbite ⛽ BP 🛏 Premier Inn P 2 hrs ✉ Norton Canes, Cannock, Staffordshire WS11 9UX
☎ 01543 272540
🖥 www.roadchef.co.uk
☾ WH Smith and shop in forecourt open 24 hrs

M6 Hilton Park
Moto

♿ 🛢 🛁 🚿 🛁 ♿ WC 👫 (())

M6 J10A and J11 · Northbound and southbound
62 D3 SJ96200500

M&S Simply Food · Fone Bitz · WH Smith · Burger King · Coffee Nation · Costa Coffee · EDC ⛽ BP 🛏 Travelodge P 2 hrs ✉ Essington, Wolverhampton, Staffordshire WV11 2AT ☎ 01922 412237 🖥 www.moto-way.co.uk
☾ Coffee shops in forecourt and WH Smith are open 24 hrs

M6 Stafford – northbound
Moto

♿ 🛢 🛁 ♿ WC 👫 (())

M6, 3 miles north of J14 · Northbound only
75 F5 SJ88613186

Fonebitz · M&S Simply Food · WH Smith · Burger King · Coffee Nation · EDC ⛽ BP, LPG available 🛏 Travelodge P 2 hrs ✉ Stone, Staffordshire ST15 0EU ☎ 01785 811188 🖥 www.moto-way.co.uk
☾ The outlets on the forecourt are open 24 hrs

M6 Stafford – southbound
RoadChef

£ 👫 (())

M6, 7.5 miles south of J15 · Southbound only
75 F5 SJ89243065

Fonebitz · WH Smith · The Burger Company · Costa Coffee · Restbite ⛽ Esso 🛏 Premier Inn P 2 hrs ✉ M6 Southbound, Stone, Staffordshire ST15 0EU ☎ 01785 826300 🖥 www.roadchef.co.uk

M6 Keele
Welcome Break

£ 👫 (())

M6, 6 miles north of J15 · Northbound and southbound
74 E5 SJ80624406

WH Smith · Burger King · Eat In · KFC · Starbucks ⛽ Shell, LPG available (southbound) P 2 hrs ✉ Three Mile Lane, Keele, Newcastle under Lyme, Staffordshire ST5 5HG ☎ 01782 634230 @ keele.enquiry@welcomebreak.co.uk
🖥 www.welcomebreak.co.uk
☾ Eat In and WH Smith are open 24 hrs

M6 Sandbach
RoadChef

£ 👫 (())

M6, just south of J17 · Northbound and southbound
74 C4 SK02290745

WH Smith · The Burger Company · Costa Coffee · Restbite ⛽ Esso P 2 hrs ✉ M6 Northbound, Sandbach, Cheshire CW11 2FZ
☎ 01270 767134
🖥 www.roadchef.co.uk
☾ The outlets in the forecourt are open 24 hrs

M6 Knutsford
Moto

🛁 🚿 ♿ WC 👫 ♿ (())

M6, between J18 and J19 · Northbound and southbound
74 B4 SJ73267826

M&S Simply Food · WH Smith · Burger King · Coffee Nation · Costa Coffee · EDC · Krispy Kreme Doughnuts ⛽ BP, LPG available 🛏 Travelodge P 2 hrs ✉ Northwich Road, Knutsford, Cheshire WA16 0TL ☎ 01565 634167 🖥 www.moto-way.co.uk
☾ Shop in forecourt open 24 hrs

M6 Charnock Richard
Welcome Break

£ ✖ 🛁 👫 (())

M6, 2.5 miles north of J27 · Northbound and southbound
86 C3 SD54411521

WH Smith · Burger King · Coffee Primo · Eat In (northbound only) · KFC ⛽ Shell (southbound, LPG available); Texaco (northbound) 🛏 Days Inn P 2 hrs ✉ Mill Lane, Chorley, Lancashire PR7 5LR ☎ 01257 791746 🖥 www.welcomebreak.co.uk
☾ Eat In and WH Smith open 24 hrs

M6 Lancaster (Forton)
Moto

♿ 🛢 🛁 🚿 👫 WC ♿ (())

M6 south of J33 · Northbound and southbound
92 D5 SD50145198

Fone Bitz · M&S Simply Food · WH Smith · Burger King · Coffee Nation · Costa Coffee · EDC ⛽ BP, LPG available 🛏 Travelodge P 2 hrs ✉ White Carr Lane, Bay Horse, Lancaster, Lancashire LA2 9DU ☎ 01524 791775
🖥 www.moto-way.co.uk
☾ WH Smith and shop in forecourt are open 24 hrs

M6 Burton-in-Kendal
Moto

♿ 🛢 🛁 ♿ WC 👫 (())

M6 between J35 and J36 · Northbound only
92 B5 SD52207617

WH Smith · Burger King · Coffee Nation Costa Coffee · EDC ⛽ BP 🛏 Travelodge P 2 hrs ✉ Burton West, Carnforth, Lancashire LA6 1JF ☎ 01524 781234 🖥 www.moto-way.co.uk

M6 Killington Lake
RoadChef

£ 👫 (())

M6 just south of J37 · Southbound only
99 E7 SD58779111

WH Smith · The Burger Company · Costa Coffee ⛽ BP, LPG available 🛏 Premier Inn P 2 hrs ✉ M6 Southbound, near Kendal, Cumbria LA8 0NW
☎ 08701 977 145
🖥 www.roadchef.co.uk
☾ WH Smith and shop in forecourt open 24 hrs

M6 Tebay – northbound
Westmorland

£ 🛁 👫 (())

M6, just north of J38 · Northbound only
99 D8 NY60510626

Farm shop · butchers counter · Cafe · cake shop ⛽ Total, LPG available
🛏 Westmorland Hotel P Yes ✉ M6, Old Tebay, Cumbria CA10 3ZA ☎ 01539 624511
🖥 www.westmorland.com
☾ Main site and shop on forecourt open 24 hrs

M6 Tebay – southbound
Westmorland

£ 🛢 👫 (())

M6, 4.5 miles south of J39 · Southbound only
99 D8 NY60790650

Butcher's counter · Cafe · coffee shop ⛽ Total P Yes ✉ M6, Old Tebay, Cumbria CA10 3SB ☎ 01539 624511
🖥 www.westmorland.com
☾ Made to Go snack bar and forecourt shop open 24 hrs

M6 Southwaite
Moto

♿ ♿ WC ♿ 🛁 🚿 👫 (()) 🐾

M6 Junctions 41-42 · Northbound and southbound
108 E4 NY44164523

M&S · Costa · Burger King · EDC · WH Smith · Coffee Nation ⛽ BP 🛏 Travelodge P 2 hrs ✉ Broadfield Road, Carlisle CA4 0NT ☎ 01697 473476
🖥 www.moto-way.co.uk
☾ WH Smith and outlets on the forecourts are open 24 hours

M11 Birchanger Green
Welcome Break

£ 🛢 👫 (())

M11 at J8/J8a · Northbound and southbound 41 B8 TL51202149

Waitrose · WH Smith · Burger King · Eat In · KFC · Starbucks ⛽ Shell, LPG available 🛏 Days Inn P 2 hrs ✉ Old Dunmow Road, Bishop's Stortford, Hertfordshire CM23 5QZ
☎ 01279 653388
🖥 www.welcomebreak.co.uk
☾ WH Smith open 24 hrs

M18 Doncaster North
Moto

🛁 🛢 ♿ WC 👫 (())

M18 J5, at the western end of the M180 · Northbound and southbound 89 C7 SE66791104

WH Smith · Burger King · Coffee Nation · Costa Coffee · EDC ⛽ BP, LPG available 🛏 Travelodge P 2 hrs ✉ Hatfield, Doncaster, South Yorkshire DN8 5GS ☎ 02920 891141 🖥 www.moto-way.co.uk
☾ WH Smith open 24 hrs

M20 Maidstone
RoadChef

£ 👫 (())

M20 J8 30 D2 TQ82455523

WH Smith · The Burger Company · Costa Coffee · Restbite ⛽ Esso 🛏 Premier Inn P 2 hrs ✉ M20 J8, Hollingbourne, Maidstone, Kent ME17 1SS
☎ 01622 739647
🖥 www.roadchef.co.uk
☾ WH Smith and shop in forecourt are open 24 hrs

M20 Stop24 (Folkestone) — Stop 24

M20 J11 19 B8 TR13283729
Julian Graves • WH Smith • Breakfast Break • Burger King • Eat • KFC • Starbucks Shell, LPG available P 2 hrs ✉ Junction 11 M20, Stanford Intersection, Stanford, Kent CT21 4BL 01303 760273 @ info@stop24.co.uk www.stop24.co.uk Outlets on forecourt are open 24 hrs

M23 Pease Pottage — Moto

M23 J11 • Northbound and southbound 28 F3 TQ26183310
M&S Simply Food • WH Smith • Burger King • Coffee Nation • Costa Coffee • EDC • Krispy Kreme Doughnuts BP, LPG available P 2 hrs ✉ Brighton Road, Pease Pottage, Crawley, West Sussex RH11 9AE 01293 562852 www.moto-way.co.uk WH Smith and outlets in forecourt open 24 hrs

M25 Clacket Lane — RoadChef

M25 between J5 and J6 • Eastbound and westbound 28 D5 TQ42335457
Fone Bitz • WH Smith • Costa Coffee (westbound only) • Restbite • Wimpy Total Premier Inn *(westbound only)* P 2hrs ✉ M25 Westbound, Westerham, Kent TN16 2ER 01959 565577 www.roadchef.com Restbite open 24 hrs

M25 Cobham — Extra MSA

M25 J9-10 (due to open July 2012) • Clockwise and anti-clockwise 28 D2 TQ11345768
Days Inn • Eat In • KFC • McDonalds • Shell • Starbucks • WH Smith Shell Days Inn @ customerservices@extraservices.co.uk http://extraservices.co.uk

M25 South Mimms — Welcome Break

M25 J23 and A1(M) J1 • Clockwise and anti-clockwise 41 D5 TL23000023
Waitrose • WH Smith • Burger King • Eat In • KFC • Starbucks BP Days Inn P 2 hrs ✉ Bignells Corner, Potters Bar, Hertfordshire EN6 3QQ 01707 621001 @ mimms.enquiry@welcomebreak.co.uk www.welcomebreak.co.uk Eat In, WH Smith and the outlets on the forecourt are open 24 hrs

M25 Thurrock — Moto

M25, signposted from J30/J31 • Clockwise and anti-clockwise 29 B6 TQ57837947
M&S Simply Food • WH Smith • Burger King • Coffee Nation • Costa Coffee • EDC • Krispy Kreme Doughnuts Esso Travelodge P 2 hrs ✉ Arterial Road, West Thurrock, Grays, Essex RM16 3BG 01708 865487 www.moto-way.co.uk WH Smith and shop on forecourt open 24 hrs

M27 Rownhams — RoadChef

M27, between J3 and J4 • Eastbound and westbound 14 C4 SU38791769
WH Smith • Costa Coffee • Restbite (both sides); Wimpy (southbound only) Esso Premier Inn P 2 hrs ✉ M27 Southbound, Southampton, Hampshire SO16 8AP 02380 734480 www.roadchef.co.uk The outlets in the forecourts are open 24 hrs

M40 Beaconsfield — Extra MSA

M40 J2 • Eastbound and westbound 40 F2 SU95098897
M&S Simply Food • WH Smith • KFC • Le Petit Four • McDonald's • Presto • Starbucks Shell, LPG available Etap Hotel P 2 hrs ✉ A355 Windsor Drive, Beaconsfield, Buckinghamshire HP9 2SE www.extraservices.co.uk McDonald's open 24 hrs

M40 Oxford — Welcome Break

M40 J8A • Northbound and southbound 39 D6 SP62440479
Waitrose • WH Smith • Burger King • Eat In • KFC • Starbucks BP Days Inn P 2 hrs ✉ M40 Junction 8A, Waterstock, Oxfordshire OX33 1JN 01865 877000 @ oxford.enquiry@welcomebreak.co.uk www.welcomebreak.co.uk WH Smith and shop in forecourt open 24 hrs

M40 Cherwell Valley — Moto

M40 J10 • Northbound and southbound 39 B5 SP55162822
M&S Simply Food • WH Smith • Burger King • Coffee Nation • Costa Coffee • EDC Esso Travelodge P 2 hrs ✉ Northampton Road, Ardley, Bicester, Oxfordshire OX27 7RD 01869 346060 www.moto-way.co.uk Coffee Nation and WH Smith open 24 hrs

M40 Warwick South — Welcome Break

M40 between J12 and J13 • Southbound 51 D8 SP34075801
WH Smith • Burger King • Eat In • KFC • Starbucks BP, LPG available Days Inn P 2 hrs ✉ Banbury Road, Ashorne, Warwick CV35 0AA 01926 651681 @ warwicksouth.enquiry@welcomebreak.co.uk www.welcomebreak.co.uk Eat In, WH Smith and forecourt outlets open 24 hrs

M40 Warwick North — Welcome Break

M40 between J12 and J13 • Northbound 51 D8 SP33885770
Waitrose • Coffee Primo • Eat In • Burger King • KFC • WH Smith Shell Days Inn P 2 hrs ✉ Banbury Road, Ashorne, Warwick CV35 0AA 01926 650681 @ warwick.rdm@welcomebreak.co.uk www.welcomebreak.co.uk

M42 Hopwood Park — Welcome Break

M42 Junction 2 • Eastbound and westbound 50 B5 SP03637389
Waitrose • Coffee Primo Lounge • EatIn Restaurant • Burger King • KFC • WH Smith Shell P 2 hrs ✉ Redditch Road, Alvechurch B48 7AU 0121 4474000 @ hopwood.training@welcomebreak.co.uk www.welcomebreak.co.uk

M42 Tamworth — Moto

M42, just north of J10 • Northbound and southbound 63 D6 SK24440112
M&S Simply Food • WH Smith • Burger King • Coffee Nation • Costa Coffee • EDC Esso Travelodge P 2 hrs ✉ Green Lane, Tamworth, Staffordshire B77 5PS 01827 260120 www.moto-way.co.uk WH Smith and outlets on forecourt are open 24 hrs

M48 Severn View — Moto

M48 J1 • Eastbound and westbound 36 F2 ST57118959
WH Smith • Burger King • Coffee Nation • Costa Coffee BP Travelodge P 2 hrs ✉ Aust, South Gloucestershire BS35 4BH 01454 623851 www.moto-way.co.uk Forecourt outlets open 24 hrs

M54 Telford — Welcome Break

M54 J4 • Eastbound and westbound 61 D7 SJ73050890
WH Smith • Burger King • Eat In • Starbucks Shell Days Inn P 2 hrs ✉ Priorslee Road, Shifnal, Telford, Shropshire TF11 8TG 01952 238400 @ telford.gm@welcomebreak.co.uk www.welcomebreak.co.uk WH Smith and shop on forecourt open 24 hrs

M56 Chester — RoadChef

M56 J14 • Eastbound and westbound 73 B8 SJ46537491
WH Smith • Costa Coffee • Restbite • The Burger Company Shell Premier Inn P 2 hrs ✉ Elton, Chester, Cheshire CH2 4QZ 01928 728500 www.roadchef.com Costa Coffee and Restbite open 24 hrs

M61 Rivington — Euro Garages

M61 between J6 and J7 • Northbound and southbound 86 C4 SD62111168
Burger King • Spar • Starbucks • Subway BP Rivington Lodge *(southbound)* P 2 hrs ✉ M61, Horwich, Bolton, Lancashire BL6 5UZ 01254 56070 @ enquiries@eurogarages.com www.eurogarages.com/rivington-services Spar shop and forecourt open 24hrs

M62 Burtonwood — Welcome Break

M62 J8 • Eastbound and westbound 86 E3 SJ57749129
WH Smith • KFC • Starbucks Shell P 2 hrs ✉ M62 Great Sankey, Warrington, Cheshire WA5 3AX 01925 651656 @ burtonwood.enquiry@welcomebreak.co.uk www.welcomebreak.co.uk WH Smith open 24 hrs

M62 Birch — Moto

M62 1.5 miles east of J18 • Eastbound and westbound 87 D6 SD84700797
Coffee Nation • M&S Simply Food • WH Smith • Burger King • Costa Coffee • Fresh Express • the Eat and Drink Co BP Travelodge P 2 hrs ✉ Heywood, Lancashire OL10 2HQ 0161 643 0911 www.moto-way.co.uk WH Smith is open 24 hrs

M62 Hartshead Moor — Welcome Break

M62, between J25 and J26 • Eastbound and westbound 88 B2 SE16892413
WH Smith • Burger King • Eat In • KFC • Starbucks Shell Days Inn Bradford P 2 hrs ✉ Clifton, Brighouse, West Yorkshire HD6 4JX 01274 876584 @ hartshead.enquiry@welcomebreak.co.uk www.welcomebreak.co.uk Eat In is open 24 hrs

M62 Ferrybridge — Moto

M62 Junction 33. Also A1(M) J40 (northbound) or J41 (southbound) • Northbound and southbound 89 B5 SE48512262
M&S Simply Food • WH Smith • Burger King • Coffee Nation • Costa Coffee • EDC Esso Travelodge P 2 hrs ✉ Ferrybridge, Knottingly, West Yorkshire WF11 0AF 01977 672767 www.moto-way.co.uk Coffee Nation and WH Smith open 24 hrs

M65 Darwen — Extra MSA

M65 J4. • Eastbound and westbound 86 B4 SD68592414
Somerfield Essentials • Le Petit Four • McDonald's Shell, LPG Travelodge P 2 hrs ✉ Darwen Motorway Services Area, Darwen, Lancashire BB3 0AT www.extraservices.co.uk Shop in forecourt is open 24 hrs

Scotland

M9 Stirling — Moto

M9 J9 • Northbound and southbound 127 F7 NS80438870
WH Smith • Burger King • Coffee Nation • Costa Coffee • EDC BP Travelodge P 2 hrs ✉ Pirnhall, Stirling FK7 8EU 01786 813614 www.moto-way.co.uk WH Smith is open 24 hrs

M74 Bothwell — RoadChef

M74, south of J4 • southbound only 119 D7 NS70855980
WH Smith • Costa • Restbite BP, LPG available P 2hrs ✉ M74 Southbound, Bothwell, Lanarkshire G71 8BG 01698 854123 www.roadchef.com Shop in forecourt is open 24 hrs

M74 Hamilton — RoadChef

M74, 1 mile north of J6 • northbound only 119 D7 NS72525672
WH Smith • Costa Coffee • Restbite BP Premier Inn P 2hrs ✉ M74 Northbound, Hamilton, South Lanarkshire ML3 6JW 01698 282176 www.welcomebreak.co.uk Shop in forecourt is open 24hrs

M74 Happendon — Cairn Lodge

M74 between J11 and J12 on B7078 • Northbound and southbound 119 F8 NS85243364
Yes • Coffee shop • restaurant Shell P 2hrs ✉ Cairn Lodge, Douglas, Lanark, South Lanarkshire ML11 0RJ 01555 851880 Shop in forecourt open 24 hrs

A74(M) Abington — Welcome Break

A74(M) J13 • Northbound and southbound 114 B2 NS93022505
WH Smith • Burger King • Eat In • Starbucks Shell, LPG available Days Inn P 2 hrs ✉ Abington, Biggar, South Lanarkshire ML12 6RG 01864 502637 @ abington.enquiry@welcomebreak.co.uk www.welcomebreak.co.uk Eat In open 24 hrs. Tourist information office

A74(M) Annandale Water — Road Chef

A74(M) J16 • Northbound and southbound 114 E4 NY10389261
WH Smith • Costa Coffee • Restbite • The Burger Company • Wild Bean Cafe BP Premier Inn P 2hrs ✉ Johnstone Bridge, near Lockerbie, Dumfries and Galloway DG11 1HD 01576 470870 www.roadchef.com Restbite and forecourt shop are open 24 hrs

A74(M) Gretna Green — Welcome Break

A74(M), just north of J22 • Northbound and southbound 108 C3 NY30746872
WH Smith • Burger King • Eat In • KFC • Starbucks BP, LPG available Days Inn P 2 hrs ✉ M74A Trunk Road, Gretna Green, Dumfries and Galloway DG16 5HQ 01461 337567 @ gretna.enquiry@welcomebreak.co.uk www.welcomebreak.co.uk Eat In and WH Smith open 24 hrs

M80 Old Inns

M80 • Eastbound and Westbound 119 B7 NS77187671
Shell Select • Old inns Cafe • Silk Cottage Cantonese buffet restaurant and takeaway Shell ✉ Castlecary Road, Cumbernauld G68 0BJ 0843 259 0190 (filling station) http://www.shell.co.uk • http://www.oldinnscafe.com

M90 Kinross — Moto

M90 J6 • Northbound and southbound 128 D3 NO10800282
WH Smith • Burger King • Coffee Nation • Costa Coffee • EDC Esso Travelodge P 2 hrs ✉ M90, Kinross, Perth and Kinross KY13 7NQ 01577 863123 www.moto-way.co.uk WH Smith and shop in forecourt open 24 hrs

Wales

M4 Magor — First

M4 J23A • Eastbound and westbound 35 F8 ST42068796
Yes • Burger King • cafe Esso Travelodge P 2 hours ✉ M4 Magor, Caldicot, Monmouthshire NP26 3YL 01633 881887 @ info@firstmotorway.co.uk www.firstmotorway.co.uk Cafe open 24 hrs

M4 Cardiff Gate — Welcome Break

M4 J30 • Eastbound and westbound 35 F6 ST21658283
Waitrose • WH Smith • Burger King • Starbucks Total, LPG available P 2 hrs ✉ Cardiff Gate Business Park, Cardiff, South Glamorgan CF23 8RA 01758 822102 www.welcomebreak.co.uk Shop in forecourt open 24 hrs

M4 Cardiff West — Moto

M4, off J33 • Eastbound and westbound 22 B2 ST09417967
Moto Shop • WH Smith • Burger King • Coffee Nation • Costa Coffee • EDC Esso Travelodge P 2 hrs ✉ Pontyclun, Mid Glamorgan CF72 8SA 02920 891141 www.moto-way.co.uk WH Smith is open 24 hrs

M4 Sarn Park — Welcome Break

M4 J36 • Eastbound and westbound 34 F3 SS90688290
WH Smith • Burger King • Eat In Shell Days Inn P 2 hrs ✉ M4 Motorway, Junction 36, Sarn Park, Bridgend CF32 9RW 01656 655332 @ sarn.enquiry@welcomebreak.co.uk www.welcomebreak.co.uk WH Smith and shop in forecourt are open 24 hrs

M4 Swansea — Moto

M4 at J47 • Eastbound and westbound 33 E7 SS62159969
WH Smith • Burger King • Coffee Nation • Costa Coffee BP Travelodge P 2 hrs ✉ Penllergaer, Swansea, West Glamorgan SA4 1GT 01792 896222 www.moto-way.co.uk The outlets on the forecourt are open 24 hrs

M4 Pont Abraham — RoadChef

M4 J49 • Eastbound and westbound 33 D6 SN57470743
WH Smith • Costa Coffee • JJ Beanos • Restbite Texaco P 2 hours ✉ Llanedi, Pontarddulais, Swansea SA4 0FU 01792 884 663 www.roadchef.co.uk Forecourt outlets open 24 hrs

The Speed Limit:
80mph or 70mph?
Or even 60mph?

By Stephen Mesquita, Philip's *On the Road* Correspondent

It was one of those moments, described in phrasebooks as 'At the Car Hire Desk'. A moment to make the heart sink and the spirit to travel wither. It was at Frankfurt airport. 'I'm very sorry, sir, we don't have the Compact you ordered.' Visions of scooters and mopeds appeared before my eyes.

'But we do have a Mercedes blah blah blah, which we can offer you in its place at no extra charge' (sorry Mercedes fans, the specification escapes me).

So there I was, on the autobahn, with over 100 miles to drive to my appointment. An autobahn with no speed limit and a Mercedes blah blah blah which also seemed to have no speed limit. It was a pleasant autumn's afternoon. The traffic was relatively light.

We have reached the stage in this tale where I need to break the flow to state my credentials. I am not a boy racer. I never have been a boy racer (except for an incident in my long lost youth which I may decide to relate later). Speed comes a very poor second to safety when I am driving. I'm normally very happy to pootle along the motorway at 70mph, if not a bit slower.

But here I was with an opportunity to conduct an experiment – purely for the sake of research, you understand. How fast could I go in this speed machine at whose wheel I now found myself? Looking in my mirror at the outside lane I could see another Merc way back on the autobahn. Within

a few seconds it passed me in a blur. Now was my chance. I put the pedal to the metal, manoeuvred into the outside lane and held on tight.

To try to answer this question, I left my house at 4.40am on a damp February morning

From a quick calculation, 240kph is 150mph. That was the stage at which I decided that my driving skills probably weren't up to going any faster. The worrying thing was that, even at 240kph, there were still cars appearing with alarming speed in my rear view mirror, impatient to overtake.

Where is all this leading?

When, last year, the government floated the idea of raising the speed limit on motorways to 80mph, my mind went back to my experience outside Frankfurt. But it also went back even further. To my first driving experience, in the mid 1970s, on

the freeways of the Mid West. It was just after the oil crisis and the speed limit, even on the freeway, was 55mph. My job entailed a lot of driving in a car with automatic everything – a car that more or less drove itself.

The freeways were, for the most part, empty and the journeys were long. 55mph seemed mind-numbingly slow. The radio played the same hits over and over. Combating boredom was nearly impossible.

So which was it to be? The German experience, the status quo or the US experience of the mid-70s?

To try to answer this question, I left my house at 4.40am on a damp February morning. The first challenge was to find a stretch of road where I could conduct my experiment. Out here, in deepest East Anglia, there are no three-lane motorways. There are also, in some area, forests of speed cameras. I needed to drive on an east-west axis to neutralise the effect of a north wind. And I needed to be out at a time of day when lorries were least likely to be overtaking each other in the outside lane and when all good law enforcement officers were tucked up in bed.

This was the plan – to drive 30 miles at 80mph and 30 miles at 60mph and a bit in between at regulation 70mph. I chose the A14, A11 and M11 from Bury St Edmunds and back. It's dual carriageway all the

M20 Stop24 (Folkestone) Stop 24

♿🚼📶

M20 J11 19 B8 TR13283729
Julian Graves • WH Smith • Breakfast Break • Burger King • Eat • KFC • Starbucks 🅿 Shell, LPG available 🅿 2 hrs ✉ Junction 11 M20, Stanford Intersection, Stanford, Kent CT21 4BL 📞 01303 760273 @ info@stop24.co.uk 🖥 www.stop24.co.uk ◐ Outlets on forecourt are open 24 hrs

M23 Pease Pottage Moto

♿🚿🅿👶🚼📶

M23 J11 · Northbound and southbound 28 F3 TQ26183310
M&S Simply Food • WH Smith • Burger King • Coffee Nation • Costa Coffee • EDC • Krispy Kreme Doughnuts 🅿 BP, LPG available 🅿 2 hrs ✉ Brighton Road, Pease Pottage, Crawley, West Sussex RH11 9AE 📞 01293 562852 🖥 www.moto-way.co.uk ◐ WH Smith and outlets in forecourt open 24 hrs

M25 Clacket Lane RoadChef

🅿🚼📶

M25 between J5 and J6 · Eastbound and westbound 28 D5 TQ42335457
Fone Bitz • WH Smith • Costa Coffee (westbound only) • Restbite • Wimpy 🅿 Total🗪 Premier Inn (westbound only) 🅿 2hrs ✉ M25 Westbound, Westerham, Kent TN16 2ER 📞 01959 565577 🖥 www.roadchef.com ◐ Restbite open 24 hrs

M25 Cobham Extra MSA

🅿🚼📶

M25 J9-10 (due to open July 2012) · Clockwise and anti-clockwise 28 D2 TQ11345768
Days Inn • Eat In • KFC • McDonalds • Shell • Starbucks • WH Smith 🅿 Shell🗪 Days Inn @ customerservices@ extraservices.co.uk 🖥 http://extraservices.co.uk

M25 South Mimms Welcome Break

🅿🚿🅿🚐📶

M25 J23 and A1(M) J1 · Clockwise and anti-clockwise 41 D5 TL23000023
Waitrose • WH Smith • Burger King • Eat In • KFC • Starbucks 🅿 BP 🗪 Days Inn 🅿 2 hrs ✉ Bignells Corner, Potters Bar, Hertfordshire EN6 3QQ 📞 01707 621001 @ mimms.enquiry@ welcomebreak.co.uk 🖥 www.welcomebreak.co.uk ◐ Eat In, WH Smith and the outlets on the forecourt are open 24 hrs

M25 Thurrock Moto

♿🅿🚿👶🚼📶

M25, signposted from J30/J31 · Clockwise and anti-clockwise 29 B6 TQ57837947
M&S Simply Food • WH Smith • Burger King • Coffee Nation • Costa Coffee • EDC • Krispy Kreme Doughnuts 🅿 Esso🗪 Travelodge 🅿 2 hrs ✉ Arterial Road, West Thurrock, Grays, Essex RM16 3BG 📞 01708 865487 🖥 www.moto-way.co.uk ◐ WH Smith and shop on forecourt open 24 hrs

---

M27 Rownhams RoadChef

🅿🅿🚼📶

M27, between J3 and J4 · Eastbound and westbound 14 C4 SU38791769
WH Smith • Costa Coffee • Restbite (both sides) • Wimpy (southbound only) 🅿 Esso🗪 Premier Inn 🅿 2 hrs ✉ M27 Southbound, Southampton, Hampshire SO16 8AP 📞 02380 734480 🖥 www.roadchef.co.uk ◐ The outlets in the forecourts are open 24 hrs

M40 Beaconsfield Extra MSA

🅿🅿🚼📶

M40 J2 · Eastbound and westbound 40 F2 SU95098897
M&S Simply Food • WH Smith • KFC • Le Petit Four • McDonald's • Presto • Starbucks 🅿 Shell, LPG available 🗪 Etap Hotel 🅿 2 hrs ✉ A355 Windsor Drive, Beaconsfield, Buckinghamshire HP9 2SE 🖥 www.extraservices. co.uk ◐ McDonald's open 24 hrs

M40 Oxford Welcome Break

🅿🚼📶

M40 J8A · Northbound and southbound 39 D6 SP62440479
Waitrose • WH Smith • Burger King • Eat In • KFC • Starbucks 🅿 BP 🗪 Days Inn 🅿 2 hrs ✉ M40 Junction 8A, Waterstock, Oxfordshire OX33 1JN 📞 01865 877000 @ oxford.enquiry@ welcomebreak.co.uk 🖥 www. welcomebreak.co.uk ◐ WH Smith and shop in forecourt open 24 hrs

M40 Cherwell Valley Moto

🅿🅿🚿👶🚃📶

M40 J10 · Northbound and southbound 39 B5 SP55162822
M&S Simply Food • WH Smith • Burger King • Coffee Nation • Costa Coffee • EDC 🅿 Esso🗪 Travelodge 🅿 2 hrs ✉ Northampton Road, Ardley, Bicester, Oxfordshire OX27 7RD 📞 01869 346060 🖥 www.moto-way.co.uk ◐ Coffee Nation and WH Smith open 24 hrs

M40 Warwick South Welcome Break

🅿🚼📶

M40 between J12 and J13 · Southbound 51 D8 SP34075801
WH Smith • Burger King • Eat In • KFC • Starbucks 🅿 BP, LPG available 🗪 Days Inn 🅿 2 hrs ✉ Banbury Road, Ashorne, Warwick CV35 0AA 📞 01926 651681 @ warwicksouth. enquiry@welcomebreak.co.uk 🖥 www.welcomebreak.co.uk ◐ Eat In, WH Smith and forecourt outlets open 24 hrs

M40 Warwick North Welcome Break

🅿🚼📶

M40 between J12 and J13 · Northbound 51 D8 SP33885770
Waitrose • Coffee Primo • Eat In • Burger King • KFC • WH Smith 🅿 Shell🗪 Days Inn 🅿 2 hrs ✉ Banbury Road, Ashorne, Warwick CV35 0AA 📞 01926 650681 @ warwick.rdm@ welcomebreak.co.uk 🖥 www.welcomebreak.co.uk

---

M42 Hopwood Park Welcome Break

M42 Junction 2 · Eastbound and westbound 50 B5 SP03637389
Waitrose • Coffee Primo Lounge • EatIn Restaurant • Burger King • KFC • WH Smith 🅿 Shell 🅿 2 hrs ✉ Redditch Road, Alvechurch B48 7AU 📞 0121 4474000 @ hopwood.training@ welcomebreak.co.uk 🖥 www.welcomebreak.co.uk

M42 Tamworth Moto

🅿🅿🚿👶🚼📶

M42, just north of J10 · Northbound and southbound 63 D6 SK24440112
M&S Simply Food • WH Smith • Burger King • Coffee Nation • Costa Coffee • EDC 🅿 Esso🗪 Travelodge 🅿 2 hrs ✉ Green Lane, Tamworth, Staffordshire B77 5PS 📞 01827 260120 🖥 www.moto-way.co.uk ◐ WH Smith and outlets on forecourt are open 24 hrs

M48 Severn View Moto

♿🅿🚿👶🚻🚼📶

M48 J1 · Eastbound and westbound 36 F2 ST57118959
WH Smith • Burger King • Coffee Nation • Costa Coffee 🅿 BP 🗪 Travelodge 🅿 2 hrs ✉ Aust, South Gloucestershire BS35 4BH 📞 01454 623851 🖥 www.moto-way.co.uk ◐ Forecourt outlets open 24 hrs

M54 Telford Welcome Break

M54 J4 · Eastbound and westbound 61 D7 SJ73050890
WH Smith • Burger King • Eat In • Starbucks 🅿 Shell🗪 Days Inn 🅿 2 hrs ✉ Priorslee Road, Shifnal, Telford, Shropshire TF11 8TG 📞 01952 238400 @ telford. gm@welcomebreak.co.uk 🖥 www.welcomebreak.co.uk ◐ WH Smith and shop on forecourt open 24 hrs

M56 Chester RoadChef

🅿🅿🚼📶

M56 J14 · Eastbound and westbound 73 B8 SJ46537491
WH Smith • Costa Coffee • Restbite • The Burger Company 🅿 Shell 🗪 Premier Inn 🅿 2 hrs ✉ Elton, Chester, Cheshire CH2 4QZ 📞 01928 728500 🖥 www.roadchef.com ◐ Costa Coffee and Restbite open 24 hrs

M61 Rivington Euro Garages

🅿🅿🚼📶

M61 between J6 and J7 · Northbound and southbound 86 C4 SD62111168
Burger King • Spar • Starbucks • Subway 🅿 BP 🗪 Rivington Lodge (southbound) 🅿 2 hrs ✉ M61, Horwich, Bolton, Lancashire BL6 5UZ 📞 01254 760120 @ enquiries@eurogarages.com 🖥 www.eurogarages.com/ rivington-services ◐ Spar shop and forecourt open 24hrs

M62 Burtonwood Welcome Break

🅿🚼📶

M62 J8 · Eastbound and westbound 86 E3 SJ57749129
WH Smith • KFC • Starbucks 🅿 Shell 🅿 2 hrs ✉ M62 Great

Sankey, Warrington, Cheshire WA5 3AX 📞 01925 651656 @ burtonwood.enquiry@ welcomebreak.co.uk 🖥 www.welcomebreak.co.uk ◐ WH Smith open 24 hrs

M62 Birch Moto

♿🅿🚿👶🚼📶

M62 1.5 miles east of J18 · Eastbound and westbound 87 D6 SD84700797
Coffee Nation • M&S Simply Food • WH Smith • Burger King • Costa Coffee • Fresh Express • the Eat and Drink Co 🅿 BP🗪 Travelodge 🅿 2 hrs ✉ Heywood, Lancashire OL10 2HQ 📞 0161 643 0911 🖥 www.moto-way.co.uk ◐ WH Smith is open 24 hrs

M62 Hartshead Moor Welcome Break

🅿✖🅿🚼📶

M62, between J25 and J26 · Eastbound and westbound 88 B2 SE16892413
WH Smith • Burger King • Eat In • KFC • Starbucks 🅿 Shell🗪 Days Inn Bradford 🅿 2 hrs ✉ Clifton, Brighouse, West Yorkshire HD6 4JX 📞 01274 876584 @ hartshead. enquiry@welcomebreak.co.uk 🖥 www.welcomebreak.co.uk ◐ Eat In is open 24 hrs

M62 Ferrybridge Moto

♿🅿🚿👶🚻🚼📶

M62 Junction 33. Also A1(M) J40 (northbound) or J41 (southbound) · Northbound and southbound 89 B5 SE48512262
M&S Simply Food • WH Smith • Burger King • Coffee Nation • Costa Coffee • EDC 🅿 Esso🗪 Travelodge 🅿 2 hrs ✉ Ferrybridge, Knottingly, West Yorkshire WF11 0AF 📞 01977 672767 🖥 www.moto-way.co.uk ◐ Coffee Nation and WH Smith open 24 hrs

M65 Darwen Extra MSA

🅿🚼📶

M65 J4. · Eastbound and westbound 86 B4 SD68592414
Somerfield Essentials • Le Petit Four • McDonald's 🅿 Shell, LPG🗪 Travelodge 🅿 2 hrs ✉ Darwen Motorway Services Area, Darwen, Lancashire BB3 0AT 🖥 www.extraservices.co.uk ◐ Shop in forecourt is open 24 hrs

---

Scotland

M9 Stirling Moto

♿🅿🚿👶🚻🚼📶

M9 J9 · Northbound and southbound 127 F7 NS80438870
WH Smith • Burger King • Coffee Nation • Costa Coffee • EDC 🅿 BP 🗪 Travelodge 🅿 2 hrs ✉ Pirnhall, Stirling FK7 8EU 📞 01786 813614 🖥 www.moto-way.co.uk ◐ WH Smith is open 24 hrs

M74 Bothwell RoadChef

🅿🚼📶

M74, south of J4 · southbound only 119 D7 NS70855980
WH Smith • Costa • Restbite 🅿 BP, LPG available 🅿 2 hrs ✉ M74 Southbound, Bothwell, Lanarkshire G71 8BG 📞 01698 854123 🖥 www.roadchef.com ◐ Shop in forecourt is open 24 hrs

---

M74 Hamilton RoadChef

🅿🅿🚼📶

M74, 1 mile north of J6 · northbound only 119 D7 NS72525672
WH Smith • Costa Coffee • Restbite 🅿 BP🗪 Premier Inn 🅿 2hrs ✉ M74 Northbound, Hamilton, South Lanarkshire ML3 6JW 📞 01698 282176 🖥 www.welcomebreak.co.uk ◐ Shop in forecourt is open 24hrs

M74 Happendon Cairn Lodge

M74 between J11 and J12 on B7078 · Northbound and southbound 119 F8 NS85243364
Yes • Coffee shop • restaurant 🅿 Shell 🅿 2 hrs ✉ Cairn Lodge, Douglas, Lanark, South Lanarkshire ML11 0RJ 📞 01555 851880 ◐ Shop in forecourt open 24 hrs

A74(M) Abington Welcome Break

🅿✖🚼📶

A74(M) J13 · Northbound and southbound 114 B2 NS93022505
WH Smith • Burger King • Eat In • Starbucks 🅿 Shell, LPG available 🗪 Days Inn 🅿 2 hrs ✉ Abington, Biggar, South Lanarkshire ML12 6RG 📞 01864 502637 @ abington.enquiry@ welcomebreak.co.uk 🖥 www.welcomebreak.co.uk ◐ Eat In open 24 hrs. Tourist information office

A74(M) Annandale Water Road Chef

🅿🅿🚼📶

A74(M) J16 · Northbound and southbound 114 E4 NY10389261
WH Smith • Costa Coffee • Restbite • The Burger Company • Wild Bean Cafe 🅿 BP🗪 Premier Inn 🅿 2hrs ✉ Johnstone Bridge, near Lockerbie, Dumfries and Galloway DG11 1HD 📞 01576 470870 🖥 www.roadchef.com ◐ Restbite and forecourt shop are open 24 hrs

A74(M) Gretna Green Welcome Break

🅿🚼📶

A74(M), just north of J22 · Northbound and southbound 108 C3 NY30746872
WH Smith • Burger King • Eat In • KFC • Starbucks 🅿 BP, LPG available 🗪 Days Inn 🅿 2 hrs ✉ M74A Trunk Road, Gretna Green, Dumfries and Galloway DG16 5HQ 📞 01461 337567 @ gretna. enquiry@welcomebreak.co.uk 🖥 www.welcomebreak.co.uk ◐ Eat In and WH Smith open 24 hrs

M80 Old Inns

🚼

M80 · Eastbound and Westbound 119 B7 NS77187671
Shell Select • Old inns Cafe • Silk Cottage Cantonese buffet restaurant and takeaway 🅿 Shell ✉ Castlecary Road, Cumbernauld G68 0BJ 📞 0843 259 0190 (filling station) 🖥 http://www.shell.co.uk/ http://www.oldinnscafe.com

---

M90 Kinross Moto

♿🅿🚿👶🚻🚼📶

M90 J6 · Northbound and southbound 128 D3 NO10800282
WH Smith • Burger King • Coffee Nation • Costa Coffee • EDC 🅿 Esso 🗪 Travelodge 🅿 2 hrs ✉ M90, Kinross, Perth and Kinross KY13 7NQ 📞 01577 863123 🖥 www.moto-way.co.uk ◐ WH Smith and shop in forecourt open 24 hrs

Wales

M4 Magor First

🅿🅿🚼

M4 J23A · Eastbound and westbound 35 F8 ST42068796
Yes • Burger King • cafe 🅿 Esso 🗪 Travelodge 🅿 2 hrs ✉ M4 Magor, Caldicot, Monmouthshire NP26 3YL 📞 01633 881887 @ info@firstmotorway.co.uk 🖥 www.firstmotorway.co.uk ◐ Cafe open 24 hrs

M4 Cardiff Gate Welcome Break

🅿🚼📶

M4 J30 · Eastbound and westbound 35 F6 ST21658283
Waitrose • WH Smith • Burger King • Starbucks 🅿 Total, LPG available 🅿 2 hrs ✉ Cardiff Gate Business Park, Cardiff, South Glamorgan CF23 8RA 📞 01758 822102 🖥 www.welcomebreak.co.uk ◐ Shop in forecourt open 24 hrs

M4 Cardiff West Moto

♿🅿🅿🚿👶🚻🚼📶

M4, off J33 · Eastbound and westbound 22 B2 ST09417967
Moto Shop • WH Smith • Burger King • Coffee Nation • Costa Coffee • EDC 🅿 Esso🗪 Travelodge 🅿 2 hrs ✉ Pontyclun, Mid Glamorgan CF72 8SA 📞 02920 891141 🖥 www.moto-way.co.uk ◐ WH Smith is open 24 hrs

M4 Sarn Park Welcome Break

🅿🚼📶

M4 J36 · Eastbound and westbound 34 F3 SS90688290
WH Smith • Burger King • Eat In 🅿 Shell🗪 Days Inn 🅿 2 hrs ✉ M4 Motorway, Junction 36, Sarn Park, Bridgend CF32 9RW 📞 01656 655332 @ sarn. enquiry@welcomebreak.co.uk 🖥 www.welcomebreak.co.uk ◐ WH Smith and shop in forecourt open 24 hrs

M4 Swansea Moto

♿🅿🅿🚿👶🚻🚼📶

M4 at J47 · Eastbound and westbound 33 E7 SS62159969
WH Smith • Burger King • Coffee Nation • Costa Coffee 🅿 BP 🗪 Travelodge 🅿 2 hrs ✉ Penllergaer, Swansea, West Glamorgan SA4 1GT 📞 01792 896222 🖥 www.moto-way.co.uk ◐ The outlets on the forecourt are open 24 hrs

M4 Pont Abraham RoadChef

🅿🅿🚼📶

M4 J49 · Eastbound and westbound 33 D6 SN57470743
WH Smith • Costa Coffee • JJ Beanos • Restbite 🅿 Texaco 🅿 2 hours ✉ Llanedi, Pontarddulais, Swansea SA4 0FH 📞 01792 884 663 🖥 www.roadchef.com ◐ Forecourt outlets open 24 hrs

The Speed Limit:
80mph or 70mph?
Or even 60mph?

By Stephen Mesquita, Philip's *On the Road* Correspondent

It was one of those moments, described in phrasebooks as 'At the Car Hire Desk'. A moment to make the heart sink and the spirit to travel wither. It was at Frankfurt airport. 'I'm very sorry, sir, we don't have the Compact you ordered.' Visions of scooters and mopeds appeared before my eyes.

'But we do have a Mercedes blah blah blah, which we can offer you in its place at no extra charge' (sorry Mercedes fans, the specification escapes me).

So there I was, on the autobahn, with over 100 miles to drive to my appointment. An autobahn with no speed limit and a Mercedes blah blah blah which also seemed to have no speed limit. It was a pleasant autumn's afternoon. The traffic was relatively light.

We have reached the stage in this tale where I need to break the flow to state my credentials. I am not a boy racer. I never have been a boy racer (except for an incident in my long lost youth which I may decide to relate later). Speed comes a very poor second to safety when I am driving. I'm normally very happy to pootle along the motorway at 70mph, if not a bit slower.

But here I was with an opportunity to conduct an experiment – purely for the sake of research, you understand. How fast could I go in this speed machine at whose wheel I now found myself? Looking in my mirror at the outside lane I could see another Merc way back on the autobahn. Within

a few seconds it passed me in a blur. Now was my chance. I put the pedal to the metal, manoeuvred into the outside lane and held on tight.

To try to answer this question, I left my house at 4.40am on a damp February morning

From a quick calculation, 240kph is 150mph. That was the stage at which I decided that my driving skills probably weren't up to going any faster. The worrying thing was that, even at 240kph, there were still cars appearing with alarming speed in my rear view mirror, impatient to overtake.

Where is all this leading?

When, last year, the government floated the idea of raising the speed limit on motorways to 80mph, my mind went back to my experience outside Frankfurt. But it also went back even further. To my first driving experience, in the mid 1970s, on

the freeways of the Mid West. It was just after the oil crisis and the speed limit, even on the freeway, was 55mph. My job entailed a lot of driving in a car with automatic everything – a car that more or less drove itself.

The freeways were, for the most part, empty and the journeys were long. 55mph seemed mind-numbingly slow. The radio played the same hits over and over. Combating boredom was nearly impossible.

So which was it to be? The German experience, the status quo or the US experience of the mid-70s?

To try to answer this question, I left my house at 4.40am on a damp February morning. The first challenge was to find a stretch of road where I could conduct my experiment. Out here, in deepest East Anglia, there are no three-lane motorways. There are also, in some area, forests of speed cameras. I needed to drive on an east-west axis to neutralise the effect of a north wind. And I needed to be out at a time of day when lorries were least likely to be overtaking each other in the outside lane and when all good law enforcement officers were tucked up in bed.

This was the plan – to drive 30 miles at 80mph and 30 miles at 60mph and a bit in between at regulation 70mph. I chose the A14, A11 and M11 from Bury St Edmunds and back. It's dual carriageway all the

way. It's comparatively speed camera free on the outward leg (at least I hope so) and, although it's busy, it's not too busy at 5.30am when I started the 80mph stretch.

The advantage of driving faster is that you get there faster. So you save time. The advantage of driving slower is that you use less petrol, so you save money. I am not qualified to talk about road safety, although the Road Safety Pressure Groups all argue that faster is more dangerous. I am also not qualified to comment on the environmental issues, although it follows that less petrol means less pollution.

I would not normally bore you with spreadsheets – but, on this occasion, it seems to be the simplest way to express the argument.

If you're a professional driver clocking up 25,000 miles a year, it totals out at nearly £1,000 more

The important thing is to understand – as all motorists surely do – that the faster you drive, the more petrol you consume. In my trusty 10-year old VW Passat Estate 1.9 TDi (I do remember the specification of my own car), I would normally expect to do about 45 miles per gallon on a long journey.

At 80mph, over 30 miles, the petrol consumption was 36.6mpg; at 70mph over 20 miles (10 miles into the wind and 10 miles with the wind behind) the average was 42.9mpg; and, at 60mph, the consumption was 47.3mpg.

Now for the maths. At the time of going to press, diesel costs £1.40 per gallon. So my 30 miles at 80mph cost me £5.21 and my 30 miles at 60mph cost me £4.03. It may not sound much – but multiply it up over a year and it turns into a sum of money that you notice. In fact, if you're a professional driver clocking up 25,000 miles a year, it totals out at nearly £1,000 more.

So here is my Ready Reckoner (table 1)

Based on my experience, if I drove at 60mph on long journeys, it could save me 23% on my fuel costs compared with driving at 80mph and 9% compared with driving at 70mph. You'll notice that the differential is greater between 70 and 80 than between 60 and 70mph.

But time is also money. Is it possible that the savings in petrol would be wiped out by the cost of the additional journey time? Back to the spreadsheet (table 2):

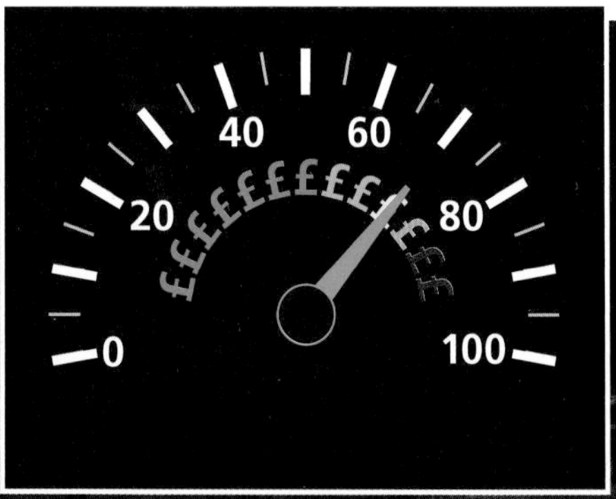

So you'll see that, although it's 23% cheaper to drive at 60mph compared with 80, it takes 32% longer. The 104 hours lost by the professional driver would cost considerably more than the £983 gained in the petrol saving.

'Hours lost' is a concept that is not always easy to quantify. How many of those hours would otherwise be downtime, so not really lost? If this is what the bean counters call a Cost Benefit Analysis, it doesn't really give us a conclusive answer.

Quite a few other drivers – and not just lorries – were also keeping to 60

Back to the A14. Here are some considerations which you can't deduce from the spreadsheets. First, I didn't actually drive at 80mph. The needle of my speedometer was at, or over, 80mph for most of the journey. But when I came to check my average speed, I had actually driven the 30 miles at 77mph. Thanks to those nice people at VW, my speedometer was set to register 3–4mph faster than I was actually driving. Anyone who uses sat nav can see this as they drive. Their speedometer registers a higher speed than the sat nav tells them they are actually driving.

But I was happy not to be averaging 80. If it had been a fine day on an empty motorway, I would probably have been very comfortable doing 80. But on a dual carriageway, with overtaking lorries which threw up spray, and in the dark, 77mph was fast enough. Actually, it was probably too fast.

And then I had a surprise when I was driving at 60mph on the return leg. Quite a few other drivers – and not just lorries – were also keeping to 60. In these tough times, many drivers have already worked out for themselves the economies of driving more slowly – without a law being needed to stop those who want or need to drive faster. The law does not force you to drive at 70.

It may make for a dull conclusion to this otherwise sparkling article (spreadsheets and all) – but my vote is to keep the speed limit at 70mph. If we were really trying to be green in this country, we would reduce it – but that's currently left to you as an individual. My dawn sortie has convinced me that raising the speed limit to 80mph on our crowded motorways does not have my vote. Sorry all you budding Jensons and Lewis's out there.

So, after breaking the law to bring you this research, I'll be going back to driving at 70mph – or, now I've done the sums, maybe a little bit slower.

Oh yes – that incident from my long lost past. I nearly forgot. Well, I didn't always keep to the 55mph speed limit during my stint on the road in the USA. In fact, on an empty freeway between Chicago and Minneapolis, I got stopped. Despite my poor impression of Bertie Wooster pleading ignorance as a foreigner, a request for $115 arrived from a court in Wisconsin. I remember thinking as I wrote the cheque, that in 1975 $115 was quite a lot of money.

1	(80)	(70)	(60)	(70)	(60)	(70)	(60)
	36.6mpg	**42.9mpg**	**47.3mpg**	**Amount saved***			**% Saved***
5,000 miles	£869	£742	£673	£127.68	£196.69	17%	23%
10,000 miles	£1,739	£1,484	£1,346	£255.37	£393.38	17%	23%
15,000 miles	£2,608	£2,225	£2,018	£383.05	£590.06	17%	23%
20,000 miles	£3,478	£2,967	£2,691	£510.74	£786.75	17%	23%
25,000 miles	£4,347	£3,709	£3,364	£638.42	£983.44	17%	23%

Price per litre – diesel: £1.40
Price per gallon – diesel: £6.36
*compared to 80mph

2	**Time taken** (hours)			**Additional time taken** (hours)			**% Additional time taken** at 60mph compared to:	
	(80)	(70)	(60)	(80)	(70)	(60)	(80)	(70)
5,000 miles	62.50	71.43	83.33	0	8.93	20.83	32%	13%
10,000 miles	125.00	142.86	166.67	0	17.86	41.67	32%	13%
15,000 miles	187.50	214.29	250.00	0	26.79	62.50	32%	13%
20,000 miles	250.00	285.71	333.33	0	35.71	83.33	32%	13%
25,000 miles	312.50	357.14	416.67	0	44.64	104.17	32%	13%

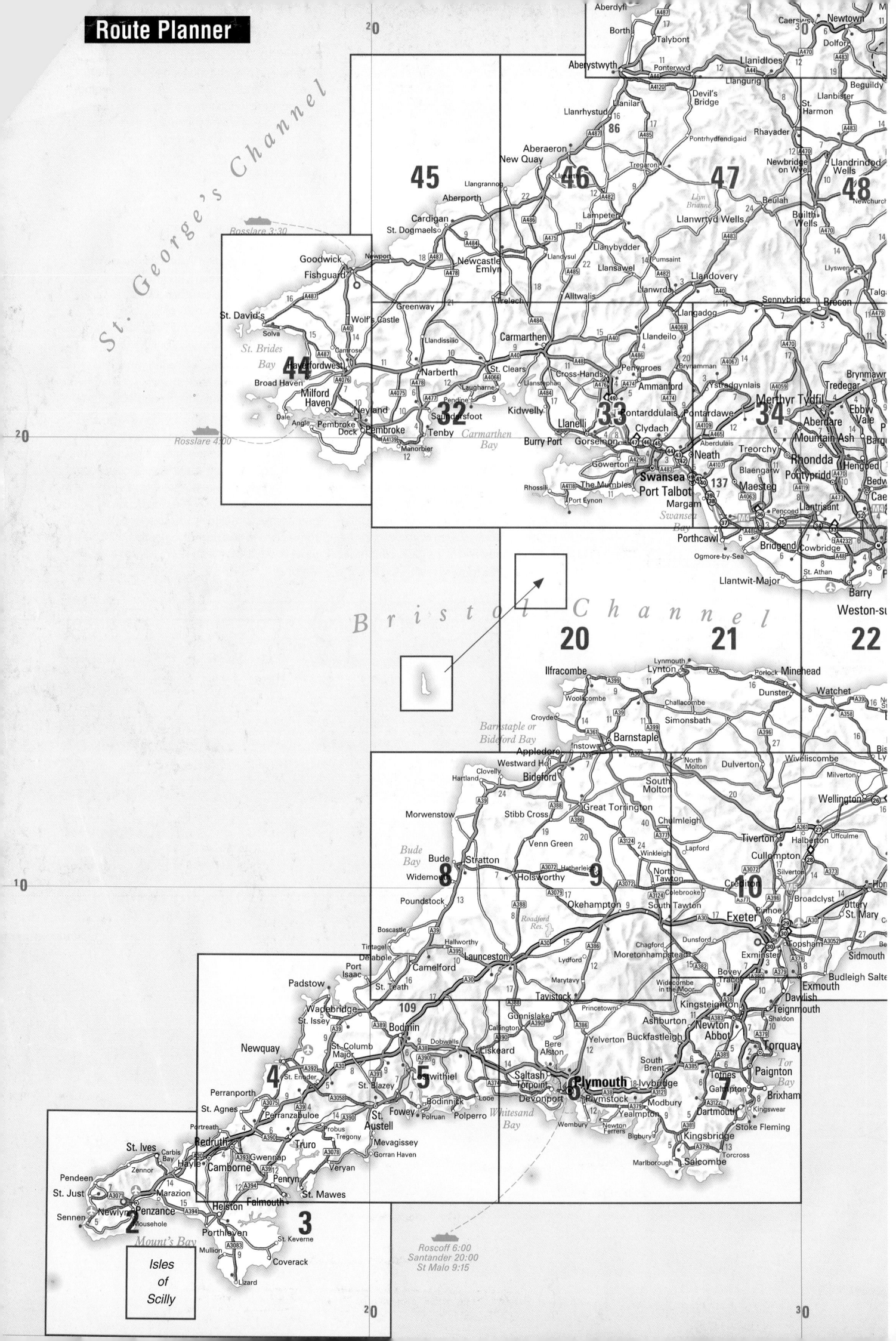

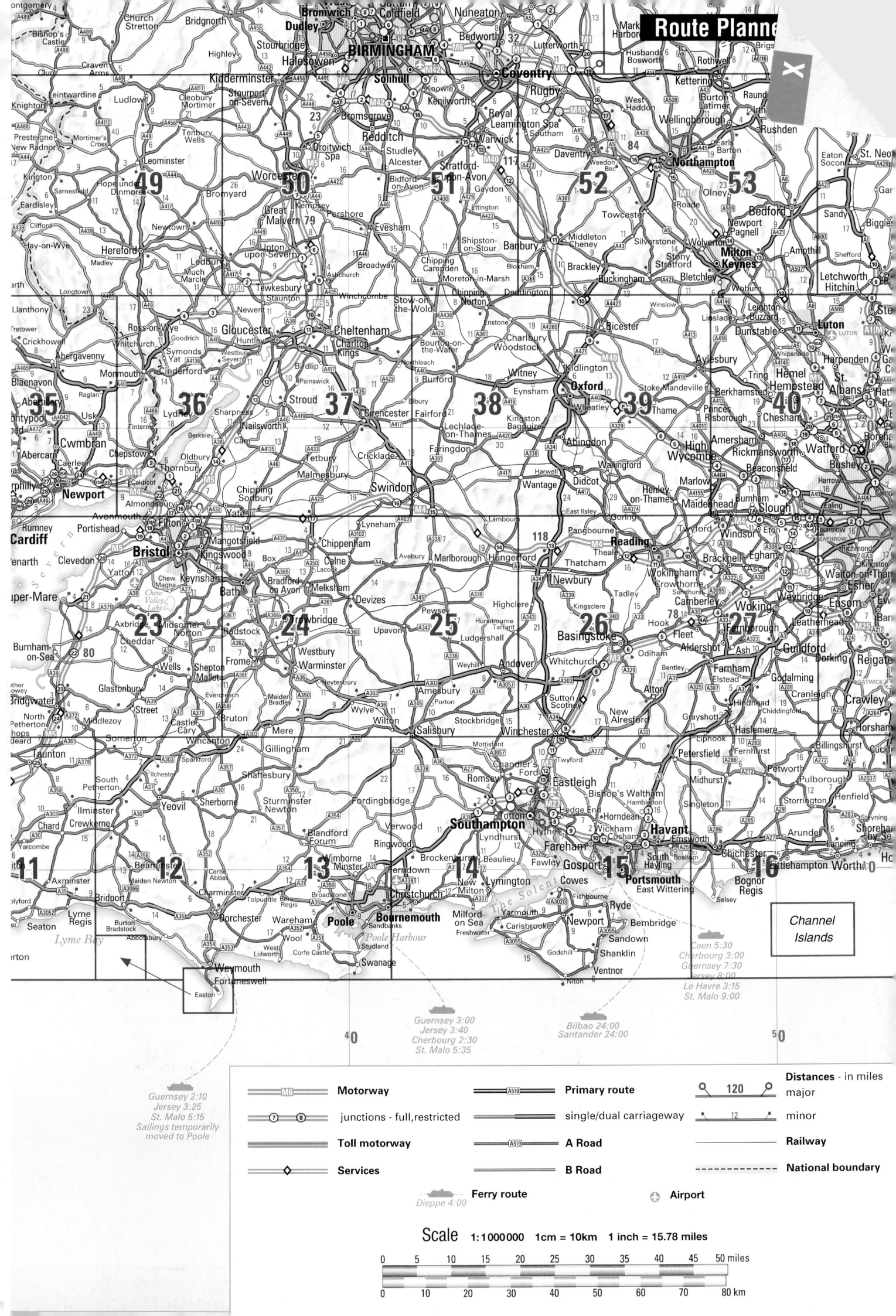

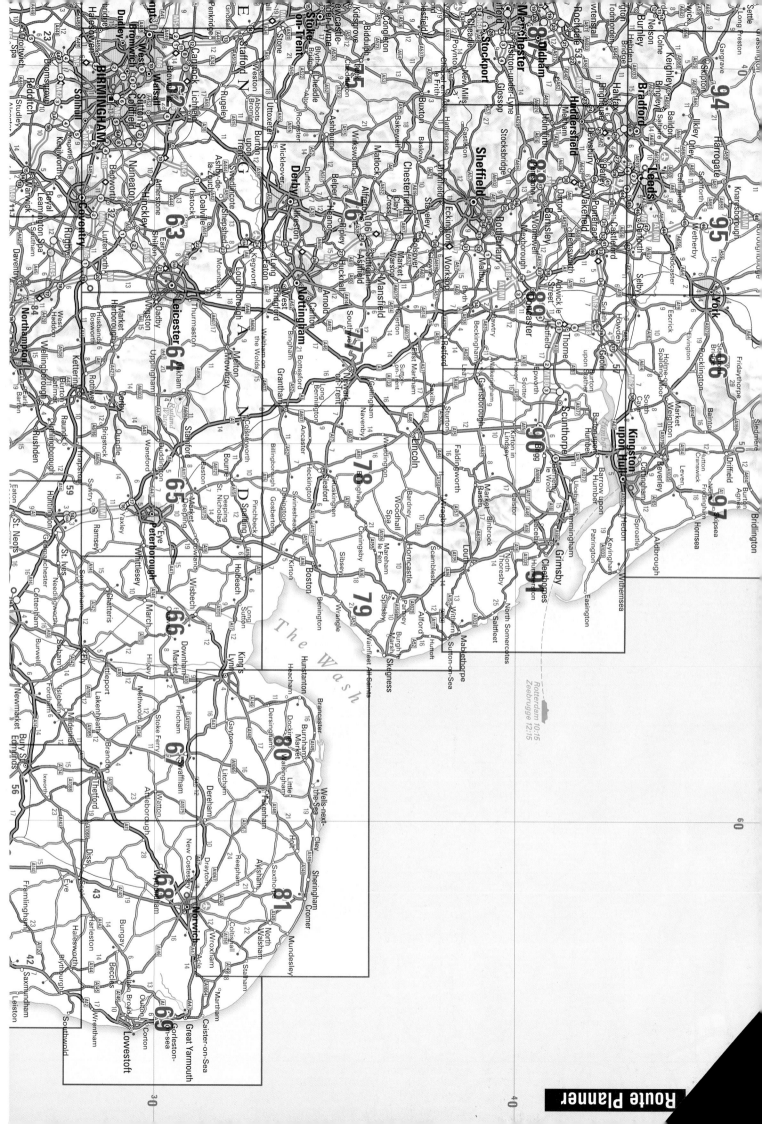

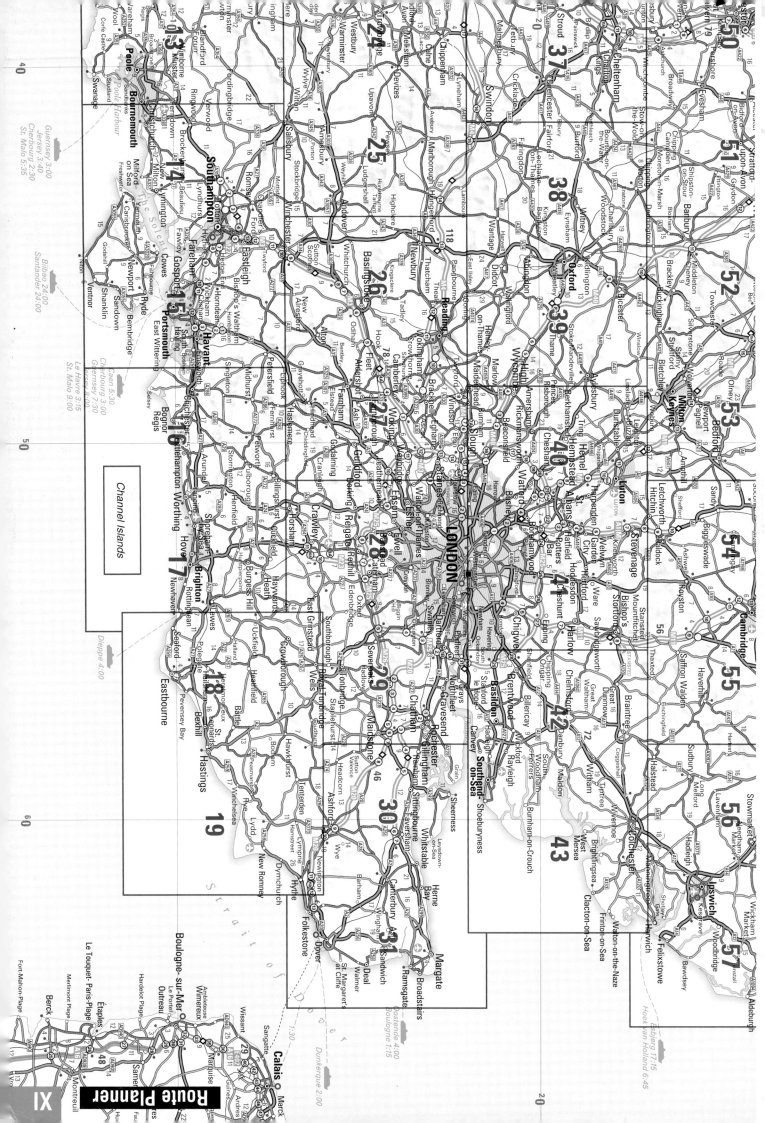

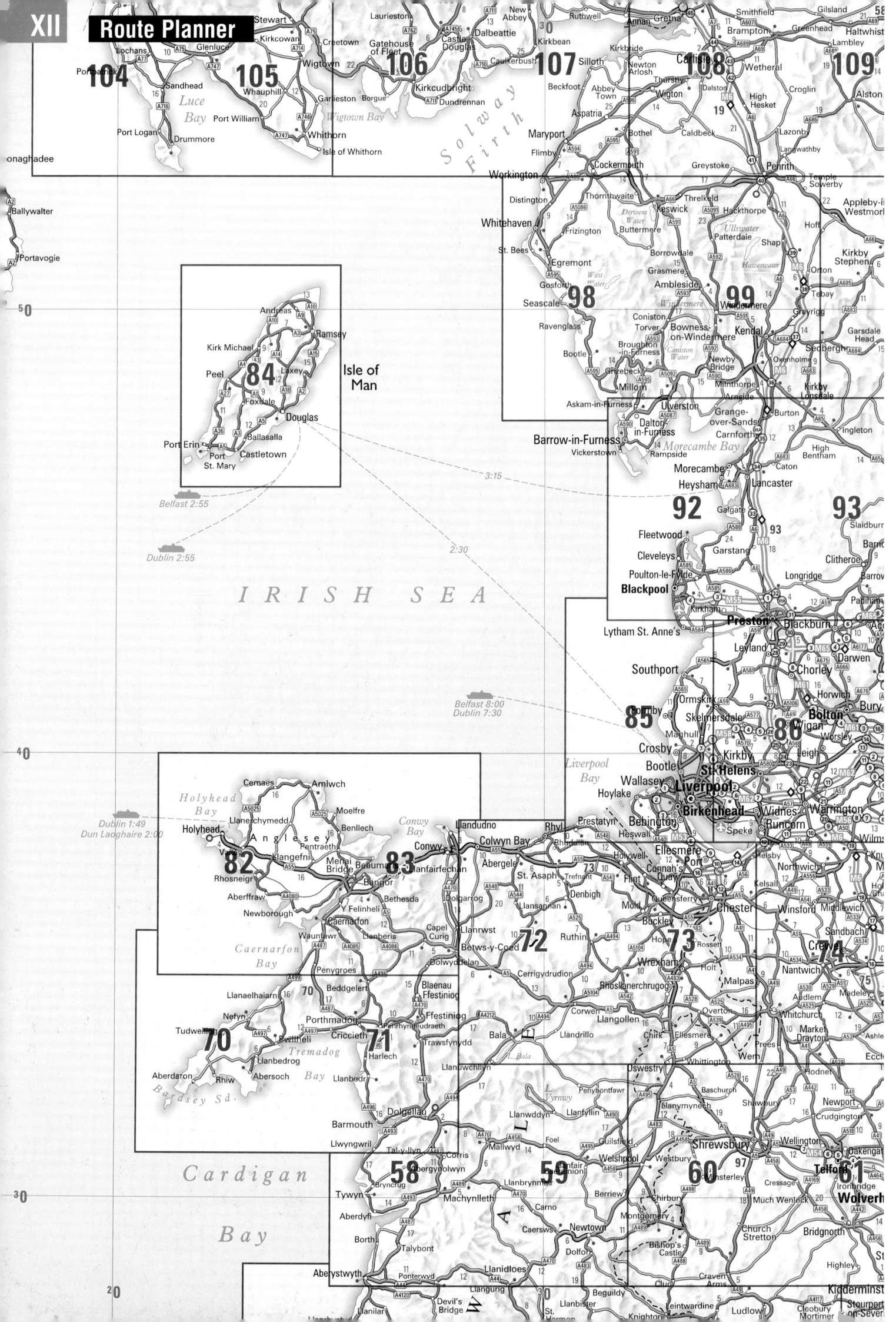

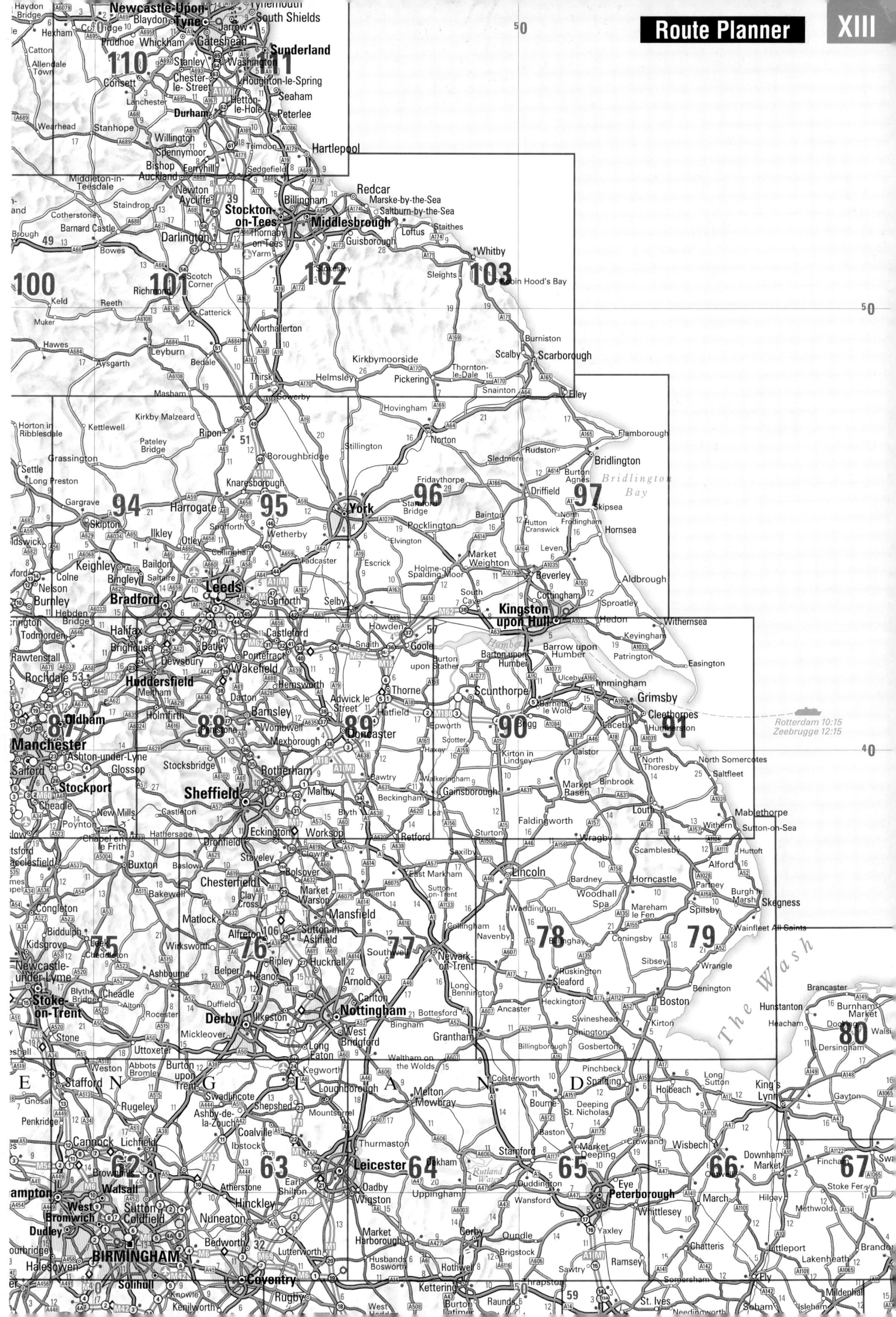

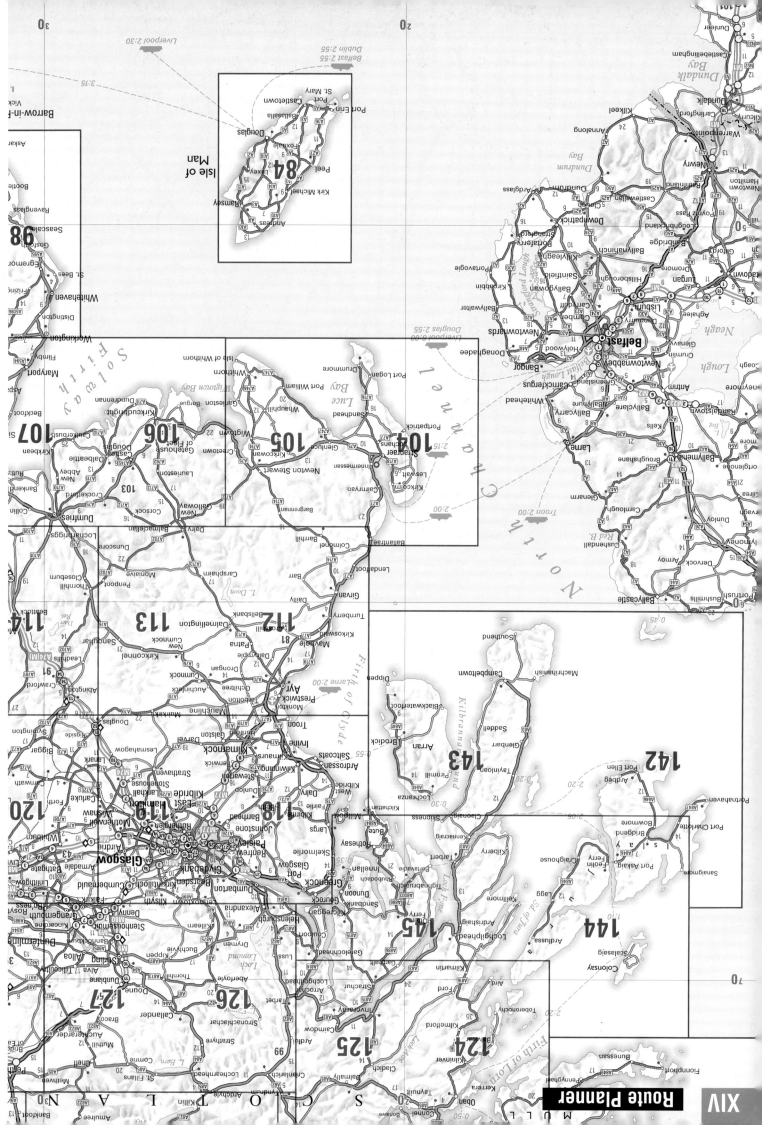

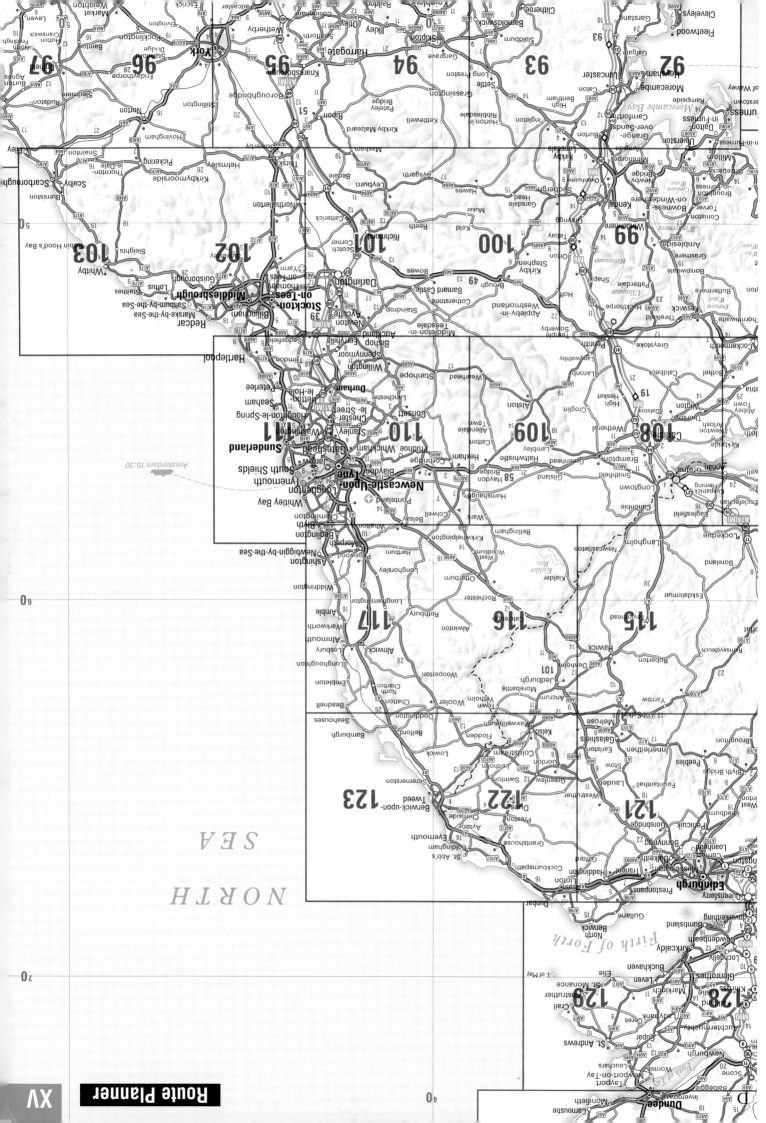

XV

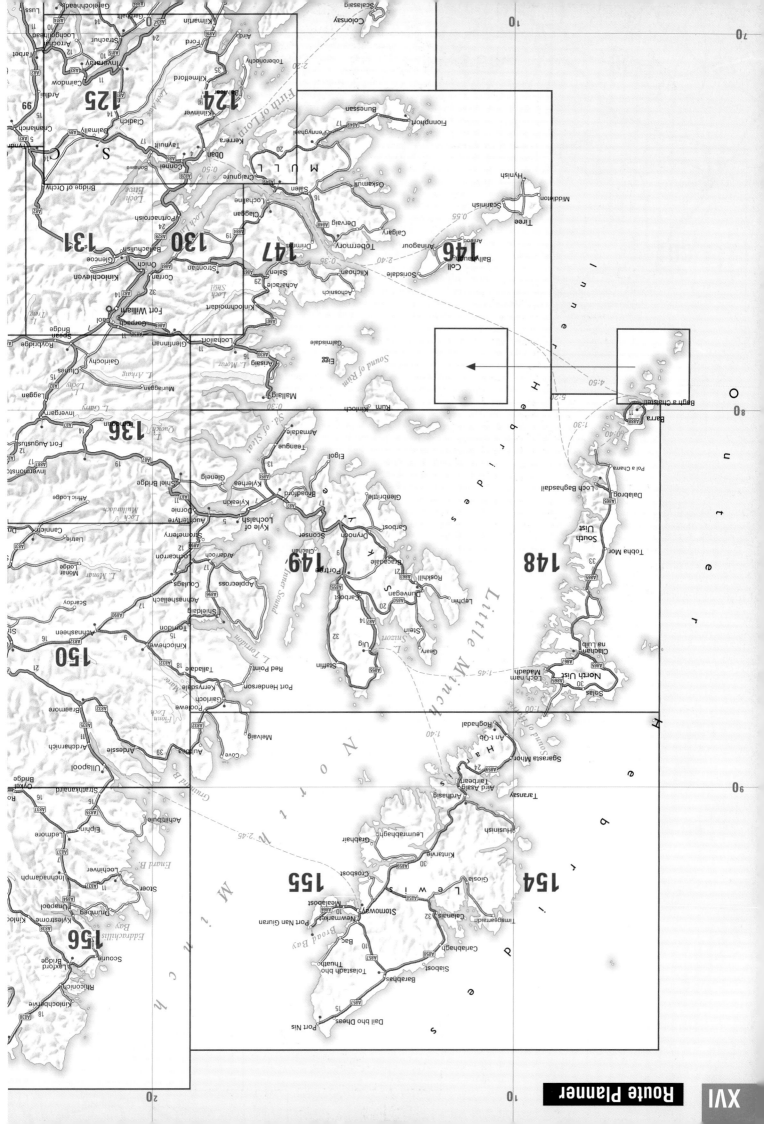

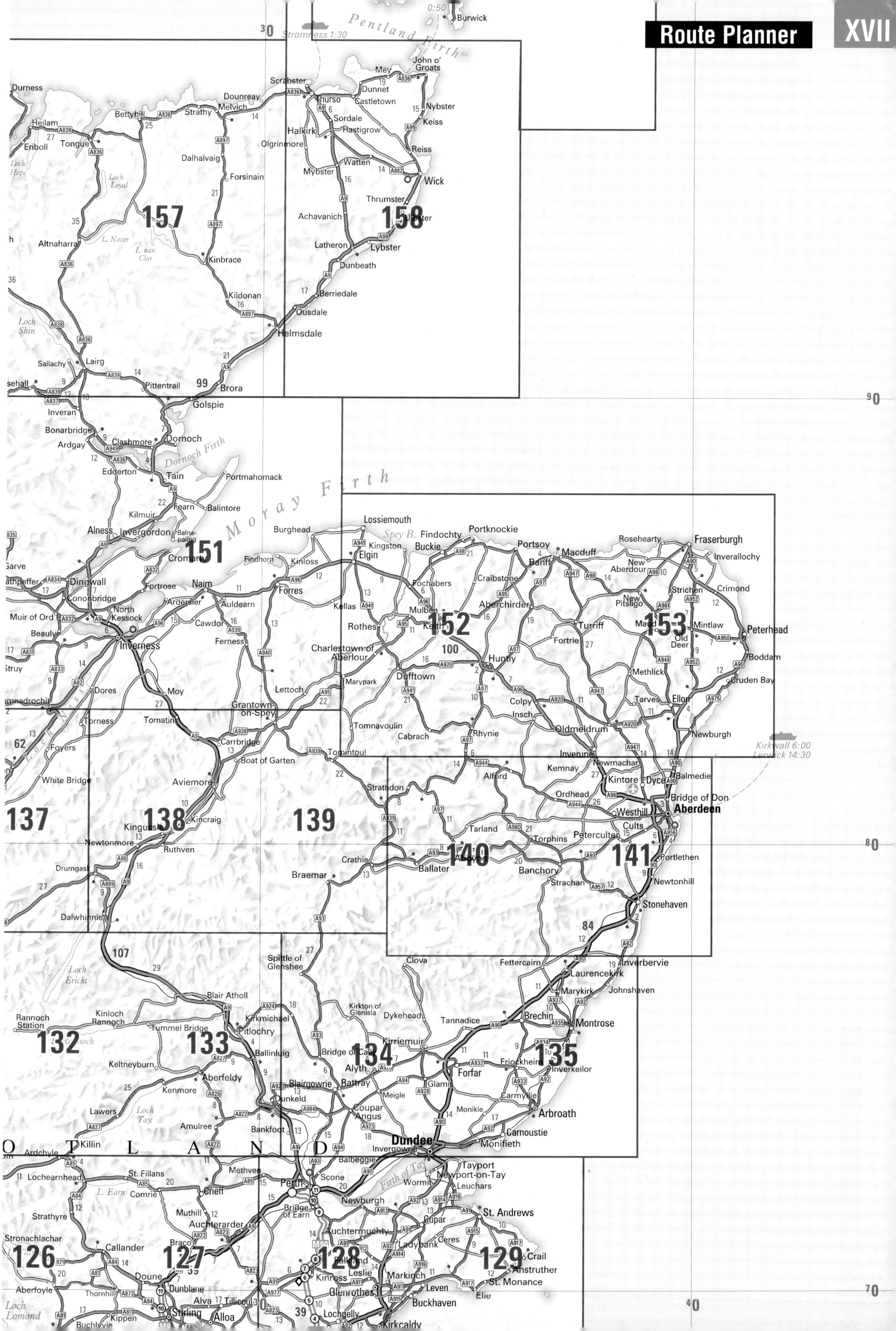
Pentland Firth
Stromness 1:30
Burwick
John o' Groats
Mey
Dunnet
Scrabster
Thurso
Castletown
Nybster
Keiss
Reiss
Wick
Durness
Dounreay
Melvich
Strathy
Bettyhill
Heilam
Tongue
Eriboll
Halkirk
Hastigrow
Sordale
Olgrinmore
Watten
Mybster
Dalhalvaig
Forsinain
Thrumster
157
158
Achavanich
Altnaharra
L. Naver
Loch Loyal
Kinbrace
Latheron
Lybster
Dunbeath
Berriedale
Kildonan
Ousdale
Helmsdale
Loch Shin
Sallachy
Lairg
Pittentrail
Brora
Golspie
Inveran
Bonarbridge
Ardgay
Clashmore
Dornoch
Dornoch Firth
Edderton
Tain
Portmahomack
Moray Firth
Fearn
Balintore
Kilmuir
Alness
Invergordon
Cromarty
151
Garve
Dingwall
Conon Bridge
Fortrose
North Kessock
Muir of Ord
Beauly
Inverness
Nairn
Ardersier
Auldearn
Cawdor
Ferness
Findhorn
Kinloss
Burghead
Forres
Lossiemouth
Elgin
Kingston
Spey B.
Findochty
Buckie
Portknockie
Portsoy
Macduff
Banff
Rosehearty
Fraserburgh
Inverallochy
New Aberdour
Crimond
Strichen
New Pitsligo
Fochabers
Craibstone
Aberchirder
Mulben
Keith
152
Kellas
Rothes
Charlestown-of-Aberlour
Maud
153
Mintlaw
Old Deer
Peterhead
Turriff
Fortrie
Huntly
Boddam
Methlick
Cruden Bay
Dufftown
Marypark
Lettoch
Dores
Moy
Tomatin
Grantown-on-Spey
Carrbridge
Boat of Garten
Tomintoul
Tomnavoulin
Cabrach
Rhynie
Colpy
Insch
Oldmeldrum
Tarves
Ellon
Newburgh
Kirkwall 6:00
Lerwick 14:30
Foyers
White Bridge
Aviemore
Kincraig
Kingussie
Newtonmore
Ruthven
137
138
139
Strathdon
Alford
Kemnay
Inverurie
Newmachar
Kintore
Dyce
Balmedie
Ordhead
Bridge of Don
Westhill
Aberdeen
Cults
Tarland
Torphins
Peterculter
Crathie
Ballater
Aboyne
140
Banchory
141
Portlethen
Braemar
Drumgask
Strachan
Newtonhill
Stonehaven
Dalwhinnie
Fettercairn
Inverbervie
Laurencekirk
Marykirk
Johnshaven
Spittle of Glenshee
Clova
Loch Ericht
Blair Atholl
Kirkton of Glenisla
Dykehead
Tannadice
Brechin
Montrose
Rannoch Station
Kinloch Rannoch
Tummel Bridge
Kirkmichael
Pitlochry
132
133
134
135
Kirriemuir
Bridge of Cally
Alyth
Friockheim
Inverkeilor
Ballinluig
Keltneyburn
Aberfeldy
Kenmore
Blairgowrie
Rattray
Glamis
Forfar
Carmyllie
Arbroath
Lawers
Loch Tay
Dunkeld
Meigle
Coupar Angus
Monikie
Amulree
Bankfoot
Carnoustie
Killin
SCOTLAND
Dundee
Invergowrie
Monifieth
Ardchyle
Balbeggie
Tayport
Newport-on-Tay
Firth of Tay
Wormit
Leuchars
Lochearnhead
St. Fillans
Methven
Perth
Scone
L. Earn
Comrie
Crieff
Newburgh
St. Andrews
Strathyre
Muthill
Bridge of Earn
Cupar
Auchterarder
Auchtermuchty
Ceres
Stronachlachar
Callander
Braco
Ladybank
Crail
126
127
128
129
Falkland
Markinch
Anstruther
Doune
Kinross
Leslie
St. Monance
Aberfoyle
Thornhill
Dunblane
Glenrothes
Leven
Elie
Loch Lomond
Alva
Tillicoultry
Buckhaven
Buchlyvie
Kippen
Stirling
Alloa
Lochgelly
Kirkcaldy

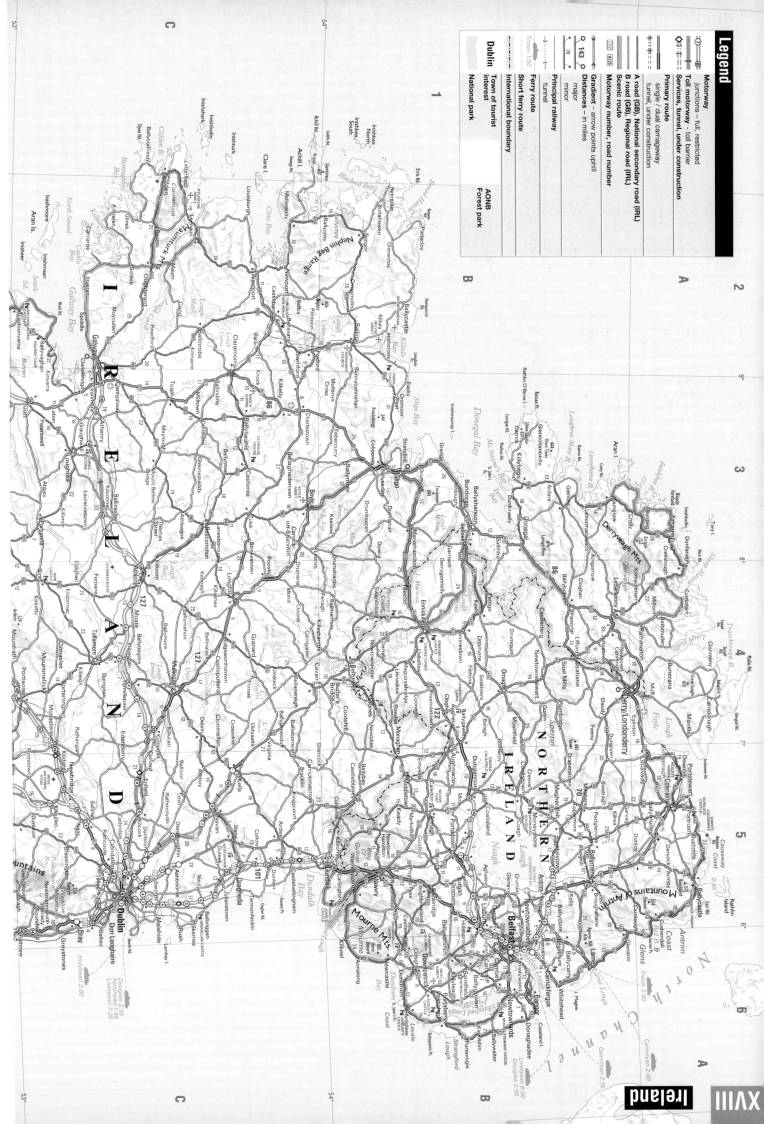

Scale ● 1 : 1 280 000

1 cm = 12.8 km   1 inch = 20 miles

0 10 20 30 40 50 km

0 10 20 30 miles

Distance table

How to use this table

Distances are shown in miles and kilometres with estimated journey times in hours and minutes.

For example: the distance between Dover and Fishguard is 331 miles or 533 kilometres with an estimated journey time of 6 hours, 20 minutes.

Estimated driving times are based on an average speed of 60mph on Motorways and 40mph on other roads. Drivers should allow extra time when driving at peak periods or through areas likely to be congested.

Worked example (upper-right sample block):

	Dover	Dundee	Edinburgh	Exeter	Fishguard
Dover					
Dundee	523 / 842 / 9:10				
Edinburgh	56 / 90 / 1:30	462 / 744 / 8:10			
Exeter	450 / 724 / 8:00	518 / 834 / 9:10	248 / 399 / 4:40		
Fishguard	230 / 370 / 4:30	399 / 642 / 7:30	460 / 740 / 8:30	331 / 533 / 6:20	
Fort William	486 / 782 / 9:30	560 / 901 / 10:20	144 / 232 / 3:30	127 / 204 / 3:10	596 / 959 / 11:00

Supporting

THINK!

Travel safe – Don't drive tired

(Map of Great Britain showing cities: John o' Groats, Kyle of Lochalsh, Inverness, Aberdeen, Braemar, Fort William, Dundee, Oban, Edinburgh, Glasgow, Ayr, Berwick-upon-Tweed, Stranraer, Carlisle, Newcastle upon Tyne, York, Leeds, Kingston upon Hull, Blackpool, Manchester, Doncaster, Liverpool, Sheffield, Lincoln, Holyhead, Nottingham, Leicester, Norwich, Great Yarmouth, Shrewsbury, Birmingham, Aberystwyth, Cambridge, Fishguard, Gloucester, Oxford, Harwich, Swansea, Cardiff, Bristol, London, Exeter, Bournemouth, Southampton, Portsmouth, Brighton, Dover, Plymouth, Land's End)

The full distance matrix lists every pair of the following locations, each cell showing miles / kilometres / hours:minutes —

London, Aberdeen, Aberystwyth, Ayr, Berwick-upon-Tweed, Birmingham, Blackpool, Bournemouth, Braemar, Brighton, Bristol, Cambridge, Cardiff, Carlisle, Doncaster, Dover, Dundee, Edinburgh, Exeter, Fishguard, Fort William, Glasgow, Gloucester, Great Yarmouth, Harwich, Holyhead, Inverness, John o' Groats, Kingston upon Hull, Kyle of Lochalsh, Land's End, Leeds, Leicester, Lincoln, Liverpool, Manchester, Newcastle upon Tyne, Norwich, Nottingham, Oban, Oxford, Plymouth, Portsmouth, Sheffield, Shrewsbury, Southampton, Stranraer, Swansea, York.

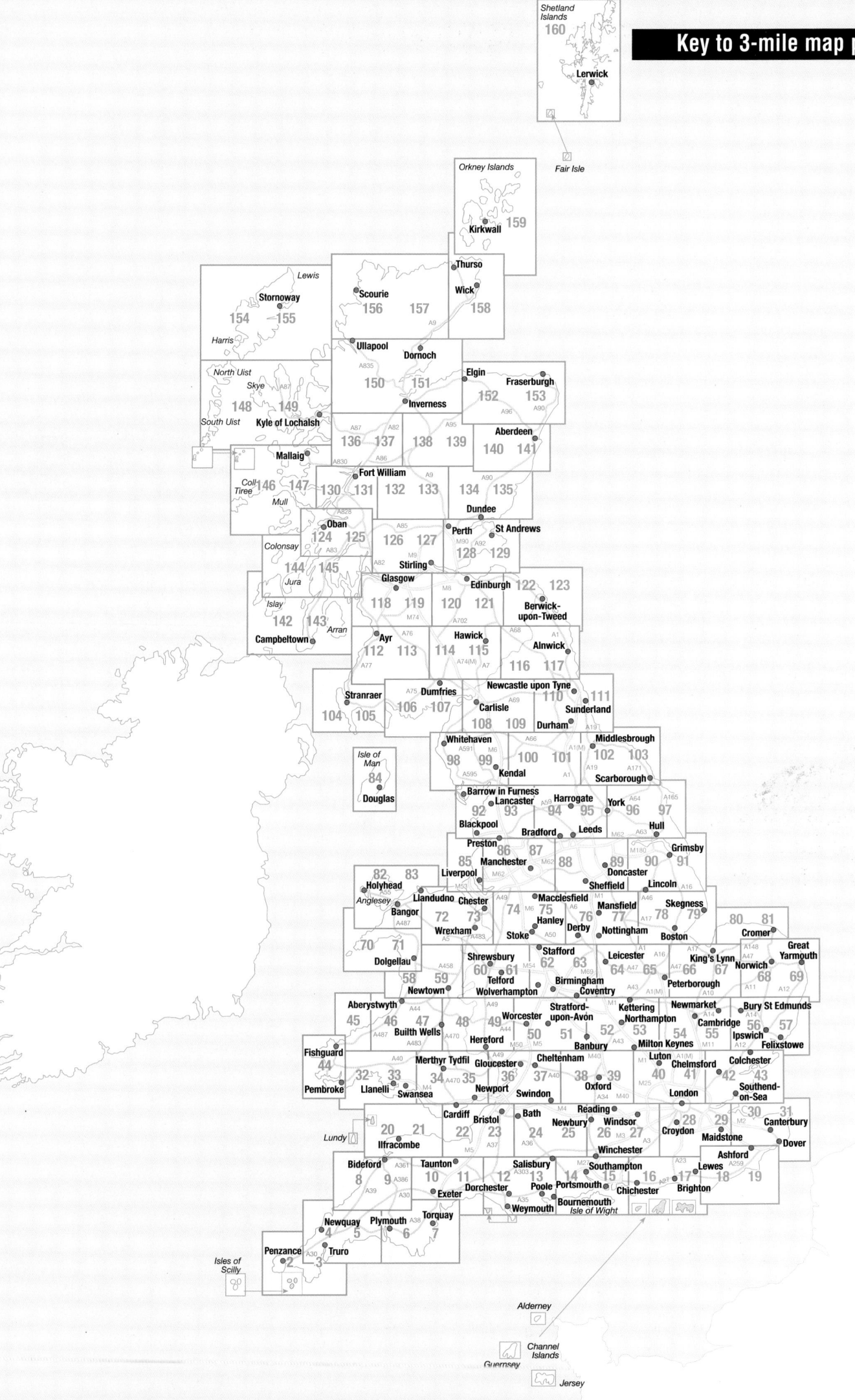

Shetland Islands
160
Lerwick

Orkney Islands
159
Kirkwall

Fair Isle

Thurso
Wick
Scourie
156 157 158

Lewis
Stornoway
154 155
Harris

Ullapool
Dornoch
150 151

Elgin
Fraserburgh
152 153

North Uist
Skye
148 149
South Uist
Kyle of Lochalsh

Inverness

Aberdeen
140 141

136 137 138 139

Mallaig
130 131 132 133 134 135
Coll
Tiree 146 147
Fort William

Mull
Dundee

Oban
124 125 126 127
Perth St Andrews
128 129

Colonsay
144 145
Stirling
Jura
Glasgow
118 119 120 121
Edinburgh 122 123

Islay
142 143
Arran
Ayr Hawick
112 113 114 115
Berwick-upon-Tweed

Campbeltown
Alnwick
116 117

Stranraer Dumfries
104 105 106 107
Carlisle
Newcastle upon Tyne
110 111
Sunderland

Isle of Man
84
Douglas

Whitehaven Middlesbrough
98 99 100 101 102 103
Kendal Scarborough

Barrow in Furness Harrogate York
92 93 94 95 96 97
Blackpool Leeds Hull

Preston 86 87
85 Manchester 88 89 90 91
Liverpool Sheffield Doncaster Grimsby
Lincoln

Bradford

82 83
Holyhead
Anglesey Llandudno
72 73 74 75 76 77 78 79
Bangor Chester Macclesfield Mansfield Skegness
Wrexham Hanley Derby Nottingham Boston
70 71 Stoke 80 81
Dolgellau Cromer

Stafford Leicester
58 59 60 61 62 63 64 65 66 67 68 69
Newtown Telford Birmingham Peterborough King's Lynn Norwich Great Yarmouth
Wolverhampton Coventry

Aberystwyth Worcester Stratford-upon-Avon Kettering Newmarket Bury St Edmunds
45 46 47 48 49 50 51 52 53 54 55 56 57
Builth Wells Northampton Cambridge Ipswich Felixstowe
Hereford Banbury Milton Keynes

Fishguard Merthyr Tydfil Cheltenham Luton Colchester
44 32 33 34 35 36 37 38 39 40 41 42 43
Pembroke Llanelli Gloucester Oxford London Southend-on-Sea
Newport Swindon Chelmsford
Swansea Maidstone

Cardiff Bath Reading Windsor Croydon Canterbury
20 21 22 23 24 25 26 27 28 29 30 31
Ilfracombe Bristol Newbury Winchester Dover
Lundy

Bideford Taunton Salisbury Southampton Ashford
8 9 10 11 12 13 14 15 16 17 18 19
Dorchester Poole Portsmouth Chichester Brighton Lewes
Exeter Weymouth Bournemouth
Newquay Plymouth Torquay *Isle of Wight*
4 5 6 7

Penzance Truro
2 3
Isles of Scilly

Alderney

Channel Islands
Guernsey
Jersey

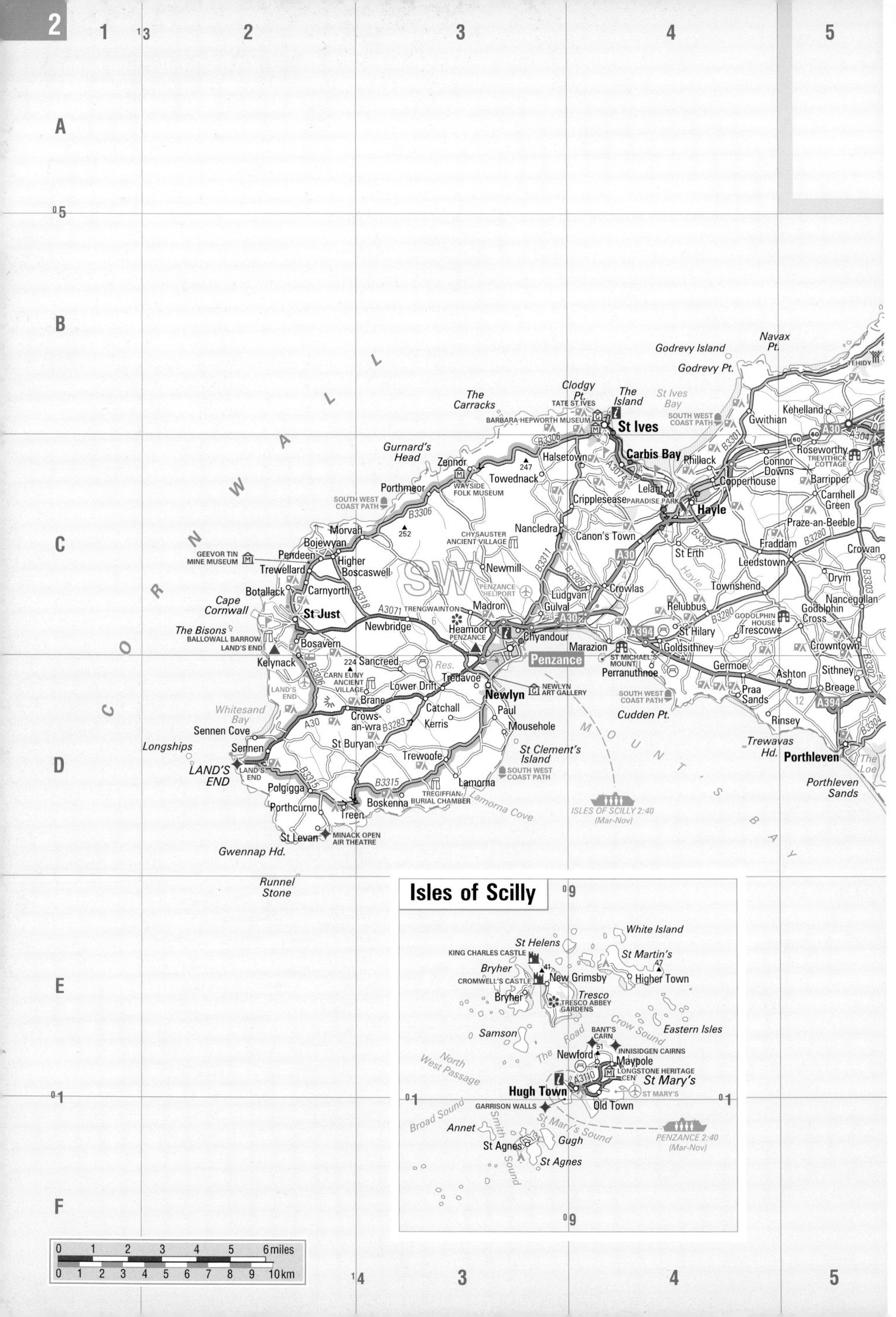

A

B

C

D

E

F

5

1

Isles of Scilly

9

St Helens

White Island

KING CHARLES CASTLE

St Martin's

Bryher

41

Higher Town

CROMWELL'S CASTLE

New Grimsby

Bryher

Tresco
TRESCO ABBEY
GARDENS

Samson

Crow Sound

Eastern Isles

North
West
Passage

The Road

BANT'S
CARN

Newford

51

INNISIDGEN CAIRNS

Maypole

LONGSTONE HERITAGE
CEN

St Mary's

Hugh Town

A3110

ST MARY'S

Old Town

GARRISON WALLS

Broad Sound

St Mary's Sound

PENZANCE 2:40
(Mar-Nov)

Annet

Smith
Sound

Gugh

St Agnes

St Agnes

9

1

CORNWALL

Navax
Pt.

Godrevy Island

Godrevy Pt.

TEHIDY

The Carracks

Clodgy
Pt.
TATE ST IVES

The
Island

St Ives
Bay

BARBARA HEPWORTH MUSEUM

St Ives

SOUTH WEST
COAST PATH

Gwithian

Gurnard's
Head

Zennor

B3306

247

Halsetown

Carbis Bay

Phillack

Kehelland

Roseworthy

A30

A3047

Porthmeor

WAYSIDE
FOLK MUSEUM

Towednack

Lelant

PARADISE PARK

Copperhouse

Connor
Downs

TREVITHICK
COTTAGE

Barripper

60

B3301

B3306

Cripplesease

Hayle

Carnhell
Green

Morvah

252

CHYSAUSTER
ANCIENT VILLAGE

Nancledra

Canon's Town

B3302

Praze-an-Beeble

Bojewyan

Higher
Boscaswell

Newmill

B3311

SW

St Erth

Fraddam

Crowan

Pendeen

GEEVOR TIN
MINE MUSEUM

Trewellard

PENZANCE
HELIPORT

Ludgvan

Crowlas

Leedstown

Townshend

Drym

B3280

B3303

Botallack

Carnyorth

Cape
Cornwall

TRENGWAINTON

Madron

Gulval

A30

Relubbus

GODOLPHIN
HOUSE

Godolphin
Cross

Nancegollan

The Bisons
BALLOWALL BARROW
LAND'S END

St Just

A3071

Newbridge

Heamoor
PENZANCE

Chyandour

A394

St Hilary

Trescowe

Growntown

Bosavern

224

Sancreed

Res.

Penzance

Marazion

ST MICHAEL'S
MOUNT

Goldsithney

Germoe

Ashton

Sithney

Kelynack

CARN EUNY
ANCIENT VILLAGE

Lower Drift

Tredavoe

Perranuthnoe

Praa
Sands

Breage

12

A394

LAND'S
END

Brane

Catchall

Newlyn

NEWLYN
ART GALLERY

SOUTH WEST
COAST PATH

Rinsey

B3304

Whitesand
Bay

A30

Crows-
an-wra

B3283

Kerris

Paul

Cudden Pt.

Trewavas
Hd.

Porthleven

Sennen Cove

St Buryan

Mousehole

MOUNT'S

The
Loe

Longships

Sennen

Trewoofe

St Clement's
Island

BAY

Porthleven
Sands

LAND'S
END

B3315

Lamorna

Porthcurno

Polgigga

B3315

Boskenna

TREGIFFIAN
BURIAL CHAMBER

SOUTH WEST
COAST PATH

Lamorna Cove

ISLES OF SCILLY 2:40
(Mar-Nov)

Treen

St Levan

MINACK OPEN
AIR THEATRE

Gwennap Hd.

Runnel
Stone

4

3

4

5

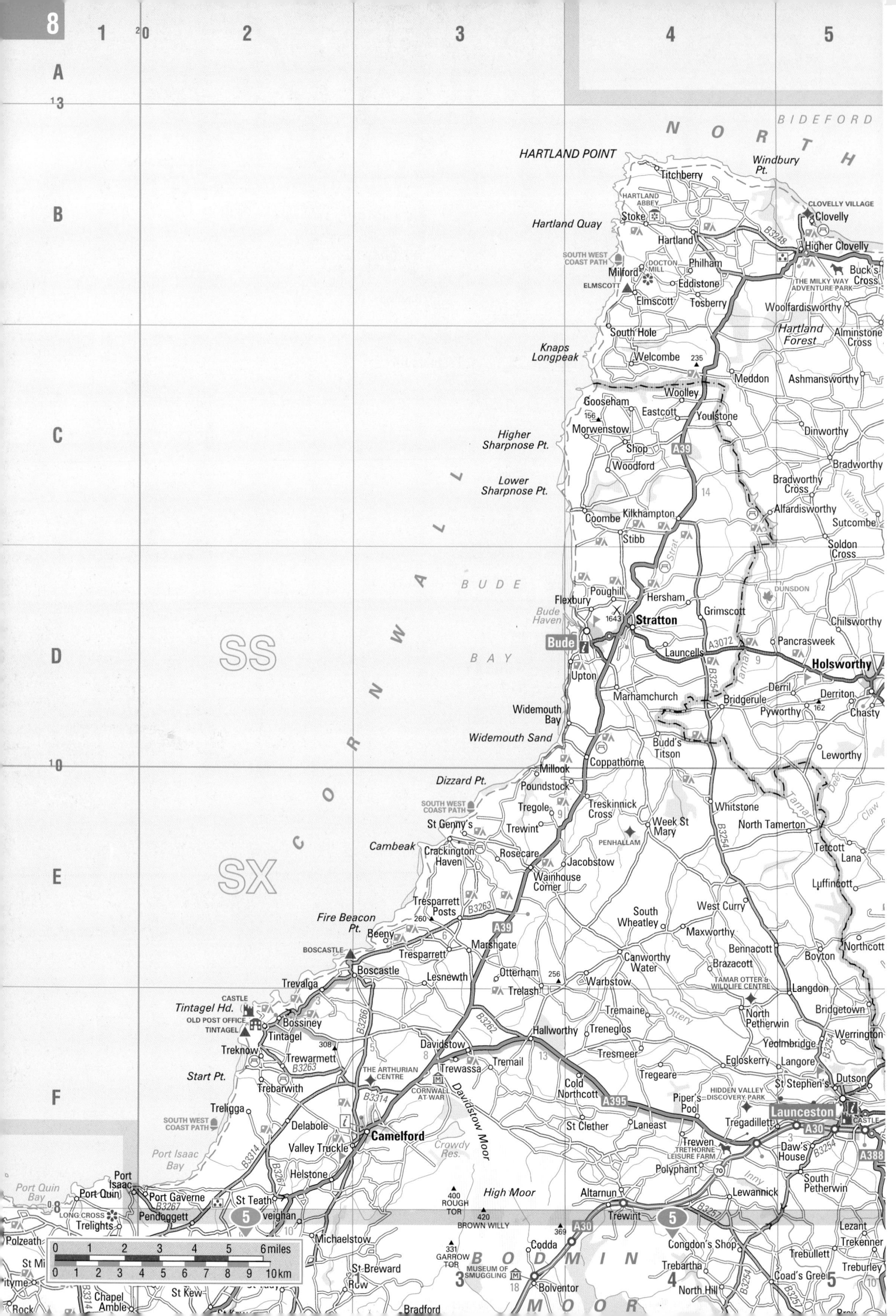

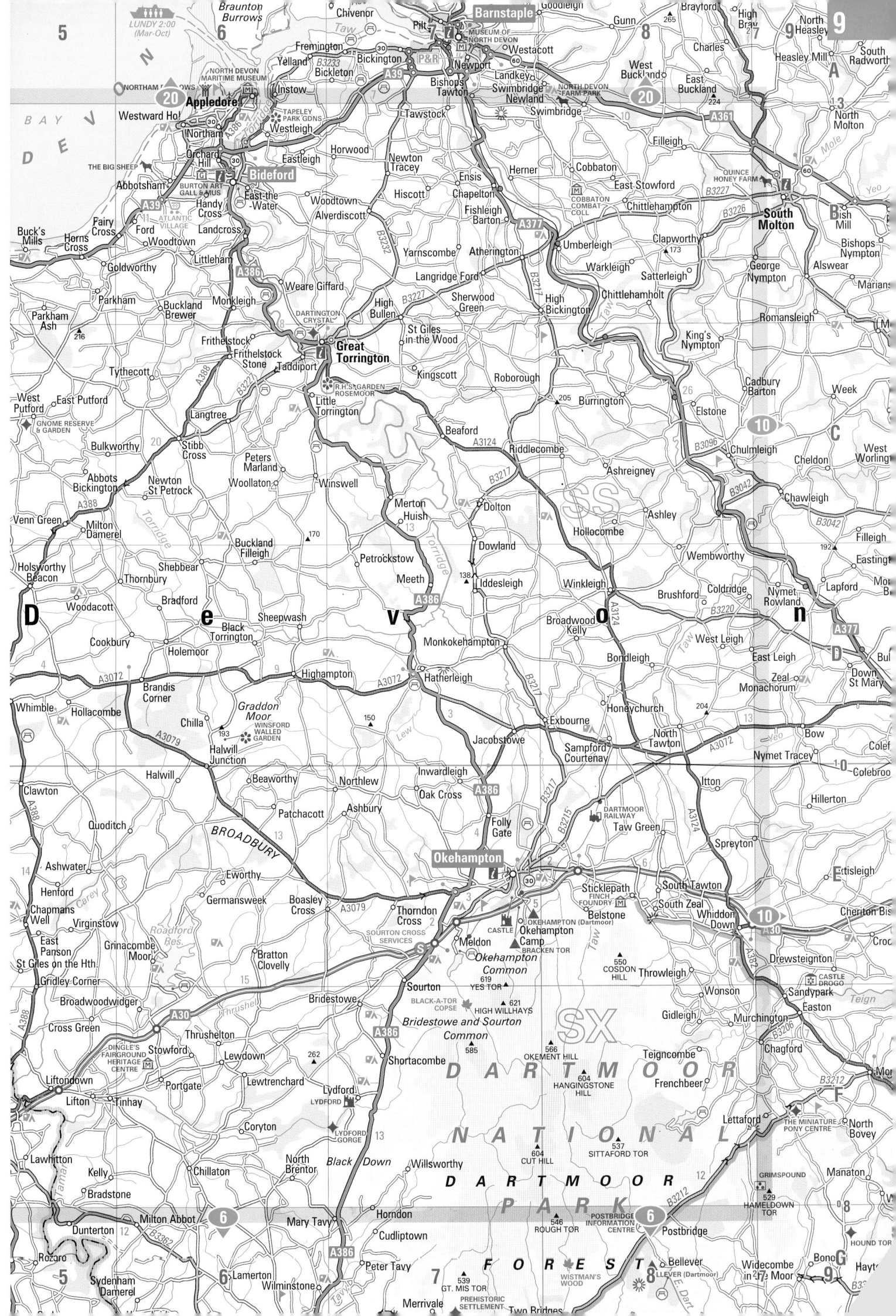

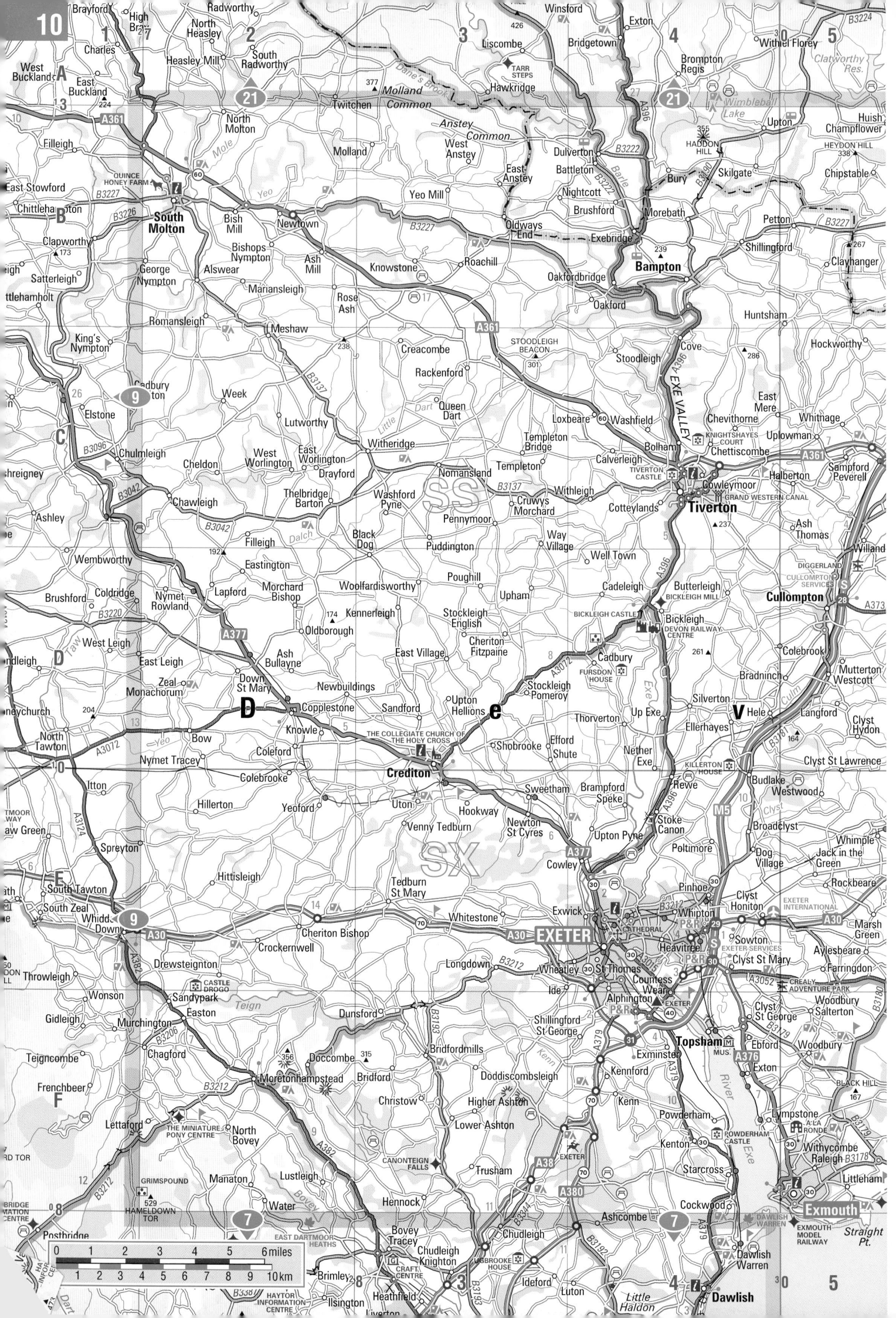

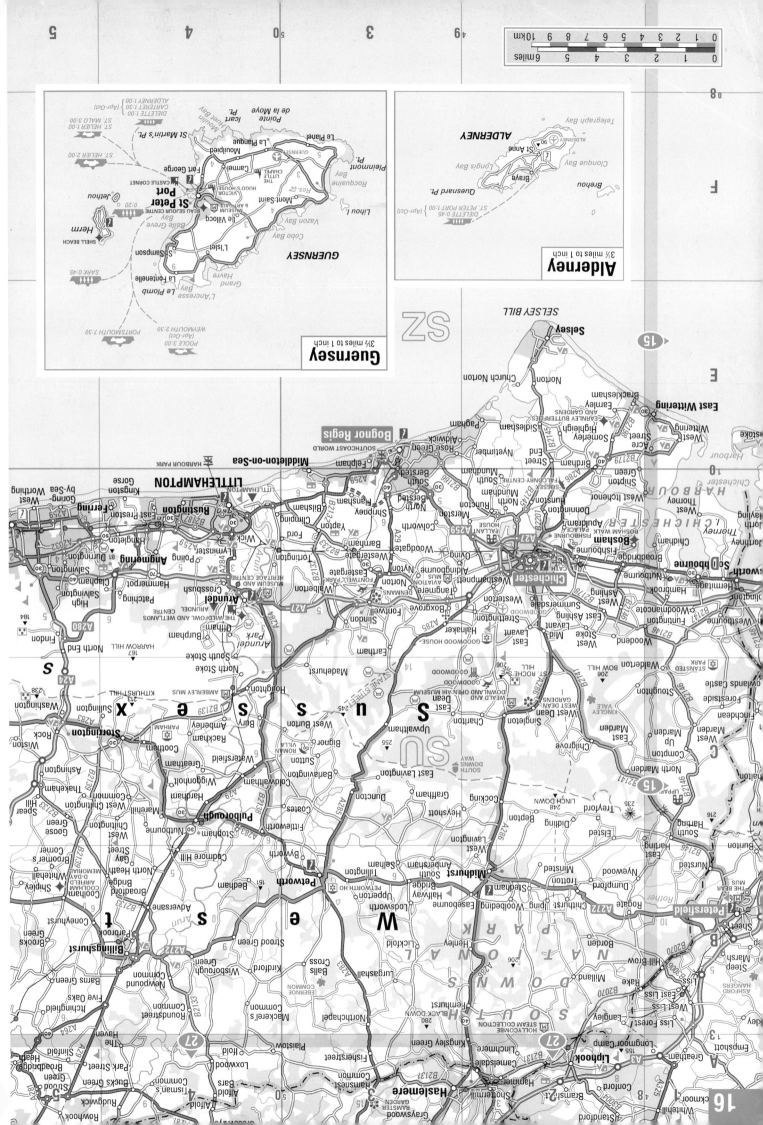

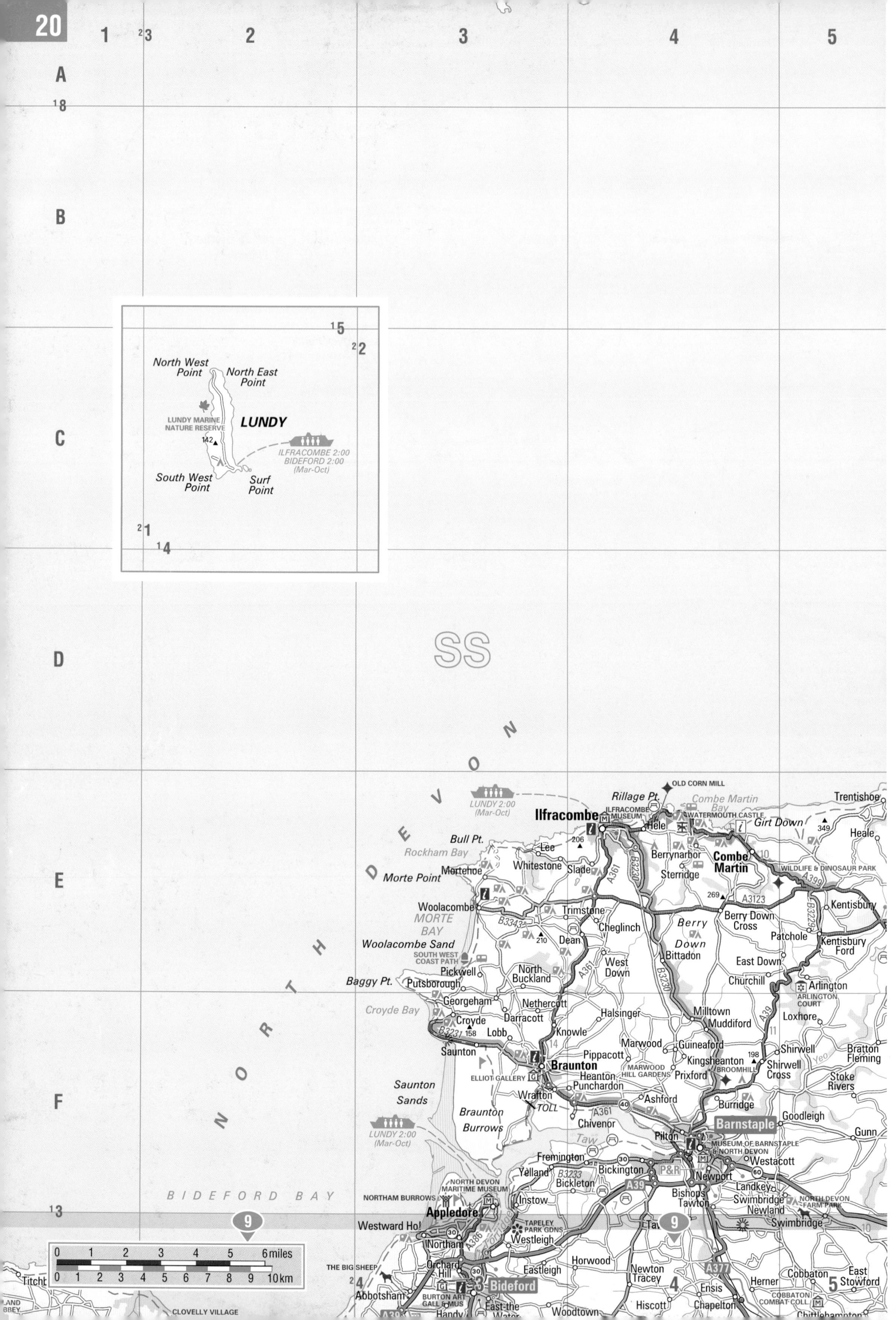

North West Point
North East Point

LUNDY

LUNDY MARINE
NATURE RESERVE

142 ▲

South West Point

Surf Point

ILFRACOMBE 2:00
BIDEFORD 2:00
(Mar-Oct)

SS

D E V O N

LUNDY 2:00
(Mar-Oct)

OLD CORN MILL

Rillage Pt.
Combe Martin Bay
Trentishoe

ILFRACOMBE MUSEUM

Ilfracombe
Hele
WATERMOUTH CASTLE

Girt Down
349 ▲
Heale

Bull Pt.

Rockham Bay
Lee
Whitestone
Slade
206 ▲
Berrynarbor
Sterridge
Combe Martin
10

WILDLIFE & DINOSAUR PARK

Mortehoe
Morte Point

A361
B3230

269 ▲
A3123
Berry Down Cross
Patchole
Kentisbury

Kentisbury Ford

Woolacombe

MORTE BAY
Trimstone
Cheglinch
Berry Down
East Down

Woolacombe Sand
210 ▲
Dean
West Down
Bittadon
Churchill

SOUTH WEST COAST PATH
Pickwell
North Buckland
✿ **Arlington**

Baggy Pt.
Putsborough
ARLINGTON COURT

Georgeham
Nethercott
Halsinger
Milltown
Muddiford
Loxhore
11

Croyde Bay
Darracott
Knowle
Marwood
Guineaford
198 ▲
Shirwell
Bratton Fleming

Croyde
B3231 158
Lobb
MARWOOD HILL GARDENS
Kingsheanton
Shirwell Cross
Stoke Rivers

Saunton
14
Pippacott
Prixford

Braunton
Heanton Punchardon
Ashford
Burridge
Goodleigh
Gunn.

ELLIOT GALLERY
Wrafton
TOLL
A361
40
Barnstaple
Westacott

Saunton Sands
Chivenor
Pilton
MUSEUM OF BARNSTAPLE & NORTH DEVON

Braunton Burrows
Taw
Fremington
Newport

LUNDY 2:00
(Mar-Oct)
Yelland
Bickleton
30
P&R
Landkey
60
NORTH DEVON FARM PARK

Instow
A39
Bishops Tawton
Swimbridge Newland

NORTH DEVON MARITIME MUSEUM

B I D E F O R D   B A Y
NORTHAM BURROWS
Swimbridge
10

13

9 ▽

Appledore
TAPELEY PARK GDNS
9

Westward Ho!
Tai.
Newton Tracey
Ensis
Herner
Cobbaton

30
Northam
Westleigh
A39
A377

LAND ABBEY

THE BIG SHEEP
Orchard Hill
Eastleigh
Horwood
Cobbaton COMBAT COLL
East Stowford

0 1 2 3 4 5 6 miles
0 1 2 3 4 5 6 7 8 9 10km

Titch.
Abbotsham
BURTON ART GALL & MUS
Bideford
Handy
Woodtown
Hiscott
Chapelton

CLOVELLY VILLAGE
East the Water
A377
Chitt

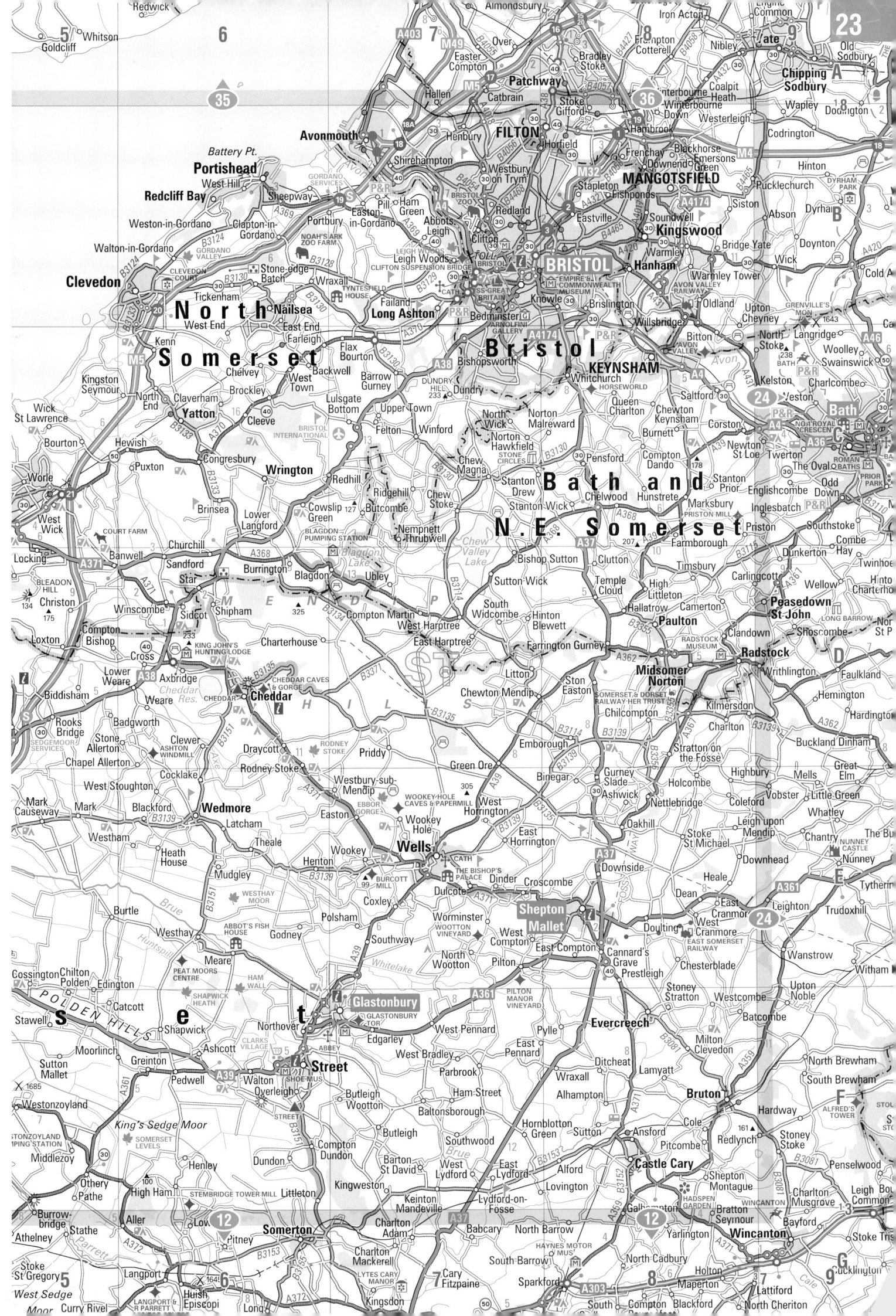

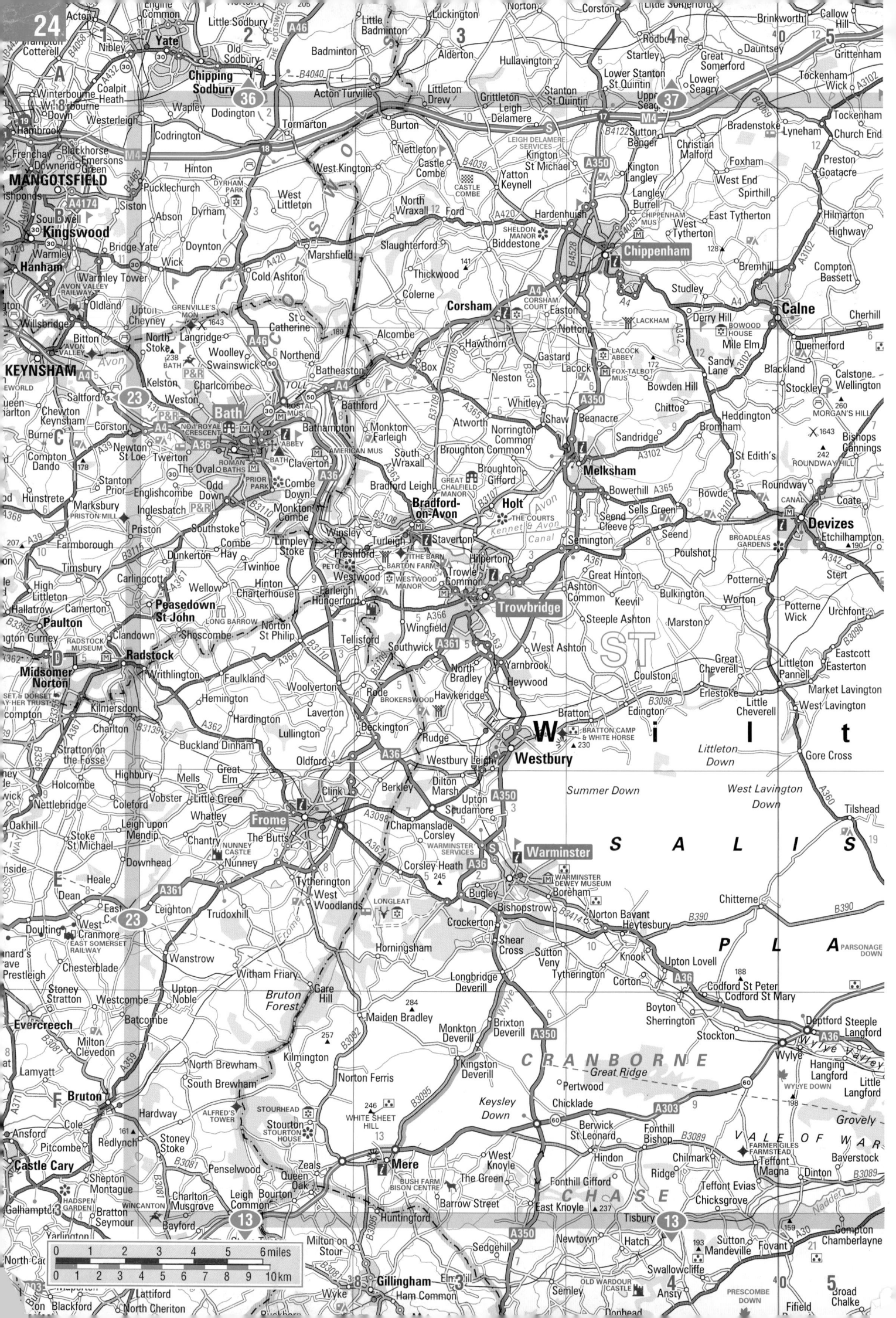

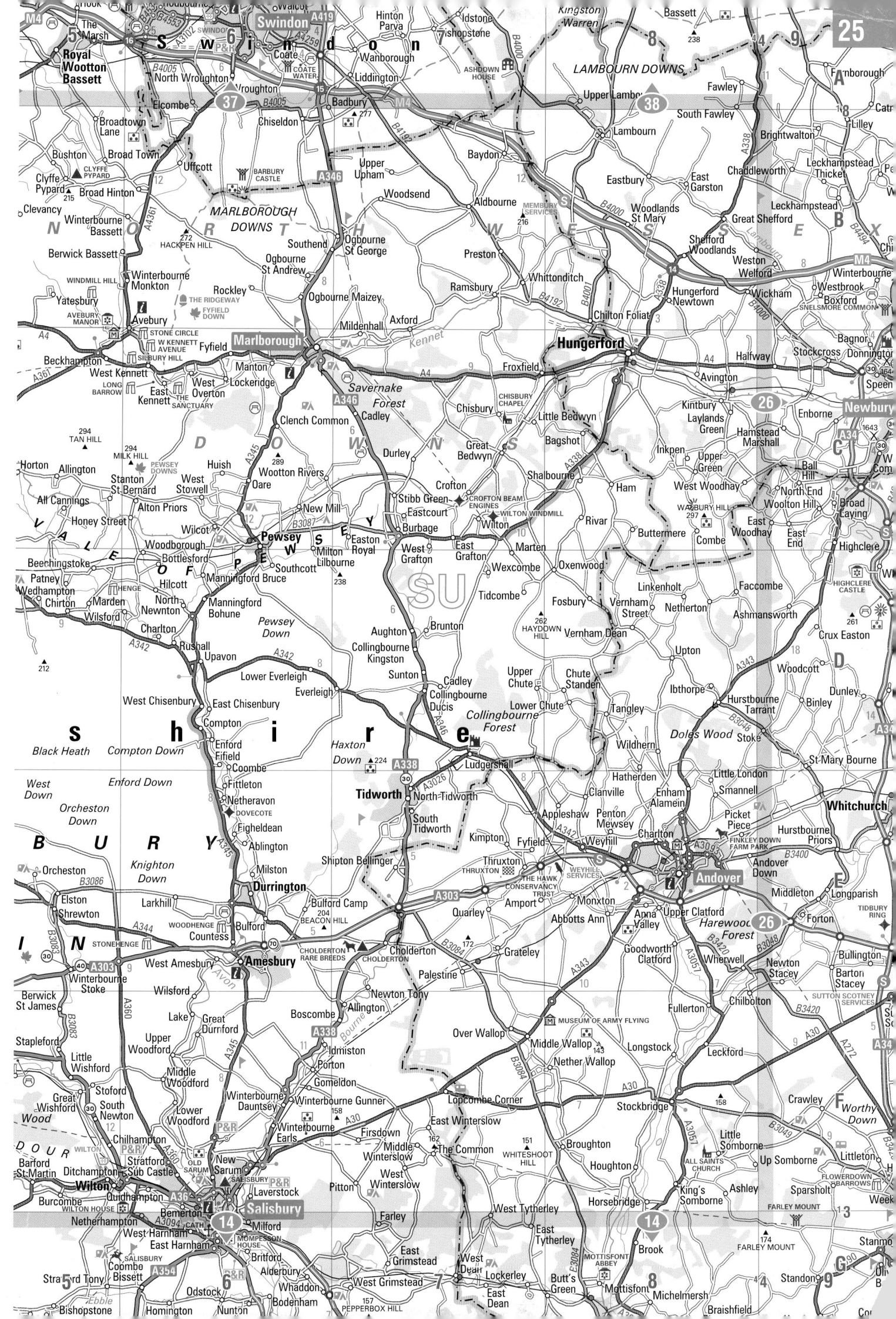

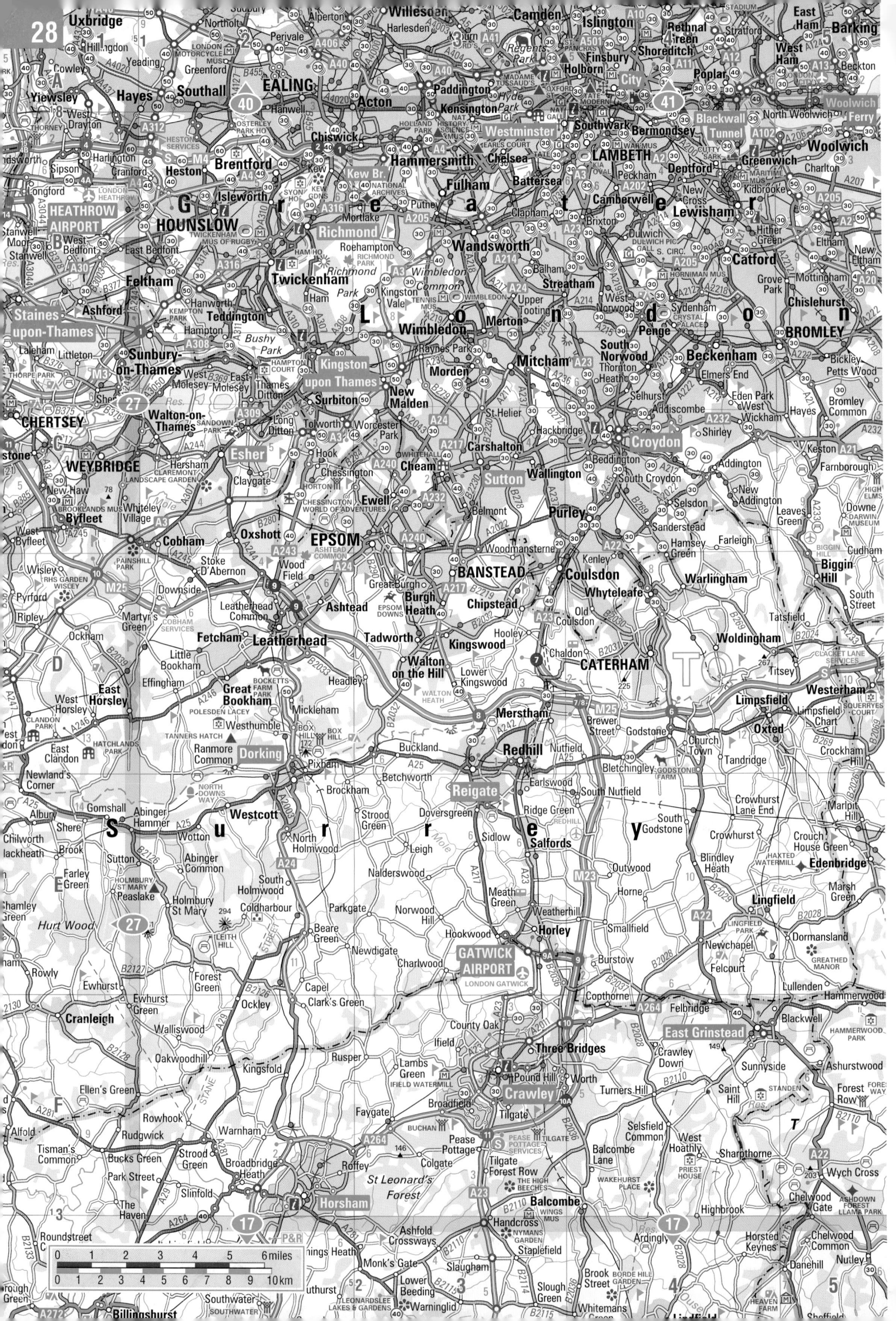

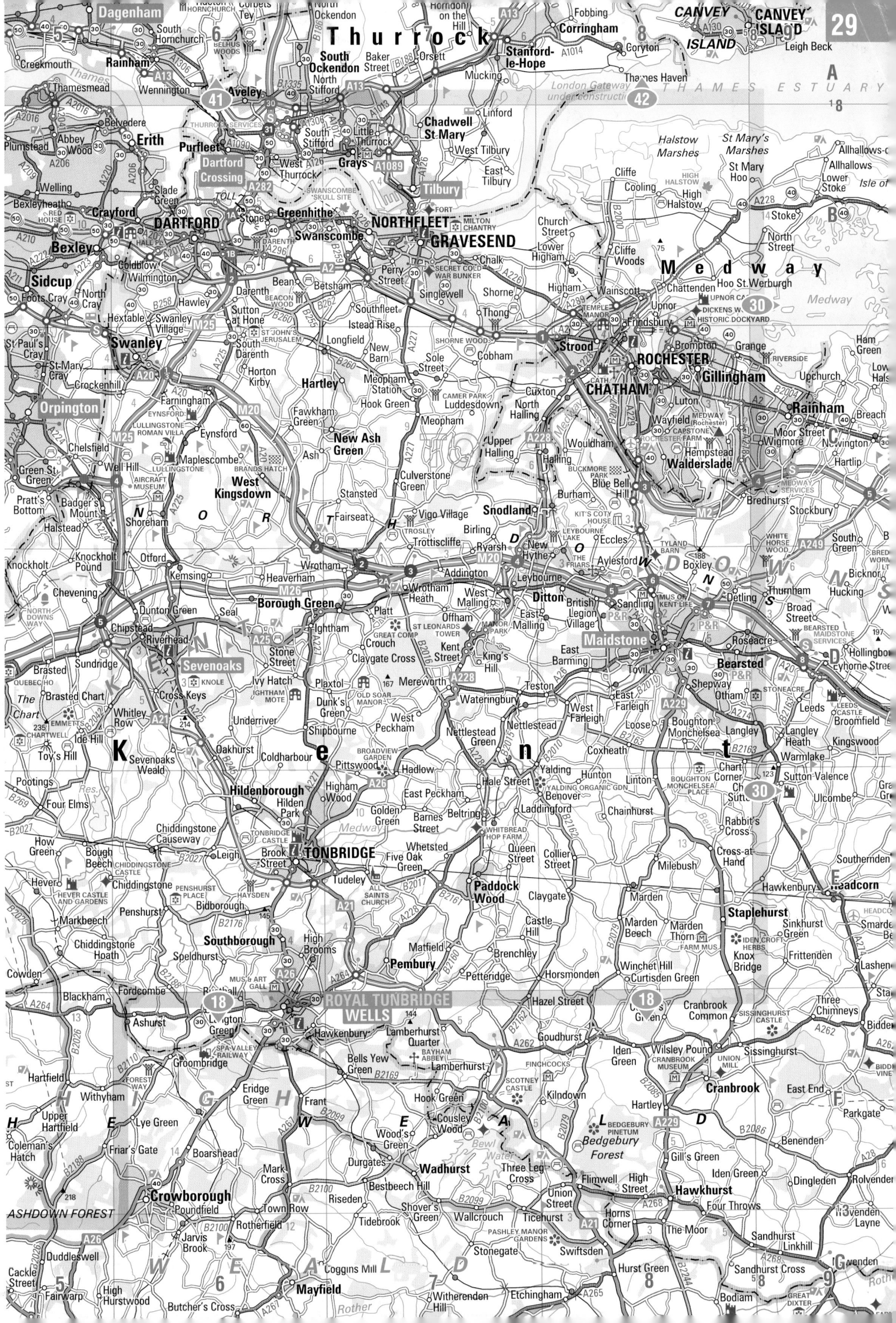

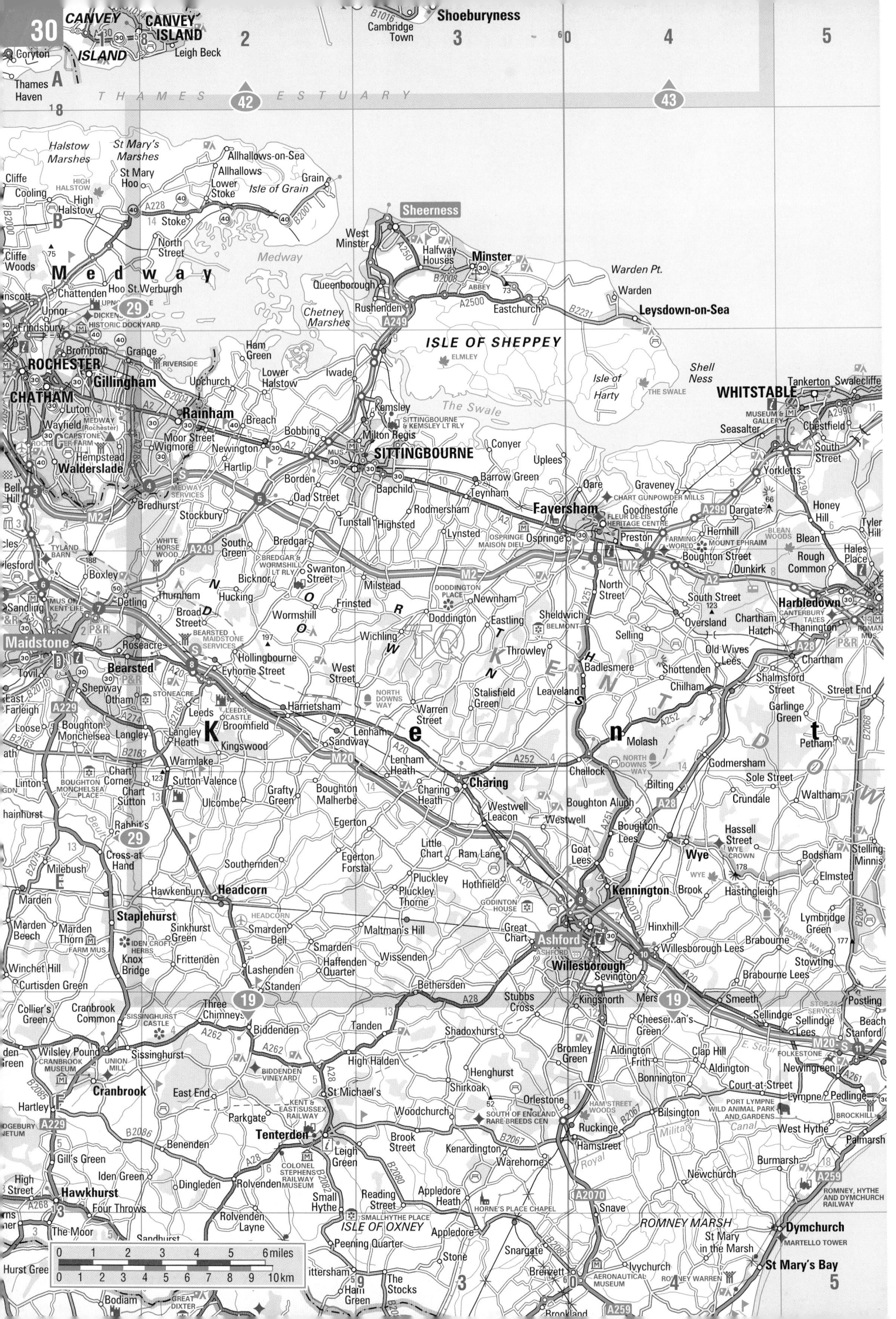

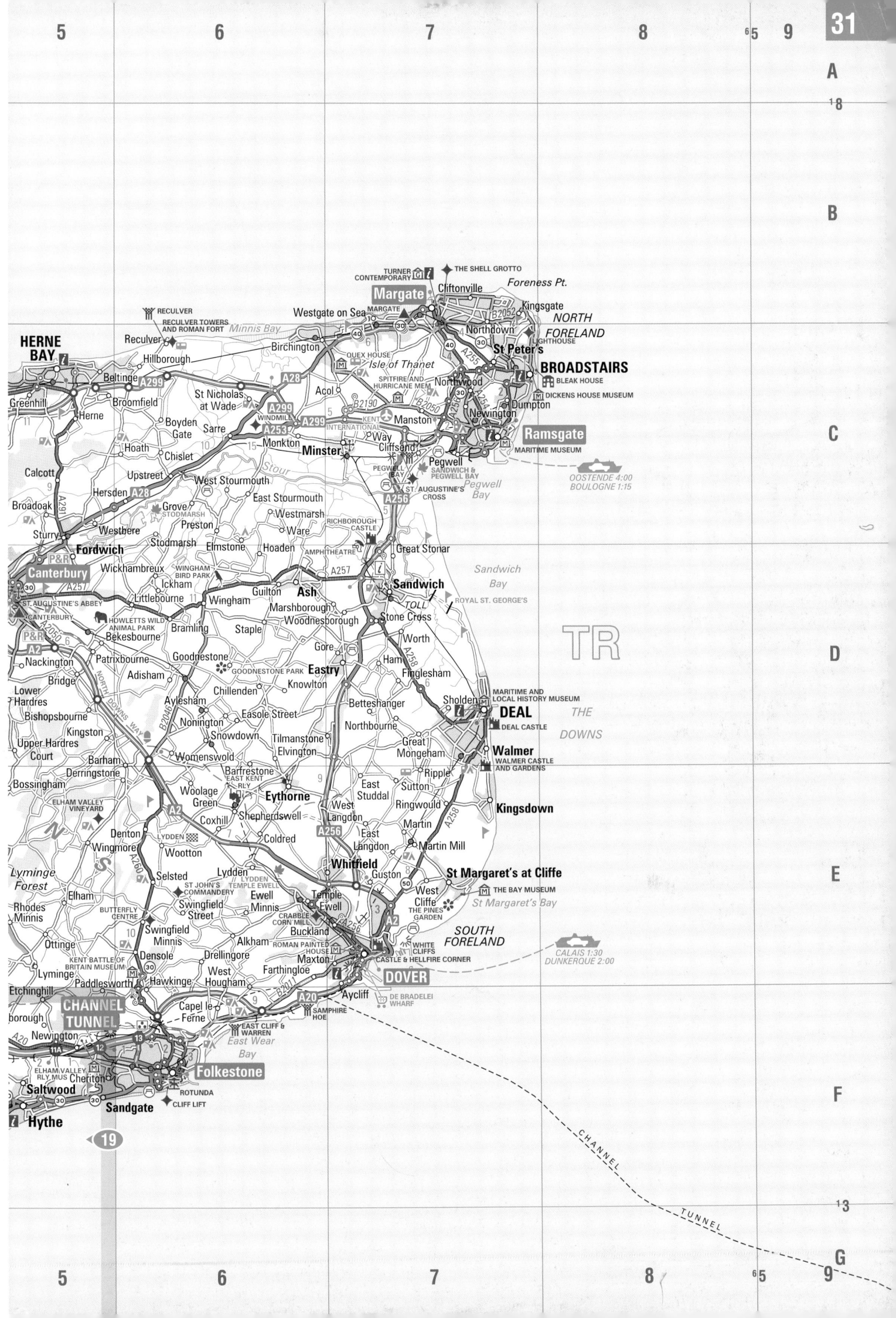

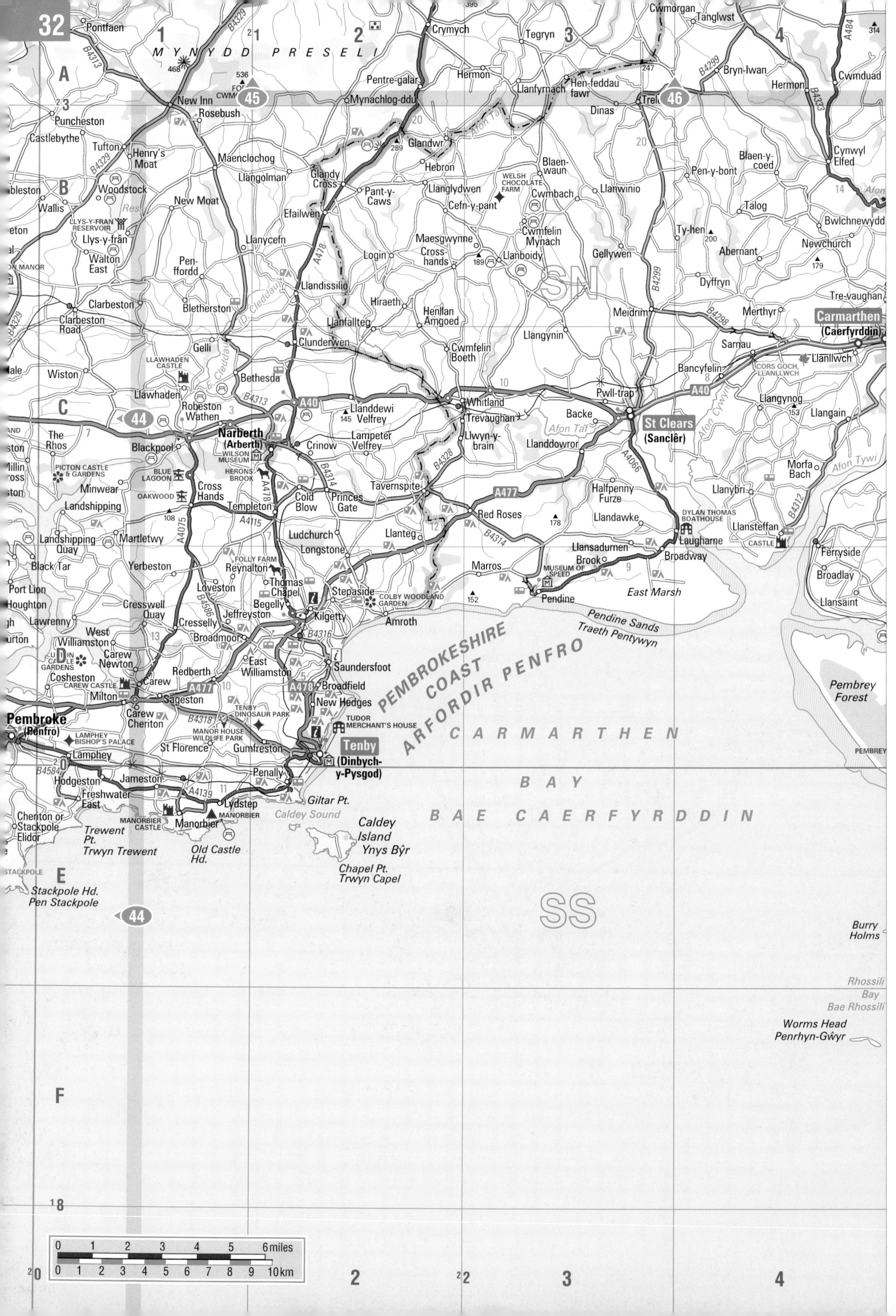

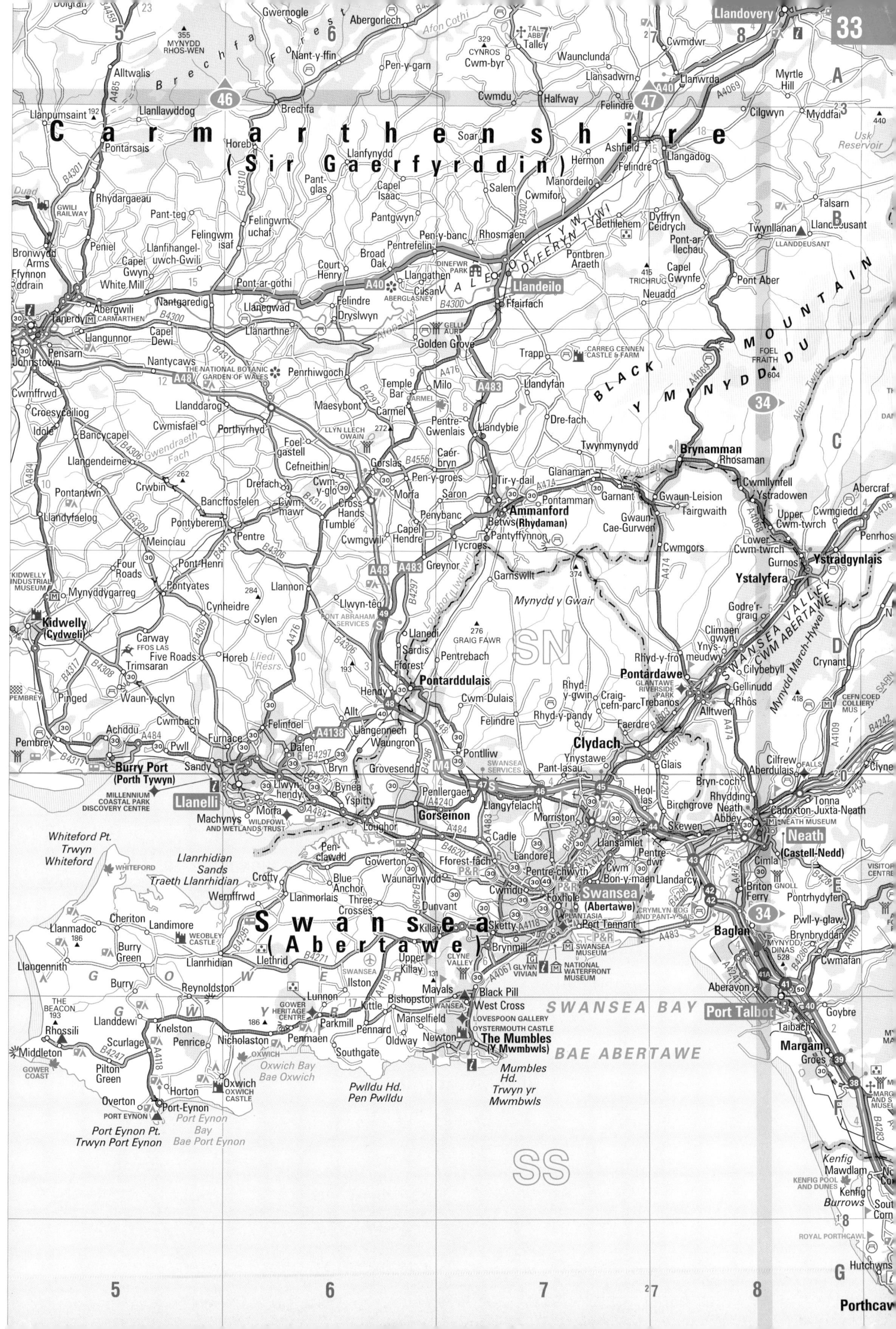

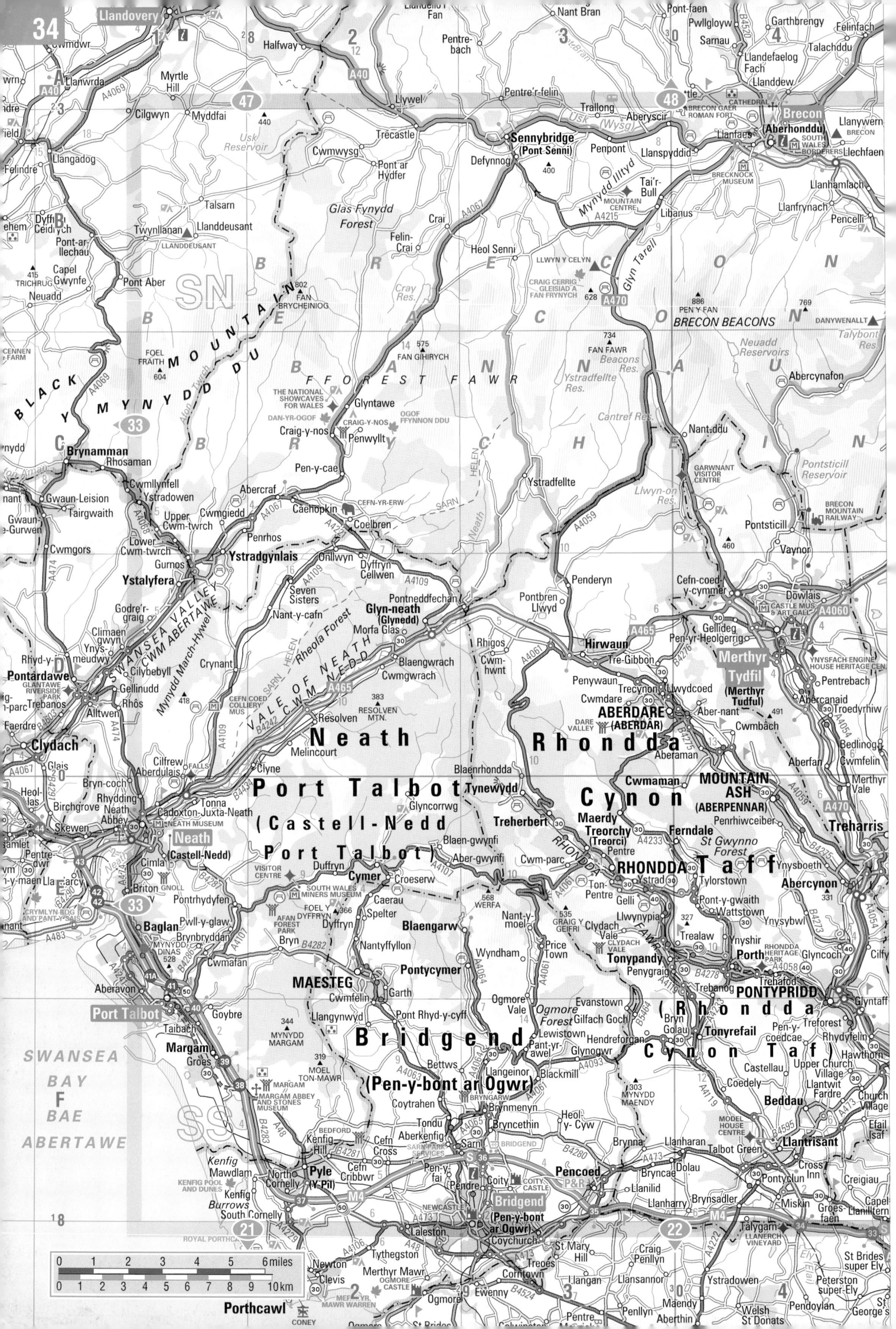

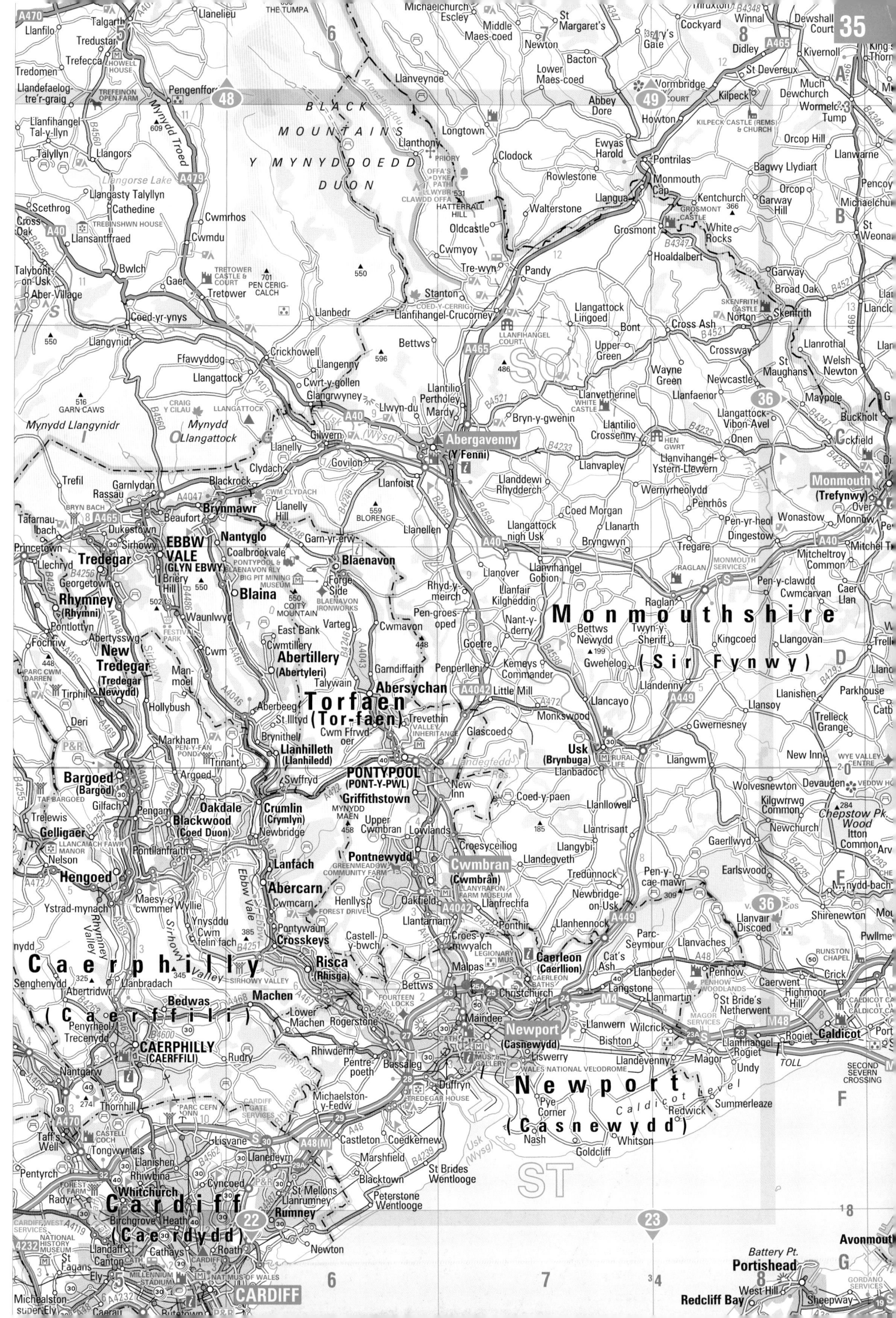

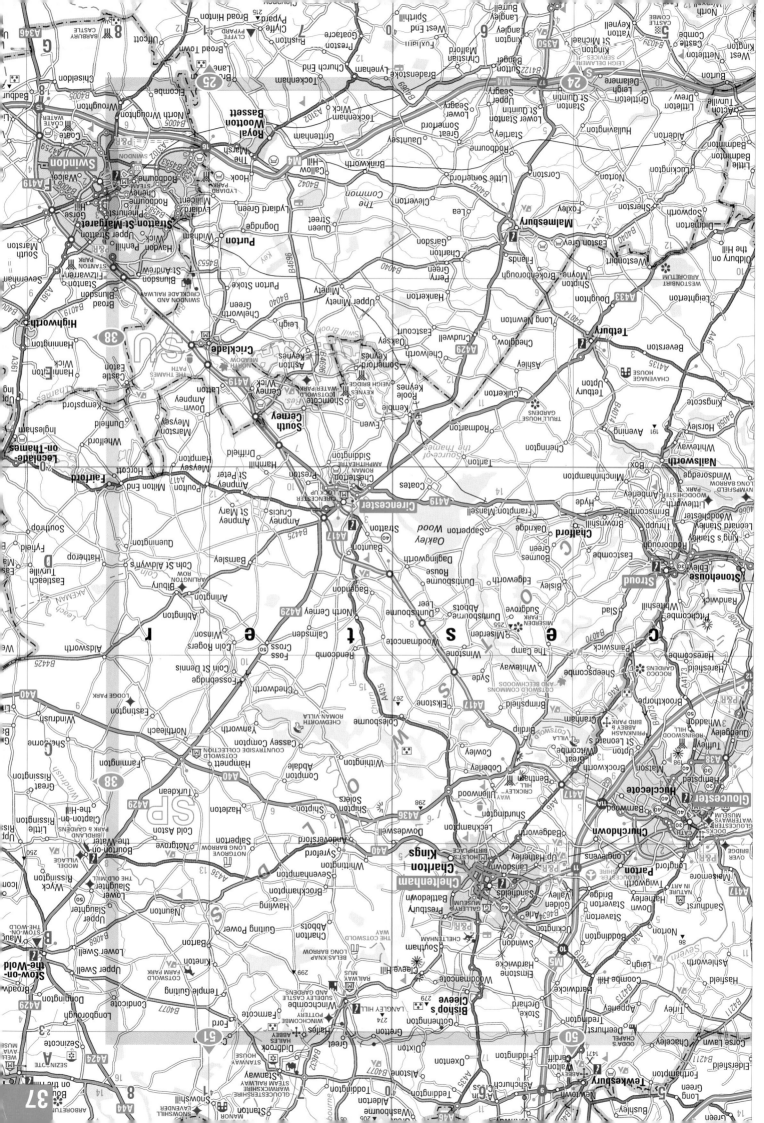

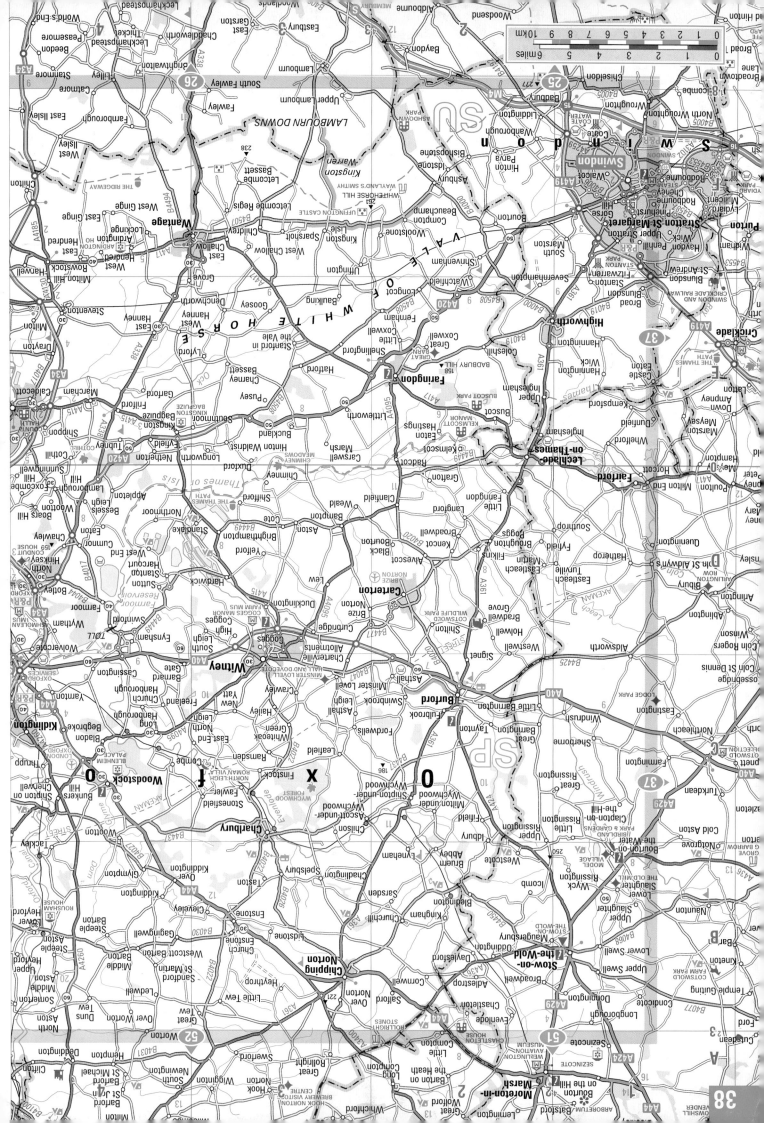

Buckingham
Bletchley
Winslow
Bicester
Aylesbury
Thame
Oxford
Headington
Cowley
Wheatley
Abingdon
Didcot
Wallingford
Goring
Henley-on-Thames
Marlow
High Wycombe
Princes Risborough
Wendover
Prestwood
Great Missenden
Chinnor
Haddenham
Maidenhead
Twyford
Sonning Common
Watlington
Nettlebed
Weston Turville
Aston Clinton
Stoke Mandeville
Waddesdon
Brill
Boarstall
Kidlington
Islip
Kirtlington
Ardley
Fritwell
Souldern
Aynho
Croughton
Mixbury
Tingewick
Gawcott
Padbury
Adstock
Great Horwood
Swanbourne
Mursley
Stewkley
Wing
Cublington
Whitchurch
Quainton
Grendon Underwood
Marsh Gibbon
Launton
Chesterton
Wendlebury
Ambrosden
Blackthorn
Kingswood
Westcott
Long Crendon
Worminghall
Tiddington
Great Milton
Garsington
Cuddesdon
Chalgrove
Benson
Ewelme
Cholsey
Blewbury
Streatley
Pangbourne
Whitchurch Hill
Woodcote
Checkendon
Stoke Row
Stonor
Turville
Fingest
Frieth
Lane End
Hambleden
Bisham
Cookham
Hurley
Wargrave
Shiplake
Stokenchurch
Radnage
West Wycombe
Hughenden Valley
Naphill
Great Kingshill
Little Kingshill
Speen
Lacey Green
Bledlow
Monks Risborough
Great Kimble
Little Kimble
Ellesborough
Halton
Bierton
Wingrave
Mentmore
Rowsham
Weedon
Hardwick
Ashendon
Dorton
Oakley
Chilton
Cuddington
Dinton
Stone
Bishopstone
Kingsey
Towersey
Emmington
Sydenham
Tetsworth
Postcombe
Lewknor
Shirburn
Pyrton
Cuxham
Easington
Stadhampton
Chiselhampton
Drayton St Leonard
Berinsfield
Dorchester
Clifton Hampden
Culham
Sutton Courtenay
Appleford
Long Wittenham
Shillingford
Warborough
Crowmarsh Gifford
North Moreton
South Moreton
East Hagbourne
West Hagbourne
Upton
Aston Upthorpe
Aston Tirrold
Moulsford
South Stoke
North Stoke
Ipsden
Nuffield
Highmoor Cross
Rotherfield Greys
Rotherfield Peppard
Kidmore End
Mapledurham
Purley
Upper Basildon
Lower Basilon
Aldworth
Compton
Ashampstead
Hampstead Norreys
SP
SU
A40
M40
A41
A418
A413
A421
A4010
A329
A4074
A34
A43
A4146
A404
A4155
B4009
B480
B4011
Chiltern Hills
Buckingham
Windsor and Maidenhead
Oxford

Central Bedfordshire

Hertfordshire

Bletchley · Tattenhoe · Fenny Stratford · Far Bletchley · Woburn · Wild Animal Kingdom · Eversholt · Bloxham · Higham Gobion · Apsley End · Pirton · Shillington · Ickleford

Little Horwood · Newton Longville · Stoke Hammond · Great Brickhill · Milton Bryan · Harlington · Sharpenhoe · Barton-le-Clay · Hexton · Pegsdon · HITCHIN

Drayton Parslow · Mursley · Soulbury · Heath and Reach · Hockliffe · Tebworth · Toddington · Upper Sundon · Streatley · Barton Hills · B655

Swanbourne · North End · South End · Leighton Buzzard · Linslade · Eggington · Wingfield · Chalton · Lower Sundon · Sundon Park · Limbury · Stopsley · Cockernhoe Green · King's Walden · St Paul's Walden

Stewkley · Cublington · Billington · Stanbridge · Tilsworth · Eaton Bray · Houghton Regis · Leagrave · Luton · Biscot · Hart Hill · Breachwood Green · Whitwell

Aston Abbots · Wing · Burcott · Ledburn · Slapton · Church End · Eaton Bray · DUNSTABLE · Caddington · Farley Hill · Peter's Green · Kimpton

Hardwick · Weedon · Mentmore · Horton · Ivinghoe Aston · Whipsnade · Kensworth Common · Slip End · Ayot St Lawrence

Rowsham · Hulcott · Wingrave · Long Marston · Ivinghoe · Dagnall · Studham · Markyate · Flamstead · HARPENDEN · Wheathampstead

AYLESBURY · Bierton · Puttenham · Marsworth · Pitstone · Ringshall · Jockey End · Trowley Bottom · Hatching Green · Marshall's Heath

Weston Turville · Aston Clinton · Halton · Drayton Beauchamp · New Mill · TRING · Aldbury · Great Gaddesden · Water End · Redbourn · Childwick Green · Sandridge

Stoke Mandeville · Wilstone · Wigginton · Hastoe · Northchurch · Potten End · Gadebridge · Piccotts End · ST ALBANS · Fleetville

North Lee · Terrick · Ellesborough · Dunsmore · BERKHAMSTED · Cholesbury · Bourne End · Boxmoor · HEMEL HEMPSTEAD · St Stephens · London Colney

Princes Risborough · Great Hampden · The Lee · Ashley Green · Bovingdon · Kings Langley · Chipperfield · Abbots Langley · Bricket Wood · Colney Street · Radlett

CHESHAM · Chesham Bois · Latimer · Chenies · Sarratt · Aldenham · Elstree · BOREHAMWOOD

Prestwood · Great Missenden · Hyde Heath · Little Missenden · Chorleywood · Croxley Green · WATFORD · Letchmore Heath

AMERSHAM · Little Chalfont · RICKMANSWORTH · Oxhey · Bushey · Stanmore · Edgware

HIGH WYCOMBE · Hazlemere · Penn · Tylers Green · Chalfont St Giles · South Oxhey · Northwood · Pinner · HARROW · Wealdstone

West Wycombe · Downley · Loudwater · Knotty Green · BEACONSFIELD · Chalfont St Peter · Harefield · Ruislip · Eastcote · Harrow on the Hill

Marlow Bottom · Flackwell Heath · Wooburn Green · Gerrards Cross · Denham · Uxbridge · Ickenham · Wembley

MARLOW · Bisham · Cookham · Burnham Beeches · Farnham Common · Stoke Poges · Denham Green · Hillingdon · Sudbury · Perivale

Windsor and Maidenhead · Hurley · Cookham Dean · Taplow · Wexham · Langley · Cowley · Yeading · Greenford · EALING

MAIDENHEAD · Bray · Dorney · SLOUGH · Iver · Richings Park · West Drayton · Hayes · Southall

WINDSOR · Eton · Datchet · Colnbrook · Poyle · Sipson · Cranford · HEATHROW · Heston · Brentford · Isleworth

Scale: 0 1 2 3 4 5 6 miles / 0 1 2 3 4 5 6 7 8 9 10km

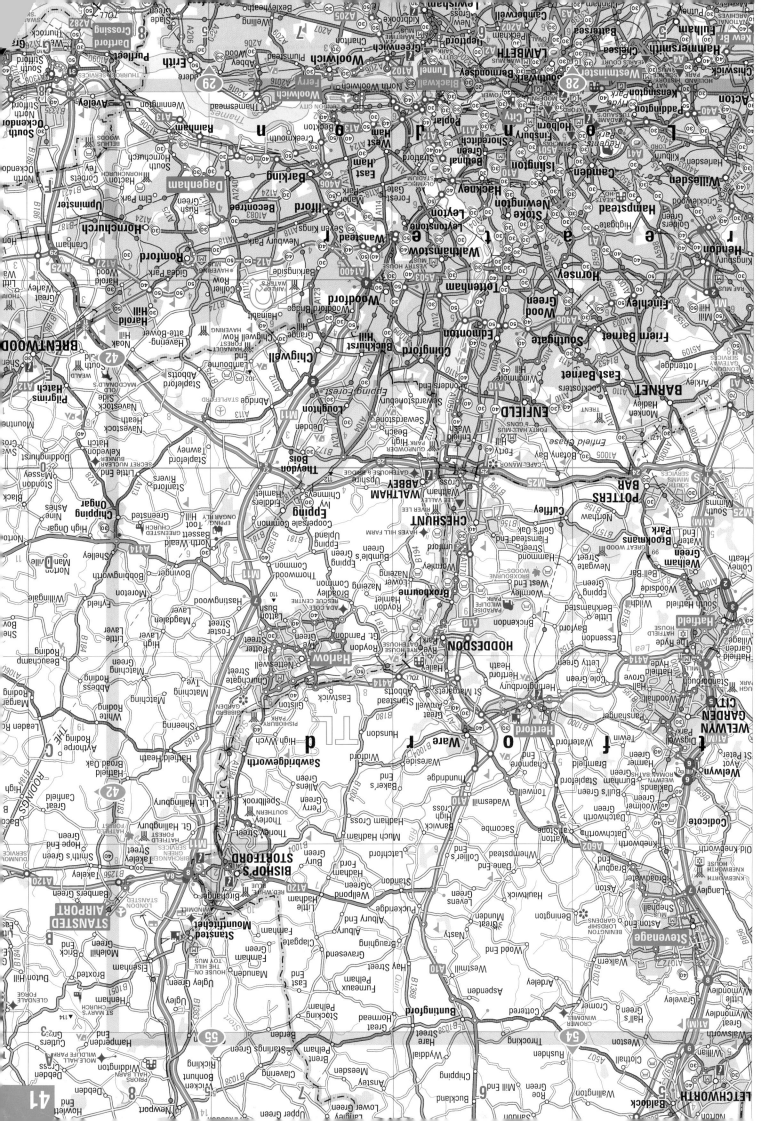

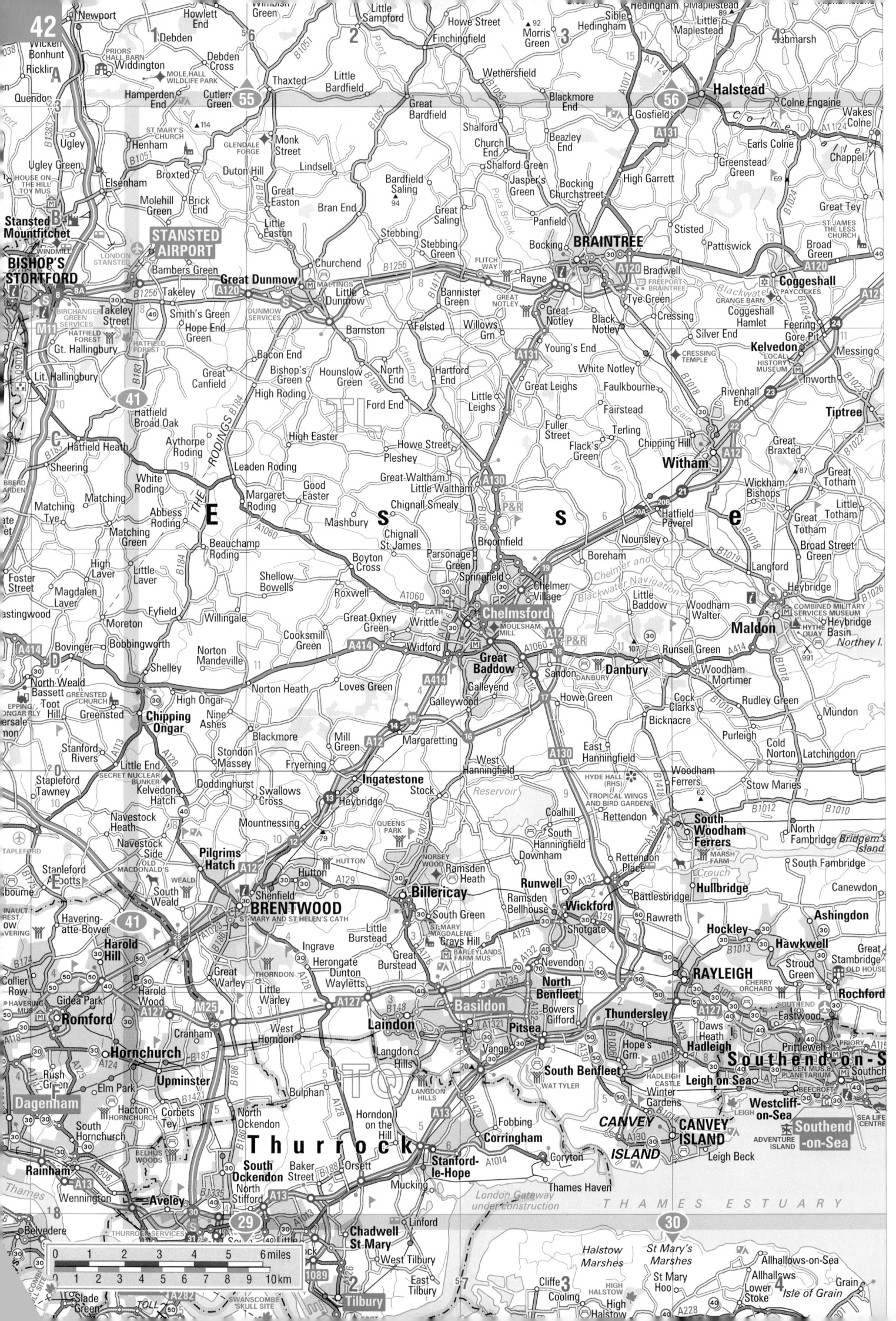

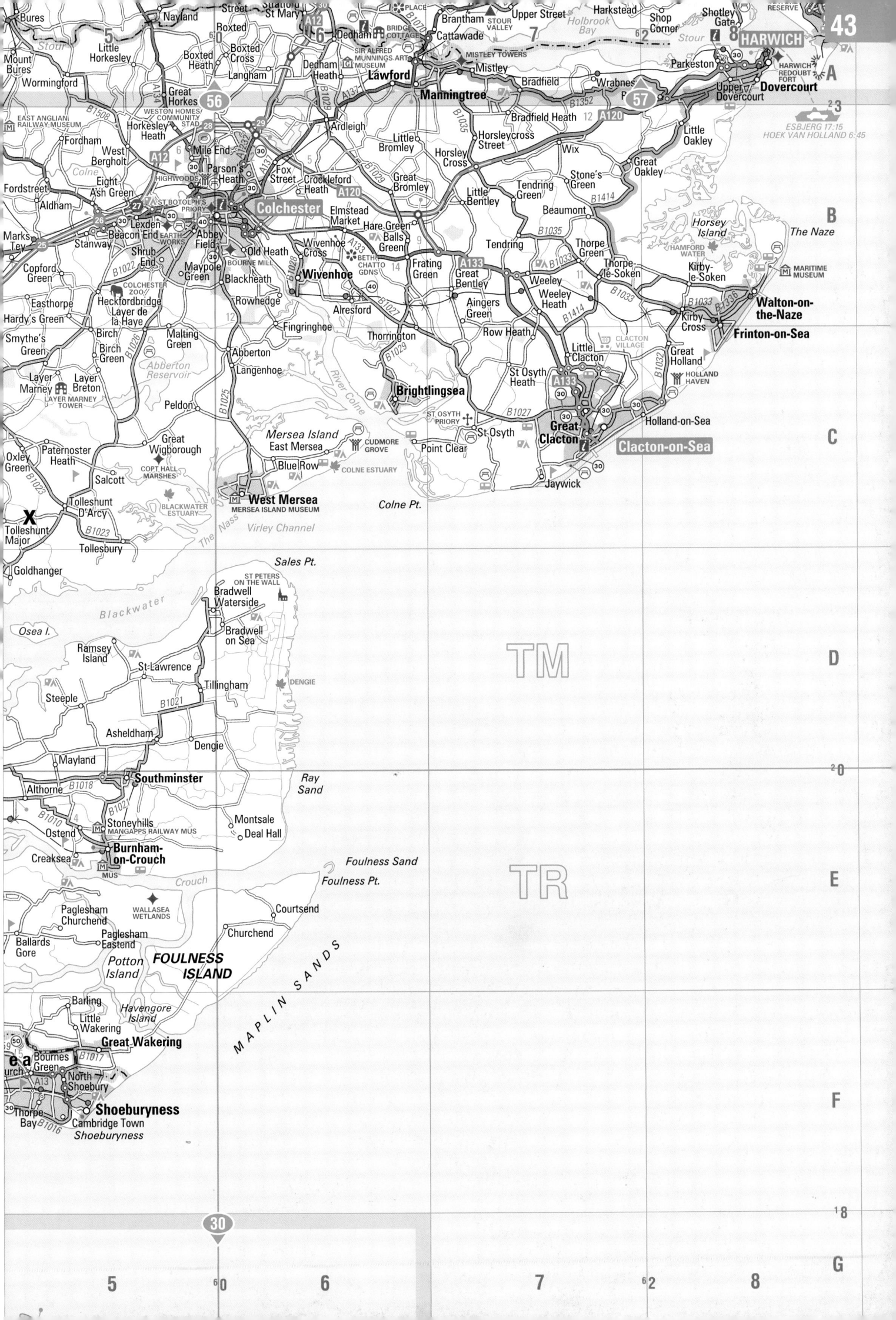

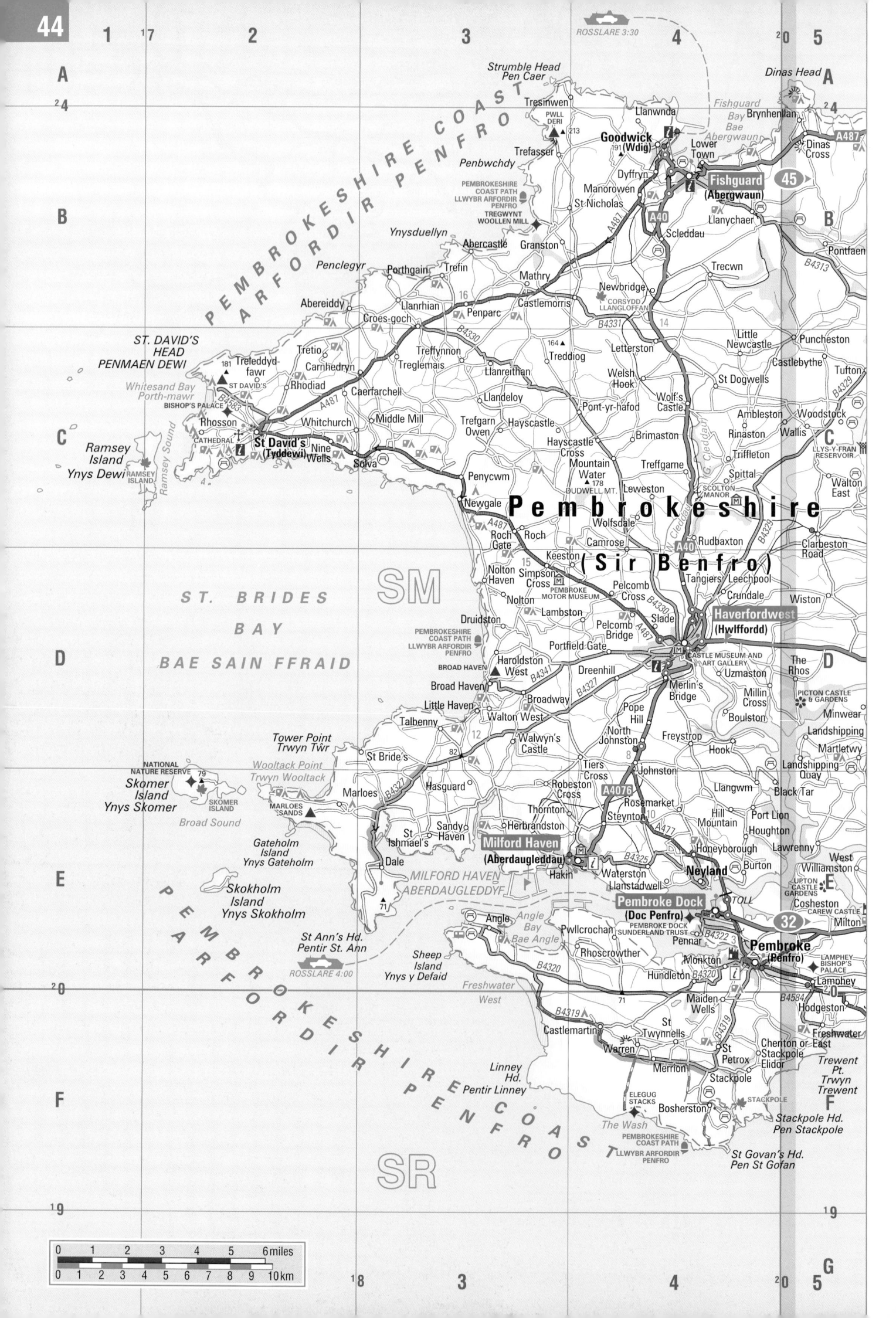

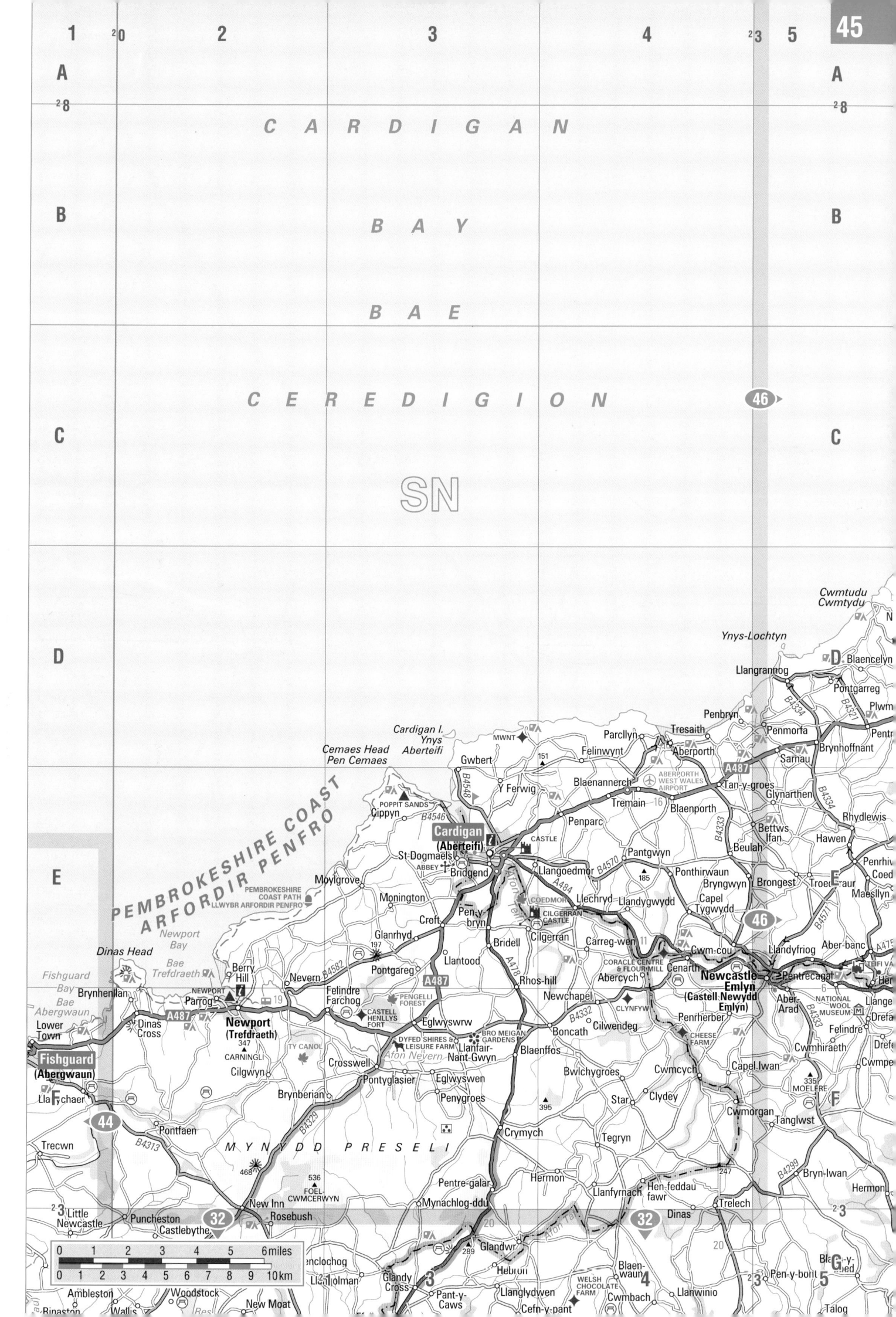

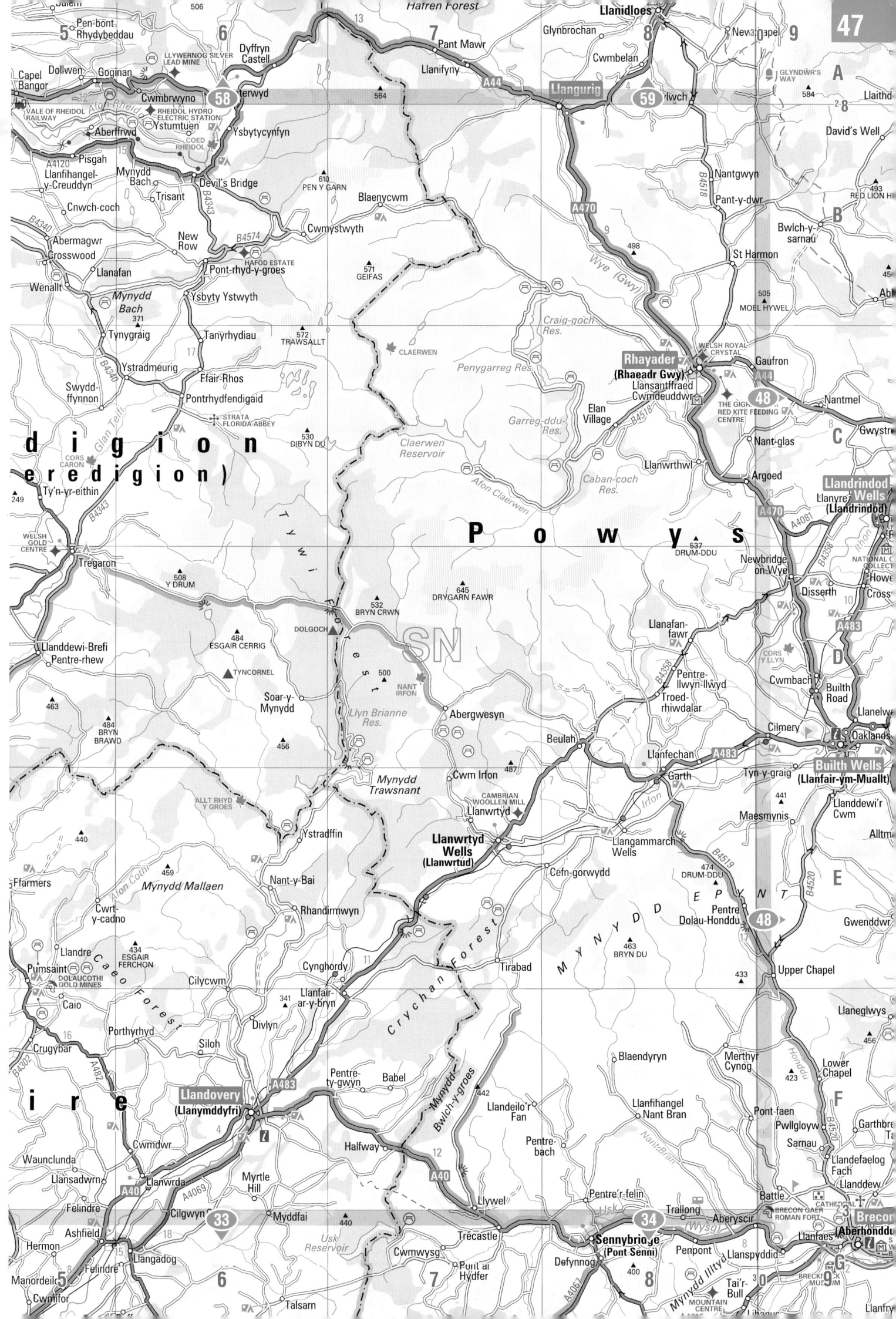

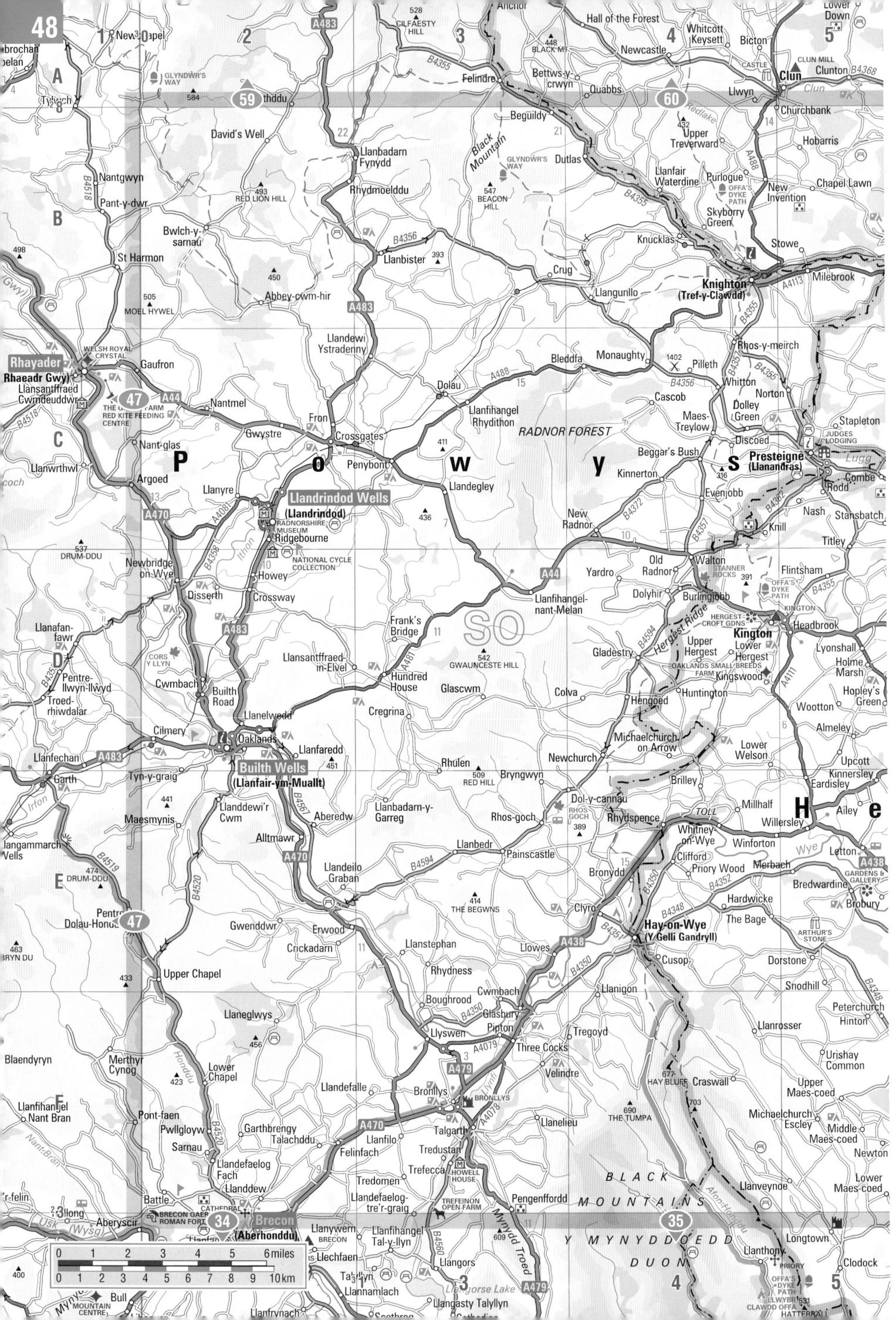

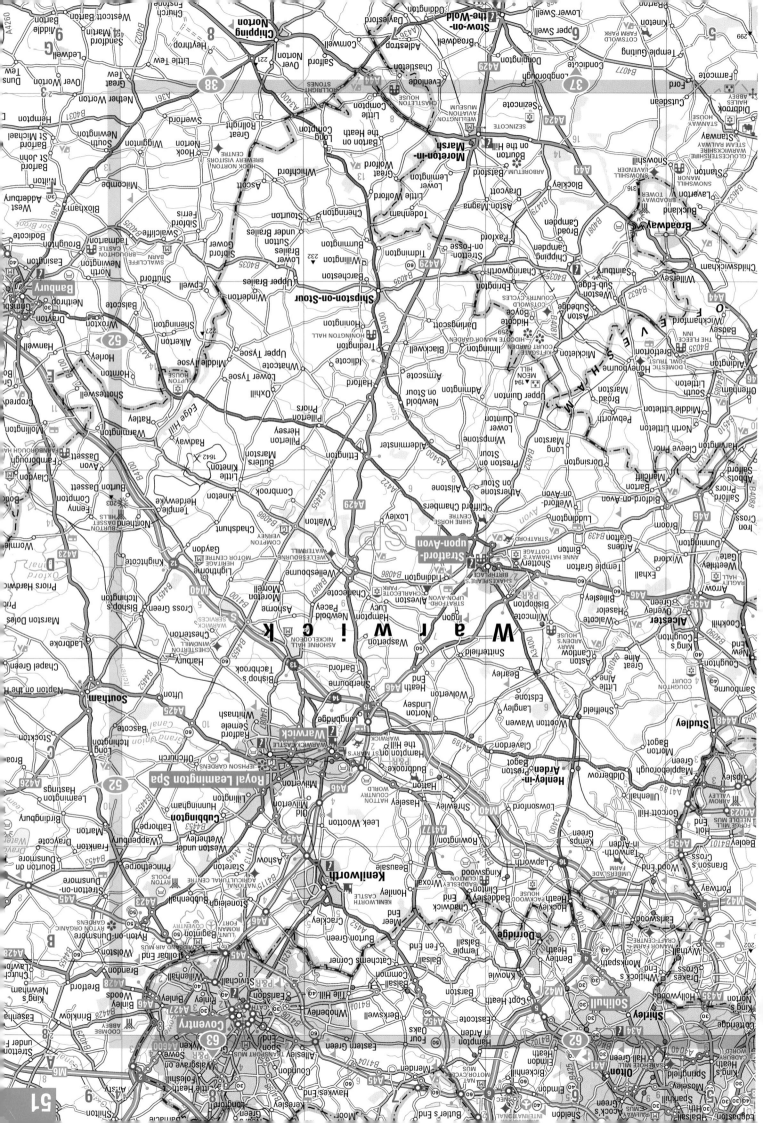

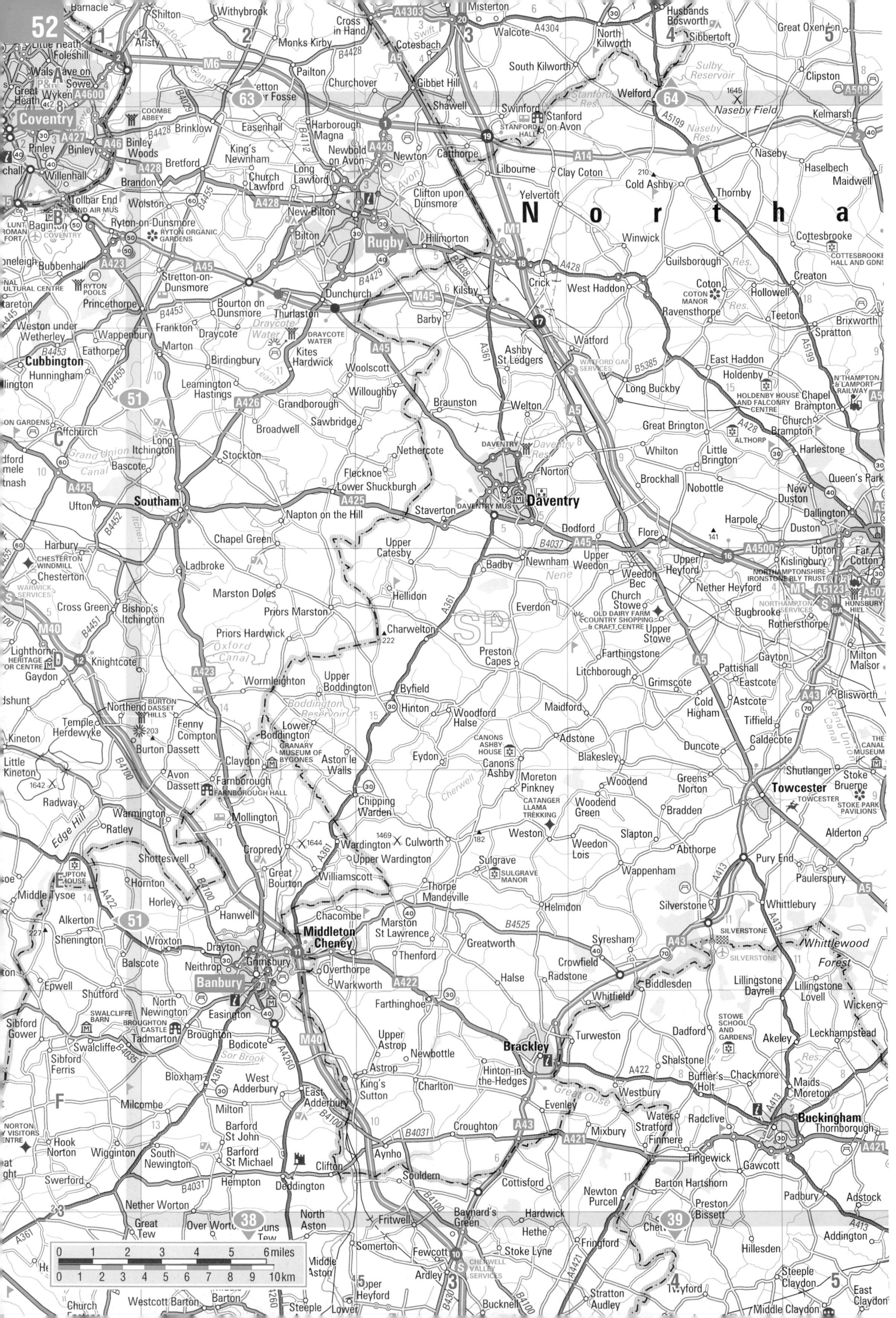

Braybrooke · Desborough · Rushton · Newton · Geddington · Eleanor Cross · Herbs · Fermyn Woods · Wadenhoe · Barnwell All Saints · Luddington in the Brook · Thurning · Great Gidding · Little Gidding

Arthingworth · Rothwell · Rushton Triangular Lodge · Weekley · A6003 · A43 · A6116 · Sudborough · Aldwincle · Achurch · Wigsthorpe · Steeple Gidding · Coppingfor · A

Harrington · Orton · Loddington · Thorpe Malsor · Kettering · Warkton · Boughton House · Grafton Underwood · Lowick · Slipton · Twywell · Islip · Thrapston · Thorpe Waterville · Titchmarsh · Clopton · Winwick · Hamerton Zoo Park · Hamerton

Draughton · Great Cransley · Broughton · Pytchley · Isham · Burton Latimer · Cranford St Andrew · Cranford St John · Woodford · Denford · Ringstead · Thrapston · Bythorn · Brington · Molesworth · Old Weston · Buckworth · Alo

Lamport · Lamport Hall · Old · Scaldwell · Mawsley · Orlinbury · Little Harrowden · Great Addington · Little Addington · Finedon · A45 · Keyston · Leighton Bromswold · Barham · Wool

Walgrave · Hannington · Holcot · Great Harrowden · Hardwick · Stanwick Lakes · Raunds · Stanwick · Chelveston · Caldecott · Shelton · Lower Dean · Upper Dean · Kimbolton · Catworth · Spaldwick · Easton · Stow Longa · West Perry · East

Pitsford Reservoir · Brixworth · Pitsford · Sywell · Wellingborough · Irthlingborough · Higham Ferrers · Warmonds Hill · Chichele College · Hargrave · Covington · Tilbrook · Dillington · Grafham Water

Boughton · Moulton · Overstone · Mears Ashby · Wilby · Little Irchester · Heritage Centre · Knuston · Rushden · Yeldon · Melchbourne · Pertenhall · Great Staughton · Staughton Hig · C

Kingsthorpe · Kingsley Park · Weston Favell · Sywell Reservoir · New Barton · Irchester · Wymington · Newton Bromswold · Swineshead · Brook End · Keysoe · Little Staughton · Hail Westo

Northampton · Little Billing · Great Billing · Billing Aquadrome · Great Doddington · Narrow Gauge Railway Mus · Farndish · Podington · Souldrop · Knotting · Riseley · Knotting Green · Keysoe Row · Duloe · Staploe

Cogenhoe · Little Houghton · Whiston · Grendon · Hinwick · Santa Pod · Bedford · Bolnhurst · Bushmead Priory · Chawston

Great Houghton · Brafield-on-the-Green · Castle Ashby · Easton Maudit · Bozeat · Sharnbrook · Odell · Felmersham · Radwell · Bletsoe · Thurleigh · Rootham's Green · Colmworth · Duck's Cross · Colesden · Roxton

Hardingstone · Wootton · Collingtree · Hackleton · Yardley Chase · Harrold · Chellington · Harrold-Odell · Carlton · Pavenham · Milton Ernest · Wilden · Ravensden · Renhold · Green End · Great Barford · Blunham

Quinton · Piddington · Horton · Warrington · Lavendon · Cold Brayfield · West End · Stevington · Oakley · Glenn Miller Museum · Bodyflight · Clapham · Salph End · Willington

Courteenhall · Roade · Hartwell · Ashton · Salcey Forest · Eakley Lanes · Weston Underwood · Ravenstone · Olney · Newton Blossomville · Turvey · Stevington Windmill · Bromham · Bedford · Goldington · Moggerhanger

Long Street · Stoke Goldington · Emberton · Clifton Reynes · A4280 · Box End · Biddenham · Queen's Park · Bedford Museum · Priory · Fenlake · Cople · Moggerhanger Park · Hatch · Thorncote Green

Grafton Regis · Hanslope · Tathall End · Gayhurst · Filgrave · Tyringham · Hardmead · Astwood · Stagsden · Great Denham · Kempston · Elstow Moot Hall · Harrowden · Shortstown · Northill · Cardington · Ickwell Green · E

Castlethorpe · Lathbury · Milton Keynes · Sherington · Chicheley · Chicheley Hall · North Crawley · Bourne End · Wootton · Keeley Green · Elstow · Kempston Hardwick · Littleworth · Cotton End · Bird of Prey Centre · Old Warden

Yardley Gobion · Potterspury · Haversham · Newport Pagnell Services · Newport Pagnell · Gullivers Land · Broad Green · Upper Shelton · Lower Shelton · Cranfield · Marston Moretaine · Stewartby · Wilstead · Haynes · Southill

Cosgrove · Old Stratford · Stony Stratford · Passenham · Great Linford · Willen · New Bradwell · Wolverton · Milton Keynes · St Lawrence's · Moulsoe · Salford · Marston Vale Millennium · Houghton Conquest · Houghton House · Haynes Church End · Central · Ampthill · Clophill · Shefford · Clifton

Calverton · Bradwell · Woughton on the Green · Woolstone · Milton Keynes Village · Wavendon · Aspley Guise · Lidlington · Millbrook · Brogborough · Maulden · Beadlow · Hoo M MAZE

Upper Weald · Beachampton · Milton Keynes National Hockey · Loughton · Shenley Church End · Shenley Brook End · Simpson · Walton · Wavendon · Aspley Heath · Husborne Crawley · Ridgmont · Steppingley · Denel End · De Grey Mausoleum · Flitton · Upper Gravenhurst · Wrest Park House · Meppershall · Inper Sundon · Shillington

Thornton · Whaddon · Nash · Bletchley · Bletchley Park · Fenny Stratford · Bow Brickhill · Woburn Sands · Wild Animal Kingdom · Eversholt · Woburn · Church End · Flitwick · Silsoe · Greenfield · Bedfordshire · Pulloxhill · Higham Gobion · Holwell

Tattenhoe · Far Bletchley · Little Brickhill · Great Brickhill · Woburn Abbey · Milton Bryan · Tingrith · Harlington · Westoning · Barton-le-Clay · Hexton · Apsley End · Pirton

Singleborough · Great Horwood · Little Horwood · Newton Longville · Drayton Parslow · Stoke Hammond · Soulbury · Potsgrove · Battlesden · Toddington · Sundon Hills · Streatley · Sharpenhoe · Knocking Hoe · Pegsdon · Great

Winslow · Mursley · Swanbourne · 6th End · Heath and Reach · Stockgrove Park · Hockliffe · Tebworth · Toddington Services · Upper Sundon · Lower Sundon · Galley Hill · Sundon · Lilley · Great Offley

Stewkley · South End · Leighton Buzzard · Eggington · Chalton · Wingfield · Kings Wood

Northampton · Milton Keynes · Bedford · Central Bedfordshire · SP · TL · YARDLEY CHASE

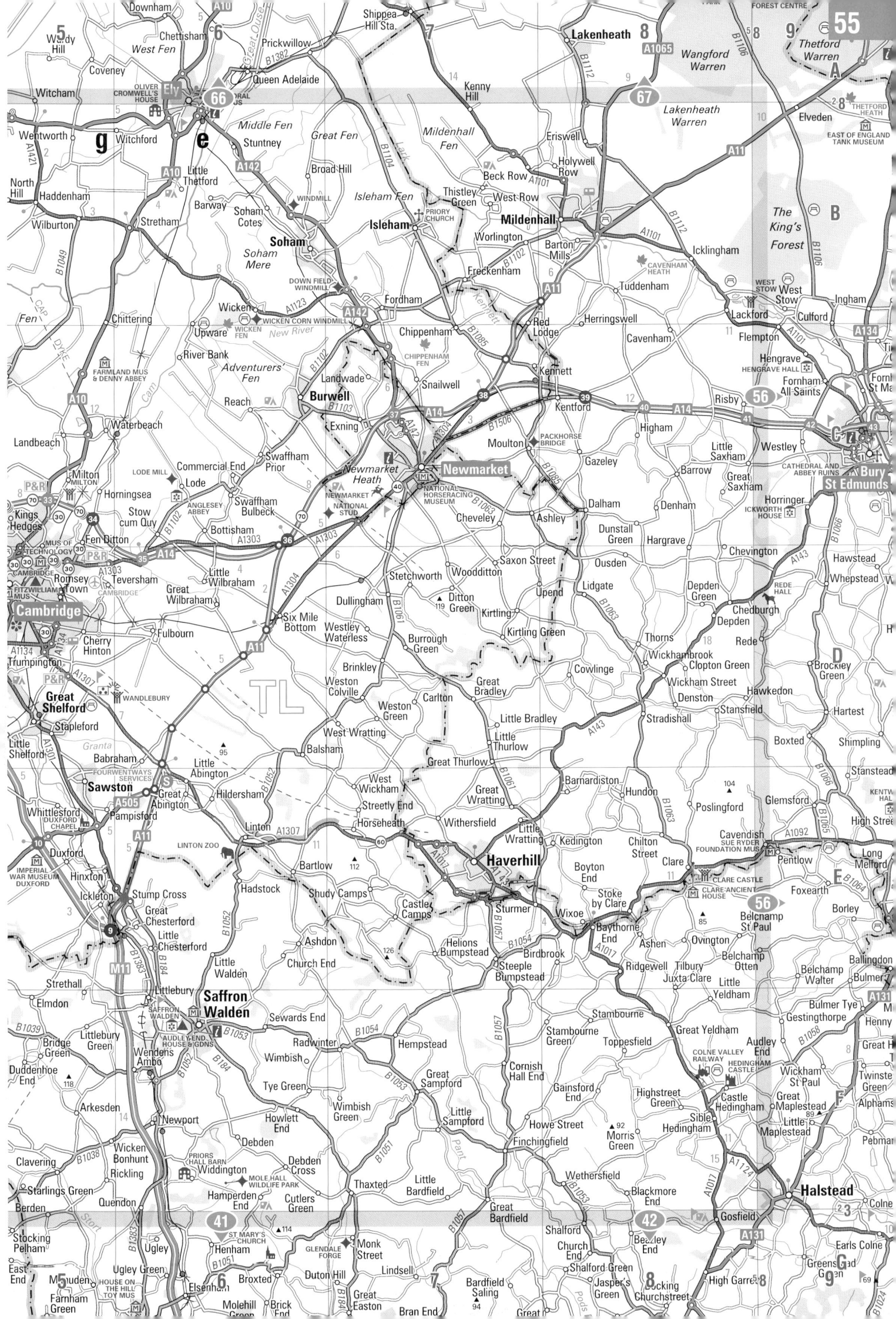

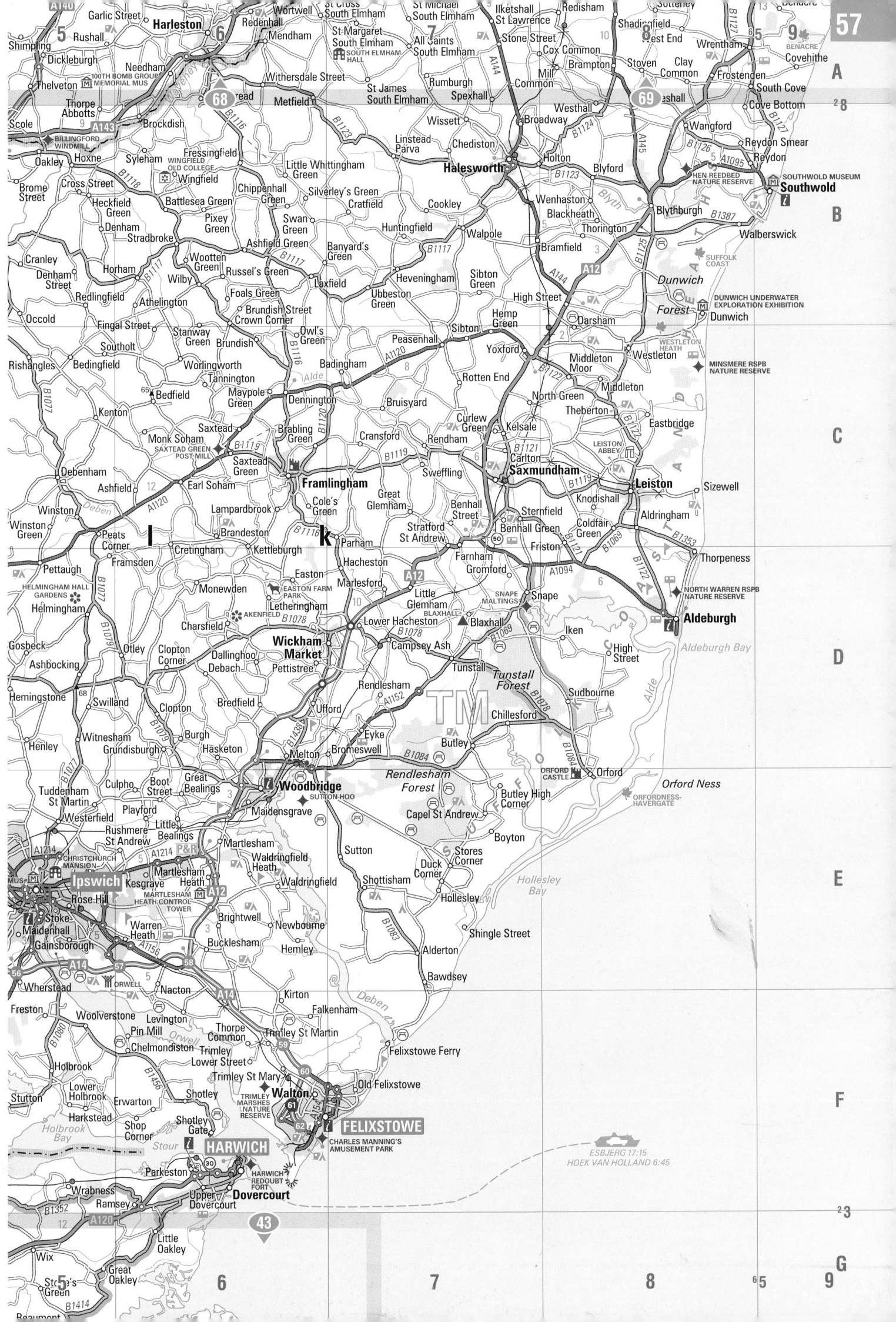

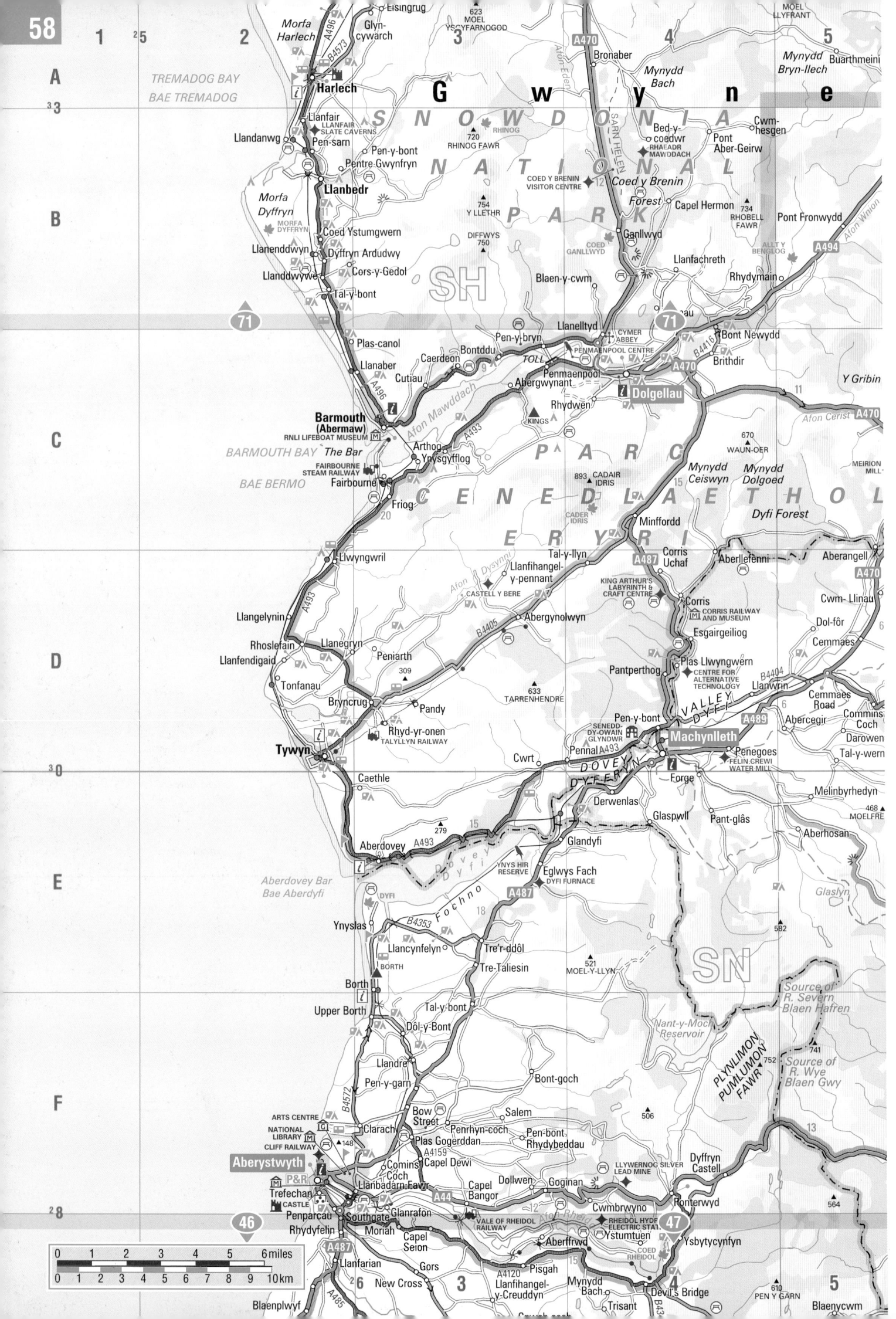

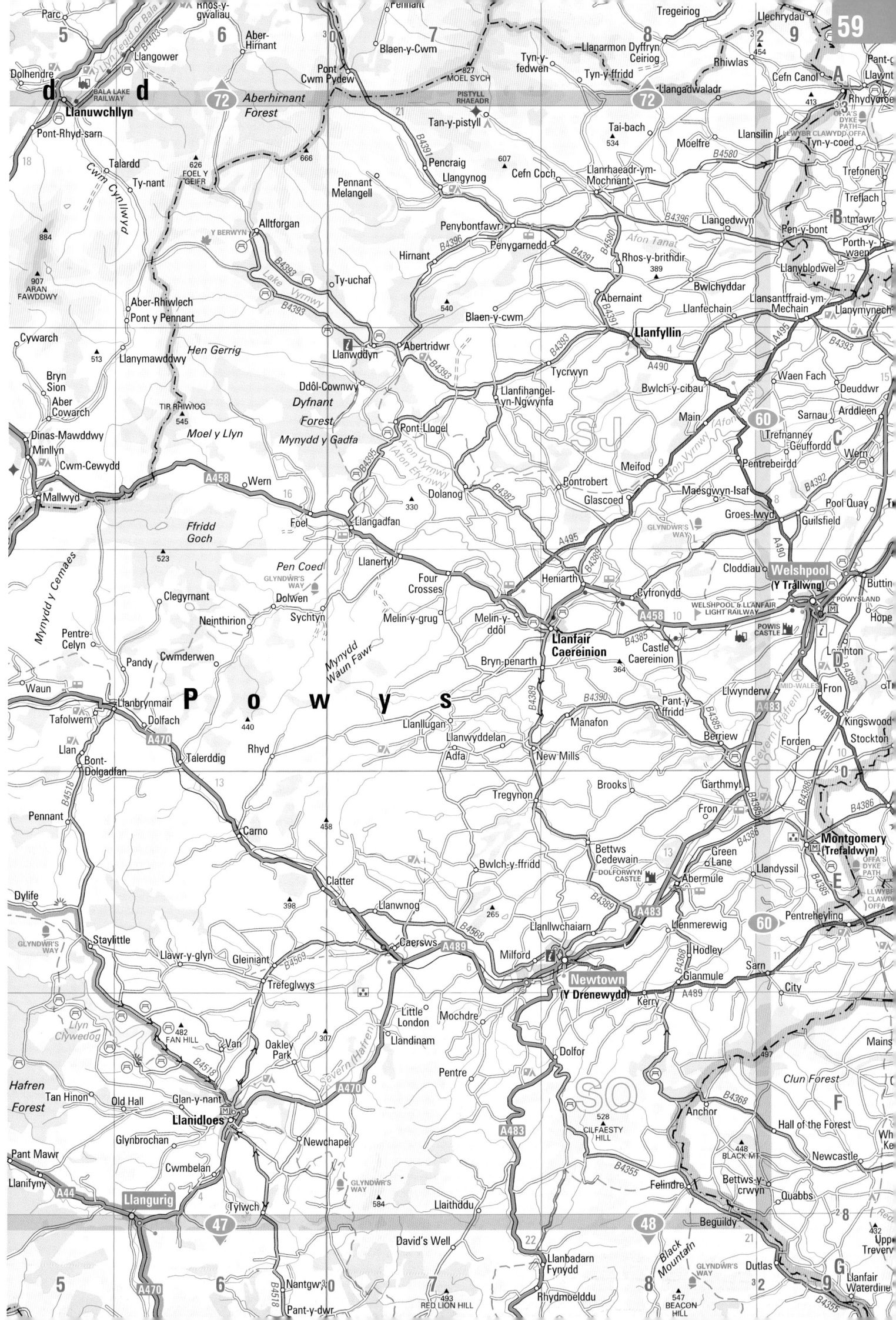

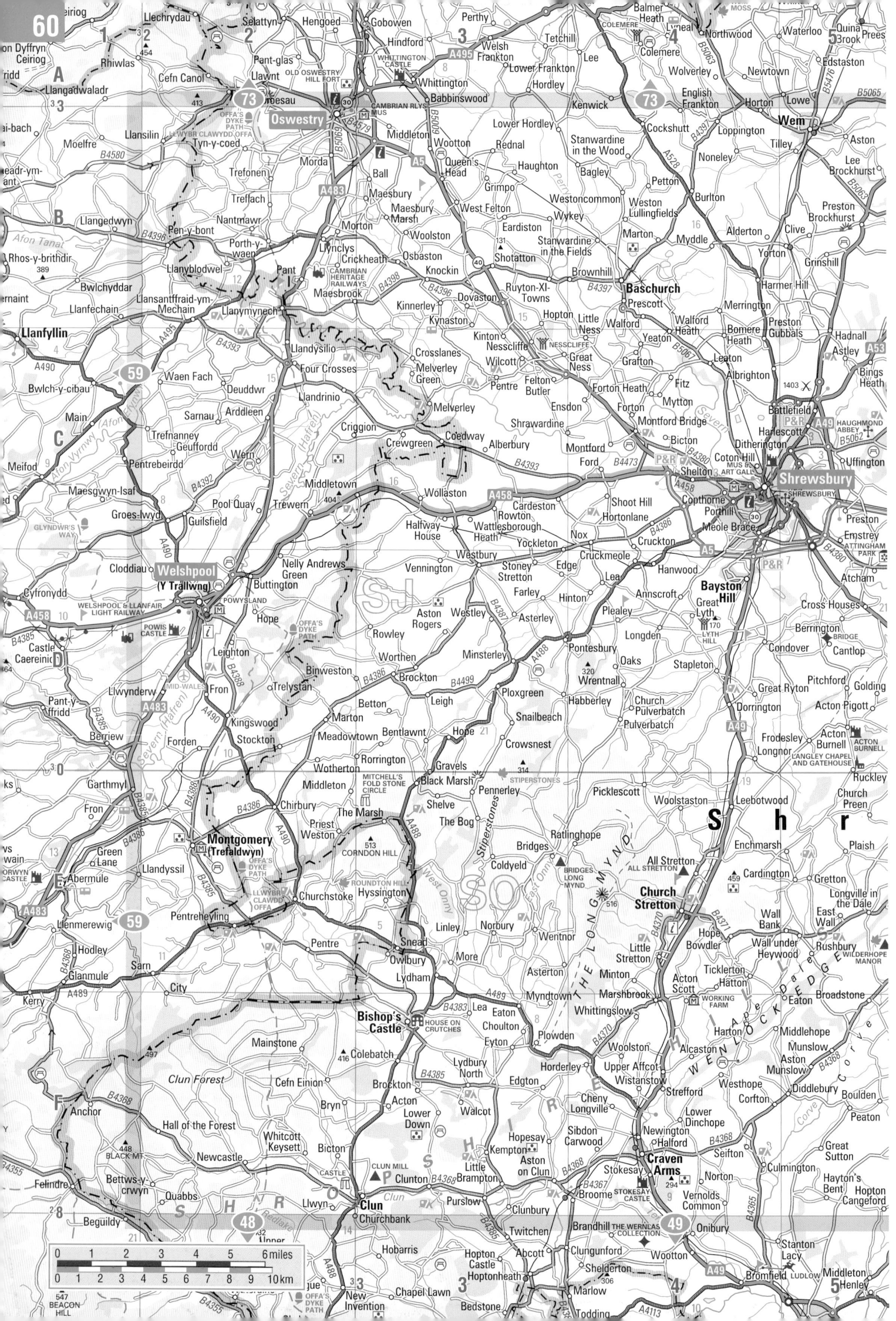

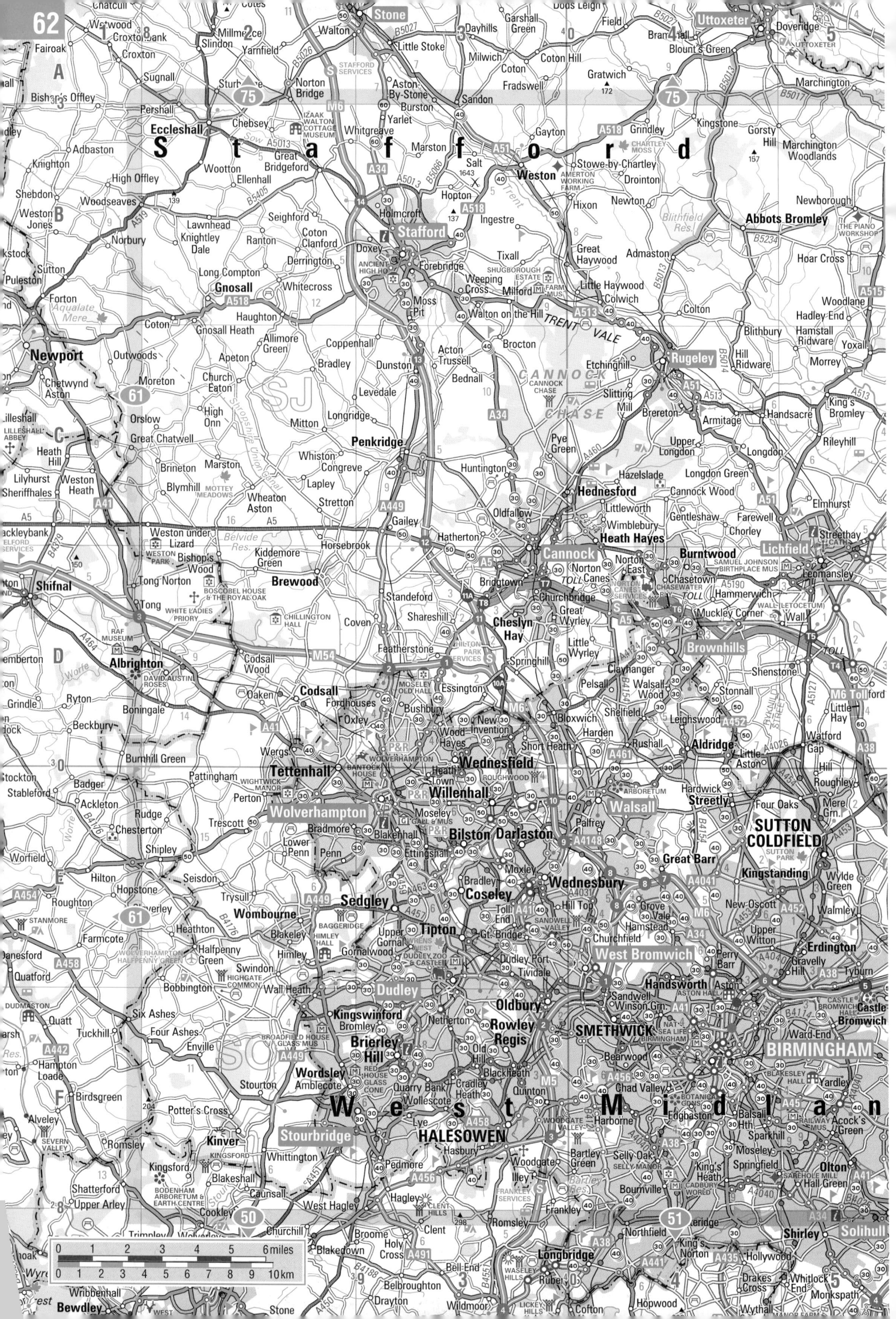

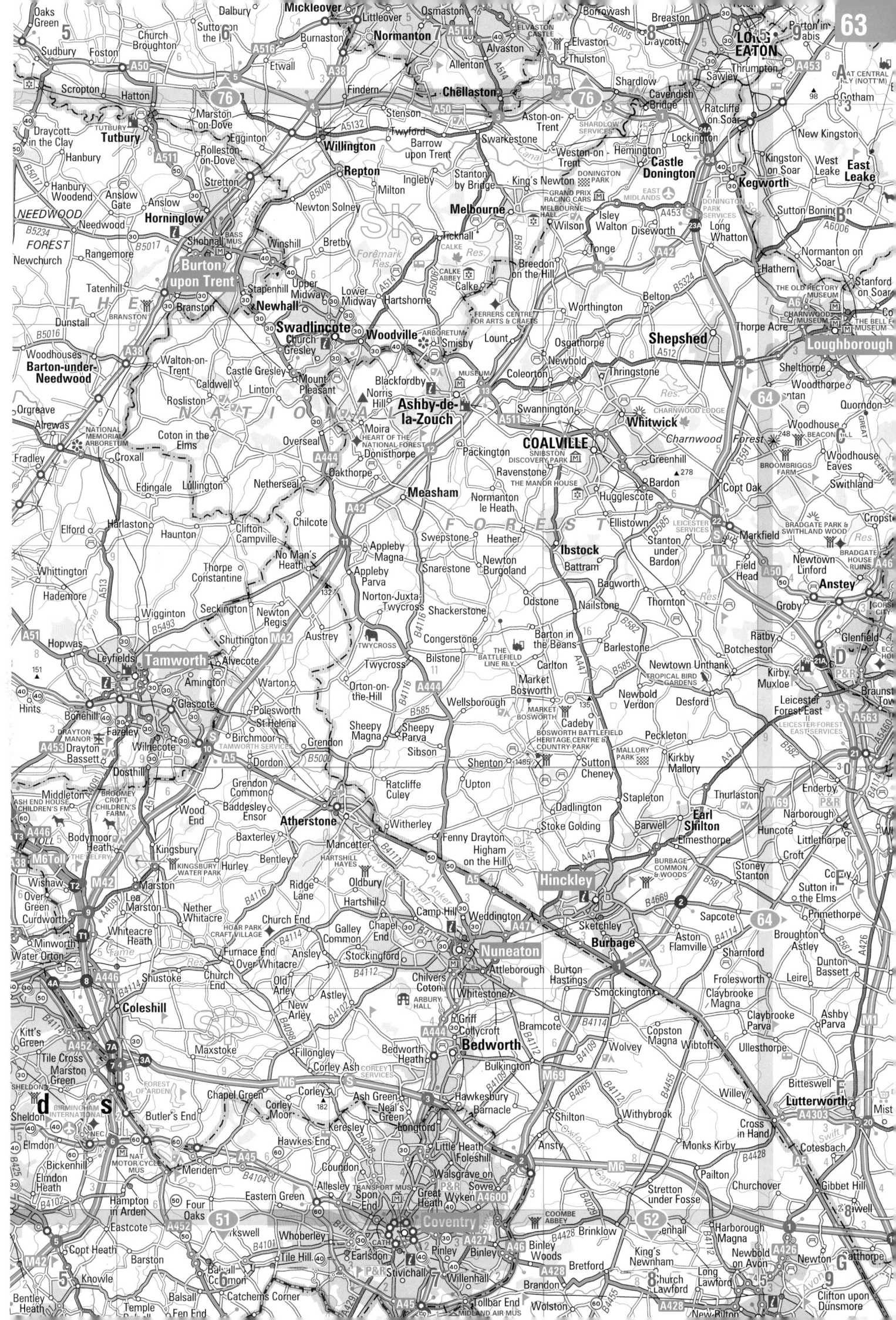

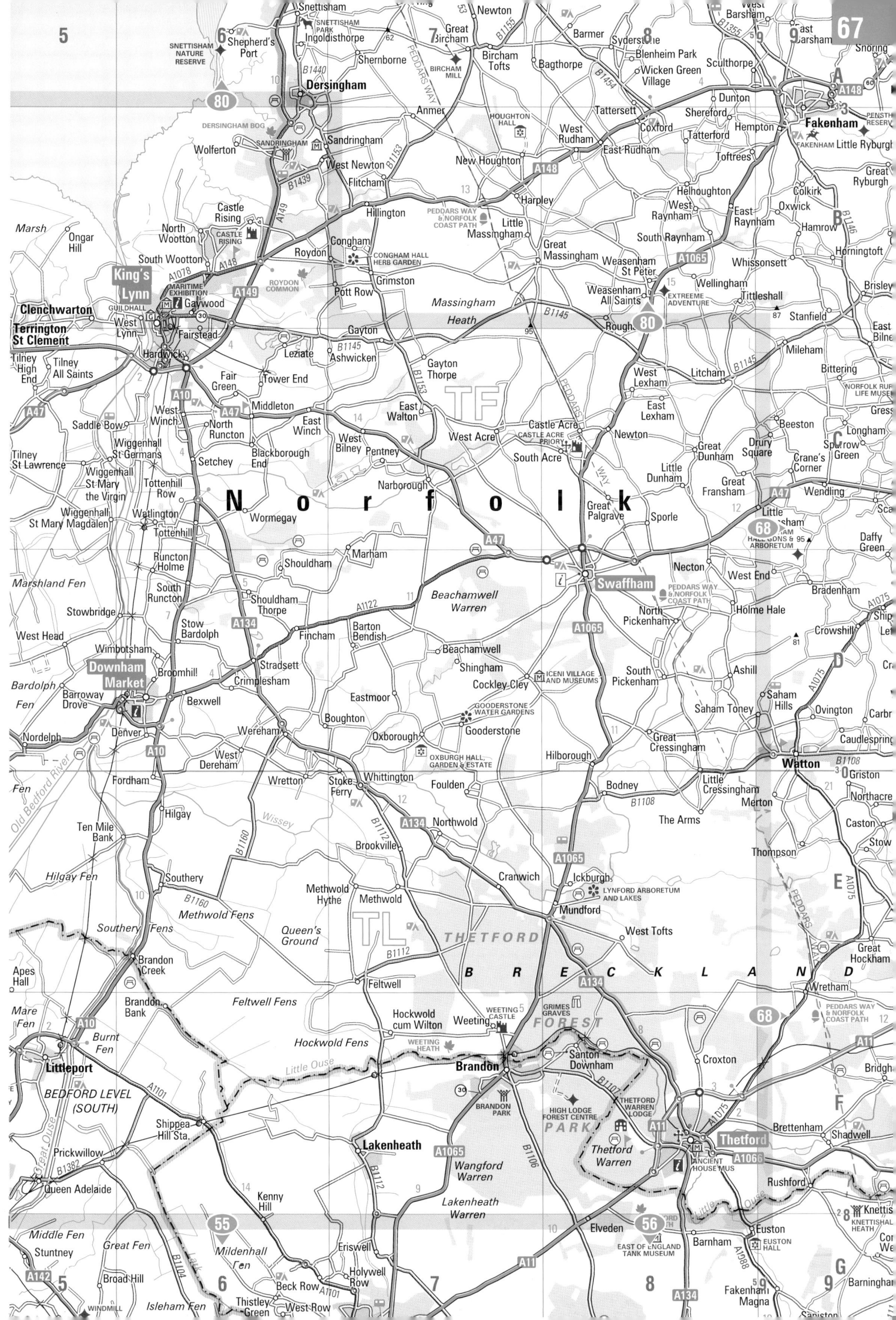

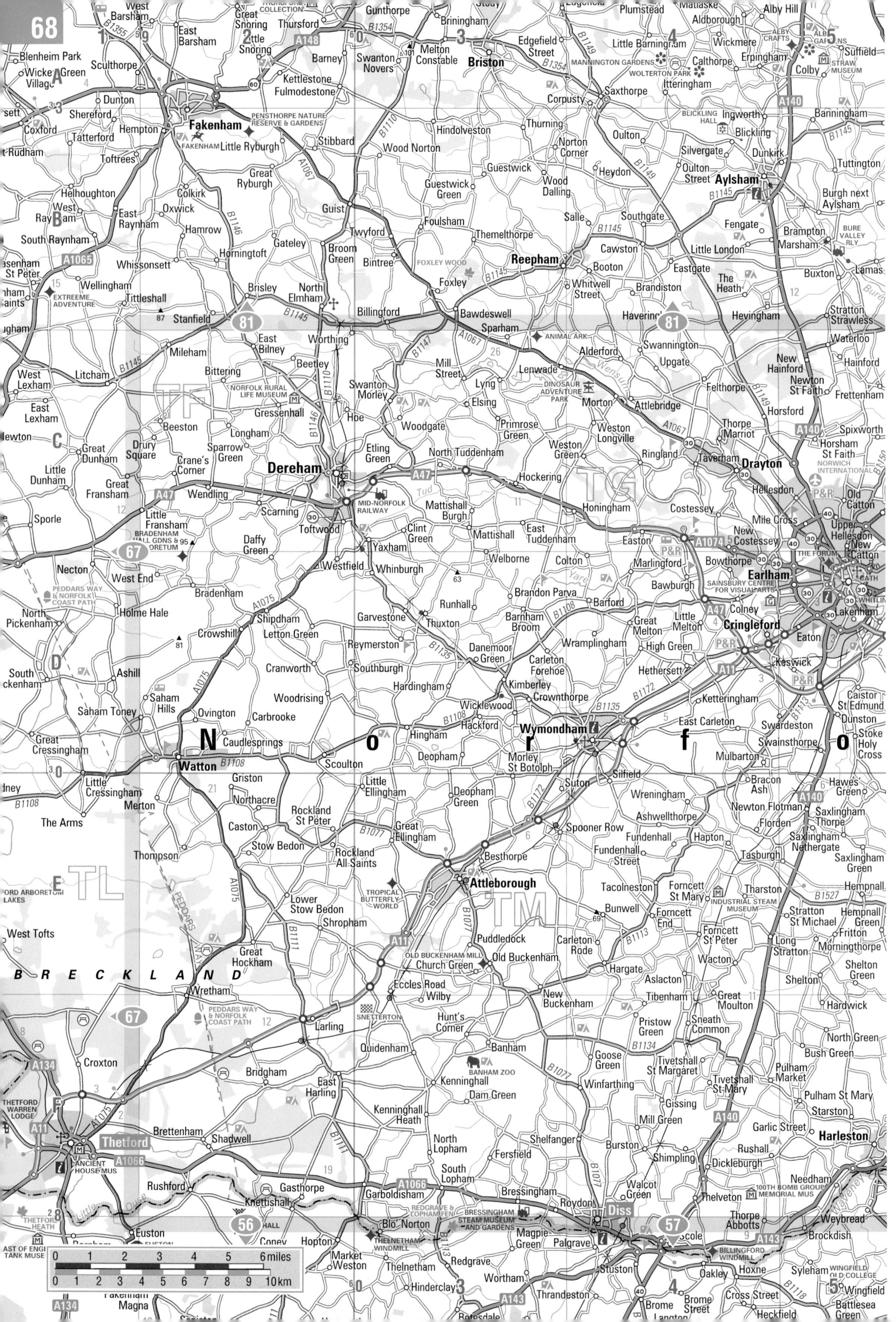

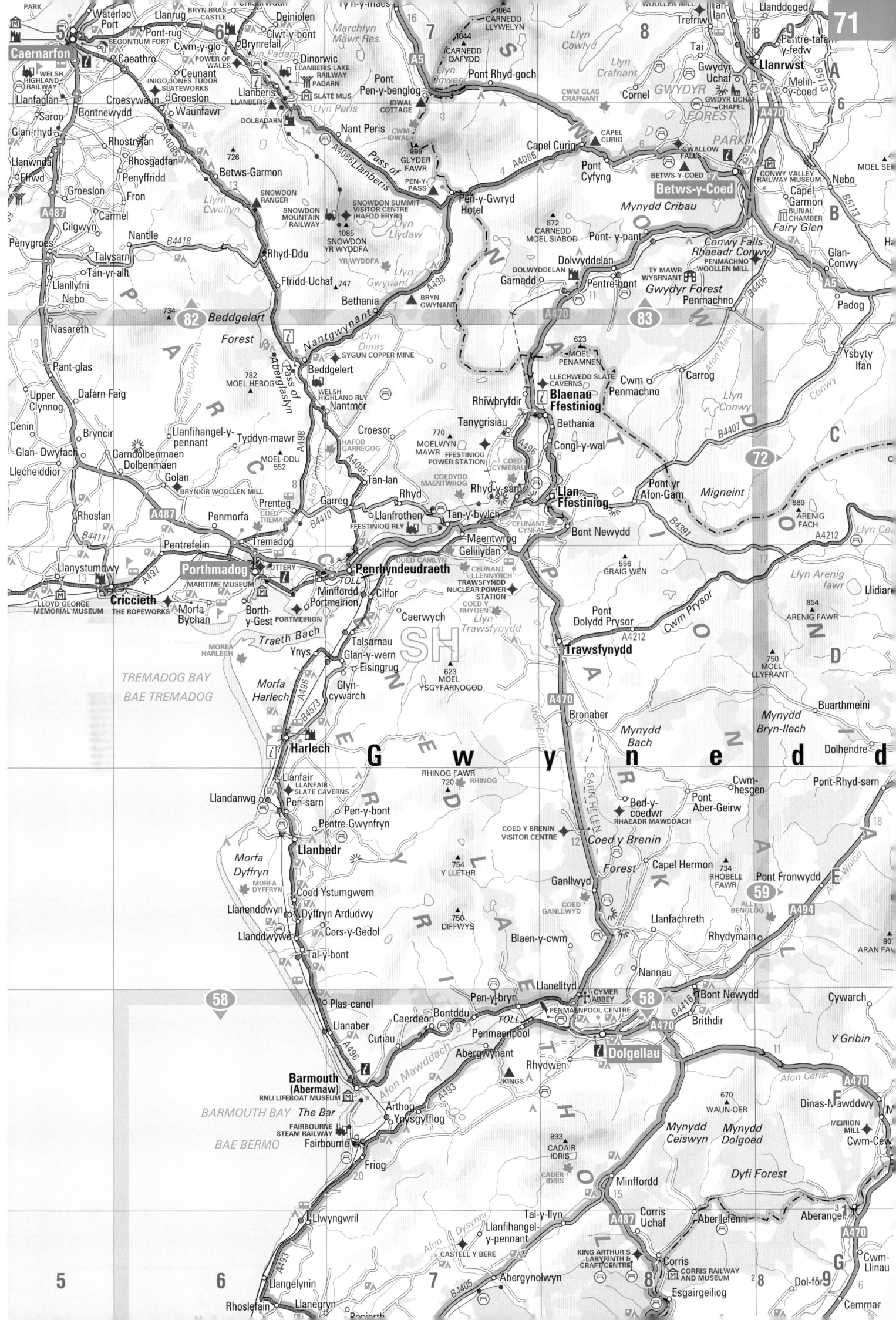

Cheshire — West and Chester

0 1 2 3 4 5 6 miles
0 1 2 3 4 5 6 7 8 9 10km

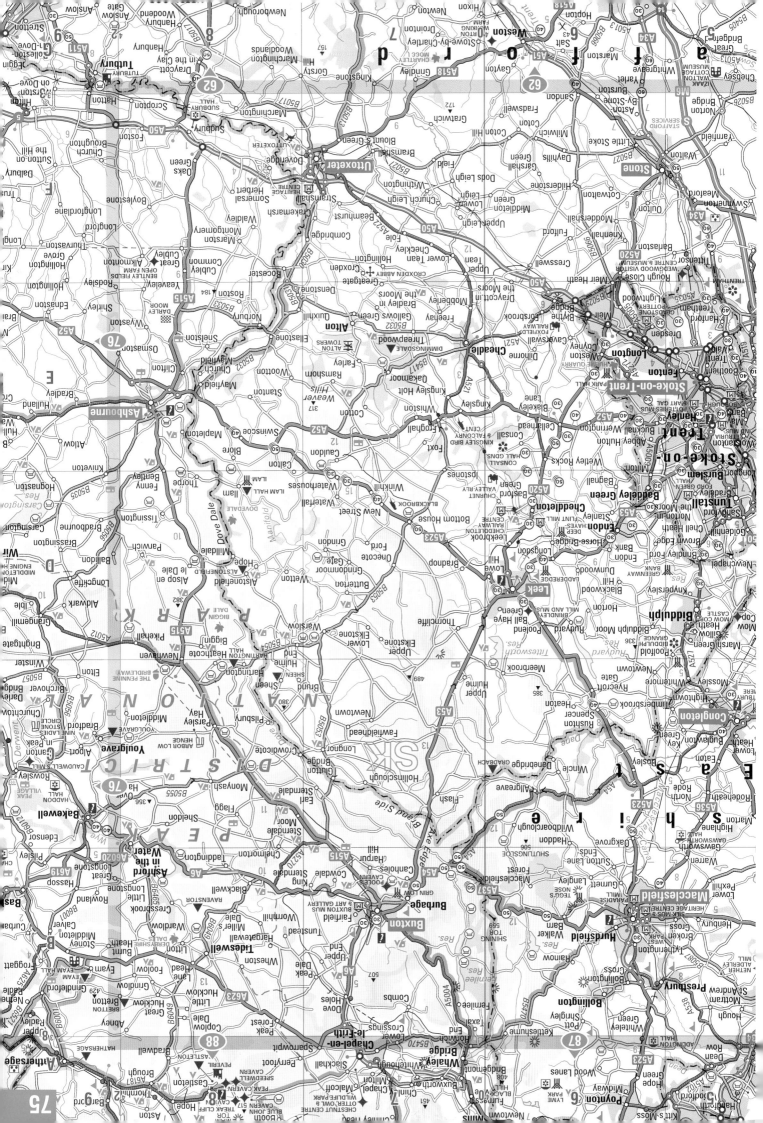

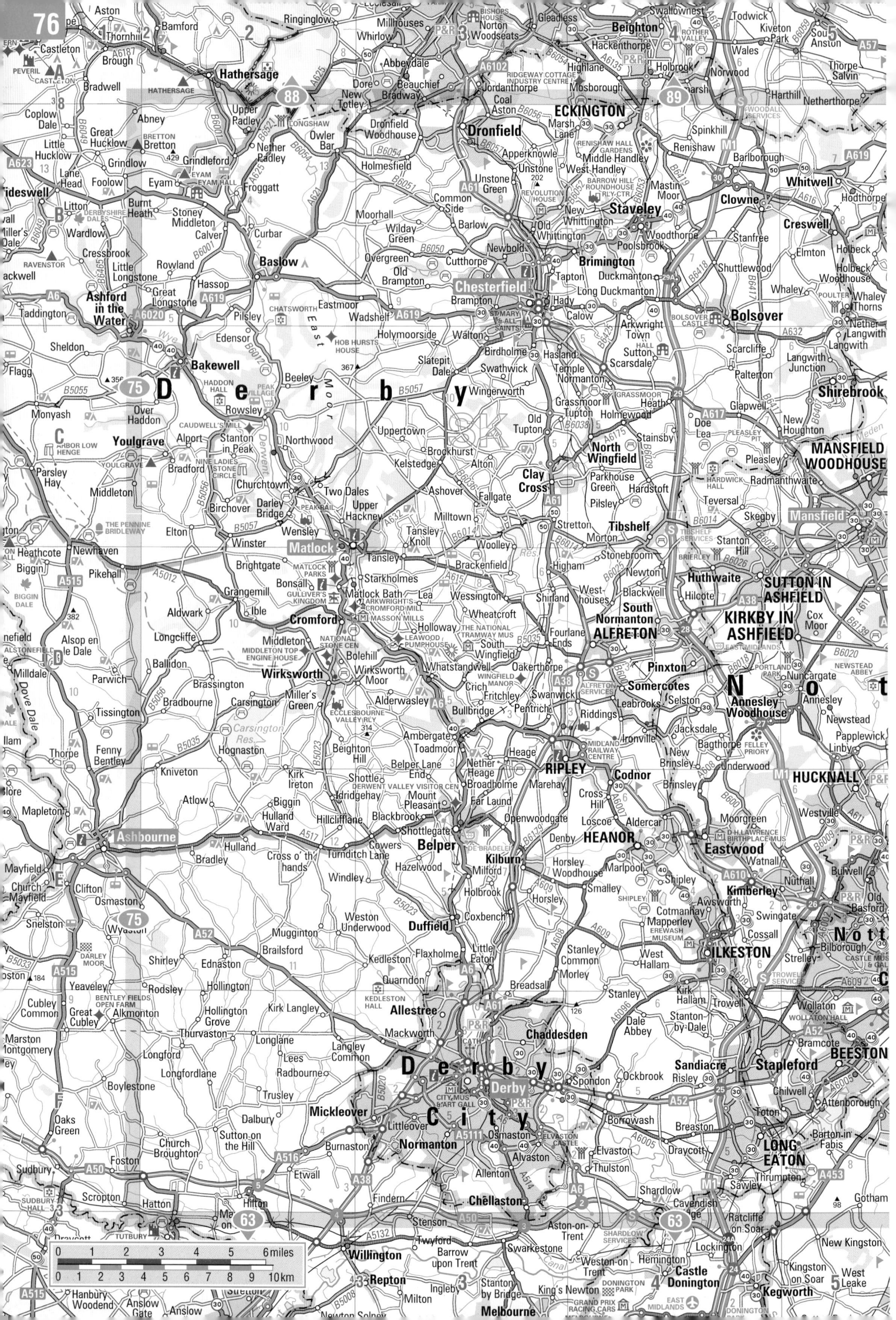

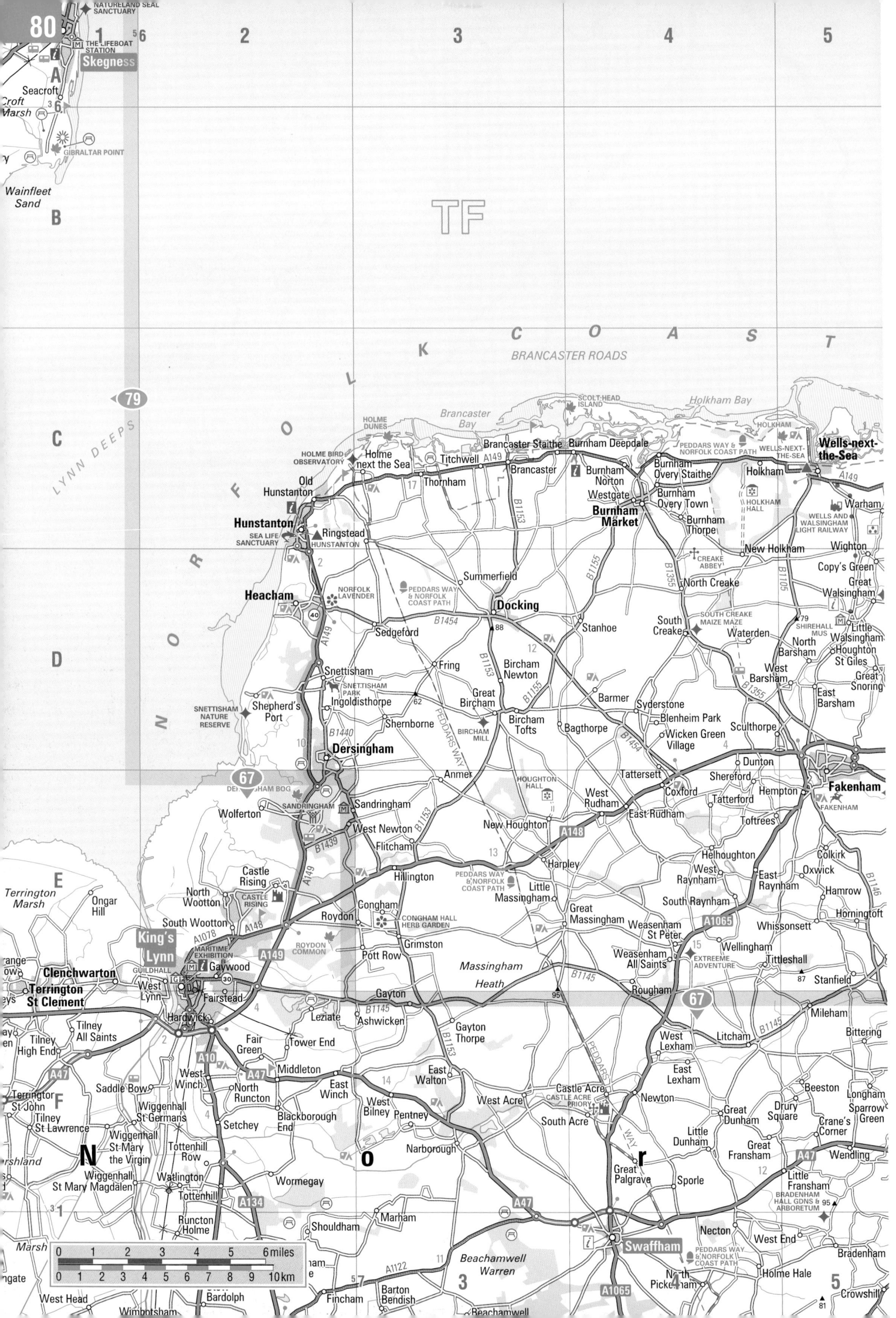

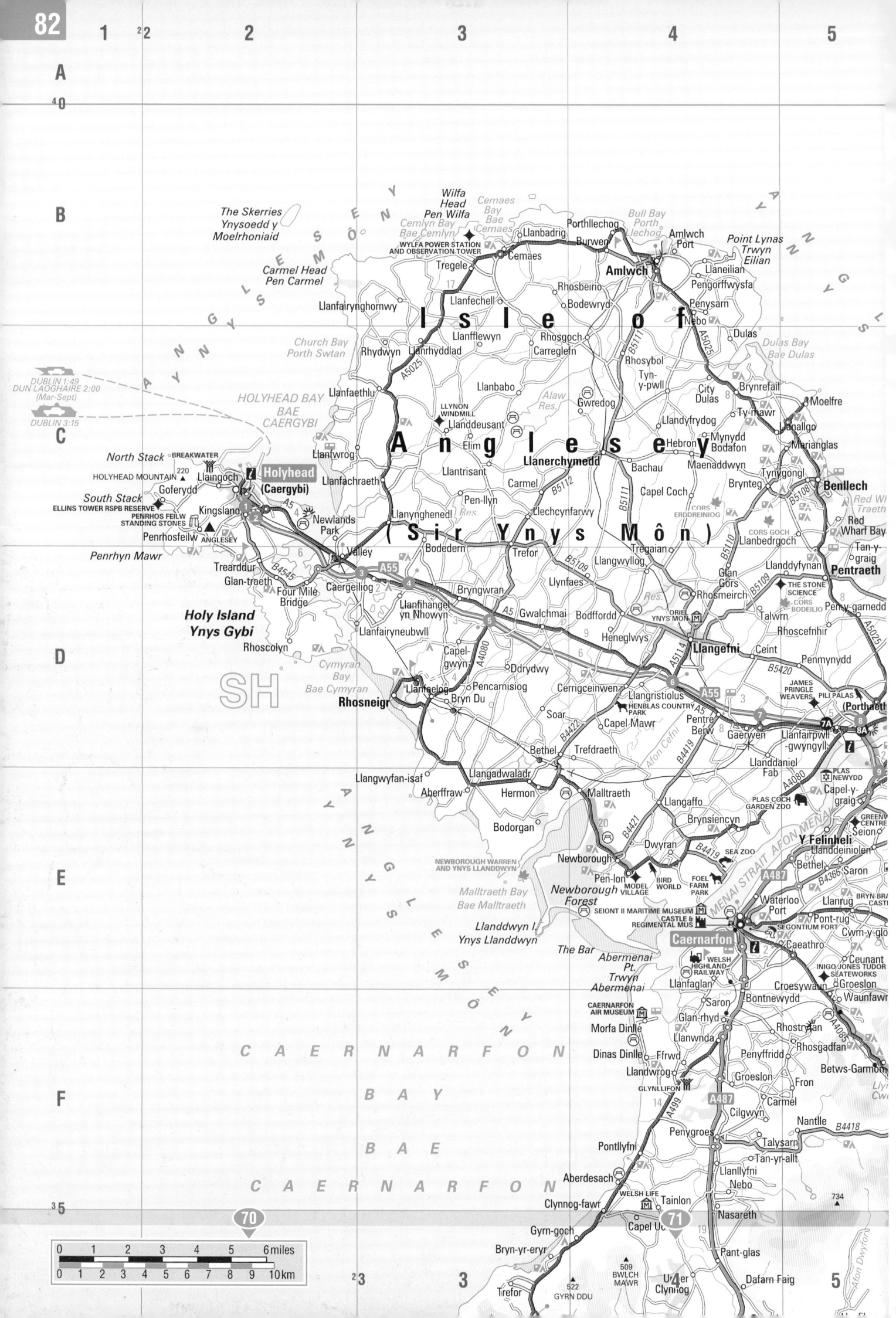

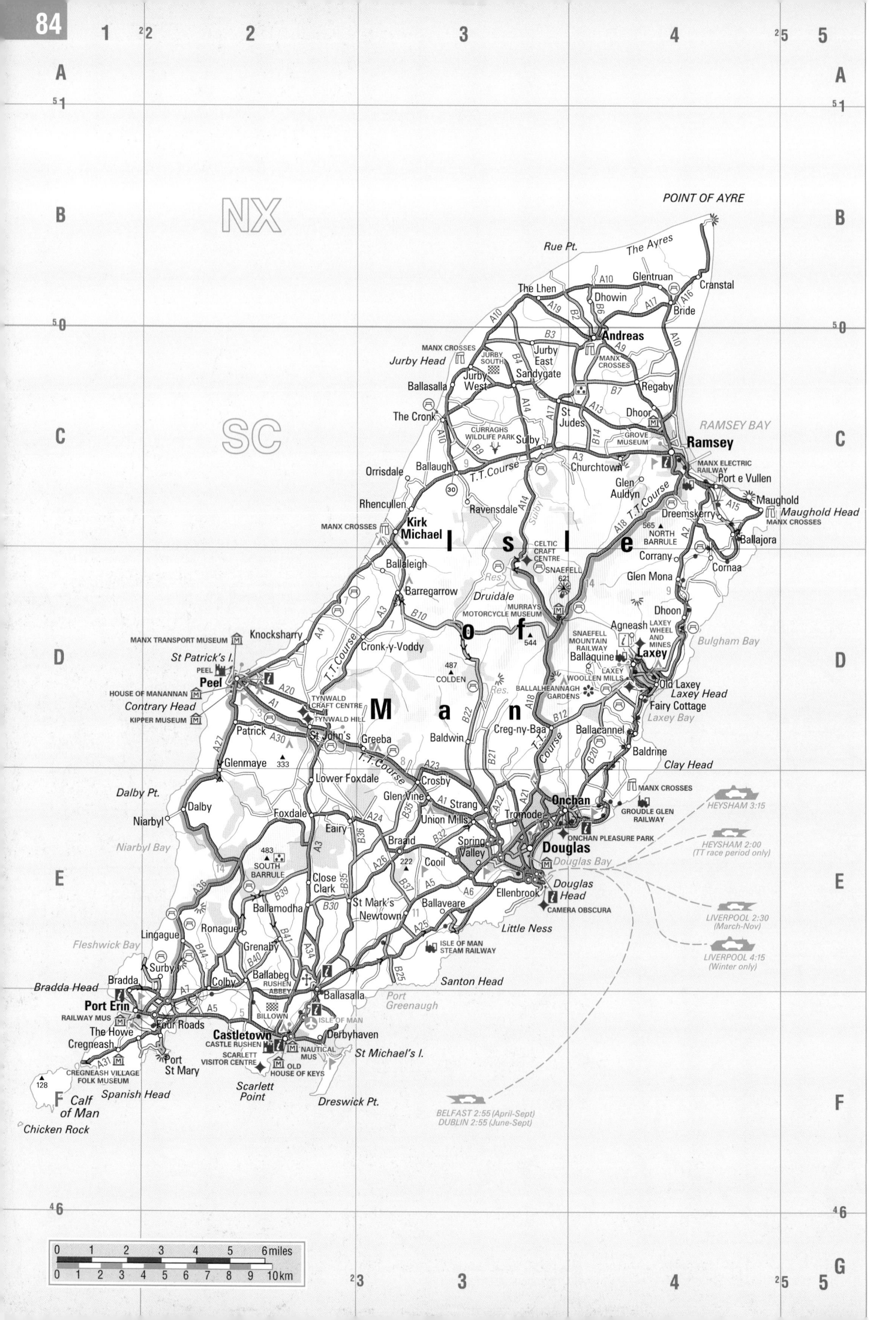

1   2   2   3   4   2   5   5

A

B

POINT OF AYRE

NX

Rue Pt. *The Ayres*

Glentruan
The Lhen   Dhowin   A16   Cranstal
A10   A19   B2   A17   Bride
MANX CROSSES   A9   Andreas   A10
Jurby Head   JURBY   Jurby   Sandygate   MANX
SOUTH   East   CROSSES
Jurby   B4   B7   Regaby
West   A14   A17   St   A13   Dhoor
Ballasalla   Judes   GROVE
The Cronk   CURRAGHS   A10   B14   MUSEUM   **Ramsey**
WILDLIFE PARK   B9   Sulby   Churchtown   MANX ELECTRIC
SC   Orrisdale   Ballaugh   A3   RAILWAY
T.T. Course   Glen   Port e Vullen
Rhencullen   30   Auldyn   A18   T.T. Course   Maughold
Ravensdale   A14   Dreemskerry   A15   *Maughold Head*
MANX CROSSES   **Kirk**   *Sulby*   565   MANX CROSSES
Michael   **I**   **s**   **l**   NORTH   A2   Ballajora
CELTIC   BARRULE   Corrany
Ballaleigh   CRAFT   **e**   Cornaa
CENTRE   SNAEFELL   Glen Mona   9
Barregarrow   *Druidale*   621   14   Dhoon
Res.   MURRAYS   Agneash   LAXEY
MANX TRANSPORT MUSEUM   B10   MOTORCYCLE MUSEUM   SNAEFELL   WHEEL
Knocksharry   A4   **o**   **f**   MOUNTAIN   AND
St Patrick's I.   Cronk-y-Voddy   544   RAILWAY   MINES
PEEL   T.T. Course   487   Ballaquine   **Laxey**
HOUSE OF MANANNAN   **Peel**   A20   COLDEN   LAXEY   Old Laxey
Contrary Head   A1   *Res.*   **M**   **a**   **n**   WOOLLEN MILLS   Fairy Cottage
KIPPER MUSEUM   TYNWALD   BALLALHEANNAGH   Laxey Head
CRAFT CENTRE   B22   GARDENS   *Laxey Bay*
Patrick   A30   TYNWALD HILL   Baldwin   A18   Ballacannel
3   St John's   Greeba   Creg-ny-Baa   B12   Baldrine
Glenmaye   333   8   A23   B21   T.T.   *Clay Head*
Lower Foxdale   Crosby   B20   7
Dalby Pt.   Glen Vine   A1   Strang   A22   *MANX CROSSES*
Dalby   Foxdale   A24   Union Mills   A21   **Onchan**   GROUDLE GLEN
Niarbyl   Eairy   B35   Tromode   RAILWAY   *HEYSHAM 3:15*
B36   Braaid   B32   Spring   ONCHAN PLEASURE PARK
Niarbyl Bay   483   A26   Valley   **Douglas**   *HEYSHAM 2:00*
SOUTH   222   Cooil   A5   *(TT race period only)*
BARRULE   14   A6   *Douglas Bay*
A36   Close   Ellenbrook   *Douglas*
Clark   St Mark's   A25   *Head*   *LIVERPOOL 2:30*
Lingague   Ronague   Newtown   11   Ballaveare   CAMERA OBSCURA   *(March-Nov)*
B39   B30   *Little Ness*
Surby   Ballamodha   A34   ISLE OF MAN   *LIVERPOOL 4:15*
B44   Grenaby   A25   STEAM RAILWAY   *(Winter only)*
Fleshwick Bay   B40   B41   *Santon Head*
Bradda Head   Bradda   A1   Ballabeg   *Port*
Port Erin   Colby   RUSHEN   B25   *Greenaugh*
RAILWAY MUS   A5   ABBEY   Ballasalla
Four Roads   5   BILLOWN   *Port Greenaugh*
The Howe   **Castletown**   ISLE OF MAN   Derbyhaven
Cregneash   A31   CASTLE RUSHEN   NAUTICAL
CREGNEASH VILLAGE   SCARLETT   MUS   *St Michael's I.*
FOLK MUSEUM   128   Port   VISITOR CENTRE   OLD
St Mary   HOUSE OF KEYS
Calf   *Spanish Head*   *Scarlett*   *Dreswick Pt.*
of Man   *Point*   *BELFAST 2:55 (April-Sept)*
Chicken Rock   *DUBLIN 2:55 (June-Sept)*

C

D

E

F

G

0   1   2   3   4   5   6 miles
0   1   2   3   4   5   6   7   8   9   10km

RAMSEY BAY

Bulgham Bay

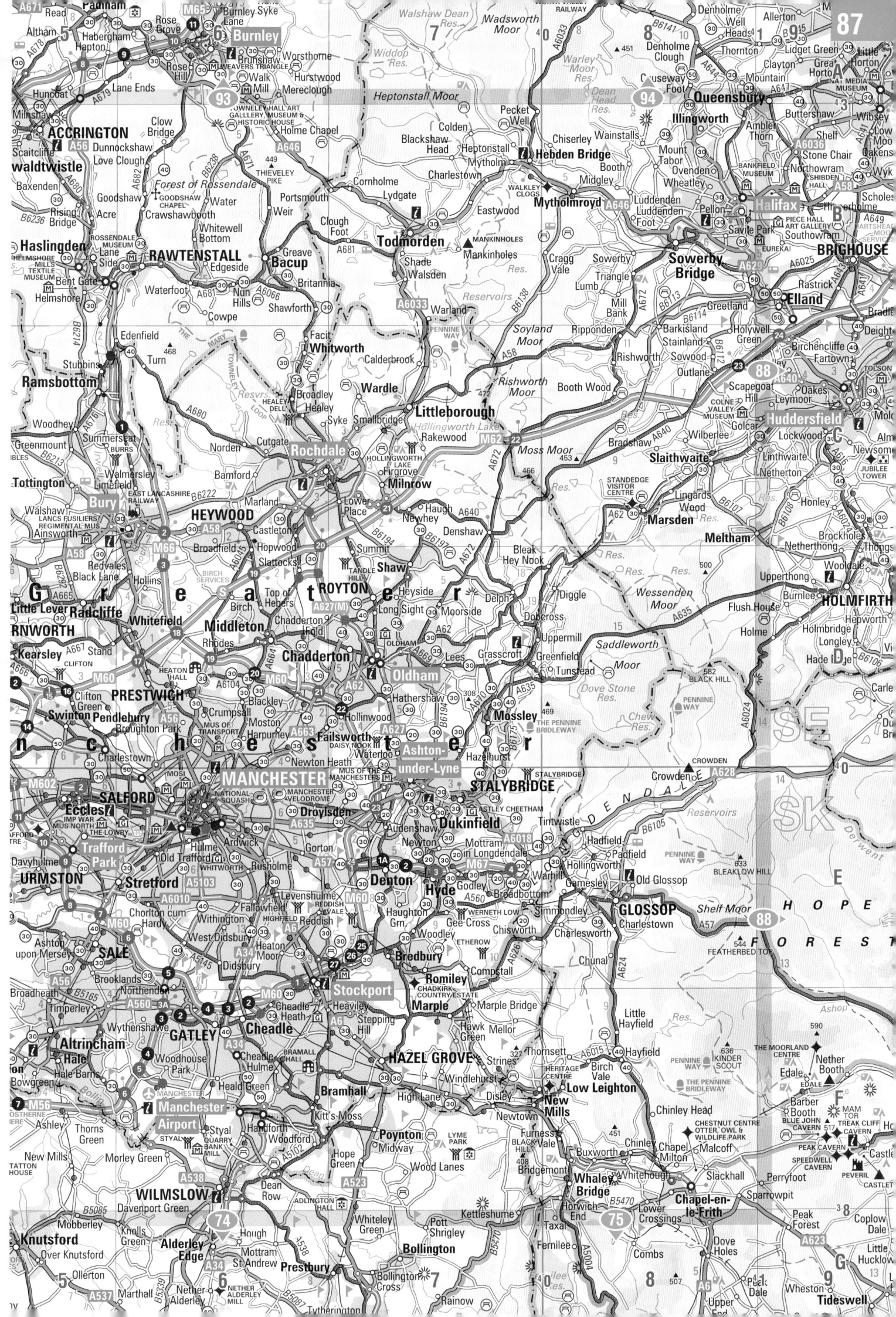

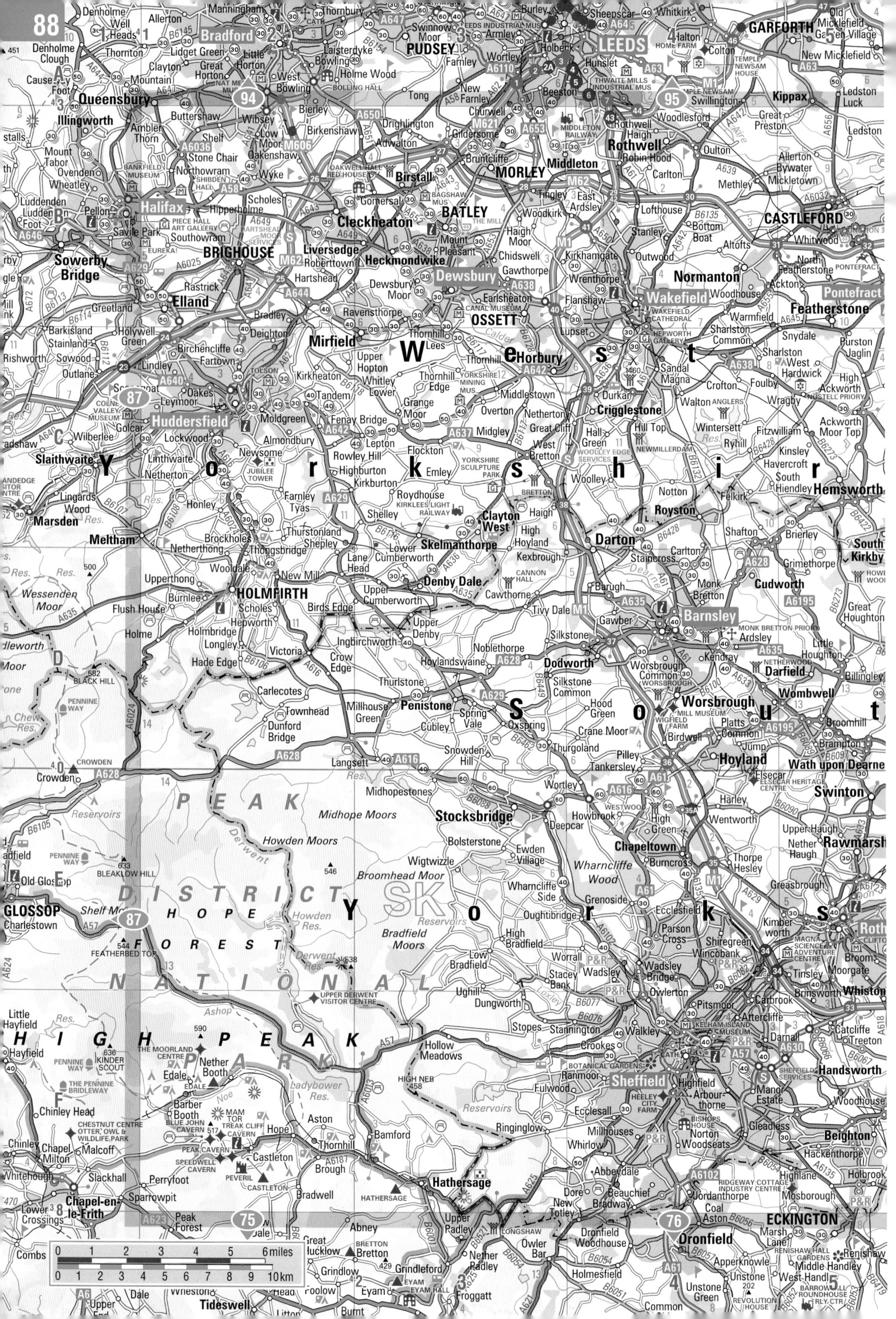

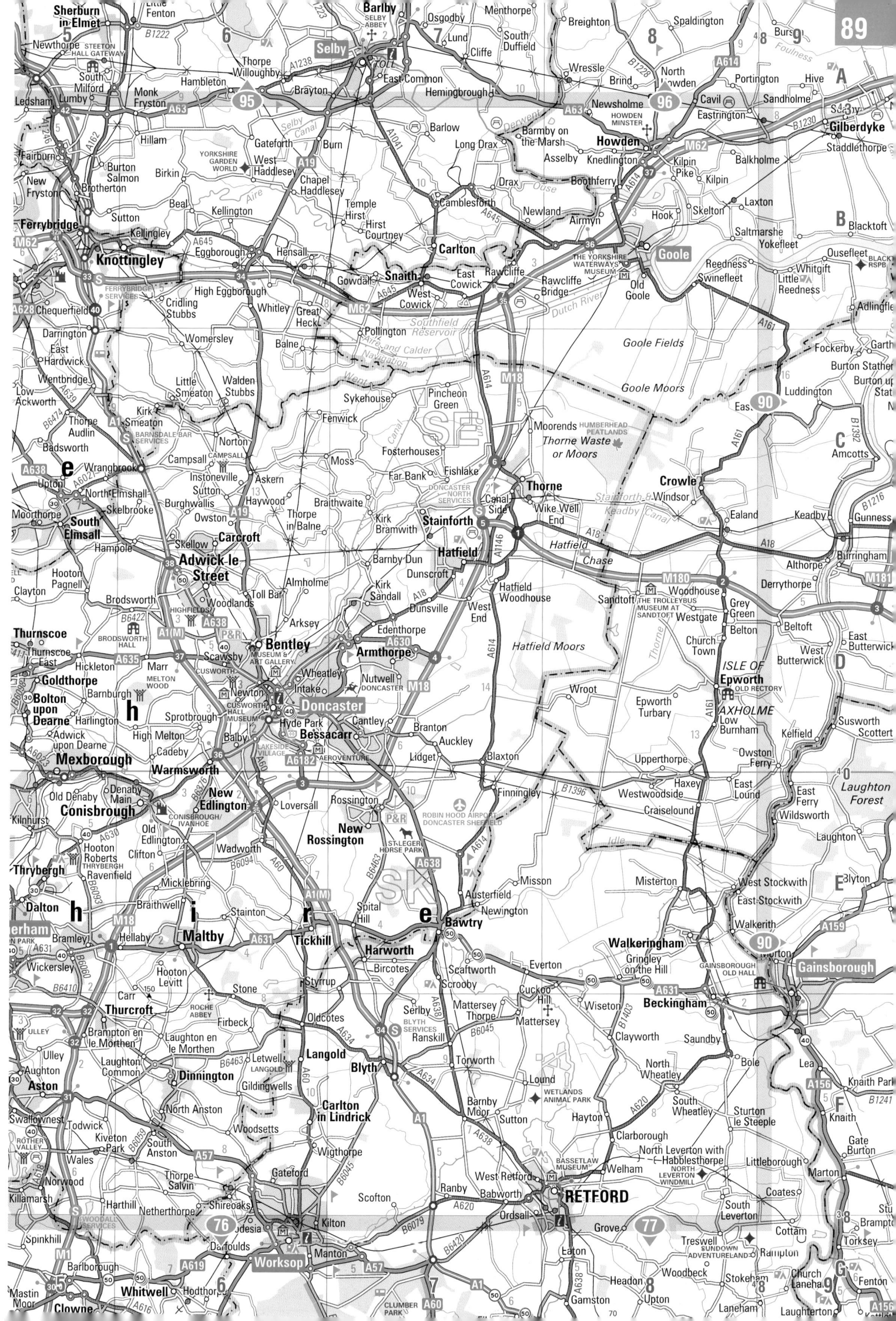

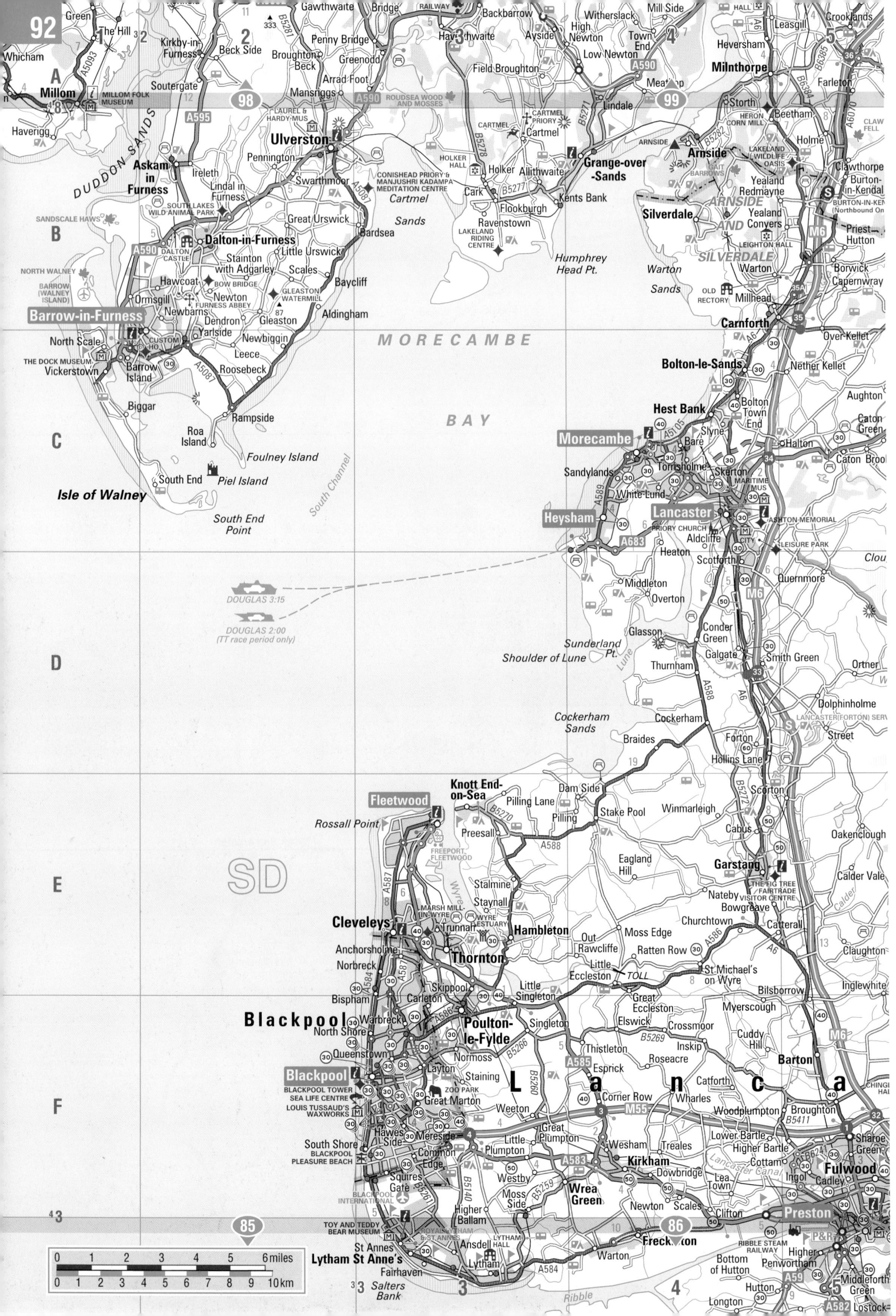

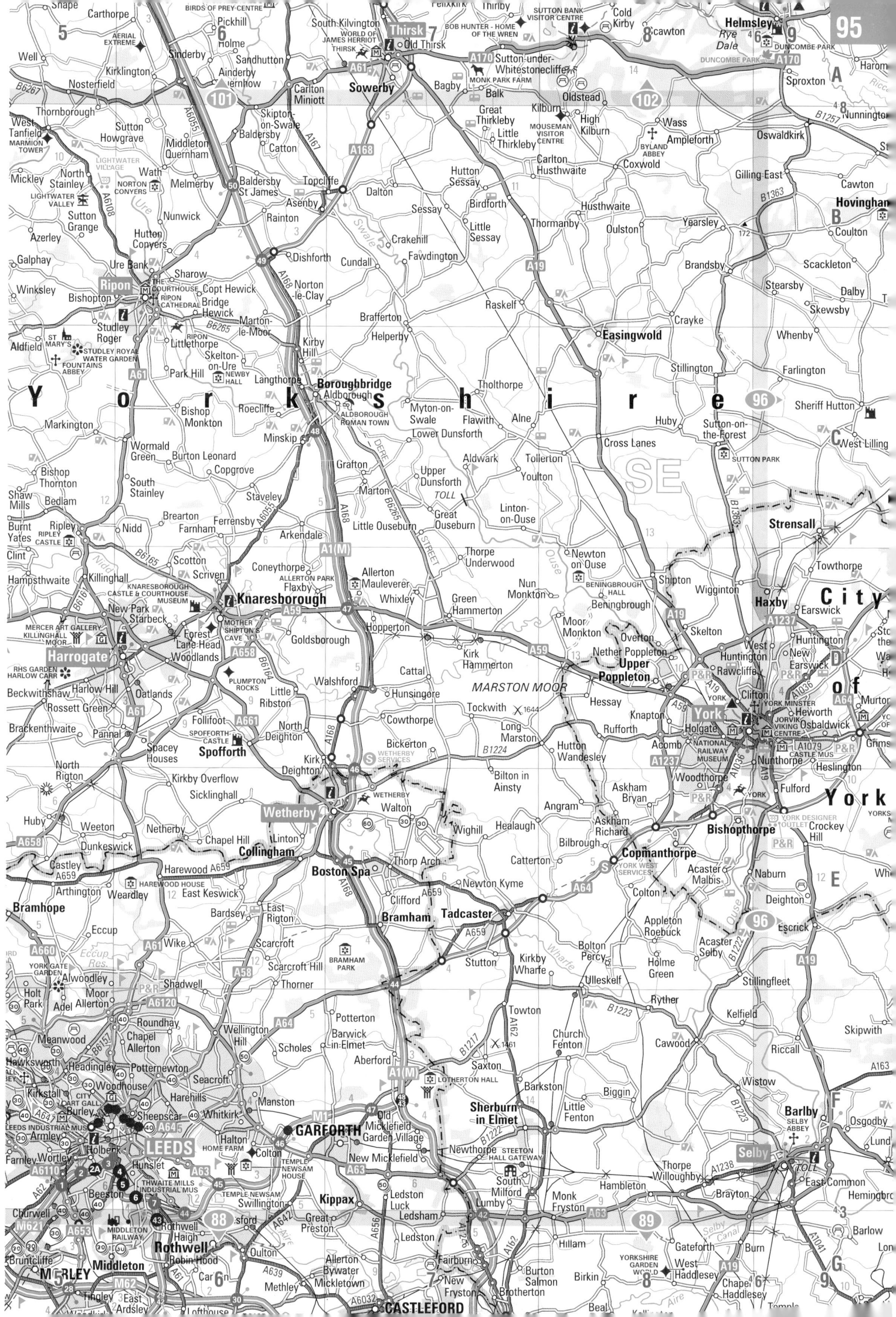

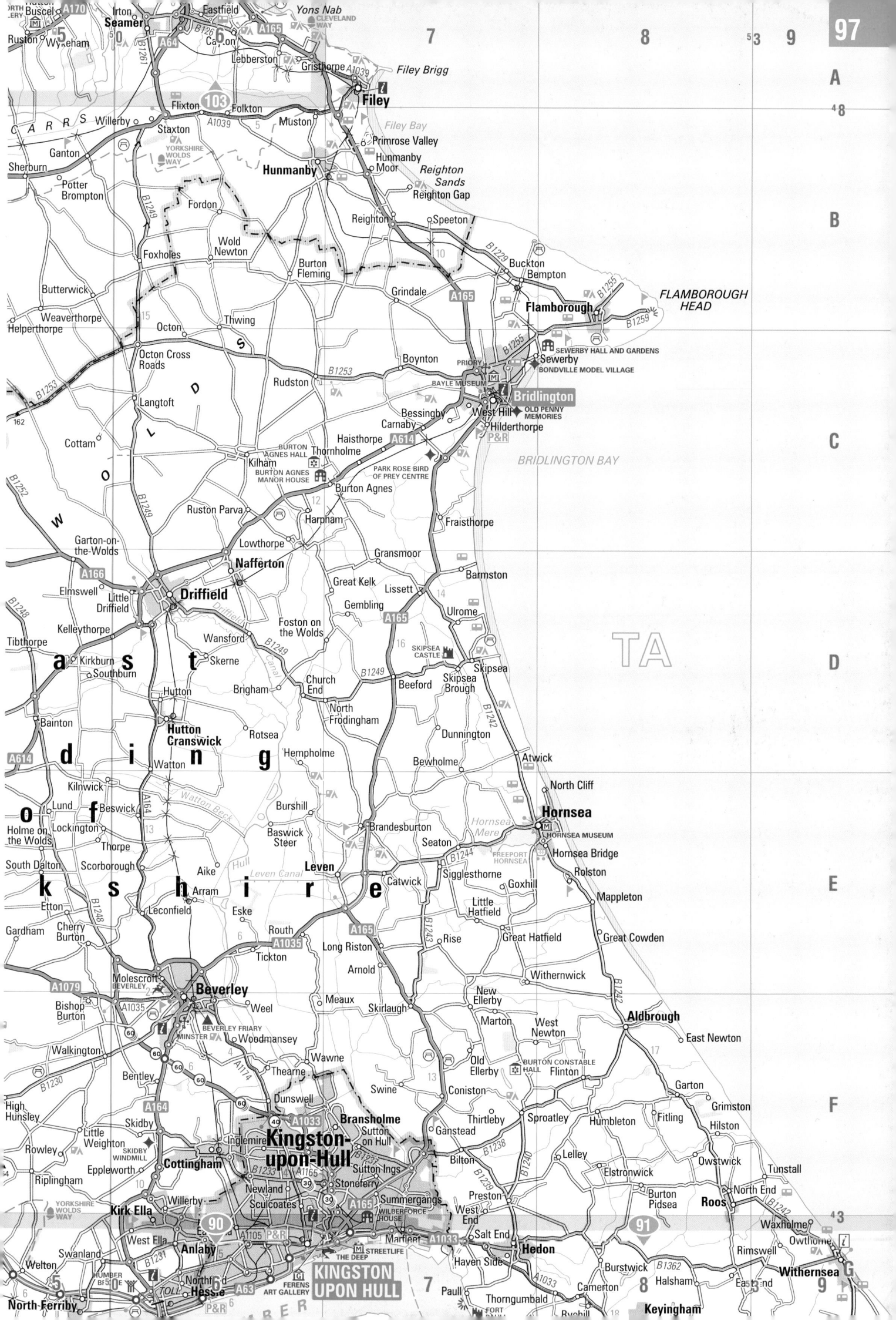

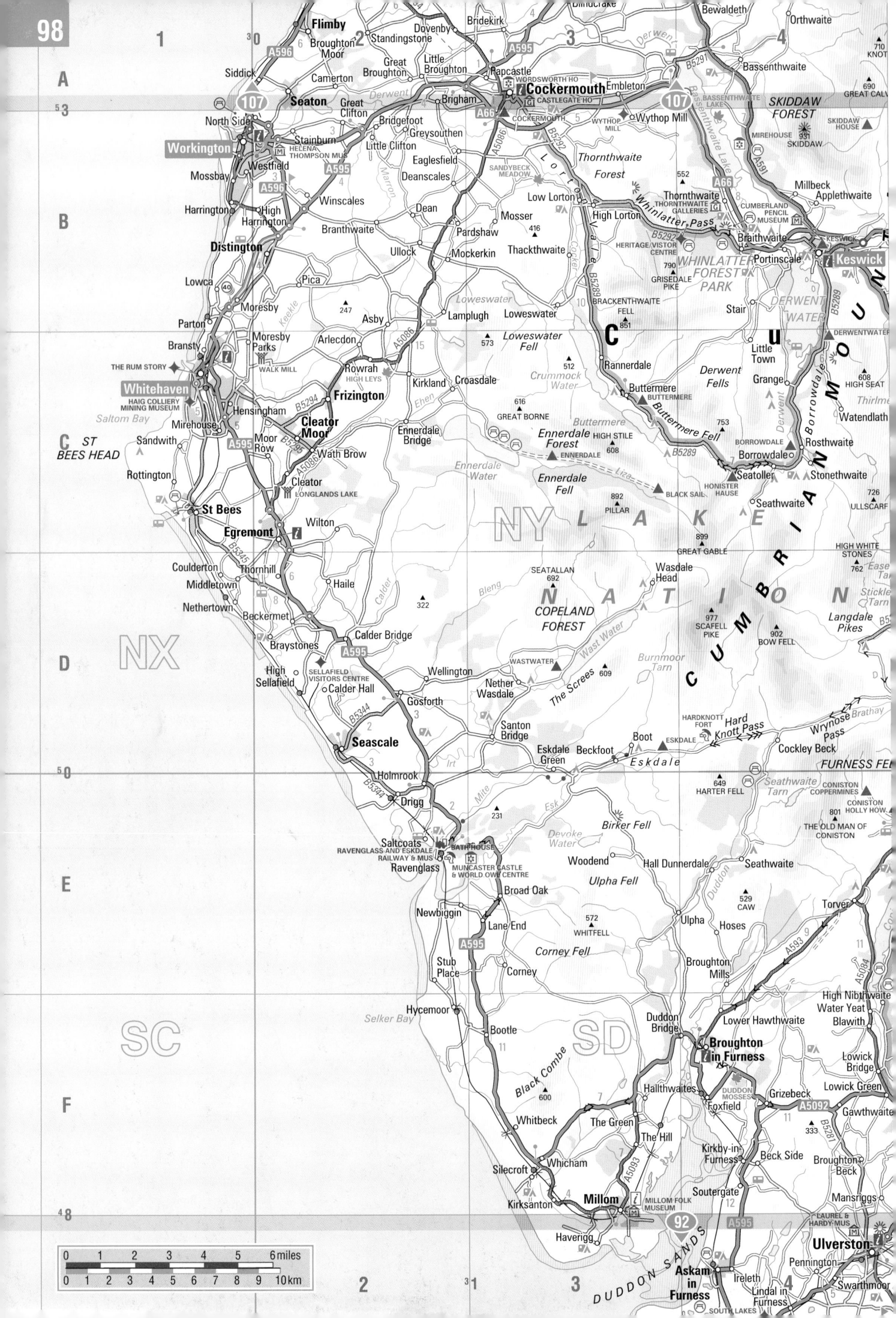

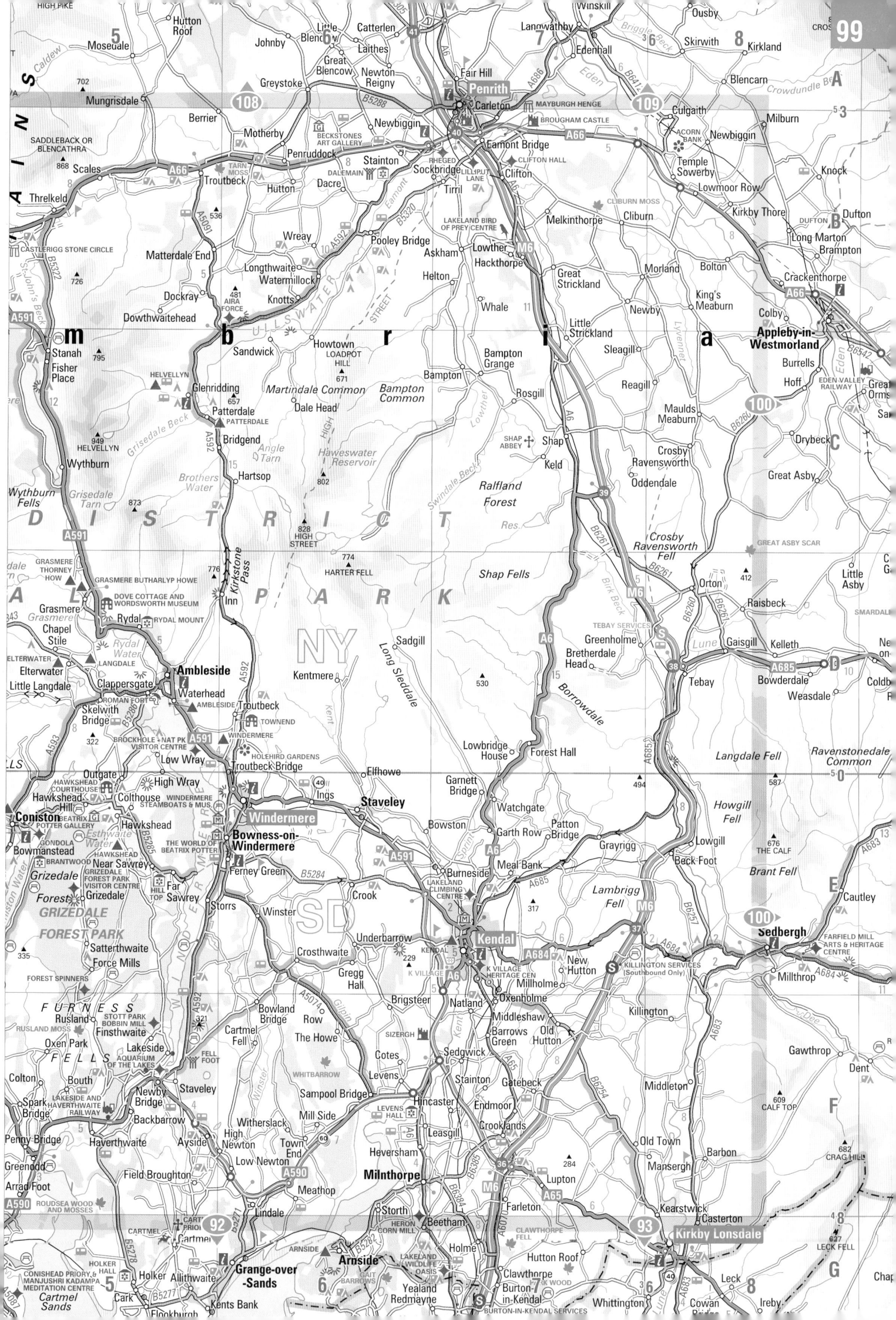

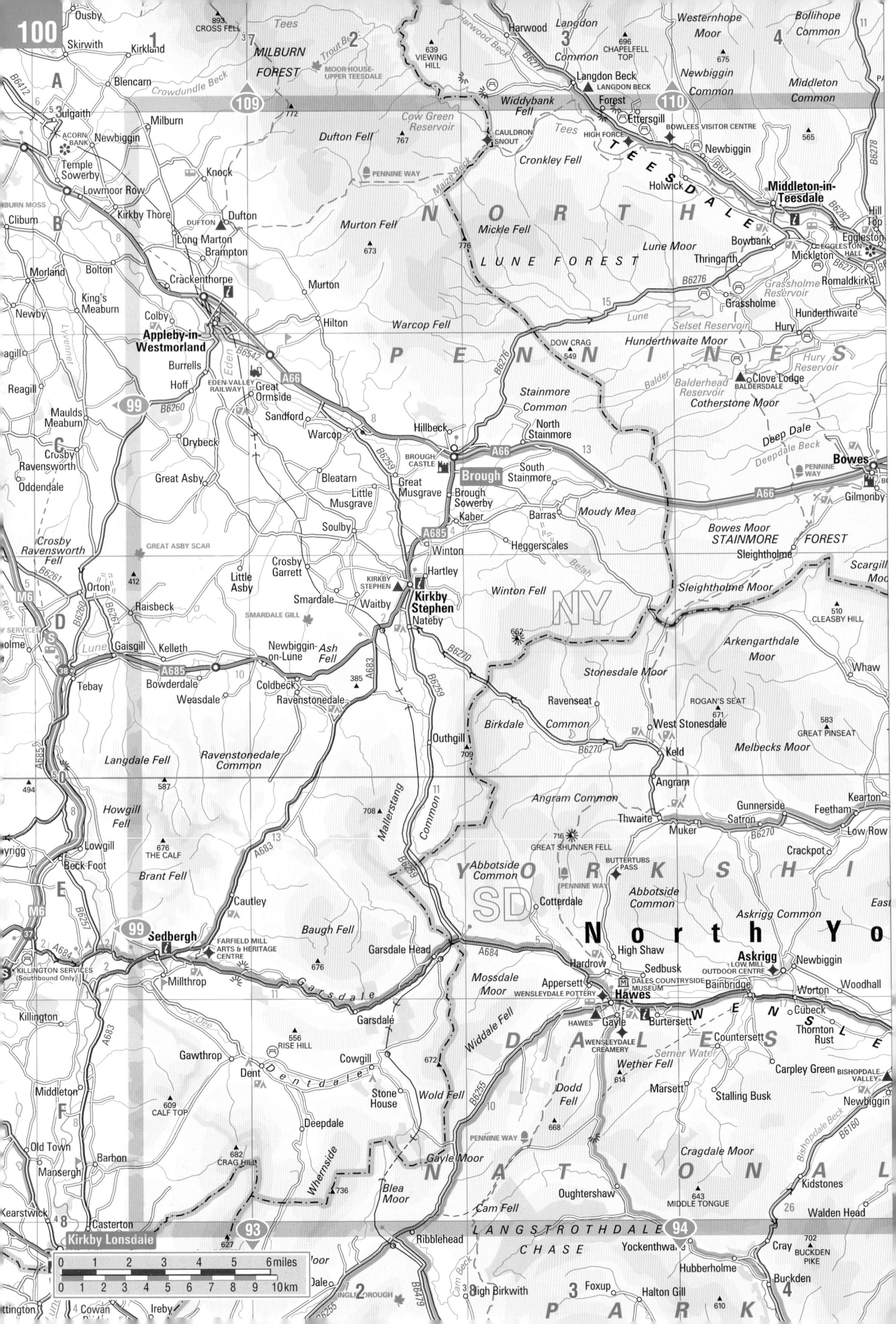

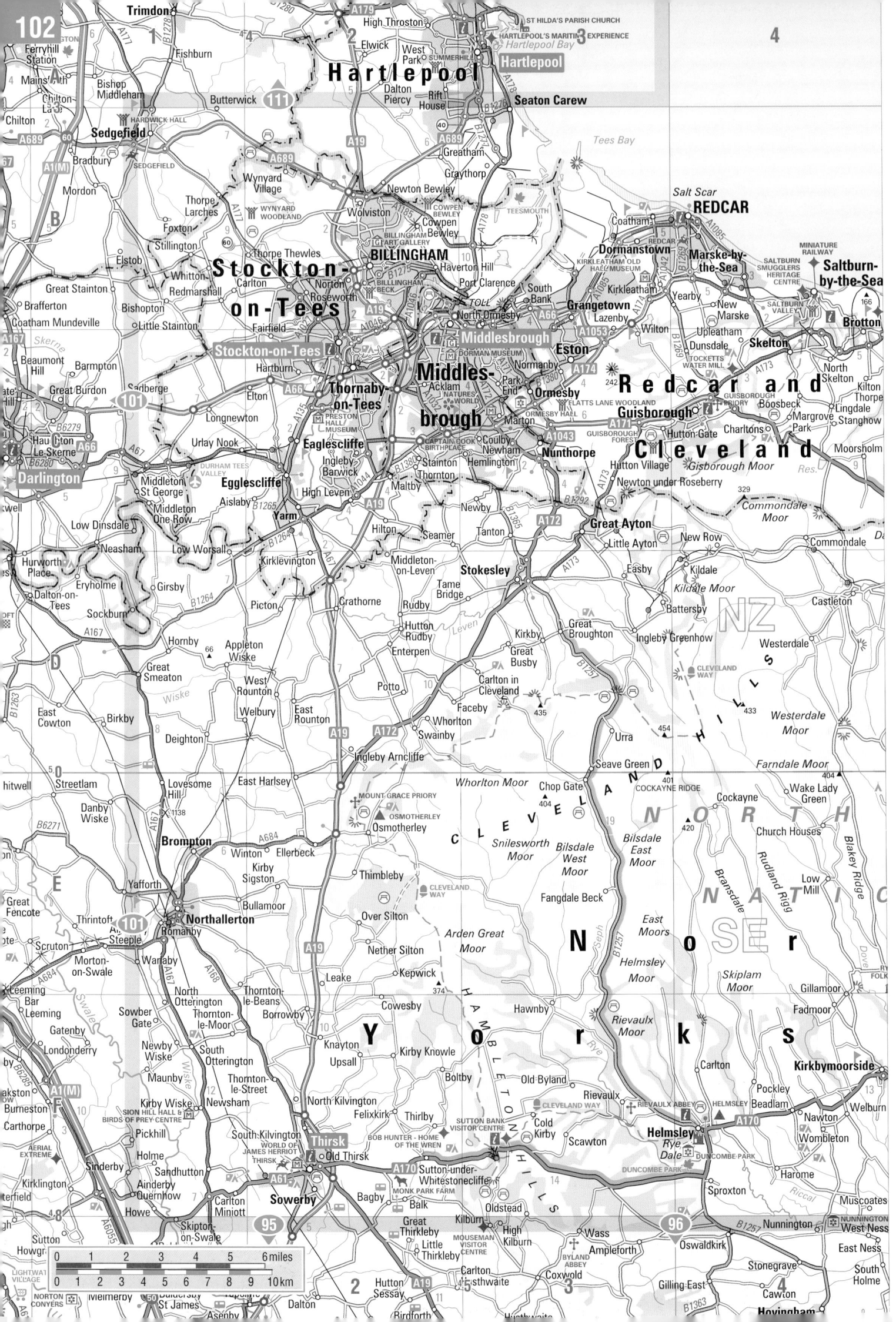

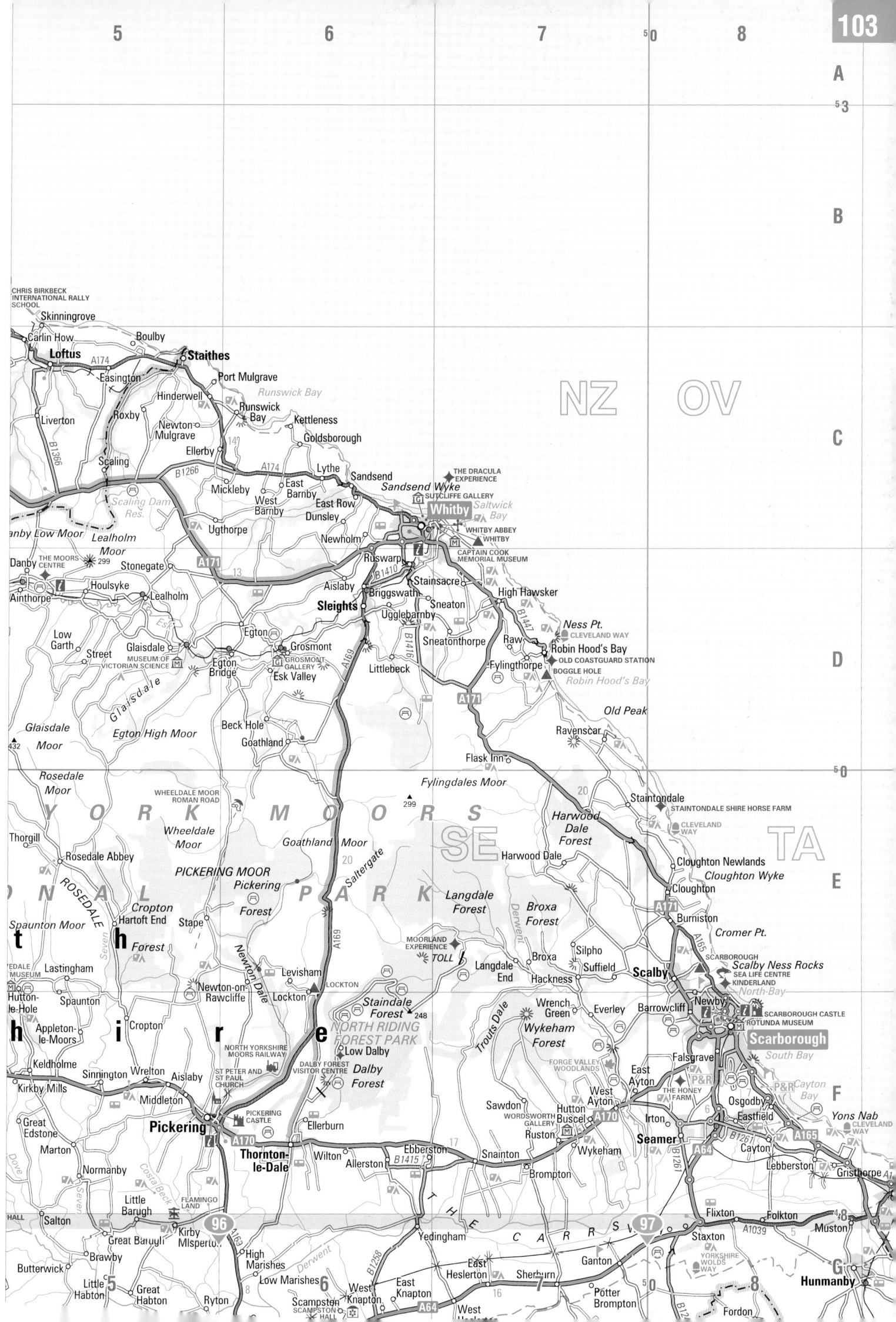

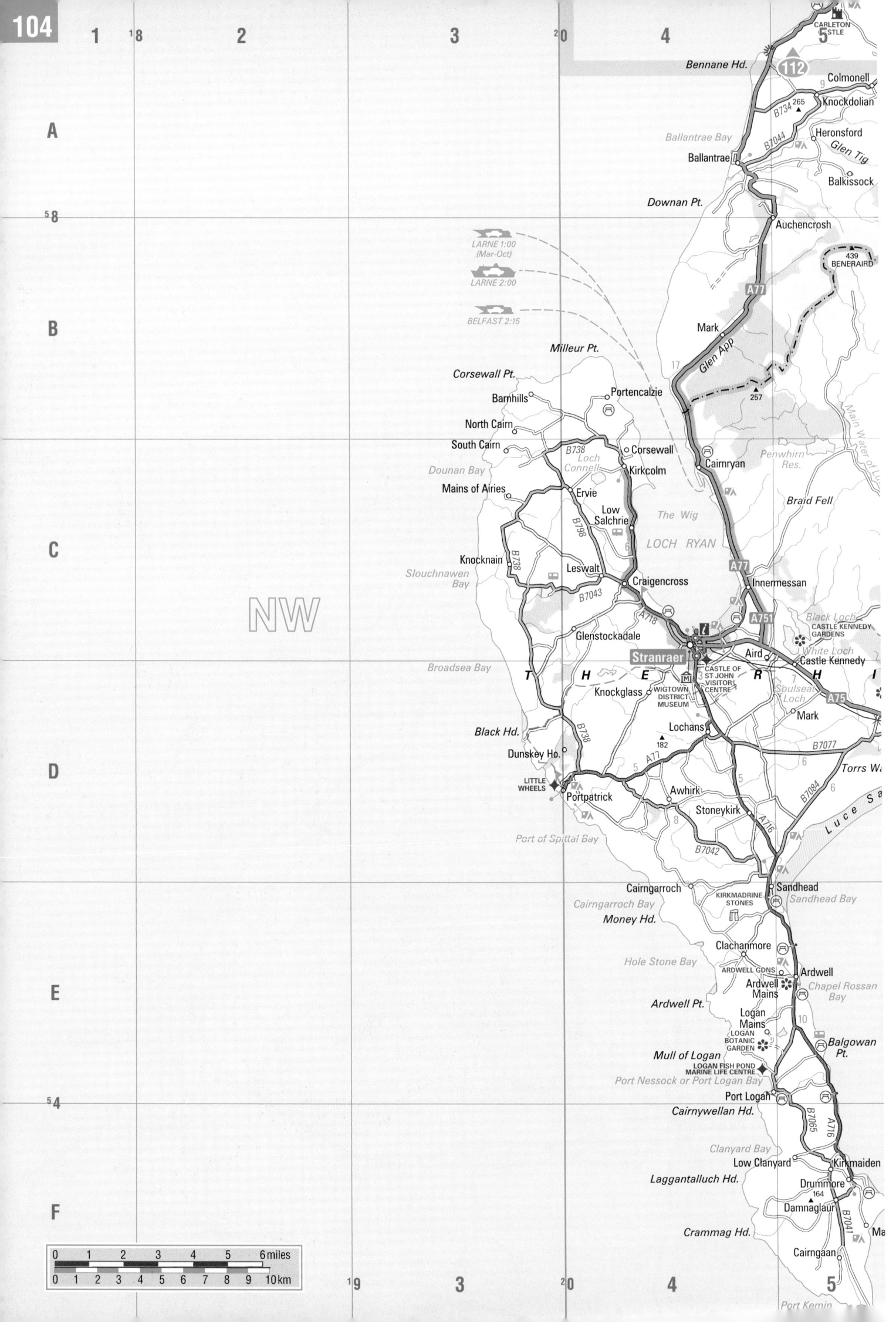

1   18   2   3   20   4   5

A

B

C

D

E

F

NW

LARNE 1:00
(Mar-Oct)

LARNE 2:00

BELFAST 2:15

Bennane Hd.

112

Colmonell

B734 265

Knockdolian

Heronsford

B7044

Glen Tig

Ballantrae

Balkissock

Ballantrae Bay

Downan Pt.

Auchencrosh

439
BENERAIRD

A77

Mark

Glen App

257

Milleur Pt.

Corsewall Pt.

Portencalzie

Barnhills

North Cairn

Corsewall

B738

South Cairn

Loch
Connell

Kirkcolm

Cairnryan

Penwhirn
Res.

Dounan Bay

Ervie

Mains of Airies

B798

Low
Salchrie

The Wig

Braid Fell

LOCH RYAN

Knocknain

B738

Leswalt

6

B7043

Craigencross

Innermessan

A77

Slouchnawen
Bay

A718

Black Loch

Glenstockadale

CASTLE KENNEDY
GARDENS

White Loch

Broadsea Bay

Stranraer

Aird

Castle Kennedy

T H E

R H I

CASTLE OF
ST JOHN
VISITOR
CENTRE

A751

Knockglass

WIGTOWN
DISTRICT
MUSEUM

Soulseat
Loch

A75

Black Hd.

B738

Lochans

Mark

Dunskey Ho.

182

A77

B7077

Torrs Wa

LITTLE
WHEELS

5

5

B7084

6

Portpatrick

Awhirk

Stoneykirk

A716

Luce Sa

8

Port of Spittal Bay

B7042

Cairngarroch

KIRKMADRINE
STONES

Sandhead

Cairngarroch Bay

Sandhead Bay

Money Hd.

Clachanmore

Hole Stone Bay

ARDWELL GDNS

Ardwell

Ardwell
Mains

Chapel Rossan
Bay

Ardwell Pt.

Logan
Mains

10

LOGAN
BOTANIC
GARDEN

Balgowan
Pt.

Mull of Logan

LOGAN FISH POND
MARINE LIFE CENTRE

Port Nessock or Port Logan Bay

Port Logan

54

Cairnywellan Hd.

B7065

A716

Clanyard Bay

Low Clanyard

Kirkmaiden

Laggantalluch Hd.

Drummore

164

Crammag Hd.

Damnaglaur

B7041

Ma

Cairngaan

Port Kemin

0 1 2 3 4 5 6 miles
0 1 2 3 4 5 6 7 8 9 10km

19   3   20   4   5

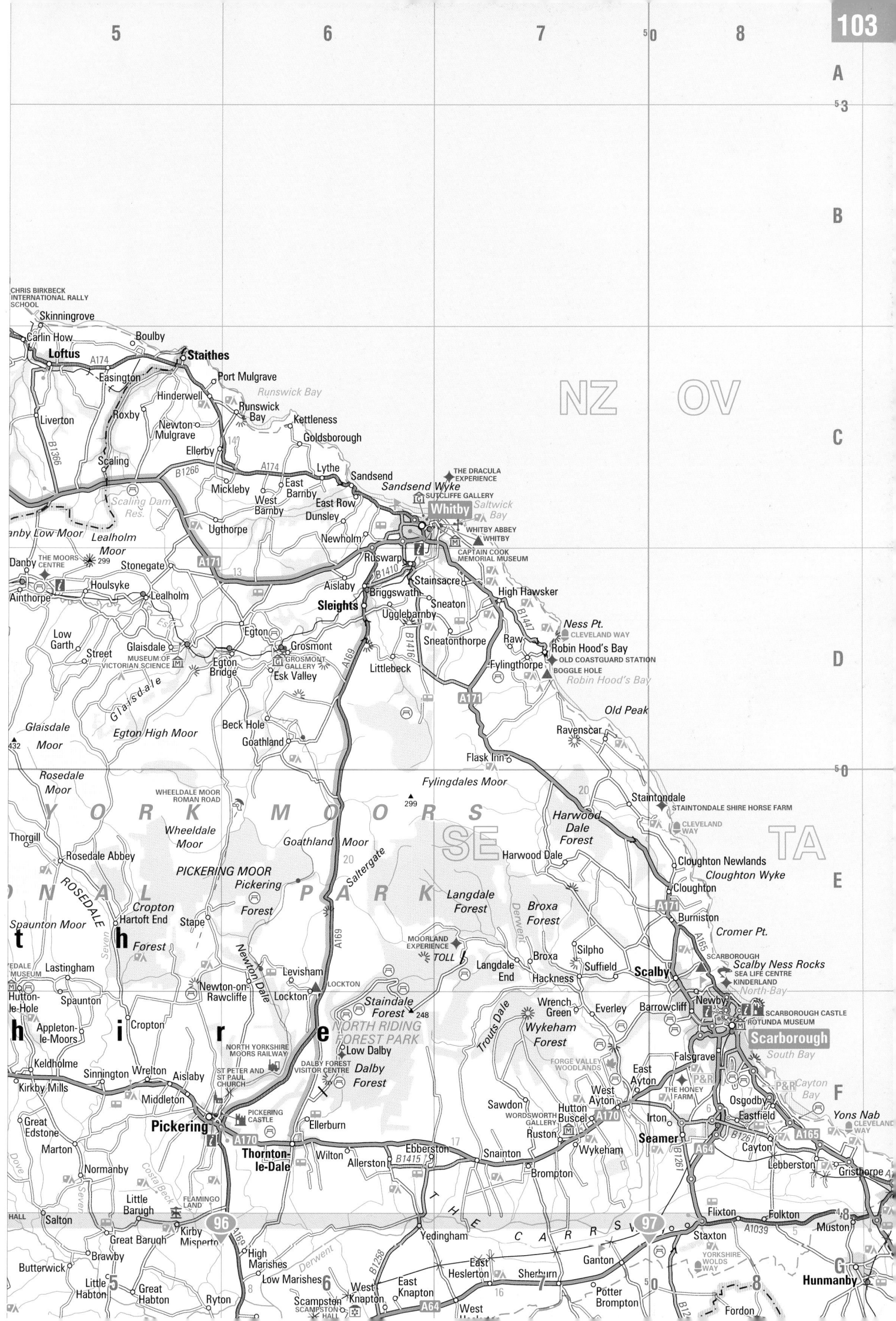

A

B

C

NW

D

E

F

CARLETON STLE

Bennane Hd.

112

Colmonell

B734 265 Knockdolian

Heronsford

B7044 Glen Tig

Ballantrae Bay

Balkissock

Ballantrae

Downan Pt.

Auchencrosh

LARNE 1:00
(Mar-Oct)

LARNE 2:00

439 BENERAIRD

BELFAST 2:15

A77

Milleur Pt.

Mark

Glen App

Corsewall Pt.

17

Barnhills

Portencalzie

257

Main Water of Ly

North Cairn

Penwhirn Res.

South Cairn

Corsewall

B738

Cairnryan

Braid Fell

Dounan Bay

Loch Connell

Kirkcolm

The Wig

Mains of Airies

Ervie

B798

LOCH RYAN

Low Salchrie

A77

Slouchnawen Bay

Knocknain

B738

Leswalt

6

B7043

Craigencross

Innermessan

Black Loch

A751

A718

CASTLE KENNEDY GARDENS

Glenstockadale

White Loch

Stranraer

Aird

Castle Kennedy

Broadsea Bay

CASTLE OF ST JOHN VISITOR CENTRE

THE

H

E

R

Knockglass

WIGTOWN DISTRICT MUSEUM

Soulseat Loch

A75

Black Hd.

Lochans

Mark

182

B7077

Dunskey Ho.

B738

A77

5

6

Torrs Wa

LITTLE WHEELS

Awhirk

B7084

6

Portpatrick

A716

Luce Sa

Stoneykirk

Port of Spittal Bay

8

B7042

Cairngarroch

Sandhead

Cairngarroch Bay

KIRKMADRINE STONES

Sandhead Bay

Money Hd.

Clachanmore

Hole Stone Bay

ARDWELL GDNS

Ardwell

Ardwell Mains

Chapel Rossan Bay

Ardwell Pt.

Logan Mains

10

LOGAN BOTANIC GARDEN

Mull of Logan

Balgowan Pt.

LOGAN FISH POND MARINE LIFE CENTRE

Port Nessock or Port Logan Bay

Port Logan

Cairnywellan Hd.

B7065

A716

Clanyard Bay

Low Clanyard

Kirkmaiden

Laggantalluch Hd.

Drummore

164

Crammag Hd.

Damnaglaur

B7041

Ma

Cairngaan

Port Kemin

0 1 2 3 4 5 6 miles

0 1 2 3 4 5 6 7 8 9 10km

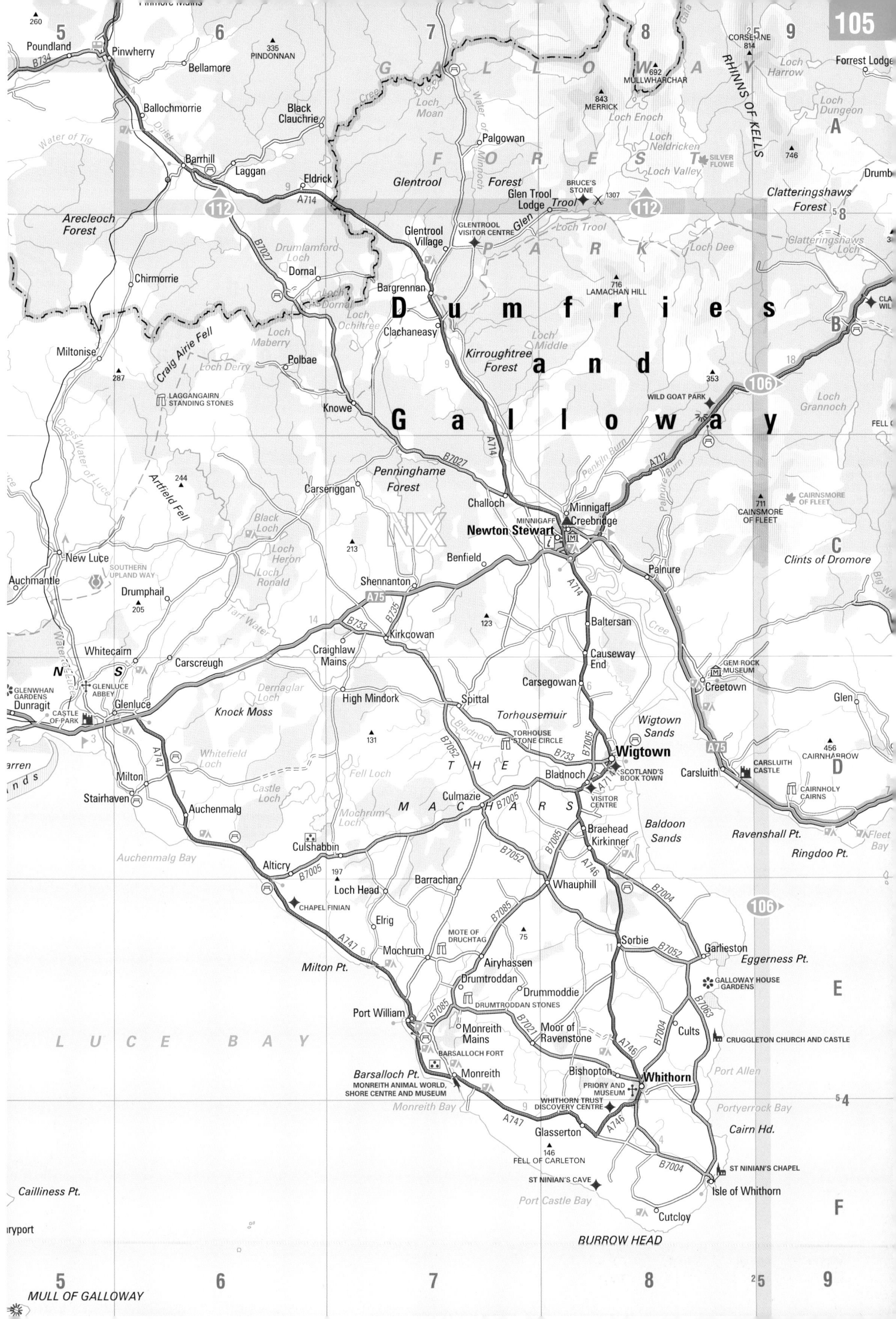

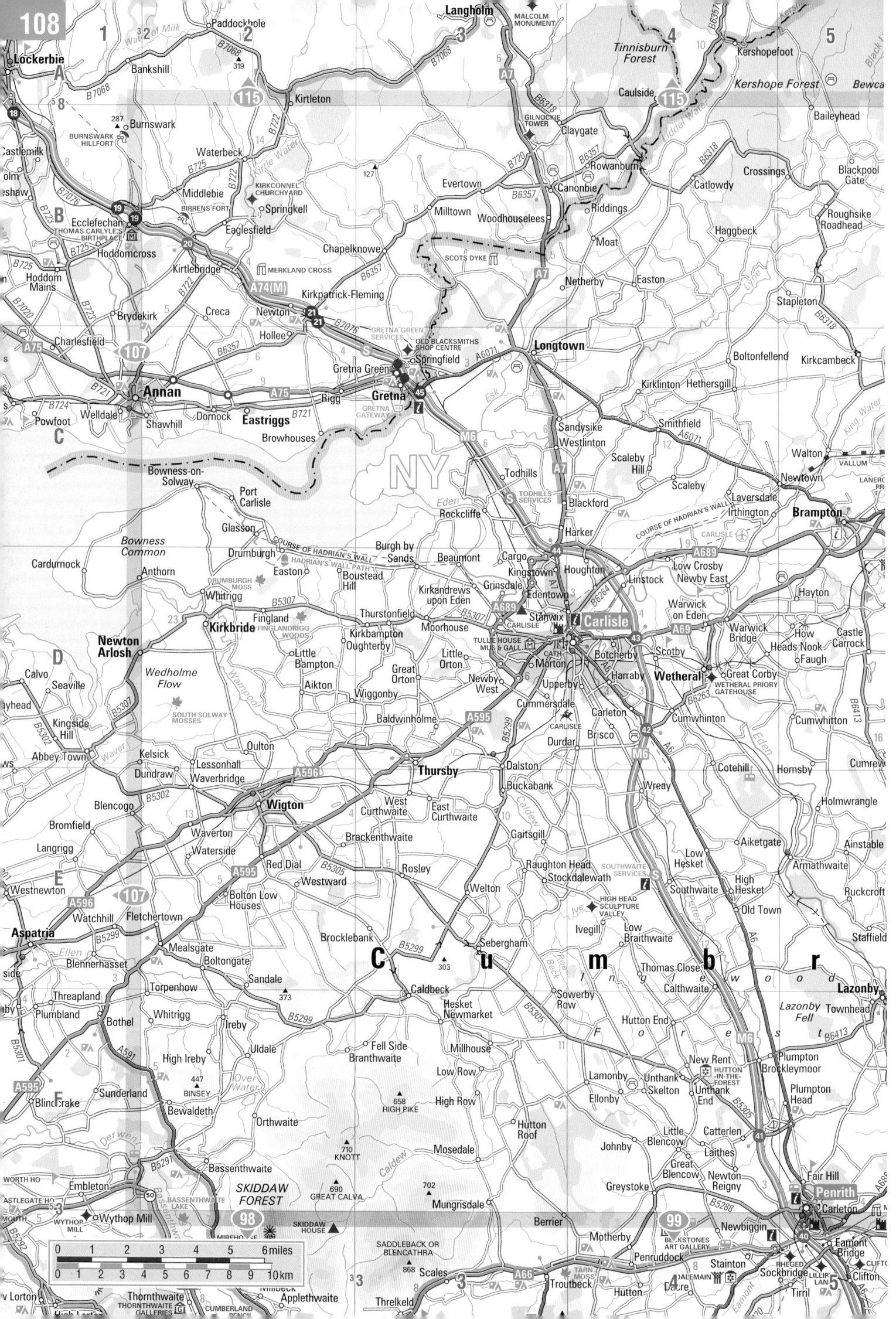

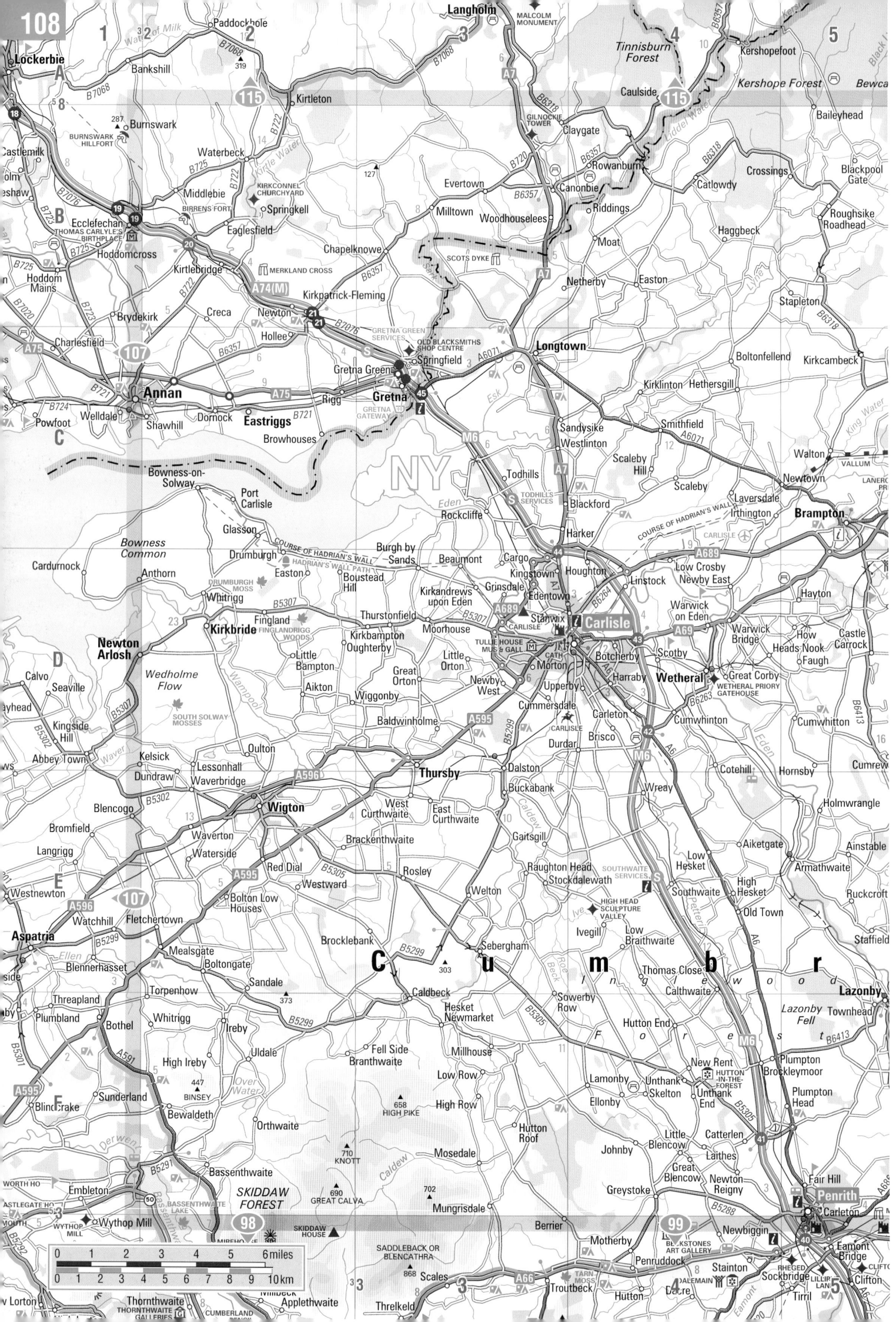

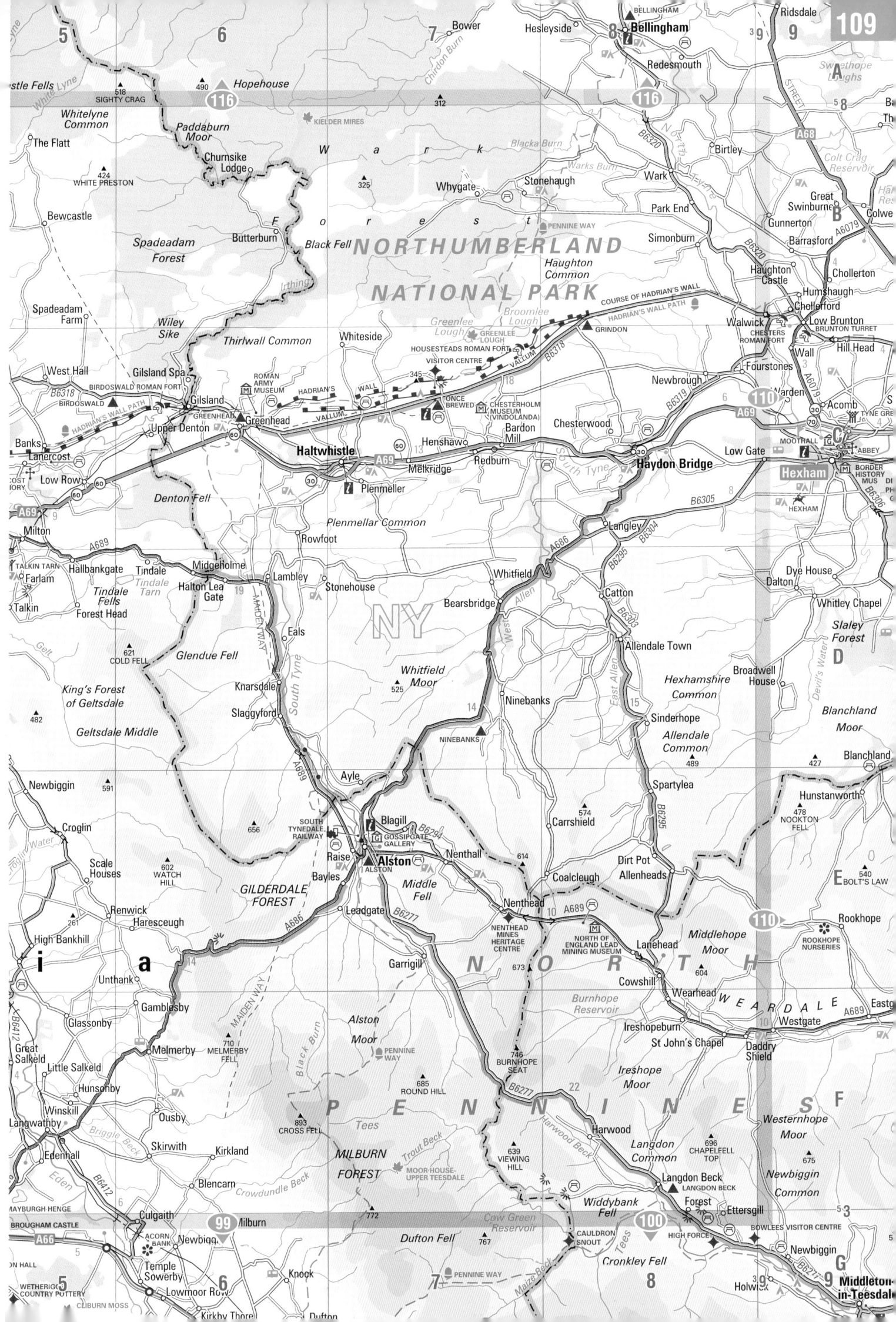

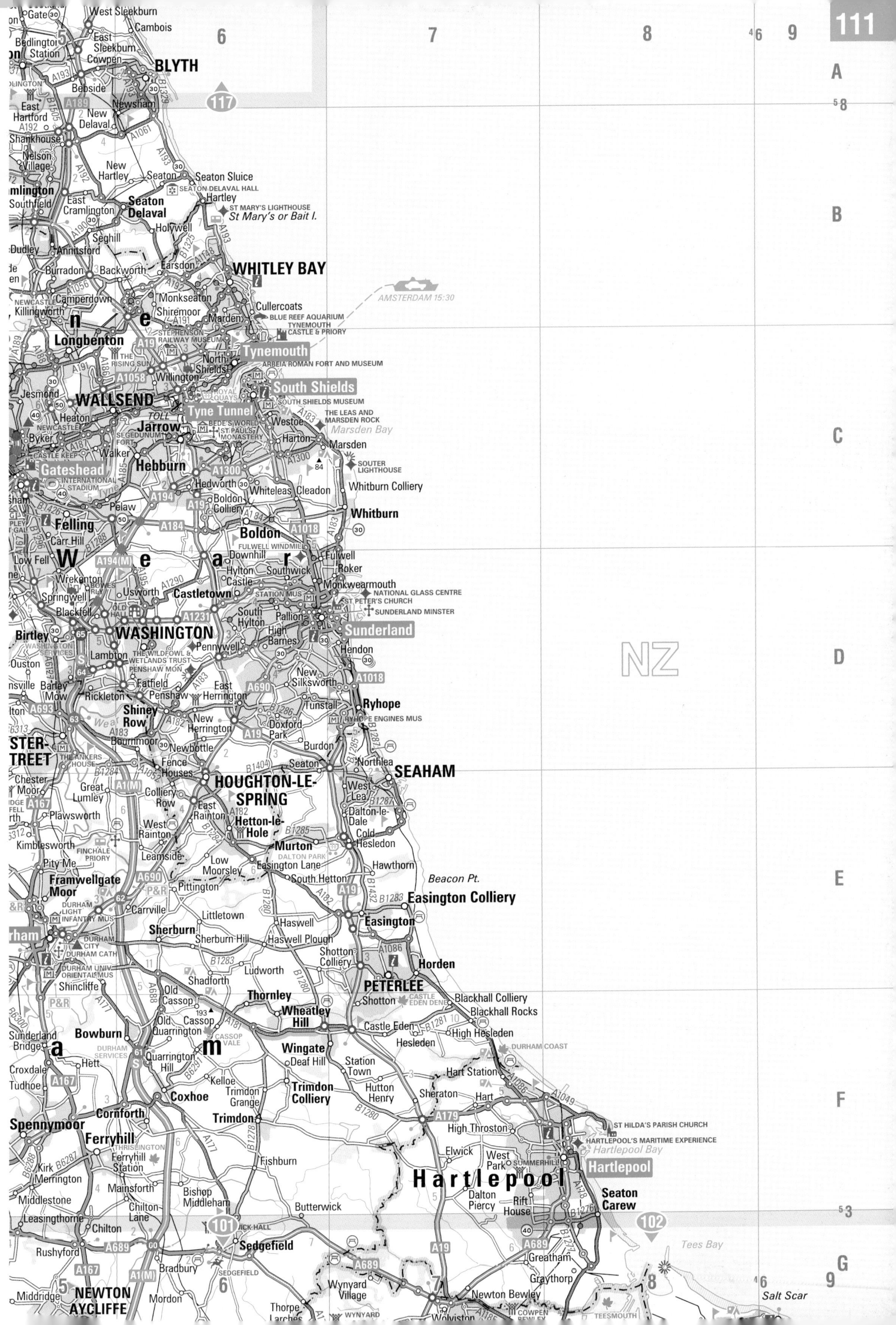

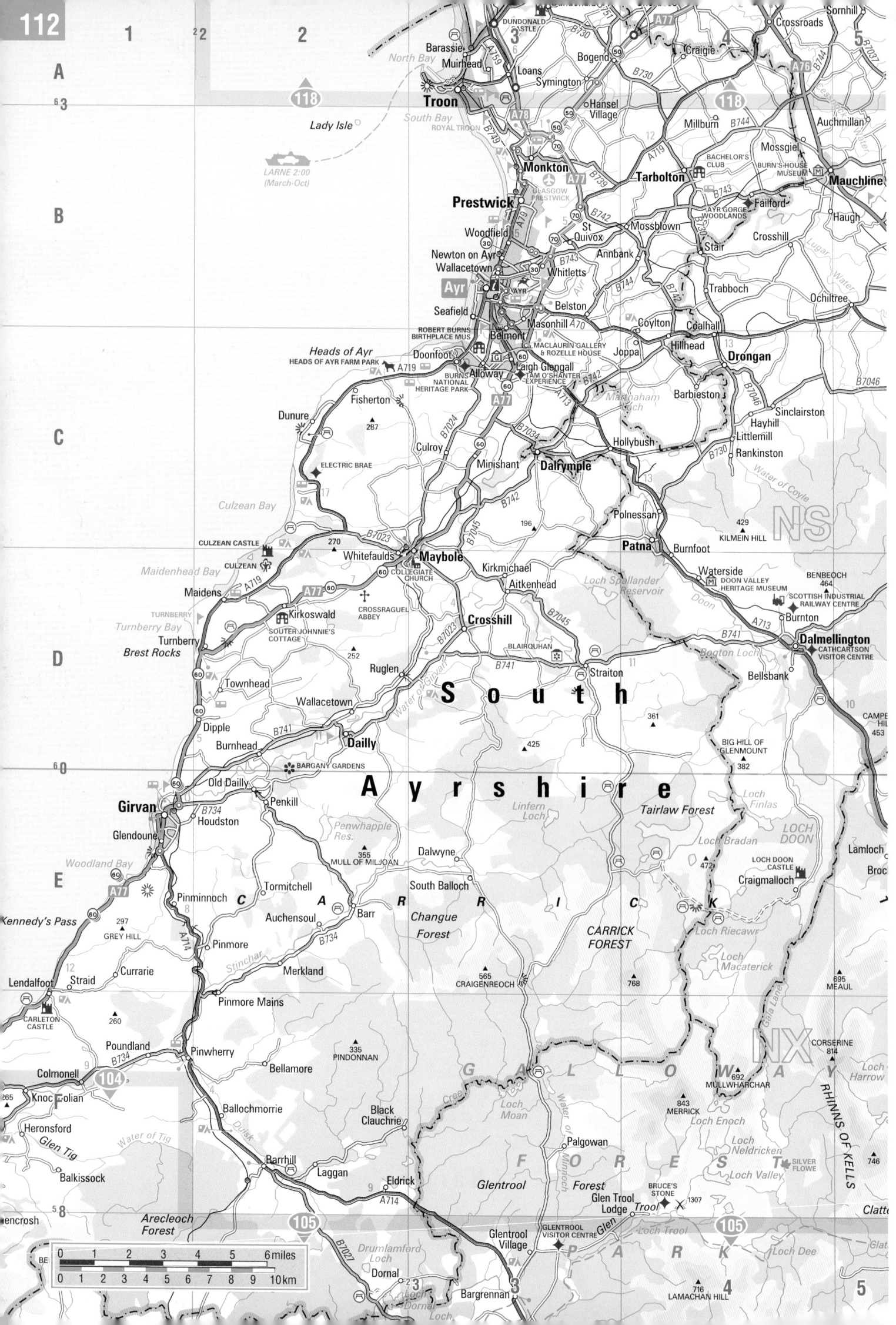

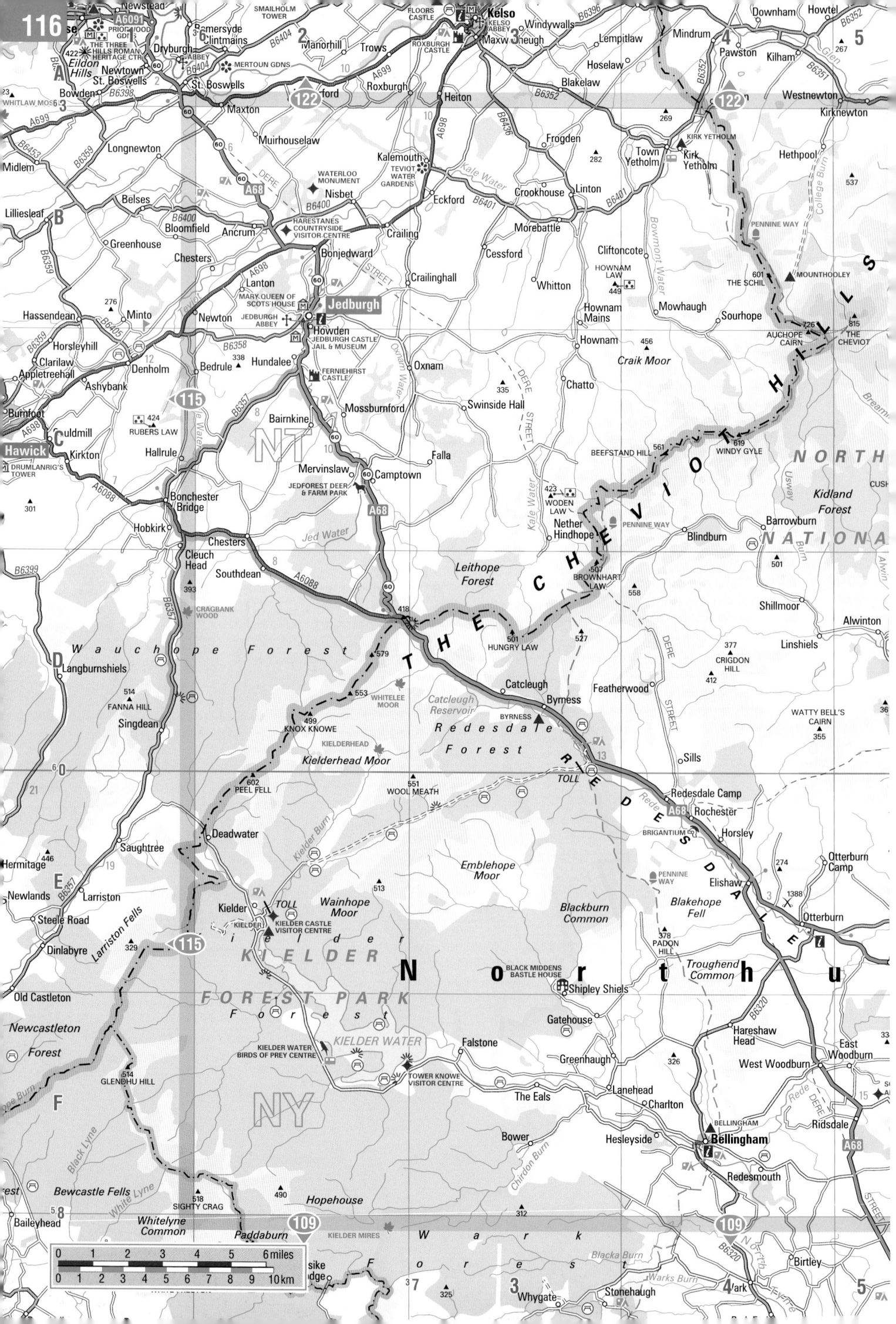

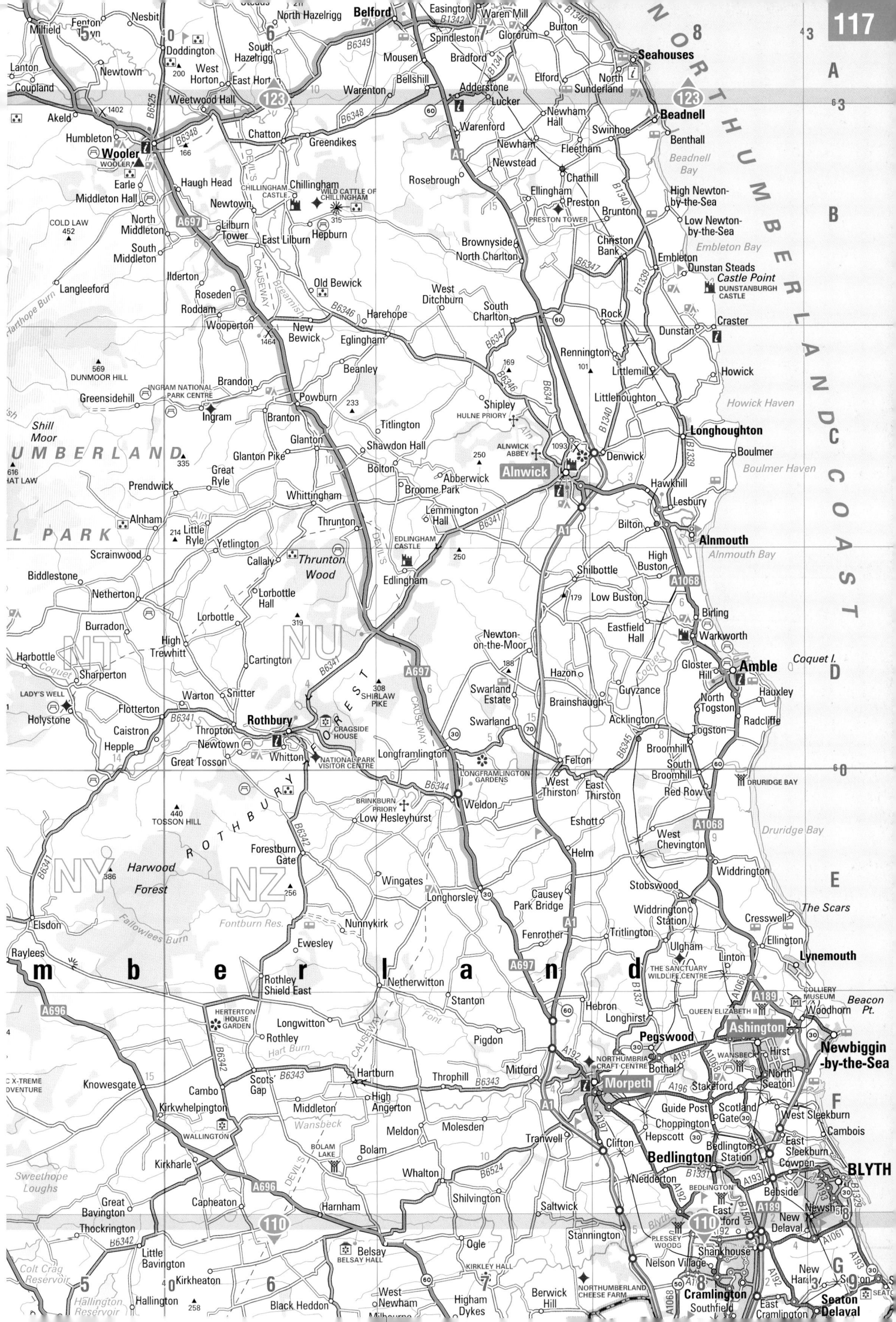

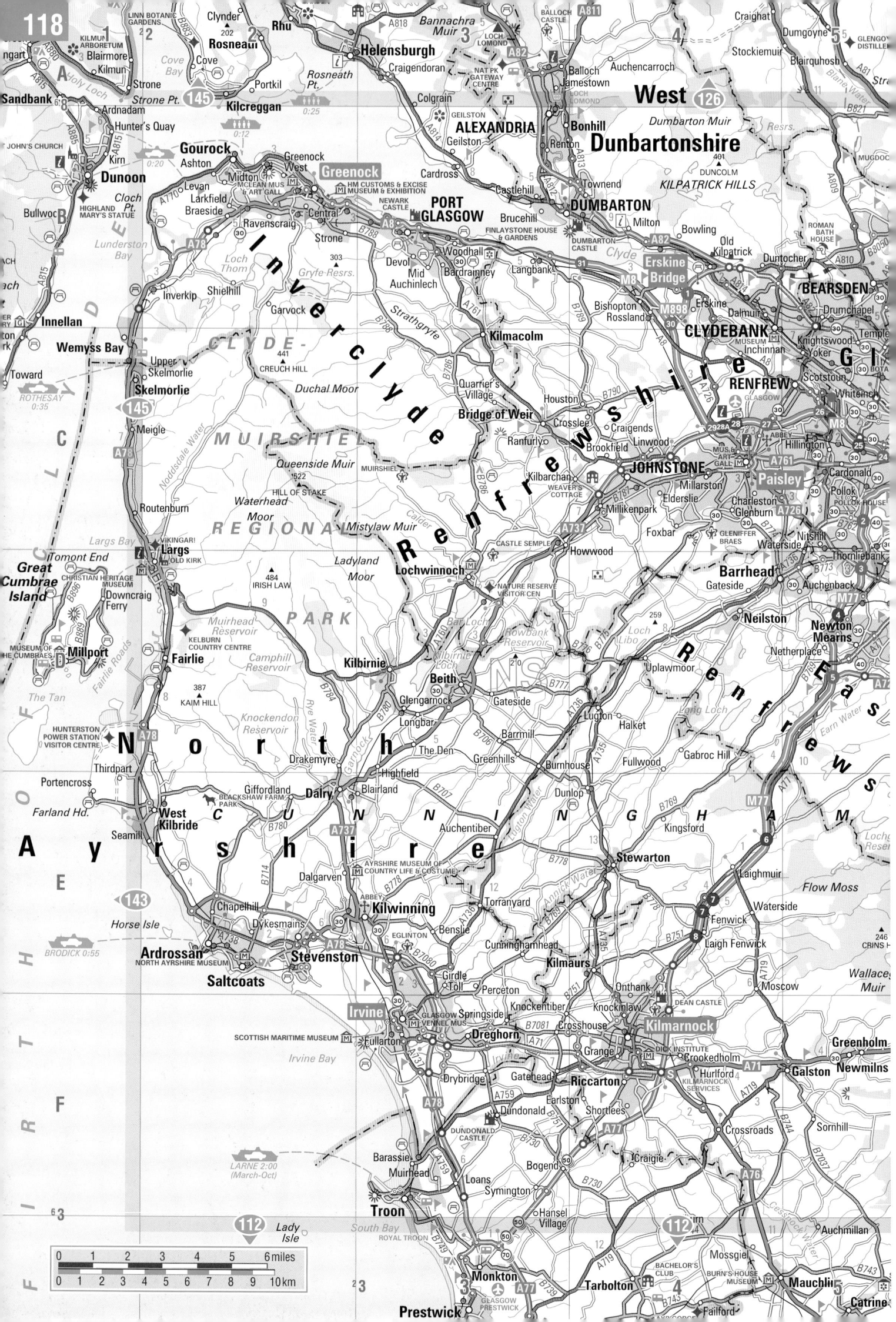

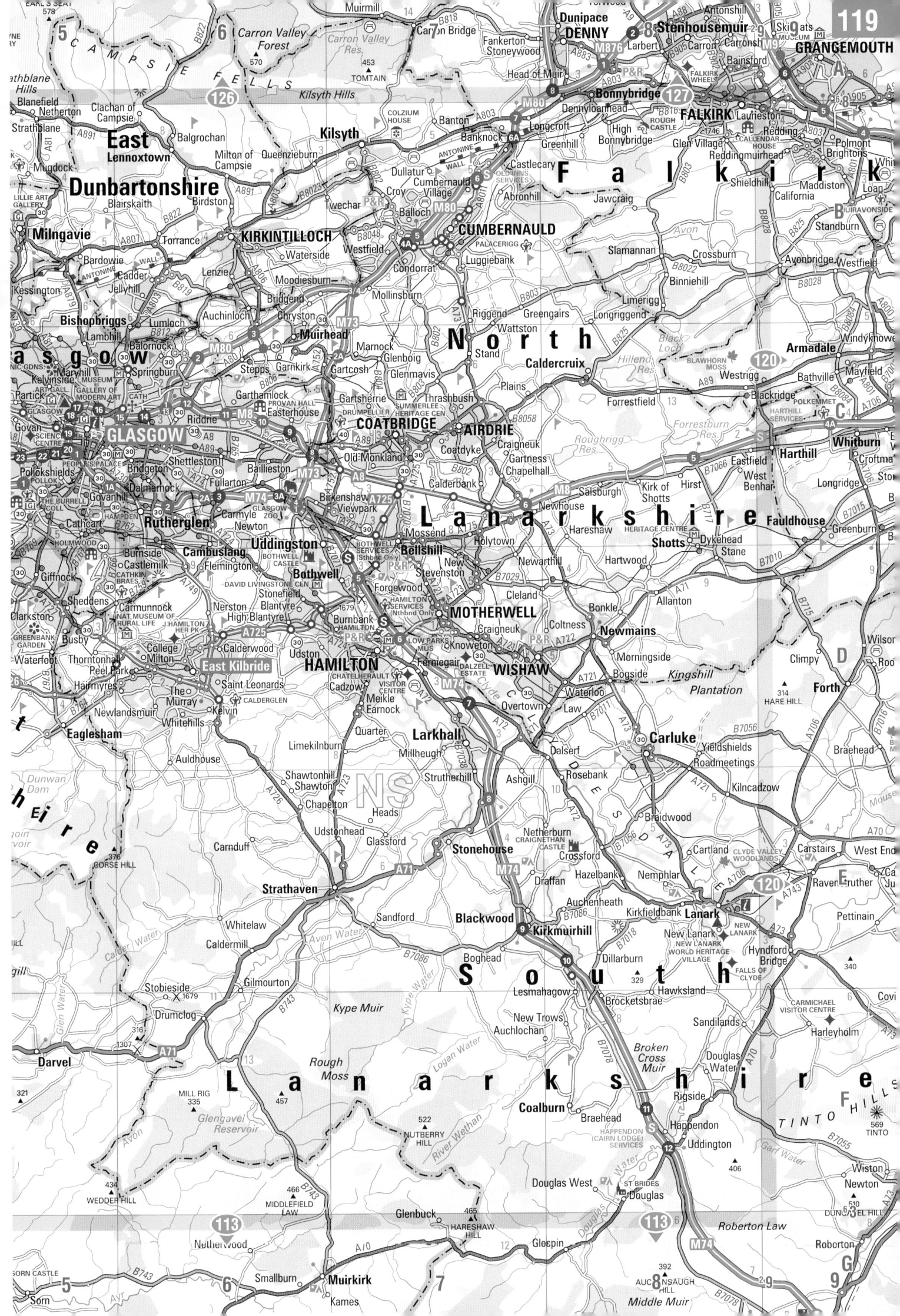

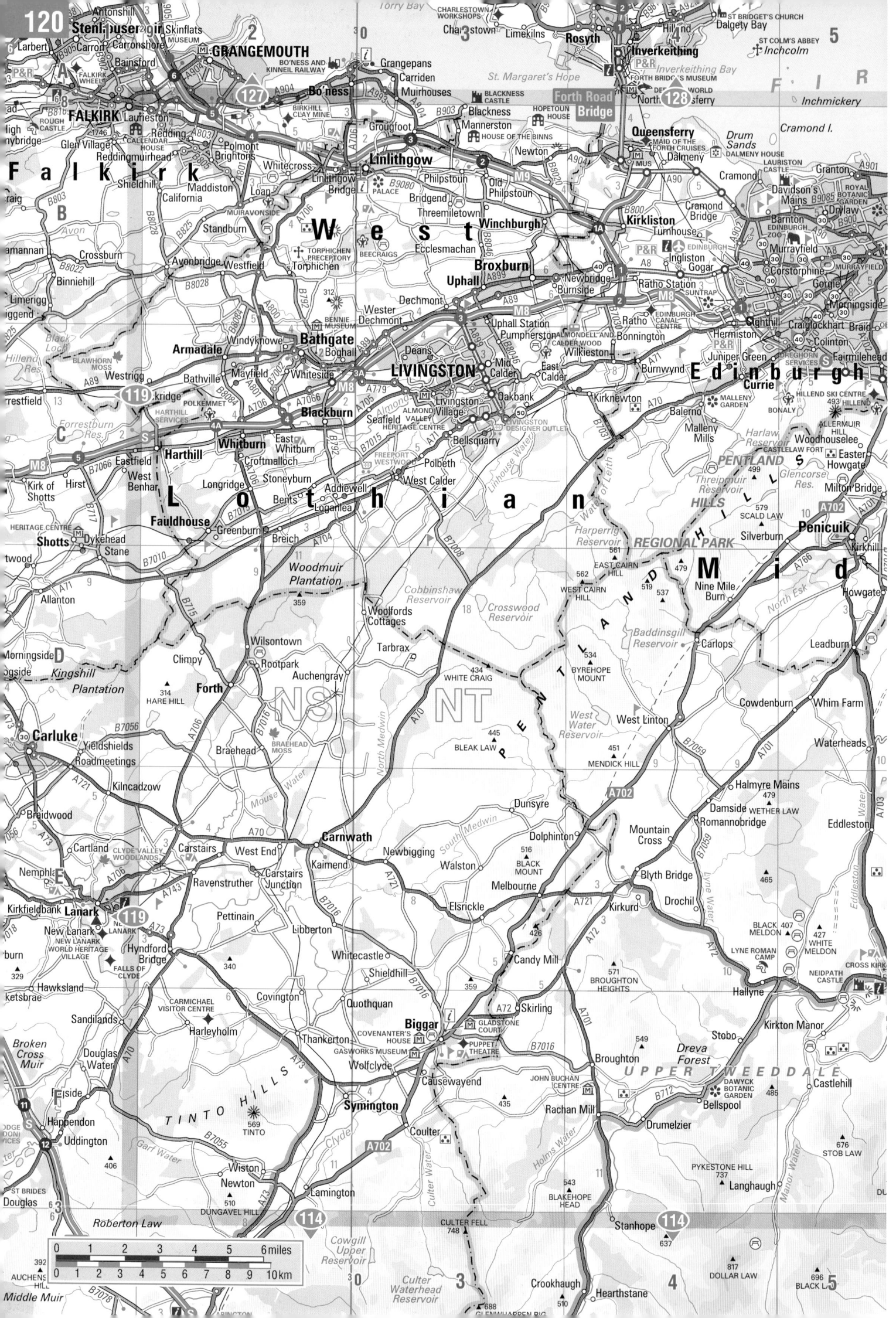

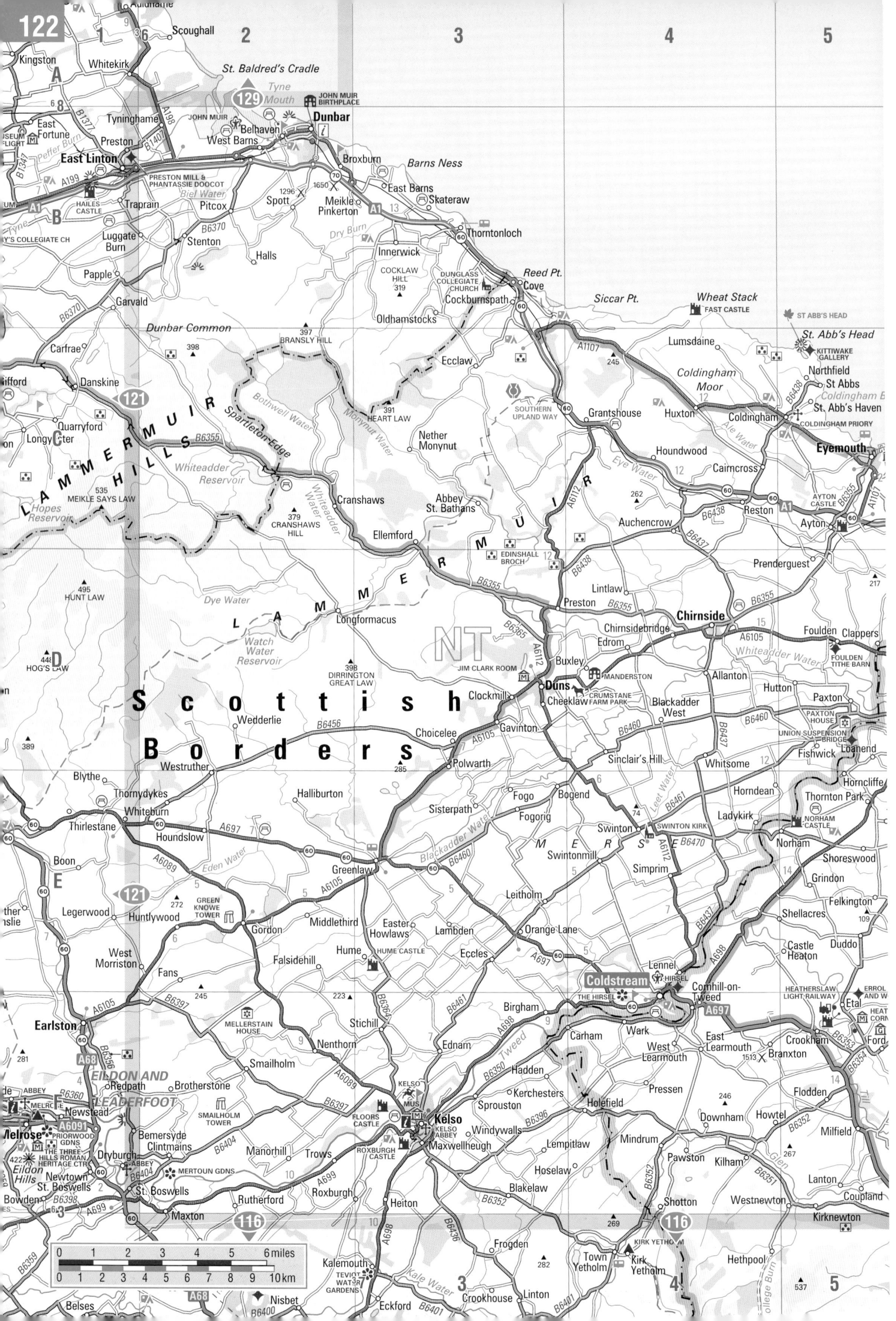

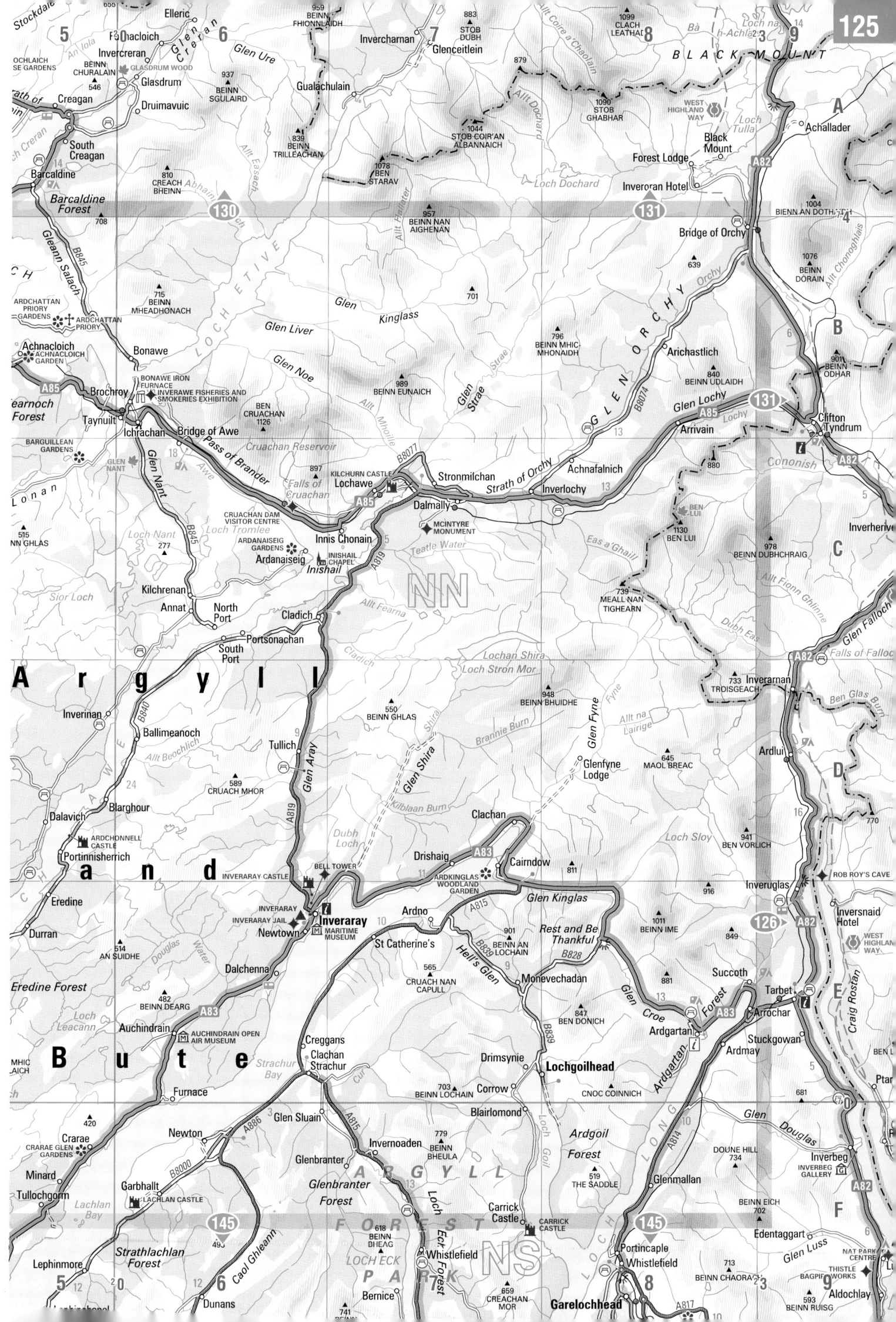

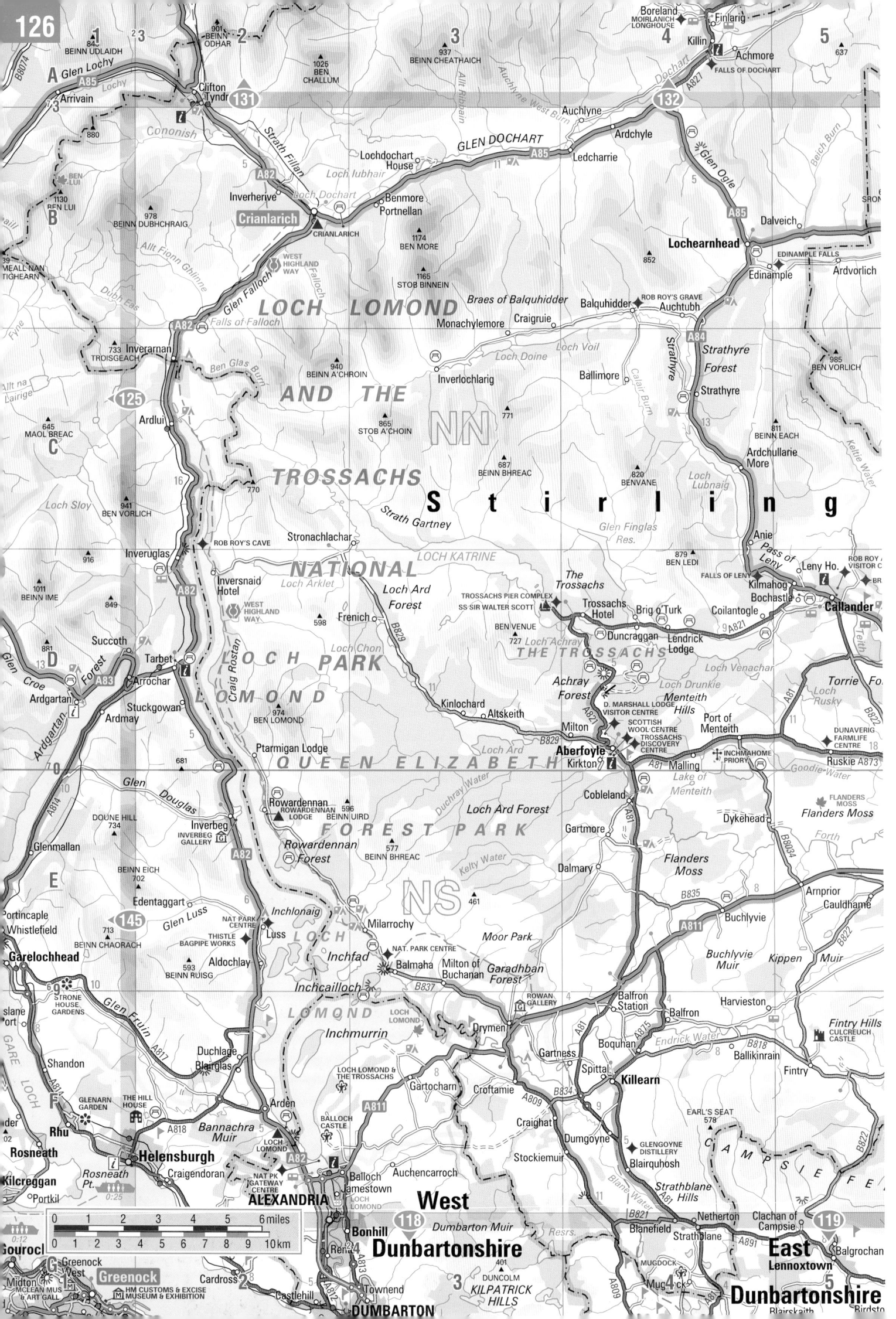

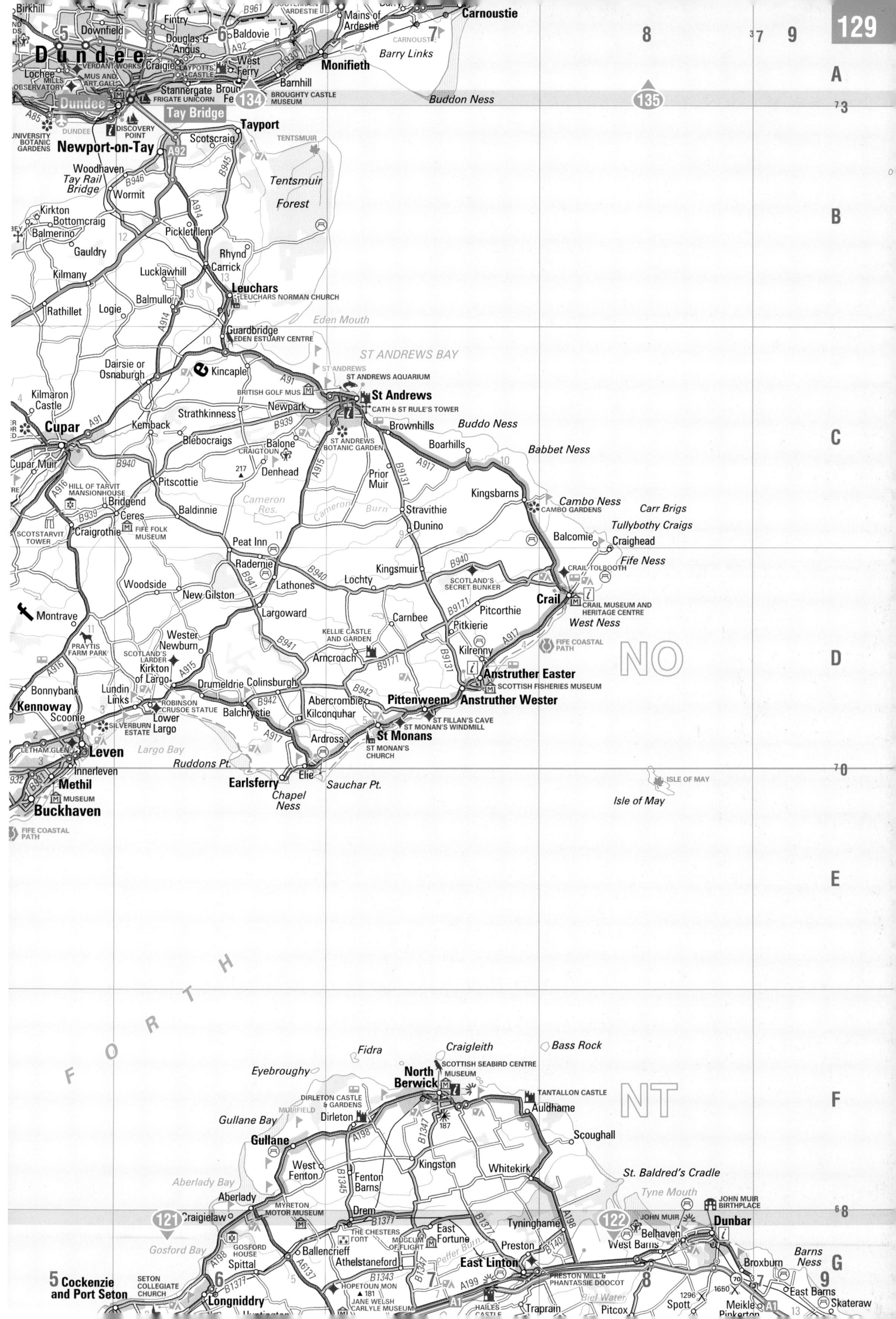

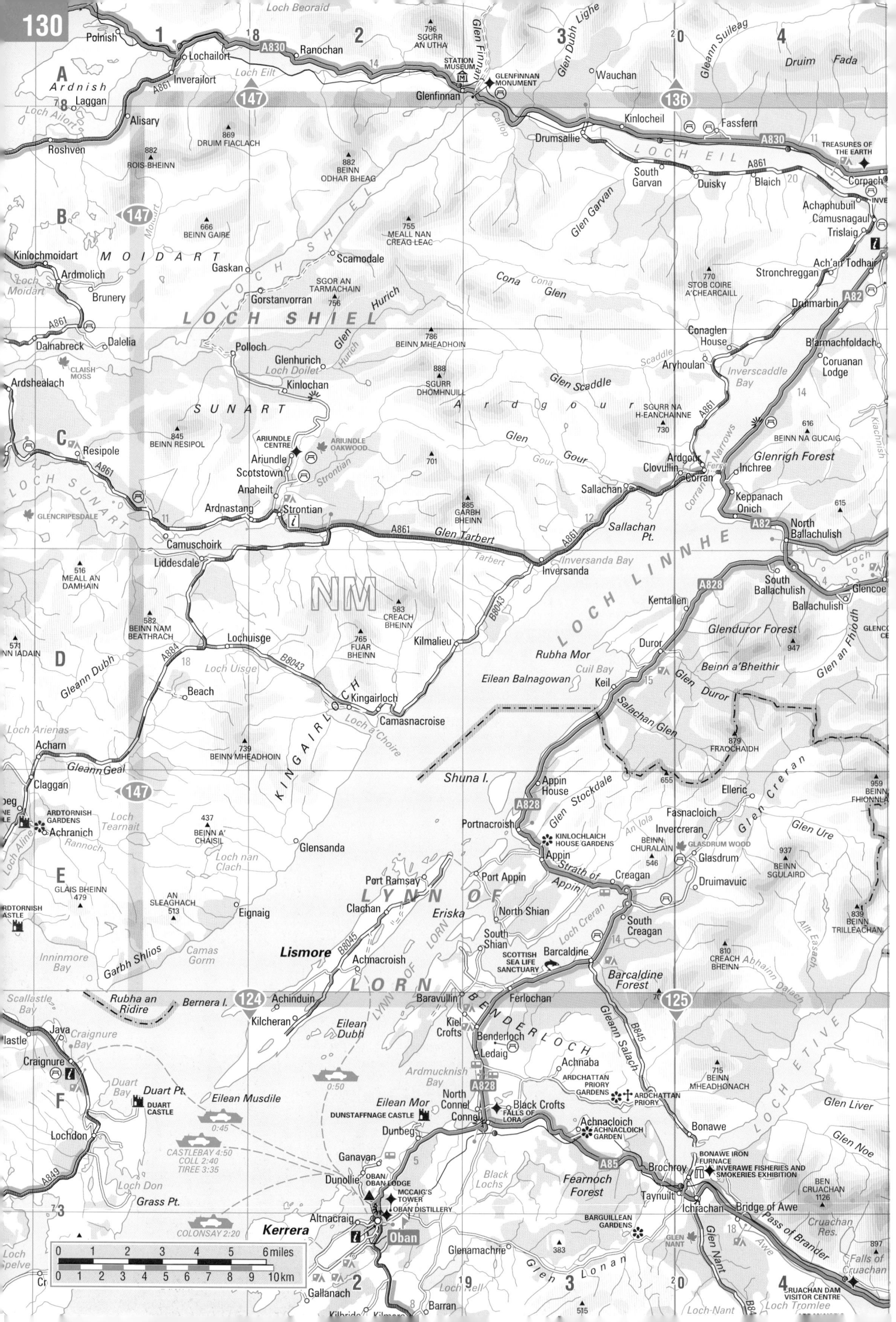

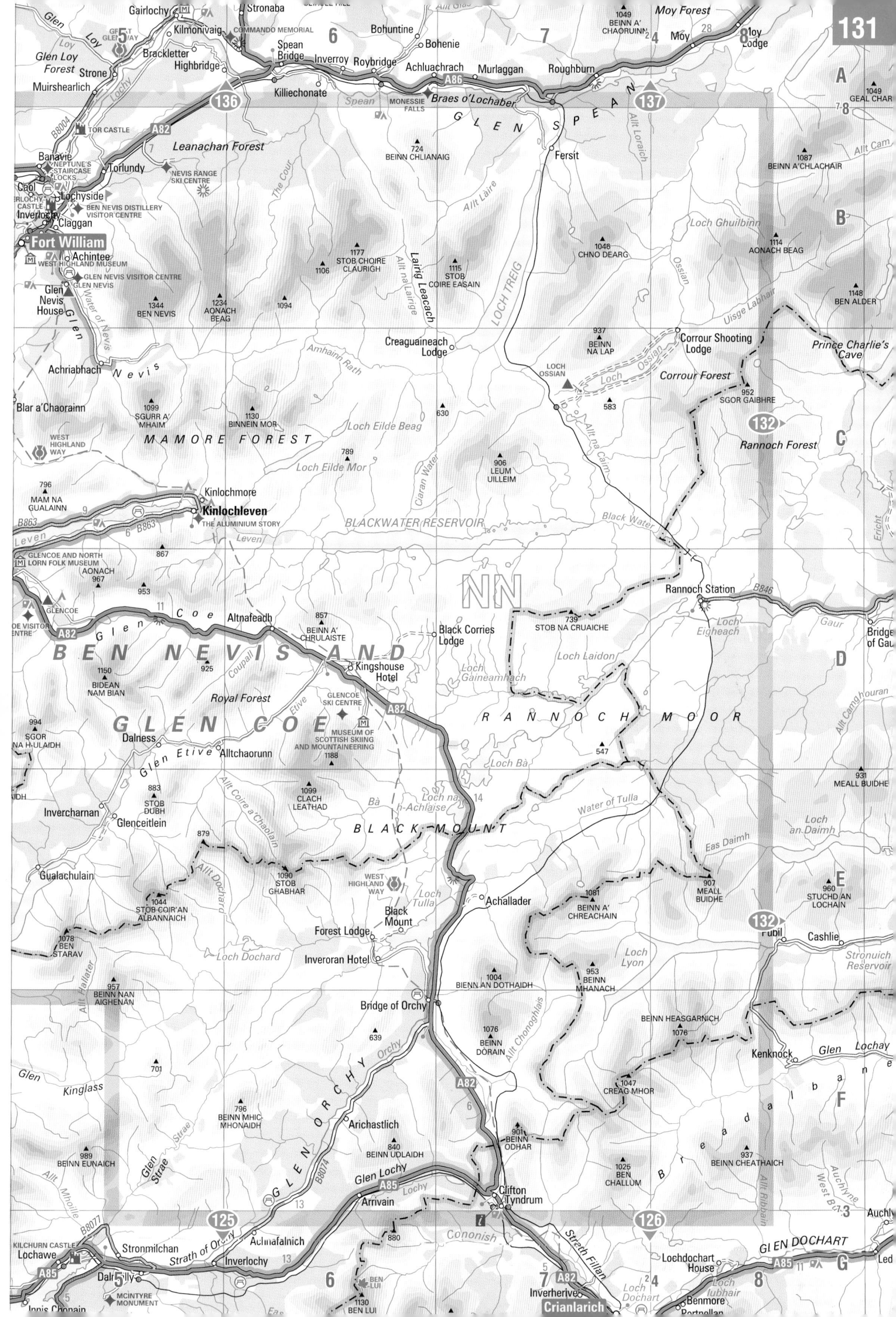

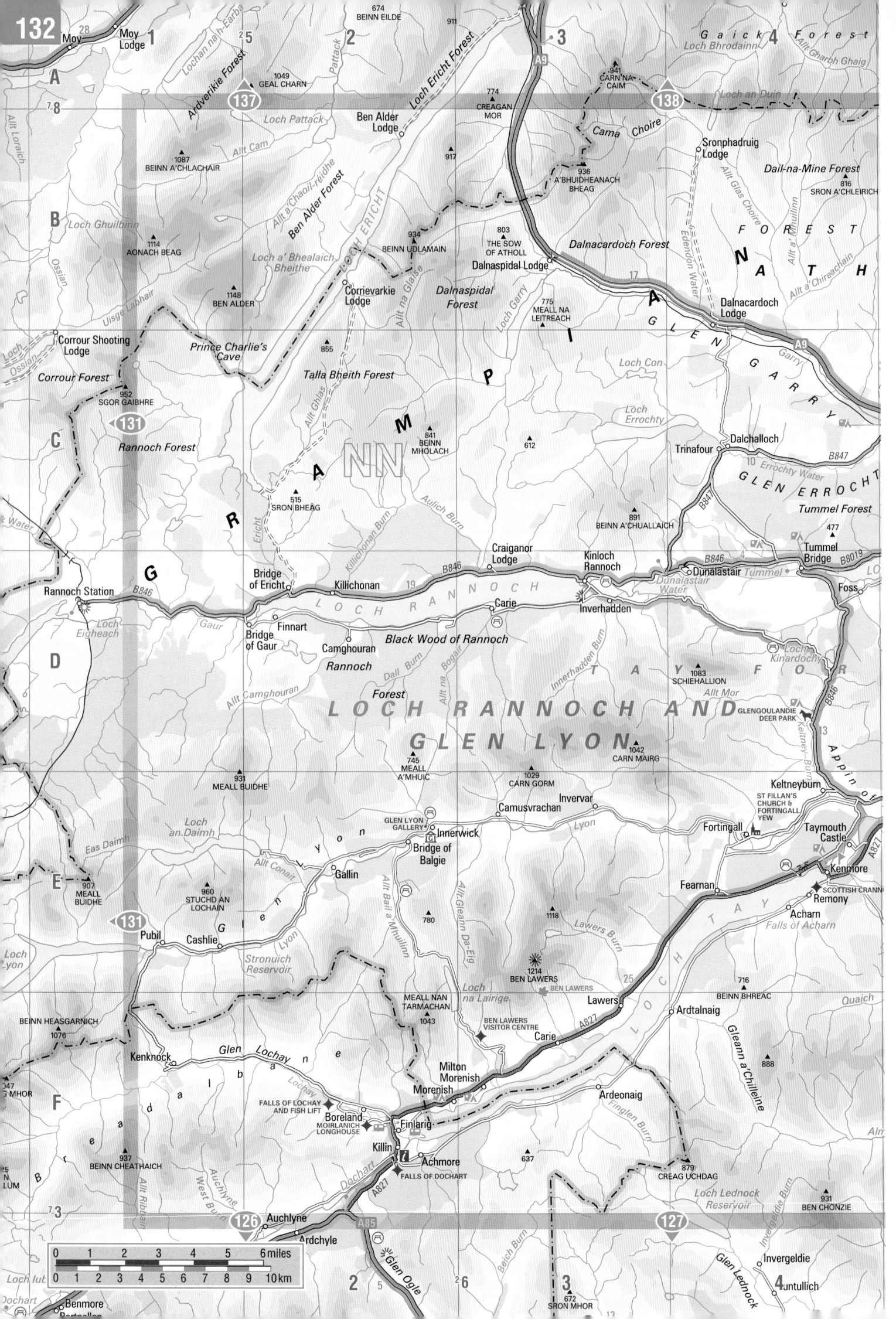

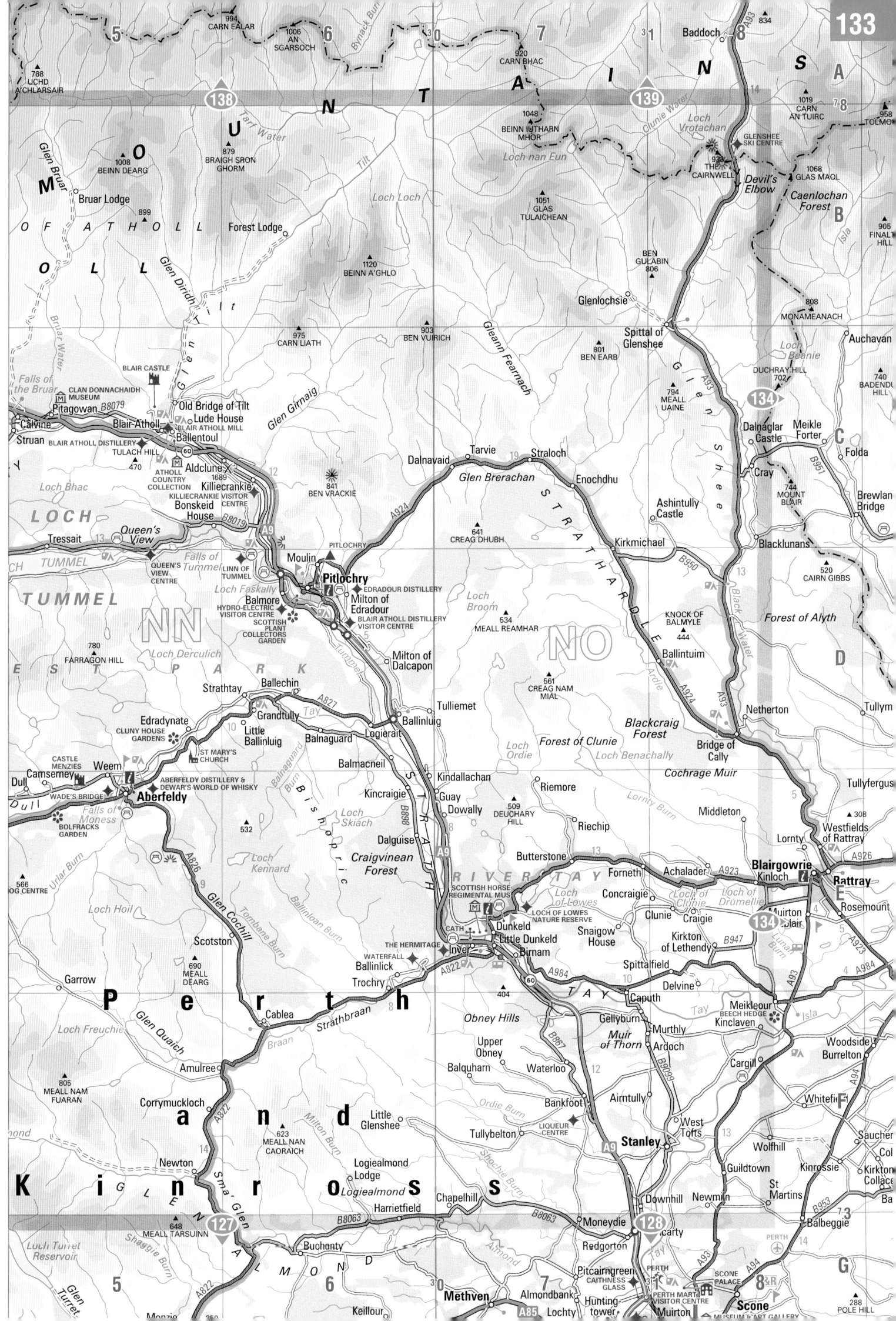

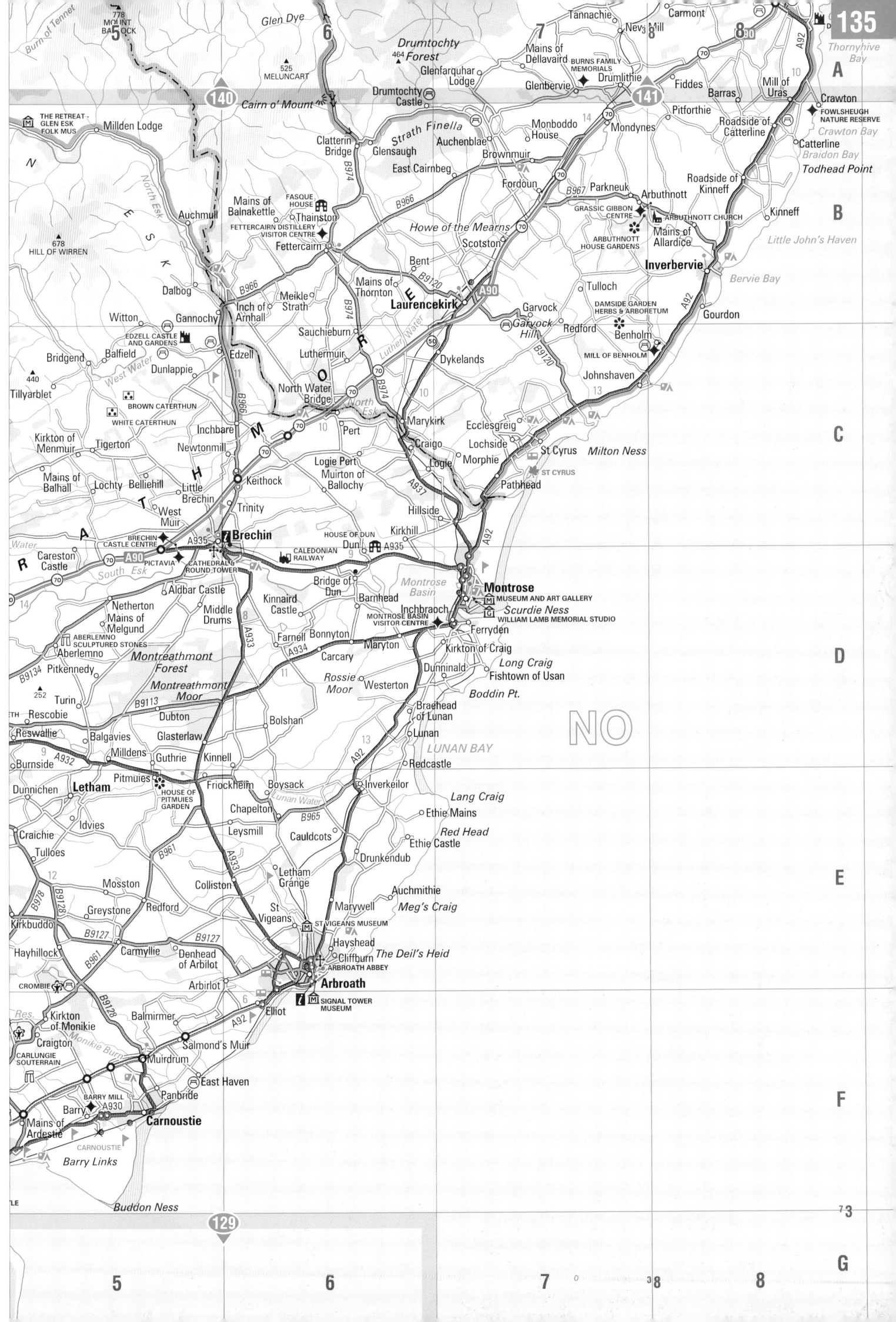

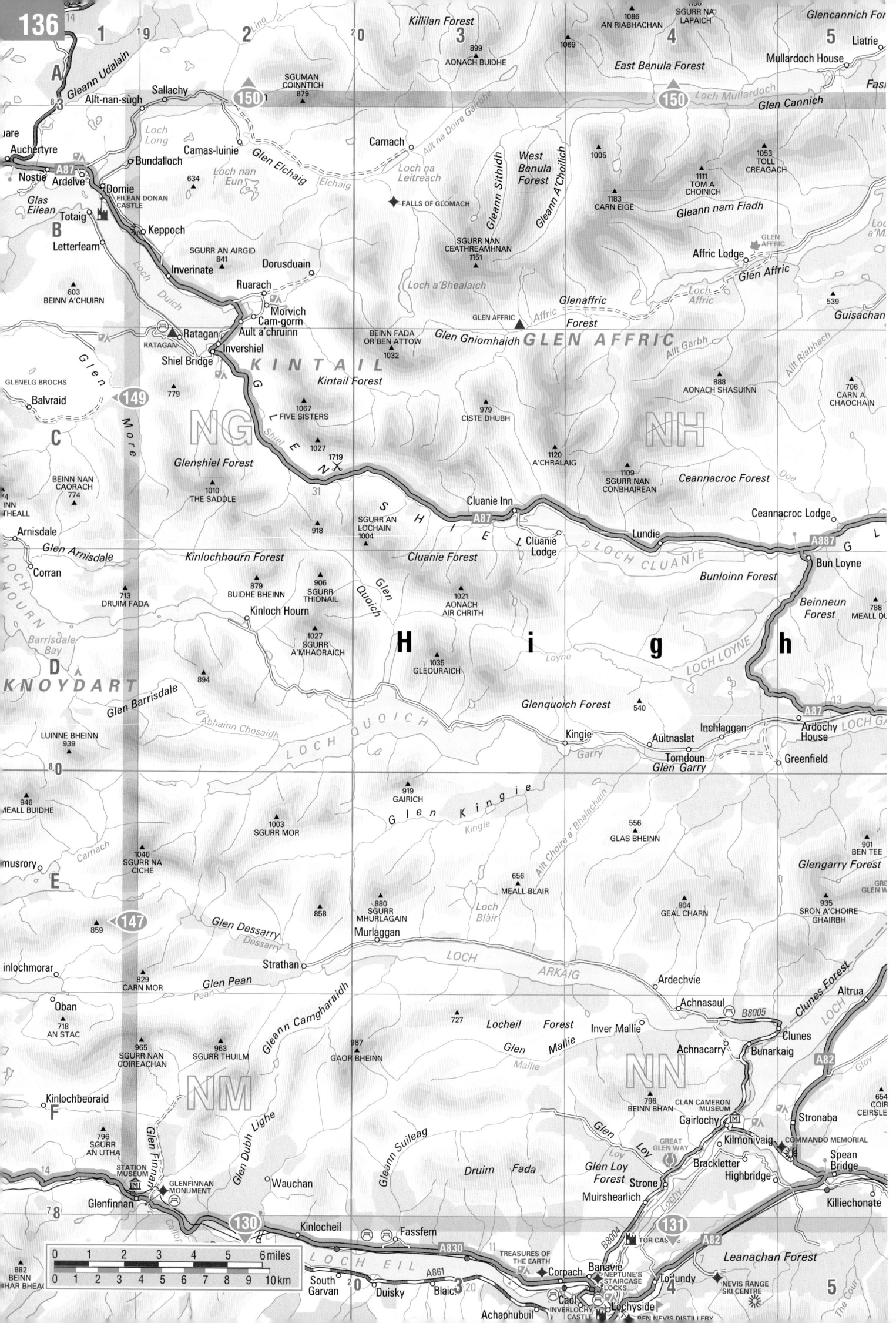

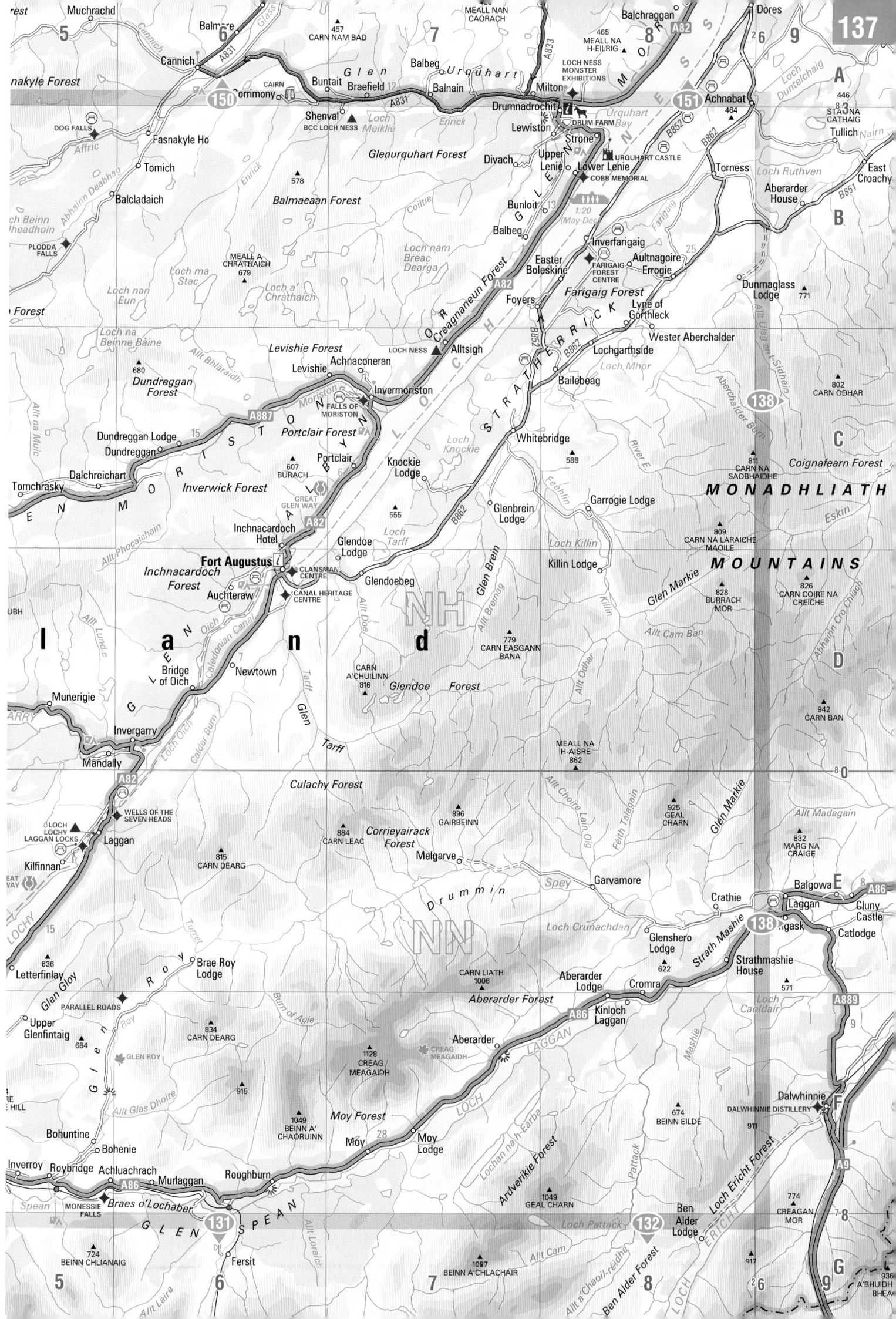

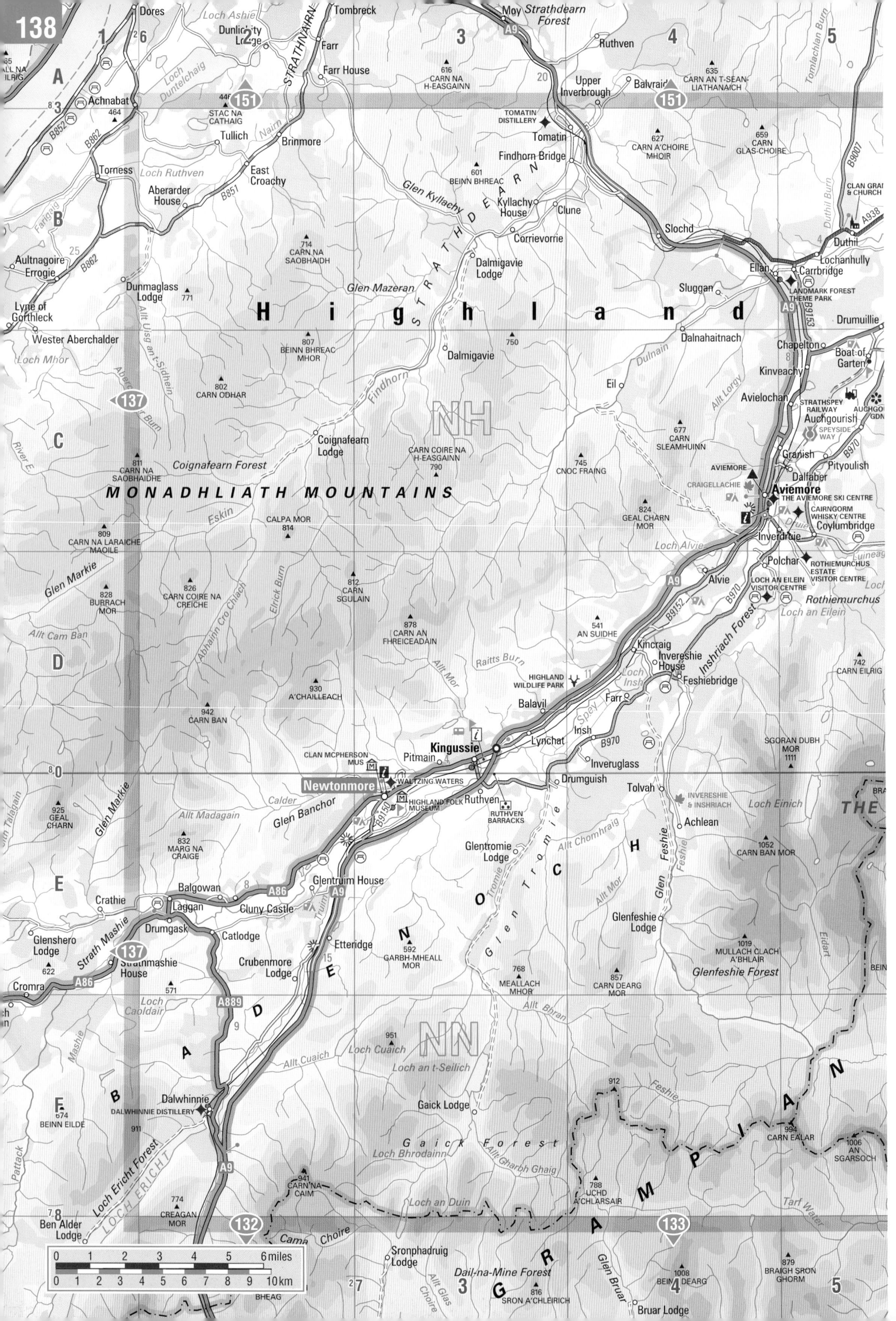

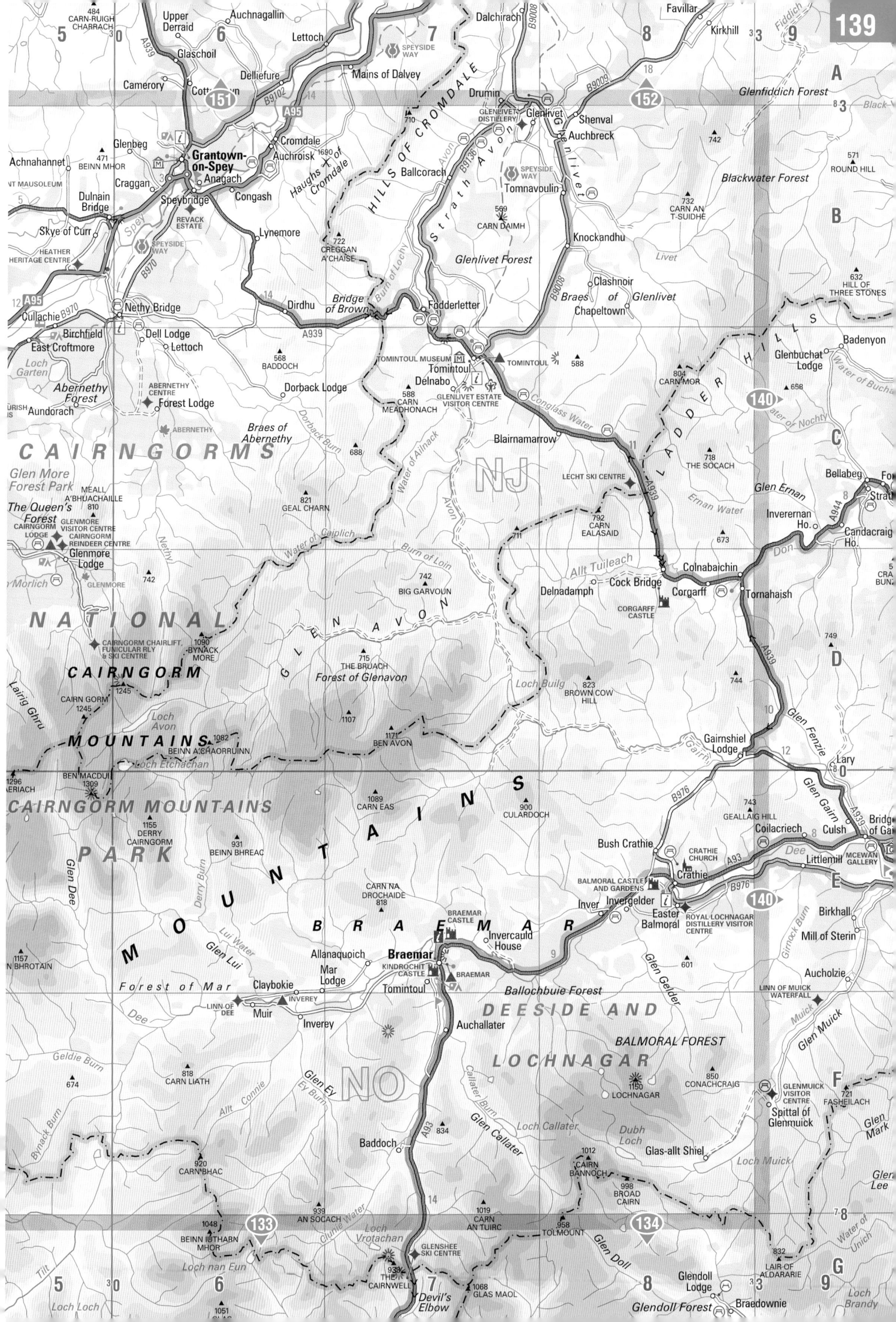

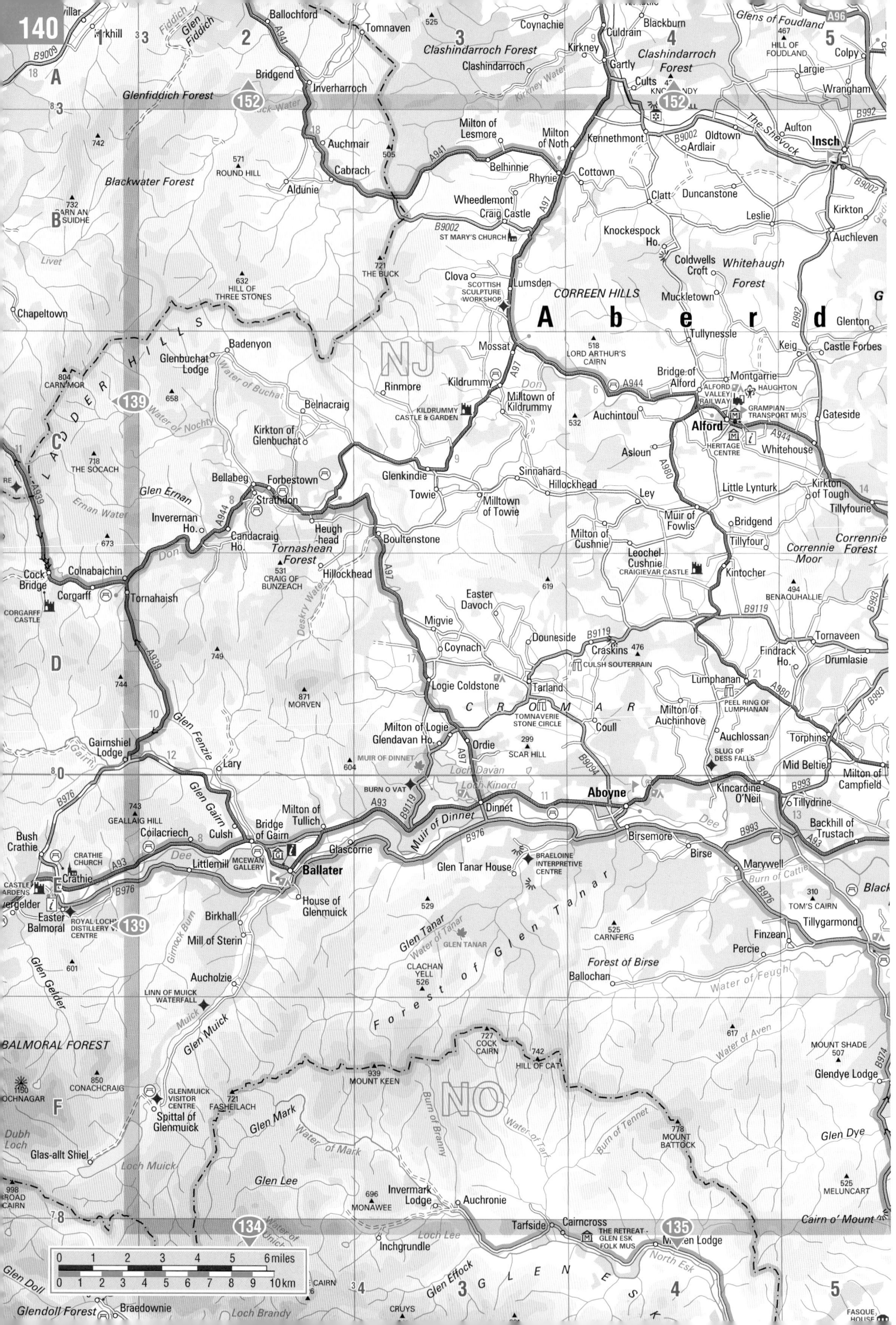

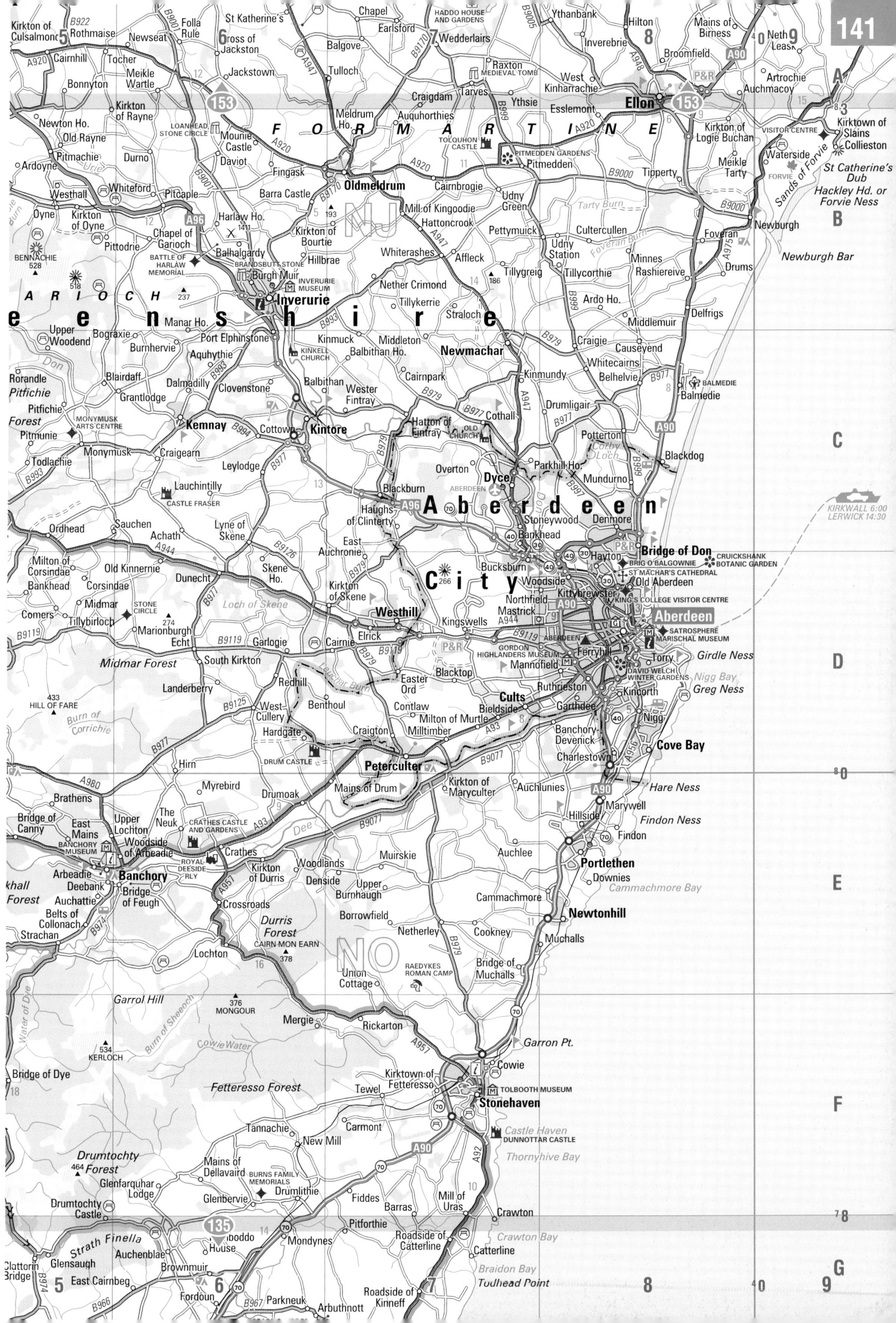

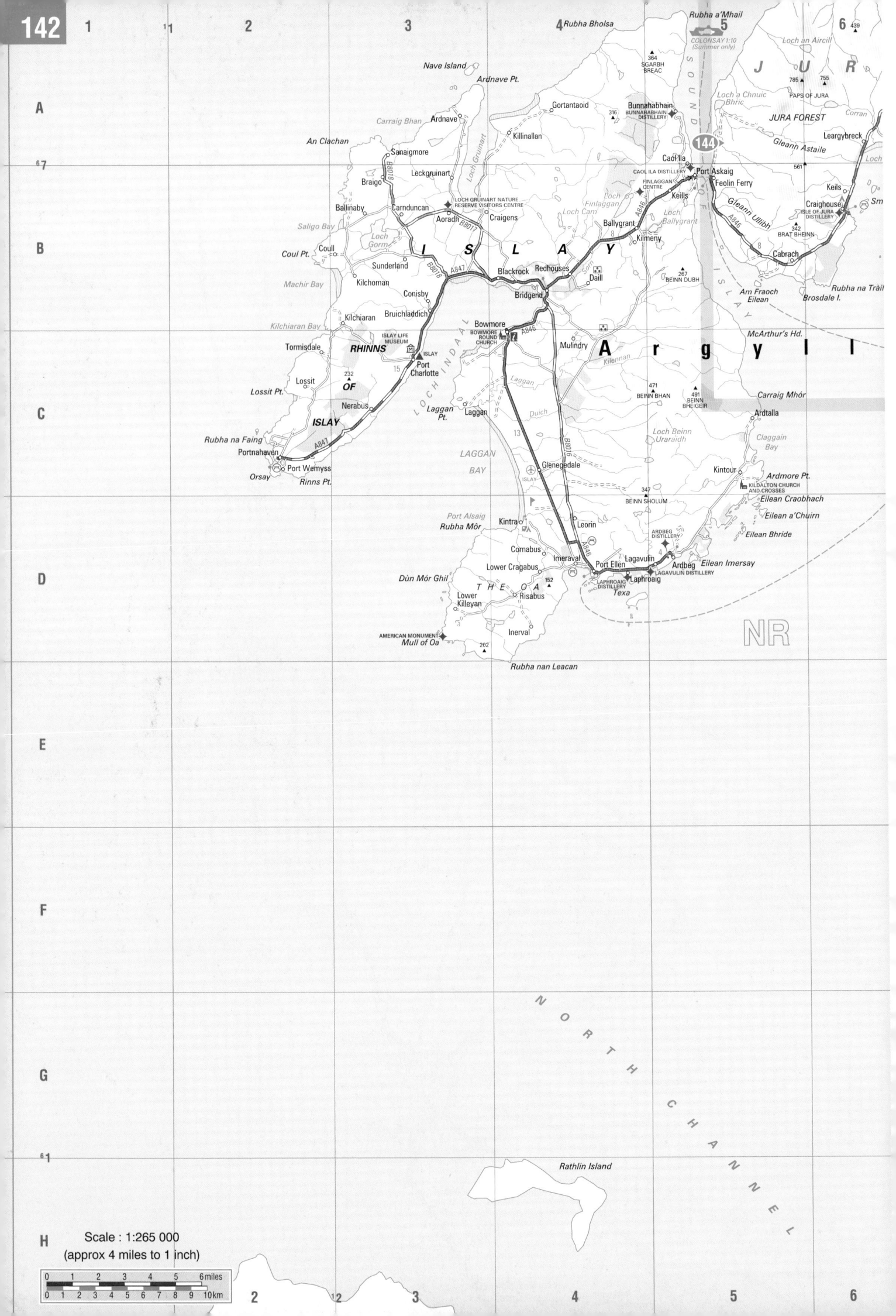

1 1 2 3 4 Rubha Bholsa 5 Rubha a'Mhail 6 439

JURA

Loch an Aircill

COLONSAY 1:10
(Summer only)

Nave Island

364
SGARBH
BREAC

Loch a Chnuic
Bhric

785 755
PAPS OF JURA

A
Ardnave Pt.

Gortantaoid

Bunnahabhain
BUNNAHABHAIN
DISTILLERY

316

JURA FOREST

Gleann Astaile

Leargybreck

Corran

7 An Clachan

Sanaigmore

Leckgruinart

Caol Ila

561

Loch

Carraig Bhan

Ardnave

Killinallan

CAOL ILA DISTILLERY

FINLAGGAN
CENTRE

Feolin Ferry

Loch
Finlaggan

Keills

Port Askaig

144

Gleann Ullibh

Keils

Sm

Braigo

Ballinaby

Carnduncan

Loch Gruinart Nature
Reserve Visitors Centre

Aoradh B8017

Craigens

ISLAY

Ballygrant

Loch
Ballygrant

Kilmeny

Craighouse
ISLE OF JURA
DISTILLERY

342
BRAT BHEINN

B Coul Pt. Coull

Sunderland

Kilchoman

Conisby

Bruichladdich

Blackrock

Redhouses

Daill

267
BEINN DUBH

Cabrach

Am Fraoch
Eilean

Rubha na Tràill

Brosdale I.

Saligo Bay

Loch
Gorm

Machir Bay

Bridgend

Kilchiaran

Kilchiaran Bay

Kilchiaran

RHINNS

Port
Charlotte

ISLAY LIFE
MUSEUM

Islay

Bowmore
BOWMORE
ROUND
CHURCH

Mulindry

A846

ARGYLL

McArthur's Hd.

Kilennan

471
BEINN BHAN

491
BEINN
BHEIGEIR

Carraig Mhór

C Tormisdale

Lossit Pt.

Lossit

OF

232

Nerabus

15

Laggan
Pt.

Laggan

Duich

Loch Beinn
Uraraidh

Ardtalla

Claggain
Bay

Rubha na Faing

Portnahaven

Port Wemyss

Orsay

Rinns Pt.

ISLAY

A847

LOCHINDAAL

13

LAGGAN
BAY

Glenegedale

ISLAY

347

Kintour

Ardmore Pt.

B8016

Eilean Craobhach

Port Alsaig
Rubha Mór

Kintra

Cornabus

Lower Cragabus

Imeraval

Leorin

Port Ellen

Lagavulin

BEINN SHOLUM

ARDBEG
DISTILLERY

Ardbeg
LAGAVULIN DISTILLERY

Eilean Imersay

Eilean a'Chuirn

Eilean Bhride

D Dùn Mór Ghil

THE OA

Lower
Killeyan

Risabus

152

LAPHROAIG
DISTILLERY

Laphroaig

Texa

NR

Inerval

AMERICAN MONUMENT
Mull of Oa

202

Rubha nan Leacan

E

F

NORTH

G

1 Rathlin Island

CHANNEL

H Scale : 1:265 000
(approx 4 miles to 1 inch)

0 1 2 3 4 5 6 miles
0 1 2 3 4 5 6 7 8 9 10km

2 2 3 4 5 6

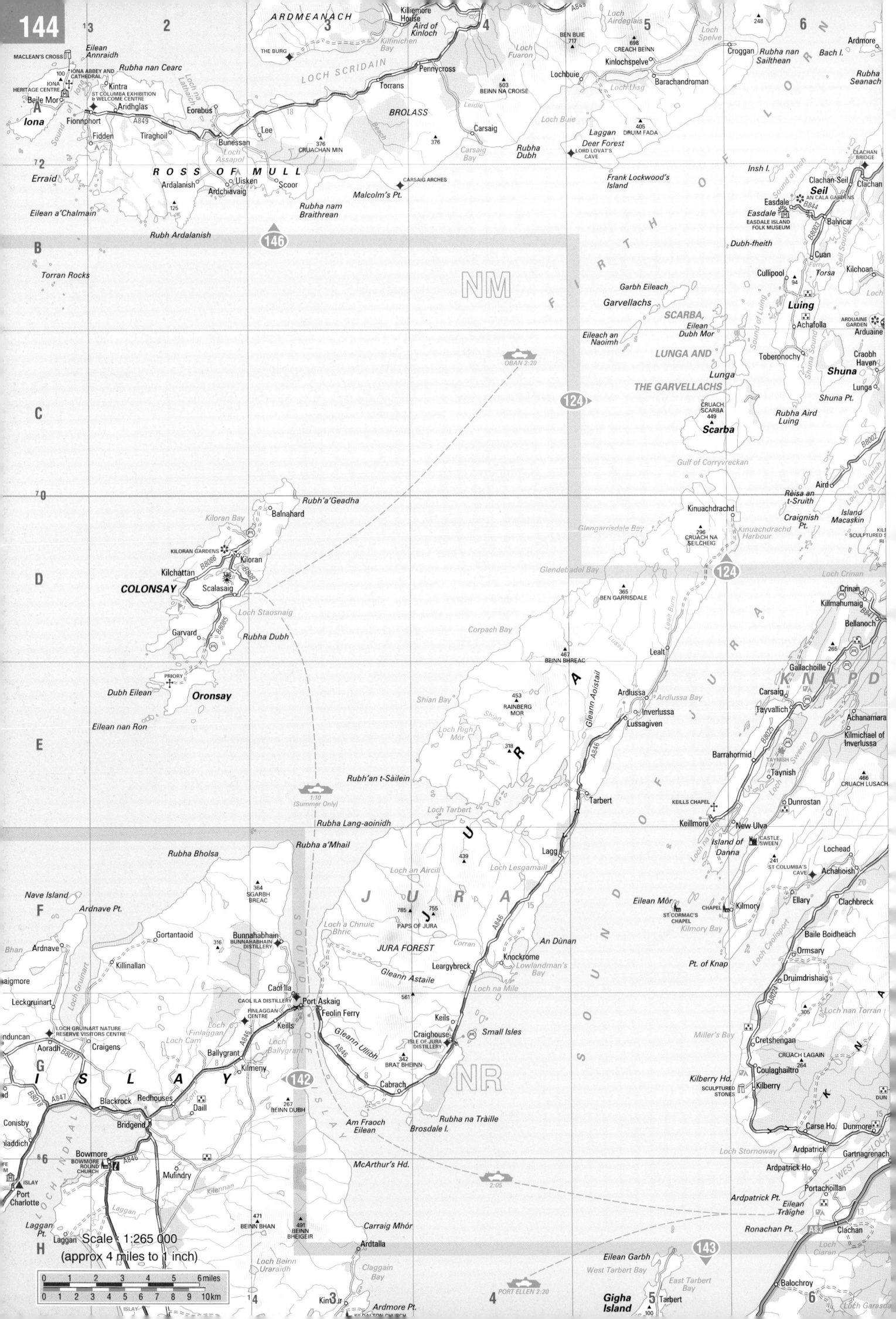

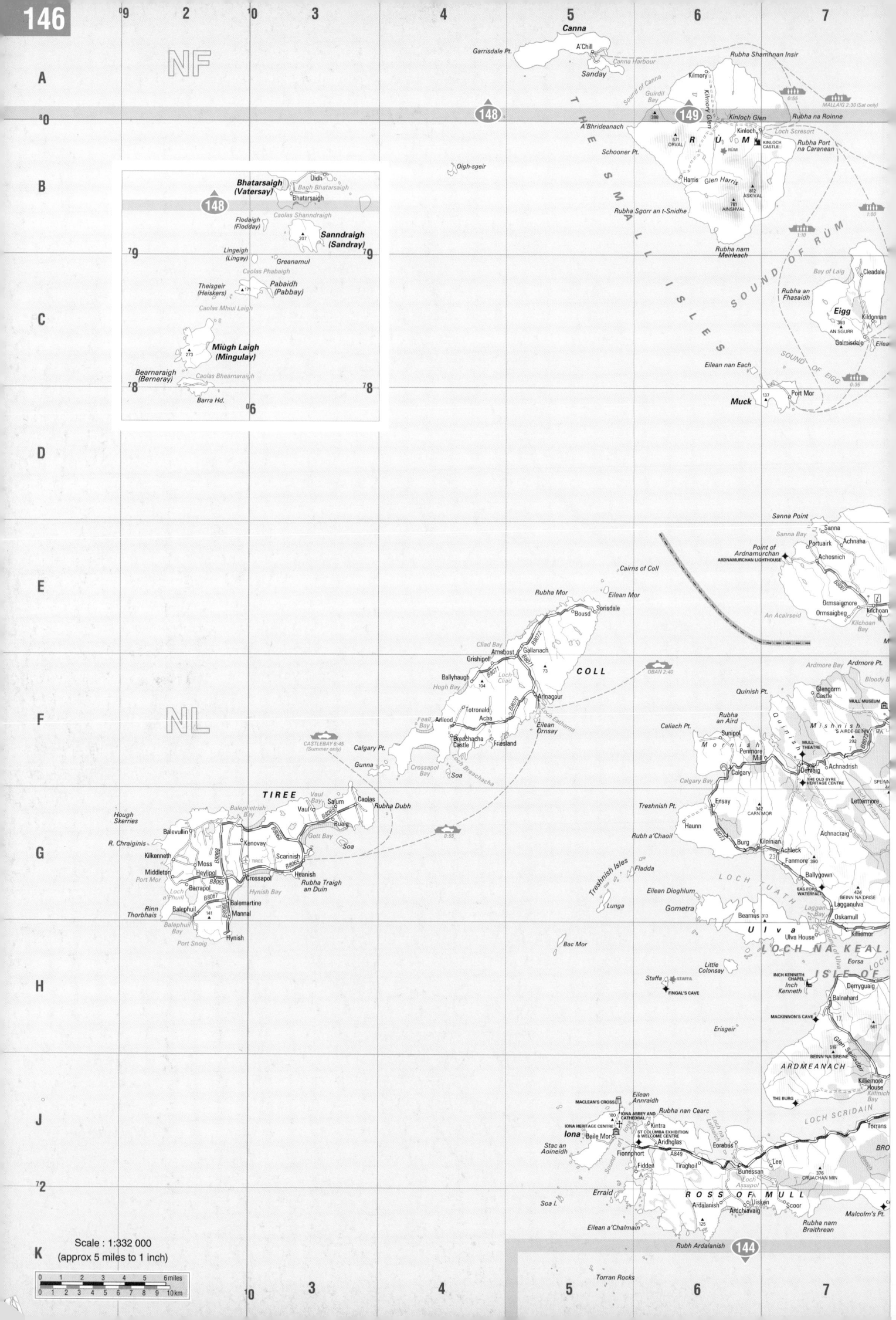

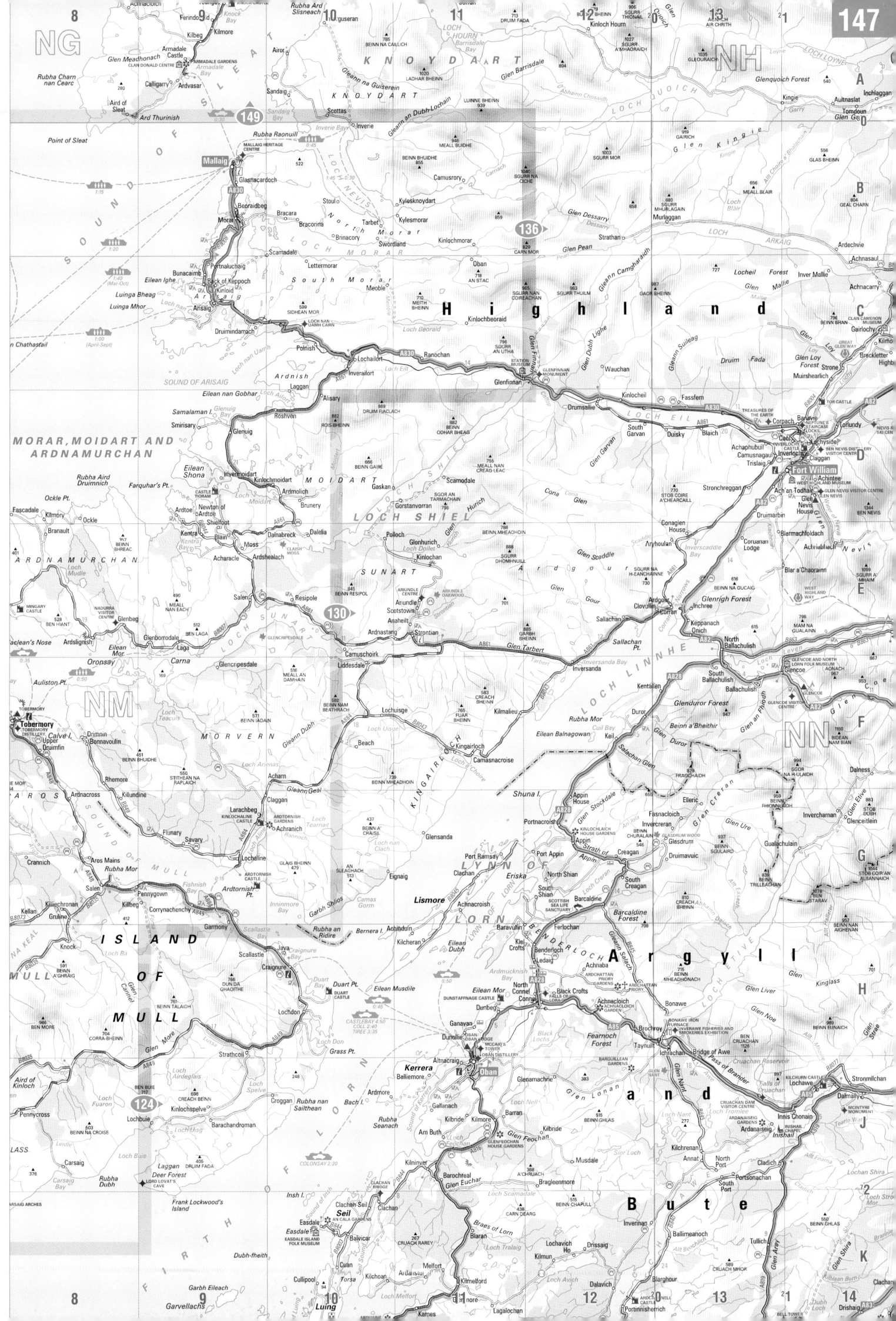

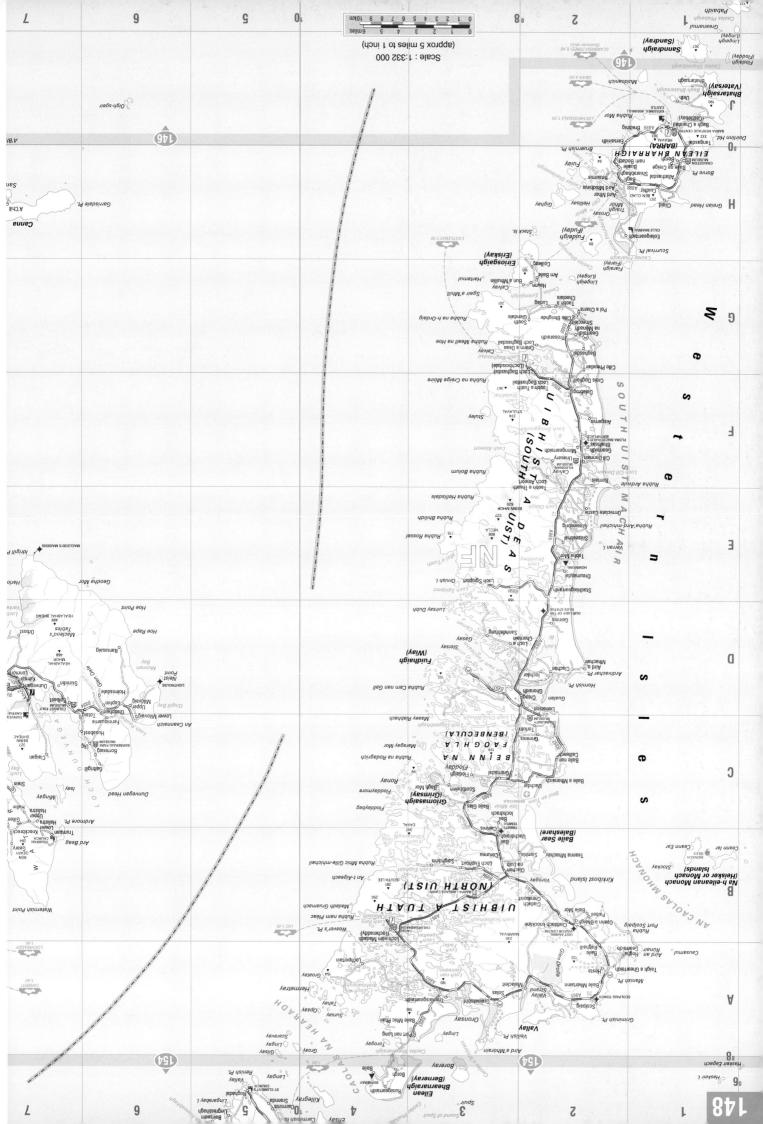

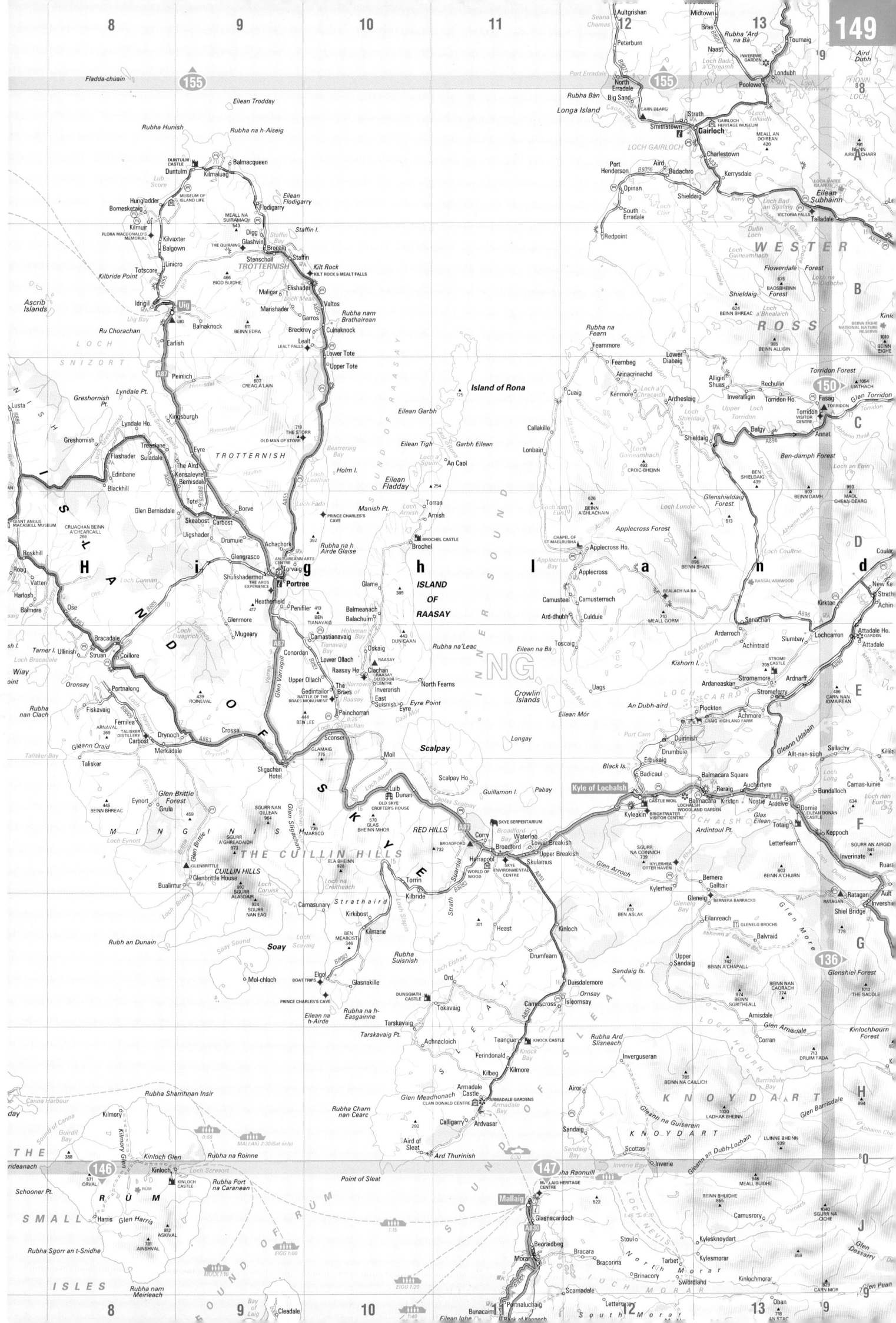

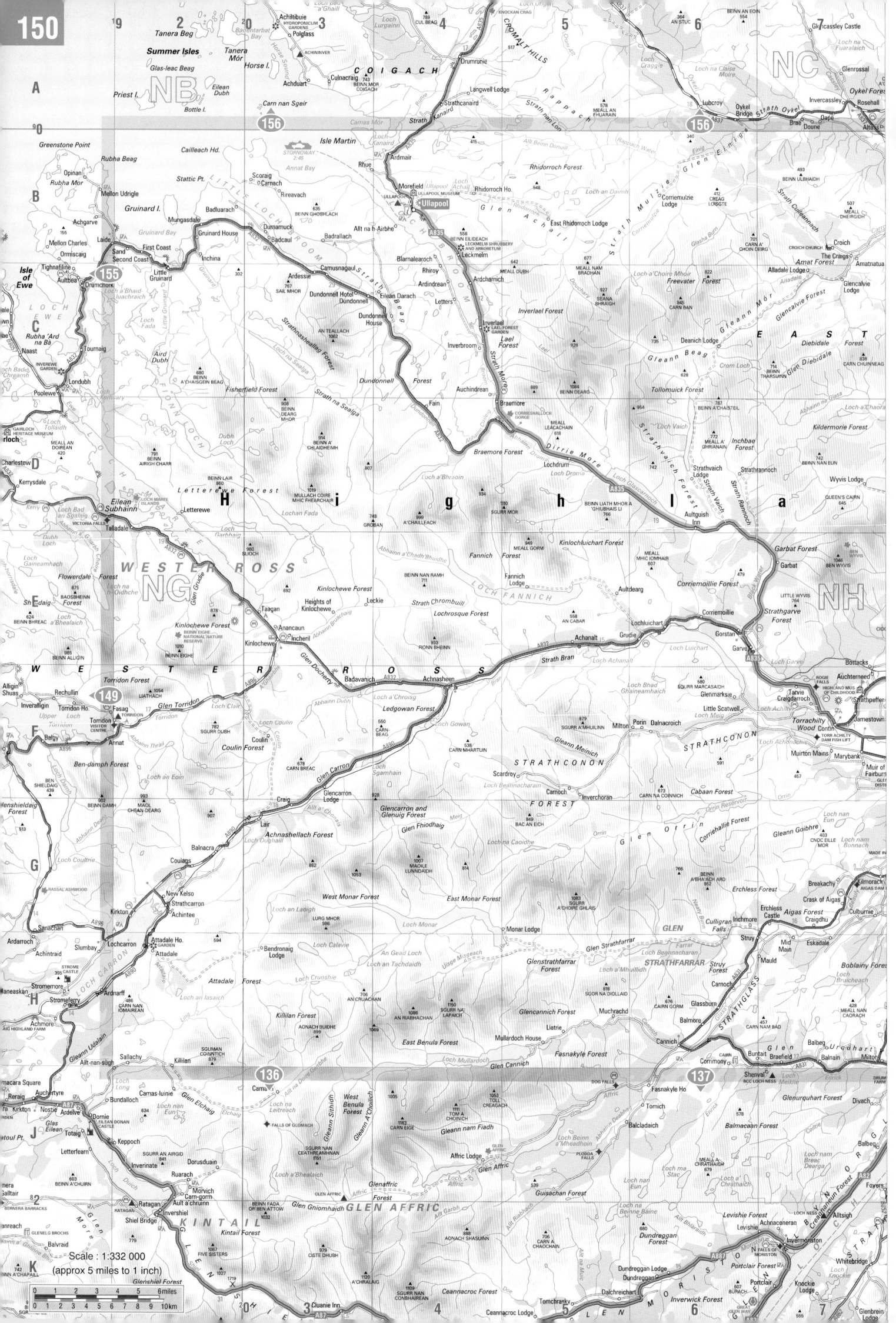

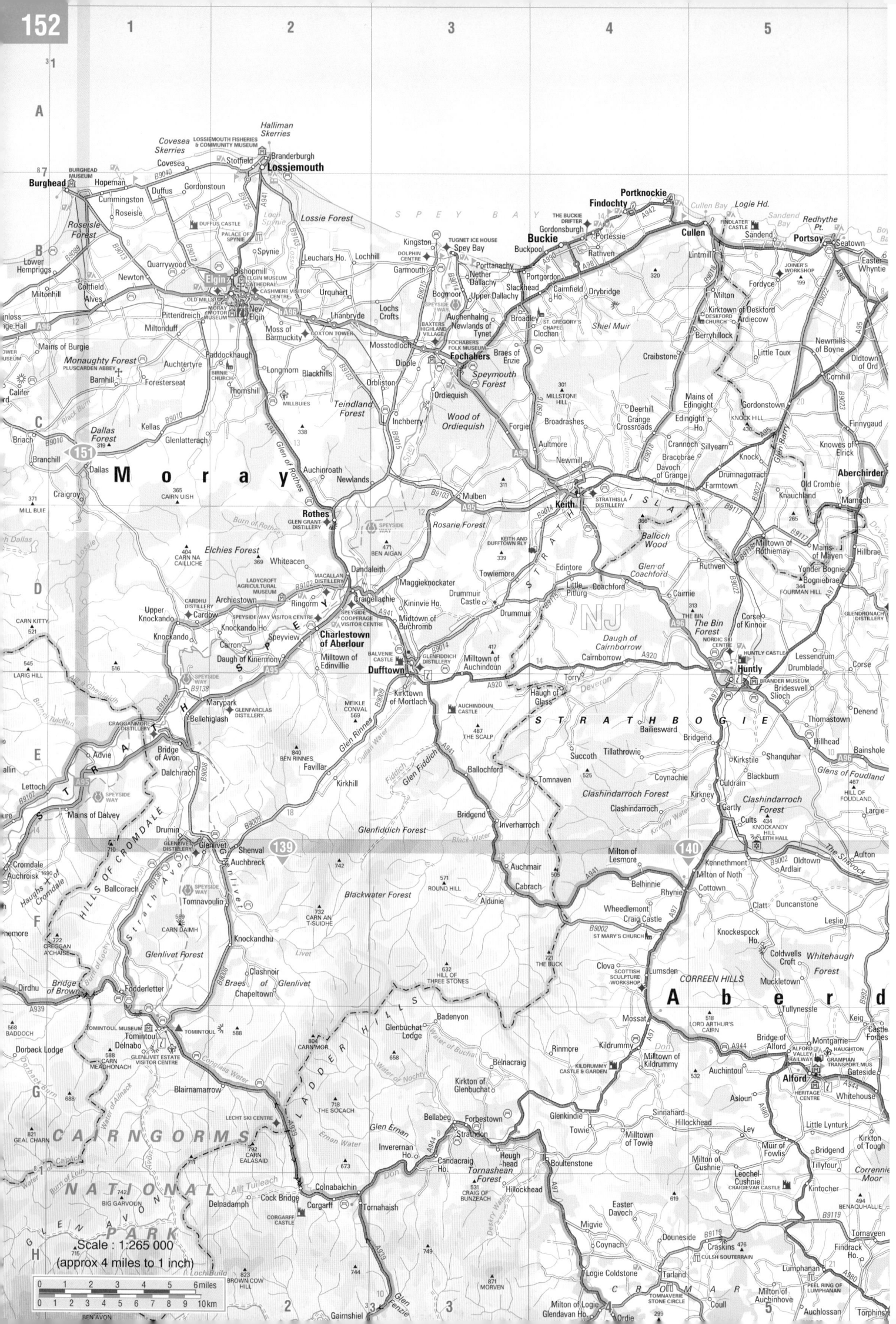

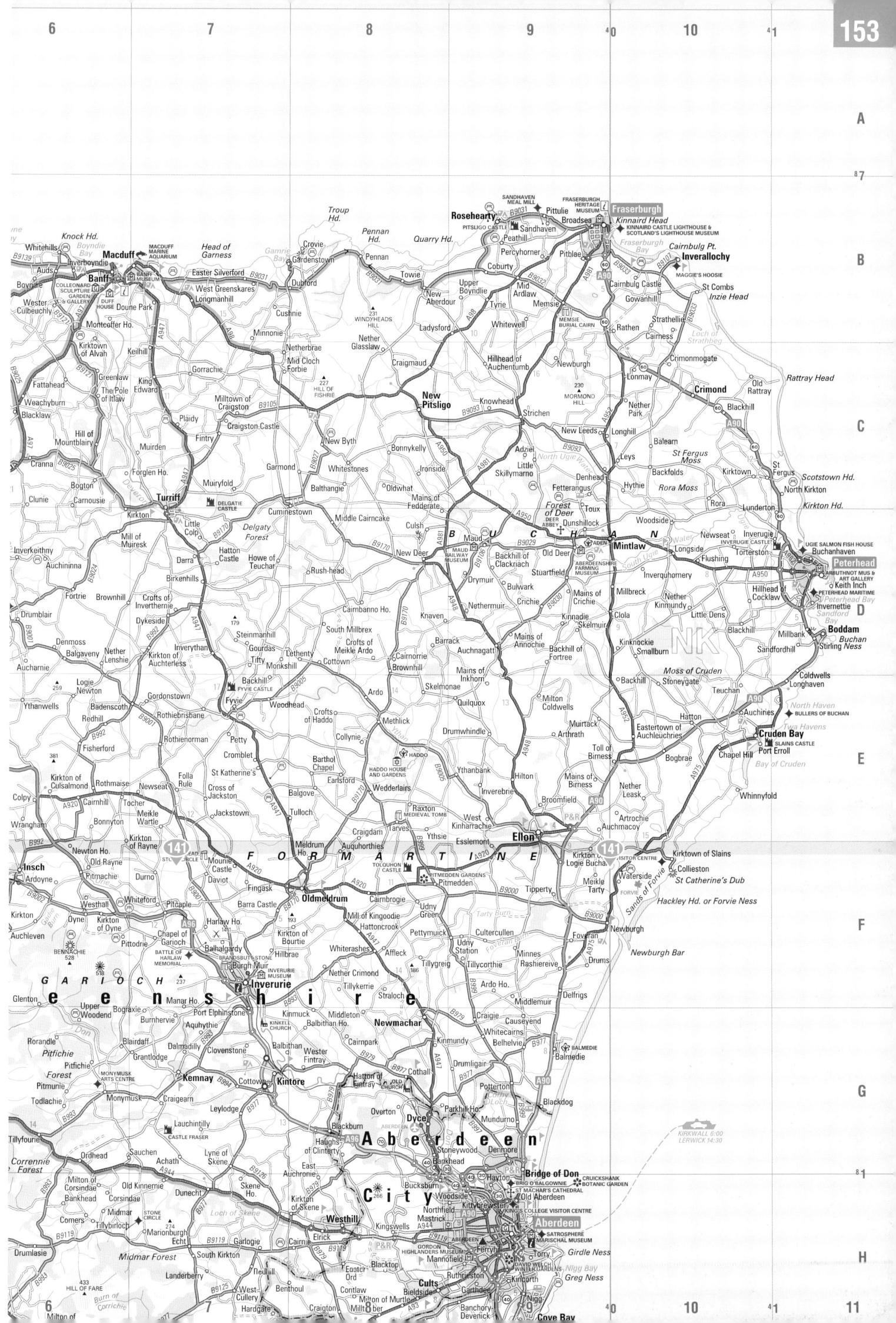

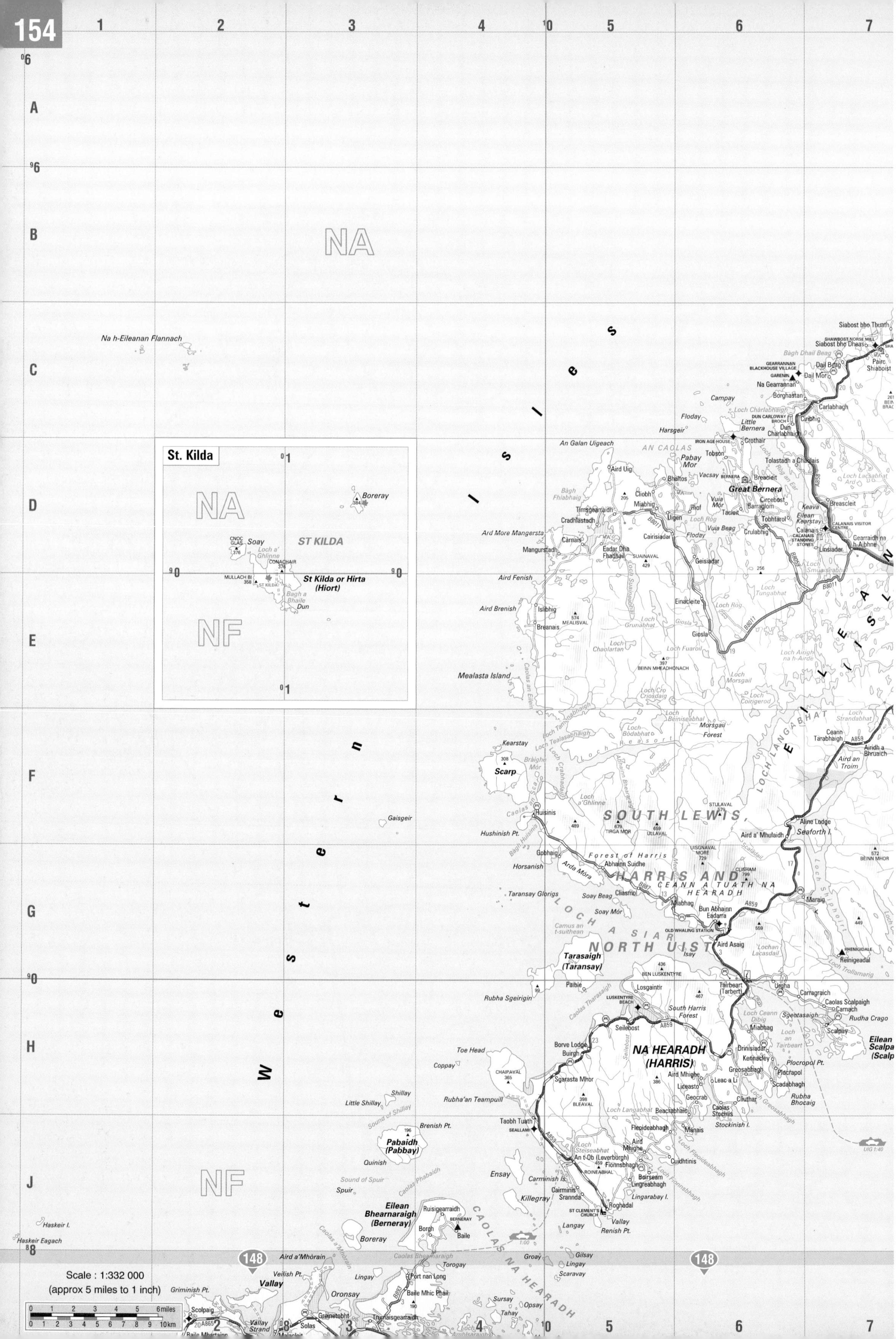

1 2 3 4 10 5 6 7

A

B

NA

C

Na h-Eileanan Flannach

Na h-Eileanan Flannach

St. Kilda

NA

Boreray
384

CNOC
GLAS
376 Soay ST KILDA
Loch a'
Ghlinne
CONACHAIR
378
MULLACH BI
358 ST KILDA St Kilda or Hirta
Bagh a' (Hiort)
Bhaile
Dun

NF

D

An Galan Uigeach

Aird Uig
Bhaltos Pabay
Timsgearraidh Mor
Cradhlastadh B8011
Ard More Mangersta
Càrnais Floday
Mangurstadh SUAINAVAL
429
Aird Fenish EADAR DHA

Aird Brenish
Islibhig 574
MEALISVAL
Breanais Loch
Chaolartan Loch
Grunavhat
Mealasta Island

SHAWBOST NORSE MILL Siabost bho Thuath
Siabost bho Dheas
Bàgh Dhail Beag Pairc
GEARRANNAN Dail Beag Shiaboist
BLACKHOUSE VILLAGE Dail Mor
GARENIN Na Gearrannan
Campay Borghastan
Floday Carlabhagh
Harsgeir Loch Charlabhaigh DUN CARLOWAY BROCH Little
IRON AGE HOUSE Bernera Dun
Tobson Charlabhaigh
Vacsay BERNERA Breacleit
Vuia Great Bernera
Mor Tacleit Circebost
Uigen Barraglom Keava
Riof Tobhtarol Eilean
Vuia Beag Crulabhig Kearstay
Geisiadar CALANAIS VISITOR
CENTRE
Cairisiadar CALANAIS
STANDING
STONES Linsiadar
Calanais
256
Loch Rog
Einacleite Loch
Tungabhat
Geàrraidh na
h-Aibhne
Loch Rog

E

NF

F

Scarp

Kearstay
308 Bràighe
Mór Gaisgeir

Gaisgeir

G

Huisinis
Hushinish Pt. 676
TIRGA MOR
489
Gobhaig Arda Móra
Horsanish Abhainn Suidhe
Soay Beag UISGNAVAL
Cliasmol MORE
Taransay Glorigs Miabhag 729
Soay Mór CLISHAM
Camus an 799
t-suitheán
Tarasaigh OLD WHALING STATION
(Taransay) Bun Abhainn
Eadarra
Paible Isay
Rubha Sgeirigin 436
BEN LUSKENTYRE
Losgaintir 467
Caolas Tharasaigh Tàirbeart
LUSKENTYRE (Tarbert)
BEACH South Harris
Forest

South Lewis,

HARRIS AND
CEANN A TUATH NA
HEARADH

North Uist,

H

Toe Head
Coppay Borve Lodge 23
Buirgh
CHAIPAVAL Aird Mhighe
365 Sgarasta Mhor 386
398 Seilebost
Little Shillay BLEAVAL
Shillay Rubha'an Teampuill
Sound of Shillay
Brenish Pt.
196 NA HEARADH
Pabaidh (HARRIS)
(Pabbay) Taobh Tuath
Quinish SEALLAM! Geocrab
Sound of Spuir An t-Ob (Leverburgh) 459
Spuir ROINEABHAL
Eilean Carminish Is.
Bhearnaraigh Cairminis Srannda
(Berneray) Killegray
Borgh BERNERA Langay
Baile ST CLEMENTS Roghadal
CHURCH Renish Pt.
Vallay

Fleodeabhagh
Manais
Stockinish I.

J

Haskeir I.

Haskeir Eagach

Aird a'Mhòrain
Veilish Pt. Lingay
Griminish Pt. Oronsay Port nan Long
Scolpaig Lingay
Vallay Valley Sursay
Strand Tahay
A865 Valley
Baile Mhic Phail
Solas

148

148

Gilsay
Groay Lingay
Scaravay

CAOLAS NA HEARADH

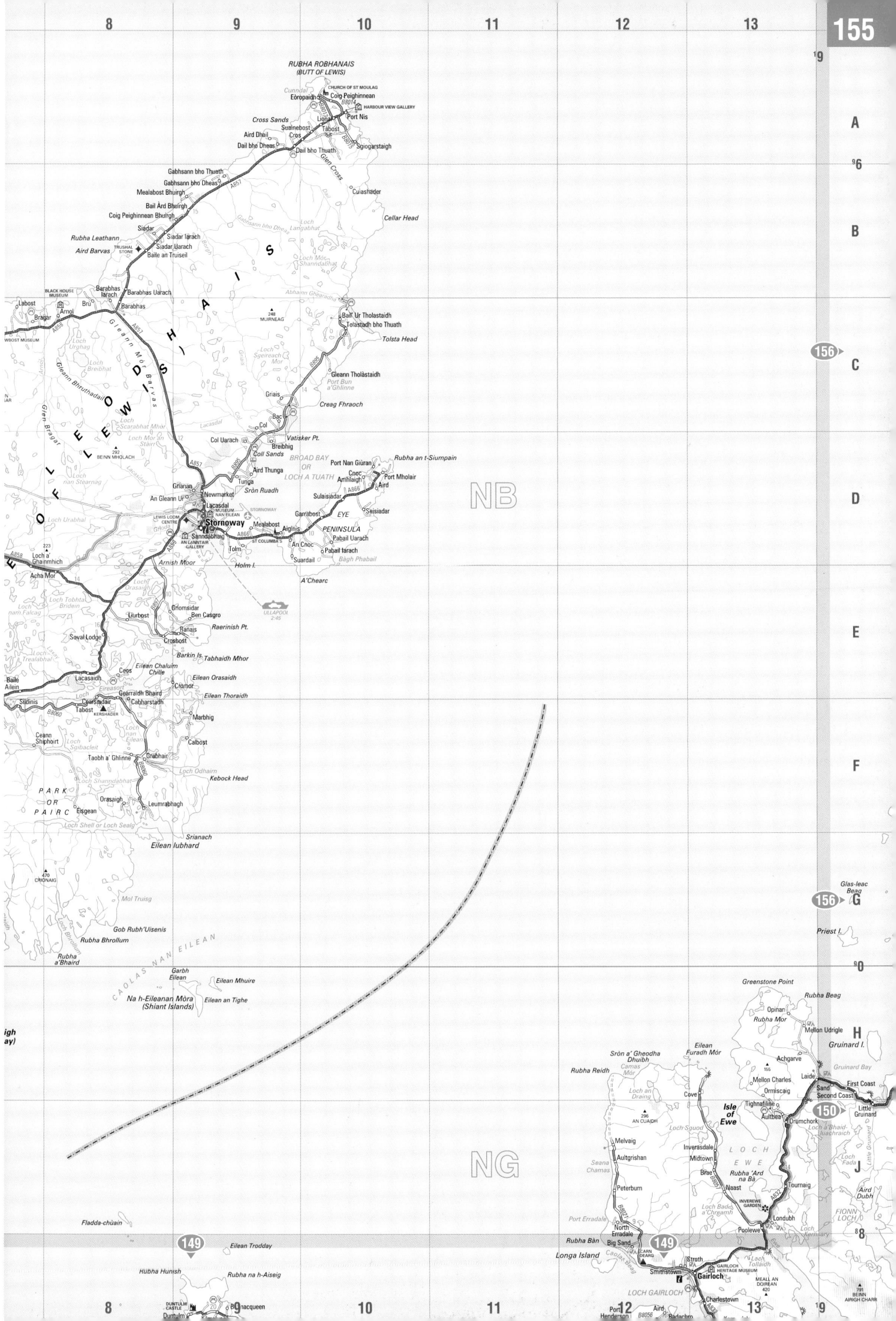

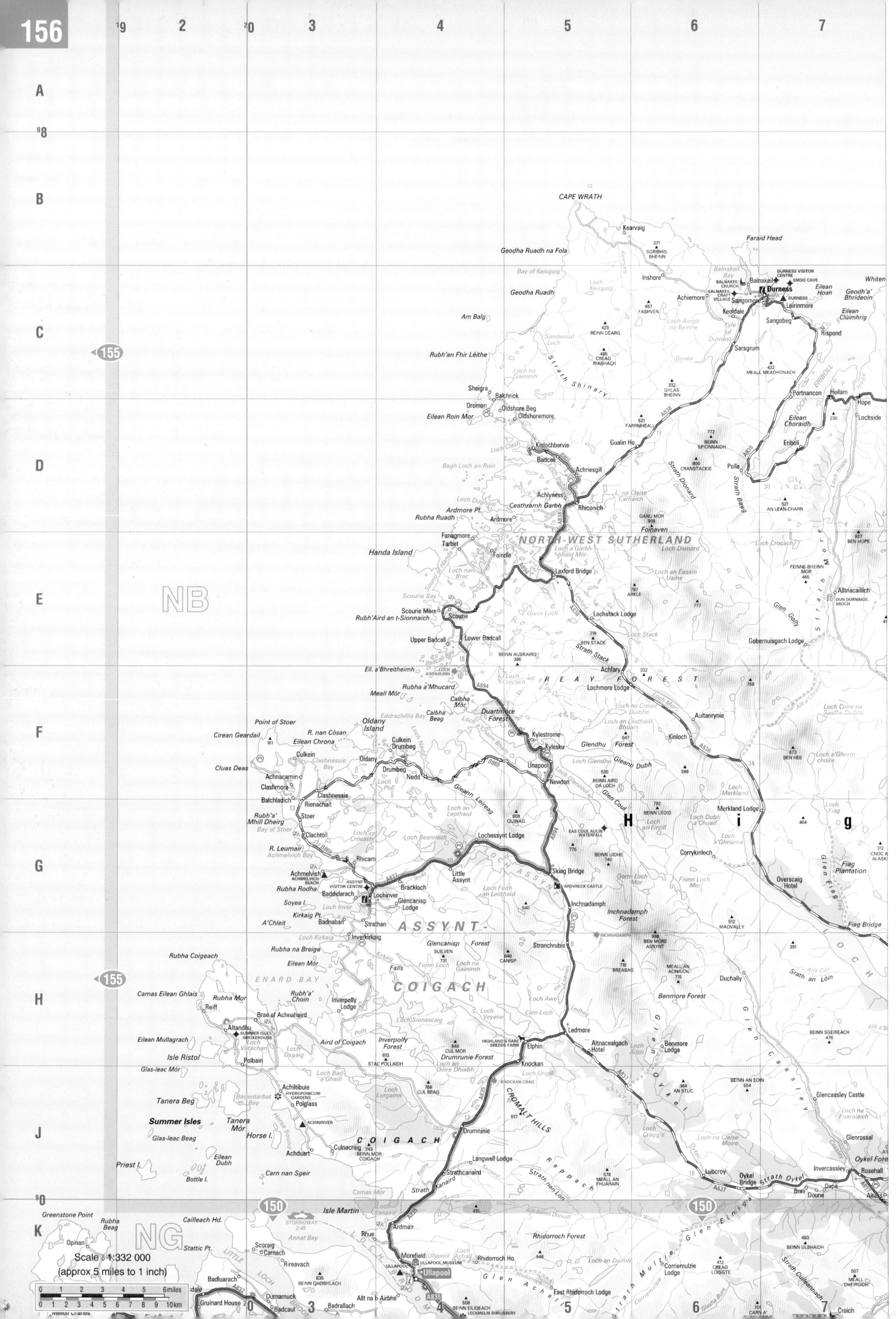

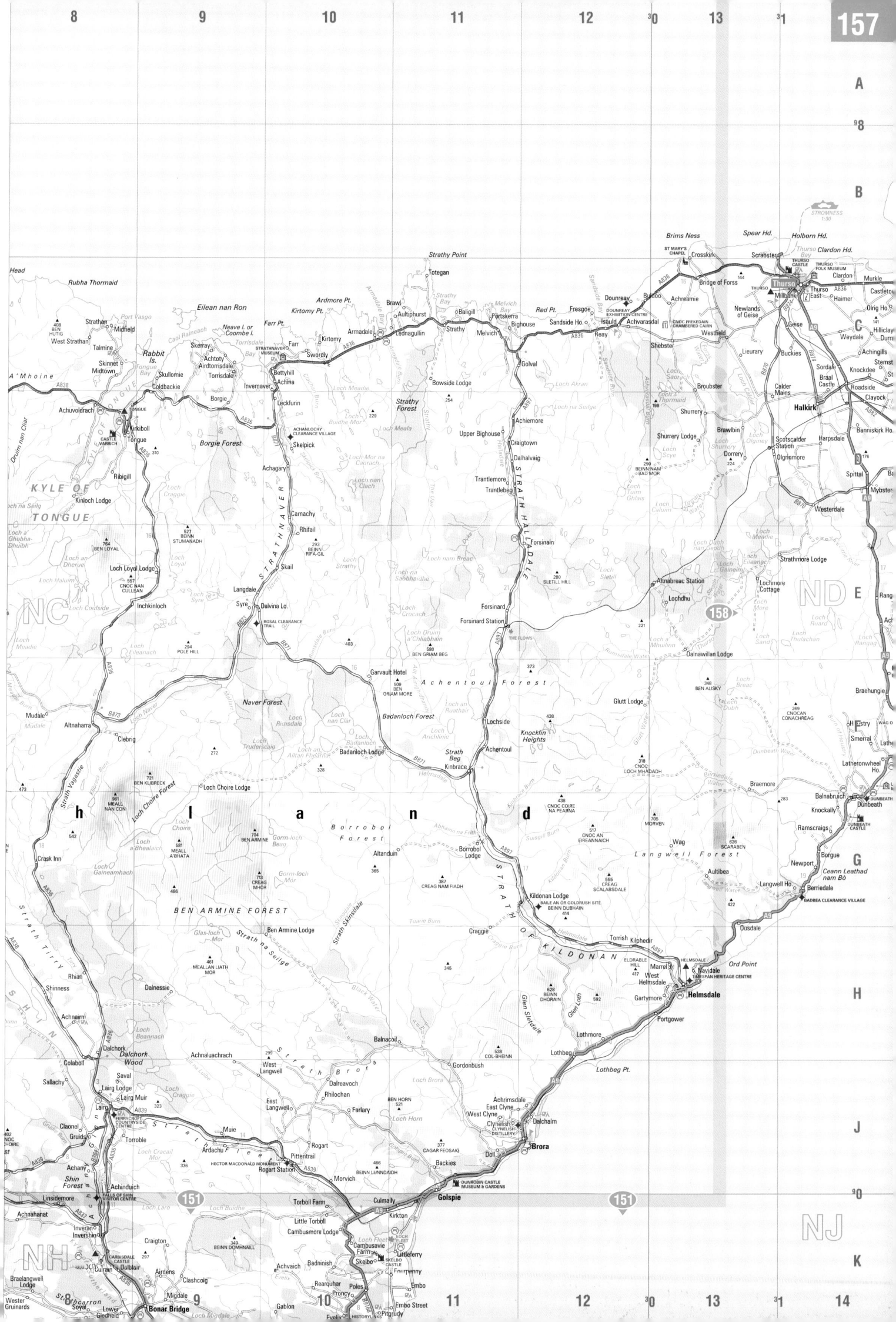

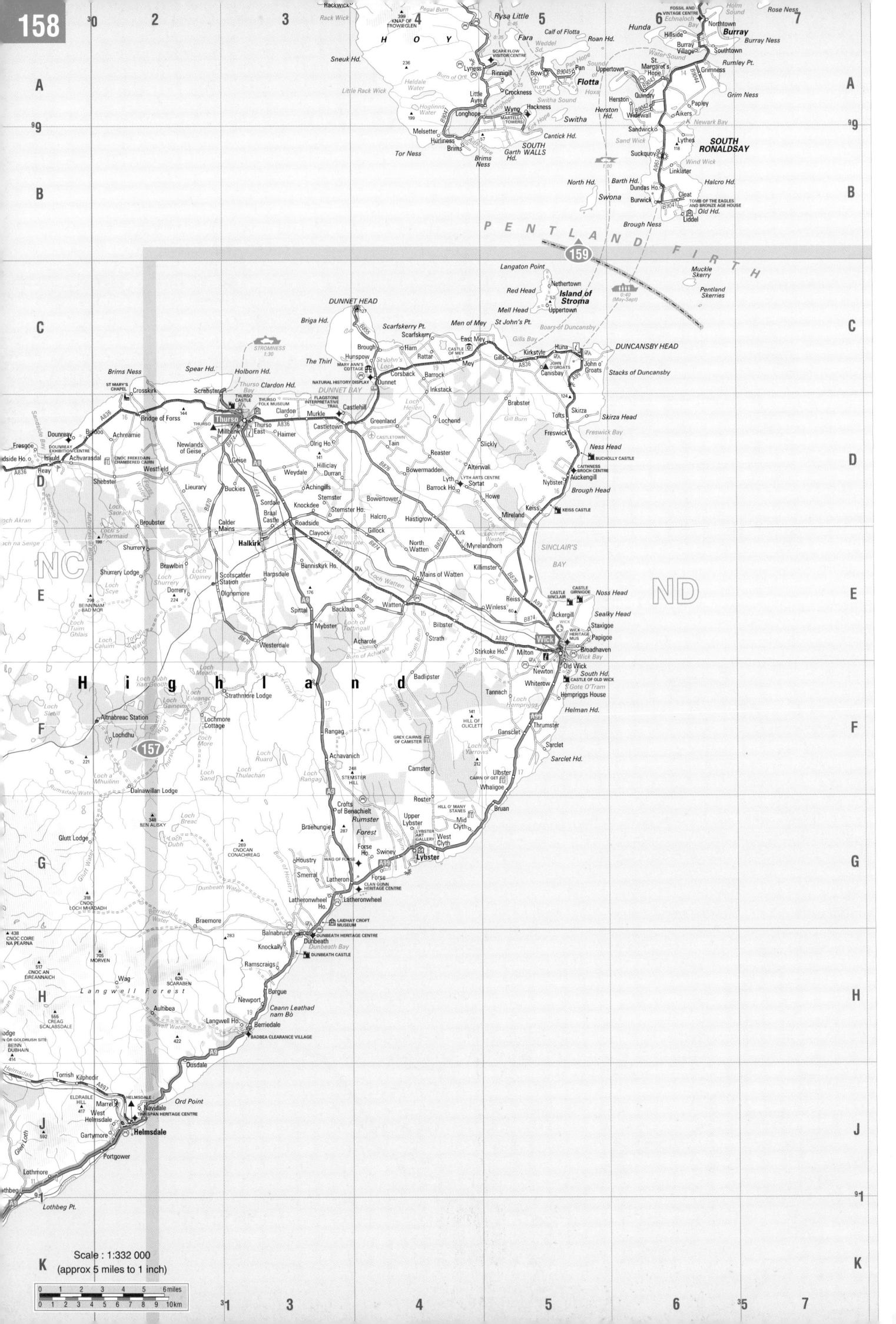

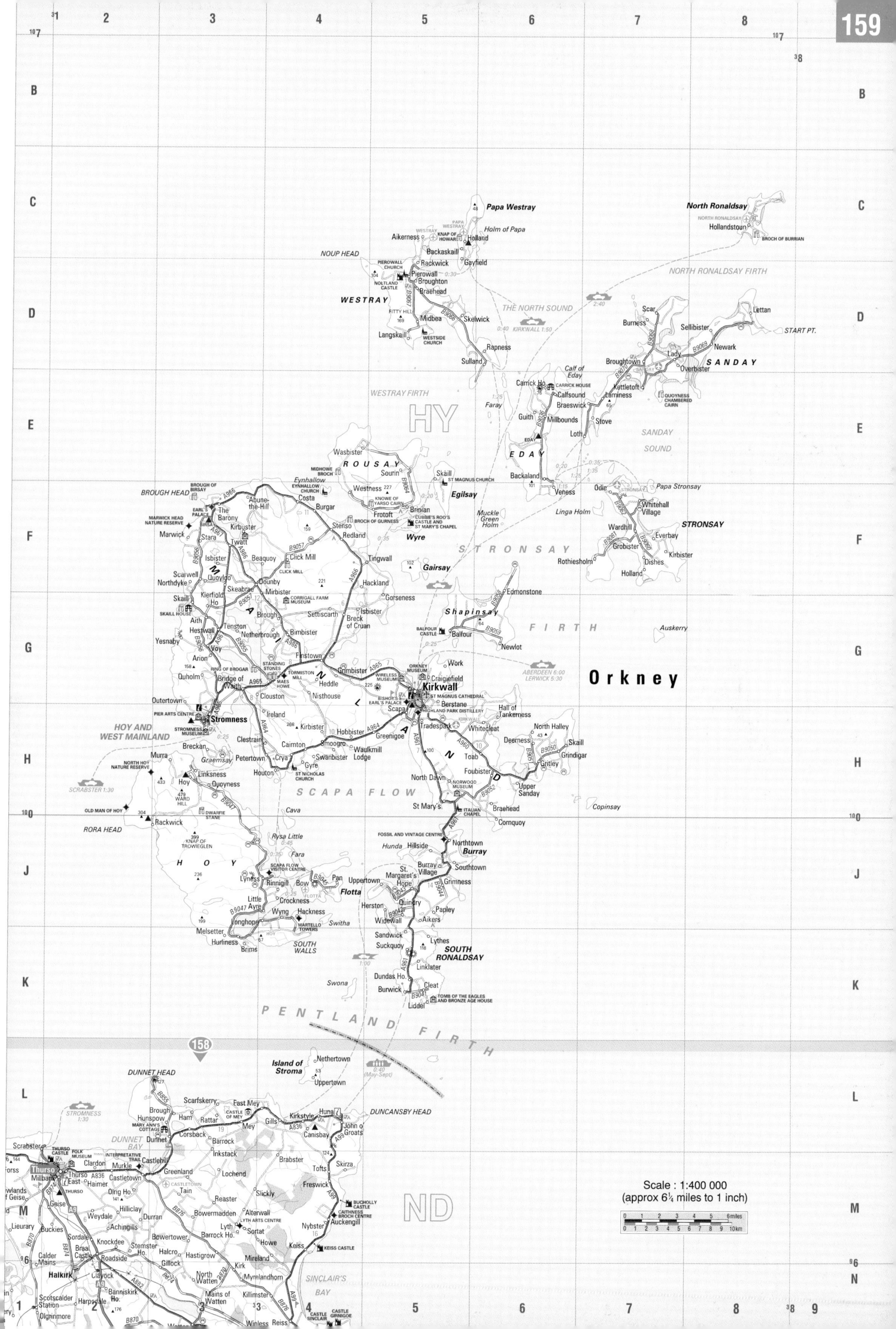

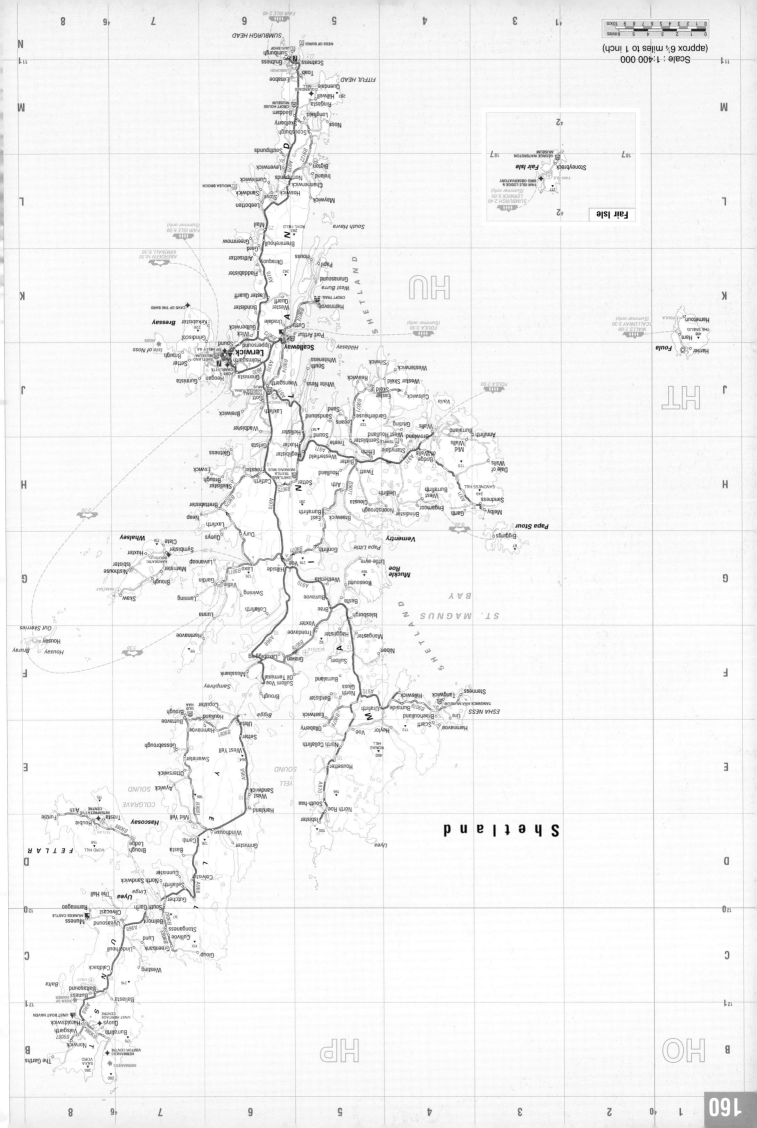

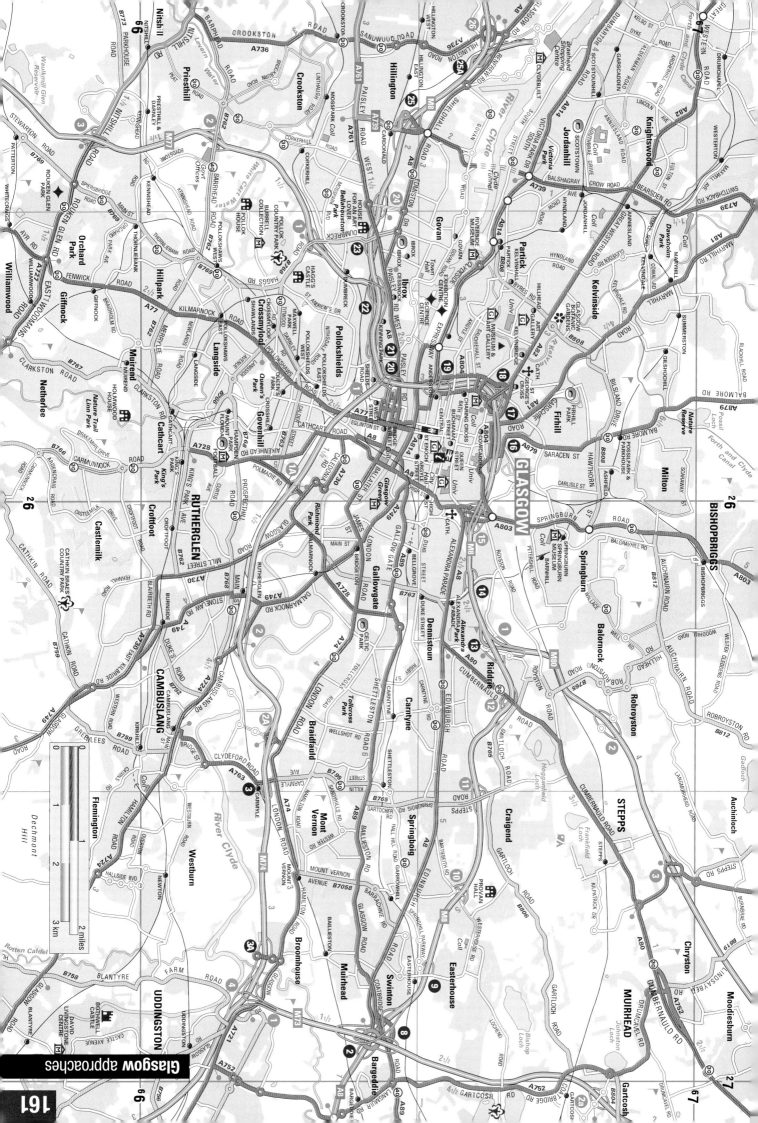

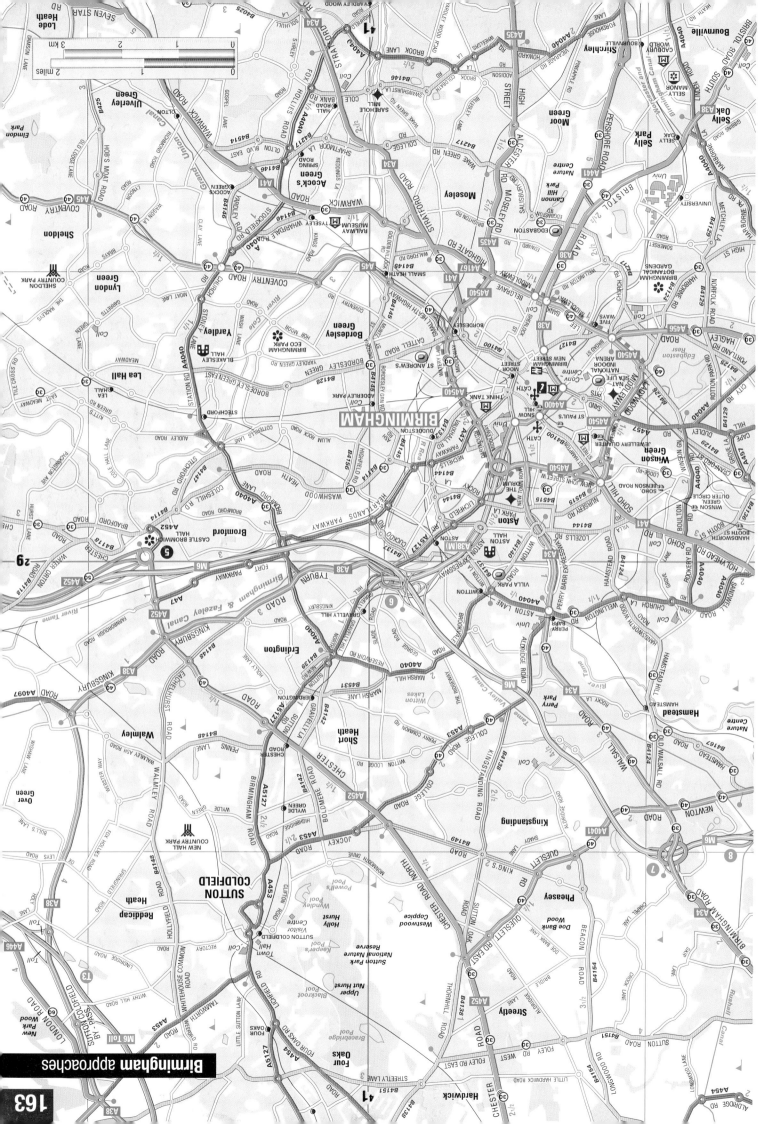

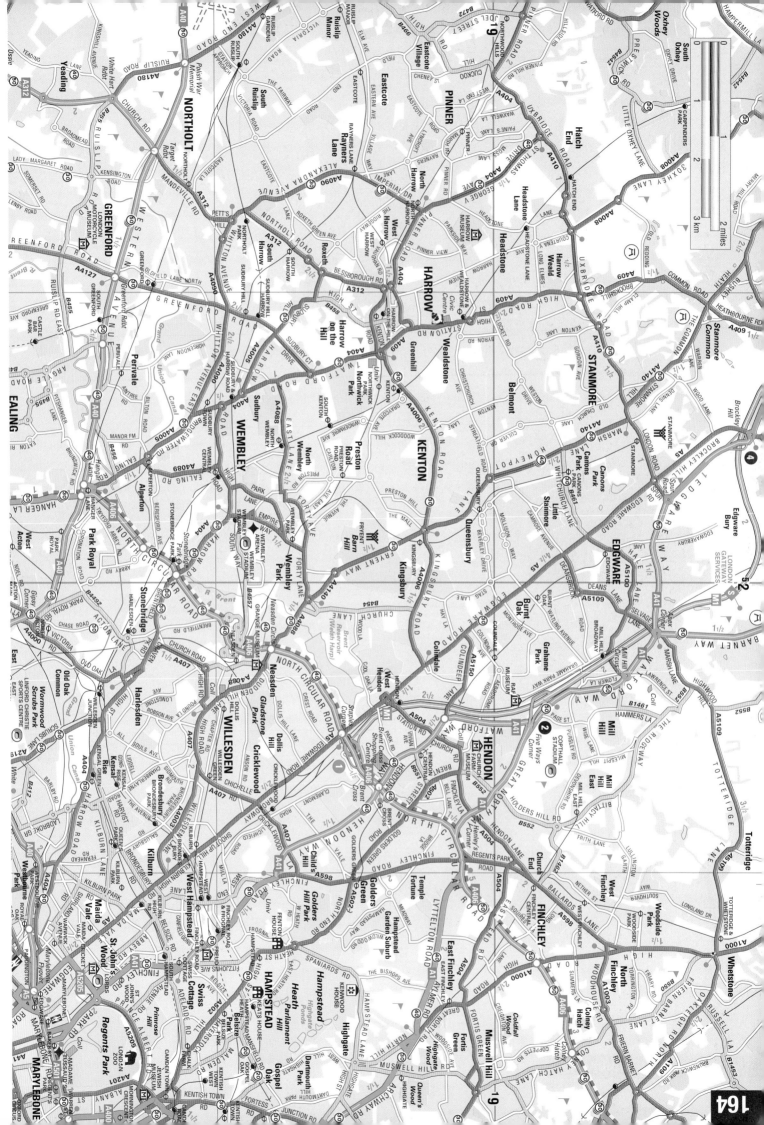

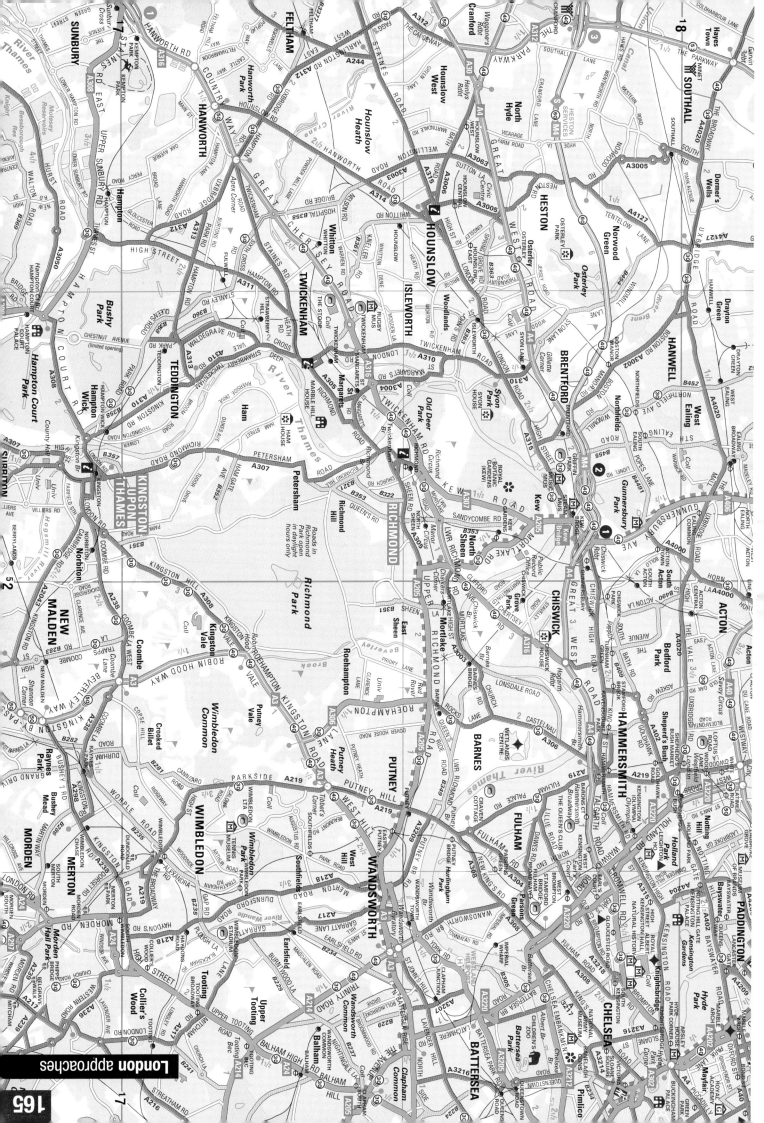

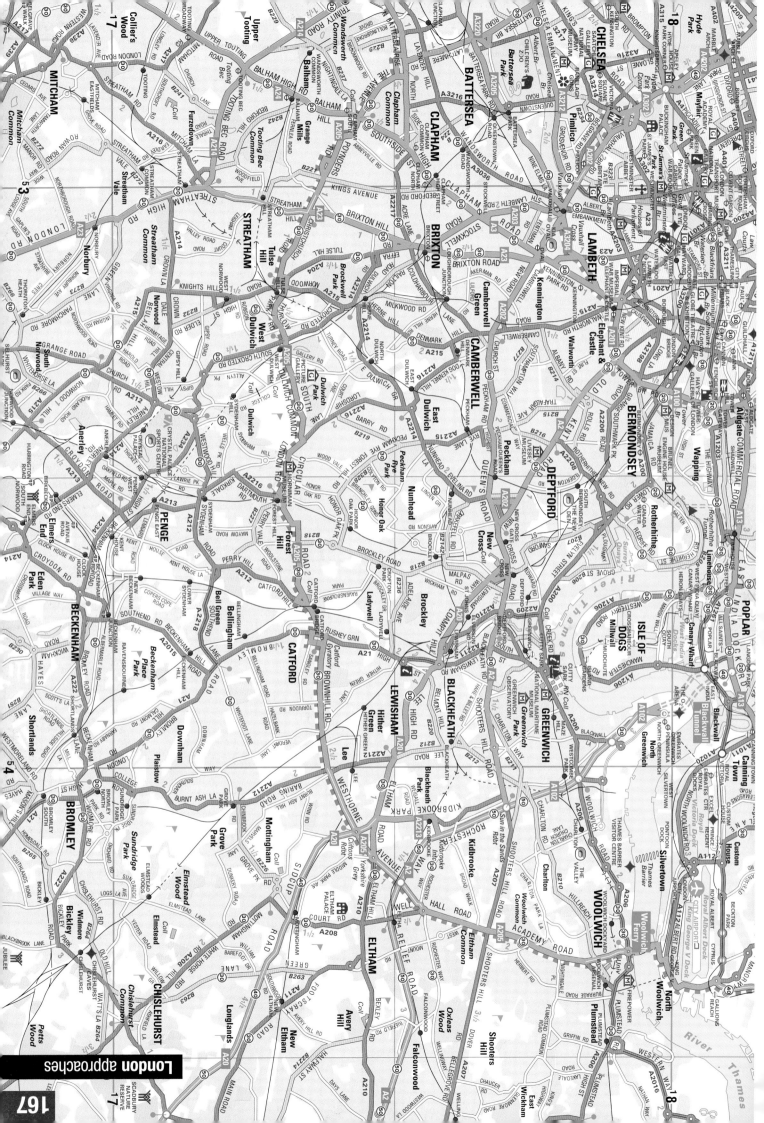

Town plan symbols

- Motorway
- **Primary route** – dual, single carriageway
- **A road** – dual, single carriageway
- **B road** – dual, single carriageway
- Minor through road
- One-way street
- Pedestrian roads
- Shopping streets
- Railway with station
- Tramway with station
- Underground or Metro station
- Hospital
- Parking
- Police, Post Office
- Shopmobility
- Youth hostel
- Bus or railway station building
- Shopping precinct or retail park
- Park
- Congestion charge zone
- Abbey or cathedral
- Ancient monument
- Aquarium
- Art gallery
- Bird collection or aviary
- Building of interest
- Castle
- Church of interest
- Cinema
- Garden
- Historic ship
- House
- House and garden
- Museum
- Preserved railway
- Roman antiquity
- Safari park
- Theatre
- Tourist information centre
- Zoo
- Other place of interest

Aberdeen

0 Miles ¼

Birmingham

0 Miles ¼

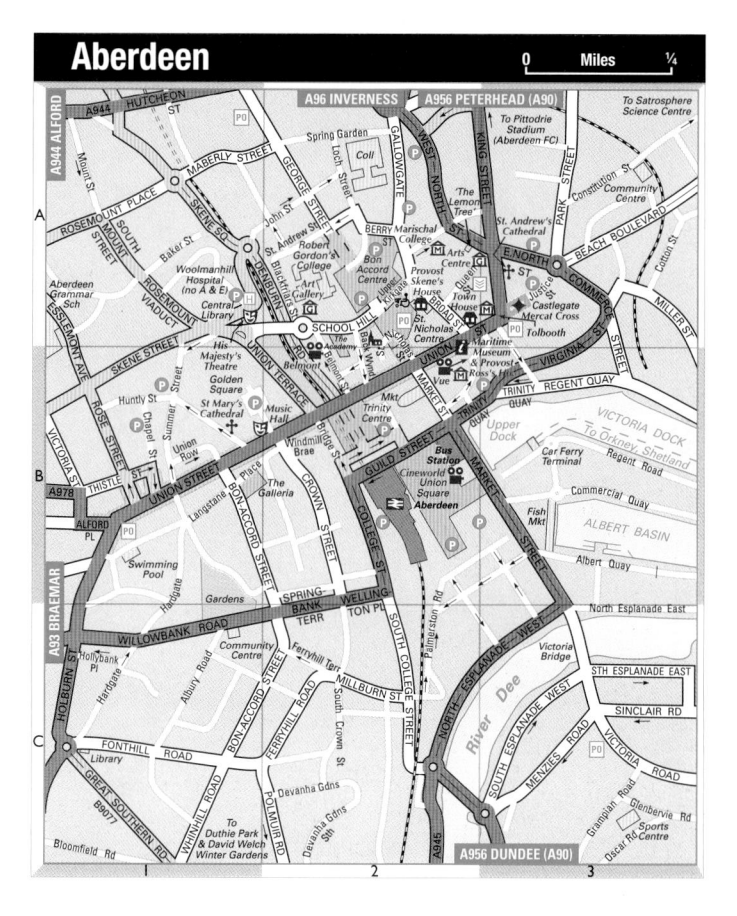

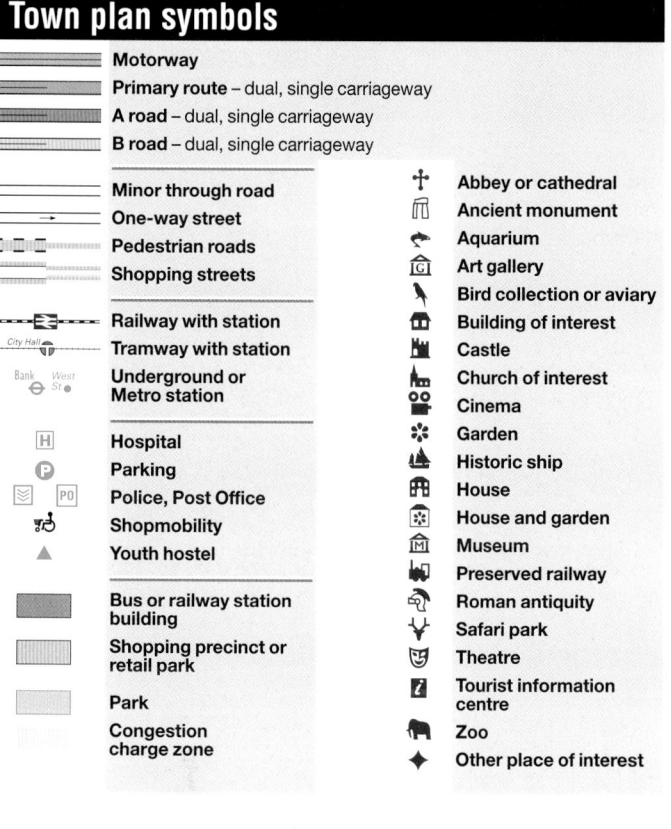

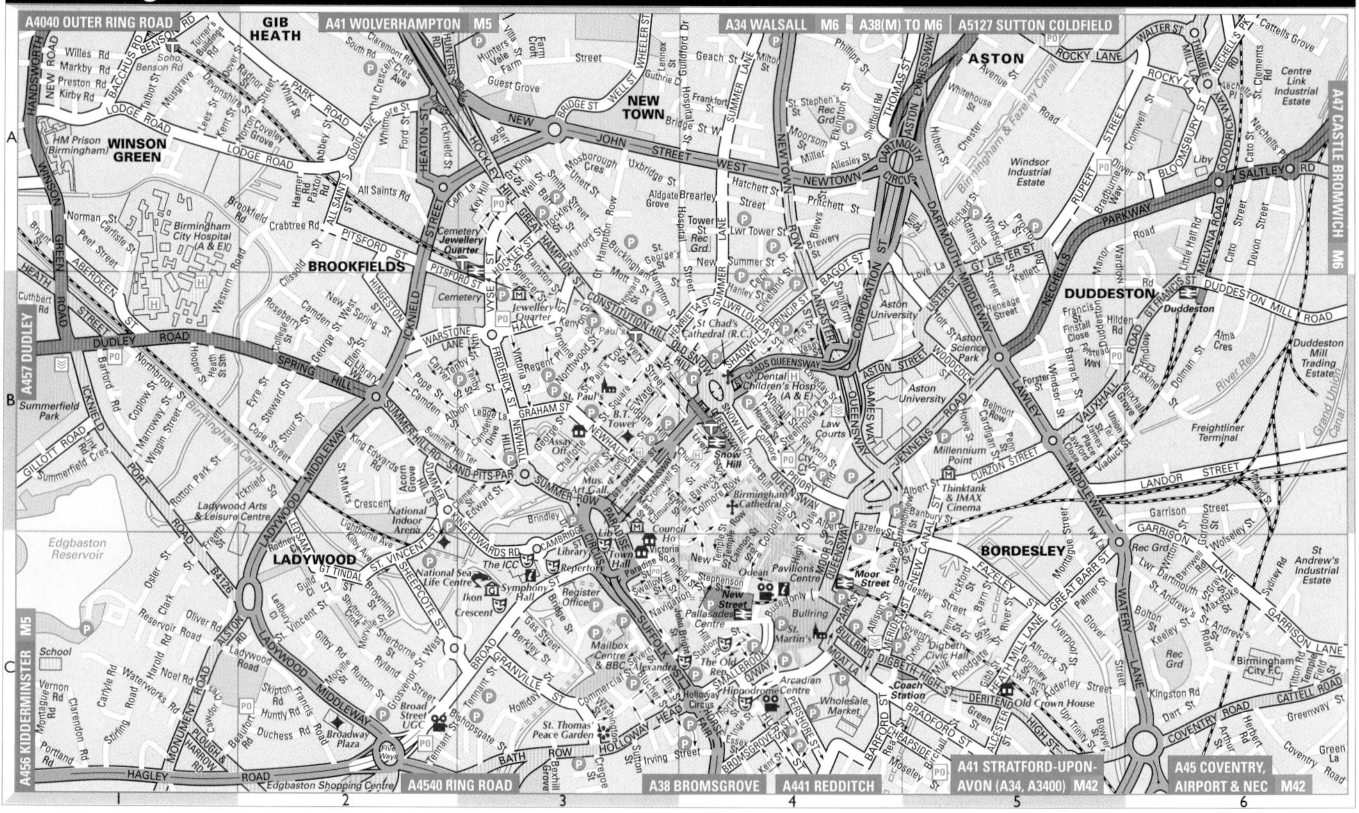

Bath

0   Miles   ¼

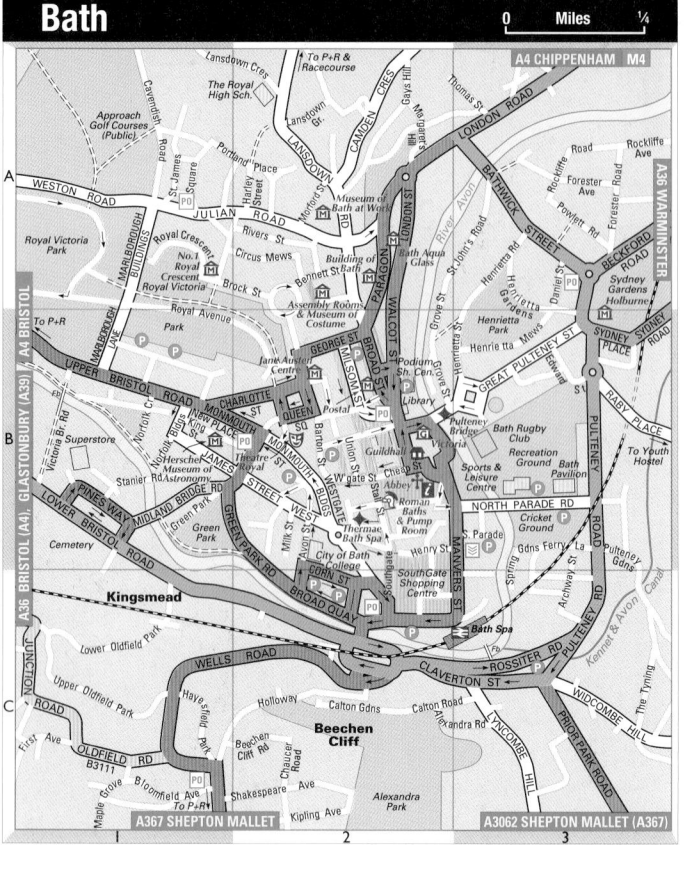

Bradford

0   Miles   ¼

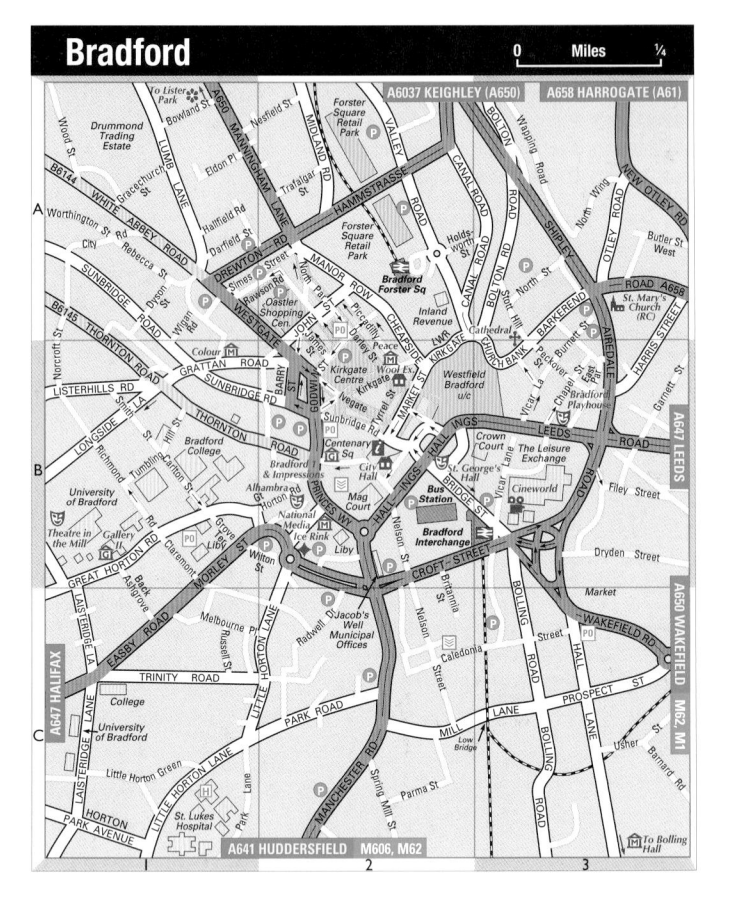

Bristol

0   Miles   ¼

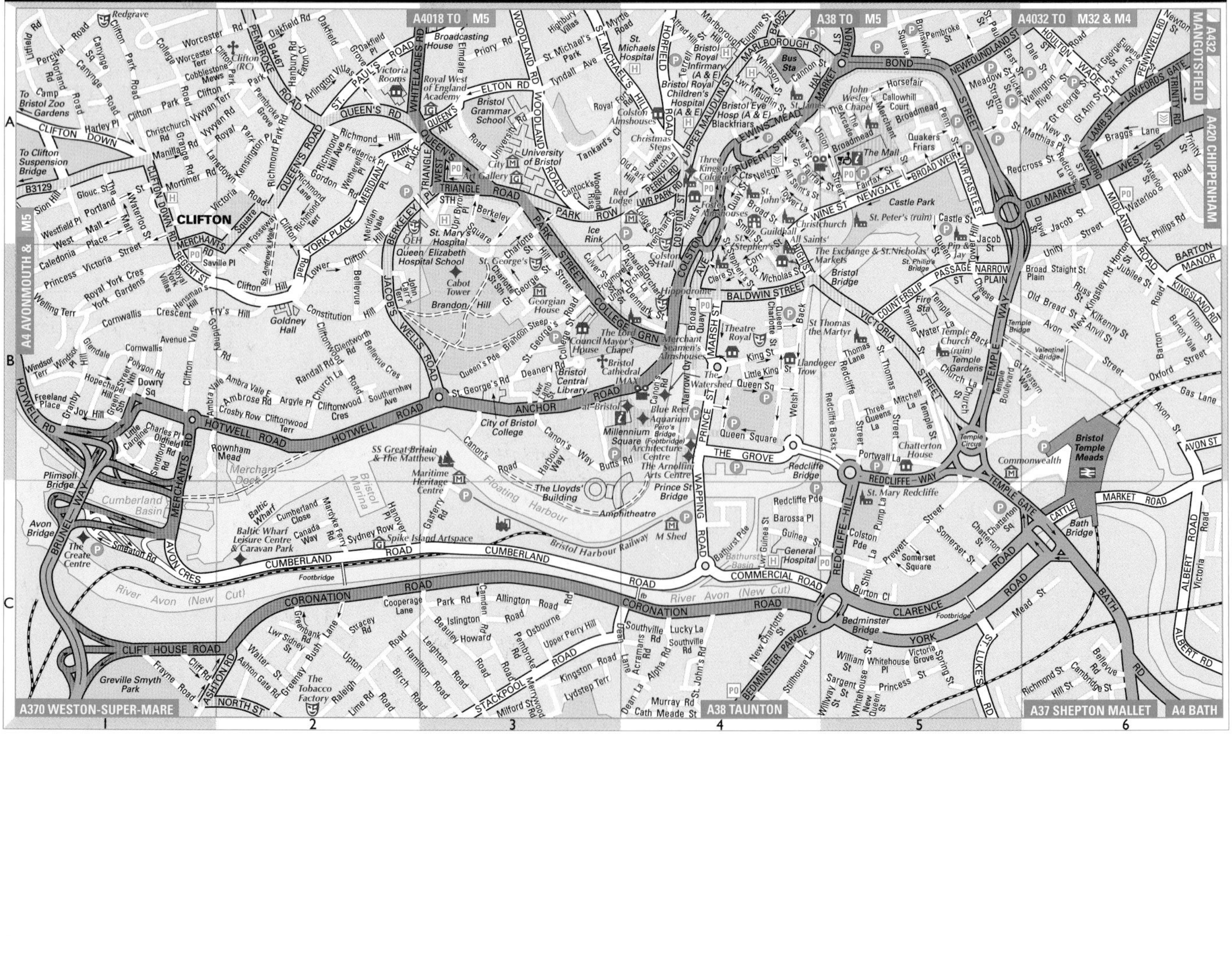

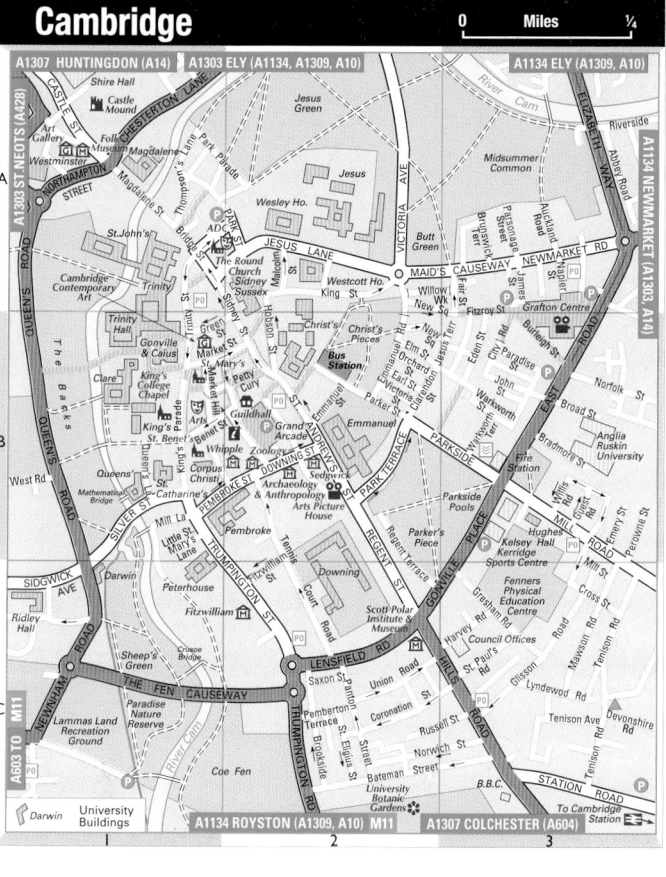
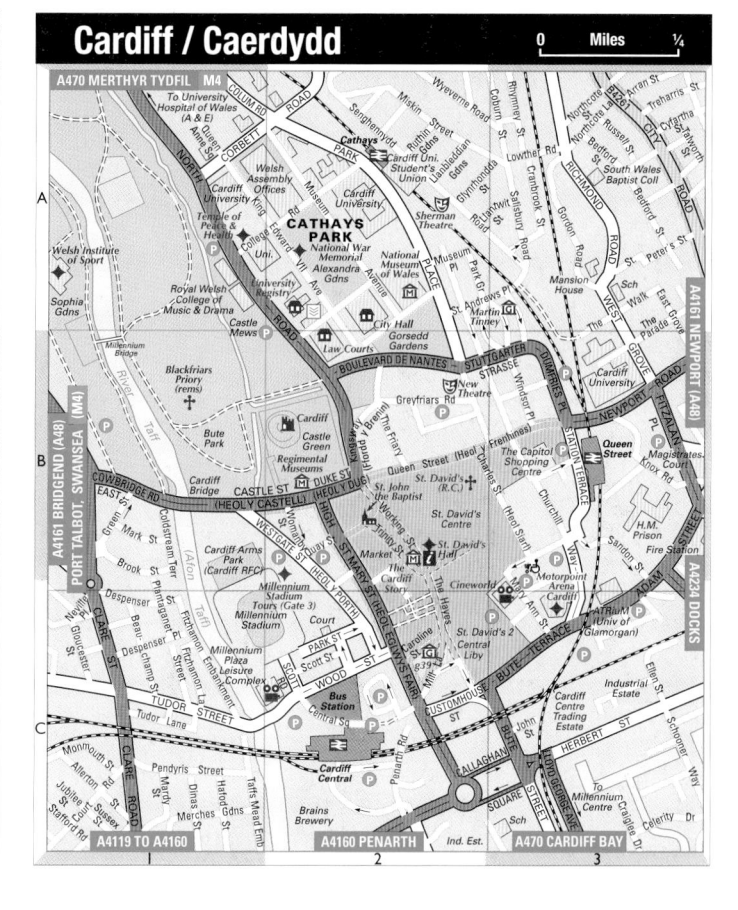
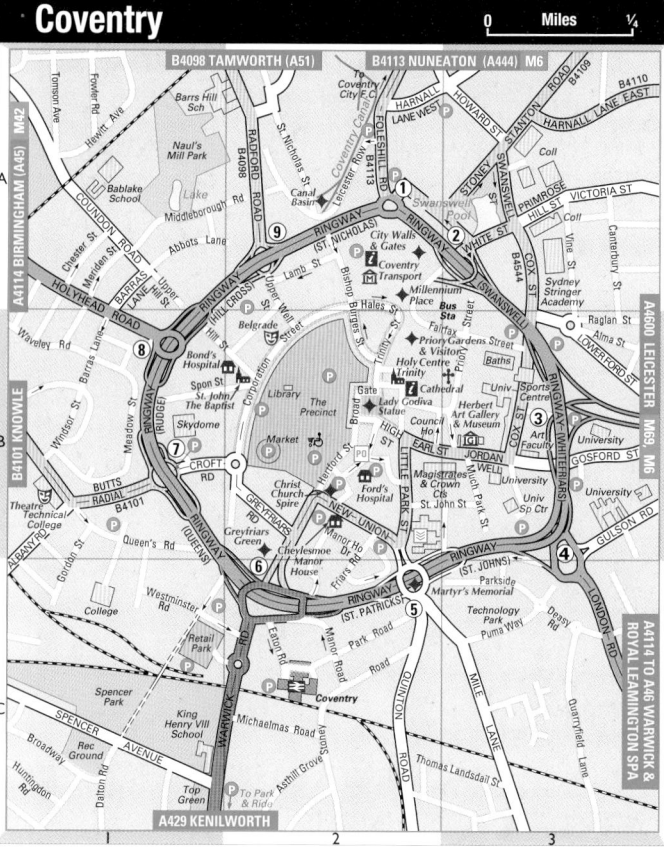
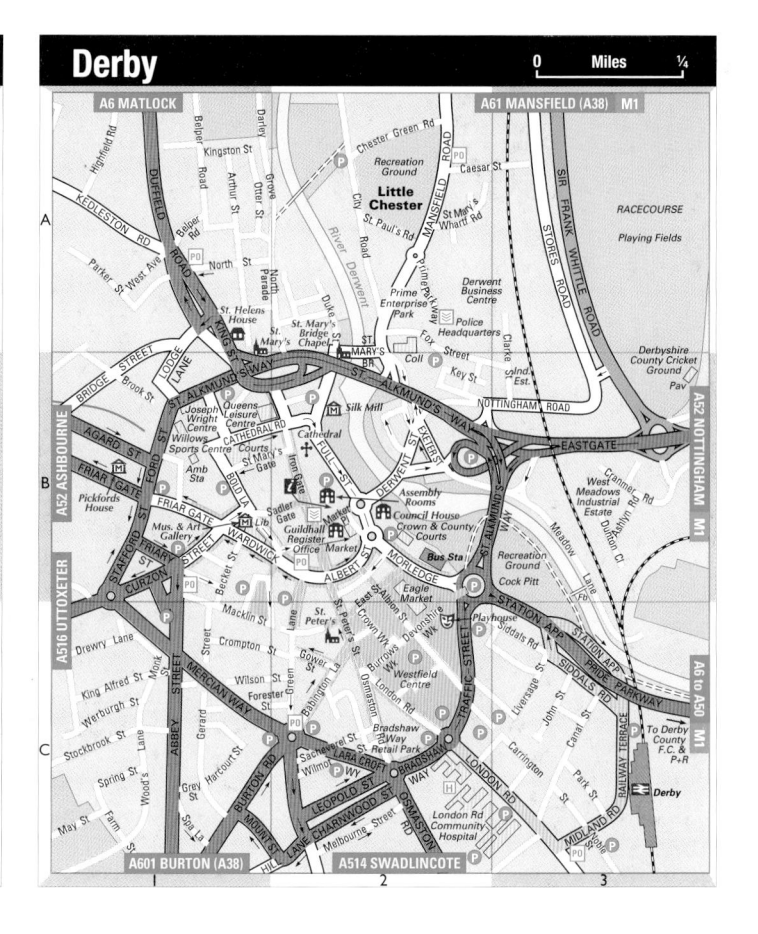

Edinburgh

0 — Miles — ¼

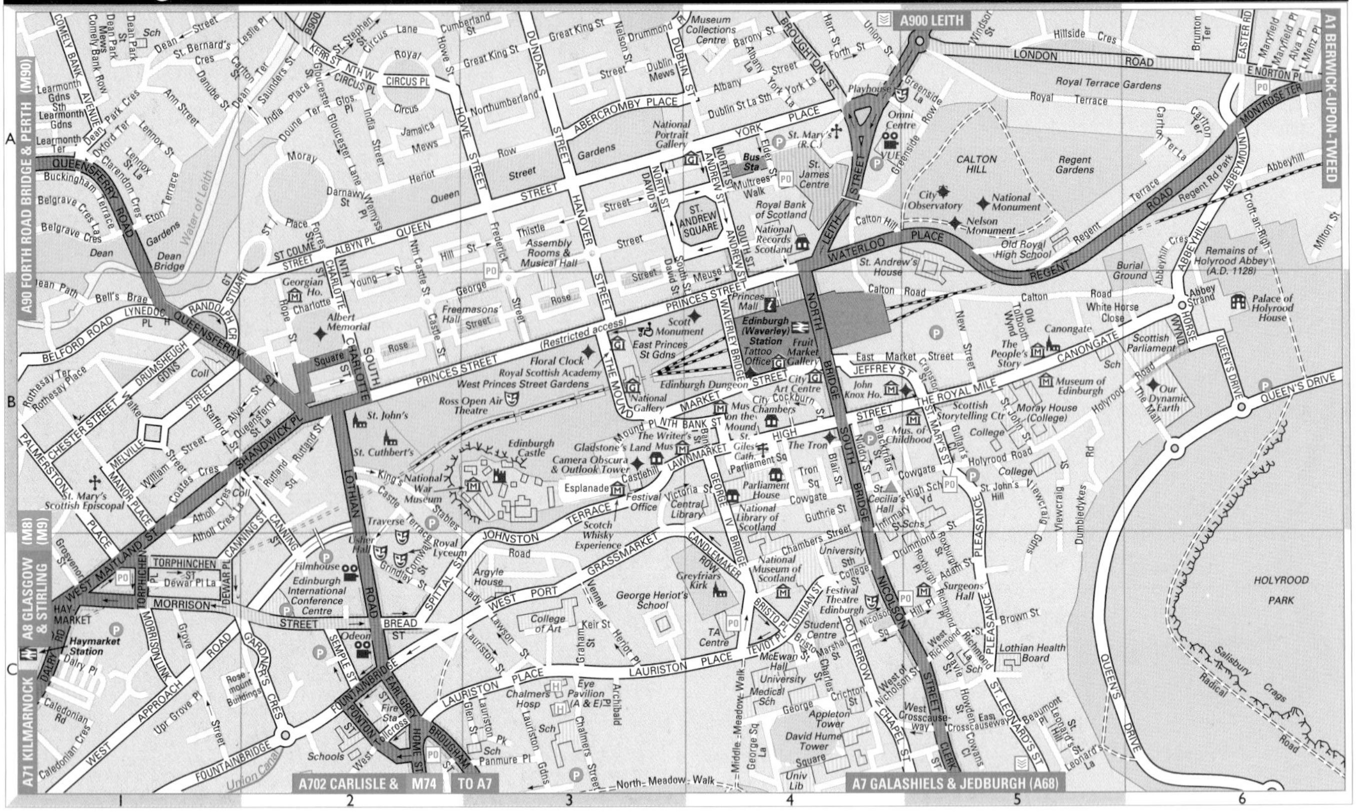

Glasgow

0 — Miles — ¼

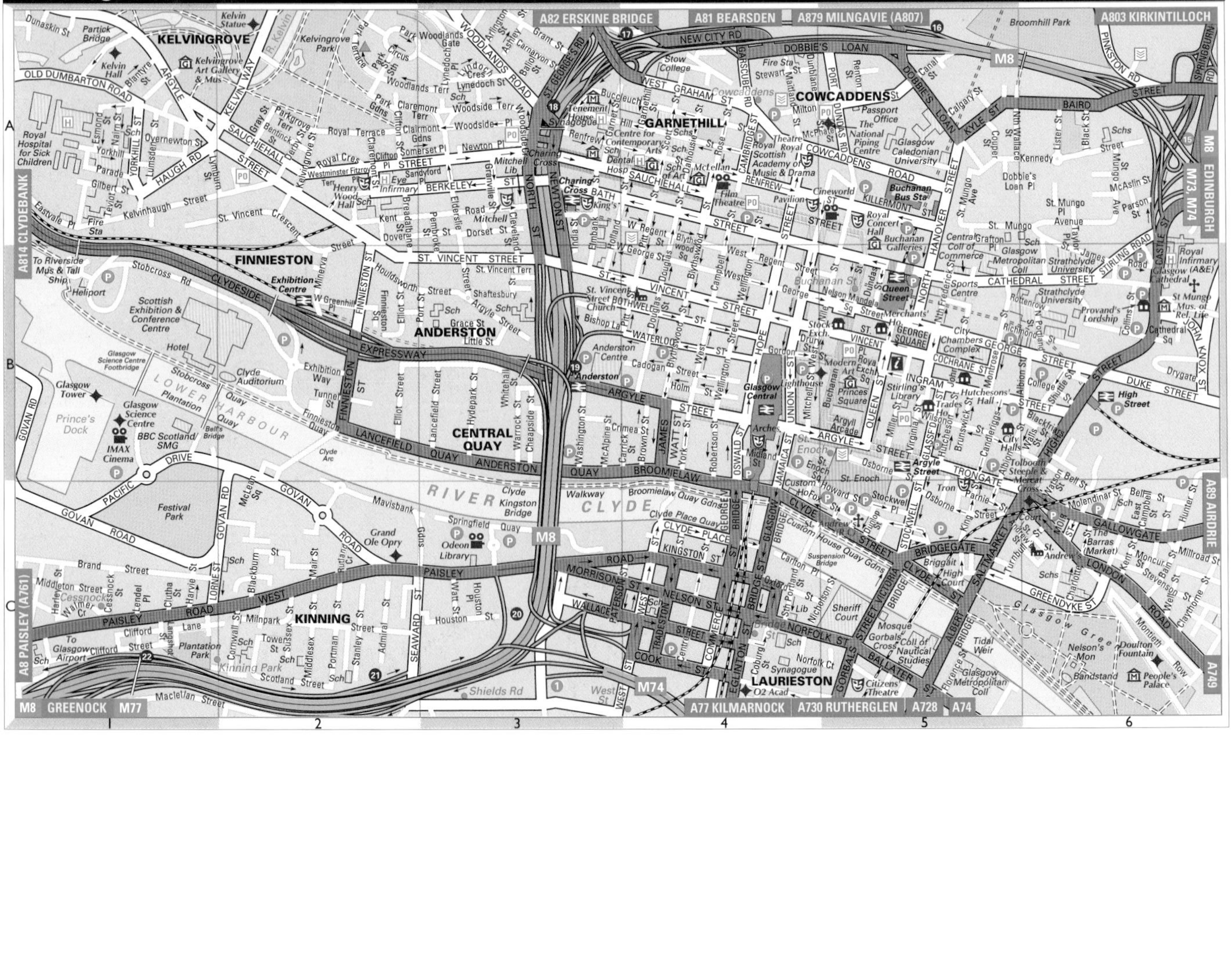

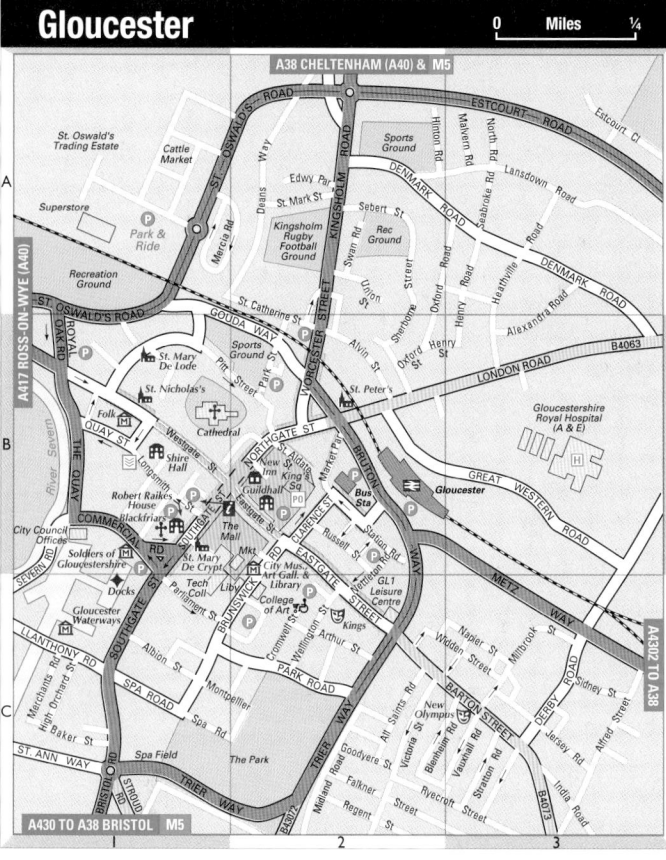

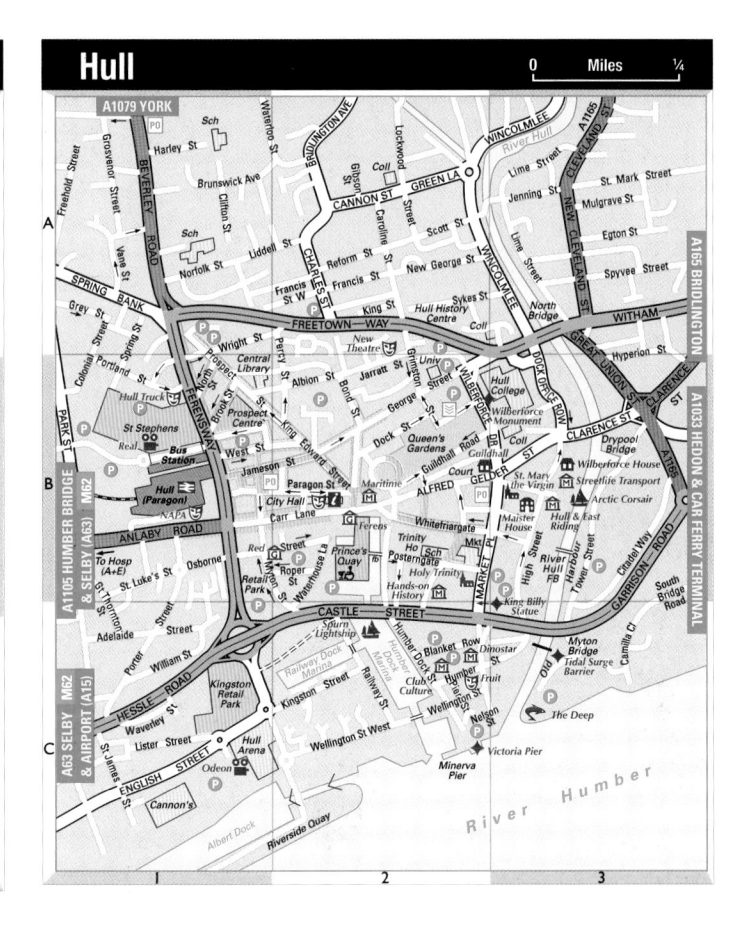

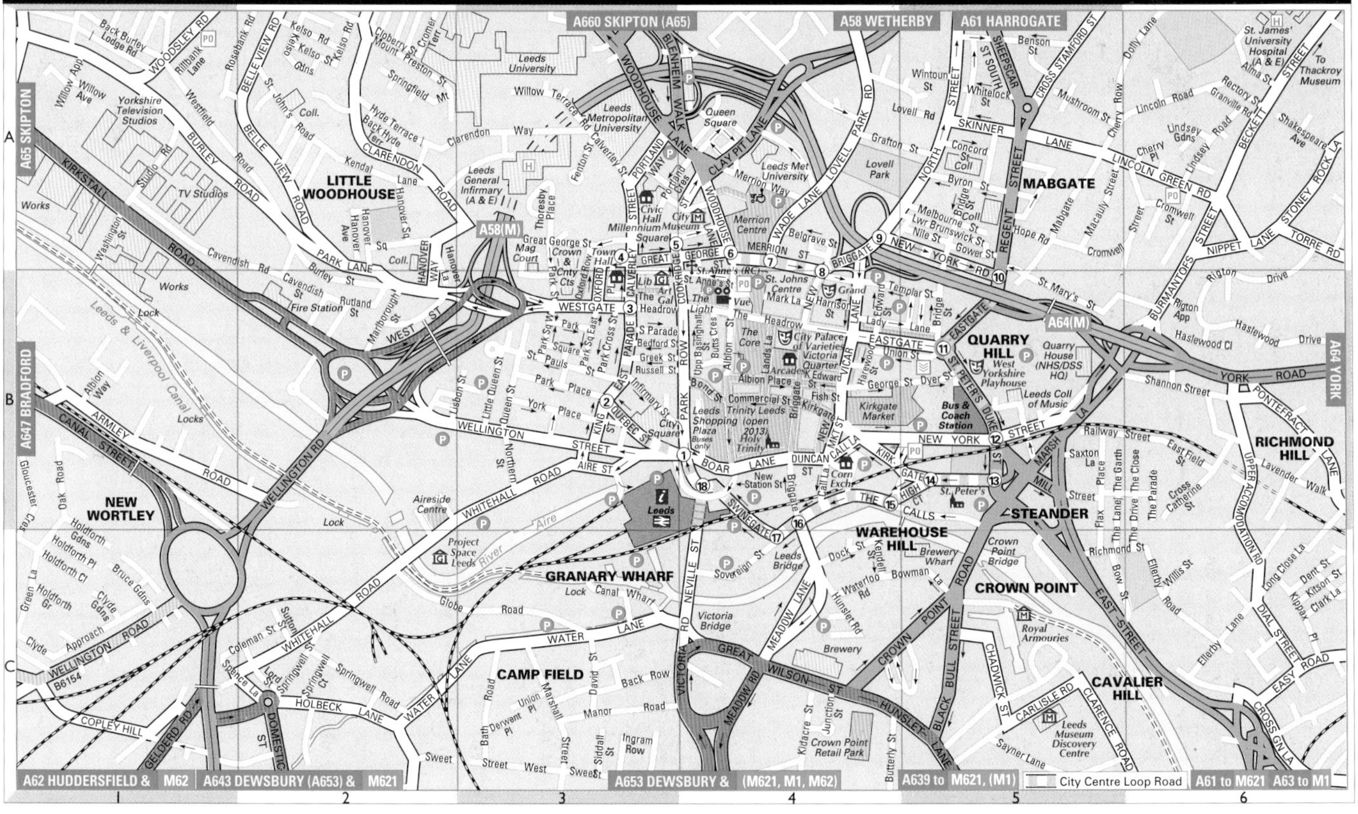

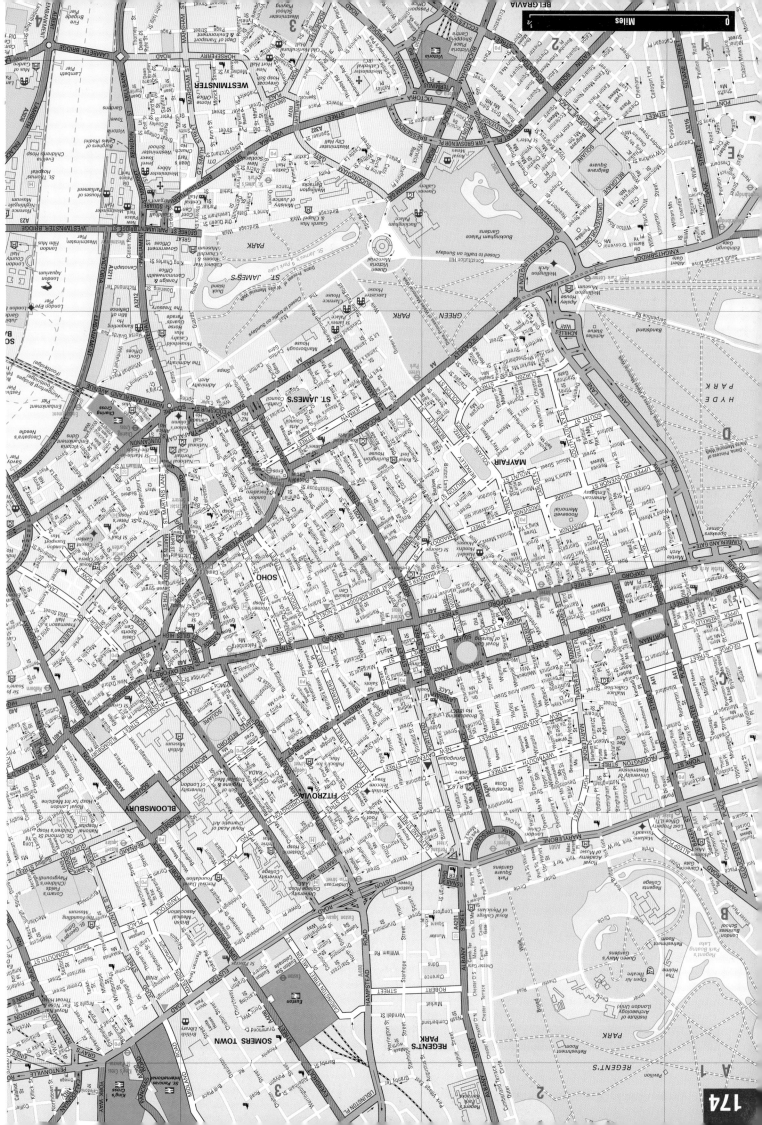

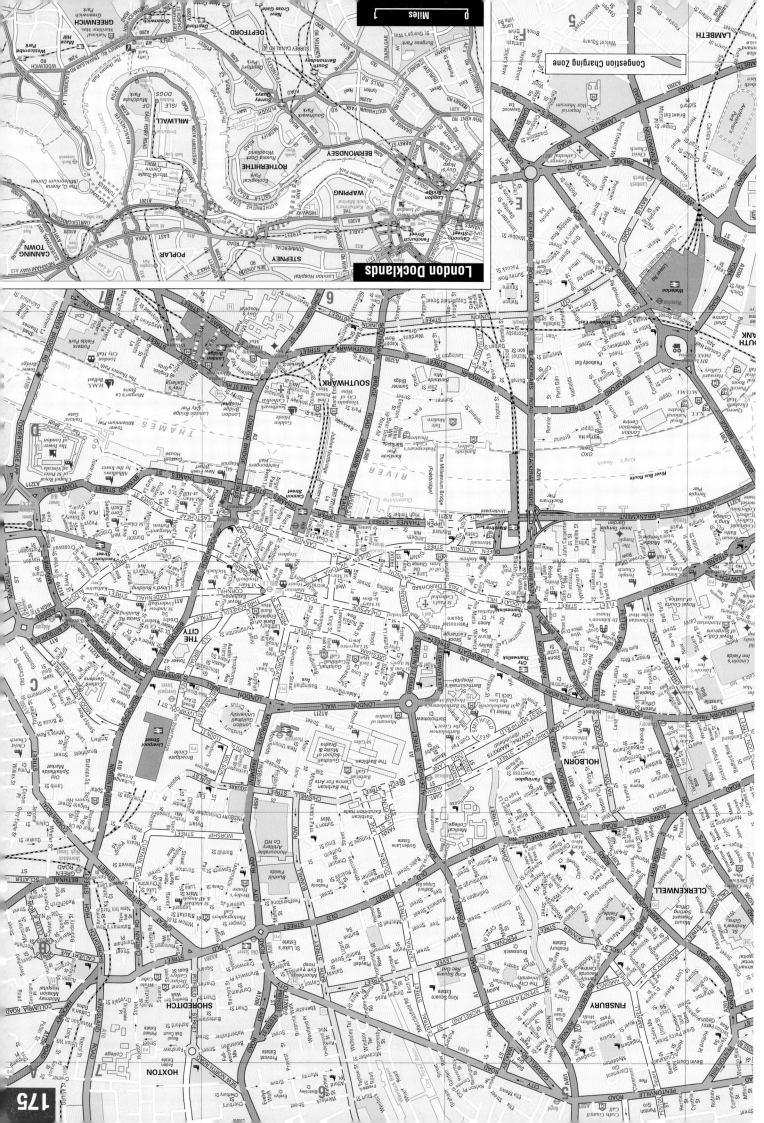

Liverpool

0   Miles   ¼

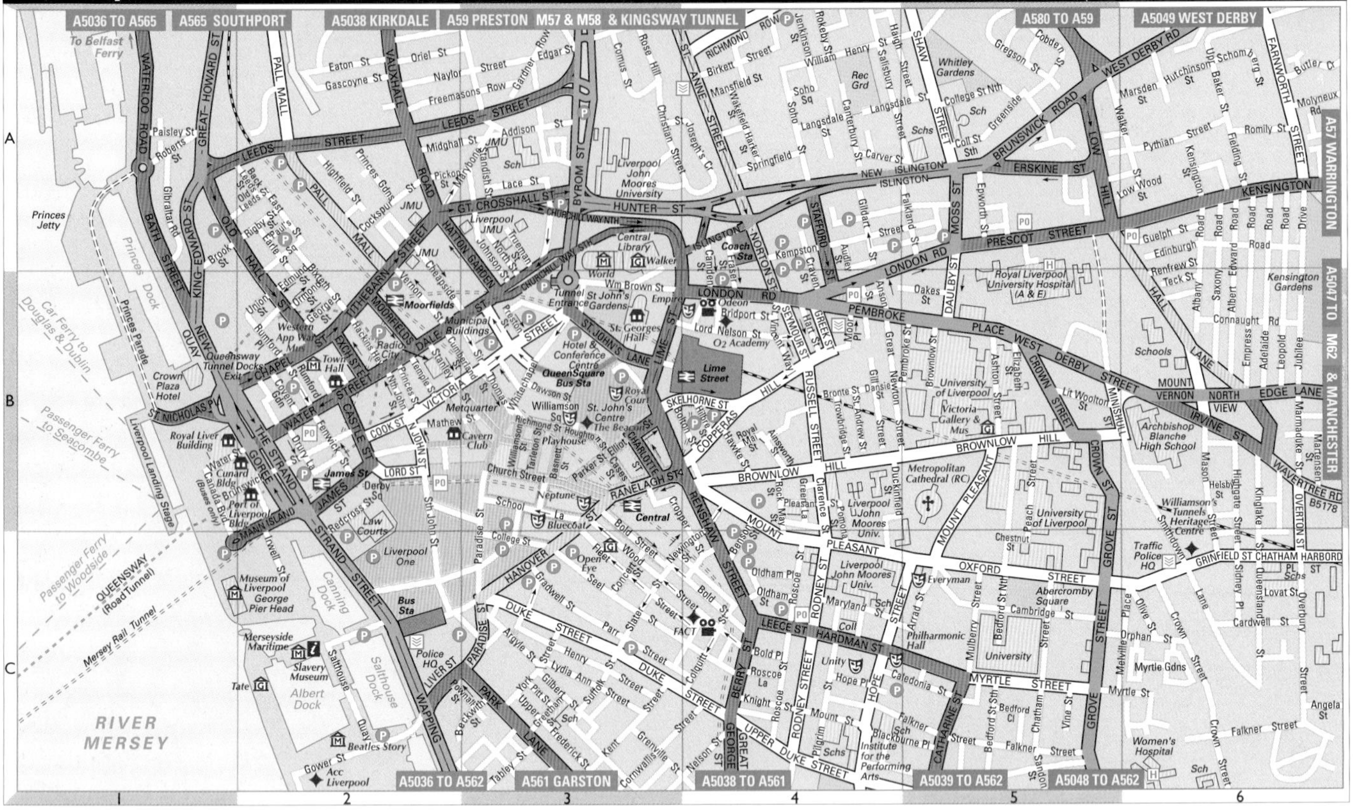

A5036 TO A565 | A565 SOUTHPORT | A5038 KIRKDALE | A59 PRESTON M57 & M58 & KINGSWAY TUNNEL | A580 TO A59 | A5049 WEST DERBY

A5036 TO A562 | A561 GARSTON | A5038 TO A561 | A5039 TO A562 | A5048 TO A562

RIVER MERSEY

Manchester

0   Miles   ¼

A6042 TO A56 | A56 BURY | A665 TO A56 | A664 ROCHDALE | A62 OLDHAM

A56 ALTRINCHAM | A6144 STRETFORD | A5103 MANCHESTER AIRPORT (M56) | A34 CONGLETON | A6 STOCKPORT | A57 DENTON

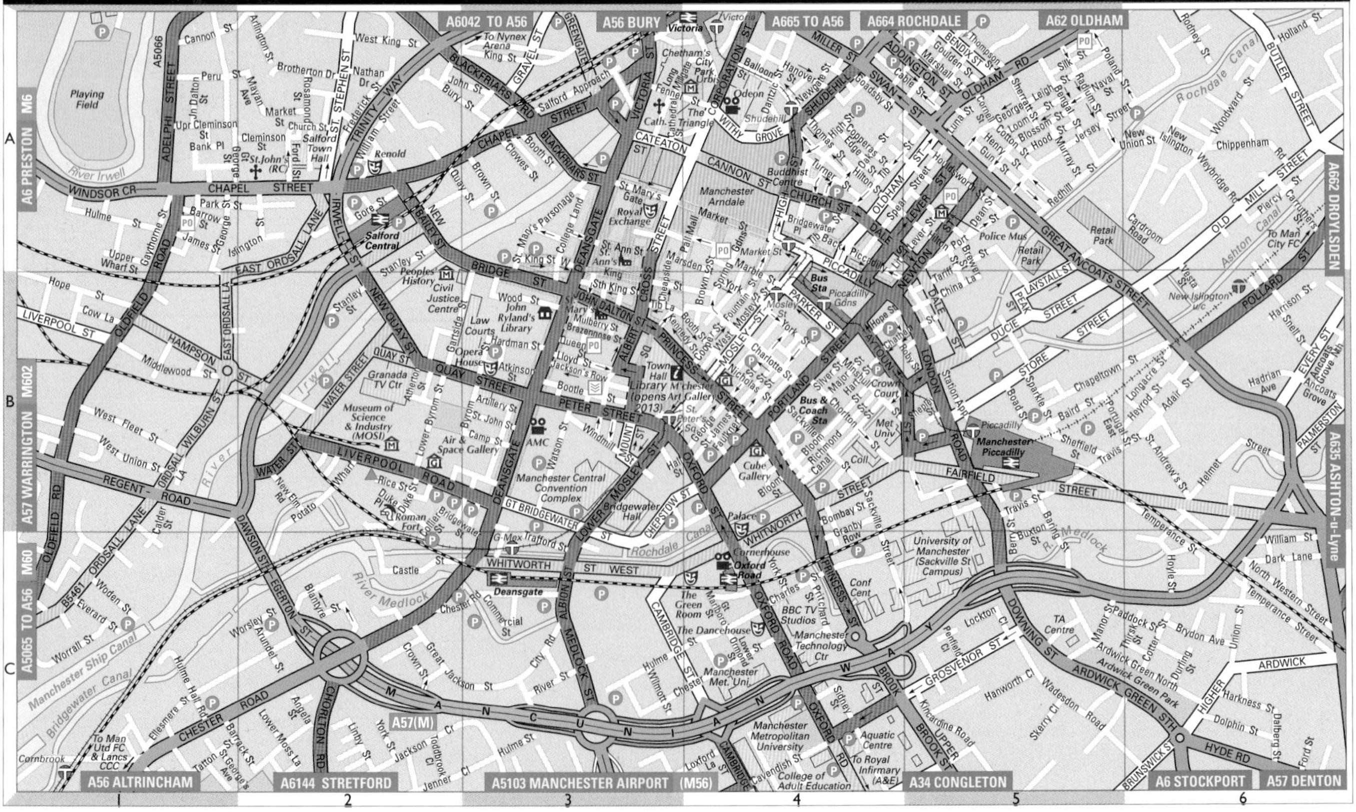

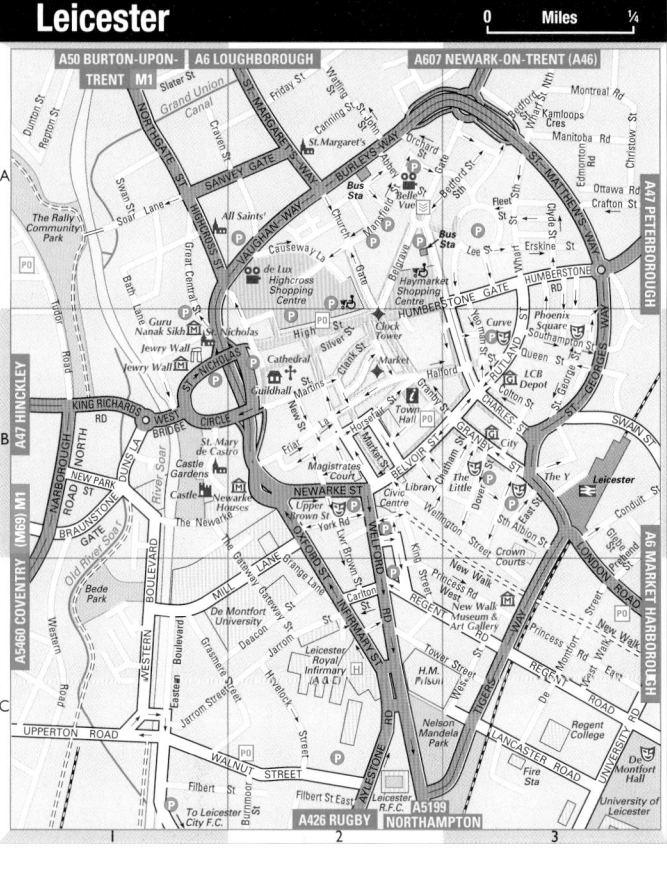

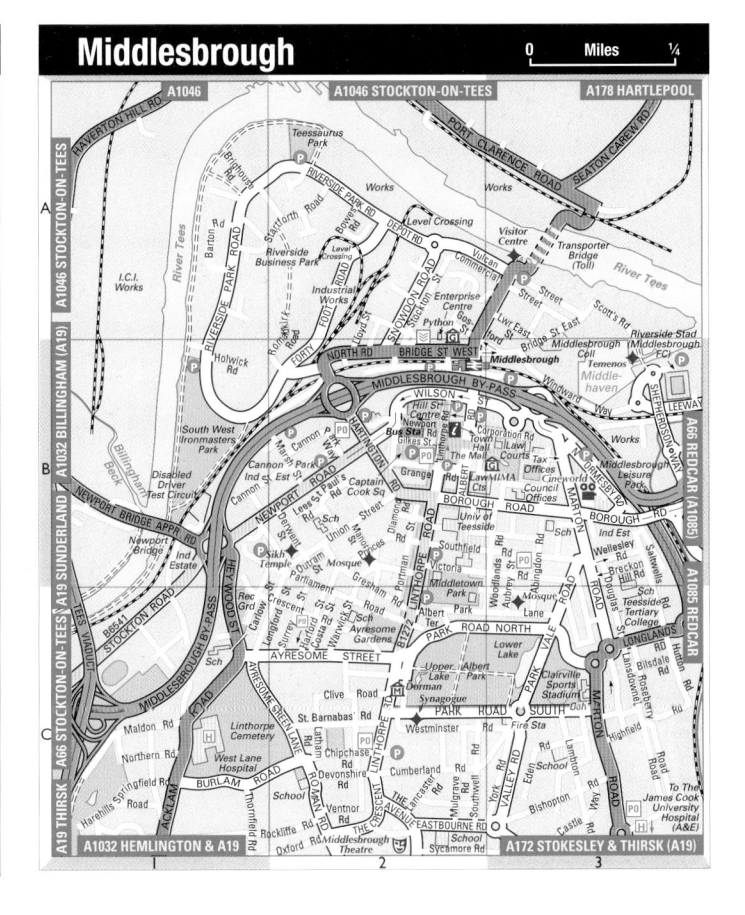

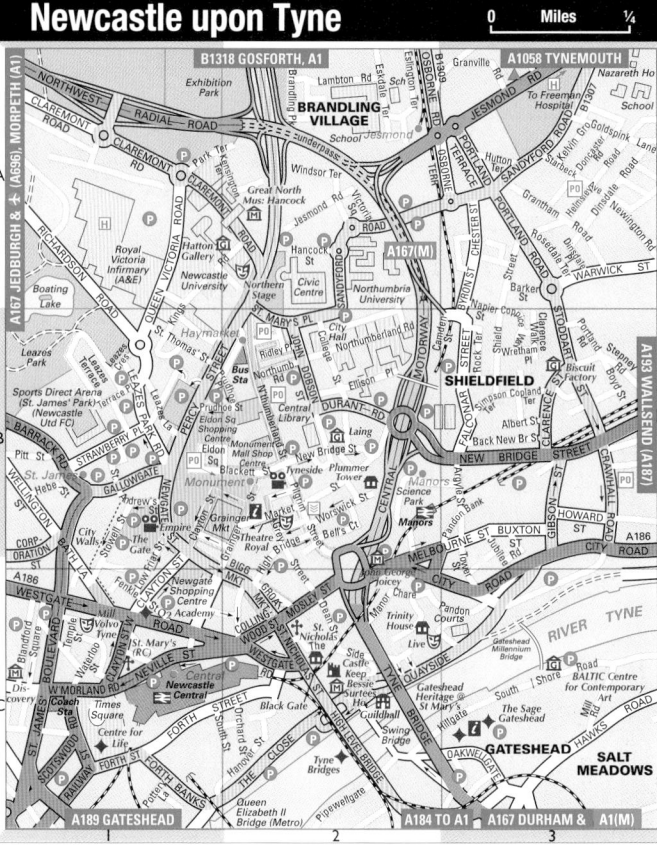

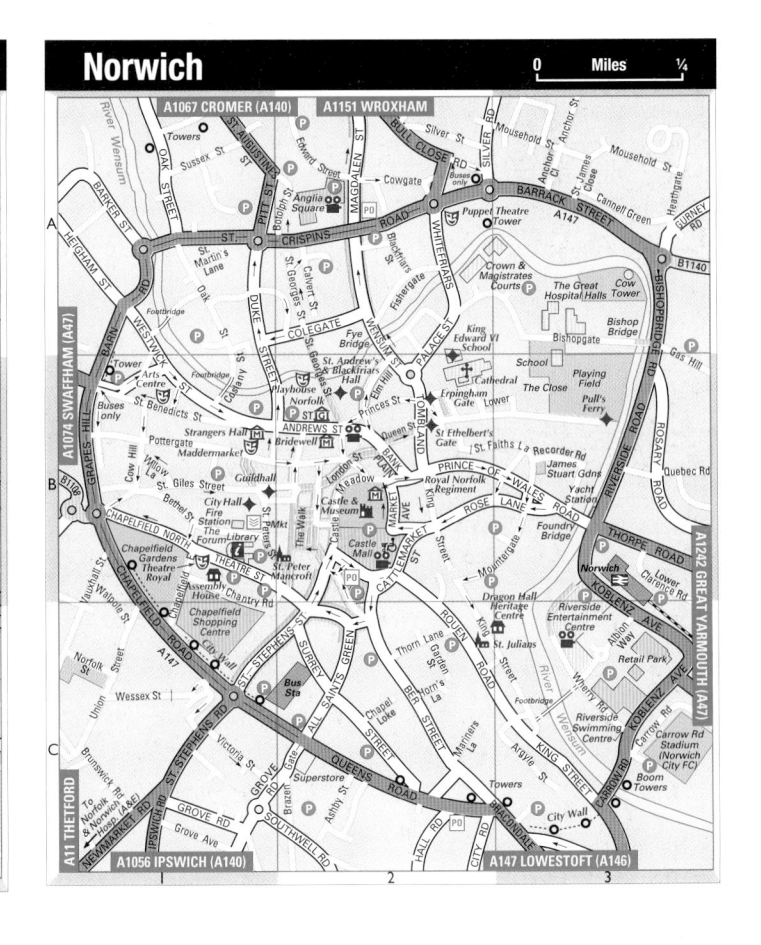

Nottingham

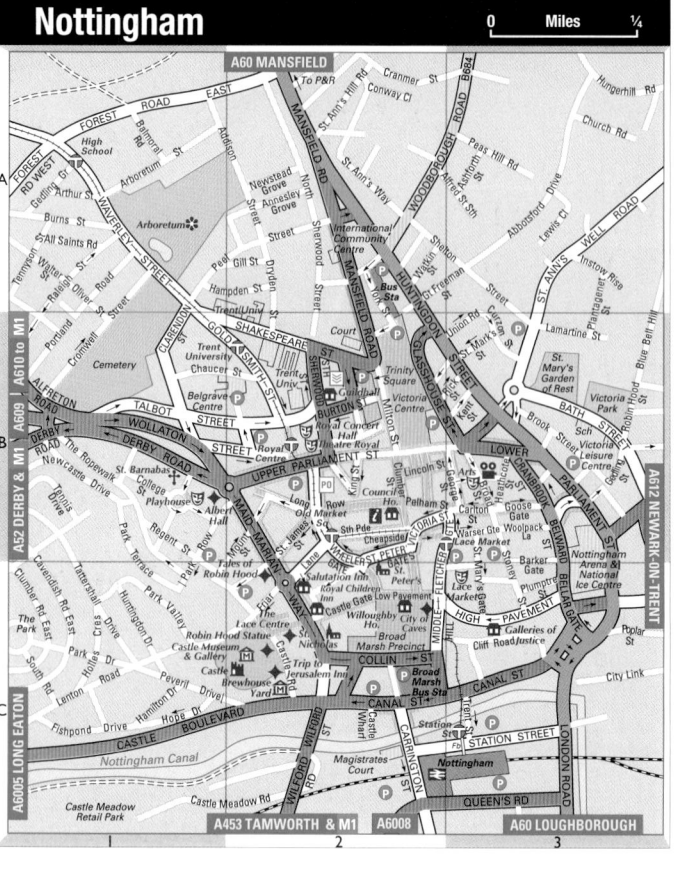

Oxford

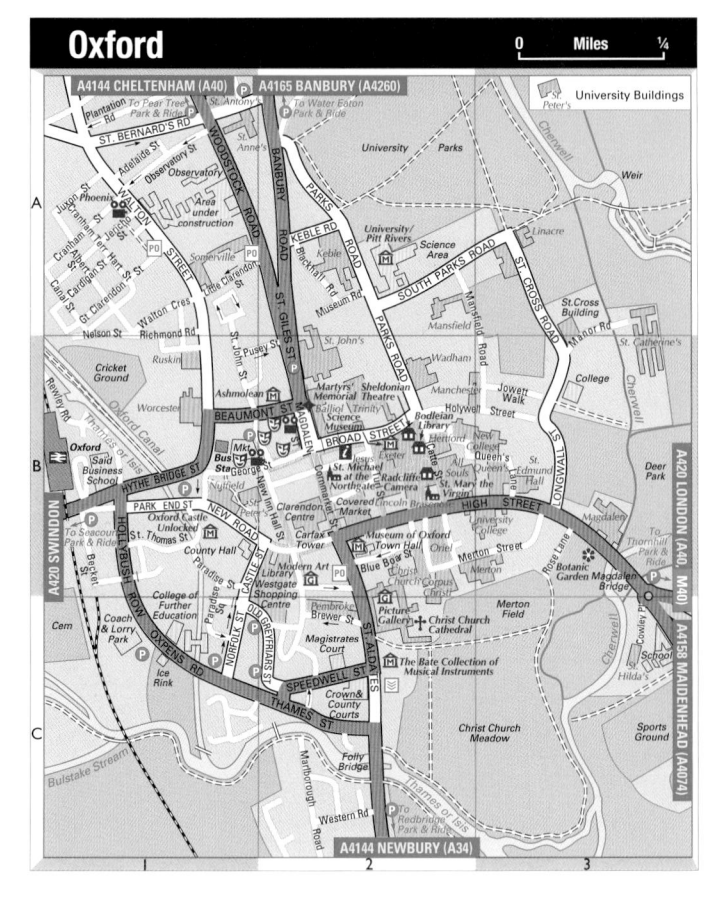

Plymouth

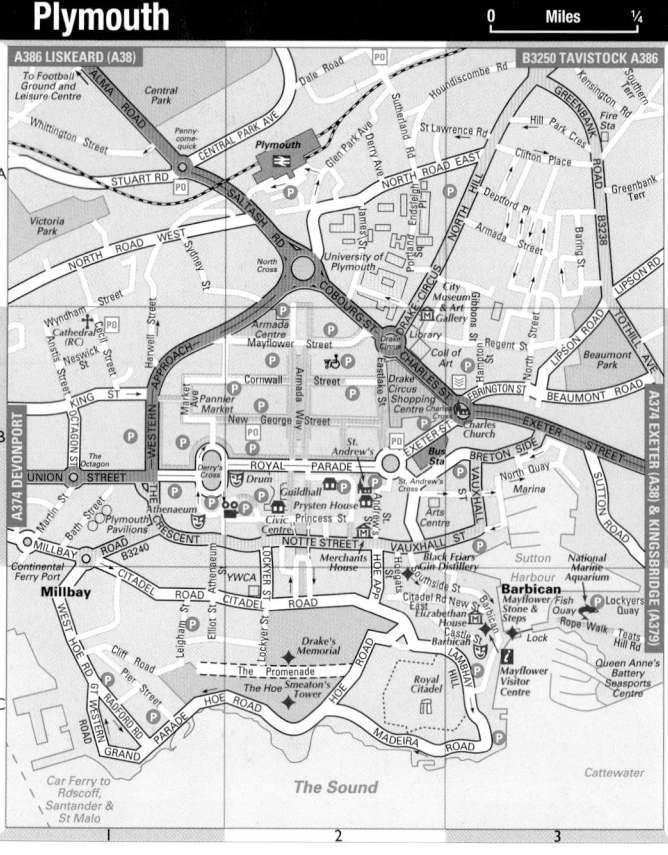

Portsmouth

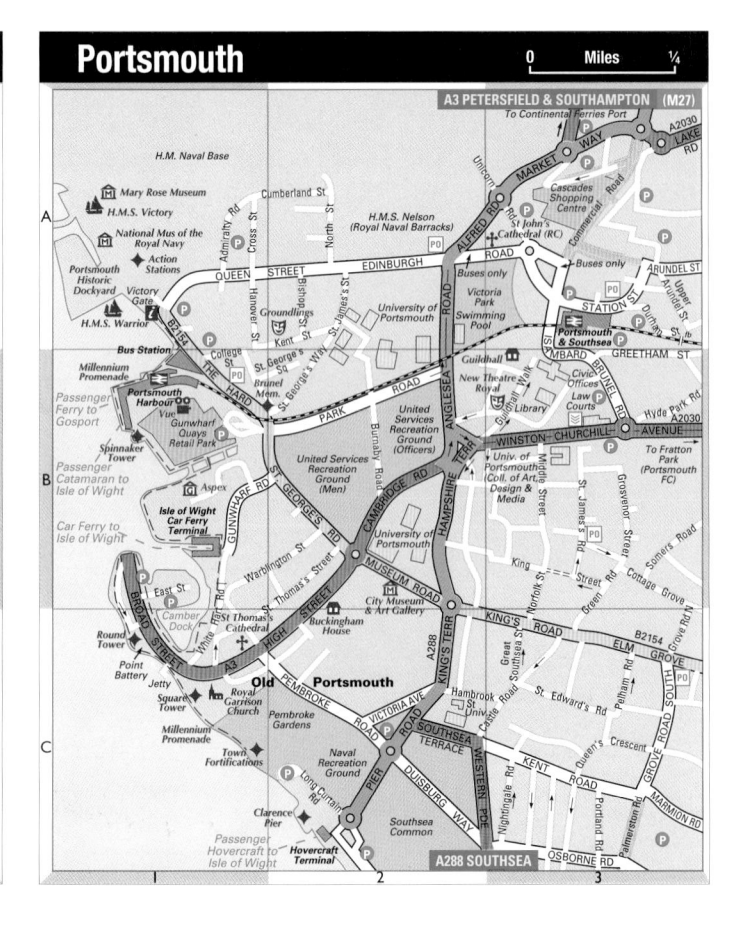

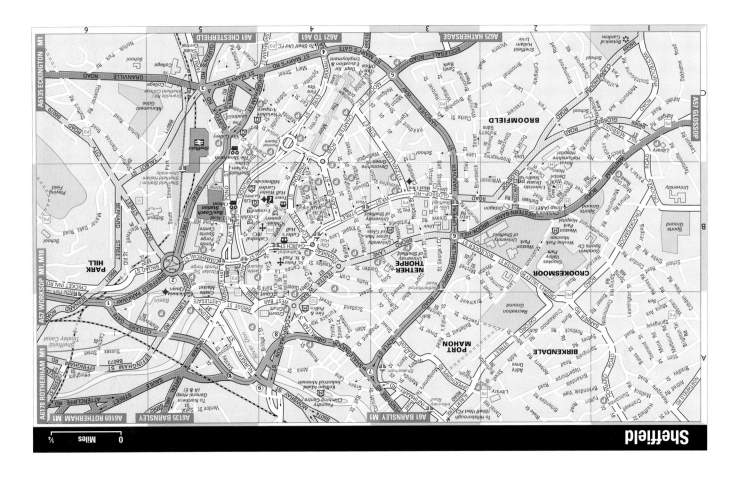

Sheffield

Miles 0 ¼

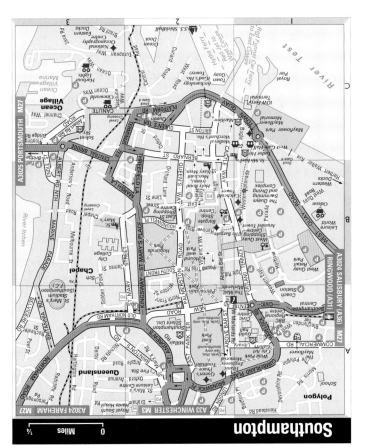

Southampton

Miles 0 ¼

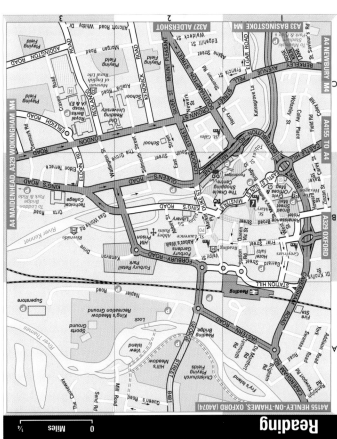

Reading

Miles 0 ¼

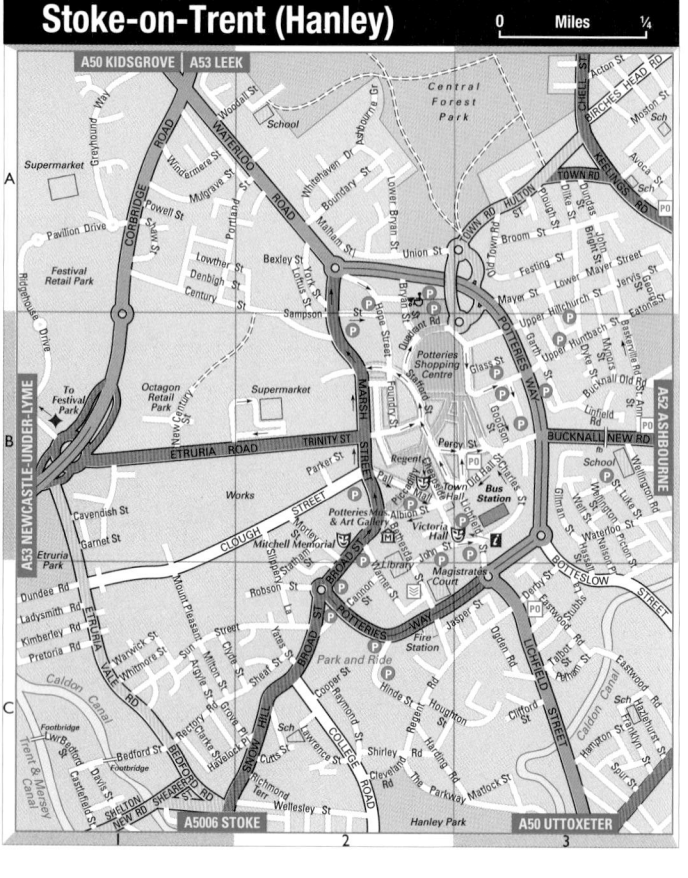

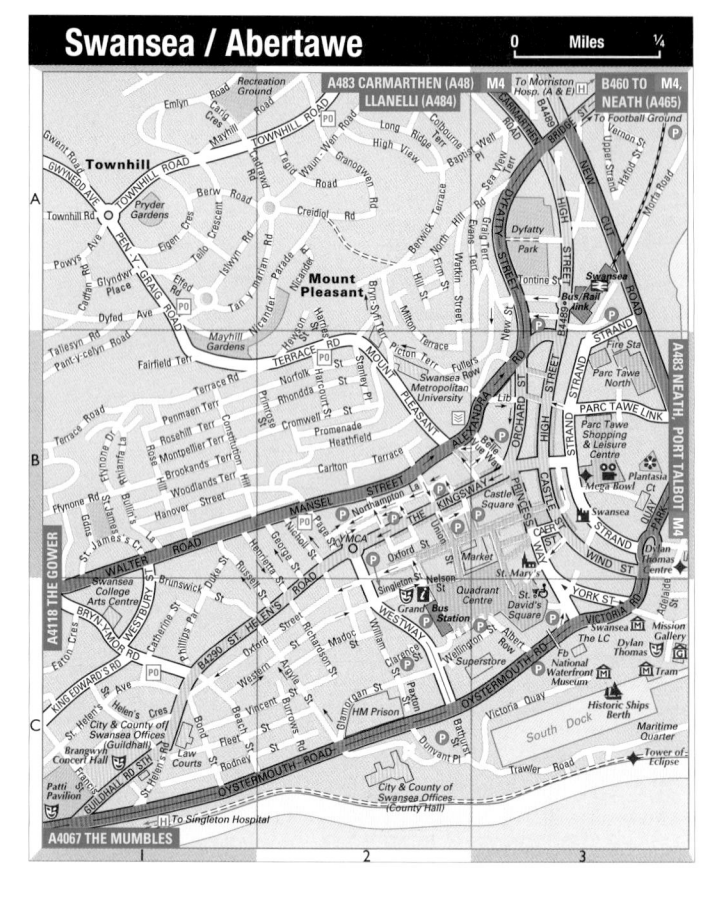

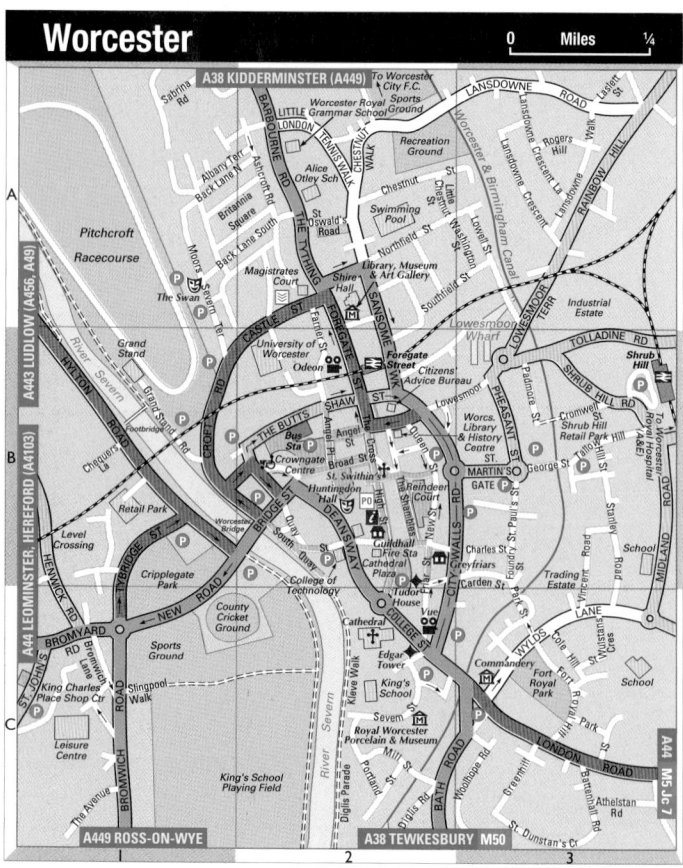

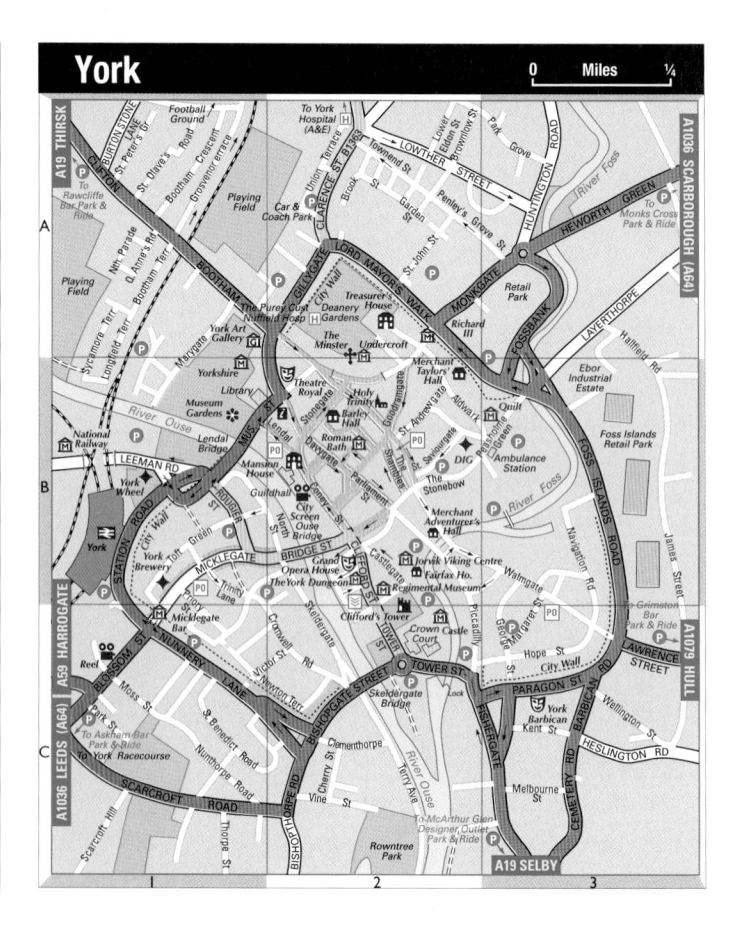

Index to road maps of Britain

Abbreviations used in the index

Aberdeen Aberdeen City
Aberds Aberdeenshire
Ald Alderney
Anglesey Isle of Anglesey
Angus Angus
Argyll Argyll and Bute
Bath Bath and North East Somerset
Bedford Bedford
Bl Gwent Blaenau Gwent
Blackburn Blackburn with Darwen
Blackpool Blackpool
Bmouth Bournemouth
Borders Scottish Borders
Brack Bracknell
Bridgend Bridgend
Brighton City of Brighton and Hove
Bristol City and County of Bristol
Bucks Buckinghamshire
C Beds Central Bedfordshire
Caerph Caerphilly
Cambs Cambridgeshire
Cardiff Cardiff
Carms Carmarthenshire
Ceredig Ceredigion
Ches E Cheshire East
Ches W Cheshire West and Chester
Clack Clackmannanshire
Conwy Conwy
Corn Cornwall
Cumb Cumbria
Darl Darlington
Denb Denbighshire
Derby City of Derby
Derbys Derbyshire
Devon Devon
Dorset Dorset
Dumfries Dumfries and Galloway
Dundee Dundee City
Durham Durham
E Ayrs East Ayrshire
E Dunb East Dunbartonshire
E Loth East Lothian
E Renf East Renfrewshire
E Sus East Sussex
E Yorks East Riding of Yorkshire
Edin City of Edinburgh
Essex Essex
Falk Falkirk
Fife Fife
Flint Flintshire
Glasgow City of Glasgow
Glos Gloucestershire
Gtr Man Greater Manchester
Guern Guernsey
Gwyn Gwynedd
Halton Halton
Hants Hampshire
Hereford Herefordshire
Herts Hertfordshire
Highld Highland
Hrtlpl Hartlepool
Hull Hull
IoM Isle of Man
IoW Isle of Wight
Invclyd Inverclyde
Jersey Jersey
Kent Kent
Lancs Lancashire
Leicester City of Leicester
Leics Leicestershire
Lincs Lincolnshire
London Greater London
Luton Luton
M Keynes Milton Keynes
M Tydf Merthyr Tydfil
Mbro Middlesbrough
Medway Medway
Mers Merseyside
Midloth Midlothian
Mon Monmouthshire
Moray Moray
N Ayrs North Ayrshire
N Lincs North Lincolnshire
N Lanark North Lanarkshire
N Som North Somerset
N Yorks North Yorkshire
NE Lincs North East Lincolnshire
Neath Neath Port Talbot
Newport City and County of Newport
Norf Norfolk
Northants Northamptonshire
Northumb Northumberland
Nottingham City of Nottingham
Notts Nottinghamshire
Orkney Orkney
Oxon Oxfordshire
Pboro Peterborough
Pembs Pembrokeshire
Perth Perth and Kinross
Plym Plymouth
Poole Poole
Powys Powys
Ptsmth Portsmouth
Reading Reading
Redcar Redcar and Cleveland
Renfs Renfrewshire
Rhondda Rhondda Cynon Taff
Rutland Rutland
S Ayrs South Ayrshire
S Glos South Gloucestershire
S Lanark South Lanarkshire
S Yorks South Yorkshire
Scilly Scilly
Shetland Shetland
Shrops Shropshire
Slough Slough
Som Somerset
Soton Southampton
Staffs Staffordshire
Southend Southend-on-Sea
Stirling Stirling
Stockton Stockton-on-Tees
Stoke Stoke-on-Trent
Suff Suffolk
Sur Surrey
Swansea Swansea
Swindon Swindon
T&W Tyne and Wear
Telford Telford and Wrekin
Thurrock Thurrock
Torbay Torbay
Torf Torfaen
V Glam The Vale of Glamorgan
W Berks West Berkshire
W Dunb West Dunbartonshire
W Isles Western Isles
W Loth West Lothian
W Mid West Midlands
W Sus West Sussex
W Yorks West Yorkshire
Warks Warwickshire
Warr Warrington
Wilts Wiltshire
Windsor Windsor and Maidenhead
Wokingham Wokingham
Worcs Worcestershire
Wrex Wrexham
York City of York

How to use the index

Example

Trudoxhill Som **24** E2

grid square
page number
county or unitary authority

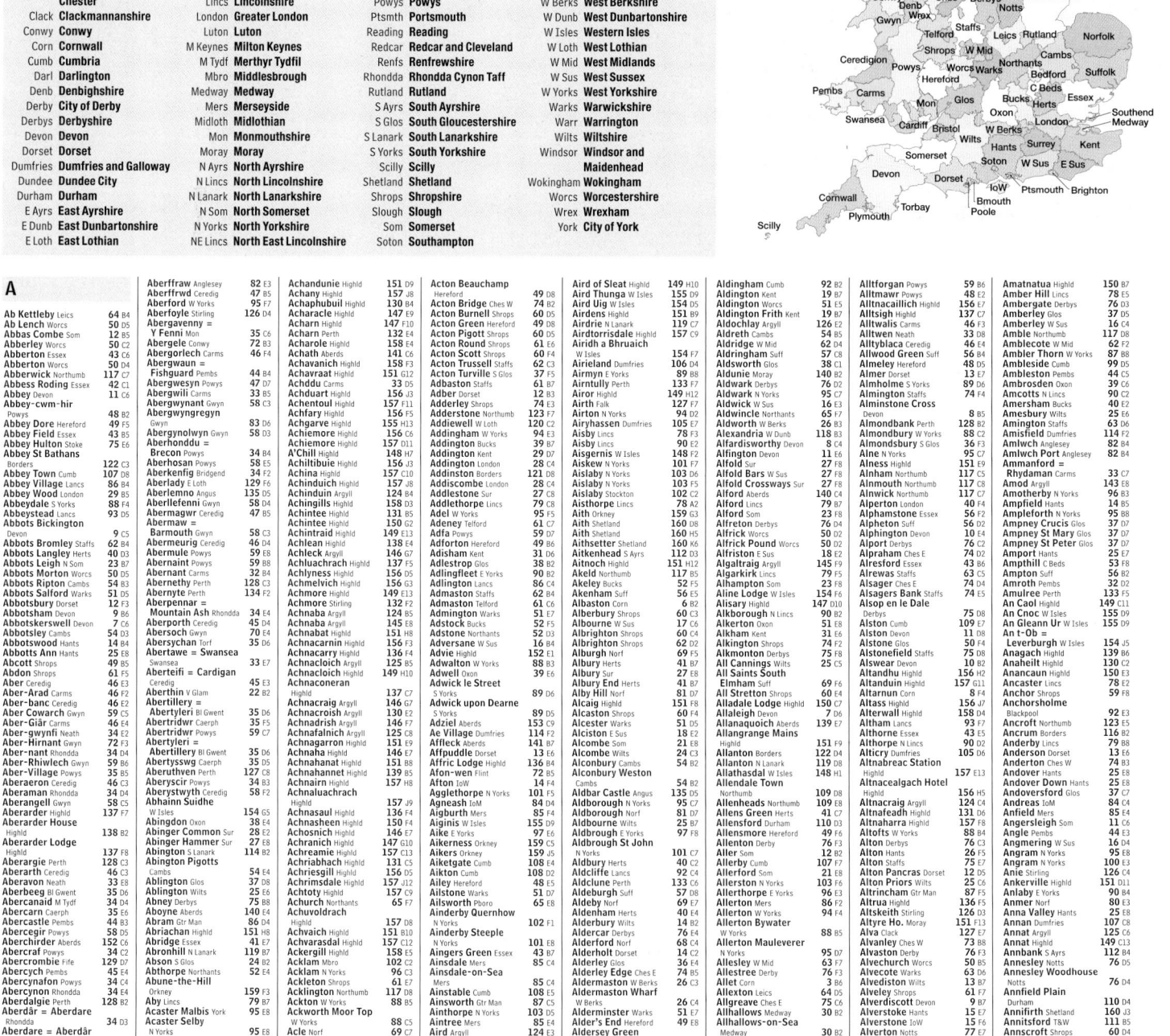

A

Ab Kettleby Leics 64 B4
Ab Lench Worcs 50 D5
Abbas Combe Som 12 B5
Abberley Worcs 50 C2
Abberton Essex 43 C6
Abberton Worcs 50 D4
Abberwick Northumb 117 C7
Abbess Roding Essex 42 C1
Abbey Devon 11 C6
Abbey-cwm-hir Powys 48 B2
Abbey Dore Hereford 49 F5
Abbey Field Essex 43 B5
Abbey Hulton Stoke 75 E6
Abbey St Bathans Borders 122 C3
Abbey Town Cumb 107 D8
Abbey Village Lancs 86 B4
Abbey Wood London 29 B5
Abbeydale S Yorks 88 F4
Abbeystead Lancs 93 D5
Abbots Bickington Devon 9 C5
Abbots Bromley Staffs 62 B4
Abbots Langley Herts 40 D3
Abbots Leigh N Som 23 B7
Abbots Morton Worcs 50 D5
Abbots Ripton Cambs 54 B3
Abbots Salford Warks 51 D5
Abbotsbury Dorset 12 F3
Abbotsham Devon 9 B6
Abbotskerswell Devon 7 C6
Abbotsley Cambs 54 D3
Abbotswood Hants 14 B4
Abbotts Ann Hants 25 E8
Abcott Shrops 49 B5
Abdon Shrops 61 F5
Aber Ceredig 46 E3
Aber-Arad Carms 46 F2
Aber-banc Ceredig 46 E2
Aber Cowarch Gwyn 59 C5
Aber-Giâr Carms 46 E4
Aber-gwynfi Neath 34 E2
Aber-Hirnant Gwyn 72 F3
Aber-nant Rhondda 34 D4
Aber-Rhiwlech Gwyn 59 B6
Aber-Village Powys 35 B5
Aberaeron Ceredig 46 C3
Aberaman Rhondda 34 D4
Aberangell Gwyn 58 C5
Aberarder Highld 137 F7
Aberarder House Highld 138 B2
Aberarder Lodge Highld 137 F8
Aberargie Perth 128 C3
Aberarth Ceredig 46 C3
Aberavon Neath 33 E8
Aberbeeg Bl Gwent 35 D6
Abercanaid M Tydf 34 D4
Abercarn Caerph 35 E6
Abercastle Pembs 44 B3
Abercegir Powys 58 D5
Aberchirder Aberds 152 C6
Abercraf Powys 34 C2
Abercrombie Fife 129 D7
Abercych Pembs 45 E4
Abercynafon Powys 34 C4
Abercynon Rhondda 34 E4
Aberdalgie Perth 128 B2
Aberdâr = Aberdare Rhondda 34 D3
Aberdare = Aberdâr Rhondda 34 D3
Aberdaron Gwyn 70 E2
Aberdaugleddau = Milford Haven Pembs 44 E4
Aberdeen Aberdeen 141 D8
Aberdesach Gwyn 82 F4
Aberdour Fife 128 F3
Aberdovey Gwyn 58 E3
Aberdulais Neath 34 D1
Aberedw Powys 48 E2
Abereiddy Pembs 44 B2
Abererch Gwyn 70 D4
Aberfan M Tydf 34 D4
Aberfeldy Perth 133 E5
Aberffraw Anglesey 82 E3
Aberffrwd Ceredig 47 B5
Aberford W Yorks 95 F7
Aberfoyle Stirling 126 D4
Abergavenny = Y Fenni Mon 35 C6
Abergele Conwy 72 B3
Abergorlech Carms 46 F4
Abergwaun = Fishguard Pembs 44 B4
Abergwesyn Powys 47 D7
Abergwili Carms 33 B5
Abergwynant Gwyn 58 C3
Abergwyngregyn Gwyn 83 D6
Abergynolwyn Gwyn 58 D3
Aberhonddu = Brecon Powys 34 B4
Aberhosan Powys 58 E5
Aberkenfig Bridgend 34 F2
Aberlady E Loth 129 F6
Aberlemno Angus 135 D5
Aberllefenni Gwyn 58 D4
Abermagwr Ceredig 47 B5
Abermaw = Barmouth Gwyn 58 C3
Abermeurig Ceredig 46 D4
Abermule Powys 59 E8
Abernaint Powys 59 B8
Abernant Carms 32 B4
Abernethy Perth 128 C3
Abernyte Perth 134 F2
Aberpennar = Mountain Ash Rhondda 34 E4
Aberporth Ceredig 45 D4
Abersoch Gwyn 70 E4
Abersychan Torf 35 D6
Abertawe = Swansea Swansea 33 E7
Aberteifi = Cardigan Ceredig 45 E3
Aberthin V Glam 22 B2
Abertillery = Abertyleri Bl Gwent 35 D6
Abertridwr Caerph 35 F5
Abertridwr Powys 59 C7
Abertyleri = Abertillery Bl Gwent 35 D6
Abertysswg Caerph 35 D5
Aberuthven Perth 127 C8
Aberyscir Powys 34 B3
Aberystwyth Ceredig 58 F2
Abhainn Suidhe W Isles 154 G5
Abingdon Oxon 38 E4
Abinger Common Sur 28 E2
Abinger Hammer Sur 27 E8
Abington S Lanark 114 B2
Abington Pigotts Cambs 54 E4
Ablington Glos 37 D8
Ablington Wilts 25 E6
Abney Derbys 75 B8
Aboyne Aberds 140 E4
Abram Gtr Man 86 D4
Abriachan Highld 151 H8
Abridge Essex 41 E7
Abronhill N Lanark 119 B7
Abson S Glos 24 B2
Abthorpe Northants 52 E4
Abune-the-Hill Orkney 159 F3
Aby Lincs 79 B7
Acaster Malbis York 95 E8
Acaster Selby N Yorks 95 E8
Accrington Lancs 87 B5
Acha Argyll 146 F4
Acha Mor W Isles 155 E8
Achabraid Argyll 145 E7
Achachork Highld 149 D9
Achafolla Argyll 124 D3
Achagary Highld 157 D10
Achahoish Argyll 144 F6
Achalader Perth 133 E8
Achallader Argyll 131 E7
Ach'an Todhair Highld 130 B4
Achanalt Highld 150 E5
Achanamara Argyll 144 E6
Achandunie Highld 151 D9
Achany Highld 157 J8
Achaphubuil Highld 130 B4
Acharacle Highld 147 E9
Acharn Highld 147 F10
Acharn Perth 132 E4
Acharole Highld 158 E4
Achath Aberds 141 C6
Achavanich Highld 158 F3
Achavraat Highld 151 G12
Achddu Carms 33 D5
Achduart Highld 156 J3
Achentoul Highld 157 F11
Achfary Highld 156 F5
Achgarve Highld 155 H13
Achiemore Highld 156 C6
Achiemore Highld 157 D11
A'Chill Highld 148 H7
Achiltibuie Highld 156 J3
Achina Highld 157 C10
Achinduich Highld 157 J8
Achinduin Argyll 124 B4
Achingills Highld 158 D3
Achintee Highld 131 B5
Achintee Highld 150 G2
Achintraid Highld 149 E13
Achlean Highld 138 E4
Achleck Argyll 146 G7
Achluachrach Highld 137 F5
Achlyness Highld 156 D5
Achmelvich Highld 156 G3
Achmore Highld 149 E13
Achmore Stirling 132 F2
Achnaba Argyll 124 B5
Achnaba Argyll 145 E8
Achnabat Highld 151 H8
Achnacarnin Highld 156 F3
Achnacarry Highld 136 F4
Achnacloich Argyll 125 B5
Achnacloich Highld 149 H10
Achnaconeran Highld 137 C7
Achnacraig Argyll 146 G7
Achnacroish Argyll 130 E2
Achnadrish Argyll 146 F7
Achnafalnich Argyll 125 C8
Achnagarron Highld 151 E9
Achnaha Highld 146 E7
Achnahanat Highld 151 B8
Achnahannet Highld 139 B5
Achnairn Highld 157 H8
Achnaluachrach Highld 157 J9
Achnasaul Highld 136 F4
Achnasheen Highld 150 F4
Achosnich Highld 146 E7
Achranich Highld 147 G10
Achreamie Highld 157 C13
Achriabhach Highld 131 C5
Achriesgill Highld 156 D5
Achrimsdale Highld 157 J12
Achtoty Highld 157 C9
Achurch Northants 65 F7
Achuvoldrach Highld 157 D8
Achvaich Highld 151 B10
Achvarasdal Highld 157 C12
Ackergill Highld 158 E5
Acklam Mbro 102 C2
Acklam N Yorks 96 C3
Ackleton Shrops 61 E7
Acklington Northumb 117 D8
Ackton W Yorks 88 B5
Ackworth Moor Top W Yorks 88 C5
Acle Norf 69 C7
Acock's Green W Mid 62 F5
Acol Kent 31 C7
Acomb Northumb 110 C2
Acomb York 95 D8
Aconbury Hereford 49 F7
Acre Lancs 87 B5
Acre Street W Sus 15 E8
Acrefair Wrex 73 E6
Acton Ches E 74 D3
Acton Dorset 13 G7
Acton London 41 F5
Acton Shrops 60 F3
Acton Suff 56 E2
Acton Wrex 73 D7
Acton Beauchamp Hereford 49 D8
Acton Bridge Ches W 74 B2
Acton Burnell Shrops 60 D5
Acton Green Hereford 49 D8
Acton Pigott Shrops 60 D5
Acton Round Shrops 61 E6
Acton Scott Shrops 60 F4
Acton Trussell Staffs 62 C3
Acton Turville S Glos 37 F5
Adbaston Staffs 61 B7
Adber Dorset 12 B3
Adderley Shrops 74 E3
Adderstone Northumb 123 F7
Addiewell W Loth 120 C2
Addingham W Yorks 94 E3
Addington Bucks 39 B7
Addington Kent 29 D7
Addington London 28 C4
Addinston Borders 121 D8
Addiscombe London 28 C4
Addlestone Sur 27 C8
Addlethorpe Lincs 79 C8
Adel W Yorks 95 F5
Adeney Telford 61 C7
Adfa Powys 59 D7
Adforton Hereford 49 B6
Adisham Kent 31 D6
Adlestrop Glos 38 B2
Adlingfleet E Yorks 90 B2
Adlington Lancs 86 C4
Admaston Staffs 62 B4
Admaston Telford 61 C6
Admington Warks 51 E7
Adstock Bucks 52 F5
Adstone Northants 52 D3
Adversane W Sus 16 B4
Advie Highld 152 E1
Adwalton W Yorks 88 B3
Adwell Oxon 39 E6
Adwick le Street S Yorks 89 D6
Adwick upon Dearne S Yorks 89 D5
Adziel Aberds 153 C9
Ae Village Dumfries 114 F2
Affleck Aberds 141 B7
Affpuddle Dorset 13 E6
Affric Lodge Highld 136 B4
Afon-wen Flint 72 B5
Afton IoW 14 F4
Agglethorpe N Yorks 101 F5
Agneash IoM 84 D4
Aigburth Mers 85 F4
Aiginis W Isles 155 D9
Aike E Yorks 97 E6
Aikerness Orkney 159 C5
Aikers Orkney 159 J5
Aiketgate Cumb 108 E4
Aikton Cumb 108 D2
Ailey Hereford 48 E5
Ailstone Warks 51 D7
Ailsworth Pboro 65 E8
Ainderby Quernhow N Yorks 102 F1
Ainderby Steeple N Yorks 101 E8
Aingers Green Essex 43 B7
Ainsdale Mers 85 C4
Ainsdale-on-Sea Mers 85 C4
Ainstable Cumb 108 E5
Ainsworth Gtr Man 87 C5
Ainthorpe N Yorks 103 D5
Aintree Mers 85 E4
Aird Argyll 124 E3
Aird Dumfries 104 C4
Aird Highld 149 A12
Aird W Isles 155 D10
Aird a Mhachair W Isles 148 D2
Aird a' Mhulaidh W Isles 154 F6
Aird Asaig W Isles 154 G6
Aird Dhail W Isles 155 A9
Aird Mhidhinis W Isles 148 H2
Aird Mhighe W Isles 154 H6
Aird Mhighe W Isles 154 J5
Aird Mhor W Isles 148 H2
Aird of Sleat Highld 149 H10
Aird Thunga W Isles 155 D9
Aird Uig W Isles 154 D5
Airdens Highld 151 B9
Airdrie N Lanark 119 C7
Airdtorrisdale Highld 157 C9
Airidh a Bhruaich W Isles 154 F7
Airieland Dumfries 106 D4
Airmyn E Yorks 89 B8
Airntully Perth 133 F7
Airor Highld 149 H12
Airth Falk 127 F7
Airton N Yorks 94 D2
Airyhassen Dumfries 105 E7
Aisby Lincs 78 F3
Aisby Lincs 90 E2
Aisgernis W Isles 148 F2
Aiskew N Yorks 101 F7
Aislaby N Yorks 103 D6
Aislaby N Yorks 103 F5
Aislaby Stockton 102 C2
Aisthorpe Lincs 78 A2
Aith Orkney 159 G3
Aith Shetland 160 D8
Aith Shetland 160 H5
Aithsetter Shetland 160 K6
Aitkenhead S Ayrs 112 D3
Aitnoch Highld 151 H12
Akeld Northumb 117 B5
Akeley Bucks 52 F5
Akenham Suff 56 E5
Albaston Corn 6 B2
Alberbury Shrops 60 C3
Albourne W Sus 17 C6
Albrighton Shrops 60 C4
Albrighton Shrops 62 D2
Alburgh Norf 69 F5
Albury Herts 41 B7
Albury Sur 27 E8
Albury End Herts 41 B7
Alby Hill Norf 81 D7
Alcaig Highld 151 F8
Alcaston Shrops 60 F4
Alcester Warks 51 D5
Alciston E Sus 18 E2
Alcombe Som 21 E8
Alcombe Wilts 24 C3
Alconbury Cambs 54 B2
Alconbury Weston Cambs 54 B2
Aldbar Castle Angus 135 D5
Aldborough N Yorks 95 C7
Aldborough Norf 81 D7
Aldbourne Wilts 25 B7
Aldbrough E Yorks 97 F8
Aldbrough St John N Yorks 101 C7
Aldbury Herts 40 C2
Aldcliffe Lancs 92 C4
Aldclune Perth 133 C6
Aldeburgh Suff 57 D8
Aldeby Norf 69 E7
Aldenham Herts 40 E4
Alderbury Wilts 14 B2
Aldercar Derbys 76 E4
Alderford Norf 68 C4
Alderholt Dorset 14 C2
Alderley Glos 36 E4
Alderley Edge Ches E 74 B5
Aldermaston W Berks 26 C3
Aldermaston Wharf W Berks 26 C4
Alderminster Warks 51 E7
Alder's End Hereford 49 E8
Aldersey Green Ches W 73 D8
Aldershot Hants 27 D6
Alderton Glos 50 F5
Alderton Northants 52 E5
Alderton Shrops 60 B4
Alderton Suff 57 E7
Alderton Wilts 37 F5
Alderwasley Derbys 76 D3
Aldfield N Yorks 95 C5
Aldford Ches W 73 D8
Aldham Essex 43 B5
Aldham Suff 56 E4
Aldie Highld 151 C10
Aldingbourne W Sus 16 D3
Aldingham Cumb 92 B2
Aldington Kent 19 B7
Aldington Worcs 51 E5
Aldington Frith Kent 19 B7
Aldochlay Argyll 126 E2
Aldreth Cambs 54 B5
Aldridge W Mid 62 D4
Aldringham Suff 57 C8
Aldsworth Glos 38 C1
Aldunie Moray 140 B2
Aldwark Derbys 76 D2
Aldwark N Yorks 95 C7
Aldwick W Sus 16 E3
Aldwincle Northants 65 F7
Aldworth W Berks 26 B3
Alexandria W Dunb 118 B3
Alfardisworthy Devon 8 C4
Alfington Devon 11 E6
Alfold Sur 27 F8
Alfold Bars W Sus 27 F8
Alfold Crossways Sur 27 F8
Alford Aberds 140 C4
Alford Lincs 79 B7
Alford Som 23 F8
Alfreton Derbys 76 D4
Alfrick Worcs 50 D2
Alfrick Pound Worcs 50 D2
Alfriston E Sus 18 E2
Algaltraig Argyll 145 F9
Algarkirk Lincs 79 F5
Alhampton Som 23 F8
Aline Lodge W Isles 154 F6
Alisary Highld 147 D10
Alkborough N Lincs 90 B2
Alkerton Oxon 51 E8
Alkham Kent 31 E6
Alkington Shrops 74 F2
Alkmonton Derbys 75 F8
All Cannings Wilts 25 C5
All Saints South Elmham Suff 69 F6
All Stretton Shrops 60 E4
Alladale Lodge Highld 150 C7
Allaleigh Devon 7 D6
Allanaquoich Aberds 139 E7
Allangrange Mains Highld 151 F9
Allanton Borders 122 D4
Allanton N Lanark 119 D8
Allathasdal W Isles 148 H1
Allendale Town Northumb 109 D8
Allenheads Northumb 109 E8
Allens Green Herts 41 C7
Allensford Durham 110 D3
Allensmore Hereford 49 F6
Allenton Derby 76 F3
Aller Som 12 B2
Allerby Cumb 107 F7
Allerford Som 21 E8
Allerston N Yorks 103 F6
Allerthorpe E Yorks 96 E3
Allerton Mers 86 F2
Allerton W Yorks 94 F4
Allerton Bywater W Yorks 88 B5
Allerton Mauleverer N Yorks 95 D7
Allesley W Mid 63 F7
Allestree Derby 76 F3
Allet Corn 3 B6
Allexton Leics 64 D5
Allgreave Ches E 75 C6
Allhallows Medway 30 B2
Allhallows-on-Sea Medway 30 B2
Alligin Shuas Highld 149 C13
Allimore Green Staffs 62 C2
Allington Lincs 77 E8
Allington Wilts 25 C5
Allington Wilts 25 F7
Allithwaite Cumb 92 B3
Alloa Clack 127 E7
Allonby Cumb 107 E7
Alloway S Ayrs 112 C3
Allt Carms 33 D6
Allt na h-Airbhe Highld 150 B4
Allt-nan-sùgh Highld 136 B2
Alltchaorunn Highld 131 D5
Alltforgan Powys 59 B6
Alltmawr Powys 48 E2
Alltnacaillich Highld 156 E7
Alltsigh Highld 137 C7
Alltwalis Carms 46 F3
Alltwen Neath 33 D8
Alltyblaca Ceredig 46 E4
Allwood Green Suff 56 B4
Almeley Hereford 48 D5
Almer Dorset 13 E7
Almholme S Yorks 89 D6
Almington Staffs 74 F4
Alminstone Cross Devon 8 B5
Almondbank Perth 128 B2
Almondbury W Yorks 88 C2
Almondsbury S Glos 36 F3
Alne N Yorks 95 C7
Alness Highld 151 E9
Alnham Northumb 117 C5
Alnmouth Northumb 117 C8
Alnwick Northumb 117 C7
Alperton London 40 F4
Alphamstone Essex 56 F2
Alpheton Suff 56 D2
Alphington Devon 10 E4
Alport Derbys 76 C2
Alpraham Ches E 74 D2
Alresford Essex 43 B6
Alrewas Staffs 63 C5
Alsager Ches E 74 D4
Alsagers Bank Staffs 74 E5
Alsop en le Dale Derbys 75 D8
Alston Cumb 109 E7
Alston Devon 11 D8
Alstone Glos 50 F4
Alstonefield Staffs 75 D8
Alswear Devon 10 B2
Altandhu Highld 156 H2
Altanduin Highld 157 G11
Altarnun Corn 8 F4
Altass Highld 156 J7
Alterwall Highld 158 D4
Altham Lancs 93 F7
Althorne Essex 43 E5
Althorpe N Lincs 90 D2
Alticry Dumfries 105 D6
Altnabreac Station Highld 157 E13
Altnacealgach Hotel Highld 156 H5
Altnacraig Argyll 124 C4
Altnafeadh Highld 131 D6
Altnaharra Highld 157 F8
Altofts W Yorks 88 B4
Alton Derbys 76 C3
Alton Hants 26 F5
Alton Staffs 75 E7
Alton Pancras Dorset 12 D5
Alton Priors Wilts 25 C6
Altrincham Gtr Man 87 F5
Altrua Highld 136 F5
Altskeith Stirling 126 D3
Altyre Ho. Moray 151 F13
Alva Clack 127 E7
Alvanley Ches W 73 B8
Alvaston Derby 76 F3
Alvechurch Worcs 50 B5
Alvecote Warks 63 D6
Alvediston Wilts 13 B7
Alveley Shrops 61 F7
Alverdiscott Devon 9 B7
Alverstoke Hants 15 E7
Alverstone IoW 15 F6
Alverton Notts 77 E7
Alves Moray 152 B1
Alvescot Oxon 38 D2
Alveston S Glos 36 F3
Alveston Warks 51 D7
Alvie Highld 138 D4
Alvingham Lincs 91 E7
Alvington Glos 36 D3
Alwalton Cambs 65 E8
Alweston Dorset 12 C4
Alwinton Northumb 116 D5
Alwoodley W Yorks 95 E5
Alyth Perth 134 E2
Am Baile W Isles 148 G2
Am Buth Argyll 124 C4
Amatnatua Highld 150 B7
Amber Hill Lincs 78 E5
Ambergate Derbys 76 D3
Amberley Glos 37 D5
Amberley W Sus 16 C4
Amble Northumb 117 D8
Amblecote W Mid 62 F2
Ambler Thorn W Yorks 87 B8
Ambleside Cumb 99 D5
Ambleston Pembs 44 C5
Ambrosden Oxon 39 C6
Amcotts N Lincs 90 C2
Amersham Bucks 40 E2
Amesbury Wilts 25 E6
Amington Staffs 63 D6
Amisfield Dumfries 114 F2
Amlwch Anglesey 82 B4
Amlwch Port Anglesey 82 B4
Ammanford = Rhydaman Carms 33 C7
Amod Argyll 143 E8
Amotherby N Yorks 96 B3
Ampfield Hants 14 B5
Ampleforth N Yorks 95 B8
Ampney Crucis Glos 37 D7
Ampney St Mary Glos 37 D7
Ampney St Peter Glos 37 D7
Amport Hants 25 E7
Ampthill C Beds 53 F8
Ampton Suff 56 B2
Amroth Pembs 32 D2
Amulree Perth 133 F5
An Caol Highld 149 C11
An Cnoc W Isles 155 D9
An Gleann Ur W Isles 155 D9
An t-Ob = Leverburgh W Isles 154 J5
Anagach Highld 139 B6
Anaheilt Highld 130 C2
Anancaun Highld 150 E3
Ancaster Lincs 78 E2
Anchor Shrops 59 F8
Anchorsholme Blackpool 92 E3
Ancroft Northumb 123 E5
Ancrum Borders 116 B2
Anderby Lincs 79 B8
Anderson Dorset 13 E6
Anderton Ches W 74 B3
Andover Hants 25 E8
Andover Down Hants 25 E8
Andoversford Glos 37 C7
Andreas IoM 84 C4
Anfield Mers 85 E4
Angersleigh Som 11 C6
Angle Pembs 44 E3
Angmering W Sus 16 D4
Angram N Yorks 95 E8
Angram N Yorks 100 E3
Anie Stirling 126 C4
Ankerville Highld 151 D11
Anlaby E Yorks 90 B4
Anmer Norf 80 E3
Anna Valley Hants 25 E8
Annan Dumfries 107 C8
Annat Argyll 125 C6
Annat Highld 149 C13
Annbank S Ayrs 112 B4
Annesley Notts 76 D5
Annesley Woodhouse Notts 76 D4
Annfield Plain Durham 110 D4
Annifirth Shetland 160 J3
Annitsford T&W 111 B5
Annscroft Shrops 60 D4
Ansdell Lancs 85 B4
Ansford Som 23 F8
Ansley Warks 63 E6
Anslow Staffs 63 B6
Anslow Gate Staffs 63 B5
Anstey Herts 54 F5
Anstey Leics 64 D2
Anstruther Easter Fife 129 D7
Anstruther Wester Fife 129 D7
Ansty Hants 26 E5
Ansty W Sus 17 B6
Ansty Warks 63 F7

Ansty Wilts 13 B7
Anthill Common Hants 15 C7
Anthorn Cumb 107 D8
Antingham Norf 81 D8
Anton's Gowt Lincs 79 E5
Antonshill Falk 127 F7
Antony Corn 5 D8
Anwick Lincs 78 D4
Anwoth Dumfries 106 D2
Aoradh Argyll 142 B3
Apes Hall Cambs 67 E5
Apethorpe Northants 65 E7
Apeton Staffs 62 C2
Apley Lincs 78 B4
Apperknowle Derbys 76 B3
Apperley Glos 37 B5
Apperley Bridge W Yorks 94 F4
Appersett N Yorks 100 E3
Appin Argyll 130 E3
Appin House Argyll 130 E3
Appleby N Lincs 90 C3
Appleby-in-Westmorland Cumb 100 B1
Appleby Magna Leics 63 D7
Appleby Parva Leics 63 D7
Applecross Highld 149 D12
Applecross Ho. Highld 149 D12
Appledore Devon 11 C5
Appledore Devon 20 F3
Appledore Kent 19 C6
Appledore Heath Kent 19 B6
Appleford Oxon 39 E5
Applegarthtown Dumfries 114 F4
Appleshaw Hants 25 E8
Applethwaite Cumb 98 B4
Appleton Halton 86 F3
Appleton Oxon 38 D4
Appleton-le-Moors N Yorks 103 F5
Appleton-le-Street N Yorks 96 B3
Appleton Roebuck N Yorks 95 E8
Appleton Thorn Warr 86 F4
Appleton Wiske N Yorks 102 D1
Appletreehall Borders 115 C8
Appletreewick N Yorks 94 C3
Appley Som 11 B5
Appley Bridge Lancs 86 D3
Apse Heath IoW 15 F6
Apsley End C Beds 54 F2
Apuldram W Sus 16 D2
Aquhythie Aberds 141 C6
Arabella Highld 151 D11
Arbeadie Aberds 141 E5
Arberth = Narberth Pembs 32 C2
Arbirlot Angus 135 E6
Arboll Highld 151 C11
Arborfield Wokingham 27 C5
Arborfield Cross Wokingham 27 C5
Arborfield Garrison Wokingham 27 C5
Arbour-thorne S Yorks 88 F4
Arbroath Angus 135 E6
Arbuthnott Aberds 135 B7
Archiestown Moray 152 D2
Arclid Ches E 74 C4
Ard-dhubh Highld 149 D12
Ardachu Highld 157 J9
Ardalanish Argyll 146 K6
Ardanaiseig Argyll 125 C6
Ardaneaskan Highld 149 E13
Ardanstur Argyll 124 D4
Ardargie House Hotel Perth 128 C2
Ardarroch Highld 149 E13
Ardbeg Argyll 142 D5
Ardbeg Argyll 145 E10
Ardcharnich Highld 150 C4
Ardchiavaig Argyll 146 K6
Ardchullarie More Stirling 126 C4
Ardchyle Stirling 126 B4
Arddleen Powys 60 C2
Ardechvie Highld 136 E4
Ardeley Herts 41 B6
Ardelve Highld 149 F13
Arden Argyll 126 F2
Ardens Grafton Warks 51 D6
Ardentinny Argyll 145 E10
Ardentraive Argyll 145 F9
Ardeonaig Stirling 132 F3
Ardersier Highld 151 F10
Ardessie Highld 150 C3
Ardfern Argyll 124 E4
Ardgartan Argyll 125 E8
Ardgay Highld 151 B8
Ardgour Highld 130 C4
Ardheslaig Highld 149 C12
Ardiecow Moray 152 B5
Ardindrean Highld 150 C4
Ardingly W Sus 17 B7
Ardington Oxon 38 F4
Ardlair Aberds 140 B4
Ardlamont Ho. Argyll 145 G8
Ardleigh Essex 43 B6
Ardler Perth 134 E2
Ardley Oxon 39 B5
Ardlui Argyll 126 C2
Ardlussa Argyll 144 E5
Ardmair Highld 150 B4
Ardmay Argyll 125 E8
Ardminish Argyll 143 D7
Ardmolich Highld 147 D10
Ardmore Argyll 124 C3
Ardmore Highld 151 C10
Ardmore Highld 156 D5
Ardnacross Argyll 147 G8
Ardnadam Argyll 145 F10
Ardnagrask Highld 151 G8
Ardnarff Highld 149 E13
Ardnastang Highld 130 C2
Ardnave Argyll 142 A3
Ardno Argyll 125 E7
Ardo Aberds 153 E8
Ardo Ho. Aberds 141 B8
Ardoch Perth 133 F7
Ardochy House Highld 136 D5
Ardoyne Aberds 141 B5
Ardpatrick Argyll 144 G6
Ardpatrick Ho. Argyll 144 H6
Ardpeaton Argyll 145 E11
Ardrishaig Argyll 145 E7
Ardross Fife 129 D7
Ardross Highld 151 D9
Ardross Castle Highld 151 D9
Ardrossan N Ayrs 118 E2
Ardshealach Highld 147 E9
Ardsley S Yorks 88 D4
Ardslignish Highld 147 E8
Ardtalla Argyll 142 C5
Ardtalnaig Perth 132 F4
Ardtoe Highld 147 D9
Ardtrostan Perth 127 B5
Arduaine Argyll 124 D3
Ardullie Highld 151 E8
Ardvasar Highld 149 H11
Ardvorlich Perth 126 B5
Ardwell Dumfries 104 E5
Ardwell Mains Dumfries 104 E5
Ardwick Gtr Man 87 E6
Areley Kings Worcs 50 B3
Arford Hants 27 F6
Argoed Caerph 35 E5
Argoed Mill Powys 47 C8
Arichamish Argyll 124 E5
Arichastlich Argyll 125 B8
Aridhglas Argyll 146 J6
Arileod Argyll 146 F4
Arinacrinachd Highld 149 C12
Arinagour Argyll 146 F5
Arion Orkney 159 G3
Arisaig Highld 147 C9
Ariundle Highld 130 C2
Arkendale N Yorks 95 C6
Arkesden Essex 55 F5
Arkholme Lancs 93 B5
Arkle Town N Yorks 101 D5
Arkleton Dumfries 115 E6
Arkley London 41 E5
Arksey S Yorks 89 D6
Arkwright Town Derbys 76 B4
Arle Glos 37 B6
Arlecdon Cumb 98 C2
Arlesey C Beds 54 F2
Arleston Telford 61 C6
Arley Ches E 86 F4
Arlingham Glos 36 C4
Arlington Devon 20 E5
Arlington E Sus 18 E2
Arlington Glos 37 D8
Armadale Highld 157 C10
Armadale W Loth 120 C2
Armadale Castle Highld 149 H11
Armathwaite Cumb 108 E5
Arminghall Norf 69 D5
Armitage Staffs 62 C4
Armley W Yorks 95 F5
Armscote Warks 51 E7
Armthorpe S Yorks 89 D7
Arnabost Argyll 146 F5
Arncliffe N Yorks 94 B2
Arncroach Fife 129 D7
Arne Dorset 13 F7
Arnesby Leics 64 E3
Arngask Perth 128 C3
Arnisdale Highld 149 G13
Arnish Highld 149 D10
Arniston Engine Midloth 121 C6
Arnol W Isles 155 C8
Arnold E Yorks 97 E7
Arnold Notts 77 E5
Arnprior Stirling 126 E5
Arnside Cumb 92 B4
Aros Mains Argyll 147 G8
Arowry Wrex 73 F8
Arpafeelie Highld 151 F9
Arrad Foot Cumb 99 F5
Arram E Yorks 97 E6
Arrathorne N Yorks 101 E7
Arreton IoW 15 F6
Arrington Cambs 54 D4
Arrivain Argyll 125 B8
Arrochar Argyll 125 E8
Arrow Warks 51 D5
Arthington W Yorks 95 E5
Arthingworth Northants 64 F4
Arthog Gwyn 58 C3
Arthrath Aberds 153 E9
Arthurstone Perth 134 E2
Artrochie Aberds 153 E10
Arundel W Sus 16 D4
Aryhoulan Highld 130 C4
Asby Cumb 98 B2
Ascog Argyll 145 G10
Ascot Windsor 27 C7
Ascott Warks 51 F8
Ascott-under-Wychwood Oxon 38 C3
Asenby N Yorks 95 B6
Asfordby Leics 64 C4
Asfordby Hill Leics 64 C4
Asgarby Lincs 78 E4
Asgarby Lincs 79 C6
Ash Kent 29 C6
Ash Kent 31 D6
Ash Som 12 B2
Ash Sur 27 D6
Ash Bullayne Devon 10 D2
Ash Green Warks 63 F7
Ash Magna Shrops 74 F2
Ash Mill Devon 10 B2
Ash Priors Som 11 B6
Ash Street Suff 56 E4
Ash Thomas Devon 10 C5
Ash Vale Sur 27 D6
Ashampstead W Berks 26 B3
Ashbocking Suff 57 D5
Ashbourne Derbys 75 E8
Ashbrittle Som 11 B5
Ashburton Devon 7 C5
Ashbury Devon 9 E7
Ashbury Oxon 38 F2
Ashby N Lincs 90 D3
Ashby by Partney Lincs 79 C7
Ashby cum Fenby NE Lincs 91 D6
Ashby de la Launde Lincs 78 D3
Ashby-de-la-Zouch Leics 63 C7
Ashby Folville Leics 64 C4
Ashby Magna Leics 64 E2
Ashby Parva Leics 64 F2
Ashby Puerorum Lincs 79 B6
Ashby St Ledgers Northants 52 C3
Ashby St Mary Norf 69 D6
Ashchurch Glos 50 F4
Ashcombe Devon 7 B7
Ashcott Som 23 F6
Ashdon Essex 55 E6
Ashe Hants 26 E3
Asheldham Essex 43 D5
Ashen Essex 55 E8
Ashendon Bucks 39 C7
Ashfield Carms 33 B7
Ashfield Stirling 127 D6
Ashfield Suff 57 C6
Ashfield Green Suff 57 B6
Ashfold Crossways W Sus 17 B6
Ashford Devon 20 F4
Ashford Hants 14 C2
Ashford Kent 30 E4
Ashford Sur 27 B8
Ashford Bowdler Shrops 49 B7
Ashford Carbonell Shrops 49 B7
Ashford Hill Hants 26 C3
Ashford in the Water Derbys 75 C8
Ashgill S Lanark 119 E7
Ashill Devon 11 C5
Ashill Norf 67 D8
Ashill Som 11 C8
Ashingdon Essex 42 E4
Ashington Northumb 117 F8
Ashington Som 12 B3
Ashington W Sus 16 C5
Ashintully Castle Perth 133 C8
Ashkirk Borders 115 B7
Ashlett Hants 15 D5
Ashleworth Glos 37 B5
Ashley Cambs 55 C7
Ashley Ches E 87 F5
Ashley Devon 9 C8
Ashley Dorset 14 D2
Ashley Glos 37 E6
Ashley Hants 14 E3
Ashley Hants 25 F8
Ashley Northants 64 E4
Ashley Staffs 74 F4
Ashley Green Bucks 40 D2
Ashley Heath Dorset 14 D2
Ashley Heath Staffs 74 F4
Ashmanhaugh Norf 69 B6
Ashmansworth Hants 26 D2
Ashmansworthy Devon 8 C5
Ashmore Dorset 13 C7
Ashorne Warks 51 D8
Ashover Derbys 76 C3
Ashow Warks 51 B8
Ashprington Devon 7 D6
Ashreigney Devon 9 C8
Ashtead Sur 28 D2
Ashton Ches W 74 C2
Ashton Corn 2 D5
Ashton Hants 15 C6
Ashton Hereford 49 C7
Ashton Invclyd 118 B2
Ashton Northants 53 E5
Ashton Northants 65 F7
Ashton Common Wilts 24 D3
Ashton-In-Makerfield Gtr Man 86 E3
Ashton Keynes Wilts 37 E7
Ashton under Hill Worcs 50 F4
Ashton-under-Lyne Gtr Man 87 E7
Ashton upon Mersey Gtr Man 87 E5
Ashurst Hants 14 C4
Ashurst Kent 18 B2
Ashurst W Sus 17 C5
Ashurstwood W Sus 28 F5
Ashwater Devon 9 E5
Ashwell Herts 54 F3
Ashwell Rutland 65 C5
Ashwell Som 11 C8
Ashwellthorpe Norf 68 E4
Ashwick Som 23 E8
Ashwicken Norf 67 C7
Ashybank Borders 115 C8
Askam in Furness Cumb 92 B2
Askern S Yorks 89 C6
Askerswell Dorset 12 E3
Askett Bucks 39 D8
Askham Cumb 99 B7
Askham Notts 77 B7
Askham Bryan York 95 E8
Askham Richard York 95 E8
Asknish Argyll 145 D8
Askrigg N Yorks 100 E4
Askwith N Yorks 94 E4
Aslackby Lincs 78 F3
Aslacton Norf 68 E4
Aslockton Notts 77 F7
Asloun Aberds 140 C4
Aspatria Cumb 107 E8
Aspenden Herts 41 B6
Asperton Lincs 79 F5
Aspley Guise C Beds 53 F7
Aspley Heath C Beds 53 F7
Aspull Gtr Man 86 D4
Asselby E Yorks 89 B8
Asserby Lincs 79 B7
Assington Suff 56 F3
Assynt Ho. Highld 151 E8
Astbury Ches E 74 C5
Astcote Northants 52 D4
Asterley Shrops 60 D3
Asterton Shrops 60 E3
Asthall Oxon 38 C2
Asthall Leigh Oxon 38 C3
Astley Shrops 60 C5
Astley Warks 63 F7
Astley Worcs 50 C2
Astley Abbotts Shrops 61 E7
Astley Bridge Gtr Man 86 C5
Astley Cross Worcs 50 C3
Astley Green Gtr Man 86 E5
Aston Ches E 74 E3
Aston Ches W 74 B2
Aston Derbys 88 F2
Aston Hereford 49 B6
Aston Herts 41 B5
Aston Oxon 38 D3
Aston S Yorks 89 F5
Aston Shrops 60 B5
Aston Staffs 74 E4
Aston Telford 61 D6
Aston W Mid 62 F4
Aston Wokingham 39 F7
Aston Abbotts Bucks 39 B8
Aston Botterell Shrops 61 F6
Aston-By-Stone Staffs 75 F6
Aston Cantlow Warks 51 D6
Aston Clinton Bucks 40 C1
Aston Crews Hereford 36 B3
Aston Cross Glos 50 F4
Aston End Herts 41 B5
Aston Eyre Shrops 61 E6
Aston Fields Worcs 50 C4
Aston Flamville Leics 63 E8
Aston Ingham Hereford 36 B3
Aston juxta Mondrum Ches E 74 D3
Aston le Walls Northants 52 D2
Aston Magna Glos 51 F6
Aston Munslow Shrops 60 F5
Aston on Clun Shrops 60 F3
Aston-on-Trent Derbys 63 B8
Aston Rogers Shrops 60 D3
Aston Rowant Oxon 39 E7
Aston Sandford Bucks 39 D7
Aston Somerville Worcs 50 F5
Aston Subedge Glos 51 E6
Aston Tirrold Oxon 39 F5
Aston Upthorpe Oxon 39 F5
Astrop Northants 52 F3
Astwick C Beds 54 F3
Astwood M Keynes 53 E7
Astwood Worcs 50 D3
Astwood Bank Worcs 50 C5
Aswarby Lincs 78 F3
Aswardby Lincs 79 B6
Atch Lench Worcs 50 D5
Atcham Shrops 60 D5
Athelhampton Dorset 13 E5
Athelington Suff 57 B6
Athelney Som 11 B8
Athelstaneford E Loth 121 B8
Atherington Devon 9 B7
Atherstone Warks 63 E7
Atherstone on Stour Warks 51 D7
Atherton Gtr Man 86 D4
Atley Hill N Yorks 101 D7
Atlow Derbys 76 E2
Attadale Highld 150 H2
Attadale Ho. Highld 150 H2
Attenborough Notts 76 F5
Atterby Lincs 90 E3
Attercliffe S Yorks 88 F4
Attleborough Norf 68 E3
Attleborough Warks 63 E7
Attlebridge Norf 68 C4
Atwick E Yorks 97 D7
Atworth Wilts 24 C3
Aubourn Lincs 78 C2
Auchagallon N Ayrs 143 E9
Auchallater Aberds 139 F7
Aucharnie Aberds 153 D6
Auchattie Aberds 141 E5
Auchavan Angus 134 C1
Auchbreck Moray 139 B8
Auchenback E Renf 118 D5
Auchenbainzie Dumfries 113 E8
Auchenblae Aberds 135 B7
Auchenbrack Dumfries 113 E7
Auchenbreck Argyll 145 E9
Auchencairn Dumfries 106 D4
Auchencairn Dumfries 114 F2
Auchencairn N Ayrs 143 F11
Auchencrosh S Ayrs 104 B5
Auchencrow Borders 122 C4
Auchendinny Midloth 121 C5
Auchengray S Lanark 120 D2
Auchenhalrig Moray 152 B3
Auchenheath S Lanark 119 E8
Auchenlochan Argyll 145 F8
Auchenmalg Dumfries 105 D6
Auchensoul S Ayrs 112 E2
Auchentiber N Ayrs 118 E3
Auchertyre Highld 149 F13
Auchgourish Highld 138 C5
Auchincarroch W Dunb 126 F3
Auchindrain Argyll 125 E6
Auchindrean Highld 150 C4
Auchininna Aberds 153 D6
Auchinleck E Ayrs 113 B5
Auchinloch N Lanark 119 B6
Auchinroath Moray 152 C2
Auchintoul Aberds 140 C4
Auchiries Aberds 153 E10
Auchlee Aberds 141 E7
Auchleven Aberds 140 B5
Auchlochan S Lanark 119 F8
Auchlossan Aberds 140 D4
Auchlunies Aberds 141 E7
Auchlyne Stirling 126 B4
Auchmacoy Aberds 153 E9
Auchmair Moray 140 B2
Auchmantle Dumfries 105 C5
Auchmillan E Ayrs 112 B5
Auchmithie Angus 135 E6
Auchmuirbridge Fife 128 D4
Auchmull Angus 135 B5
Auchnacree Angus 134 C4
Auchnagallin Highld 151 H13
Auchnagatt Aberds 153 D9
Auchnaha Argyll 145 E8
Auchnashelloch Perth 127 C6
Aucholzie Aberds 140 E2
Auchrannie Angus 134 D2
Auchroisk Highld 139 B6
Auchronie Angus 140 F3
Auchterarder Perth 127 C8
Auchteraw Highld 137 D6
Auchterderran Fife 128 E4
Auchterhouse Angus 134 F3
Auchtermuchty Fife 128 C4
Auchterneed Highld 150 F7
Auchtertool Fife 128 E4
Auchtertyre Moray 152 C1
Auchtubh Stirling 126 B4
Auckengill Highld 158 D5
Auckley S Yorks 89 D7
Audenshaw Gtr Man 87 E7
Audlem Ches E 74 E3
Audley Staffs 74 D4
Audley End Essex 56 F2
Auds Aberds 153 B6
Aughton E Yorks 96 F3
Aughton Lancs 85 D4
Aughton Lancs 93 C5
Aughton S Yorks 89 F5
Aughton Wilts 25 D7
Aughton Park Lancs 86 D2
Auldearn Highld 151 F12
Aulden Hereford 49 D6
Auldgirth Dumfries 114 F2
Auldhame E Loth 129 F7
Auldhouse S Lanark 119 D6
Ault a'chruinn Highld 136 B2
Aultanrynie Highld 156 F6
Aultbea Highld 155 J13
Aultdearg Highld 150 E5
Aultgrishan Highld 155 J12
Aultguish Inn Highld 150 D6
Aultibea Highld 157 G13
Aultiphurst Highld 157 C11
Aultmore Moray 152 C4
Aultnagoire Highld 137 B8
Aultnamain Inn Highld 151 C9
Aultnaslat Highld 136 D4
Aulton Aberds 140 B5
Aundorach Highld 139 C5
Aunsby Lincs 78 F3
Auquhorthies Aberds 141 B7
Aust S Glos 36 F2
Austendike Lincs 66 B2
Austerfield S Yorks 89 E7
Austrey Warks 63 D6
Austwick N Yorks 93 C7
Authorpe Lincs 91 F8
Authorpe Row Lincs 79 B8
Avebury Wilts 25 C6
Aveley Thurrock 42 F1
Avening Glos 37 E5
Averham Notts 77 D7
Aveton Gifford Devon 6 E4
Avielochan Highld 138 C5
Aviemore Highld 138 C4
Avington Hants 26 F3
Avington W Berks 25 C8
Avoch Highld 151 F10
Avon Hants 14 E2
Avon Dassett Warks 52 E2
Avonbridge Falk 120 B2
Avonmouth Bristol 23 B7
Avonwick Devon 6 D5
Awbridge Hants 14 B4
Awhirk Dumfries 104 D4
Awkley S Glos 36 F2
Awliscombe Devon 11 D6
Awre Glos 36 D4
Awsworth Notts 76 E4
Axbridge Som 23 D6
Axford Hants 26 E4
Axford Wilts 25 B7
Axminster Devon 11 E7
Axmouth Devon 11 E7
Axton Flint 85 F2
Aycliff Kent 31 E7
Aycliffe Durham 101 B7
Aydon Northumb 110 C3
Aylburton Glos 36 D3
Ayle Northumb 109 E7
Aylesbeare Devon 10 E5
Aylesbury Bucks 39 C8
Aylesby NE Lincs 91 D6
Aylesford Kent 29 D8
Aylesham Kent 31 D6
Aylestone Leicester 64 D2
Aylmerton Norf 81 D7
Aylsham Norf 81 E7
Aylton Hereford 49 F8
Aymestrey Hereford 49 C6
Aynho Northants 52 F3
Ayot St Lawrence Herts 40 C4
Ayot St Peter Herts 41 C5
Ayr S Ayrs 112 B3
Aysgarth N Yorks 101 F5
Ayside Cumb 99 F5
Ayston Rutland 65 D5
Aythorpe Roding Essex 42 C1
Ayton Borders 122 C5
Aywick Shetland 160 E7
Azerley N Yorks 95 B5

B

Babbacombe Torbay 7 C7
Babbinswood Shrops 73 F7
Babcary Som 12 B3
Babel Carms 47 F7
Babell Flint 73 B5
Babraham Cambs 55 D6
Babworth Notts 89 F7
Bac W Isles 155 C9
Bachau Anglesey 82 C4
Back of Keppoch Highld 147 C9
Back Rogerton E Ayrs 113 B5
Backaland Orkney 159 E6
Backaskaill Orkney 159 C5
Backbarrow Cumb 99 F5
Backe Carms 32 C3
Backfolds Aberds 153 C10
Backford Ches W 73 B8
Backford Cross Ches W 73 B7
Backhill Aberds 153 E7
Backhill Aberds 153 E10
Backhill of Clackriach Aberds 153 D9
Backhill of Fortree Aberds 153 D9
Backhill of Trustach Aberds 140 E5
Backies Highld 157 J11
Backlass Highld 158 E4
Backwell N Som 23 C6
Backworth T&W 111 B6
Bacon End Essex 42 C2
Baconsthorpe Norf 81 D7
Bacton Hereford 49 F5
Bacton Norf 81 D9
Bacton Suff 56 C4
Bacton Green Suff 56 C4
Bacup Lancs 87 B6
Badachro Highld 149 A12
Badanloch Lodge Highld 157 F10
Badavanich Highld 150 F4
Badbury Swindon 38 F1
Badby Northants 52 D3
Badcall Highld 156 D5
Badcaul Highld 150 B3
Baddeley Green Stoke 75 D6
Baddesley Clinton Warks 51 B7
Baddesley Ensor Warks 63 E6
Baddidarach Highld 156 G3
Baddoch Aberds 139 F7
Baddock Highld 151 F10
Badenscoth Aberds 153 E7
Badenyon Aberds 140 C2
Badger Shrops 61 E7
Badger's Mount Kent 29 C5
Badgeworth Glos 37 C6
Badgworth Som 23 D5
Badicaul Highld 149 F12
Badingham Suff 57 C7
Badlesmere Kent 30 D4
Badlipster Highld 158 F4
Badluarach Highld 150 B2
Badminton S Glos 37 F5
Badnaban Highld 156 G3
Badninish Highld 151 B10
Badrallach Highld 150 B3
Badsey Worcs 51 E5
Badshot Lea Sur 27 E6
Badsworth W Yorks 89 C5
Badwell Ash Suff 56 C3
Bae Colwyn = Colwyn Bay Conwy 83 D8
Bag Enderby Lincs 79 B6
Bagby N Yorks 102 F2
Bagendon Glos 37 D7
Bagh a Chaisteil = Castlebay W Isles 148 J1
Bagh Mor W Isles 148 C3
Bagh Shiarabhagh W Isles 148 H2
Baghasdal W Isles 148 G2
Bagillt Flint 73 B6
Baginton Warks 51 B8
Baglan Neath 33 E8
Bagley Shrops 60 B4
Bagnall Staffs 75 D6
Bagnor W Berks 26 C2
Bagshot Sur 27 C7
Bagshot Wilts 25 C8
Bagthorpe Norf 80 D3
Bagthorpe Notts 76 D4
Bagworth Leics 63 D8
Bagwy Llydiart Hereford 35 B8
Bail Àrd Bhuirgh W Isles 155 B9
Bail Uachdraich W Isles 148 B3
Baildon W Yorks 94 F4
Baile W Isles 154 J4
Baile a Mhanaich W Isles 148 C2
Baile Ailein W Isles 155 E7
Baile an Truiseil W Isles 155 B8
Baile Boidheach Argyll 144 F6
Baile Glas W Isles 148 C3
Baile Mhartainn W Isles 148 A2
Baile Mhic Phail W Isles 148 A3
Baile Mor Argyll 146 J5
Baile Mor W Isles 148 B2
Baile na Creige W Isles 148 H1
Baile nan Cailleach W Isles 148 C2
Baile Raghaill W Isles 148 A2
Bailebeag Highld 137 C8
Baileyhead Cumb 108 B5
Bailiesward Aberds 152 E4
Baillieston Glasgow 119 C6
Bail'lochdrach W Isles 148 C3
Bail'Ur Tholastaidh W Isles 155 C10
Bainbridge N Yorks 100 E4
Bainsford Falk 127 F7
Bainshole Aberds 152 E6
Bainton E Yorks 97 D5
Bainton Pboro 65 D7
Bairnkine Borders 116 C2
Baker Street Thurrock 42 F2
Baker's End Herts 41 C6
Bakewell Derbys 76 C2
Bala = Y Bala Gwyn 72 F3
Balachuirn Highld 149 D10
Balavil Highld 138 D3
Balbeg Highld 137 B7
Balbeg Highld 150 H7
Balbeggie Perth 128 B3
Balbithan Aberds 141 C6
Balbithan Ho. Aberds 141 C7
Balblair Highld 151 B8
Balblair Highld 151 E10
Balby S Yorks 89 D6
Balchladich Highld 156 F3
Balchraggan Highld 151 G8
Balchraggan Highld 151 H8
Balchrick Highld 156 D4
Balchrystie Fife 129 D6
Balcladaich Highld 137 B5
Balcombe W Sus 28 F4
Balcombe Lane W Sus 28 F4
Balcomie Fife 129 C8
Balcurvie Fife 128 D5
Baldersby N Yorks 95 B6
Baldersby St James N Yorks 95 B6
Balderstone Lancs 93 F6
Balderton Ches W 73 C7
Balderton Notts 77 D8
Baldhu Corn 3 B6
Baldinnie Fife 129 C6
Baldock Herts 54 F3
Baldovie Dundee 134 F4
Baldrine IoM 84 D4
Baldslow E Sus 18 D4
Baldwin IoM 84 D3
Baldwinholme Cumb 108 D3
Baldwin's Gate Staffs 74 E4
Bale Norf 81 D6
Balearn Aberds 153 C10
Balemartine Argyll 146 G2
Balephuil Argyll 146 G2
Balerno Edin 120 C4
Balevullin Argyll 146 G2
Balfield Angus 135 C5
Balfour Orkney 159 G5
Balfron Stirling 126 F4
Balfron Station Stirling 126 F4
Balgaveny Aberds 153 D6
Balgavies Angus 135 D5
Balgonar Fife 128 E2
Balgove Aberds 153 E8
Balgowan Highld 138 E2
Balgown Highld 149 B8
Balgrochan E Dunb 119 B6
Balgy Highld 149 C13
Balhaldie Stirling 127 D7
Balhalgardy Aberds 141 B6
Balham London 28 B3
Balhary Perth 134 E2
Baliasta Shetland 160 C8
Baligill Highld 157 C11
Balintore Angus 134 D2
Balintore Highld 151 D11
Balintraid Highld 151 D10
Balk N Yorks 102 F2
Balkeerie Angus 134 E3
Balkemback Angus 134 F3
Balkholme E Yorks 89 B8
Balkissock S Ayrs 104 A5
Ball Shrops 60 B3
Ball Haye Green Staffs 75 D6
Ball Hill Hants 26 C2
Ballabeg IoM 84 E2
Ballacannel IoM 84 D4
Ballachulish Highld 130 D4
Ballajora IoM 84 C4
Ballaleigh IoM 84 D3
Ballamodha IoM 84 E2
Ballantrae S Ayrs 104 A4
Ballaquine IoM 84 D4
Ballards Gore Essex 43 E5
Ballasalla IoM 84 C3
Ballasalla IoM 84 E2
Ballater Aberds 140 E2
Ballaugh IoM 84 C3
Ballaveare IoM 84 E3
Ballcorach Moray 139 B7
Ballechin Perth 133 D6
Balleigh Highld 151 C10
Ballencrieff E Loth 121 B7
Ballentoul Perth 133 C5
Ballidon Derbys 76 D2
Balliemore Argyll 124 C4
Balliemore Argyll 145 E9
Ballikinrain Stirling 126 F4
Ballimeanoch Argyll 125 D6
Ballimore Argyll 145 E8
Ballimore Stirling 126 C4
Ballinaby Argyll 142 B3
Ballindean Perth 128 B4
Ballingdon Suff 56 E2
Ballinger Common Bucks 40 D2
Ballingham Hereford 49 F7
Ballingry Fife 128 E3
Ballinlick Perth 133 E6
Ballinluig Perth 133 D6
Ballintuim Perth 133 D8
Balloch Angus 134 D3
Balloch Highld 151 G10
Balloch N Lanark 119 B7
Balloch W Dunb 126 F2
Ballochan Aberds 140 E4
Ballochford Moray 152 E3
Ballochmorrie S Ayrs 112 F2
Balls Cross W Sus 16 B3
Balls Green Essex 43 B6
Ballygown Argyll 146 G7
Ballygrant Argyll 142 B4
Ballyhaugh Argyll 146 F4
Balmacara Highld 149 F13
Balmacara Square Highld 149 F13
Balmaclellan Dumfries 106 B3
Balmacneil Perth 133 D6
Balmacqueen Highld 149 A9
Balmae Dumfries 106 E3
Balmaha Stirling 126 E3
Balmalcolm Fife 128 D5
Balmeanach Highld 149 D10
Balmedie Aberds 141 C8
Balmer Heath Shrops 73 F8
Balmerino Fife 129 B5
Balmerlawn Hants 14 D4
Balmichael N Ayrs 143 E10
Balmirmer Angus 135 F5
Balmore Highld 149 D7
Balmore Highld 150 H6
Balmore Highld 151 G11
Balmore Perth 133 D6
Balmule Fife 128 F4
Balmullo Fife 129 B6
Balmungie Highld 151 F10
Balnaboth Angus 134 C3
Balnabruaich Highld 151 E10
Balnabruich Highld 158 H3
Balnacoil Highld 157 H11
Balnacra Highld 150 G2
Balnafoich Highld 151 H9
Balnagall Highld 151 C11
Balnaguard Perth 133 D6
Balnahard Argyll 144 D3
Balnahard Argyll 146 H7
Balnain Highld 150 H7
Balnakeil Highld 156 C6
Balnaknock Highld 149 B9
Balnapaling Highld 151 E10
Balne N Yorks 89 C6
Balochroy Argyll 143 C8
Balone Fife 129 C6
Balornock Glasgow 119 C6
Balquharn Perth 133 F7
Balquhidder Stirling 126 B4
Balsall W Mid 51 B7
Balsall Common W Mid 51 B7
Balsall Heath W Mid 62 F4
Balscott Oxon 51 E8
Balsham Cambs 55 D6
Baltasound Shetland 160 C8
Balterley Staffs 74 D4
Baltersan Dumfries 105 C8
Balthangie Aberds 153 C8
Baltonsborough Som 23 F7
Balvaird Highld 151 F8
Balvicar Argyll 124 D3
Balvraid Highld 149 G13
Balvraid Highld 151 H11
Bamber Bridge Lancs 86 B3
Bambers Green Essex 42 B1
Bamburgh Northumb 123 F7
Bamff Perth 134 D2
Bamford Derbys 88 F3
Bamford Gtr Man 87 C6
Bampton Cumb 99 C7
Bampton Devon 10 B4
Bampton Oxon 38 D3
Bampton Grange Cumb 99 C7
Banavie Highld 131 B5
Banbury Oxon 52 E2
Bancffosfelen Carms 33 C5
Banchory Aberds 141 E5
Banchory-Devenick Aberds 141 D8
Bancycapel Carms 33 C5
Bancyfelin Carms 32 C4
Bancyffordd Carms 46 F3
Bandirran Perth 134 F2
Banff Aberds 153 B6
Bangor Gwyn 83 D5
Bangor-is-y-coed Wrex 73 E7
Banham Norf 68 F3
Bank Hants 14 D3
Bank Newton N Yorks 94 D2
Bank Street Worcs 49 C8
Bankend Dumfries 107 C7
Bankfoot Perth 133 F7
Bankglen E Ayrs 113 C6
Bankhead Aberdeen 141 C7
Bankhead Aberds 141 D5
Banknock Falk 119 B7
Banks Cumb 109 C5
Banks Lancs 85 B4
Bankshill Dumfries 114 F4
Banningham Norf 81 E8
Banniskirk Ho. Highld 158 E3
Bannister Green Essex 42 B2
Bannockburn Stirling 127 E7
Banstead Sur 28 D3
Bantham Devon 6 E4
Banton N Lanark 119 B7
Banwell N Som 23 D5
Banyard's Green Suff 57 B6
Bapchild Kent 30 C3
Bar Hill Cambs 54 C4
Barabhas W Isles 155 C8
Barabhas Iarach W Isles 155 C8
Barabhas Uarach W Isles 155 B8
Barachandroman Argyll 124 C2
Barassie S Ayrs 118 F3
Baravullin Argyll 124 E4
Barbaraville Highld 151 D10
Barber Booth Derbys 88 F2
Barbieston S Ayrs 112 C4
Barbon Cumb 99 F8
Barbridge Ches E 74 D3
Barbrook Devon 21 E6
Barby Northants 52 B3
Barcaldine Argyll 130 E3
Barcheston Warks 51 F7
Barcombe E Sus 17 C8
Barcombe Cross E Sus 17 C8
Barden N Yorks 101 E6
Barden Scale N Yorks 94 D3
Bardennoch Dumfries 113 E5
Bardfield Saling Essex 42 B2
Bardister Shetland 160 F5
Bardney Lincs 78 C4
Bardon Leics 63 C8
Bardon Mill Northumb 109 C7
Bardowie E Dunb 119 B5
Bardrainney Invclyd 118 B3
Bardsea Cumb 92 B3
Bardsey W Yorks 95 E6
Bardwell Suff 56 B3
Bare Lancs 92 C4
Barfad Argyll 145 G7
Barford Norf 68 D4
Barford Warks 51 C7
Barford St John Oxon 52 F2
Barford St Martin Wilts 25 F5
Barford St Michael Oxon 52 F2
Barfrestone Kent 31 D6
Bargod = Bargoed Caerph 35 E5
Bargoed = Bargod Caerph 35 E5
Bargrennan Dumfries 105 B7
Barham Cambs 54 B2
Barham Kent 31 D6
Barham Suff 56 D5
Barharrow Dumfries 106 D3
Barhill Dumfries 106 C5
Barholm Lincs 65 C7
Barkby Leics 64 D3
Barkestone-le-Vale Leics 77 F7
Barkham Wokingham 27 C5
Barking London 41 F7
Barking Suff 56 D4
Barking Tye Suff 56 D4
Barkingside London 41 F7
Barkisland W Yorks 87 C8
Barkston Lincs 78 E2
Barkston N Yorks 95 F7
Barkway Herts 54 F4
Barlaston Staffs 75 F5
Barlavington W Sus 16 C3
Barlborough Derbys 76 B4
Barlby N Yorks 96 F2
Barlestone Leics 63 D8
Barley Herts 54 F4
Barley Lancs 93 E8
Barley Mow T&W 111 D5
Barleythorpe Rutland 64 D5
Barling Essex 43 F5
Barlow Derbys 76 B3
Barlow N Yorks 89 B7
Barlow T&W 110 C4
Barmby Moor E Yorks 96 E3
Barmby on the Marsh E Yorks 89 B7
Barmer Norf 80 D4
Barmoor Castle Northumb 123 F5
Barmoor Lane End Northumb 123 F6
Barmouth = Abermaw Gwyn 58 C3
Barmpton Darl 101 C8
Barmston E Yorks 97 D7
Barnack Pboro 65 D7
Barnacle Warks 63 F7
Barnard Castle Durham 101 C5
Barnard Gate Oxon 38 C4
Barnardiston Suff 55 E8
Barnbarroch Dumfries 106 D5
Barnburgh S Yorks 89 D5
Barnby Suff 69 F7
Barnby Dun S Yorks 89 D7
Barnby in the Willows Notts 77 D8
Barnby Moor Notts 89 F7
Barnes Street Kent 29 E7
Barnet London 41 E5
Barnetby le Wold N Lincs 90 D4
Barney Norf 81 D5
Barnham Suff 56 B2
Barnham W Sus 16 D3
Barnham Broom Norf 68 D3
Barnhead Angus 135 D6
Barnhill Ches W 73 D8
Barnhill Dundee 134 F4
Barnhill Moray 152 C1
Barnhills Dumfries 104 B3
Barningham Durham 101 C5
Barningham Suff 56 B3
Barnoldby le Beck NE Lincs 91 D6
Barnoldswick Lancs 93 E8
Barns Green W Sus 16 B5
Barnsley Glos 37 D7
Barnsley S Yorks 88 D4
Barnstaple Devon 20 F4
Barnston Essex 42 C2
Barnston Mers 85 F3
Barnstone Notts 77 F7
Barnt Green Worcs 50 B5
Barnton Ches W 74 B3
Barnton Edin 120 B4
Barnwell All Saints Northants 65 F7
Barnwell St Andrew Northants 65 F7
Barnwood Glos 37 C5
Barochreal Argyll 124 C4
Barons Cross Hereford 49 D6
Barr S Ayrs 112 E2
Barra Castle Aberds 141 B6
Barrachan Dumfries 105 E7
Barrack Aberds 153 D8
Barraglom W Isles 154 D6
Barrahormid Argyll 144 E6
Barran Argyll 124 C4
Barrapol Argyll 146 G2
Barras Aberds 141 F7
Barras Cumb 100 C3
Barrasford Northumb 110 B2
Barravullin Argyll 124 E4
Barregarrow IoM 84 D3
Barrhead E Renf 118 D4
Barrhill S Ayrs 112 F2
Barrington Cambs 54 E4
Barrington Som 11 C8
Barripper Corn 2 C5
Barrmill N Ayrs 118 D3
Barrock Highld 158 C4
Barrock Ho. Highld 158 D4
Barrow Lancs 93 F7
Barrow Rutland 65 C5
Barrow Suff 55 C8
Barrow Green Kent 30 C3
Barrow Gurney N Som 23 C7
Barrow Haven N Lincs 90 B4
Barrow-in-Furness Cumb 92 C2
Barrow Island Cumb 92 C1
Barrow Nook Lancs 86 D2
Barrow Street Wilts 24 F3
Barrow upon Humber N Lincs 90 B4
Barrow upon Soar Leics 64 C2
Barrow upon Trent Derbys 63 B7
Barroway Drove Norf 67 D5
Barrowburn Northumb 116 C4
Barrowby Lincs 77 F8
Barrowcliff N Yorks 103 F8
Barrowden Rutland 65 D6
Barrowford Lancs 93 F8
Barrows Green Ches E 74 D3
Barrows Green Cumb 99 F7
Barrow's Green Mers 86 F3
Barry Angus 135 F5
Barry = Y Barri V Glam 22 C3
Barry Island V Glam 22 C3
Barsby Leics 64 C3
Barsham Suff 69 F6
Barston W Mid 51 B7
Bartestree Hereford 49 E7
Barthol Chapel Aberds 153 E8
Barthomley Ches E 74 D4
Bartley Hants 14 C4
Bartley Green W Mid 62 F4
Bartlow Cambs 55 E6
Barton Cambs 54 D5
Barton Ches W 73 D8
Barton Glos 37 B8
Barton Lancs 85 D4
Barton Lancs 92 F5
Barton N Yorks 101 D7
Barton Oxon 39 D5
Barton Torbay 7 C7
Barton Warks 51 D6
Barton Bendish Norf 67 D7
Barton Hartshorn Bucks 52 F4
Barton in Fabis Notts 76 F5
Barton in the Beans Leics 63 D7
Barton-le-Clay C Beds 53 F8
Barton-le-Street N Yorks 96 B3
Barton-le-Willows N Yorks 96 C3
Barton Mills Suff 55 B8
Barton on Sea Hants 14 E3
Barton on the Heath Warks 51 F7
Barton St David Som 23 F7
Barton Seagrave Northants 53 B6
Barton Stacey Hants 26 E2
Barton Turf Norf 69 B6
Barton-under-Needwood Staffs 63 C5
Barton-upon-Humber N Lincs 90 B4
Barton Waterside N Lincs 90 B4
Barugh S Yorks 88 D4
Barway Cambs 55 B6
Barwell Leics 63 E8
Barwick Herts 41 C6
Barwick Som 12 C3
Barwick in Elmet W Yorks 95 F6
Baschurch Shrops 60 B4
Bascote Warks 52 C2
Basford Green Staffs 75 D6
Bashall Eaves Lancs 93 E6
Bashley Hants 14 E3
Basildon Essex 42 F3
Basingstoke Hants 26 D4
Baslow Derbys 76 B2
Bason Bridge Som 22 E5
Bassaleg Newport 35 F6
Bassenthwaite Cumb 108 F2
Bassett Soton 14 C5
Bassingbourn Cambs 54 E4
Bassingfield Notts 77 F6
Bassingham Lincs 78 C2
Bassingthorpe Lincs 65 B6
Basta Shetland 160 D7
Baston Lincs 65 C8
Bastwick Norf 69 C7
Baswick Steer E Yorks 97 E6
Batchworth Heath Herts 40 E3
Batcombe Dorset 12 D4
Batcombe Som 23 F8
Bate Heath Ches E 74 B3
Batford Herts 40 C4
Bath Bath 24 C2
Bathampton Bath 24 C2
Bathealton Som 11 B5
Batheaston Bath 24 C2
Bathford Bath 24 C2
Bathgate W Loth 120 C2
Bathley Notts 77 D7
Bathpool Corn 5 B7
Bathpool Som 11 B7
Bathville W Loth 120 C2
Batley W Yorks 88 B3
Batsford Glos 51 F6
Battersby N Yorks 102 D3
Battersea London 28 B3
Battisborough Cross Devon 6 E3
Battisford Suff 56 D4
Battisford Tye Suff 56 D4
Battle E Sus 18 D4
Battle Powys 48 F2
Battledown Glos 37 B6
Battlefield Shrops 60 C5
Battlesbridge Essex 42 E3
Battlesden C Beds 40 B2
Battlesea Green Suff 57 B6
Battleton Som 10 B4
Battram Leics 63 D8
Battramsley Hants 14 E4
Baughton Worcs 50 E3
Baughurst Hants 26 D3

Baulking Oxon 38 E3
Baumber Lincs 78 B5
Baunton Glos 37 D7
Baverstock Wilts 24 F5
Bawburgh Norf 68 D4
Bawdeswell Norf 81 E6
Bawdrip Som 22 F5
Bawdsey Suff 57 E7
Bawtry S Yorks 89 E7
Baxenden Lancs 87 B5
Baxterley Warks 63 E6
Baybridge Hants 15 B6
Baycliff Cumb 92 B2
Baydon Wilts 25 B7
Bayford Herts 41 D6
Bayford Som 12 B5
Bayles Cumb 109 E7
Baylham Suff 56 D5
Baynard's Green Oxon 39 B5
Bayston Hill Shrops 60 D4
Baythorn End Essex 55 E8
Bayton Worcs 49 B8
Beach Highld 130 D1
Beachampton Bucks 53 F5
Beachamwell Norf 67 D7
Beachans Moray 151 G13
Beacharr Argyll 143 D7
Beachborough Kent 19 B8
Beachley Glos 36 E2
Beacon Devon 11 D6
Beacon End Essex 43 B5
Beacon Hill Sur 27 F6
Beacon's Bottom Bucks 39 E7
Beaconsfield Bucks 40 F2
Beacrabhaic W Isles 154 H6
Beadlam N Yorks 102 F4
Beadlow C Beds 54 F2
Beadnell Northumb 117 B8
Beaford Devon 9 C7
Beal N Yorks 89 B6
Beal Northumb 123 E6
Beamhurst Staffs 75 F7
Beaminster Dorset 12 D2
Beamish Durham 110 D5
Beamsley N Yorks 94 D3
Bean Kent 29 B6
Beanacre Wilts 24 C4
Beanley Northumb 117 C6
Beaquoy Orkney 159 F4
Bear Cross Bmouth 13 E8
Beardwood Blackburn 86 B4
Beare Green Sur 28 E2
Bearley Warks 51 C6
Bearnus Argyll 146 G6
Bearpark Durham 110 E5
Bearsbridge Northumb 109 D7
Bearsden E Dunb 118 B5
Bearsted Kent 29 D8
Bearstone Shrops 74 F4
Bearwood Hereford 49 D5
Bearwood Poole 13 E8
Bearwood W Mid 62 F4
Beattock Dumfries 114 D3
Beauchamp Roding Essex 42 C1
Beauchief S Yorks 88 F4
Beaufort Bl Gwent 35 C5
Beaufort Castle Highld 151 G8
Beaulieu Hants 14 D4
Beauly Highld 151 G8
Beaumaris Anglesey 83 D6
Beaumont Cumb 108 D3
Beaumont Essex 43 B7
Beaumont Hill Darl 101 C7
Beausale Warks 51 B7
Beauworth Hants 15 B6
Beaworthy Devon 9 E6
Beazley End Essex 42 B3
Bebington Mers 85 F4
Bebside Northumb 117 F8
Beccles Suff 69 E7
Becconsall Lancs 86 B2
Beck Foot Cumb 99 E8
Beck Hole N Yorks 103 D6
Beck Row Suff 55 B7
Beck Side Cumb 98 F4
Beckbury Shrops 61 D7
Beckenham London 28 C4
Beckermet Cumb 98 D2
Beckfoot Cumb 98 D3
Beckfoot Cumb 107 E7
Beckford Worcs 50 F4
Beckhampton Wilts 25 C5
Beckingham Lincs 77 D8
Beckingham Notts 89 F8
Beckington Som 24 D3
Beckley E Sus 19 C5
Beckley Hants 14 E3
Beckley Oxon 39 C5
Beckton London 41 F7
Beckwithshaw N Yorks 95 D5
Becontree London 41 F7
Bed-y-coedwr Gwyn 71 E8
Bedale N Yorks 101 F7
Bedburn Durham 110 F4
Bedchester Dorset 13 C6
Beddau Rhondda 34 F4
Beddgelert Gwyn 71 C6
Beddingham E Sus 17 D8
Beddington London 28 C4
Bedfield Suff 57 C6
Bedford Bedford 53 D8
Bedham W Sus 16 B4
Bedhampton Hants 15 D8
Bedingfield Suff 57 C5
Bedlam N Yorks 95 C5
Bedlington Northumb 117 F8
Bedlington Station Northumb 117 F8
Bedlinog M Tydf 34 D4
Bedminster Bristol 23 B7
Bedmond Herts 40 D3
Bednall Staffs 62 C3
Bedrule Borders 116 C2
Bedstone Shrops 49 B5
Bedwas Caerph 35 F5
Bedworth Warks 63 F7
Bedworth Heath Warks 63 F7
Beeby Leics 64 D3
Beech Hants 26 F4
Beech Staffs 75 F5
Beech Hill Gtr Man 86 D3
Beech Hill W Berks 26 C4
Beechingstoke Wilts 25 D5
Beedon W Berks 26 B2
Beeford E Yorks 97 D7
Beeley Derbys 76 C2
Beelsby NE Lincs 91 D6
Beenham W Berks 26 C3
Beeny Corn 8 E3
Beer Devon 11 F7
Beer Hackett Dorset 12 C3
Beercrocombe Som 11 B8
Beesands Devon 7 E6
Beesby Lincs 91 F8
Beeson Devon 7 E6
Beeston C Beds 54 E2
Beeston Ches W 74 D2
Beeston Norf 68 C2
Beeston Notts 76 F5
Beeston W Yorks 95 F5
Beeston Regis Norf 81 C7
Beeswing Dumfries 107 C5
Beetham Cumb 92 B4
Beetley Norf 68 C2
Begbroke Oxon 38 C4
Begelly Pembs 32 D2
Beggar's Bush Powys 48 C4
Beguildy Powys 48 B3
Beighton Norf 69 D6
Beighton S Yorks 88 F5
Beighton Hill Derbys 76 D2
Beith N Ayrs 118 D3
Bekesbourne Kent 31 D5
Belaugh Norf 69 C5
Belbroughton Worcs 50 B4
Belchamp Otten Essex 56 E2
Belchamp St Paul Essex 55 E8
Belchamp Walter Essex 56 E2
Belchford Lincs 79 B5
Belford Northumb 123 F7
Belhaven E Loth 122 B2
Belhelvie Aberds 141 C8
Belhinnie Aberds 140 B3
Bell Bar Herts 41 D5
Bell Busk N Yorks 94 D2
Bell End Worcs 50 B4
Bell o'th'Hill Ches W 74 E2
Bellabeg Aberds 140 C2
Bellamore S Ayrs 112 F2
Bellanoch Argyll 144 D6
Bellaty Angus 134 D2
Belleau Lincs 79 B7
Bellehiglash Moray 152 E1
Bellerby N Yorks 101 E6
Bellever Devon 6 B4
Belliehill Angus 135 C5
Bellingdon Bucks 40 D2
Bellingham Northumb 116 F4
Belloch Argyll 143 E7
Bellochantuy Argyll 143 E7
Bells Yew Green E Sus 18 B3
Bellsbank E Ayrs 112 D4
Bellshill N Lanark 119 C7
Bellshill Northumb 123 F7
Bellspool Borders 120 F4
Bellsquarry W Loth 120 C3
Belmaduthy Highld 151 F9
Belmesthorpe Rutland 65 C7
Belmont Blackburn 86 C4
Belmont London 28 C3
Belmont S Ayrs 112 B3
Belmont Shetland 160 C7
Belnacraig Aberds 140 C2
Belowda Corn 4 C4
Belper Derbys 76 E3
Belper Lane End Derbys 76 E3
Belsay Northumb 110 B4
Belses Borders 115 B8
Belsford Devon 7 D5
Belstead Suff 56 E5
Belston S Ayrs 112 B3
Belstone Devon 9 E8
Belthorn Blackburn 86 B5
Beltinge Kent 31 C5
Beltoft N Lincs 90 D2
Belton Leics 63 B8
Belton Lincs 78 F2
Belton N Lincs 89 D8
Belton Norf 69 D7
Belton in Rutland Rutland 64 D5
Beltring Kent 29 E7
Belts of Collonach Aberds 141 E5
Belvedere London 29 B5
Belvoir Leics 77 F8
Bembridge IoW 15 F7
Bemersyde Borders 121 F8
Bemerton Wilts 25 F6
Bempton E Yorks 97 B7
Ben Alder Lodge Highld 132 B2
Ben Armine Lodge Highld 157 H10
Ben Casgro W Isles 155 E9
Benacre Suff 69 F8
Benbuie Dumfries 113 E7
Benderloch Argyll 124 B5
Bendronaig Lodge Highld 150 H3
Benenden Kent 18 B5
Benfield Dumfries 105 C7
Bengate Norf 69 B6
Bengeworth Worcs 50 E5
Benhall Green Suff 57 C7
Benhall Street Suff 57 C7
Benholm Aberds 135 C8
Beningbrough N Yorks 95 D8
Benington Herts 41 B5
Benington Lincs 79 E6
Benllech Anglesey 82 C5
Benmore Argyll 145 E10
Benmore Stirling 126 B3
Benmore Lodge Highld 156 H6
Bennacott Corn 8 E4
Bennan N Ayrs 143 F10
Benniworth Lincs 91 F6
Benover Kent 29 E8
Bensham T&W 110 C5
Benslie N Ayrs 118 E3
Benson Oxon 39 E6
Bent Aberds 135 B6
Bent Gate Lancs 87 B5
Benthall Northumb 117 B8
Benthall Shrops 61 D6
Bentham Glos 37 C6
Benthoul Aberdeen 141 D7
Bentlawnt Shrops 60 D3
Bentley E Yorks 97 F6
Bentley Hants 27 E5
Bentley S Yorks 89 D6
Bentley Suff 56 F5
Bentley Warks 63 E6
Bentley Worcs 50 C4
Bentley Heath W Mid 51 B6
Benton Devon 21 F5
Bentpath Dumfries 115 E6
Bents W Loth 120 C2
Bentworth Hants 26 E4
Benvie Dundee 134 F3
Benwick Cambs 66 E3
Beoley Worcs 51 C5
Beoraidbeg Highld 147 B9
Bepton W Sus 16 C2
Berden Essex 41 B7
Bere Alston Devon 6 C2
Bere Ferrers Devon 6 C2
Bere Regis Dorset 13 E6
Berepper Corn 3 D5
Bergh Apton Norf 69 D6
Berinsfield Oxon 39 E5
Berkeley Glos 36 E3
Berkhamsted Herts 40 D2
Berkley Som 24 E3
Berkswell W Mid 51 B7
Bermondsey London 28 B4
Bernera Highld 149 F13
Bernice Argyll 145 D10
Bernisdale Highld 149 C9
Berrick Salome Oxon 39 E6
Berriedale Highld 158 H3
Berrier Cumb 99 B5
Berriew Powys 59 D8
Berrington Northumb 123 E6
Berrington Shrops 60 D5
Berrow Som 22 D5
Berrow Green Worcs 50 D2
Berry Down Cross Devon 20 E4
Berry Hill Glos 36 C2
Berry Hill Pembs 45 E2
Berry Pomeroy Devon 7 C6
Berryhillock Moray 152 B5
Berrynarbor Devon 20 E4
Bersham Wrex 73 E7
Berstane Orkney 159 G5
Berwick E Sus 18 E2
Berwick Bassett Wilts 25 B5
Berwick Hill Northumb 110 B4
Berwick St James Wilts 25 F5
Berwick St John Wilts 13 B7
Berwick St Leonard Wilts 24 F4
Berwick-upon-Tweed Northumb 123 D5
Bescar Lancs 85 C4
Besford Worcs 50 E4
Bessacarr S Yorks 89 D7
Bessels Leigh Oxon 38 D4
Bessingby E Yorks 97 C7
Bessingham Norf 81 D7
Bestbeech Hill E Sus 18 B3
Besthorpe Norf 68 E3
Besthorpe Notts 77 C8
Bestwood Nottingham 77 E5
Bestwood Village Notts 77 E5
Beswick E Yorks 97 E6
Betchworth Sur 28 E3
Bethania Ceredig 46 C4
Bethania Gwyn 71 C8
Bethania Gwyn 83 F6
Bethel Anglesey 82 D3
Bethel Gwyn 72 F3
Bethel Gwyn 82 E5
Bethersden Kent 30 E3
Bethesda Gwyn 83 E6
Bethesda Pembs 32 C1
Bethlehem Carms 33 B7
Bethnal Green London 41 F6
Betley Staffs 74 E4
Betsham Kent 29 B7
Betteshanger Kent 31 D7
Bettiscombe Dorset 11 E8
Bettisfield Wrex 73 F8
Betton Shrops 60 D3
Betton Shrops 74 F3
Bettws Bridgend 34 F3
Bettws Mon 35 C6
Bettws Newport 35 E6
Bettws Cedewain Powys 59 E8
Bettws Gwerfil Goch Denb 72 E4
Bettws Ifan Ceredig 46 E2
Bettws Newydd Mon 35 D7
Bettws-y-crwyn Shrops 60 F2
Bettyhill Highld 157 C10
Betws Carms 33 C7
Betws Bledrws Ceredig 46 D4
Betws-Garmon Gwyn 82 F5
Betws-y-Coed Conwy 83 F7
Betws-yn-Rhos Conwy 72 B3
Beulah Ceredig 45 E4
Beulah Powys 47 D8
Bevendean Brighton 17 D7
Bevercotes Notts 77 B6
Beverley E Yorks 97 F6
Beverston Glos 37 E5
Bevington Glos 36 E3
Bewaldeth Cumb 108 F2
Bewcastle Cumb 109 B5
Bewdley Worcs 50 B2
Bewerley N Yorks 94 C4
Bewholme E Yorks 97 D7
Bexhill E Sus 18 E4
Bexley London 29 B5
Bexleyheath London 29 B5
Bexwell Norf 67 D6
Beyton Suff 56 C3
Bhaltos W Isles 154 D5
Bhatarsaigh W Isles 148 J1
Bibury Glos 37 D8
Bicester Oxon 39 B5
Bickenhall Som 11 C7
Bickenhill W Mid 63 F5
Bicker Lincs 78 F5
Bickershaw Gtr Man 86 D4
Bickerstaffe Lancs 86 D2
Bickerton Ches E 74 D2
Bickerton N Yorks 95 D7
Bickington Devon 7 B5
Bickington Devon 20 F4
Bickleigh Devon 6 C3
Bickleigh Devon 10 D4
Bickleton Devon 20 F4
Bickley London 28 C5
Bickley Moss Ches W 74 E2
Bicknacre Essex 42 D3
Bicknoller Som 22 F3
Bicknor Kent 30 D2
Bickton Hants 14 C2
Bicton Shrops 60 C4
Bicton Shrops 60 F2
Bidborough Kent 29 E6
Biddenden Kent 19 B5
Biddenham Bedford 53 E8
Biddestone Wilts 24 B3
Biddisham Som 23 D5
Biddlesden Bucks 52 E4
Biddlestone Northumb 117 D5
Biddulph Staffs 75 D5
Biddulph Moor Staffs 75 D6
Bideford Devon 9 B6
Bidford-on-Avon Warks 51 D6
Bidston Mers 85 E3
Bielby E Yorks 96 E3
Bieldside Aberdeen 141 D7
Bierley IoW 15 G6
Bierley W Yorks 94 F4
Bierton Bucks 39 C8
Big Sand Highld 149 A12
Bigbury Devon 6 E4
Bigbury on Sea Devon 6 E4
Bigby Lincs 90 D4
Biggar Cumb 92 C1
Biggar S Lanark 120 F3
Biggin Derbys 75 D8
Biggin Derbys 76 E2
Biggin N Yorks 95 F8
Biggin Hill London 28 D5
Biggings Shetland 160 G3
Biggleswade C Beds 54 E2
Bighouse Highld 157 C11
Bighton Hants 26 F4
Bignor W Sus 16 C3
Bigton Shetland 160 L5
Bilberry Corn 4 C5
Bilborough Nottingham 76 E5
Bilbrook Som 22 E2
Bilbrough N Yorks 95 E8
Bilbster Highld 158 E4
Bildershaw Durham 101 B7
Bildeston Suff 56 E3
Billericay Essex 42 E2
Billesdon Leics 64 D4
Billesley Warks 51 D6
Billingborough Lincs 78 F4
Billinge Mers 86 D3
Billingford Norf 81 E6
Billingham Stockton 102 B2
Billinghay Lincs 78 D4
Billingley S Yorks 88 D5
Billingshurst W Sus 16 B4
Billingsley Shrops 61 F7
Billington C Beds 40 B2
Billington Lancs 93 F7
Billockby Norf 69 C7
Billy Row Durham 110 F4
Bilsborrow Lancs 92 F5
Bilsby Lincs 79 B7
Bilsham W Sus 16 D3
Bilsington Kent 19 B7
Bilson Green Glos 36 C3
Bilsthorpe Notts 77 C6
Bilsthorpe Moor Notts 77 D6
Bilston Midloth 121 C5
Bilston W Mid 62 E3
Bilstone Leics 63 D7
Bilting Kent 30 E4
Bilton E Yorks 97 F7
Bilton Northumb 117 C8
Bilton Warks 52 B2
Bilton in Ainsty N Yorks 95 E7
Bimbister Orkney 159 G4
Binbrook Lincs 91 E6
Binchester Blocks Durham 110 F5
Bincombe Dorset 12 F4
Bindal Highld 151 C12
Binegar Som 23 E8
Binfield Brack 27 B6
Binfield Heath Oxon 26 B5
Bingfield Northumb 110 B2
Bingham Notts 77 F7
Bingley W Yorks 94 F4
Bings Heath Shrops 60 C5
Binham Norf 81 D5
Binley Hants 26 D2
Binley W Mid 51 B8
Binley Woods Warks 51 B8
Binniehill Falk 119 B8
Binsoe N Yorks 94 B5
Binstead IoW 15 E6
Binsted Hants 27 E5
Binton Warks 51 D6
Bintree Norf 81 E6
Binweston Shrops 60 D3
Birch Essex 43 C5
Birch Gtr Man 87 D6
Birch Green Essex 43 C5
Birch Heath Ches W 74 C2
Birch Hill Ches W 74 B2
Birch Vale Derbys 87 F8
Bircham Newton Norf 80 D3
Bircham Tofts Norf 80 D3
Birchanger Essex 41 B8
Birchencliffe W Yorks 88 C2
Bircher Hereford 49 C6
Birchgrove Cardiff 22 B3
Birchgrove Swansea 33 E8
Birchington Kent 31 C6
Birchmoor Warks 63 D6
Birchover Derbys 76 C2
Birchwood Lincs 78 C2
Birchwood Warr 86 E4
Bircotes Notts 89 E7
Birdbrook Essex 55 E8
Birdforth N Yorks 95 B7
Birdham W Sus 16 E2
Birdholme Derbys 76 C3
Birdingbury Warks 52 C2
Birdlip Glos 37 C6
Birds Edge W Yorks 88 D3
Birdsall N Yorks 96 C4
Birdsgreen Shrops 61 F7
Birdsmoor Gate Dorset 11 D8
Birdston E Dunb 119 B6
Birdwell S Yorks 88 D4
Birdwood Glos 36 C4
Birgham Borders 122 F3
Birkby N Yorks 101 D8
Birkdale Mers 85 C4
Birkenhead Mers 85 F4
Birkenhills Aberds 153 D7
Birkenshaw N Lanark 119 C6
Birkenshaw W Yorks 88 B3
Birkhall Aberds 140 E2
Birkhill Angus 134 F3
Birkhill Borders 114 C5
Birkholme Lincs 65 B6
Birkin N Yorks 89 B6
Birley Hereford 49 D6
Birling Kent 29 C7
Birling Northumb 117 D8
Birling Gap E Sus 18 F2
Birlingham Worcs 50 E4
Birmingham W Mid 62 F4
Birnam Perth 133 E7
Birse Aberds 140 E4
Birsemore Aberds 140 E4
Birstall Leics 64 D2
Birstall W Yorks 88 B3
Birstwith N Yorks 94 D5
Birthorpe Lincs 78 F4
Birtley Hereford 49 C5
Birtley Northumb 109 B8
Birtley T&W 111 D5
Birts Street Worcs 50 F2
Bisbrooke Rutland 65 E5
Biscathorpe Lincs 91 F6
Biscot Luton 40 B3
Bish Mill Devon 10 B2
Bisham Windsor 39 F8
Bishampton Worcs 50 D4
Bishop Auckland Durham 101 B7
Bishop Burton E Yorks 97 F5
Bishop Middleham Durham 111 F6
Bishop Monkton N Yorks 95 C6
Bishop Norton Lincs 90 E3
Bishop Sutton Bath 23 D7
Bishop Thornton N Yorks 95 C5
Bishop Wilton E Yorks 96 D3
Bishopbridge Lincs 90 E4
Bishopbriggs E Dunb 119 C6
Bishopmill Moray 152 B2
Bishops Cannings Wilts 24 C5
Bishop's Castle Shrops 60 F3
Bishop's Caundle Dorset 12 C4
Bishop's Cleeve Glos 37 B6
Bishops Frome Hereford 49 E8
Bishop's Green Essex 42 C2
Bishop's Hull Som 11 B7
Bishop's Itchington Warks 51 D8
Bishops Lydeard Som 11 B6
Bishops Nympton Devon 10 B2
Bishop's Offley Staffs 61 B7
Bishop's Stortford Herts 41 B7
Bishop's Sutton Hants 26 F4
Bishop's Tachbrook Warks 51 C8
Bishops Tawton Devon 20 F4
Bishop's Waltham Hants 15 C6
Bishop's Wood Staffs 62 D2
Bishopsbourne Kent 31 D5
Bishopsteignton Devon 7 B7
Bishopstoke Hants 15 C5
Bishopston Swansea 33 F6
Bishopstone Bucks 39 C8
Bishopstone E Sus 17 D8
Bishopstone Hereford 49 E6
Bishopstone Swindon 38 F2
Bishopstone Wilts 13 B8
Bishopstrow Wilts 24 E3
Bishopswood Som 11 C7
Bishopsworth Bristol 23 C7
Bishopthorpe York 95 E8
Bishopton Darl 102 B1
Bishopton Dumfries 105 E8
Bishopton N Yorks 95 B6
Bishopton Renfs 118 B4
Bishopton Warks 51 D6
Bishton Newport 35 F7
Bisley Glos 37 D6
Bisley Sur 27 D7
Bispham Blackpool 92 E3
Bispham Green Lancs 86 C2
Bissoe Corn 3 B6
Bisterne Close Hants 14 D3
Bitchfield Lincs 65 B6
Bittadon Devon 20 E4
Bittaford Devon 6 D4
Bittering Norf 68 C2
Bitterley Shrops 49 B7
Bitterne Soton 15 C5
Bitteswell Leics 64 F2
Bitton S Glos 23 C8
Bix Oxon 39 F7
Bixter Shetland 160 H5
Blaby Leics 64 E2
Black Bourton Oxon 38 D2
Black Callerton T&W 110 C4
Black Clauchrie S Ayrs 112 F2
Black Corries Lodge Highld 131 D6
Black Crofts Argyll 124 B5
Black Dog Devon 10 D3
Black Heddon Northumb 110 B3
Black Lane Gtr Man 87 D5
Black Marsh Shrops 60 E3
Black Mount Argyll 131 E6
Black Notley Essex 42 B3
Black Pill Swansea 33 E7
Black Tar Pembs 44 E4
Black Torrington Devon 9 D6
Blackacre Dumfries 114 E3
Blackadder West Borders 122 D4
Blackawton Devon 7 D6
Blackborough Devon 11 D5
Blackborough End Norf 67 C6
Blackboys E Sus 18 C2
Blackbrook Derbys 76 E3
Blackbrook Mers 86 E3
Blackbrook Staffs 74 F4
Blackburn Aberds 141 C7
Blackburn Aberds 152 E5
Blackburn Blackburn 86 B4
Blackburn W Loth 120 C2
Blackcraig Dumfries 113 F7
Blackden Heath Ches E 74 B4
Blackdog Aberds 141 C8
Blackfell T&W 111 D5
Blackfield Hants 14 D5
Blackford Cumb 108 C3
Blackford Perth 127 D7
Blackford Som 12 B4
Blackford Som 23 E6
Blackfordby Leics 63 C7
Blackgang IoW 15 G5
Blackhall Colliery Durham 111 F7
Blackhall Mill T&W 110 D4
Blackhall Rocks Durham 111 F7
Blackham E Sus 29 F5
Blackhaugh Borders 121 F7
Blackheath Essex 43 B6
Blackheath Suff 57 B8
Blackheath Sur 27 E8
Blackheath W Mid 62 F3
Blackhill Aberds 153 C10
Blackhill Aberds 153 D10
Blackhill Highld 149 C8
Blackhills Highld 151 F12
Blackhills Moray 152 C2
Blackhorse S Glos 23 B8
Blackland Wilts 24 C5
Blacklaw Aberds 153 C6
Blackley Gtr Man 87 D6
Blacklunans Perth 134 C1
Blackmill Bridgend 34 F3
Blackmoor Hants 27 F5
Blackmoor Gate Devon 21 E5
Blackmore Essex 42 D2
Blackmore End Essex 55 F8
Blackmore End Herts 40 C4
Blackness Falk 120 B3
Blacknest Hants 27 E5
Blacko Lancs 93 E8
Blackpool Blackpool 92 F3
Blackpool Devon 7 E6
Blackpool Pembs 32 C1
Blackpool Gate Cumb 108 B5
Blackridge W Loth 119 C8
Blackrock Argyll 142 B4
Blackrock Mon 35 C6
Blackrod Gtr Man 86 C4
Blackshaw Dumfries 107 C7
Blackshaw Head W Yorks 87 B7
Blacksmith's Green Suff 56 C5
Blackstone W Sus 17 C6
Blackthorn Oxon 39 C6
Blackthorpe Suff 56 C3
Blacktoft E Yorks 90 B2
Blacktop Aberdeen 141 D7
Blacktown Newport 35 F6
Blackwall Tunnel London 41 F6
Blackwater Corn 3 B6
Blackwater Hants 27 D6
Blackwater IoW 15 F6
Blackwaterfoot N Ayrs 143 F9
Blackwell Darl 101 C7
Blackwell Derbys 75 B8
Blackwell Derbys 76 D4
Blackwell W Sus 28 F4
Blackwell Warks 51 E7
Blackwell Worcs 50 B4
Blackwood = Coed Duon Caerph 35 E5
Blackwood S Lanark 119 E7
Blackwood Hill Staffs 75 D6
Blacon Ches W 73 C7
Bladnoch Dumfries 105 D8
Bladon Oxon 38 C4
Blaen-gwynfi Neath 34 E2
Blaen-waun Carms 32 B3
Blaen-y-coed Carms 32 B4
Blaen-y-Cwm Denb 72 F4
Blaen-y-cwm Gwyn 71 E8
Blaen-y-cwm Powys 59 B7
Blaenannerch Ceredig 45 E4
Blaenau Ffestiniog Gwyn 71 C8
Blaenavon Torf 35 D6
Blaencelyn Ceredig 46 D2
Blaendyryn Powys 47 F8
Blaenffos Pembs 45 F3
Blaengarw Bridgend 34 E3
Blaengwrach Neath 34 D2
Blaenpennal Ceredig 46 C5
Blaenplwyf Ceredig 46 B4
Blaenporth Ceredig 45 E4
Blaenrhondda Rhondda 34 D3
Blaenycwm Ceredig 47 B7
Blagdon N Som 23 D7
Blagdon Torbay 7 C6
Blagdon Hill Som 11 C7
Blagill Cumb 109 E7
Blaguegate Lancs 86 D2
Blaich Highld 130 B4
Blain Highld 147 E9
Blaina Bl Gwent 35 D6
Blair Atholl Perth 133 C5
Blair Drummond Stirling 127 E6
Blairbeg N Ayrs 143 E11
Blairdaff Aberds 141 C5
Blairglas Argyll 126 F2
Blairgowrie Perth 134 E1
Blairhall Fife 128 F2
Blairingone Perth 127 E8
Blairland N Ayrs 118 E3
Blairlogie Stirling 127 E7
Blairlomond Argyll 125 F7
Blairmore Argyll 145 E10
Blairnamarrow Moray 139 C8
Blairquhosh Stirling 126 F4
Blair's Ferry Argyll 145 G8
Blairskaith E Dunb 119 B5
Blaisdon Glos 36 C4
Blakebrook Worcs 50 B3
Blakedown Worcs 50 B3
Blakelaw Borders 122 F3
Blakeley Staffs 62 E2
Blakeley Lane Staffs 75 E6
Blakemere Hereford 49 E5
Blakeney Glos 36 D3
Blakeney Norf 81 C6
Blakenhall Ches E 74 E4
Blakenhall W Mid 62 E3
Blakeshall Worcs 62 F2
Blakesley Northants 52 D4
Blanchland Northumb 110 D2
Bland Hill N Yorks 94 D5
Blandford Forum Dorset 13 D6
Blandford St Mary Dorset 13 D6
Blanefield Stirling 119 B5
Blankney Lincs 78 C3
Blantyre S Lanark 119 D6
Blar a'Chaorainn Highld 131 C5
Blaran Argyll 124 D4
Blarghour Argyll 125 D5
Blarmachfoldach Highld 130 C4
Blarnalearoch Highld 150 B4
Blashford Hants 14 D2
Blaston Leics 64 E5
Blatherwycke Northants 65 E6
Blawith Cumb 98 F4
Blaxhall Suff 57 D7
Blaxton S Yorks 89 D7
Blaydon T&W 110 C4
Bleadon N Som 22 D5
Bleak Hey Nook Gtr Man 87 D8
Blean Kent 30 C5
Bleasby Lincs 90 F5
Bleasby Notts 77 E7
Bleasdale Lancs 93 E5
Bleatarn Cumb 100 C2
Blebocraigs Fife 129 C6
Bleddfa Powys 48 C4
Bledington Glos 38 B2
Bledlow Bucks 39 D7
Bledlow Ridge Bucks 39 E7
Blegbie E Loth 121 C7
Blencarn Cumb 109 F6
Blencogo Cumb 107 E8
Blendworth Hants 15 C8
Blenheim Park Norf 80 D4
Blennerhasset Cumb 107 E8
Blervie Castle Moray 151 F13
Bletchingdon Oxon 39 C5
Bletchingley Sur 28 D4
Bletchley M Keynes 53 F6
Bletchley Shrops 74 F3
Bletherston Pembs 32 B1
Bletsoe Bedford 53 D8
Blewbury Oxon 39 F5
Blickling Norf 81 E7
Blidworth Notts 77 D5
Blindburn Northumb 116 C4
Blindcrake Cumb 107 F8
Blindley Heath Sur 28 E4
Blisland Corn 5 B6
Bliss Gate Worcs 50 B2
Blissford Hants 14 C2
Blisworth Northants 52 D5
Blithbury Staffs 62 B4
Blitterlees Cumb 107 D8
Blockley Glos 51 F6
Blofield Norf 69 D6
Blofield Heath Norf 69 C6
Blo' Norton Norf 56 B4
Bloomfield Borders 115 B8
Blore Staffs 75 E8
Blount's Green Staffs 75 F7
Blowick Mers 85 C4
Bloxham Oxon 52 F2
Bloxholm Lincs 78 D3
Bloxwich W Mid 62 D3
Bloxworth Dorset 13 E6
Blubberhouses N Yorks 94 D4
Blue Anchor Som 22 E2
Blue Anchor Swansea 33 E6
Blue Row Essex 43 C6
Blundeston Suff 69 E8
Blunham C Beds 54 D2
Blunsdon St Andrew Swindon 37 F8
Bluntington Worcs 50 B3
Bluntisham Cambs 54 B4
Blunts Corn 5 C8
Blyborough Lincs 90 E3
Blyford Suff 57 B8
Blymhill Staffs 62 C2
Blyth Northumb 117 F9
Blyth Notts 89 F7
Blyth Bridge Borders 120 E4
Blythburgh Suff 57 B8
Blythe Borders 121 E8
Blythe Bridge Staffs 75 E6
Blyton Lincs 90 E2
Boarhills Fife 129 C7
Boarhunt Hants 15 D7
Boars Head Gtr Man 86 D3
Boars Hill Oxon 38 D4
Boarshead E Sus 18 B2
Boarstall Bucks 39 C6
Boasley Cross Devon 9 E6
Boat of Garten Highld 138 C5
Boath Highld 151 D8
Bobbing Kent 30 C2
Bobbington Staffs 62 E2
Bobbingworth Essex 41 D8
Bocaddon Corn 5 D6
Bochastle Stirling 126 D5
Bocking Essex 42 B3
Bocking Churchstreet Essex 42 B3
Boddam Aberds 153 D11
Boddam Shetland 160 M5
Boddington Glos 37 B5
Bodedern Anglesey 82 C3
Bodelwyddan Denb 72 B4
Bodenham Hereford 49 D7
Bodenham Wilts 14 B2
Bodenham Moor Hereford 49 D7
Bodermid Gwyn 70 E2
Bodewryd Anglesey 82 B3
Bodfari Denb 72 B4
Bodffordd Anglesey 82 D4
Bodham Norf 81 C7
Bodiam E Sus 18 C4
Bodicote Oxon 52 F2
Bodieve Corn 4 B4
Bodinnick Corn 5 D6
Bodle Street Green E Sus 18 D3
Bodmin Corn 5 C5
Bodney Norf 67 E8
Bodorgan Anglesey 82 E3
Bodsham Kent 30 E5
Boduan Gwyn 70 D4
Bodymoor Heath Warks 63 E5
Bogallan Highld 151 F9
Bogbrae Aberds 153 E10
Bogend Borders 122 E3
Bogend S Ayrs 118 F3
Boghall W Loth 120 C2
Boghead S Lanark 119 E7
Bogmoor Moray 152 B3
Bogniebrae Aberds 152 D5
Bognor Regis W Sus 16 E3
Bograxie Aberds 141 C6
Bogside N Lanark 119 D8
Bogton Aberds 153 C6
Bogue Dumfries 113 F6
Bohenie Highld 137 F5
Bohortha Corn 3 C7
Bohuntine Highld 137 F5
Boirseam W Isles 154 J5
Bojewyan Corn 2 C2
Bolam Durham 101 B6
Bolam Northumb 117 F6
Bolberry Devon 6 F4
Bold Heath Mers 86 F3
Boldon T&W 111 C6
Boldon Colliery T&W 111 C6
Boldre Hants 14 E4
Boldron Durham 101 C5
Bole Notts 89 F8
Bolehill Derbys 76 D2
Boleside Borders 121 F7
Bolham Devon 10 C4
Bolham Water Devon 11 C6
Bolingey Corn 4 D2
Bollington Ches E 75 B6
Bollington Cross Ches E 75 B6
Bolney W Sus 17 B6
Bolnhurst Bedford 53 D8
Bolshan Angus 135 D6
Bolsover Derbys 76 B4
Bolsterstone S Yorks 88 E3
Bolstone Hereford 49 F7
Boltby N Yorks 102 F2
Bolter End Bucks 39 E7
Bolton Cumb 99 B8
Bolton E Loth 121 B8
Bolton E Yorks 96 D3
Bolton Gtr Man 86 D5
Bolton Northumb 117 C7
Bolton Abbey N Yorks 94 D3
Bolton Bridge N Yorks 94 D3
Bolton-by-Bowland Lancs 93 E7
Bolton-le-Sands Lancs 92 C4
Bolton Low Houses Cumb 108 E2
Bolton-on-Swale N Yorks 101 E7
Bolton Percy N Yorks 95 E8
Bolton Town End Lancs 92 C4
Bolton upon Dearne S Yorks 89 D5
Boltonfellend Cumb 108 C4
Boltongate Cumb 108 E2
Bolventor Corn 5 B6
Bomere Heath Shrops 60 C4
Bon-y-maen Swansea 33 E7
Bonar Bridge Highld 151 B9
Bonawe Argyll 125 B6
Bonby N Lincs 90 C4
Boncath Pembs 45 F4
Bonchester Bridge Borders 115 C8
Bonchurch IoW 15 G6
Bondleigh Devon 9 D8
Bonehill Devon 6 B5
Bonehill Staffs 63 D5
Bo'ness Falk 127 F8
Bonhill W Dunb 118 B3
Boningale Shrops 62 D2
Bonjedward Borders 116 B2
Bonkle N Lanark 119 D8
Bonnavoulin Highld 147 F8
Bonnington Edin 120 C4
Bonnington Kent 19 B7
Bonnybank Fife 129 D5
Bonnybridge Falk 127 F7
Bonnykelly Aberds 153 C8
Bonnyrigg and Lasswade Midloth 121 C6
Bonnyton Aberds 153 E6
Bonnyton Angus 134 F3
Bonnyton Angus 135 D6
Bonsall Derbys 76 D2
Bonskeid House Perth 133 C5
Bont Mon 35 C7
Bont-Dolgadfan Powys 59 D5
Bont-goch Ceredig 58 F3
Bont-newydd Conwy 72 B4
Bont Newydd Gwyn 71 C8
Bont Newydd Gwyn 71 E8
Bontddu Gwyn 58 C3
Bonthorpe Lincs 79 B7
Bontnewydd Ceredig 46 C5
Bontnewydd Gwyn 82 F4
Bontuchel Denb 72 D4
Bonvilston V Glam 22 B2
Booker Bucks 39 E8
Boon Borders 121 E8
Boosbeck Redcar 102 C4
Boot Cumb 98 D3
Boot Street Suff 57 E6
Booth W Yorks 87 B8
Booth Wood W Yorks 87 C8
Boothby Graffoe Lincs 78 D2
Boothby Pagnell Lincs 78 F2
Boothen Stoke 75 E5
Boothferry E Yorks 89 B8
Boothville Northants 53 C5
Bootle Cumb 98 F3
Bootle Mers 85 E4
Booton Norf 81 E7
Boquhan Stirling 126 F4
Boraston Shrops 49 B8
Borden Kent 30 C2
Borden W Sus 16 B2
Bordley N Yorks 94 C2
Bordon Hants 27 F6
Bordon Camp Hants 27 F5
Boreham Essex 42 D3
Boreham Wilts 24 E3
Boreham Street E Sus 18 D3
Borehamwood Herts 40 E4
Boreland Dumfries 114 E4
Boreland Stirling 132 F2
Borgh W Isles 148 H1
Borgh W Isles 154 J4
Borghastan W Isles 154 C7
Borgie Highld 157 D9
Borgue Dumfries 106 E3
Borgue Highld 158 H3
Borley Essex 56 E2
Bornais W Isles 148 F2
Bornesketaig Highld 149 A8
Borness Dumfries 106 E3
Borough Green Kent 29 D7
Boroughbridge N Yorks 95 C6
Borras Head Wrex 73 D7
Borreraig Highld 148 C6
Borrobol Lodge Highld 157 G11
Borrowash Derbys 76 F4
Borrowby N Yorks 102 F2
Borrowdale Cumb 98 C4
Borrowfield Aberds 141 E7
Borth Ceredig 58 E3
Borth-y-Gest Gwyn 71 D6
Borthwickbrae Borders 115 C7
Borthwickshiels Borders 115 C7
Borve Highld 149 D9
Borve Lodge W Isles 154 H5
Borwick Lancs 92 B5
Bosavern Corn 2 C2
Bosbury Hereford 49 E8
Boscastle Corn 8 E3
Boscombe Bmouth 14 E2
Boscombe Wilts 25 F7
Boscoppa Corn 4 D5
Bosham W Sus 16 D2
Bosherston Pembs 44 F4
Boskenna Corn 2 D3
Bosley Ches E 75 C6
Bossall N Yorks 96 C3
Bossiney Corn 8 F2
Bossingham Kent 31 E5
Bossington Som 21 E7
Bostock Green Ches W 74 C3
Boston Lincs 79 E6
Boston Long Hedges Lincs 79 E6
Boston Spa W Yorks 95 E7
Boston West Lincs 79 E5
Boswinger Corn 3 B8
Botallack Corn 2 C2
Botany Bay London 41 E5
Botcherby Cumb 108 D4
Botcheston Leics 63 D8
Botesdale Suff 56 B4
Bothal Northumb 117 F8
Bothamsall Notts 77 B6
Bothel Cumb 107 F8
Bothenhampton Dorset 12 E2
Bothwell S Lanark 119 D7
Botley Bucks 40 D2
Botley Hants 15 C6
Botley Oxon 38 D4
Botolph Claydon Bucks 39 B7
Botolphs W Sus 17 D5
Bottacks Highld 150 E7
Bottesford Leics 77 F8
Bottesford N Lincs 90 D2
Bottisham Cambs 55 C6
Bottlesford Wilts 25 D6
Bottom Boat W Yorks 88 B4
Bottom House Staffs 75 D7
Bottom o'th'Moor Gtr Man 86 C4
Bottom of Hutton Lancs 86 B2
Bottomcraig Fife 129 B5
Botusfleming Corn 6 C2
Botwnnog Gwyn 70 D3
Bough Beech Kent 29 E5
Boughrood Powys 48 F3
Boughspring Glos 36 E2
Boughton Norf 67 D6
Boughton Northants 53 C5
Boughton Notts 77 C6
Boughton Aluph Kent 30 E4
Boughton Lees Kent 30 E4
Boughton Malherbe Kent 30 E2
Boughton Monchelsea Kent 29 D8
Boughton Street Kent 30 D4
Boulby Redcar 103 C5
Boulden Shrops 60 F5
Boulmer Northumb 117 C8
Boulston Pembs 44 D4
Boultenstone Aberds 140 C3
Boultham Lincs 78 C2
Bourn Cambs 54 D4
Bourne Lincs 65 B7
Bourne End Bucks 40 F1
Bourne End C Beds 53 E7
Bourne End Herts 40 D3
Bournemouth Bmouth 13 E8
Bournes Green Glos 37 D6
Bournes Green Southend 43 F5
Bournheath Worcs 50 B4
Bournmoor Durham 111 D6
Bournville W Mid 62 F4
Bourton Dorset 24 F2
Bourton N Som 23 C5
Bourton Oxon 38 F2
Bourton Shrops 61 E5
Bourton on Dunsmore Warks 52 B2
Bourton on the Hill Glos 51 F6
Bourton-on-the-Water Glos 38 B1
Bousd Argyll 146 E5
Boustead Hill Cumb 108 D2
Bouth Cumb 99 F5
Bouthwaite N Yorks 94 B4
Boveney Bucks 27 B7
Boverton V Glam 21 C8
Bovey Tracey Devon 7 B6
Bovingdon Herts 40 D3
Bovingdon Green Bucks 39 F8
Bovingdon Green Herts 40 D3
Bovinger Essex 41 D8
Bovington Camp Dorset 13 F6
Bow Borders 121 E7
Bow Devon 10 D2
Bow Orkney 159 J4
Bow Brickhill M Keynes 53 F7
Bow of Fife Fife 128 C5
Bow Street Ceredig 58 F3
Bowbank Durham 100 B4
Bowburn Durham 111 F6
Bowcombe IoW 15 F5
Bowd Devon 11 E6
Bowden Borders 121 F8
Bowden Devon 7 E6
Bowden Hill Wilts 24 C4
Bowderdale Cumb 100 D1
Bowdon Gtr Man 87 F5
Bower Northumb 116 F3
Bower Hinton Som 12 C2
Bowerchalke Wilts 13 B8
Bowerhill Wilts 24 C4
Bowermadden Highld 158 D4
Bowers Gifford Essex 42 F3
Bowershall Fife 128 E2
Bowertower Highld 158 D4
Bowes Durham 100 C4
Bowgreave Lancs 92 E4
Bowgreen Gtr Man 87 F5
Bowhill Borders 115 B7
Bowhouse Dumfries 107 C7
Bowland Bridge Cumb 99 F6
Bowley Hereford 49 D7
Bowlhead Green Sur 27 F7
Bowling W Dunb 118 B4
Bowling W Yorks 94 F4
Bowling Bank Wrex 73 E7
Bowling Green Worcs 50 D3
Bowmanstead Cumb 99 E5
Bowmore Argyll 142 C4
Bowness-on-Solway Cumb 108 C2
Bowness-on-Windermere Cumb 99 E6
Bowsden Northumb 123 E5
Bowside Lodge Highld 157 C11
Bowston Cumb 99 E6
Bowthorpe Norf 68 D4
Box Glos 37 D5
Box Wilts 24 C3
Box End Bedford 53 E8
Boxbush Glos 36 C4
Boxford Suff 56 E3
Boxford W Berks 26 B2
Boxgrove W Sus 16 D3
Boxley Kent 29 D8
Boxmoor Herts 40 D3
Boxted Essex 56 F4
Boxted Suff 56 D2
Boxted Cross Essex 56 F4
Boxted Heath Essex 56 F4
Boxworth Cambs 54 C4
Boxworth End Cambs 54 C4
Boyden Gate Kent 31 C6
Boylestone Derbys 75 F8
Boyndie Aberds 153 B6
Boynton E Yorks 97 C7
Boysack Angus 135 E6
Boyton Corn 8 E5
Boyton Suff 57 E7
Boyton Wilts 24 F4
Boyton Cross Essex 42 D2
Boyton End Suff 55 E8
Bozeat Northants 53 D7

184 Bra–Bux

Braaid IoM 84 E3
Braal Castle Highld 158 D3
Brabling Green Suff 57 C6
Brabourne Kent 30 E4
Brabourne Lees Kent 30 E4
Brabster Highld 158 D5
Bracadale Highld 149 E8
Bracara Highld 147 B10
Braceborough Lincs 65 C7
Bracebridge Lincs 78 C2
Bracebridge Heath Lincs 78 C2
Bracebridge Low Fields Lincs 78 C2
Braceby Lincs 78 F3
Bracewell Lancs 93 E8
Brackenfield Derbys 76 D3
Brackenthwaite Cumb 108 E2
Brackenthwaite N Yorks 95 D5
Bracklesham W Sus 16 E2
Brackletter Highld 136 F4
Brackley Argyll 143 D8
Brackley Northants 52 F3
Brackloch Highld 156 G4
Bracknell Brack 27 C6
Braco Perth 127 D7
Bracobrae Moray 152 C5
Bracon Ash Norf 68 E4
Bracorina Highld 147 B10
Bradbourne Derbys 76 D2
Bradbury Durham 101 B8
Bradda IoM 84 F1
Bradden Northants 52 E4
Braddock Corn 5 C6
Bradeley Stoke 75 D5
Bradenham Bucks 39 E8
Bradenham Norf 68 D2
Bradenstoke Wilts 24 B5
Bradfield Essex 56 F5
Bradfield Norf 81 D8
Bradfield W Berks 26 B4
Bradfield Combust Suff 56 D2
Bradfield Green Ches E 74 D3
Bradfield Heath Essex 43 B7
Bradfield St Clare Suff 56 D3
Bradfield St George Suff 56 C3
Bradford Corn 5 B6
Bradford Derbys 76 C2
Bradford Devon 9 D6
Bradford Northumb 123 F7
Bradford W Yorks 94 F4
Bradford Abbas Dorset 12 C3
Bradford Leigh Wilts 24 C3
Bradford-on-Avon Wilts 24 C3
Bradford-on-Tone Som 11 B6
Bradford Peverell Dorset 12 E4
Brading IoW 15 F7
Bradley Derbys 76 E2
Bradley Hants 26 E4
Bradley NE Lincs 91 D6
Bradley Staffs 62 C2
Bradley W Mid 62 E3
Bradley W Yorks 88 B2
Bradley Green Worcs 50 C4
Bradley in the Moors Staffs 75 E7
Bradley Stoke S Glos 36 F3
Bradlow Hereford 50 F2
Bradmore Notts 77 F5
Bradmore W Mid 62 E2
Bradninch Devon 10 D5
Bradnop Staffs 75 D7
Bradpole Dorset 12 E2
Bradshaw Gtr Man 86 C5
Bradshaw W Yorks 87 C8
Bradstone Devon 9 F5
Bradwall Green Ches E 74 C4
Bradway S Yorks 88 F4
Bradwell Derbys 88 F2
Bradwell Essex 42 B4
Bradwell M Keynes 53 F6
Bradwell Norf 69 D8
Bradwell Staffs 74 E5
Bradwell Grove Oxon 38 D2
Bradwell on Sea Essex 43 D6
Bradwell Waterside Essex 43 D5
Bradworthy Devon 8 C5
Bradworthy Cross Devon 8 C5
Brae Dumfries 107 B5
Brae Highld 155 J13
Brae Highld 156 J7
Brae Shetland 160 G5
Brae of Achnahaird Highld 156 H3
Brae Roy Lodge Highld 137 E6
Braeantra Highld 151 D8
Braedownie Angus 134 B2
Braefield Highld 150 H7
Braegrum Perth 128 B2
Braehead Dumfries 105 D8
Braehead Orkney 159 D5
Braehead Orkney 159 H6
Braehead S Lanark 119 F8
Braehead S Lanark 120 D2
Braehead of Lunan Angus 135 D6
Braehoulland Shetland 160 F4
Braehungie Highld 158 G3
Braelangwell Lodge Highld 151 B8
Braemar Aberds 139 E7
Braemore Highld 150 D4
Braemore Highld 158 G2
Braes of Enzie Moray 152 C3
Braeside Invclyd 118 B2
Braeswick Orkney 159 E7
Braewick Shetland 160 H5
Brafferton Darl 101 B7
Brafferton N Yorks 95 B7
Brafield-on-the-Green Northants 53 D6
Bragar W Isles 155 C7
Bragbury End Herts 41 B5
Bragleenmore Argyll 124 C5
Braichmelyn Gwyn 83 E6
Braid Edin 120 C5
Braides Lancs 92 D4
Braidley N Yorks 101 F5
Braidwood S Lanark 119 E8
Braigo Argyll 142 B3
Brailsford Derbys 76 E2
Brainshaugh Northumb 117 D8
Braintree Essex 42 B3
Braiseworth Suff 56 B5
Braishfield Hants 14 B4
Braithwaite Cumb 98 B4
Braithwaite S Yorks 89 C7
Braithwaite W Yorks 94 E3
Braithwell S Yorks 89 E6
Bramber W Sus 17 C5
Bramcote Notts 76 F5
Bramcote Warks 63 F8
Bramdean Hants 15 B7
Bramerton Norf 69 D5
Bramfield Herts 41 C5
Bramfield Suff 57 B7
Bramford Suff 56 E5
Bramhall Gtr Man 87 F6
Bramham W Yorks 95 E7
Bramhope W Yorks 95 E5
Bramley Hants 26 D4
Bramley S Yorks 89 E5
Bramley Sur 27 E8
Bramley W Yorks 94 F5
Bramling Kent 31 D6
Brampford Speke Devon 10 E4
Brampton Cambs 54 B3
Brampton Cumb 100 B1
Brampton Cumb 108 C5
Brampton Derbys 76 B3
Brampton Hereford 49 F6
Brampton Lincs 77 B8
Brampton Norf 81 E8
Brampton S Yorks 88 D5
Brampton Suff 69 F7
Brampton Abbotts Hereford 36 B3
Brampton Ash Northants 64 F4
Brampton Bryan Hereford 49 B5
Brampton en le Morthen S Yorks 89 F5
Bramshall Staffs 75 F7
Bramshaw Hants 14 C3
Bramshill Hants 26 C5
Bramshott Hants 27 F6
Bran End Essex 42 B2
Branault Highld 147 E8
Brancaster Norf 80 C3
Brancaster Staithe Norf 80 C3
Brancepeth Durham 110 F5
Branch End Northumb 110 C3
Branchill Moray 151 F13
Brand Green Glos 36 B4
Branderburgh Moray 152 A2
Brandesburton E Yorks 97 E7
Brandeston Suff 57 C6
Brandhill Shrops 49 B6
Brandis Corner Devon 9 D6
Brandiston Norf 81 E7
Brandon Durham 110 F5
Brandon Lincs 78 E2
Brandon Northumb 117 C6
Brandon Suff 67 F7
Brandon Warks 52 B2
Brandon Bank Cambs 67 F6
Brandon Creek Norf 67 E6
Brandon Parva Norf 68 D3
Brandsby N Yorks 95 B8
Brandy Wharf Lincs 90 E4
Brane Corn 2 D3
Branksome Poole 13 E8
Branksome Park Poole 13 E8
Bransby Lincs 77 B8
Branscombe Devon 11 F6
Bransford Worcs 50 D2
Bransgore Hants 14 E2
Branshill Clack 127 E7
Bransholme Hull 97 F7
Branson's Cross Worcs 51 B5
Branston Leics 64 B5
Branston Lincs 78 C3
Branston Staffs 63 B6
Branston Booths Lincs 78 C3
Branstone IoW 15 F6
Bransty Cumb 98 C1
Brant Broughton Lincs 78 D2
Brantham Suff 56 F5
Branthwaite Cumb 98 B2
Branthwaite Cumb 108 F2
Brantingham E Yorks 90 B3
Branton Northumb 117 C6
Branton S Yorks 89 D7
Branxholm Park Borders 115 C7
Branxholme Borders 115 C7
Branxton Northumb 122 F4
Brassey Green Ches W 74 C2
Brassington Derbys 76 D2
Brasted Kent 29 D5
Brasted Chart Kent 29 D5
Brathens Aberds 141 E5
Bratoft Lincs 79 C7
Brattleby Lincs 90 F3
Bratton Telford 61 C6
Bratton Wilts 24 D4
Bratton Clovelly Devon 9 E6
Bratton Fleming Devon 20 F5
Bratton Seymour Som 12 B4
Braughing Herts 41 B6
Braunston Northants 52 C3
Braunston-in-Rutland Rutland 64 D5
Braunstone Town Leicester 64 D2
Braunton Devon 20 F3
Brawby N Yorks 96 B3
Brawl Highld 157 C11
Brawlbin Highld 158 E2
Bray Windsor 27 B7
Bray Shop Corn 5 B8
Bray Wick Windsor 27 B6
Braybrooke Northants 64 F4
Braye Ald 16
Brayford Devon 21 F5
Braystones Cumb 98 D2
Braythorn N Yorks 94 E5
Brayton N Yorks 95 F9
Brazacott Corn 8 E4
Breach Kent 30 C2
Breachacha Castle Argyll 146 F4
Breachwood Green Herts 40 B4
Breacleit W Isles 154 D6
Breaden Heath Shrops 73 F8
Breadsall Derbys 76 F3
Breadstone Glos 36 D4
Breage Corn 2 D5
Breakachy Highld 150 G7
Bream Glos 36 D3
Breamore Hants 14 C2
Brean Som 22 D4
Breanais W Isles 154 E4
Brearton N Yorks 95 C6
Breascleit W Isles 154 D7
Breaston Derbys 76 F4
Brechfa Carms 46 F4
Brechin Angus 135 C5
Breck of Cruan Orkney 159 G4
Breckan Orkney 159 H3
Breckrey Highld 149 B10
Brecon = Aberhonddu Powys 34 B4
Bredbury Gtr Man 87 E7
Brede E Sus 18 D5
Bredenbury Hereford 49 D8
Bredfield Suff 57 D6
Bredgar Kent 30 C2
Bredhurst Kent 29 C8
Bredicot Worcs 50 D4
Bredon Worcs 50 F4
Bredon's Norton Worcs 50 F4
Bredwardine Hereford 48 E5
Breedon on the Hill Leics 63 B8
Breibhig W Isles 148 J1
Breibhig W Isles 155 D9
Breich W Loth 120 C2
Breightmet Gtr Man 86 D5
Breighton E Yorks 96 F3
Breinton Hereford 49 F6
Breinton Common Hereford 49 E6
Breiwick Shetland 160 J6
Bremhill Wilts 24 B4
Bremirehoull Shetland 160 L6
Brenchley Kent 29 E7
Brendon Devon 21 E6
Brenkley T&W 110 B5
Brent Eleigh Suff 56 E3
Brent Knoll Som 22 D5
Brent Pelham Herts 54 F5
Brentford London 28 B2
Brentingby Leics 64 C4
Brentwood Essex 42 E1
Brenzett Kent 19 C7
Brereton Staffs 62 C4
Brereton Green Ches E 74 C4
Brereton Heath Ches E 74 C5
Bressingham Norf 68 F3
Bretby Derbys 63 B6
Bretford Warks 52 B2
Bretforton Worcs 51 E5
Bretherdale Head Cumb 99 D7
Bretherton Lancs 86 B2
Brettabister Shetland 160 H6
Brettenham Norf 68 F2
Brettenham Suff 56 D3
Bretton Derbys 76 B2
Bretton Flint 73 C7
Brewer Street Sur 28 D4
Brewlands Bridge Angus 134 C1
Brewood Staffs 62 D2
Briach Moray 151 F13
Briants Puddle Dorset 13 E6
Brick End Essex 42 B1
Brickendon Herts 41 D6
Bricket Wood Herts 40 D4
Bricklehampton Worcs 50 E4
Bride IoM 84 B4
Bridekirk Cumb 107 F8
Bridell Pembs 45 E3
Bridestowe Devon 9 F7
Brideswell Aberds 152 E5
Bridford Devon 10 F3
Bridfordmills Devon 10 F3
Bridge Kent 31 D5
Bridge End Lincs 78 F4
Bridge Green Essex 55 F5
Bridge Hewick N Yorks 95 B6
Bridge of Alford Aberds 140 C4
Bridge of Allan Stirling 127 E6
Bridge of Avon Moray 152 E1
Bridge of Awe Argyll 125 C6
Bridge of Balgie Perth 132 E2
Bridge of Cally Perth 133 D8
Bridge of Canny Aberds 141 E5
Bridge of Craigisla Angus 134 D2
Bridge of Dee Dumfries 106 D4
Bridge of Don Aberdeen 141 C8
Bridge of Dun Angus 135 D6
Bridge of Dye Aberds 141 F5
Bridge of Earn Perth 128 C3
Bridge of Ericht Perth 132 D2
Bridge of Feugh Aberds 141 E6
Bridge of Forss Highld 157 C13
Bridge of Gairn Aberds 140 E2
Bridge of Gaur Perth 132 D2
Bridge of Muchalls Aberds 141 E7
Bridge of Oich Highld 137 D6
Bridge of Orchy Argyll 125 B8
Bridge of Waith Orkney 159 G3
Bridge of Walls Shetland 160 H4
Bridge of Weir Renfs 118 C3
Bridge Sollers Hereford 49 E6
Bridge Street Suff 56 E2
Bridge Trafford Ches W 73 B8
Bridge Yate S Glos 23 B8
Bridgefoot Angus 134 F3
Bridgefoot Cumb 98 B2
Bridgehampton Som 12 B3
Bridgehill Durham 110 D3
Bridgemary Hants 15 D6
Bridgemont Derbys 87 F8
Bridgend Aberds 140 C4
Bridgend Aberds 152 E5
Bridgend Angus 135 C5
Bridgend Argyll 142 B4
Bridgend Argyll 143 E8
Bridgend Argyll 145 D7
Bridgend = Pen-Y-Bont Ar Ogwr Bridgend 21 B8
Bridgend Cumb 99 C5
Bridgend Fife 129 C5
Bridgend Moray 152 E3
Bridgend N Lanark 119 B6
Bridgend Pembs 45 E3
Bridgend W Loth 120 B3
Bridgend of Lintrathen Angus 134 D2
Bridgerule Devon 8 D4
Bridges Shrops 60 E3
Bridgeton Glasgow 119 C6
Bridgetown Corn 8 F5
Bridgetown Som 21 F8
Bridgham Norf 68 F2
Bridgnorth Shrops 61 E7
Bridgtown Staffs 62 D3
Bridgwater Som 22 F5
Bridlington E Yorks 97 C7
Bridport Dorset 12 E2
Bridstow Hereford 36 B2
Brierfield Lancs 93 F8
Brierley Glos 36 C3
Brierley Hereford 49 D6
Brierley S Yorks 88 C5
Brierley Hill W Mid 62 F3
Briery Hill Bl Gwent 35 D5
Brig o'Turk Stirling 126 D4
Brigg N Lincs 90 D4
Briggswath N Yorks 103 D6
Brigham Cumb 107 F7
Brigham E Yorks 97 D6
Brighouse W Yorks 88 B2
Brighstone IoW 14 F5
Brightgate Derbys 76 D2
Brighthampton Oxon 38 D3
Brightling E Sus 18 C3
Brightlingsea Essex 43 C6
Brighton Brighton 17 D7
Brighton Corn 4 D4
Brighton Hill Hants 26 E4
Brightons Falk 120 B2
Brightwalton W Berks 26 B2
Brightwell Suff 57 E6
Brightwell Baldwin Oxon 39 E6
Brightwell cum Sotwell Oxon 39 E5
Brignall Durham 101 C5
Brigsley NE Lincs 91 D6
Brigsteer Cumb 99 F6
Brigstock Northants 65 F6
Brill Bucks 39 C6
Brilley Hereford 48 E4
Brimaston Pembs 44 C4
Brimfield Hereford 49 C7
Brimington Derbys 76 B4
Brimley Devon 7 B5
Brimpsfield Glos 37 C6
Brimpton W Berks 26 C3
Brims Orkney 159 K3
Brimscombe Glos 37 D5
Brimstage Mers 85 F4
Brinacory Highld 147 B10
Brind E Yorks 96 F3
Brindister Shetland 160 H4
Brindister Shetland 160 K6
Brindle Lancs 86 B4
Brindley Ford Stoke 75 D5
Brineton Staffs 62 C2
Bringhurst Leics 64 E5
Brington Cambs 53 B8
Brinian Orkney 159 F5
Briningham Norf 81 D6
Brinkhill Lincs 79 B6
Brinkley Cambs 55 D7
Brinklow Warks 52 B2
Brinkworth Wilts 37 F7
Brinmore Highld 138 B2
Brinscall Lancs 86 B4
Brinsea N Som 23 C6
Brinsley Notts 76 E4
Brinsop Hereford 49 E6
Brinsworth S Yorks 88 F5
Brinton Norf 81 D6
Brisco Cumb 108 D4
Brisley Norf 81 E5
Brislington Bristol 23 B8
Bristol Bristol 23 B7
Briston Norf 81 D6
Britannia Lancs 87 B6
Britford Wilts 14 B2
Brithdir Gwyn 58 C4
British Legion Village Kent 29 D8
Briton Ferry Neath 33 E8
Britwell Salome Oxon 39 E6
Brixham Torbay 7 D7
Brixton Devon 6 D3
Brixton London 28 B4
Brixton Deverill Wilts 24 F3
Brixworth Northants 52 B5
Brize Norton Oxon 38 D3
Broad Blunsdon Swindon 38 E1
Broad Campden Glos 51 F6
Broad Chalke Wilts 13 B8
Broad Green C Beds 53 E7
Broad Green Essex 42 B4
Broad Green Worcs 50 D2
Broad Haven Pembs 44 D3
Broad Heath Worcs 49 C8
Broad Hill Cambs 55 B6
Broad Hinton Wilts 25 B6
Broad Laying Hants 26 C2
Broad Marston Worcs 51 E6
Broad Oak Carms 33 B6
Broad Oak Cumb 98 E3
Broad Oak Dorset 12 E2
Broad Oak Dorset 13 C5
Broad Oak E Sus 18 C3
Broad Oak E Sus 18 D5
Broad Oak Hereford 36 B1
Broad Oak Mers 86 E3
Broad Street Kent 30 D2
Broad Street Green Essex 42 D4
Broad Town Wilts 25 B5
Broadbottom Gtr Man 87 E7
Broadbridge W Sus 16 D2
Broadbridge Heath W Sus 28 F2
Broadclyst Devon 10 E4
Broadfield Gtr Man 87 C6
Broadfield Lancs 86 B3
Broadfield Pembs 32 D2
Broadfield W Sus 28 F3
Broadford Highld 149 F11
Broadford Bridge W Sus 16 B4
Broadhaugh Borders 115 D7
Broadhaven Highld 158 E5
Broadheath Gtr Man 87 F5
Broadhembury Devon 11 D6
Broadhempston Devon 7 C6
Broadholme Derbys 76 E3
Broadholme Lincs 77 B8
Broadland Row E Sus 18 D5
Broadlay Carms 32 D4
Broadley Lancs 87 C6
Broadley Moray 152 B3
Broadley Common Essex 41 D7
Broadmayne Dorset 12 F5
Broadmeadows Borders 121 F7
Broadmere Hants 26 E4
Broadmoor Pembs 32 D1
Broadoak Kent 31 C5
Broadrashes Moray 152 C4
Broadsea Aberds 153 B9
Broadstairs Kent 31 C7
Broadstone Poole 13 E8
Broadstone Shrops 60 F5
Broadtown Lane Wilts 25 B5
Broadwas Worcs 50 D2
Broadwater Herts 41 B5
Broadwater W Sus 17 D5
Broadway Carms 32 D3
Broadway Pembs 44 D3
Broadway Som 11 C8
Broadway Suff 57 B7
Broadway Worcs 51 F5
Broadwell Glos 36 C2
Broadwell Glos 38 B2
Broadwell Oxon 38 D2
Broadwell Warks 52 C2
Broadwell House Northumb 110 D2
Broadwey Dorset 12 F4
Broadwindsor Dorset 12 D2
Broadwood Kelly Devon 9 D8
Broadwoodwidger Devon 9 F6
Brobury Hereford 48 E5
Brochel Highld 149 D10
Brochloch Dumfries 113 E5
Brochroy Argyll 125 B6
Brockamin Worcs 50 D2
Brockbridge Hants 15 C7
Brockdam Northumb 117 B7
Brockdish Norf 57 B6
Brockenhurst Hants 14 D4
Brocketsbrae S Lanark 119 F8
Brockford Street Suff 56 C5
Brockhall Northants 52 C4
Brockham Sur 28 E2
Brockhampton Glos 37 B7
Brockhampton Hereford 49 F7
Brockholes W Yorks 88 C2
Brockhurst Derbys 76 C3
Brockhurst Hants 15 D7
Brocklebank Cumb 108 E3
Brocklesby Lincs 90 C5
Brockley N Som 23 C6
Brockley Green Suff 56 D2
Brockleymoor Cumb 108 F4
Brockton Shrops 60 D3
Brockton Shrops 60 F3
Brockton Shrops 61 D7
Brockton Shrops 61 E5
Brockton Telford 61 C7
Brockweir Glos 36 D2
Brockwood Hants 15 B7
Brockworth Glos 37 C5
Brocton Staffs 62 C3
Brodick N Ayrs 143 E11
Brodsworth S Yorks 89 D6
Brogaig Highld 149 B9
Brogborough C Beds 53 F7
Broken Cross Ches E 75 B5
Broken Cross Ches W 74 B3
Brokenborough Wilts 37 F6
Bromborough Mers 85 F4
Brome Suff 56 B5
Brome Street Suff 57 B5
Bromeswell Suff 57 D7
Bromfield Cumb 107 E8
Bromfield Shrops 49 B6
Bromham Bedford 53 D8
Bromham Wilts 24 C4
Bromley London 28 C5
Bromley W Mid 62 F3
Bromley Common London 28 C5
Bromley Green Kent 19 B6
Brompton Medway 29 C8
Brompton N Yorks 102 E1
Brompton N Yorks 103 F7
Brompton-on-Swale N Yorks 101 E7
Brompton Ralph Som 22 F2
Brompton Regis Som 21 F8
Bromsash Hereford 36 B3
Bromsberrow Heath Glos 50 F2
Bromsgrove Worcs 50 B4
Bromyard Hereford 49 D8
Bromyard Downs Hereford 49 D8
Bronaber Gwyn 71 D8
Brongest Ceredig 46 E2
Bronington Wrex 73 F8
Bronllys Powys 48 F3
Bronnant Ceredig 46 C5
Bronwydd Arms Carms 33 B5
Bronydd Powys 48 E4
Bronygarth Shrops 73 F6
Brook Carms 32 D3
Brook Hants 14 B4
Brook Hants 14 C3
Brook IoW 14 F4
Brook Kent 30 E4
Brook Sur 27 E8
Brook Sur 27 F7
Brook End Bedford 53 C8
Brook Hill Hants 14 C3
Brook Street Kent 19 B6
Brook Street Kent 29 E6
Brook Street W Sus 17 B7
Brooke Norf 69 E5
Brooke Rutland 64 D5
Brookenby Lincs 91 E6
Brookend Glos 36 E2
Brookfield Renfs 118 C4
Brookhouse Lancs 92 C5
Brookhouse Green Ches E 74 C5
Brookland Kent 19 C6
Brooklands Dumfries 106 B5
Brooklands Gtr Man 87 E5
Brooklands Shrops 74 E2
Brookmans Park Herts 41 D5
Brooks Powys 59 E8
Brooks Green W Sus 16 B5
Brookthorpe Glos 37 C5
Brookville Norf 67 E7
Brookwood Sur 27 D7
Broom C Beds 54 E2
Broom S Yorks 88 E5
Broom Warks 51 D5
Broom Worcs 50 B4
Broom Green Norf 81 E5
Broom Hill Dorset 13 D8
Broome Norf 69 E6
Broome Shrops 60 F4
Broome Park Northumb 117 C7
Broomedge Warr 86 F5
Broomer's Corner W Sus 16 B5
Broomfield Aberds 153 E9
Broomfield Essex 42 C3
Broomfield Kent 30 D2
Broomfield Kent 31 C5
Broomfield Som 22 F4
Broomfleet E Yorks 90 B2
Broomhall Ches E 74 E3
Broomhall Windsor 27 C7
Broomhaugh Northumb 110 C3
Broomhill Norf 67 D6
Broomhill Northumb 117 D8
Broomhill S Yorks 88 D5
Broomholm Norf 81 D9
Broomley Northumb 110 C3
Broompark Durham 110 E5
Broom's Green Glos 50 F2
Broomy Lodge Hants 14 C3
Brora Highld 157 J12
Broseley Shrops 61 D6
Brotherhouse Bar Lincs 66 C2
Brotherstone Borders 122 F2
Brothertoft Lincs 79 E5
Brotherton N Yorks 89 B5
Brotton Redcar 102 C4
Broubster Highld 157 C13
Brough Cumb 100 C2
Brough Derbys 88 F2
Brough E Yorks 90 B3
Brough Highld 158 C4
Brough Notts 77 D8
Brough Orkney 159 G4
Brough Shetland 160 F6
Brough Shetland 160 F7
Brough Shetland 160 G7
Brough Shetland 160 H6
Brough Shetland 160 J7
Brough Lodge Shetland 160 D7
Brough Sowerby Cumb 100 C2
Broughall Shrops 74 E2
Broughton Borders 120 F4
Broughton Cambs 54 B3
Broughton Flint 73 C7
Broughton Hants 25 F8
Broughton Lancs 92 F5
Broughton M Keynes 53 E6
Broughton N Lincs 90 D3
Broughton N Yorks 94 D2
Broughton N Yorks 96 B3
Broughton Northants 53 B6
Broughton Orkney 159 D5
Broughton Oxon 52 F2
Broughton V Glam 21 B8
Broughton Astley Leics 64 E2
Broughton Beck Cumb 98 F4
Broughton Common Wilts 24 C3
Broughton Gifford Wilts 24 C3
Broughton Hackett Worcs 50 D4
Broughton in Furness Cumb 98 F4
Broughton Mills Cumb 98 E4
Broughton Moor Cumb 107 F7
Broughton Park Gtr Man 87 D6
Broughton Poggs Oxon 38 D2
Broughtown Orkney 159 D7
Broughty Ferry Dundee 134 F4
Browhouses Dumfries 108 C2
Browland Shetland 160 H4
Brown Candover Hants 26 F3
Brown Edge Lancs 85 C4
Brown Edge Staffs 75 D6
Brown Heath Ches W 73 C8
Brownhill Aberds 153 D6
Brownhill Aberds 153 D8
Brownhill Blackburn 93 F6
Brownhill Shrops 60 B4
Brownhills Fife 129 C7
Brownhills W Mid 62 D4
Brownlow Ches E 74 C5
Brownlow Heath Ches E 74 C5
Brownmuir Aberds 135 B7
Brown's End Glos 50 F2
Brownshill Glos 37 D5
Brownston Devon 6 D4
Brownyside Northumb 117 B7
Broxa N Yorks 103 E7
Broxbourne Herts 41 D6
Broxburn E Loth 122 B2
Broxburn W Loth 120 B3
Broxholme Lincs 78 B2
Broxted Essex 42 B1
Broxton Ches W 73 D8
Broxwood Hereford 49 D5
Broyle Side E Sus 17 C8
Brù W Isles 155 C8
Bruairnis W Isles 148 H2
Bruan Highld 158 G5
Bruar Lodge Perth 133 B5
Brucehill W Dunb 118 B3
Bruera Ches W 73 C8
Bruern Abbey Oxon 38 B2
Bruichladdich Argyll 142 B3
Bruisyard Suff 57 C7
Brumby N Lincs 90 D2
Brund Staffs 75 C8
Brundall Norf 69 D6
Brundish Suff 57 C6
Brundish Street Suff 57 B6
Brunery Highld 147 D10
Brunshaw Lancs 93 F8
Brunswick Village T&W 110 B5
Bruntcliffe W Yorks 88 B3
Bruntingthorpe Leics 64 E3
Brunton Fife 128 B5
Brunton Northumb 117 B8
Brunton Wilts 25 D7
Brushford Devon 9 D8
Brushford Som 10 B4
Bruton Som 23 F8
Bryanston Dorset 13 D6
Brydekirk Dumfries 107 B8
Bryher Scilly 2 E3
Brymbo Wrex 73 D6
Brympton Som 12 C3
Bryn Carms 33 D6
Bryn Gtr Man 86 D3
Bryn Neath 34 E2
Bryn Shrops 60 F2
Bryn-coch Neath 33 E8
Bryn Du Anglesey 82 D3
Bryn Gates Gtr Man 86 D3
Bryn-glas Conwy 83 E8
Bryn Golau Rhondda 34 F3
Bryn-Iwan Carms 46 F2
Bryn-mawr Gwyn 70 D3
Bryn-nantllech Conwy 72 C3
Bryn-penarth Powys 59 D8
Bryn Rhyd-yr-Arian Conwy 72 C3
Bryn Saith Marchog Denb 72 D4
Bryn Sion Gwyn 59 C5
Bryn-y-gwenin Mon 35 C7
Bryn-y-maen Conwy 83 D8
Bryn-yr-eryr Gwyn 70 C4
Brynamman Carms 33 C8
Brynberian Pembs 45 F3
Brynbryddan Neath 34 E1
Brynbuga = Usk Mon 35 D7
Bryncae Rhondda 34 F3
Bryncethin Bridgend 34 F3
Bryncir Gwyn 71 C5
Bryncroes Gwyn 70 D3
Bryncrug Gwyn 58 D3
Bryneglwys Denb 72 E5
Brynford Flint 73 B5
Bryngwran Anglesey 82 D3
Bryngwyn Ceredig 45 E4
Bryngwyn Mon 35 D7
Bryngwyn Powys 48 E3
Brynhenllan Pembs 45 F2
Brynhoffnant Ceredig 46 D2
Brynithel Bl Gwent 35 D6
Brynmawr Bl Gwent 35 C5
Brynmenyn Bridgend 34 F3
Brynmill Swansea 33 E7
Brynna Rhondda 34 F3
Brynrefail Anglesey 82 C4
Brynrefail Gwyn 83 E5
Brynsadler Rhondda 34 F4
Brynsiencyn Anglesey 82 E4
Brynteg Anglesey 82 C4
Brynteg Ceredig 46 E3
Buaile nam Bodach W Isles 148 H2
Bualintur Highld 149 F9
Buarthmeini Gwyn 72 F2
Bubbenhall Warks 51 B8
Bubwith E Yorks 96 F3
Buccleuch Borders 115 C6
Buchanhaven Aberds 153 D11
Buchanty Perth 127 B8
Buchlyvie Stirling 126 E4
Buckabank Cumb 108 E3
Buckden Cambs 54 C2
Buckden N Yorks 94 B2
Buckenham Norf 69 D6
Buckerell Devon 11 D6
Buckfast Devon 6 C5
Buckfastleigh Devon 6 C5
Buckhaven Fife 129 E5
Buckholm Borders 121 F7
Buckholt Mon 36 C2
Buckhorn Weston Dorset 13 B5
Buckhurst Hill Essex 41 E7
Buckie Moray 152 B4
Buckies Highld 158 D3
Buckingham Bucks 52 F4
Buckland Bucks 40 C1
Buckland Devon 6 E4
Buckland Glos 51 F5
Buckland Hants 14 E4
Buckland Herts 54 F4
Buckland Kent 31 E7
Buckland Oxon 38 E3
Buckland Sur 28 D3
Buckland Brewer Devon 9 B6
Buckland Common Bucks 40 D2
Buckland Dinham Som 24 D2
Buckland Filleigh Devon 9 D6
Buckland in the Moor Devon 6 B5
Buckland Monachorum Devon 6 C2
Buckland Newton Dorset 12 D4
Buckland St Mary Som 11 C7
Bucklebury W Berks 26 B3
Bucklegate Lincs 79 F6
Bucklerheads Angus 134 F4
Bucklers Hard Hants 14 E5
Bucklesham Suff 57 E6
Buckley = Bwcle Flint 73 C6
Bucklow Hill Ches E 86 F5
Buckminster Leics 65 B5
Bucknall Lincs 78 C4
Bucknall Stoke 75 E6
Bucknell Oxon 39 B5
Bucknell Shrops 49 B5
Buckpool Moray 152 B4
Buck's Cross Devon 8 B5
Bucks Green W Sus 27 F8
Bucks Horn Oak Hants 27 E6
Buck's Mills Devon 9 B5
Bucksburn Aberdeen 141 D7
Buckshaw Village Lancs 86 B3
Buckskin Hants 26 D4
Buckton E Yorks 97 B7
Buckton Hereford 49 B5
Buckton Northumb 123 F6
Buckworth Cambs 54 B2
Budbrooke Warks 51 C7
Budby Notts 77 C6
Budd's Titson Corn 8 D4
Bude Corn 8 D4
Budlake Devon 10 E4
Budle Northumb 123 F7
Budleigh Salterton Devon 11 F5
Budock Water Corn 3 C6
Buerton Ches E 74 E3
Buffler's Holt Bucks 52 F4
Bugbrooke Northants 52 D4
Buglawton Ches E 75 C5
Bugle Corn 4 D5
Bugley Wilts 24 E3
Bugthorpe E Yorks 96 D3
Buildwas Shrops 61 D6
Builth Road Powys 48 D2
Builth Wells = Llanfair-Ym-Muallt Powys 48 D2
Buirgh W Isles 154 H5
Bulby Lincs 65 B7
Bulcote Notts 77 E6
Buldoo Highld 157 C12
Bulford Wilts 25 E6
Bulford Camp Wilts 25 E6
Bulkeley Ches E 74 D2
Bulkington Warks 63 F7
Bulkington Wilts 24 D4
Bulkworthy Devon 9 C5
Bull Hill Hants 14 E4
Bullamoor N Yorks 102 E1
Bullbridge Derbys 76 D3
Bullbrook Brack 27 C6
Bulley Glos 36 C4
Bullgill Cumb 107 F7
Bullington Hants 26 E2
Bullington Lincs 78 B3
Bull's Green Herts 41 C5
Bullwood Argyll 145 F10
Bulmer Essex 56 E2
Bulmer N Yorks 96 C2
Bulmer Tye Essex 56 F2
Bulphan Thurrock 42 F2
Bulverhythe E Sus 18 E4
Bulwark Aberds 153 D9
Bulwell Nottingham 76 E5
Bulwick Northants 65 E6
Bumble's Green Essex 41 D7
Bun a'Mhuillin W Isles 148 G2
Bun Abhainn Eadarra W Isles 154 G6
Bun Loyne Highld 136 D5
Bunacaimb Highld 147 C9
Bunarkaig Highld 136 F4
Bunbury Ches E 74 D2
Bunbury Heath Ches E 74 D2
Bunchrew Highld 151 G9
Bundalloch Highld 149 F13
Buness Shetland 160 C8
Bunessan Argyll 146 J6
Bungay Suff 69 F6
Bunker's Hill Lincs 78 B2
Bunker's Hill Lincs 79 D5
Bunkers Hill Oxon 38 C4
Bunloit Highld 137 B8
Bunnahabhain Argyll 142 A5
Bunny Notts 64 B2
Buntait Highld 150 H6
Buntingford Herts 41 B6
Bunwell Norf 68 E4
Burbage Derbys 75 B7
Burbage Leics 63 E8
Burbage Wilts 25 C7
Burchett's Green Windsor 39 F8
Burcombe Wilts 25 F5
Burcot Oxon 39 E5
Burcott Bucks 40 B1
Burdon T&W 111 D6
Bures Suff 56 F3
Bures Green Suff 56 F3
Burford Ches E 74 D3
Burford Oxon 38 C2
Burford Shrops 49 C7
Burg Argyll 146 G6
Burgar Orkney 159 F4
Burgate Hants 14 C2
Burgate Suff 56 B4
Burgess Hill W Sus 17 C7
Burgh Suff 57 D6
Burgh by Sands Cumb 108 D3
Burgh Castle Norf 69 D7
Burgh Heath Sur 28 D3
Burgh le Marsh Lincs 79 C8
Burgh Muir Aberds 141 B6
Burgh next Aylsham Norf 81 E8
Burgh on Bain Lincs 91 F6
Burgh St Margaret Norf 69 C7
Burgh St Peter Norf 69 E7
Burghclere Hants 26 C2
Burghead Moray 151 E14
Burghfield W Berks 26 C4
Burghfield Common W Berks 26 C4
Burghfield Hill W Berks 26 C4
Burghill Hereford 49 E6
Burghwallis S Yorks 89 C6
Burham Kent 29 C8
Buriton Hants 15 B8
Burland Ches E 74 D3
Burlawn Corn 4 B4
Burleigh Brack 27 C6
Burlescombe Devon 11 C5
Burleston Dorset 13 E5
Burley Hants 14 D3
Burley Rutland 65 C5
Burley W Yorks 95 F5
Burley Gate Hereford 49 E7
Burley in Wharfedale W Yorks 94 E4
Burley Lodge Hants 14 D3
Burley Street Hants 14 D3
Burleydam Ches E 74 E3
Burlingjobb Powys 48 D4
Burlow E Sus 18 D2
Burlton Shrops 60 B4
Burmarsh Kent 19 B7
Burmington Warks 51 F7
Burn N Yorks 89 B6
Burn of Cambus Stirling 127 D6
Burnaston Derbys 76 F2
Burnbank S Lanark 119 D7
Burnby E Yorks 96 E4
Burncross S Yorks 88 E4
Burneside Cumb 99 E7
Burness Orkney 159 D7
Burneston N Yorks 101 F8
Burnett Bath 23 C8
Burnfoot Borders 115 C7
Burnfoot Borders 115 C8
Burnfoot E Ayrs 112 D4
Burnfoot Perth 127 D8
Burnham Bucks 40 F2
Burnham N Lincs 90 C4
Burnham Deepdale Norf 80 C4
Burnham Green Herts 41 C5
Burnham Market Norf 80 C4
Burnham Norton Norf 80 C4
Burnham-on-Crouch Essex 43 E5
Burnham-on-Sea Som 22 E5
Burnham Overy Staithe Norf 80 C4
Burnham Overy Town Norf 80 C4
Burnham Thorpe Norf 80 C4
Burnhead Dumfries 113 E8
Burnhead S Ayrs 112 D2
Burnhervie Aberds 141 C6
Burnhill Green Staffs 61 D7
Burnhope Durham 110 E4
Burnhouse N Ayrs 118 D3
Burniston N Yorks 103 E8
Burnlee W Yorks 88 D2
Burnley Lancs 93 F8
Burnley Lane Lancs 93 F8
Burnmouth Borders 123 C5
Burnopfield Durham 110 D4
Burnsall N Yorks 94 C3
Burnside Angus 135 D5
Burnside E Ayrs 113 C5
Burnside Fife 128 D3
Burnside S Lanark 119 C6
Burnside Shetland 160 F4
Burnside W Loth 120 B3
Burnside of Duntrune Angus 134 F4
Burnswark Dumfries 107 B8
Burnt Heath Derbys 76 B2
Burnt Houses Durham 101 B6
Burnt Yates N Yorks 95 C5
Burntcommon Sur 27 D8
Burnthouse Corn 3 C6
Burntisland Fife 128 F4
Burnton E Ayrs 112 D4
Burntwood Staffs 62 D4
Burnwynd Edin 120 C4
Burpham Sur 27 D8
Burpham W Sus 16 D4
Burradon Northumb 117 D5
Burradon T&W 111 B5
Burrafirth Shetland 160 B8
Burraland Shetland 160 F5
Burraland Shetland 160 J4
Burras Corn 3 C5
Burravoe Shetland 160 F7
Burravoe Shetland 160 G5
Burray Village Orkney 159 J5
Burrells Cumb 100 C1
Burrelton Perth 134 F2
Burridge Devon 20 F4
Burridge Hants 15 C6
Burrill N Yorks 101 F7
Burringham N Lincs 90 D2
Burrington Devon 9 C8
Burrington Hereford 49 B6
Burrington N Som 23 D6
Burrough Green Cambs 55 D7
Burrough on the Hill Leics 64 C4
Burrow-bridge Som 11 B8
Burrowhill Sur 27 C7
Burry Swansea 33 E5
Burry Green Swansea 33 E5
Burry Port = Porth Tywyn Carms 33 D5
Burscough Lancs 86 C2
Burscough Bridge Lancs 86 C2
Bursea E Yorks 96 F4
Burshill E Yorks 97 E6
Bursledon Hants 15 D5
Burslem Stoke 75 E5
Burstall Suff 56 E4
Burstock Dorset 12 D2
Burston Norf 68 F4
Burston Staffs 75 F6
Burstow Sur 28 E4
Burstwick E Yorks 91 B6
Burtersett N Yorks 100 F3
Burtle Som 23 E5
Burton Ches W 73 B7
Burton Ches W 74 C2
Burton Dorset 14 E2
Burton Lincs 78 B2
Burton Northumb 123 F7
Burton Pembs 44 E4
Burton Som 22 E3
Burton Wilts 24 B3
Burton Agnes E Yorks 97 C7
Burton Bradstock Dorset 12 F2
Burton Dassett Warks 51 D8
Burton Fleming E Yorks 97 B6
Burton Green W Mid 51 B7
Burton Green Wrex 73 D7
Burton Hastings Warks 63 E8
Burton-in-Kendal Cumb 92 B5
Burton in Lonsdale N Yorks 93 B6
Burton Joyce Notts 77 E6
Burton Latimer Northants 53 B7
Burton Lazars Leics 64 C4
Burton-le-Coggles Lincs 65 B6
Burton Leonard N Yorks 95 C6
Burton on the Wolds Leics 64 B2
Burton Overy Leics 64 E3
Burton Pedwardine Lincs 78 E4
Burton Pidsea E Yorks 97 F8
Burton Salmon N Yorks 89 B5
Burton Stather N Lincs 90 C2
Burton upon Stather N Lincs 90 C2
Burton upon Trent Staffs 63 B6
Burtonwood Warr 86 E3
Burwardsley Ches W 74 D2
Burwarton Shrops 61 F6
Burwash E Sus 18 C3
Burwash Common E Sus 18 C3
Burwash Weald E Sus 18 C3
Burwell Cambs 55 C6
Burwell Lincs 79 B6
Burwen Anglesey 82 B4
Burwick Orkney 159 K5
Bury Cambs 66 F2
Bury Gtr Man 87 C6
Bury Som 10 B4
Bury W Sus 16 C4
Bury Green Herts 41 B7
Bury St Edmunds Suff 56 C2
Burythorpe N Yorks 96 C3
Busby E Renf 119 D5
Buscot Oxon 38 E2
Bush Bank Hereford 49 D6
Bush Crathie Aberds 139 E8
Bush Green Norf 68 F5
Bushbury W Mid 62 D3
Bushby Leics 64 D3
Bushey Herts 40 E4
Bushey Heath Herts 40 E4
Bushley Worcs 50 F3
Bushton Wilts 25 B5
Buslingthorpe Lincs 90 F4
Busta Shetland 160 G5
Butcher's Cross E Sus 18 C2
Butcombe N Som 23 C7
Butetown Cardiff 22 B3
Butleigh Som 23 F7
Butleigh Wootton Som 23 F7
Butler's Cross Bucks 39 D8
Butler's End Warks 63 F6
Butlers Marston Warks 51 E8
Butley Suff 57 D7
Butley High Corner Suff 57 E7
Butt Green Ches E 74 D3
Butterburn Cumb 109 B6
Buttercrambe N Yorks 96 D3
Butterknowle Durham 101 B6
Butterleigh Devon 10 D4
Buttermere Cumb 98 C3
Buttermere Wilts 25 C8
Buttershaw W Yorks 88 B2
Butterstone Perth 133 E7
Butterton Staffs 75 D7
Butterwick Durham 102 B1
Butterwick Lincs 79 E6
Butterwick N Yorks 96 B3
Butterwick N Yorks 97 B5
Buttington Powys 60 D2
Buttonoak Worcs 50 B2
Butt's Green Hants 14 B4
Buttsash Hants 14 D5
Buxhall Suff 56 D4
Buxhall Fen Street Suff 56 D4
Buxley Borders 122 D4
Buxted E Sus 17 B8
Buxton Derbys 75 B7

Buxton Norf 81 E8
Buxworth Derbys 87 F8
Bwcle = Buckley Flint 73 C6
Bwlch Powys 35 B5
Bwlch-Llan Ceredig 46 D4
Bwlch-y-cibau Powys 59 C8
Bwlch-y-fadfa Ceredig 46 E3
Bwlch-y-ffridd Powys 59 E7
Bwlch-y-sarnau Powys 48 B2
Bwlchgwyn Wrex 73 D6
Bwlchnewydd Carms 32 B4
Bwlchtocyn Gwyn 70 E4
Bwlchyddar Powys 59 B8
Bwlchygroes Pembs 45 F4
Byermoor T&W 110 D4
Byers Green Durham 110 F5
Byfield Northants 52 D3
Byfleet Sur 27 C8
Byford Hereford 49 E5
Bygrave Herts 54 F3
Byker T&W 111 C5
Bylchau Conwy 72 C3
Byley Ches W 74 C4
Bynea Carms 33 E6
Byrness Northumb 116 D3
Bythorn Cambs 53 B8
Byton Hereford 49 C5
Byworth W Sus 16 B3

C

Cabharstadh W Isles 155 E8
Cablea Perth 133 F6
Cabourne Lincs 90 D5
Cabrach Argyll 144 G3
Cabrach Moray 140 B2
Cabrich Highld 151 G8
Cabus Lancs 92 E4
Cackle Street E Sus 17 B8
Cadbury Devon 10 D4
Cadbury Barton Devon 9 C8
Cadder E Dunb 119 B6
Caddington C Beds 40 C3
Caddonfoot Borders 121 F7
Cade Street E Sus 18 C3
Cadeby Leics 63 D8
Cadeby S Yorks 89 D6
Cadeleigh Devon 10 D4
Cadgwith Corn 3 E6
Cadham Fife 128 D4
Cadishead Gtr Man 86 E5
Cadle Swansea 33 E7
Cadley Lancs 92 F5
Cadley Wilts 25 C7
Cadley Wilts 25 D7
Cadmore End Bucks 39 E7
Cadnam Hants 14 C3
Cadney N Lincs 90 D4
Cadole Flint 73 C6
Cadoxton V Glam 22 C3
Cadoxton-Juxta-Neath Neath 34 E1
Cadshaw Blackburn 86 C5
Cadzow S Lanark 119 D7
Caeathro Gwyn 82 E4
Caehopkin Powys 34 C2
Caenby Lincs 90 F4
Caenby Corner Lincs 90 F3
Caér-bryn Carms 33 C6
Caer Llan Mon 36 D1
Caerau Bridgend 34 E2
Caerau Cardiff 22 B3
Caerdeon Gwyn 58 C3
Caerdydd = Cardiff Cardiff 22 B3
Caerfarchell Pembs 44 C2
Caerffili = Caerphilly Caerph 35 F5
Caerfyrddin = Carmarthen Carms 33 B5
Caergeiliog Anglesey 82 D3
Caergwrle Flint 73 D7
Caergybi = Holyhead Anglesey 82 C2
Caerleon = Caerllion Newport 35 E7
Caerllion = Caerleon Newport 35 E7
Caernarfon Gwyn 82 E4
Caerphilly = Caerffili Caerph 35 F5
Caersws Powys 59 E7
Caerwedros Ceredig 46 D2
Caerwent Mon 36 E1
Caerwych Gwyn 71 D7
Caerwys Flint 72 B5
Caethle Gwyn 58 E3
Caim Anglesey 83 C6
Caio Carms 47 F5
Cairinis W Isles 148 B3
Cairisiadar W Isles 154 D5
Cairminis W Isles 154 J5
Cairnbaan Argyll 145 D7
Cairnbanno Ho. Aberds 153 D8
Cairnborrow Aberds 152 D4
Cairnbrogie Aberds 141 B7
Cairnbulg Castle Aberds 153 B10
Cairncross Angus 134 B4
Cairncross Borders 122 C4
Cairndow Argyll 125 D7
Cairness Aberds 153 B10
Cairneyhill Fife 128 F2
Cairnfield Ho. Moray 152 B4
Cairngaan Dumfries 104 F5
Cairngarroch Dumfries 104 E4
Cairnhill Aberds 153 E6
Cairnie Aberds 141 D7
Cairnie Aberds 152 D4
Cairnorrie Aberds 153 D8
Cairnpark Aberds 141 C7
Cairnryan Dumfries 104 C4
Cairnton Orkney 159 H4
Caister-on-Sea Norf 69 C8
Caistor Lincs 90 D5
Caistor St Edmund Norf 68 D5
Caistron Northumb 117 D5
Caitha Bowland Borders 121 E7
Calais Street Suff 56 F3
Calanais W Isles 154 D7
Calbost W Isles 155 F9
Calbourne IoW 14 F5
Calceby Lincs 79 B6
Calcot Row W Berks 26 B4
Calcott Kent 31 C5
Caldback Shetland 160 C8
Caldbeck Cumb 108 F3
Caldbergh N Yorks 101 F5
Caldecote Cambs 54 D4
Caldecote Cambs 65 F8
Caldecote Herts 54 F3
Caldecote Northants 52 D4
Caldecott Northants 53 C7
Caldecott Oxon 38 E4
Caldecott Rutland 65 E5
Calder Bridge Cumb 98 D2
Calder Hall Cumb 98 D2
Calder Mains Highld 158 E2
Calder Vale Lancs 92 E5
Calderbank N Lanark 119 C7
Calderbrook Gtr Man 87 C7
Caldercruix N Lanark 119 C8
Caldermill S Lanark 119 E6
Calderwood S Lanark 119 D6
Caldhame Angus 134 E4
Caldicot Mon 36 F1
Caldwell Derbys 63 C6
Caldwell N Yorks 101 C6
Caldy Mers 85 F3
Caledrhydiau Ceredig 46 D3
Calfsound Orkney 159 E6
Calgary Argyll 146 F6
Califer Moray 151 F13
California Falk 120 B2
California Norf 69 C8
Calke Derbys 63 B7
Callakille Highld 149 C11
Callaly Northumb 117 D6
Callander Stirling 126 D5
Callaughton Shrops 61 E6
Callestick Corn 4 D2
Calligarry Highld 149 H11
Callington Corn 5 C8
Callow Hereford 49 F6
Callow End Worcs 50 E3
Callow Hill Wilts 37 F7
Callow Hill Worcs 50 B2
Callows Grave Worcs 49 C7
Calmore Hants 14 C4
Calmsden Glos 37 D7
Calne Wilts 24 B5
Calow Derbys 76 B4
Calshot Hants 15 D5
Calstock Corn 6 C2
Calstone Wellington Wilts 24 C5
Calthorpe Norf 81 D7
Calthwaite Cumb 108 E4
Calton N Yorks 94 D2
Calton Staffs 75 D8
Calveley Ches E 74 D2
Calver Derbys 76 B2
Calver Hill Hereford 49 E5
Calverhall Shrops 74 F3
Calverleigh Devon 10 C4
Calverley W Yorks 94 F5
Calvert Bucks 39 B6
Calverton M Keynes 53 F5
Calverton Notts 77 E6
Calvine Perth 133 C5
Calvo Cumb 107 D8
Cam Glos 36 E4
Camas-luinie Highld 136 B2
Camasnacroise Highld 130 D2
Camastianavaig Highld 149 E10
Camasunary Highld 149 G10
Camault Muir Highld 151 G8
Camb Shetland 160 D7
Camber E Sus 19 D6
Camberley Sur 27 C6
Camberwell London 28 B4
Camblesforth N Yorks 89 B7
Cambo Northumb 117 F6
Cambois Northumb 117 F9
Camborne Corn 3 B5
Cambourne Cambs 54 D4
Cambridge Cambs 55 D5
Cambridge Glos 36 D4
Cambridge Town Southend 43 F5
Cambus Clack 127 E7
Cambusavie Farm Highld 151 B10
Cambusbarron Stirling 127 E6
Cambuskenneth Stirling 127 E7
Cambuslang S Lanark 119 C6
Cambusmore Lodge Highld 151 B10
Camden London 41 F5
Camelford Corn 8 F3
Camelsdale Sur 27 F6
Camerory Highld 151 H13
Camer's Green Worcs 50 F2
Camerton Bath 23 D8
Camerton Cumb 107 F7
Camerton E Yorks 91 B6
Camghouran Perth 132 D2
Cammachmore Aberds 141 E8
Cammeringham Lincs 90 F3
Camore Highld 151 B10
Camp Hill Warks 63 E7
Campbeltown Argyll 143 F8
Camperdown T&W 111 B5
Campmuir Perth 134 F2
Campsall S Yorks 89 C6
Campsey Ash Suff 57 D7
Campton C Beds 54 F2
Camptown Borders 116 C2
Camrose Pembs 44 C4
Camserney Perth 133 E5
Camster Highld 158 F4
Camuschoirk Highld 130 C1
Camuscross Highld 149 G11
Camusnagaul Highld 130 B4
Camusnagaul Highld 150 C3
Camusrory Highld 147 B11
Camusteel Highld 149 D12
Camusterrach Highld 149 D12
Camusvrachan Perth 132 E3
Canada Hants 14 C3
Canadia E Sus 18 D4
Canal Side S Yorks 89 C7
Candacraig Ho. Aberds 140 C2
Candlesby Lincs 79 C7
Candy Mill S Lanark 120 E3
Cane End Oxon 26 B4
Canewdon Essex 42 E4
Canford Bottom Dorset 13 D8
Canford Cliffs Poole 13 F8
Canford Magna Poole 13 E8
Canham's Green Suff 56 C4
Canholes Derbys 75 B7
Canisbay Highld 158 C5
Cann Dorset 13 B6
Cann Common Dorset 13 B6
Cannard's Grave Som 23 E8
Cannich Highld 150 H6
Cannington Som 22 F4
Cannock Staffs 62 D3
Cannock Wood Staffs 62 C4
Canon Bridge Hereford 49 E6
Canon Frome Hereford 49 E8
Canon Pyon Hereford 49 E6
Canonbie Dumfries 108 B3
Canons Ashby Northants 52 D3
Canonstown Corn 2 C4
Canterbury Kent 30 D5
Cantley Norf 69 D6
Cantley S Yorks 89 D7
Cantlop Shrops 60 D5
Canton Cardiff 22 B3
Cantraybruich Highld 151 G10
Cantraydoune Highld 151 G10
Cantraywood Highld 151 G10
Cantsfield Lancs 93 B6
Canvey Island Essex 42 F3
Canwick Lincs 78 C2
Canworthy Water Corn 8 E4
Caol Highld 131 B5
Caol Ila Argyll 142 A5
Caolas Argyll 146 G3
Caolas Scalpaigh W Isles 154 H7
Caolas Stocinis W Isles 154 H6
Capel Sur 28 E2
Capel Bangor Ceredig 58 F3
Capel Betws Lleucu Ceredig 46 D5
Capel Carmel Gwyn 70 E2
Capel Coch Anglesey 82 C4
Capel Curig Conwy 83 F7
Capel Cynon Ceredig 46 E2
Capel Dewi Carms 33 B5
Capel Dewi Ceredig 46 E3
Capel Dewi Ceredig 58 F3
Capel Garmon Conwy 83 F8
Capel-gwyn Anglesey 82 D3
Capel Gwyn Carms 33 B5
Capel Gwynfe Carms 33 B8
Capel Hendre Carms 33 C6
Capel Hermon Gwyn 71 E8
Capel Isaac Carms 33 B6
Capel Iwan Carms 45 F4
Capel le Ferne Kent 31 F6
Capel Llanilltern Cardiff 34 F4
Capel Mawr Anglesey 82 D4
Capel St Andrew Suff 57 E7
Capel St Mary Suff 56 F4
Capel Seion Ceredig 46 B5
Capel Tygwydd Ceredig 45 E4
Capel Uchaf Gwyn 70 C5
Capel-y-graig Gwyn 82 E5
Capelulo Conwy 83 D7
Capenhurst Ches W 73 B7
Capernwray Lancs 92 B5
Capheaton Northumb 117 F6
Cappercleuch Borders 115 B5
Capplegill Dumfries 114 D4
Capton Devon 7 D6
Caputh Perth 133 F7
Car Colston Notts 77 E7
Carbis Bay Corn 2 C4
Carbost Highld 149 D9
Carbost Highld 149 E8
Carbrook S Yorks 88 F4
Carbrooke Norf 68 D2
Carburton Notts 77 B6
Carcant Borders 121 D6
Carcary Angus 135 D6
Carclaze Corn 4 D5
Carcroft S Yorks 89 C6
Cardenden Fife 128 E4
Cardeston Shrops 60 C3
Cardiff = Caerdydd Cardiff 22 B3
Cardigan = Aberteifi Ceredig 45 E3
Cardington Bedford 53 E8
Cardington Shrops 60 E5
Cardinham Corn 5 C6
Cardonald Glasgow 118 C5
Cardow Moray 152 D1
Cardrona Borders 121 F6
Cardross Argyll 118 B3
Cardurnock Cumb 107 D8
Careby Lincs 65 C7
Careston Castle Angus 135 D5
Carew Pembs 32 D1
Carew Cheriton Pembs 32 D1
Carew Newton Pembs 32 D1
Carey Hereford 49 F7
Carfrae E Loth 121 C8
Cargenbridge Dumfries 107 B6
Cargill Perth 134 F1
Cargo Cumb 108 D3
Cargreen Corn 6 C2
Carham Northumb 122 F4
Carhampton Som 22 E2
Carharrack Corn 3 B6
Carie Perth 132 D3
Carie Perth 132 F3
Carines Corn 4 D2
Carisbrooke IoW 15 F5
Cark Cumb 92 B3
Carlabhagh W Isles 154 C7
Carland Cross Corn 4 D3
Carlby Lincs 65 C7
Carlecotes S Yorks 88 D2
Carlesmoor N Yorks 94 B4
Carleton Cumb 99 B7
Carleton Cumb 108 D4
Carleton Lancs 92 F3
Carleton N Yorks 94 E2
Carleton Forehoe Norf 68 D3
Carleton Rode Norf 68 E4
Carlin How Redcar 103 C5
Carlingcott Bath 23 D8
Carlisle Cumb 108 D4
Carlops Borders 120 D4
Carlton Bedford 53 D7
Carlton Cambs 55 D7
Carlton Leics 63 D7
Carlton N Yorks 89 B7
Carlton N Yorks 101 C6
Carlton N Yorks 101 F5
Carlton N Yorks 102 F4
Carlton Notts 77 E6
Carlton S Yorks 88 C4
Carlton Stockton 102 B1
Carlton Suff 57 C7
Carlton W Yorks 88 B4
Carlton Colville Suff 69 F8
Carlton Curlieu Leics 64 E3
Carlton Husthwaite N Yorks 95 B7
Carlton in Cleveland N Yorks 102 D3
Carlton in Lindrick Notts 89 F6
Carlton le Moorland Lincs 78 D2
Carlton Miniott N Yorks 102 F1
Carlton on Trent Notts 77 C7
Carlton Scroop Lincs 78 E2
Carluke S Lanark 119 D8
Carmarthen = Caerfyrddin Carms 33 B5
Carmel Anglesey 82 C3
Carmel Carms 33 C6
Carmel Flint 73 B5
Carmel Guern 16
Carmel Gwyn 82 F4
Carmont Aberds 141 F7
Carmunnock Glasgow 119 D6
Carmyle Glasgow 119 C6
Carmyllie Angus 135 E5
Carn-gorm Highld 136 B2
Carnaby E Yorks 97 C7
Carnach Highld 136 B3
Carnach Highld 150 B3
Carnach W Isles 154 H7
Carnachy Highld 157 D10
Càrnais W Isles 154 D5
Carnbee Fife 129 D7
Carnbo Perth 128 D2
Carnbrea Corn 3 B5
Carnduff S Lanark 119 E6
Carnduncan Argyll 142 B3
Carne Corn 3 C8
Carnforth Lancs 92 B4
Carnhedryn Pembs 44 C3
Carnhell Green Corn 2 C5
Carnkie Corn 3 C5
Carnkie Corn 3 C6
Carno Powys 59 E6
Carnoch Highld 150 F5
Carnoch Highld 150 H6
Carnock Fife 128 F2
Carnon Downs Corn 3 B6
Carnousie Aberds 153 C6
Carnoustie Angus 135 F5
Carnwath S Lanark 120 E2
Carnyorth Corn 2 C2
Carperby N Yorks 101 F5
Carpley Green N Yorks 100 F4
Carr S Yorks 89 E6
Carr Hill T&W 111 C5
Carradale Argyll 143 E9
Carragraich W Isles 154 H6
Carrbridge Highld 138 B5
Carrefour Selous Jersey 17
Carreg-wen Pembs 45 E4
Carreglefn Anglesey 82 C3
Carrick Argyll 145 E8
Carrick Fife 129 B6
Carrick Castle Argyll 145 D10
Carrick Ho. Orkney 159 E6
Carriden Falk 128 F2
Carrington Gtr Man 86 E5
Carrington Lincs 79 D6
Carrington Midloth 121 C6
Carrog Conwy 71 C8
Carrog Denb 72 E5
Carron Falk 127 F7
Carron Moray 152 D2
Carron Bridge Stirling 127 F6
Carronbridge Dumfries 113 E8
Carronshore Falk 127 F7
Carrshield Northumb 109 E8
Carrutherstown Dumfries 107 B8
Carrville Durham 111 E6
Carsaig Argyll 144 E6
Carsaig Argyll 147 J8
Carscreugh Dumfries 105 D6
Carse Gray Angus 134 D4
Carse Ho. Argyll 144 G6
Carsegowan Dumfries 105 D8
Carseriggan Dumfries 105 C7
Carsethorn Dumfries 107 D6
Carshalton London 28 C3
Carsington Derbys 76 D2
Carskiey Argyll 143 H7
Carsluith Dumfries 105 D8
Carsphairn Dumfries 113 E5
Carstairs S Lanark 120 E2
Carstairs Junction S Lanark 120 E2
Carswell Marsh Oxon 38 E3
Carter's Clay Hants 14 B4
Carterton Oxon 38 D2
Carterway Heads Northumb 110 D3
Carthew Corn 4 D5
Carthorpe N Yorks 101 F8
Cartington Northumb 117 D6
Cartland S Lanark 119 E8
Cartmel Cumb 92 B3
Cartmel Fell Cumb 99 F6
Carway Carms 33 D5
Cary Fitzpaine Som 12 B3
Cas-gwent = Chepstow Mon 36 E2
Cascob Powys 48 C4
Cashlie Perth 132 E1
Cashmoor Dorset 13 C7
Casnewydd = Newport Newport 35 F7
Cassey Compton Glos 37 C7
Cassington Oxon 38 C4
Cassop Durham 111 F6
Castell Denb 72 C5
Castell-Howell Ceredig 46 E3
Castell-Nedd = Neath Neath 33 E8
Castell Newydd Emlyn = Newcastle Emlyn Carms 46 E2
Castell-y-bwch Torf 35 E6
Castellau Rhondda 34 F4
Casterton Cumb 93 B6
Castle Acre Norf 67 C8
Castle Ashby Northants 53 D6
Castle Bolton N Yorks 101 E5
Castle Bromwich W Mid 62 F5
Castle Bytham Lincs 65 C6
Castle Caereinion Powys 59 D8
Castle Camps Cambs 55 E7
Castle Carrock Cumb 108 D5
Castle Cary Som 23 F8
Castle Combe Wilts 24 B3
Castle Donington Leics 63 B8
Castle Douglas Dumfries 106 C4
Castle Eaton Swindon 37 E8
Castle Eden Durham 111 F7
Castle Forbes Aberds 140 C5
Castle Frome Hereford 49 E8
Castle Green Sur 27 C7
Castle Gresley Derbys 63 C6
Castle Heaton Northumb 122 E5
Castle Hedingham Essex 55 F8
Castle Hill Kent 29 E7
Castle Huntly Perth 128 B5
Castle Kennedy Dumfries 104 D5
Castle O'er Dumfries 115 E5
Castle Pulverbatch Shrops 60 D4
Castle Rising Norf 67 B6
Castle Stuart Highld 151 G10
Castlebay = Bagh a Chaisteil W Isles 148 J1
Castlebythe Pembs 32 B1
Castlecary N Lanark 119 B7
Castlecraig Highld 151 E11
Castlefairn Dumfries 113 F7
Castleford W Yorks 88 B5
Castlehill Borders 120 F5
Castlehill Highld 158 D3
Castlehill W Dunb 118 B3
Castlemaddy Dumfries 113 F5
Castlemartin Pembs 44 F4
Castlemilk Dumfries 107 B8
Castlemilk Glasgow 119 D6
Castlemorris Pembs 44 B4
Castlemorton Worcs 50 F2
Castleside Durham 110 E3
Castlethorpe M Keynes 53 E6
Castleton Angus 134 E3
Castleton Argyll 145 E7
Castleton Derbys 88 F2
Castleton Gtr Man 87 C6
Castleton N Yorks 102 D4
Castleton Newport 35 F6
Castletown Ches W 73 D8
Castletown Highld 151 G10
Castletown Highld 158 D3
Castletown IoM 84 F2
Castletown T&W 111 D6
Castleweary Borders 115 D7
Castley N Yorks 95 E5
Caston Norf 68 E2
Castor Pboro 65 E8
Catacol N Ayrs 143 D10
Catbrain S Glos 36 F2
Catbrook Mon 36 D2
Catchall Corn 2 D3
Catchems Corner W Mid 51 B7
Catchgate Durham 110 D4
Catcleugh Northumb 116 D3
Catcliffe S Yorks 88 F5
Catcott Som 23 F5
Caterham Sur 28 D4
Catfield Norf 69 B6
Catfirth Shetland 160 H6
Catford London 28 B4
Catforth Lancs 92 F4
Cathays Cardiff 22 B3
Cathcart Glasgow 119 C5
Cathedine Powys 35 B5
Catherington Hants 15 C7
Catherton Shrops 49 B8
Catlodge Highld 138 E2
Catlowdy Cumb 108 B4
Catmore W Berks 38 F4
Caton Lancs 92 C5
Caton Green Lancs 92 C5
Catrine E Ayrs 113 B5
Cat's Ash Newport 35 E7
Catsfield E Sus 18 D4
Catshill Worcs 50 B4
Cattal N Yorks 95 D7
Cattawade Suff 56 F5
Catterall Lancs 92 E4
Catterick N Yorks 101 E7
Catterick Bridge N Yorks 101 E7
Catterick Garrison N Yorks 101 E6
Catterlen Cumb 108 F4
Catterline Aberds 135 B8
Catterton N Yorks 95 E8
Catthorpe Leics 52 B3
Cattistock Dorset 12 E3
Catton N Yorks 95 B6
Catton Northumb 109 D8
Catwick E Yorks 97 E7
Catworth Cambs 53 B8
Caudlesprings Norf 68 D2
Caulcott Oxon 39 B5
Cauldcots Angus 135 E6
Cauldhame Stirling 126 E5
Cauldmill Borders 115 C8
Cauldon Staffs 75 E7
Caulkerbush Dumfries 107 D6
Caulside Dumfries 115 F7
Caunsall Worcs 62 F2
Caunton Notts 77 D7
Causeway End Dumfries 105 C8
Causeway Foot W Yorks 94 F3
Causeway-head Stirling 127 E6
Causewayend S Lanark 120 F3
Causewayhead Cumb 107 D8
Causey Park Bridge Northumb 117 E7
Causeyend Aberds 141 C8
Cautley Cumb 100 E1
Cavendish Suff 56 E2
Cavendish Bridge Leics 63 B8
Cavenham Suff 55 C8
Caversfield Oxon 39 B5
Caversham Reading 26 B5
Caverswall Staffs 75 E6
Cavil E Yorks 96 F3
Cawdor Highld 151 F11
Cawkwell Lincs 79 B5
Cawood N Yorks 95 F8
Cawsand Corn 6 D2
Cawston Norf 81 E7
Cawthorne S Yorks 88 D3
Cawthorpe Lincs 65 B7
Cawton N Yorks 96 B2
Caxton Cambs 54 D4
Caynham Shrops 49 B7
Caythorpe Lincs 78 E2
Caythorpe Notts 77 E6
Cayton N Yorks 103 F8
Ceann a Bhaigh W Isles 148 B2
Ceann a Deas Loch Baghasdail W Isles 148 G2
Ceann Shiphoirt W Isles 155 F7
Ceann Tarabhaigh W Isles 154 F7
Ceannacroc Lodge Highld 136 C5
Cearsiadair W Isles 155 E8
Cefn Berain Conwy 72 C3
Cefn-brith Conwy 72 D3
Cefn Canol Powys 73 F6
Cefn-coch Conwy 83 E8
Cefn Coch Powys 59 B8
Cefn-coed-y-cymmer M Tydf 34 D4
Cefn Cribbwr Bridgend 34 F2
Cefn Cross Bridgend 34 F2
Cefn-ddwysarn Gwyn 72 F3
Cefn Einion Shrops 60 F2
Cefn-gorwydd Powys 47 E8
Cefn-mawr Wrex 73 E6
Cefn-y-bedd Flint 73 D7
Cefn-y-pant Carms 32 B2
Cefneithin Carms 33 C6
Cei-bach Ceredig 46 D3
Ceinewydd = New Quay Ceredig 46 D2
Ceint Anglesey 82 D4
Cellan Ceredig 46 E5
Cellarhead Staffs 75 E6
Cemaes Anglesey 82 B3
Cemmaes Powys 58 D5
Cemmaes Road Powys 58 D5
Cenarth Carms 45 E4
Cenin Gwyn 71 C5
Central Invclyd 118 B2
Ceos W Isles 155 E8
Ceres Fife 129 C6
Cerne Abbas Dorset 12 D4
Cerney Wick Glos 37 E7
Cerrigceinwen Anglesey 82 D4
Cerrigydrudion Conwy 72 E3
Cessford Borders 116 B3
Ceunant Gwyn 82 E5
Chaceley Glos 50 F3
Chacewater Corn 3 B6
Chackmore Bucks 52 F4
Chacombe Northants 52 E2
Chad Valley W Mid 62 F4
Chadderton Gtr Man 87 D7
Chadderton Fold Gtr Man 87 D6
Chaddesden Derby 76 F3
Chaddesley Corbett Worcs 50 B3
Chaddleworth W Berks 26 B2
Chadlington Oxon 38 B3
Chadshunt Warks 51 D8
Chadwell Leics 64 B4
Chadwell St Mary Thurrock 29 B7
Chadwick End W Mid 51 B7
Chadwick Green Mers 86 E3
Chaffcombe Som 11 C8
Chagford Devon 10 F2
Chailey E Sus 17 C7
Chain Bridge Lincs 79 E6
Chainbridge Cambs 66 D4
Chainhurst Kent 29 E8
Chalbury Dorset 13 D8
Chalbury Common Dorset 13 D8
Chaldon Sur 28 D4
Chaldon Herring Dorset 13 F5
Chale IoW 15 G5
Chale Green IoW 15 G5
Chalfont Common Bucks 40 E3
Chalfont St Giles Bucks 40 E2
Chalfont St Peter Bucks 40 E3
Chalford Glos 37 D5
Chalgrove Oxon 39 E6
Chalk Kent 29 B7
Challacombe Devon 21 E5
Challoch Dumfries 105 C7
Challock Kent 30 D4
Chalton C Beds 40 B3
Chalton Hants 15 C8
Chalvington E Sus 18 E2
Chancery Ceredig 46 B4
Chandler's Ford Hants 14 B5
Channel Tunnel Kent 19 B8
Channerwick Shetland 160 L6
Chantry Som 24 E2
Chantry Suff 56 E5
Chapel Fife 128 E4
Chapel Allerton Som 23 D6
Chapel Allerton W Yorks 95 F6
Chapel Amble Corn 4 B4
Chapel Brampton Northants 52 C5
Chapel Chorlton Staffs 74 F5
Chapel-en-le-Frith Derbys 87 F8
Chapel End Warks 63 E7
Chapel Green Warks 52 C2
Chapel Green Warks 63 F6
Chapel Haddlesey N Yorks 89 B6
Chapel Head Cambs 66 F3
Chapel Hill Aberds 153 E10
Chapel Hill Lincs 78 D5
Chapel Hill Mon 36 E2
Chapel Hill N Yorks 95 E6
Chapel Lawn Shrops 48 B5
Chapel-le-Dale N Yorks 93 B7
Chapel Milton Derbys 87 F8
Chapel of Garioch Aberds 141 B6
Chapel Row W Berks 26 C3
Chapel St Leonards Lincs 79 B8
Chapel Stile Cumb 99 D5
Chapelgate Lincs 66 B4
Chapelhall N Lanark 119 C7
Chapelhill Dumfries 114 E3
Chapelhill Highld 151 D11
Chapelhill N Ayrs 118 E2
Chapelhill Perth 128 B4
Chapelhill Perth 133 F7
Chapelknowe Dumfries 108 B3
Chapelton Angus 135 E6
Chapelton Devon 9 B7
Chapelton Highld 138 C5
Chapelton S Lanark 119 E6
Chapeltown Blackburn 86 C5
Chapeltown Moray 139 B8
Chapeltown S Yorks 88 E4
Chapmans Well Devon 9 E5
Chapmanslade Wilts 24 E3
Chapmore End Herts 41 C6
Chappel Essex 42 B4
Chard Som 11 D8
Chardstock Devon 11 D8
Charfield S Glos 36 E4
Charford Worcs 50 C4
Charing Kent 30 E3
Charing Cross Dorset 14 C2
Charing Heath Kent 30 E3
Charingworth Glos 51 F7
Charlbury Oxon 38 C3
Charlcombe Bath 24 C2
Charlecote Warks 51 D7
Charles Devon 21 F5
Charles Tye Suff 56 D4
Charlesfield Dumfries 107 C8
Charleston Angus 134 E3
Charleston Renfs 118 C4
Charlestown Aberdeen 141 D8
Charlestown Corn 4 D5
Charlestown Derbys 87 E8
Charlestown Dorset 12 G4
Charlestown Fife 128 F2
Charlestown Gtr Man 87 D6
Charlestown Highld 149 A13
Charlestown Highld 151 G9
Charlestown W Yorks 87 B7
Charlestown of Aberlour Moray 152 D2
Charlesworth Derbys 87 E8
Charleton Devon 7 E5
Charlton Hants 25 E8
Charlton Herts 40 B4
Charlton London 28 B5
Charlton Northants 52 F3
Charlton Northumb 116 F4
Charlton Som 23 D8
Charlton Telford 61 C5
Charlton W Sus 16 C2
Charlton Wilts 13 B7
Charlton Wilts 25 D6
Charlton Wilts 37 F6
Charlton Worcs 50 E5
Charlton Abbots Glos 37 B7
Charlton Adam Som 12 B3
Charlton-All-Saints Wilts 14 B2
Charlton Down Dorset 12 E4
Charlton Horethorne Som 12 B4
Charlton Kings Glos 37 B6
Charlton Mackerell Som 12 B3
Charlton Marshall Dorset 13 D6
Charlton Musgrove Som 12 B5
Charlton on Otmoor Oxon 39 C5
Charltons Redcar 102 C4
Charlwood Sur 28 E3
Charlynch Som 22 F4
Charminster Dorset 12 E4
Charmouth Dorset 11 E8
Charndon Bucks 39 B6
Charney Bassett Oxon 38 E3
Charnock Richard Lancs 86 C3
Charsfield Suff 57 D6
Chart Corner Kent 29 D8
Chart Sutton Kent 30 E2
Charter Alley Hants 26 D3
Charterhouse Som 23 D6
Charterville Allotments Oxon 38 C3
Chartham Kent 30 D5
Chartham Hatch Kent 30 D5
Chartridge Bucks 40 D2
Charvil Wokingham 27 B5
Charwelton Northants 52 D3
Chasetown Staffs 62 D4
Chastleton Oxon 38 B2
Chasty Devon 8 D5
Chatburn Lancs 93 E7
Chatcull Staffs 74 F4
Chatham Medway 29 C8
Chathill Northumb 117 B7
Chattenden Medway 29 B8
Chatteris Cambs 66 F3
Chattisham Suff 56 E4
Chatto Borders 116 C3
Chatton Northumb 117 B6
Chawleigh Devon 10 C2
Chawley Oxon 38 D4
Chawston Bedford 54 D2
Chawton Hants 26 F5
Cheadle Gtr Man 87 F6
Cheadle Staffs 75 E7
Cheadle Heath Gtr Man 87 F6
Cheadle Hulme Gtr Man 87 F6
Cheam London 28 C3
Cheapside Sur 27 D8
Chearsley Bucks 39 C7
Chebsey Staffs 62 B2
Checkendon Oxon 39 F6
Checkley Ches E 74 E4
Checkley Hereford 49 F7
Checkley Staffs 75 F7
Chedburgh Suff 55 D8
Cheddar Som 23 D6
Cheddington Bucks 40 C2
Cheddleton Staffs 75 D6
Cheddon Fitzpaine Som 11 B7
Chedglow Wilts 37 E6
Chedgrave Norf 69 E6
Chedington Dorset 12 D2
Chediston Suff 57 B7
Chedworth Glos 37 C7
Chedzoy Som 22 F5
Cheeklaw Borders 122 D3
Cheeseman's Green Kent 19 B7
Cheglinch Devon 20 E4
Cheldon Devon 10 C2
Chelford Ches E 74 B5
Chell Heath Stoke 75 D5
Chellaston Derby 76 F3
Chellington Bedford 53 D7
Chelmarsh Shrops 61 F7
Chelmer Village Essex 42 D3
Chelmondiston Suff 57 F6
Chelmorton Derbys 75 C8
Chelmsford Essex 42 D3
Chelsea London 28 B3
Chelsfield London 29 C5
Chelsworth Suff 56 E3
Cheltenham Glos 37 B6
Chelveston Northants 53 C7
Chelvey N Som 23 C6
Chelwood Bath 23 C8
Chelwood Common E Sus 17 B8
Chelwood Gate E Sus 17 B8
Chelworth Wilts 37 E6
Chelworth Green Wilts 37 E7
Chemistry Shrops 74 E2
Chenies Bucks 40 E3
Cheny Longville Shrops 60 F4
Chepstow = Cas-gwent Mon 36 E2
Chequerfield W Yorks 89 B5
Cherhill Wilts 24 B5
Cherington Glos 37 E6
Cherington Warks 51 F7
Cheriton Devon 21 E6
Cheriton Hants 15 B6
Cheriton Kent 19 B8
Cheriton Swansea 33 E5
Cheriton Bishop Devon 10 E2
Cheriton Fitzpaine Devon 10 D3
Cheriton or Stackpole Elidor Pembs 44 F4
Cherrington Telford 61 B6
Cherry Burton E Yorks 97 E5
Cherry Hinton Cambs 55 D5
Cherry Orchard Worcs 50 D3
Cherry Willingham Lincs 78 B3
Cherrybank Perth 128 B3
Chertsey Sur 27 C8
Cheselbourne Dorset 13 E5
Chesham Bucks 40 D2
Chesham Bois Bucks 40 E2
Cheshunt Herts 41 D6
Cheslyn Hay Staffs 62 D3
Chessington London 28 C2
Chester Ches W 73 C8
Chester-Le-Street Durham 111 D5
Chester Moor Durham 111 E5
Chesterblade Som 23 E8
Chesterfield Derbys 76 B3
Chesters Borders 116 B2
Chesters Borders 116 C2
Chesterton Cambs 55 C5
Chesterton Cambs 65 E8
Chesterton Glos 37 D7
Chesterton Oxon 39 B5
Chesterton Shrops 61 E7
Chesterton Staffs 74 E5
Chesterton Warks 51 D8
Chesterwood Northumb 109 C8
Chestfield Kent 30 C5
Cheston Devon 6 D4
Cheswardine Shrops 61 B7
Cheswick Northumb 123 E6
Chetnole Dorset 12 D4
Chettiscombe Devon 10 C4
Chettisham Cambs 66 F5
Chettle Dorset 13 C7
Chetton Shrops 61 E6
Chetwode Bucks 39 B6
Chetwynd Aston Telford 61 C7
Cheveley Cambs 55 C7
Chevening Kent 29 D5
Chevington Suff 55 D8
Chevithorne Devon 10 C4
Chew Magna Bath 23 C7
Chew Stoke Bath 23 C7
Chewton Keynsham Bath 23 C8
Chewton Mendip Som 23 D7
Chicheley M Keynes 53 E7
Chichester W Sus 16 D2
Chickerell Dorset 12 F4
Chicklade Wilts 24 F4
Chicksgrove Wilts 24 F4
Chidden Hants 15 C7
Chiddingfold Sur 27 F7
Chiddingly E Sus 18 D2
Chiddingstone Kent 29 E5
Chiddingstone Causeway Kent 29 E6
Chiddingstone Hoath Kent 29 E5
Chideock Dorset 12 E2
Chidham W Sus 15 D8
Chidswell W Yorks 88 B3
Chieveley W Berks 26 B2
Chignall Smealy Essex 42 C2
Chignall St James Essex 42 D2
Chigwell Essex 41 E7
Chigwell Row Essex 41 E7
Chilbolton Hants 25 F8
Chilcomb Hants 15 B6
Chilcombe Dorset 12 E3
Chilcompton Som 23 D8
Chilcote Leics 63 C6
Child Okeford Dorset 13 C6
Childer Thornton Ches W 73 B7
Childrey Oxon 38 F3
Child's Ercall Shrops 61 B6
Childswickham Worcs 51 F5
Childwall Mers 86 F2
Childwick Green Herts 40 C4
Chilfrome Dorset 12 E3
Chilgrove W Sus 16 C2
Chilham Kent 30 D4
Chilhampton Wilts 25 F5
Chilla Devon 9 D6
Chillaton Devon 9 F6
Chillenden Kent 31 D6
Chillerton IoW 15 F5
Chillesford Suff 57 D7
Chillingham Northumb 117 B6
Chillington Devon 7 E5
Chillington Som 11 C8
Chilmark Wilts 24 F4
Chilson Oxon 38 C3
Chilsworthy Corn 6 B2
Chilsworthy Devon 8 D5
Chilthorne Domer Som 12 C3
Chiltington E Sus 17 C7
Chilton Bucks 39 C6
Chilton Durham 101 B7
Chilton Oxon 38 F4
Chilton Cantelo Som 12 B3
Chilton Foliat Wilts 25 B8
Chilton Lane Durham 111 F6
Chilton Polden Som 23 F5
Chilton Street Suff 55 E8
Chilton Trinity Som 22 F4
Chilvers Coton Warks 63 E7
Chilwell Notts 76 F5
Chilworth Hants 14 C5
Chilworth Sur 27 E8
Chimney Oxon 38 D3
Chineham Hants 26 D4
Chingford London 41 E6
Chinley Derbys 87 F8
Chinley Head Derbys 87 F8
Chinnor Oxon 39 D7
Chipnall Shrops 74 F4
Chippenhall Green Suff 57 B6
Chippenham Cambs 55 C7
Chippenham Wilts 24 B4
Chipperfield Herts 40 D3
Chipping Herts 54 F4
Chipping Lancs 93 E6
Chipping Campden Glos 51 F6
Chipping Hill Essex 42 C4
Chipping Norton Oxon 38 B3
Chipping Ongar Essex 42 D1
Chipping Sodbury S Glos 36 F4
Chipping Warden Northants 52 E2
Chipstable Som 10 B5
Chipstead Kent 29 D5
Chipstead Sur 28 D3
Chirbury Shrops 60 E2
Chirk = Y Waun Wrex 73 F6
Chirk Bank Shrops 73 F6
Chirmorrie S Ayrs 105 B6
Chirnside Borders 122 D4
Chirnsidebridge Borders 122 D4
Chirton Wilts 25 D5
Chisbury Wilts 25 C7
Chiselborough Som 12 C2
Chiseldon Swindon 25 B6
Chiserley W Yorks 87 B8
Chislehampton Oxon 39 E5
Chislehurst London 28 B5
Chislet Kent 31 C6
Chiswell Green Herts 40 D4
Chiswick London 28 B3
Chiswick End Cambs 54 E4
Chisworth Derbys 87 E7
Chithurst W Sus 16 B2
Chittering Cambs 55 B5
Chitterne Wilts 24 E4
Chittlehamholt Devon 9 B8
Chittlehampton Devon 9 B8
Chittoe Wilts 24 C4
Chivenor Devon 20 F4
Chobham Sur 27 C7
Choicelee Borders 122 D3
Cholderton Wilts 25 E7
Cholesbury Bucks 40 D2
Chollerford Northumb 110 B2
Chollerton Northumb 110 B2
Cholmondeston Ches E 74 C3
Cholsey Oxon 39 F5
Cholstrey Hereford 49 D6
Chop Gate N Yorks 102 E3
Choppington Northumb 117 F8
Chopwell T&W 110 D4
Chorley Ches E 74 D2
Chorley Lancs 86 C3
Chorley Shrops 61 F6
Chorley Staffs 62 C4
Chorleywood Herts 40 E3
Chorlton cum Hardy Gtr Man 87 E6
Chorlton Lane Ches W 73 E8
Choulton Shrops 60 F3
Chowdene T&W 111 D5
Chowley Ches W 73 D8
Chrishall Essex 54 F5
Christchurch Cambs 66 E4
Christchurch Dorset 14 E2
Christchurch Glos 36 C2
Christchurch Newport 35 F7
Christian Malford Wilts 24 B4
Christleton Ches W 73 C8
Christmas Common Oxon 39 E7
Christon N Som 23 D5
Christon Bank Northumb 117 B8
Christow Devon 10 F3
Chryston N Lanark 119 B6
Chudleigh Devon 7 B6
Chudleigh Knighton Devon 7 B6
Chulmleigh Devon 9 C8
Chunal Derbys 87 E8
Church Lancs 86 B5
Church Aston Telford 61 C7
Church Brampton Northants 52 C5
Church Broughton Derbys 76 F2
Church Crookham Hants 27 D6
Church Eaton Staffs 62 C2
Church End C Beds 40 B2
Church End C Beds 53 F7
Church End C Beds 54 F2
Church End Cambs 66 D3
Church End Cambs 66 F2
Church End E Yorks 97 D6
Church End Essex 42 B3
Church End Essex 55 E6
Church End Hants 26 D4
Church End Lincs 78 F5
Church End Warks 63 E6
Church End Warks 63 E6
Church End Wilts 24 B5
Church Enstone Oxon 38 B3
Church Fenton N Yorks 95 F8
Church Green Devon 11 E6
Church Green Norf 68 E3
Church Gresley Derbys 63 C6
Church Hanborough Oxon 38 C4
Church Hill Ches W 74 C3
Church Houses N Yorks 102 E4
Church Knowle Dorset 13 F7
Church Laneham Notts 77 B8
Church Langton Leics 64 E4
Church Lawford Warks 52 B2
Church Lawton Ches E 74 D5
Church Leigh Staffs 75 F7
Church Lench Worcs 50 D5
Church Mayfield Staffs 75 E8
Church Minshull Ches E 74 C3
Church Norton W Sus 16 E2
Church Preen Shrops 60 E5
Church Pulverbatch Shrops 60 D4
Church Stoke Powys 60 E2
Church Stowe Northants 52 D4
Church Street Kent 29 B8
Church Stretton Shrops 60 E4
Church Town N Lincs 89 D8
Church Town Sur 28 D4
Church Village Rhondda 34 F4
Church Warsop Notts 77 C5
Churcham Glos 36 C4
Churchbank Shrops 48 B4
Churchbridge Staffs 62 D3
Churchdown Glos 37 C5
Churchend Essex 42 B2
Churchend Essex 43 E6
Churchend S Glos 36 E4
Churchfield W Mid 62 E4
Churchgate Street Essex 41 C7
Churchill Devon 11 D8
Churchill Devon 20 E4
Churchill N Som 23 D6
Churchill Oxon 38 B2
Churchill Worcs 50 B3
Churchill Worcs 50 D4
Churchinford Som 11 C7
Churchover Warks 64 F2
Churchstanton Som 11 C6
Churchstow Devon 6 E5
Churchtown Derbys 76 C2
Churchtown IoM 84 C4
Churchtown Lancs 92 E4

Crofton Wilts 25 C7
Crofts of Benachielt Highld 158 G3
Crofts of Haddo Aberds 153 E8
Crofts of Inverthernie Aberds 153 D7
Crofts of Meikle Ardo Aberds 153 D8
Crofty Swansea 33 E6
Croggan Argyll 124 C3
Croglin Cumb 109 E5
Croich Highld 150 B7
Crois Dughaill W Isles 148 F2
Cromarty Highld 151 E10
Cromblet Aberds 153 E7
Cromdale Highld 139 B6
Cromer Herts 41 B5
Cromer Norf 81 C8
Cromford Derbys 76 D2
Cromhall S Glos 36 E3
Cromhall Common S Glos 36 F3
Cromor W Isles 155 E9
Cromra Highld 137 E8
Cromwell Notts 77 C7
Cronberry E Ayrs 113 B6
Crondall Hants 27 E5
Cronk-y-Voddy IoM 84 D3
Cronton Mers 86 F2
Crook Cumb 99 E6
Crook Durham 110 F4
Crook of Devon Perth 128 D2
Crookedholm E Ayrs 118 F4
Crookes S Yorks 88 F4
Crookham Northumb 122 F5
Crookham W Berks 26 C3
Crookham Village Hants 27 D5
Crookhaugh Borders 114 B4
Crookhouse Borders 116 B3
Crooklands Cumb 99 F7
Cropredy Oxon 52 E2
Cropston Leics 64 C2
Cropthorne Worcs 50 E4
Cropton N Yorks 103 F5
Cropwell Bishop Notts 77 F6
Cropwell Butler Notts 77 F6
Cros W Isles 155 A10
Crosbost W Isles 155 E8
Crosby Cumb 107 F7
Crosby IoM 84 E3
Crosby N Lincs 90 C2
Crosby Garrett Cumb 100 D2
Crosby Ravensworth Cumb 99 C8
Crosby Villa Cumb 107 F7
Croscombe Som 23 E7
Cross Som 23 D6
Cross Ash Mon 35 C8
Cross-at-Hand Kent 29 E8
Cross Green Devon 9 F5
Cross Green Suff 56 D2
Cross Green Suff 56 D3
Cross Green Warks 51 D8
Cross-hands Carms 32 B2
Cross Hands Carms 33 C6
Cross Hands Pembs 32 C1
Cross Hill Derbys 76 E4
Cross Houses Shrops 60 D5
Cross in Hand E Sus 18 C2
Cross in Hand Leics 64 F2
Cross Inn Ceredig 46 C4
Cross Inn Ceredig 46 D2
Cross Inn Rhondda 34 F4
Cross Keys Kent 29 D6
Cross Lane Head Shrops 61 E7
Cross Lanes Corn 3 D5
Cross Lanes N Yorks 95 C8
Cross Lanes Wrex 73 E7
Cross Oak Powys 35 B5
Cross of Jackston Aberds 153 E7
Cross o'th'hands Derbys 76 E2
Cross Street Suff 57 B5
Crossaig Argyll 143 C9
Crossal Highld 149 E9
Crossapol Argyll 146 G2
Crossburn Falk 119 B8
Crossbush W Sus 16 D4
Crosscanonby Cumb 107 F7
Crossdale Street Norf 81 D8
Crossens Mers 85 C4
Crossflatts W Yorks 94 E4
Crossford Fife 128 F2
Crossford S Lanark 119 E8
Crossgate Lincs 66 B2
Crossgatehall E Loth 121 C6
Crossgates Fife 128 F3
Crossgates Powys 48 C2
Crossgill Lancs 93 C5
Crosshill E Ayrs 112 B4
Crosshill Fife 128 E3
Crosshill S Ayrs 112 D3
Crosshouse E Ayrs 118 F3
Crossings Cumb 108 B5
Crosskeys Caerph 35 E6
Crosskirk Highld 157 B13
Crosslanes Shrops 60 C3
Crosslee Borders 115 C6
Crosslee Renfs 118 C4
Crossmichael Dumfries 106 C4
Crossmoor Lancs 92 F4
Crossroads Aberds 141 E6
Crossroads E Ayrs 118 F4
Crossway Hereford 49 F8
Crossway Mon 35 C8
Crossway Powys 48 D2
Crossway Green Worcs 50 C3
Crossways Dorset 13 F5
Crosswell Pembs 45 F3
Crosswood Ceredig 47 B5
Crosthwaite Cumb 99 E6
Croston Lancs 86 C2
Crostwick Norf 69 C5
Crostwight Norf 69 B6
Crothair W Isles 154 D6
Crouch Kent 29 D7
Crouch Hill Dorset 12 C5
Crouch House Green Kent 28 E5
Croucheston Wilts 13 B8
Croughton Northants 52 F3
Crovie Aberds 153 B8
Crow Edge S Yorks 88 D2
Crow Hill Hereford 36 B3
Crowan Corn 2 C5
Crowborough E Sus 18 B2
Crowcombe Som 22 F3
Crowdecote Derbys 75 C8
Crowden Derbys 87 E8
Crowell Oxon 39 E7
Crowfield Northants 52 E4
Crowfield Suff 56 D5
Crowhurst E Sus 18 D4
Crowhurst Sur 28 E4
Crowhurst Lane End Sur 28 E4
Crowland Lincs 66 C2
Crowlas Corn 2 C4
Crowle N Lincs 89 C8
Crowle Worcs 50 D4
Crowmarsh Gifford Oxon 39 F6
Crown Corner Suff 57 B6
Crownhill Plym 6 D2
Crownland Suff 56 C4
Crownthorpe Norf 68 D3
Crowntown Corn 2 C5
Crows-an-wra Corn 2 D2
Crowshill Norf 68 D2
Crowsnest Shrops 60 D3
Crowthorne Brack 27 C6
Crowton Ches W 74 B2
Croxall Staffs 63 C5
Croxby Lincs 91 E5
Croxdale Durham 111 F5
Croxden Staffs 75 F7
Croxley Green Herts 40 E3
Croxton Cambs 54 C3
Croxton N Lincs 90 C4
Croxton Norf 67 F8
Croxton Staffs 74 F4
Croxton Kerrial Leics 64 B5
Croxtonbank Staffs 74 F4
Croy Highld 151 G10
Croy N Lanark 119 B7
Croyde Devon 20 F3
Croydon Cambs 54 E4
Croydon London 28 C4
Crubenmore Lodge Highld 138 E2
Cruckmeole Shrops 60 D4
Cruckton Shrops 60 C4
Cruden Bay Aberds 153 E10
Crudgington Telford 61 C6
Crudwell Wilts 37 E6
Crug Powys 48 B3
Crugmeer Corn 4 B4
Crugybar Carms 47 F5
Crulabhig W Isles 154 D6
Crumlin = Crymlyn Caerph 35 E6
Crumpsall Gtr Man 87 D6
Crundale Kent 30 E4
Crundale Pembs 44 D4
Cruwys Morchard Devon 10 C3
Crux Easton Hants 26 D2
Crwbin Carms 33 C5
Crya Orkney 159 H4
Cryers Hill Bucks 40 E1
Crymlyn = Crumlin Caerph 35 E6
Crymlyn Gwyn 83 D6
Crymych Pembs 45 F3
Crynant Neath 34 D1
Crynfryn Ceredig 46 C4
Cuaig Highld 149 C12
Cuan Argyll 124 D3
Cubbington Warks 51 C8
Cubeck N Yorks 100 F4
Cubert Corn 4 D2
Cubley S Yorks 88 D3
Cubley Common Derbys 75 F8
Cublington Bucks 39 B8
Cublington Hereford 49 F6
Cuckfield W Sus 17 B7
Cucklington Som 13 B5
Cuckney Notts 77 B5
Cuckoo Hill Notts 89 E8
Cuddesdon Oxon 39 D6
Cuddington Bucks 39 C7
Cuddington Ches W 74 B3
Cuddington Heath Ches W 73 E8
Cuddy Hill Lancs 92 F4
Cudham London 28 D5
Cudliptown Devon 6 B3
Cudworth S Yorks 88 D4
Cudworth Som 11 C8
Cuffley Herts 41 D6
Cuiashader W Isles 155 B10
Cuidhir W Isles 148 H1
Cuidhtinis W Isles 154 J5
Culbo Highld 151 E9
Culbokie Highld 151 F9
Culburnie Highld 150 G7
Culcabock Highld 151 G9
Culcairn Highld 151 E9
Culcharry Highld 151 F11
Culcheth Warr 86 E4
Culdrain Aberds 152 E5
Culduie Highld 149 D12
Culford Suff 56 B2
Culgaith Cumb 99 B8
Culham Oxon 39 E5
Culkein Highld 156 F3
Culkein Drumbeg Highld 156 F4
Culkerton Glos 37 E6
Cullachie Highld 139 B5
Cullen Moray 152 B5
Cullercoats T&W 111 B6
Cullicudden Highld 151 E9
Cullingworth W Yorks 94 F3
Cullipool Argyll 124 D3
Cullivoe Shetland 160 C7
Culloch Perth 127 C6
Culloden Highld 151 G10
Cullompton Devon 10 D5
Culmaily Highld 151 B11
Culmazie Dumfries 105 D7
Culmington Shrops 60 F4
Culmstock Devon 11 C6
Culnacraig Highld 156 J3
Culnaknock Highld 149 B10
Culpho Suff 57 E6
Culrain Highld 151 B8
Culross Fife 127 F8
Culroy S Ayrs 112 C3
Culsh Aberds 140 E2
Culsh Aberds 153 D8
Culshabbin Dumfries 105 D7
Culswick Shetland 160 J4
Cultercullen Aberds 141 B8
Cults Aberdeen 141 D7
Cults Aberds 152 E5
Cults Dumfries 105 E8
Culverstone Green Kent 29 C7
Culverthorpe Lincs 78 E3
Culworth Northants 52 E3
Culzie Lodge Highld 151 D8
Cumbernauld N Lanark 119 B7
Cumbernauld Village N Lanark 119 B7
Cumberworth Lincs 79 B8
Cuminestown Aberds 153 C8
Cumlewick Shetland 160 L6
Cummersdale Cumb 108 D3
Cummertrees Dumfries 107 C8
Cummingston Moray 152 B1
Cumnock E Ayrs 113 B5
Cumnor Oxon 38 D4
Cumrew Cumb 108 D5
Cumwhinton Cumb 108 D4
Cumwhitton Cumb 108 D5
Cundall N Yorks 95 B7
Cunninghamhead N Ayrs 118 E3
Cunnister Shetland 160 D7
Cupar Fife 129 C5
Cupar Muir Fife 129 C5
Cupernham Hants 14 B4
Curbar Derbys 76 B2
Curbridge Hants 15 C6
Curbridge Oxon 38 D3
Curdridge Hants 15 C6
Curdworth Warks 63 E5
Curland Som 11 C7
Curlew Green Suff 57 C7
Currarie S Ayrs 112 E1
Curridge W Berks 26 B2
Currie Edin 120 C4
Curry Mallet Som 11 B8
Curry Rivel Som 11 B8
Curtisden Green Kent 29 E8
Curtisknowle Devon 6 D5
Cury Corn 3 D5
Cushnie Aberds 153 B7
Cushuish Som 22 F3
Cusop Hereford 48 E4
Cutcloy Dumfries 105 F8
Cutcombe Som 21 F8
Cutgate Gtr Man 87 C6
Cutiau Gwyn 58 C3
Cutlers Green Essex 55 F6
Cutnall Green Worcs 50 C3
Cutsdean Glos 51 F5
Cutthorpe Derbys 76 B3
Cutts Shetland 160 K6
Cuxham Oxon 39 E6
Cuxton Medway 29 C8
Cuxwold Lincs 91 D5
Cwm Bl Gwent 35 D5
Cwm Denb 72 B4
Cwm Swansea 33 E7
Cwm-byr Carms 46 F5
Cwm-Cewydd Gwyn 59 C5
Cwm-cou Ceredig 45 E4
Cwm-Dulais Swansea 33 D7
Cwm-felin-fach Caerph 35 E5
Cwm Ffrwd-oer Torf 35 D6
Cwm-hesgen Gwyn 71 E8
Cwm-hwnt Rhondda 34 D3
Cwm Irfon Powys 47 E7
Cwm-Llinau Powys 58 D5
Cwm-mawr Carms 33 C6
Cwm-parc Rhondda 34 E3
Cwm Penmachno Conwy 71 C8
Cwm-y-glo Carms 33 C6
Cwm-y-glo Gwyn 82 E5
Cwmafan Neath 34 E1
Cwmaman Rhondda 34 E4
Cwmann Carms 46 E4
Cwmavon Torf 35 D6
Cwmbâch Rhondda 34 D4
Cwmbach Carms 32 B3
Cwmbach Carms 33 D5
Cwmbach Powys 48 D2
Cwmbach Powys 48 F3
Cwmbelan Powys 59 F6
Cwmbrân = Cwmbran Torf 35 E6
Cwmbran = Cwmbrân Torf 35 E6
Cwmbrwyno Ceredig 58 F4
Cwmcarn Caerph 35 E6
Cwmcarvan Mon 36 D1
Cwmcych Carms 45 F4
Cwmdare Rhondda 34 D3
Cwmderwen Powys 59 D6
Cwmdu Carms 46 F5
Cwmdu Powys 35 B5
Cwmdu Swansea 33 E7
Cwmduad Carms 46 F2
Cwmdwr Carms 47 F6
Cwmfelin Bridgend 34 F2
Cwmfelin M Tydf 34 D4
Cwmfelin Boeth Carms 32 C2
Cwmfelin Mynach Carms 32 B3
Cwmffrwd Carms 33 C5
Cwmgiedd Powys 34 C1
Cwmgors Neath 33 C8
Cwmgwili Carms 33 C6
Cwmgwrach Neath 34 D2
Cwmhiraeth Carms 46 F2
Cwmifor Carms 33 B7
Cwmisfael Carms 33 C5
Cwmllynfell Neath 33 C8
Cwmorgan Pembs 45 F4
Cwmpengraig Carms 46 F2
Cwmrhos Powys 35 B5
Cwmsychpant Ceredig 46 E3
Cwmtillery Bl Gwent 35 D6
Cwmwysg Powys 34 B2
Cwmyoy Mon 35 B6
Cwmystwyth Ceredig 47 B6
Cwrt Gwyn 58 D3
Cwrt-newydd Ceredig 46 E3
Cwrt-y-cadno Carms 47 E5
Cwrt-y-gollen Powys 35 C6
Cydweli = Kidwelly Carms 33 D5
Cyffordd Llandudno = Llandudno Junction Conwy 83 D7
Cyffylliog Denb 72 D4
Cyfronydd Powys 59 D8
Cymer Neath 34 E2
Cyncoed Cardiff 35 F5
Cynghordy Carms 47 E7
Cynheidre Carms 33 D5
Cynwyd Denb 72 E4
Cynwyl Elfed Carms 32 B4
Cywarch Gwyn 59 C5

D

Dacre Cumb 99 B6
Dacre N Yorks 94 C4
Dacre Banks N Yorks 94 C4
Daddry Shield Durham 109 F8
Dadford Bucks 52 F4
Dadlington Leics 63 E8
Dafarn Faig Gwyn 71 C5
Dafen Carms 33 D6
Daffy Green Norf 68 D2
Dagenham London 41 F7
Daglingworth Glos 37 D6
Dagnall Bucks 40 C2
Dail Beag W Isles 154 C7
Dail bho Dheas W Isles 155 A9
Dail bho Thuath W Isles 155 A9
Dail Mor W Isles 154 C7
Daill Argyll 142 B4
Dailly S Ayrs 112 D2
Dairsie or Osnaburgh Fife 129 C6
Daisy Hill Gtr Man 86 D4
Dalabrog W Isles 148 F2
Dalavich Argyll 125 D5
Dalbeattie Dumfries 106 C5
Dalblair E Ayrs 113 C6
Dalbog Angus 135 B5
Dalbury Derbys 76 F2
Dalby IoM 84 E2
Dalby N Yorks 96 B2
Dalchalloch Perth 132 C4
Dalchalm Highld 157 J12
Dalchenna Argyll 125 E6
Dalchirach Moray 152 E1
Dalchork Highld 157 H8
Dalchreichart Highld 137 C5
Dalchruin Perth 127 C6
Dalderby Lincs 78 C5
Dale Pembs 44 E3
Dale Abbey Derbys 76 F4
Dale Head Cumb 99 C6
Dale of Walls Shetland 160 H3
Dalelia Highld 147 E10
Daless Highld 151 H11
Dalfaber Highld 138 C5
Dalgarven N Ayrs 118 E2
Dalgety Bay Fife 128 F3
Dalginross Perth 127 B6
Dalguise Perth 133 E6
Dalhalvaig Highld 157 D11
Dalham Suff 55 C8
Dalinlongart Argyll 145 E10
Dalkeith Midloth 121 C6
Dallam Warr 86 E3
Dallas Moray 151 F14
Dalleagles E Ayrs 113 C5
Dallinghoo Suff 57 D6
Dallington E Sus 18 D3
Dallington Northants 52 C5
Dallow N Yorks 94 B4
Dalmadilly Aberds 141 C6
Dalmally Argyll 125 C7
Dalmarnock Glasgow 119 C6
Dalmary Stirling 126 E4
Dalmellington E Ayrs 112 D4
Dalmeny Edin 120 B4
Dalmigavie Highld 138 C3
Dalmigavie Lodge Highld 138 B3
Dalmore Highld 151 E9
Dalmuir W Dunb 118 B4
Dalnabreck Highld 147 E9
Dalnacardoch Lodge Perth 132 B4
Dalnacroich Highld 150 F6
Dalnaglar Castle Perth 133 C8
Dalnahaitnach Highld 138 B4
Dalnaspidal Lodge Perth 132 B3
Dalnavaid Perth 133 C7
Dalnavie Highld 151 D9
Dalnawillan Lodge Highld 157 E13
Dalness Highld 131 D5
Dalnessie Highld 157 H9
Dalqueich Perth 128 D2
Dalreavoch Highld 157 J10
Dalry N Ayrs 118 E2
Dalrymple E Ayrs 112 C3
Dalserf S Lanark 119 D8
Dalston Cumb 108 D3
Dalswinton Dumfries 114 F2
Dalton Dumfries 107 B8
Dalton Lancs 86 D2
Dalton N Yorks 95 B7
Dalton N Yorks 101 D6
Dalton Northumb 110 B4
Dalton Northumb 110 D2
Dalton S Yorks 89 E5
Dalton-in-Furness Cumb 92 B2
Dalton-le-Dale Durham 111 E7
Dalton-on-Tees N Yorks 101 D7
Dalton Piercy Hrtlpl 111 F7
Dalveich Stirling 126 B5
Dalvina Lodge Highld 157 E9
Dalwhinnie Highld 138 F2
Dalwood Devon 11 D7
Dalwyne S Ayrs 112 E3
Dam Green Norf 68 F3
Dam Side Lancs 92 E4
Damerham Hants 14 C2
Damgate Norf 69 D7
Damnaglaur Dumfries 104 F5
Damside Borders 120 E4
Danbury Essex 42 D3
Danby N Yorks 103 D5
Danby Wiske N Yorks 101 E8
Dandaleith Moray 152 D2
Danderhall Midloth 121 C6
Dane End Herts 41 B6
Danebridge Ches E 75 C6
Danehill E Sus 17 B8
Danemoor Green Norf 68 D3
Danesford Shrops 61 E7
Daneshill Hants 26 D4
Dangerous Corner Lancs 86 C3
Danskine E Loth 121 C8
Darcy Lever Gtr Man 86 D5
Darenth Kent 29 B6
Daresbury Halton 86 F3
Darfield S Yorks 88 D5
Darfoulds Notts 77 B5
Dargate Kent 30 C4
Darite Corn 5 C7
Darlaston W Mid 62 E3
Darley N Yorks 94 D5
Darley Bridge Derbys 76 C2
Darley Head N Yorks 94 D4
Darlingscott Warks 51 E7
Darlington Darl 101 C7
Darliston Shrops 74 F2
Darlton Notts 77 B7
Darnall S Yorks 88 F4
Darnick Borders 121 F8
Darowen Powys 58 D5
Darra Aberds 153 D7
Darracott Devon 20 F3
Darras Hall Northumb 110 B4
Darrington W Yorks 89 B5
Darsham Suff 57 C8
Dartford Kent 29 B6
Dartford Crossing Kent 29 B6
Dartington Devon 7 C5
Dartmeet Devon 6 B4
Dartmouth Devon 7 D6
Darton S Yorks 88 D4
Darvel E Ayrs 119 F5
Darwell Hole E Sus 18 D3
Darwen Blackburn 86 B4
Datchet Windsor 27 B7
Datchworth Herts 41 C5
Datchworth Green Herts 41 C5
Daubhill Gtr Man 86 D5
Daugh of Kinermony Moray 152 D2
Dauntsey Wilts 37 F6
Dava Moray 151 H13
Davenham Ches W 74 B3
Davenport Green Ches E 74 B5
Daventry Northants 52 C3
David's Well Powys 48 B2
Davidson's Mains Edin 120 B5
Davidstow Corn 8 F3
Davington Dumfries 115 D5
Daviot Aberds 141 B6
Daviot Highld 151 H10
Davoch of Grange Moray 152 C4
Davyhulme Gtr Man 87 E5
Daw's House Corn 8 F5
Dawley Telford 61 D6
Dawlish Devon 7 B7
Dawlish Warren Devon 7 B7
Dawn Conwy 83 D8
Daws Heath Essex 42 F4
Daw's House Corn 8 F5
Dawsmere Lincs 79 F7
Dayhills Staffs 75 F6
Daylesford Glos 38 B2
Ddôl-Cownwy Powys 59 C7
Ddrydwy Anglesey 82 D3
Deadwater Northumb 116 E2
Deaf Hill Durham 111 F6
Deal Kent 31 D7
Deal Hall Essex 43 E6
Dean Cumb 98 B2
Dean Devon 6 C5
Dean Devon 20 E4
Dean Dorset 13 C7
Dean Hants 15 C6
Dean Som 23 E8
Dean Prior Devon 6 C5
Dean Row Ches E 87 F6
Deanburnhaugh Borders 115 C6
Deane Gtr Man 86 D4
Deane Hants 26 D3
Deanich Lodge Highld 150 C6
Deanland Dorset 13 C7
Deans W Loth 120 C3
Deanscales Cumb 98 B2
Deanshanger Northants 53 F5
Deanston Stirling 127 D6
Dearham Cumb 107 F7
Debach Suff 57 D6
Debden Essex 41 E7
Debden Essex 55 F6
Debden Cross Essex 55 F6
Debenham Suff 57 C5
Dechmont W Loth 120 B3
Deddington Oxon 52 F2
Dedham Essex 56 F4
Dedham Heath Essex 56 F4
Deebank Aberds 141 E5
Deene Northants 65 E6
Deenethorpe Northants 65 E6
Deepcar S Yorks 88 E3
Deepcut Sur 27 D7
Deepdale Cumb 100 F2
Deeping Gate Lincs 65 D8
Deeping St James Lincs 65 D8
Deeping St Nicholas Lincs 66 C2
Deerhill Moray 152 C4
Deerhurst Glos 37 B5
Deerness Orkney 159 H6
Defford Worcs 50 E4
Defynnog Powys 34 B3
Deganwy Conwy 83 D7
Deighton N Yorks 102 D1
Deighton W Yorks 88 C2
Deighton York 96 E2
Deiniolen Gwyn 83 E5
Delabole Corn 8 F2
Delamere Ches W 74 C2
Delfrigs Aberds 141 B8
Dell Lodge Highld 139 C6
Delliefure Highld 151 H13
Delnabo Moray 139 C7
Delnadamph Aberds 139 D8
Delph Gtr Man 87 D7
Delves Durham 110 E4
Delvine Perth 133 E8
Dembleby Lincs 78 F3
Denaby Main S Yorks 89 E5
Denbigh = Dinbych Denb 72 C4
Denbury Devon 7 C6
Denby Derbys 76 E3
Denby Dale W Yorks 88 D3
Denchworth Oxon 38 E3
Dendron Cumb 92 B2
Denel End C Beds 53 F8
Denend Aberds 152 E6
Denford Northants 53 B7
Dengie Essex 43 D5
Denham Bucks 40 F3
Denham Suff 55 C8
Denham Suff 57 B5
Denham Street Suff 57 B5
Denhead Aberds 153 C9
Denhead Fife 129 C6
Denhead of Arbilot Angus 135 E5
Denhead of Gray Dundee 134 F3
Denholm Borders 115 C8
Denholme W Yorks 94 F3
Denholme Clough W Yorks 94 F3
Denio Gwyn 70 D4
Denmead Hants 15 C7
Denmore Aberdeen 141 C8
Denmoss Aberds 153 D6
Dennington Suff 57 C6
Denny Falk 127 F7
Denny Lodge Hants 14 D4
Dennyloanhead Falk 127 F7
Denshaw Gtr Man 87 C7
Denside Aberds 141 E7
Densole Kent 31 E6
Denston Suff 55 D8
Denstone Staffs 75 E8
Dent Cumb 100 F2
Denton Cambs 65 F8
Denton Darl 101 C7
Denton E Sus 17 D8
Denton Gtr Man 87 E7
Denton Kent 31 E6
Denton Lincs 77 F8
Denton N Yorks 94 E4
Denton Norf 69 F5
Denton Northants 53 D6
Denton Oxon 39 D5
Denton's Green Mers 86 E2
Denver Norf 67 D6
Denwick Northumb 117 C8
Deopham Norf 68 D3
Deopham Green Norf 68 E3
Depden Suff 55 D8
Depden Green Suff 55 D8
Deptford London 28 B4
Deptford Wilts 24 F5
Derby Derby 76 F3
Derbyhaven IoM 84 F2
Dereham Norf 68 C2
Deri Caerph 35 D5
Derril Devon 8 D5
Derringstone Kent 31 E6
Derrington Staffs 62 B2
Derriton Devon 8 D5
Derry Hill Wilts 24 B4
Derryguaig Argyll 146 H7
Derrythorpe N Lincs 90 D2
Dersingham Norf 80 D2
Dervaig Argyll 146 F7
Derwen Denb 72 D4
Derwenlas Powys 58 E4
Desborough Northants 64 F5
Desford Leics 63 D8
Detchant Northumb 123 F6
Detling Kent 29 D8
Deuddwr Powys 60 C2
Devauden Mon 36 E1
Devil's Bridge Ceredig 47 B6
Devizes Wilts 24 C5
Devol Invclyd 118 B3
Devonport Plym 6 D2
Devonside Clack 127 E8
Devoran Corn 3 C6
Dewar Borders 121 E6
Dewlish Dorset 13 E5
Dewsbury W Yorks 88 B3
Dewsbury Moor W Yorks 88 B3
Dewshall Court Hereford 49 F6
Dhoon IoM 84 D4
Dhoor IoM 84 C4
Dhowin IoM 84 B4
Dial Post W Sus 17 C5
Dibden Hants 14 D5
Dibden Purlieu Hants 14 D5
Dickleburgh Norf 68 F4
Didbrook Glos 51 F5
Didcot Oxon 39 F5
Diddington Cambs 54 C2
Diddlebury Shrops 60 F5
Didley Hereford 49 F6
Didling W Sus 16 C2
Didmarton Glos 37 F5
Didsbury Gtr Man 87 E6
Didworthy Devon 6 C4
Digby Lincs 78 D3
Digg Highld 149 B9
Diggle Gtr Man 87 D8
Digmoor Lancs 86 D2
Digswell Park Herts 41 C5
Dihewyd Ceredig 46 D3
Dilham Norf 69 B6
Dilhorne Staffs 75 E6
Dillarburn S Lanark 119 E8
Dillington Cambs 54 C2
Dilston Northumb 110 C2
Dilton Marsh Wilts 24 E3
Dilwyn Hereford 49 D6
Dinas Carms 45 F4
Dinas Gwyn 70 D3
Dinas Cross Pembs 45 F2
Dinas Dinlle Gwyn 82 F4
Dinas-Mawddwy Gwyn 59 C5
Dinas Powys V Glam 22 B3
Dinbych = Denbigh Denb 72 C4
Dinbych-Y-Pysgod = Tenby Pembs 32 D2
Dinder Som 23 E7
Dinedor Hereford 49 F7
Dingestow Mon 36 C1
Dingle Mers 85 F4
Dingleden Kent 18 B5
Dingley Northants 64 F4
Dingwall Highld 151 F8
Dinlabyre Borders 115 E8
Dinmael Conwy 72 E4
Dinnet Aberds 140 E3
Dinnington S Yorks 89 F6
Dinnington Som 12 C2
Dinnington T&W 110 B5
Dinorwic Gwyn 83 E5
Dinton Bucks 39 C7
Dinton Wilts 24 F5
Dinwoodie Mains Dumfries 114 E4
Dinworthy Devon 8 C5
Dippen N Ayrs 143 F11
Dippenhall Sur 27 E6
Dipple Moray 152 C3
Dipple S Ayrs 112 D2
Diptford Devon 6 D5
Dipton Durham 110 D4
Dirdhu Highld 139 B6
Dirleton E Loth 129 F7
Dirt Pot Northumb 109 E8
Discoed Powys 48 C4
Diseworth Leics 63 B8
Dishes Orkney 159 F7
Dishforth N Yorks 95 B6
Disley Ches E 87 F7
Diss Norf 56 B5
Disserth Powys 48 D2
Distington Cumb 98 B2
Ditchampton Wilts 25 F5
Ditcheat Som 23 F8
Ditchingham Norf 69 E6
Ditchling E Sus 17 C7
Ditherington Shrops 60 C5
Dittisham Devon 7 D6
Ditton Halton 86 F2
Ditton Kent 29 D8
Ditton Green Cambs 55 D7
Ditton Priors Shrops 61 F6
Divach Highld 137 B7
Divlyn Carms 47 F6
Dixton Glos 50 F4
Dixton Mon 36 C2
Dobcross Gtr Man 87 D7
Dobwalls Corn 5 C7
Doc Penfro = Pembroke Dock Pembs 44 E4
Doccombe Devon 10 F2
Dochfour Ho. Highld 151 H9
Dochgarroch Highld 151 G9
Docking Norf 80 D3
Docklow Hereford 49 D7
Dockray Cumb 99 B5
Dockroyd W Yorks 94 F3
Dodburn Borders 115 D7
Doddinghurst Essex 42 E1
Doddington Cambs 66 E3
Doddington Kent 30 D3
Doddington Lincs 78 B2
Doddington Northumb 123 F5
Doddington Shrops 49 B8
Doddiscombsleigh Devon 10 F3
Dodford Northants 52 C4
Dodford Worcs 50 B4
Dodington S Glos 24 A2
Dodleston Ches W 73 C7
Dods Leigh Staffs 75 F7
Dodworth S Yorks 88 D4
Doe Green Warr 86 F3
Doe Lea Derbys 76 C4
Dog Village Devon 10 E4
Dogdyke Lincs 78 D5
Dogmersfield Hants 27 D5
Dogridge Wilts 37 F7
Dogsthorpe Pboro 65 D8
Dol-fôr Powys 58 D5
Dôl-y-Bont Ceredig 58 F3
Dol-y-cannau Powys 48 E4
Dolanog Powys 59 C7
Dolau Powys 48 C3
Dolau Rhondda 34 F3
Dolbenmaen Gwyn 71 C6
Dolfach Powys 59 D6
Dolfor Powys 59 F8
Dolgarrog Conwy 83 E7
Dolgellau Gwyn 58 C4
Dolgran Carms 46 F3
Dolhendre Gwyn 72 F2
Doll Highld 157 J11
Dollar Clack 127 E8
Dolley Green Powys 48 C4
Dollwen Ceredig 58 F3
Dolphin Flint 73 B5
Dolphinholme Lancs 92 D5
Dolphinton S Lanark 120 E4
Dolton Devon 9 C7
Dolwen Conwy 83 D8
Dolwen Powys 59 D6
Dolwyd Conwy 83 D8
Dolwyddelan Conwy 83 F7
Dolyhir Powys 48 D4
Doncaster S Yorks 89 D6
Dones Green Ches W 74 B3
Donhead St Andrew Wilts 13 B7
Donhead St Mary Wilts 13 B7
Donibristle Fife 128 F3
Donington Lincs 78 F5
Donington on Bain Lincs 91 F6
Donington South Ing Lincs 78 F5
Donisthorpe Leics 63 C7
Donkey Town Sur 27 C7
Donnington Glos 38 B1
Donnington Hereford 50 F2
Donnington Shrops 61 D5
Donnington Telford 61 C7
Donnington W Berks 26 C2
Donnington W Sus 16 D2
Donnington Wood Telford 61 C7
Donyatt Som 11 C8
Doonfoot S Ayrs 112 C3
Dorback Lodge Highld 139 C6
Dorchester Dorset 12 E4
Dorchester Oxon 39 E5
Dordon Warks 63 D6
Dore S Yorks 88 F4
Dores Highld 151 H8
Dorking Sur 28 E2
Dormansland Sur 28 E5
Dormanstown Redcar 102 B3
Dormington Hereford 49 E7
Dormston Worcs 50 D4
Dornal S Ayrs 105 B6
Dorney Bucks 27 B7
Dornie Highld 149 F13
Dornoch Highld 151 C10
Dornock Dumfries 108 C2
Dorrery Highld 158 E2
Dorridge W Mid 51 B6
Dorrington Lincs 78 D3
Dorrington Shrops 60 D4
Dorsington Warks 51 E6
Dorstone Hereford 48 E5
Dorton Bucks 39 C6
Dorusduain Highld 136 B2
Dosthill Staffs 63 E6
Dottery Dorset 12 E2
Doublebois Corn 5 C6
Dougarie N Ayrs 143 E9
Doughton Glos 37 E5
Douglas IoM 84 E3
Douglas S Lanark 119 F8
Douglas & Angus Dundee 134 F4
Douglas Water S Lanark 119 F8
Douglas West S Lanark 119 F8
Douglastown Angus 134 E4
Doulting Som 23 E8
Dounby Orkney 159 F3
Doune Highld 156 J7
Doune Stirling 127 D6
Doune Park Aberds 153 B7
Douneside Aberds 140 D3
Dounie Highld 151 B8
Dounreay Highld 157 C12
Dousland Devon 6 C3
Dovaston Shrops 60 B3
Dove Holes Derbys 75 B7
Dovenby Cumb 107 F7
Dover Kent 31 E7
Dovercourt Essex 57 F6
Doverdale Worcs 50 C3
Doveridge Derbys 75 F8
Doversgreen Sur 28 E3
Dowally Perth 133 E7
Dowbridge Lancs 92 F4
Dowdeswell Glos 37 C6
Dowlais M Tydf 34 D4
Dowland Devon 9 C7
Dowlish Wake Som 11 C8
Down Ampney Glos 37 E8
Down Hatherley Glos 37 B5
Down St Mary Devon 10 D2
Down Thomas Devon 6 D3
Downcraig Ferry N Ayrs 145 H10
Downderry Corn 5 D8
Downe London 28 C5
Downend IoW 15 F6
Downend S Glos 23 B8
Downend W Berks 26 B2
Downfield Dundee 134 F3
Downgate Corn 5 B8
Downham Essex 42 E3
Downham Lancs 93 E7
Downham Northumb 122 F4
Downham Market Norf 67 D6
Downhead Som 23 E8
Downhill Perth 133 F7
Downhill T&W 111 D6
Downholland Cross Lancs 85 D4
Downholme N Yorks 101 E6
Downies Aberds 141 E8
Downley Bucks 39 E8
Downside Som 23 E8
Downside Sur 28 D2
Downton Hants 14 E3
Downton Wilts 14 B2
Downton on the Rock Hereford 49 B6
Dowsby Lincs 65 B8
Dowsdale Lincs 66 C2
Dowthwaitehead Cumb 99 B5
Doxey Staffs 62 B3
Doxford Northumb 117 B7
Doxford Park T&W 111 D6
Doynton S Glos 24 B2
Draffan S Lanark 119 E7
Dragonby N Lincs 90 C3
Drakeland Corner Devon 6 D3
Drakemyre N Ayrs 118 D2
Drake's Broughton Worcs 50 E4
Drakes Cross Worcs 51 B5
Drakewalls Corn 6 B2
Draughton N Yorks 94 D3
Draughton Northants 53 B5
Drax N Yorks 89 B7
Draycote Warks 52 B2
Draycott Derbys 76 F4
Draycott Glos 51 F6
Draycott Som 23 D6
Draycott in the Clay Staffs 63 B5
Draycott in the Moors Staffs 75 E6
Drayford Devon 10 C2
Drayton Leics 64 E5
Drayton Lincs 78 F5
Drayton Norf 68 C4
Drayton Oxon 38 E4
Drayton Oxon 52 E2
Drayton Ptsmth 15 D7
Drayton Som 12 B2
Drayton Worcs 50 B4
Drayton Bassett Staffs 63 D5
Drayton Beauchamp Bucks 40 C2
Drayton Parslow Bucks 39 B8
Drayton St Leonard Oxon 39 E5
Dre-fach Carms 33 C7
Dre-fach Ceredig 46 E4
Drebley N Yorks 94 D3
Dreemskerry IoM 84 C4
Dreenhill Pembs 44 D4
Drefach Carms 33 C6
Drefach Carms 46 F2
Drefelin Carms 46 F2
Dreghorn N Ayrs 118 F3
Drellingore Kent 31 E6
Drem E Loth 121 B8
Dresden Stoke 75 E6
Dreumasdal W Isles 148 E2
Drewsteignton Devon 10 E2
Driby Lincs 79 B6
Driffield E Yorks 97 D6
Driffield Glos 37 E7
Drigg Cumb 98 E2
Drighlington W Yorks 88 B3
Drimnin Highld 147 F8
Drimpton Dorset 12 D2
Drimsynie Argyll 125 E7
Drinisiadar W Isles 154 H6
Drinkstone Suff 56 C3
Drinkstone Green Suff 56 C3
Drishaig Argyll 125 D7
Drissaig Argyll 124 D5
Drochil Borders 120 E4
Drointon Staffs 62 B4
Droitwich Spa Worcs 50 C3
Droman Highld 156 D4
Dron Perth 128 C3
Dronfield Derbys 76 B3
Dronfield Woodhouse Derbys 76 B3
Drongan E Ayrs 112 C4
Dronley Angus 134 F3
Droxford Hants 15 C7
Droylsden Gtr Man 87 E7
Druid Denb 72 E4
Druidston Pembs 44 D3
Druimarbin Highld 130 B4
Druimavuic Argyll 130 E4
Druimdrishaig Argyll 144 F6
Druimindarroch Highld 147 C9
Druimyeon More Argyll 143 C7
Drum Argyll 145 F8
Drum Perth 128 D2
Drumbeg Highld 156 F4
Drumblade Aberds 152 D5
Drumblair Aberds 153 D6
Drumbuie Dumfries 113 F5
Drumbuie Highld 149 E12
Drumburgh Cumb 108 D2
Drumburn Dumfries 107 C6
Drumchapel Glasgow 118 B5
Drumchardine Highld 151 G8
Drumchork Highld 155 J13
Drumclog S Lanark 119 F6
Drumderfit Highld 151 F9
Drumeldrie Fife 129 D6
Drumelzier Borders 120 F4
Drumfearn Highld 149 G11
Drumgask Highld 138 E2
Drumgley Angus 134 D4
Drumguish Highld 138 E3
Drumin Moray 152 E1
Drumlasie Aberds 140 D5
Drumlemble Argyll 143 G7
Drumligair Aberds 141 C8
Drumlithie Aberds 141 F6
Drummoddie Dumfries 105 E7
Drummond Highld 151 E9
Drummore Dumfries 104 F5
Drummuir Moray 152 D3
Drummuir Castle Moray 152 D3
Drumnadrochit Highld 137 B8
Drumnagorrach Moray 152 C5
Drumoak Aberds 141 E6
Drumpark Dumfries 107 A5
Drumphail Dumfries 105 C6
Drumrash Dumfries 106 B3
Drumrunie Highld 156 J4
Drums Aberds 141 B8
Drumsallie Highld 130 B3
Drumstinchall Dumfries 107 D5
Drumsturdy Angus 134 F4
Drumtochty Castle Aberds 135 B6
Drumtroddan Dumfries 105 E7
Drumuie Highld 149 D9
Drumuillie Highld 138 B5
Drumvaich Stirling 127 D5
Drumwhindle Aberds 153 E9
Drunkendub Angus 135 E6
Drury Flint 73 C6
Drury Square Norf 68 C2
Dry Doddington Lincs 77 E8
Dry Drayton Cambs 54 C4
Drybeck Cumb 100 C1
Drybridge Moray 152 B4
Drybridge N Ayrs 118 F3
Drybrook Glos 36 C3
Dryburgh Borders 121 F8
Dryhope Borders 115 B5
Drylaw Edin 120 B5
Drym Corn 2 C5
Drymen Stirling 126 F3
Drymuir Aberds 153 D9
Drynoch Highld 149 E9
Dryslwyn Carms 33 B6
Dryton Shrops 61 D5
Dubford Aberds 153 B8
Dubton Angus 135 D5
Duchally Highld 156 H6
Duchlage Argyll 126 F2
Duck Corner Suff 57 E7
Duckington Ches W 73 D8
Ducklington Oxon 38 D3
Duckmanton Derbys 76 B4
Duck's Cross Bedford 54 D2
Duddenhoe End Essex 55 F5
Duddingston Edin 121 B5
Duddington Northants 65 D6
Duddleswell E Sus 17 B8
Duddo Northumb 122 E5
Duddon Ches W 74 C2
Duddon Bridge Cumb 98 F4
Dudleston Shrops 73 F7
Dudleston Heath Shrops 73 F7
Dudley T&W 111 B5
Dudley W Mid 62 E3
Dudley Port W Mid 62 E3
Duffield Derbys 76 E3
Duffryn Neath 34 E2
Duffryn Newport 35 F6
Dufftown Moray 152 E3
Duffus Moray 152 B1
Dufton Cumb 100 B1
Duggleby N Yorks 96 C4
Duirinish Highld 149 E12
Duisdalemore Highld 149 G12
Duisky Highld 130 B4
Dukestown Bl Gwent 35 C5
Dukinfield Gtr Man 87 E7
Dulas Anglesey 82 C4
Dulcote Som 23 E7
Dulford Devon 11 D5
Dull Perth 133 E5
Dullatur N Lanark 119 B7
Dullingham Cambs 55 D7
Dulnain Bridge Highld 139 B5
Duloe Bedford 54 C2
Duloe Corn 5 D7
Dulsie Highld 151 G12
Dulverton Som 10 B4
Dulwich London 28 B4
Dumbarton W Dunb 118 B3
Dumbleton Glos 50 F5
Dumcrieff Dumfries 114 D4
Dumfries Dumfries 107 B6
Dumgoyne Stirling 126 F4
Dummer Hants 26 E3
Dumpford W Sus 16 B2
Dumpton Kent 31 C7
Dun Angus 135 D6
Dun Charlabhaigh W Isles 154 C6
Dunain Ho. Highld 151 G9
Dunalastair Perth 132 D4
Dunan Highld 149 F10
Dunans Argyll 145 D9
Dunball Som 22 E5
Dunbar E Loth 122 B2
Dunbeath Highld 158 H3
Dunbeg Argyll 124 B4
Dunblane Stirling 127 D6
Dunbog Fife 128 C4
Duncanston Highld 151 F8
Duncanstone Aberds 140 B4
Dunchurch Warks 52 B2
Duncote Northants 52 D4
Duncow Dumfries 114 F2
Duncraggan Stirling 126 D4
Duncrievie Perth 128 D3
Duncton W Sus 16 C3
Dundas Ho. Orkney 159 K5
Dundee Dundee 134 F4
Dundeugh Dumfries 113 F5
Dundon Som 23 F6
Dundonald S Ayrs 118 F3
Dundonnell Highld 150 C3
Dundonnell Hotel Highld 150 C3
Dundonnell House Highld 150 C4
Dundraw Cumb 108 E2
Dundreggan Highld 137 C6
Dundreggan Lodge Highld 137 C6
Dundrennan Dumfries 106 E4
Dundry N Som 23 C7
Dunecht Aberds 141 D6
Dunfermline Fife 128 F2
Dunfield Glos 37 E8
Dunford Bridge S Yorks 88 D2
Dungworth S Yorks 88 F3
Dunham Notts 77 B8
Dunham-on-the-Hill Ches W 73 B8

Dunham Town Gtr Man 86 F5
Dunhampton Worcs 50 C3
Dunholme Lincs 78 B3
Dunino Fife 129 C7
Dunipace Falk 127 F7
Dunira Perth 127 B6
Dunkeld Perth 133 E7
Dunkerton Bath 24 D2
Dunkeswell Devon 11 D6
Dunkeswick N Yorks 95 E6
Dunkirk Kent 30 D4
Dunkirk Norf 81 E8
Dunk's Green Kent 29 D7
Dunlappie Angus 135 C5
Dunley Hants 26 D2
Dunley Worcs 50 C2
Dunlichity Lodge Highld 151 H9
Dunlop E Ayrs 118 E4
Dunmaglass Lodge Highld 137 B8
Dunmore Argyll 144 G6
Dunmore Falk 127 F7
Dunnet Highld 158 C4
Dunnichen Angus 135 E5
Dunninald Angus 135 D7
Dunning Perth 128 C2
Dunnington E Yorks 97 D7
Dunnington Warks 51 D5
Dunnington York 96 D2
Dunnockshaw Lancs 87 B6
Dunollie Argyll 124 B4
Dunoon Argyll 145 F10
Dunragit Dumfries 105 D5
Dunrostan Argyll 144 E6
Duns Borders 122 D3
Duns Tew Oxon 38 B4
Dunsby Lincs 65 B8
Dunscore Dumfries 113 F8
Dunscroft S Yorks 89 D7
Dunsdale Redcar 102 C4
Dunsden Green Oxon 26 B5
Dunsfold Sur 27 F8
Dunsford Devon 10 F3
Dunshalt Fife 128 C4
Dunshillock Aberds 153 D9
Dunskey Ho. Dumfries 104 D4
Dunsley N Yorks 103 C6
Dunsmore Bucks 40 D1
Dunsop Bridge Lancs 93 D6
Dunstable C Beds 40 B3
Dunstall Staffs 63 B5
Dunstall Common Worcs 50 E3
Dunstall Green Suff 55 C8
Dunstan Northumb 117 C8
Dunstan Steads Northumb 117 B8
Dunster Som 21 E8
Dunston Lincs 78 C3
Dunston Norf 68 D5
Dunston Staffs 62 C3
Dunston T&W 110 C5
Dunsville S Yorks 89 D7
Dunswell E Yorks 97 F6
Dunsyre S Lanark 120 E3
Dunterton Devon 5 B8
Duntisbourne Abbots Glos 37 D6
Duntisbourne Leer Glos 37 D6
Duntisbourne Rouse Glos 37 D6
Duntish Dorset 12 D4
Duntocher W Dunb 118 B4
Dunton Bucks 39 B8
Dunton C Beds 54 E3
Dunton Norf 80 D4
Dunton Bassett Leics 64 E2
Dunton Green Kent 29 D6
Dunton Wayletts Essex 42 E2
Duntulm Highld 149 A9
Dunure S Ayrs 112 C2
Dunvant Swansea 33 E6
Dunvegan Highld 148 D7
Dunwich Suff 57 B8
Dunwood Staffs 75 D6
Dupplin Castle Perth 128 C2
Durdar Cumb 108 D4
Durgates E Sus 18 B3
Durham Durham 111 E5
Durisdeer Dumfries 113 D8
Durisdeermill Dumfries 113 D8
Durkar W Yorks 88 C4
Durleigh Som 22 F4
Durley Hants 15 C6
Durley Wilts 25 C7
Durnamuck Highld 150 B3
Durness Highld 156 C7
Durno Aberds 141 B6
Duror Highld 130 D3
Durran Argyll 125 E5
Durran Highld 158 D3
Durrington W Sus 16 D5
Durrington Wilts 25 E6
Dursley Glos 36 E4
Durston Som 11 B7
Durweston Dorset 13 D6
Dury Shetland 160 G6
Duston Northants 52 C5
Duthil Highld 138 B5
Dutlas Powys 48 B4
Duton Hill Essex 42 B2
Dutson Corn 8 F5
Dutton Ches W 74 B2
Duxford Cambs 55 E5
Duxford Oxon 38 E3
Dwygyfylchi Conwy 83 D7
Dwyran Anglesey 82 E4
Dyce Aberdeen 141 C7
Dye House Northumb 110 D2
Dyffryn Bridgend 34 E2
Dyffryn Carms 32 B4
Dyffryn Pembs 44 B4
Dyffryn Ardudwy Gwyn 71 E6
Dyffryn Castell Ceredig 58 F4
Dyffryn Ceidrych Carms 33 B8
Dyffryn Cellwen Neath 34 D2
Dyke Lincs 65 B8
Dyke Moray 151 F12
Dykehead Angus 134 C3
Dykehead N Lanark 119 D8
Dykehead Stirling 126 E4
Dykelands Aberds 135 C7
Dykends Angus 134 D2
Dykeside Aberds 153 D7
Dykesmains N Ayrs 118 E2
Dylife Powys 59 E5
Dymchurch Kent 19 C7
Dymock Glos 50 F2
Dyrham S Glos 24 B2
Dysart Fife 128 E5
Dyserth Denb 72 B4

E

Eachwick Northumb 110 B4
Eadar Dha Fhadhail W Isles 154 D5
Eagland Hill Lancs 92 E4
Eagle Lincs 77 C8
Eagle Barnsdale Lincs 77 C8
Eagle Moor Lincs 77 C8
Eaglescliffe Stockton 102 C2
Eaglesfield Cumb 98 B2
Eaglesfield Dumfries 108 B2
Eaglesham E Renf 119 D5
Eaglethorpe Northants 65 E7
Eairy IoM 84 E2
Eakley Lanes M Keynes 53 D6
Eakring Notts 77 C6
Ealand N Lincs 89 C8
Ealing London 40 F4
Eals Northumb 109 D6
Eamont Bridge Cumb 99 B7
Earby Lancs 94 E2
Earcroft Blackburn 86 B4
Eardington Shrops 61 E7
Eardisland Hereford 49 D6
Eardisley Hereford 48 E5
Eardiston Shrops 60 B3
Eardiston Worcs 49 C8
Earith Cambs 54 B4
Earl Shilton Leics 63 E8
Earl Soham Suff 57 C6
Earl Sterndale Derbys 75 C7
Earl Stonham Suff 56 D5
Earle Northumb 117 B5
Earley Wokingham 27 B5
Earlham Norf 68 D5
Earlish Highld 149 B8
Earls Barton Northants 53 C6
Earls Colne Essex 42 B4
Earl's Croome Worcs 50 E3
Earl's Green Suff 56 C4
Earlsdon W Mid 51 B8
Earlsferry Fife 129 E6
Earlsfield Lincs 78 F2
Earlsford Aberds 153 E8
Earlsheaton W Yorks 88 B3
Earlsmill Moray 151 F12
Earlston Borders 121 F8
Earlston E Ayrs 118 F4
Earlswood Mon 36 E1
Earlswood Sur 28 E3
Earlswood Warks 51 B6
Earnley W Sus 16 E2
Earsairidh W Isles 148 J2
Earsdon T&W 111 B6
Earsham Norf 69 F6
Earswick York 96 D2
Eartham W Sus 16 D3
Easby N Yorks 101 D6
Easby N Yorks 102 D3
Easdale Argyll 124 D3
Easebourne W Sus 16 B2
Easenhall Warks 52 B2
Eashing Sur 27 E7
Easington Bucks 39 C6
Easington Durham 111 E7
Easington E Yorks 91 C7
Easington Northumb 123 F7
Easington Oxon 39 E6
Easington Oxon 52 F2
Easington Redcar 103 C5
Easington Colliery Durham 111 E7
Easington Lane T&W 111 E6
Easingwold N Yorks 95 C8
Easole Street Kent 31 D6
Eassie Angus 134 E3
East Aberthaw V Glam 22 C2
East Adderbury Oxon 52 F2
East Allington Devon 7 E5
East Anstey Devon 10 B3
East Appleton N Yorks 101 E7
East Ardsley W Yorks 88 B4
East Ashling W Sus 16 D2
East Auchronie Aberds 141 D7
East Ayton N Yorks 103 F7
East Bank Bl Gwent 35 D6
East Barkwith Lincs 91 F5
East Barming Kent 29 D8
East Barnby N Yorks 103 C6
East Barnet London 41 E5
East Barns E Loth 122 B3
East Barsham Norf 80 D5
East Beckham Norf 81 D7
East Bedfont London 27 B8
East Bergholt Suff 56 F4
East Bilney Norf 68 C2
East Blatchington E Sus 17 D8
East Boldre Hants 14 D4
East Brent Som 22 D5
East Bridgford Notts 77 E6
East Buckland Devon 21 F5
East Budleigh Devon 11 F5
East Burrafirth Shetland 160 H5
East Burton Dorset 13 F6
East Butsfield Durham 110 E4
East Butterwick N Lincs 90 D2
East Cairnbeg Aberds 135 B7
East Calder W Loth 120 C3
East Carleton Norf 68 D4
East Carlton Northants 64 F5
East Carlton W Yorks 94 E5
East Chaldon Dorset 13 F5
East Challow Oxon 38 F3
East Chiltington E Sus 17 C7
East Chinnock Som 12 C2
East Chisenbury Wilts 25 D6
East Clandon Sur 27 D8
East Claydon Bucks 39 B7
East Clyne Highld 157 J12
East Coker Som 12 C3
East Combe Som 22 F3
East Common N Yorks 96 F2
East Compton Som 23 E8
East Cottingwith E Yorks 96 E3
East Cowes IoW 15 E6
East Cowick E Yorks 89 B7
East Cowton N Yorks 101 D8
East Cramlington Northumb 111 B5
East Cranmore Som 23 E8
East Creech Dorset 13 F7
East Croachy Highld 138 B2
East Croftmore Highld 139 C5
East Curthwaite Cumb 108 E3
East Dean E Sus 18 F2
East Dean Hants 14 B3
East Dean W Sus 16 C3
East Down Devon 20 E5
East Drayton Notts 77 B7
East Ella Hull 90 B4
East End Dorset 13 E7
East End E Yorks 91 B6
East End Hants 14 E4
East End Hants 15 B7
East End Hants 26 C2
East End Herts 41 B7
East End Kent 18 B5
East End N Som 23 B6
East End Oxon 38 C3
East Farleigh Kent 29 D8
East Farndon Northants 64 F4
East Ferry Lincs 90 E2
East Fortune E Loth 121 B8
East Garston W Berks 25 B8
East Ginge Oxon 38 F4
East Goscote Leics 64 C3
East Grafton Wilts 25 C7
East Grimstead Wilts 14 B3
East Grinstead W Sus 28 F4
East Guldeford E Sus 19 C6
East Haddon Northants 52 C4
East Hagbourne Oxon 39 F5
East Halton N Lincs 90 C5
East Ham London 41 F7
East Hanney Oxon 38 E4
East Hanningfield Essex 42 D3
East Hardwick W Yorks 89 C5
East Harling Norf 68 F2
East Harlsey N Yorks 102 E2
East Harnham Wilts 14 B2
East Harptree Bath 23 D7
East Hartford Northumb 111 B5
East Harting W Sus 15 C8
East Hatley Cambs 54 D3
East Hauxwell N Yorks 101 E6
East Haven Angus 135 F5
East Heckington Lincs 78 E4
East Hedleyhope Durham 110 E4
East Hendred Oxon 38 F4
East Herrington T&W 111 D6
East Heslerton N Yorks 96 B5
East Hoathly E Sus 18 D2
East Horrington Som 23 E7
East Horsley Sur 27 D8
East Horton Northumb 123 F6
East Huntspill Som 22 E5
East Hyde C Beds 40 C4
East Ilkerton Devon 21 E6
East Ilsley W Berks 38 F4
East Keal Lincs 79 C6
East Kennett Wilts 25 C6
East Keswick W Yorks 95 E6
East Kilbride S Lanark 119 D6
East Kirkby Lincs 79 C6
East Knapton N Yorks 96 B4
East Knighton Dorset 13 F6
East Knoyle Wilts 24 F3
East Kyloe Northumb 123 F6
East Lambrook Som 12 C2
East Lamington Highld 151 D10
East Langdon Kent 31 E7
East Langton Leics 64 E4
East Langwell Highld 157 J10
East Lavant W Sus 16 D2
East Lavington W Sus 16 C3
East Layton N Yorks 101 D6
East Leake Notts 64 B2
East Learmouth Northumb 122 F4
East Leigh Devon 9 D8
East Lexham Norf 67 C8
East Lilburn Northumb 117 B6
East Linton E Loth 121 B8
East Liss Hants 15 B8
East Looe Corn 5 D7
East Lound N Lincs 89 E8
East Lulworth Dorset 13 F6
East Lutton N Yorks 96 C5
East Lydford Som 23 F7
East Mains Aberds 141 E5
East Malling Kent 29 D8
East March Angus 134 F4
East Marden W Sus 16 C2
East Markham Notts 77 B7
East Marton N Yorks 94 D2
East Meon Hants 15 B7
East Mere Devon 10 C4
East Mersea Essex 43 C6
East Mey Highld 158 C5
East Molesey Sur 28 C2
East Morden Dorset 13 E7
East Morton W Yorks 94 E3
East Ness N Yorks 96 B2
East Newton E Yorks 97 F8
East Norton Leics 64 D4
East Nynehead Som 11 B6
East Oakley Hants 26 D3
East Ogwell Devon 7 B6
East Orchard Dorset 13 C6
East Ord Northumb 123 D5
East Panson Devon 9 E5
East Peckham Kent 29 E7
East Pennard Som 23 F7
East Perry Cambs 54 C2
East Portlemouth Devon 6 F5
East Prawle Devon 7 F5
East Preston W Sus 16 D4
East Putford Devon 9 C5
East Quantoxhead Som 22 E3
East Rainton T&W 111 E6
East Ravendale NE Lincs 91 E6
East Raynham Norf 80 E4
East Rhidorroch Lodge Highld 150 B5
East Rigton W Yorks 95 E6
East Rounton N Yorks 102 D2
East Row N Yorks 103 C6
East Rudham Norf 80 E4
East Runton Norf 81 C7
East Ruston Norf 69 B6
East Saltoun E Loth 121 C7
East Sleekburn Northumb 117 F8
East Somerton Norf 69 C7
East Stockwith Lincs 89 E8
East Stoke Dorset 13 F6
East Stoke Notts 77 E7
East Stour Dorset 13 B6
East Stourmouth Kent 31 C6
East Stowford Devon 9 B8
East Stratton Hants 26 F3
East Studdal Kent 31 E7
East Suisnish Highld 149 E10
East Taphouse Corn 5 C6
East-the-Water Devon 9 B6
East Thirston Northumb 117 E7
East Tilbury Thurrock 29 B7
East Tisted Hants 26 F5
East Torrington Lincs 90 F5
East Tuddenham Norf 68 C3
East Tytherley Hants 14 B3
East Tytherton Wilts 24 B4
East Village Devon 10 D3
East Wall Shrops 60 E5
East Walton Norf 67 C7
East Wellow Hants 14 B4
East Wemyss Fife 128 E5
East Whitburn W Loth 120 C2
East Williamston Pembs 32 D1
East Winch Norf 67 C6
East Winterslow Wilts 25 F7
East Wittering W Sus 15 E8
East Witton N Yorks 101 F6
East Woodburn Northumb 116 F5
East Woodhay Hants 26 C2
East Worldham Hants 26 F5
East Worlington Devon 10 C2
East Worthing W Sus 17 D5
Eastbourne E Sus 18 F3
Eastbridge Suff 57 C8
Eastburn W Yorks 94 E3
Eastbury London 40 E3
Eastbury W Berks 25 B8
Eastby N Yorks 94 D3
Eastchurch Kent 30 B3
Eastcombe Glos 37 D5
Eastcote London 40 F4
Eastcote Northants 52 D4
Eastcote W Mid 51 B6
Eastcott Corn 8 C4
Eastcott Wilts 24 D5
Eastcourt Wilts 25 C7
Eastcourt Wilts 37 E6
Easter Ardross Highld 151 D9
Easter Balmoral Aberds 139 E8
Easter Boleskine Highld 137 B8
Easter Compton S Glos 36 F2
Easter Cringate Stirling 127 F6
Easter Davoch Aberds 140 D3
Easter Earshaig Dumfries 114 D3
Easter Fearn Highld 151 C9
Easter Galcantray Highld 151 G11
Easter Howgate Midloth 120 C5
Easter Howlaws Borders 122 E3
Easter Kinkell Highld 151 F8
Easter Lednathie Angus 134 C3
Easter Milton Highld 151 F12
Easter Moniack Highld 151 G8
Easter Ord Aberdeen 141 D7
Easter Quarff Shetland 160 K6
Easter Rhynd Perth 128 C3
Easter Row Stirling 127 E6
Easter Silverford Aberds 153 B7
Easter Skeld Shetland 160 J5
Easter Whyntie Aberds 152 B6
Eastergate W Sus 16 D3
Easterhouse Glasgow 119 C6
Eastern Green W Mid 63 F6
Easterton Wilts 24 D5
Eastertown Som 22 D5
Eastertown of Auchleuchries Aberds 153 E10
Eastfield N Lanark 119 C8
Eastfield N Yorks 103 F8
Eastfield Hall Northumb 117 D8
Eastgate Durham 110 F2
Eastgate Norf 81 E7
Eastham Mers 85 F4
Eastham Ferry Mers 85 F4
Easthampstead Brack 27 C6
Eastheath Wokingham 27 C6
Easthope Shrops 61 E5
Easthorpe Essex 43 B5
Easthorpe Leics 77 F8
Easthorpe Notts 77 D7
Easthouses Midloth 121 C6
Eastington Devon 10 D2
Eastington Glos 36 D4
Eastington Glos 37 C8
Eastleach Martin Glos 38 D2
Eastleach Turville Glos 38 D1
Eastleigh Devon 9 B6
Eastleigh Hants 14 C5
Eastling Kent 30 D3
Eastmoor Derbys 76 B3
Eastmoor Norf 67 D7
Eastney Ptsmth 15 E7
Eastnor Hereford 50 F2
Eastoft N Lincs 90 C2
Eastoke Hants 15 E8
Easton Cambs 54 B2
Easton Cumb 108 B4
Easton Cumb 108 D2
Easton Devon 10 F2
Easton Dorset 12 G4
Easton Hants 26 F3
Easton Lincs 65 B6
Easton Norf 68 C4
Easton Som 23 E7
Easton Suff 57 D6
Easton Wilts 24 B3
Easton Grey Wilts 37 F5
Easton-in-Gordano N Som 23 B7
Easton Maudit Northants 53 D6
Easton on the Hill Northants 65 D7
Easton Royal Wilts 25 C7
Eastpark Dumfries 107 C7
Eastrea Cambs 66 E2
Eastriggs Dumfries 108 C2
Eastrington E Yorks 89 B8
Eastry Kent 31 D7
Eastville Bristol 23 B8
Eastville Lincs 79 D7
Eastwell Leics 64 B4
Eastwick Herts 41 C7
Eastwick Shetland 160 F5
Eastwood Notts 76 E4
Eastwood Southend 42 F4
Eastwood W Yorks 87 B7
Eathorpe Warks 51 C8
Eaton Ches E 75 C5
Eaton Ches W 74 C2
Eaton Leics 64 B4
Eaton Norf 68 D5
Eaton Notts 77 B7
Eaton Oxon 38 D4
Eaton Shrops 60 F3
Eaton Shrops 60 F5
Eaton Bishop Hereford 49 F6
Eaton Bray C Beds 40 B2
Eaton Constantine Shrops 61 D5
Eaton Green C Beds 40 B2
Eaton Hastings Oxon 38 E2
Eaton on Tern Shrops 61 B6
Eaton Socon Cambs 54 D2
Eavestone N Yorks 94 C5
Ebberston N Yorks 103 F6
Ebbesbourne Wake Wilts 13 B7
Ebbw Vale = Glyn Ebwy Bl Gwent 35 D5
Ebchester Durham 110 D4
Ebford Devon 10 F4
Ebley Glos 37 D5
Ebnal Ches W 73 E8
Ebrington Glos 51 E6
Ecchinswell Hants 26 D2
Ecclaw Borders 122 C3
Ecclefechan Dumfries 107 B8
Eccles Borders 122 E3
Eccles Gtr Man 87 E5
Eccles Kent 29 C8
Eccles on Sea Norf 69 B7
Eccles Road Norf 68 E3
Ecclesall S Yorks 88 F4
Ecclesfield S Yorks 88 E4
Ecclesgreig Aberds 135 C7
Eccleshall Staffs 62 B2
Eccleshill W Yorks 94 F4
Ecclesmachan W Loth 120 B3
Eccleston Ches W 73 C8
Eccleston Lancs 86 C3
Eccleston Mers 86 E2
Eccleston Park Mers 86 E2
Eccup W Yorks 95 E5
Echt Aberds 141 D6
Eckford Borders 116 B3
Eckington Derbys 76 B4
Eckington Worcs 50 E4
Ecton Northants 53 C6
Edale Derbys 88 F2
Edburton W Sus 17 C6
Edderside Cumb 107 E7
Edderton Highld 151 C10
Eddistone Devon 8 B4
Eddleston Borders 120 E5
Eden Park London 28 C4
Edenbridge Kent 28 E5
Edenfield Lancs 87 C5
Edenhall Cumb 109 F5
Edenham Lincs 65 B7
Edensor Derbys 76 C2
Edentaggart Argyll 126 E2
Edenthorpe S Yorks 89 D7
Edentown Cumb 108 D3
Ederline Argyll 124 E4
Edern Gwyn 70 D3
Edgarley Som 23 F7
Edgbaston W Mid 62 F4
Edgcott Bucks 39 B6
Edgcott Som 21 F7
Edge Shrops 60 D3
Edge End Glos 36 C2
Edge Green Ches W 73 D8
Edge Hill Mers 85 F4
Edgebolton Shrops 61 B5
Edgefield Norf 81 D6
Edgefield Street Norf 81 D6
Edgeside Lancs 87 B6
Edgeworth Glos 37 D6
Edgmond Telford 61 C7
Edgmond Marsh Telford 61 B7
Edgton Shrops 60 F3
Edgware London 40 E4
Edgworth Blackburn 86 C5
Edinample Stirling 126 B4
Edinbane Highld 149 C8
Edinburgh Edin 121 B5
Edingale Staffs 63 C6
Edingight Ho. Moray 152 C5
Edingley Notts 77 D6
Edingthorpe Norf 69 A6
Edingthorpe Green Norf 69 A6
Edington Som 23 F5
Edington Wilts 24 D4
Edintore Moray 152 D4
Edith Weston Rutland 65 D6
Edithmead Som 22 E5
Edlesborough Bucks 40 C2
Edlingham Northumb 117 D7
Edlington Lincs 78 B5
Edmondsham Dorset 13 C8
Edmondsley Durham 110 E5
Edmondthorpe Leics 65 C5
Edmonstone Orkney 159 F6
Edmonton London 41 E6
Edmundbyers Durham 110 D3
Ednam Borders 122 F3
Ednaston Derbys 76 E2
Edradynate Perth 133 D5
Edrom Borders 122 D4
Edstaston Shrops 74 F2
Edstone Warks 51 C6
Edvin Loach Hereford 49 D8
Edwalton Notts 77 F5
Edwardstone Suff 56 E3
Edwinsford Carms 46 F5
Edwinstowe Notts 77 C6
Edworth C Beds 54 E3
Edwyn Ralph Hereford 49 D8
Edzell Angus 135 C5
Efail Isaf Rhondda 34 F4
Efailnewydd Gwyn 70 D4
Efailwen Carms 32 B2
Efenechtyd Denb 72 D5
Effingham Sur 28 D2
Effirth Shetland 160 H5
Efford Devon 10 D3
Egdon Worcs 50 D4
Egerton Gtr Man 86 C5
Egerton Kent 30 E3
Egerton Forstal Kent 30 E2
Eggborough N Yorks 89 B6
Eggbuckland Plym 6 D3
Eggington C Beds 40 B2
Egginton Derbys 63 B6
Egglescliffe Stockton 102 C2
Eggleston Durham 100 B4
Egham Sur 27 B8
Egleton Rutland 65 D5
Eglingham Northumb 117 C7
Egloshayle Corn 4 B5
Egloskerry Corn 8 F4
Eglwys-Brewis V Glam 22 C2
Eglwys Cross Wrex 73 E8
Eglwys Fach Ceredig 58 E3
Eglwysbach Conwy 83 D8
Eglwyswen Pembs 45 F3
Eglwyswrw Pembs 45 F3
Egmanton Notts 77 C7
Egremont Cumb 98 C2
Egremont Mers 85 E4
Egton N Yorks 103 D6
Egton Bridge N Yorks 103 D6
Eight Ash Green Essex 43 B5
Eignaig Highld 130 E1
Eil Highld 138 C4
Eilanreach Highld 149 G13
Eilean Darach Highld 150 C4
Eileanach Lodge Highld 151 E8
Einacleite W Isles 154 E6
Eisgean W Isles 155 F8
Eisingrug Gwyn 71 D7
Elan Village Powys 47 C8
Elberton S Glos 36 F3
Elburton Plym 6 D3
Elcho Perth 128 B3
Elcombe Swindon 37 F8
Eldernell Cambs 66 E3
Eldersfield Worcs 50 F3
Elderslie Renfs 118 C4
Eldon Durham 101 B7
Eldrick S Ayrs 112 F2
Eldroth N Yorks 93 C7
Eldwick W Yorks 94 E4
Elfhowe Cumb 99 E6
Elford Northumb 123 F7
Elford Staffs 63 C5
Elgin Moray 152 B2
Elgol Highld 149 G10
Elham Kent 31 E5
Elie Fife 129 D6
Elim Anglesey 82 C3
Eling Hants 14 C4
Elishader Highld 149 B10
Elishaw Northumb 116 E4
Elkesley Notts 77 B6
Elkstone Glos 37 C6
Ellan Highld 138 B4
Elland W Yorks 88 B2
Ellary Argyll 144 F6
Ellastone Staffs 75 E8
Ellemford Borders 122 C3
Ellenbrook IoM 84 E3
Ellenhall Staffs 62 B2
Ellen's Green Sur 27 F8
Ellerbeck N Yorks 102 E2
Ellerburn N Yorks 103 F6
Ellerby N Yorks 103 C5
Ellerdine Heath Telford 61 B6
Ellerhayes Devon 10 D4
Elleric Argyll 130 E4
Ellerker E Yorks 90 B3
Ellerton E Yorks 96 F3
Ellerton Shrops 61 B7
Ellesborough Bucks 39 D8
Ellesmere Shrops 73 F8
Ellesmere Port Ches W 73 B8
Ellingham Norf 69 E6
Ellingham Northumb 117 B7
Ellingstring N Yorks 101 F6
Ellington Cambs 54 B2
Ellington Northumb 117 E8
Elliot Angus 135 F6
Ellisfield Hants 26 E4
Ellistown Leics 63 C8
Ellon Aberds 153 E9
Ellonby Cumb 108 F4
Ellough Suff 69 F7
Elloughton E Yorks 90 B3
Ellwood Glos 36 D2
Elm Cambs 66 D4
Elm Hill Dorset 13 B6
Elm Park London 41 F8
Elmbridge Worcs 50 C4
Elmdon Essex 55 F5
Elmdon W Mid 63 F5
Elmdon Heath W Mid 63 F5
Elmers End London 28 C4
Elmesthorpe Leics 63 E8
Elmfield IoW 15 E7
Elmhurst Staffs 62 C5
Elmley Castle Worcs 50 E4
Elmley Lovett Worcs 50 C3
Elmore Glos 36 C4
Elmore Back Glos 36 C4
Elmscott Devon 8 B4
Elmsett Suff 56 E4
Elmstead Market Essex 43 B6
Elmsted Kent 30 E5
Elmstone Kent 31 C6
Elmstone Hardwicke Glos 37 B6
Elmswell E Yorks 97 D5
Elmswell Suff 56 C3
Elmton Derbys 76 B5
Elphin Highld 156 H5
Elphinstone E Loth 121 B6
Elrick Aberds 141 D7
Elrig Dumfries 105 E7
Elsdon Northumb 117 E5
Elsecar S Yorks 88 E4
Elsenham Essex 41 B8
Elsfield Oxon 39 C5
Elsham N Lincs 90 C4
Elsing Norf 68 C3
Elslack N Yorks 94 E2
Elson Shrops 73 F7
Elsrickle S Lanark 120 E3
Elstead Sur 27 E7
Elsted W Sus 16 C2
Elsthorpe Lincs 65 B7
Elstob Durham 101 B8
Elston Notts 77 E7
Elston Wilts 25 E5
Elstone Devon 9 C8
Elstow Bedford 53 E8
Elstree Herts 40 E4
Elstronwick E Yorks 97 F8
Elswick Lancs 92 F4
Elsworth Cambs 54 C4
Elterwater Cumb 99 D5
Eltham London 28 B5
Eltisley Cambs 54 D3
Elton Cambs 65 E7
Elton Ches W 73 B8
Elton Derbys 76 C2
Elton Glos 36 C4
Elton Hereford 49 B6
Elton Notts 77 F7
Elton Stockton 102 C2
Elton Green Ches W 73 B8
Elvanfoot S Lanark 114 C2
Elvaston Derbys 76 F4
Elveden Suff 56 B2
Elvingston E Loth 121 B7
Elvington Kent 31 D6
Elvington York 96 E2
Elwick Hrtlpl 111 F7
Elwick Northumb 123 F7
Elworth Ches E 74 C4
Elworthy Som 22 F2
Ely Cambs 66 F5
Ely Cardiff 22 B3
Emberton M Keynes 53 E6
Embleton Cumb 107 F8
Embleton Northumb 117 B8
Embo Highld 151 B11
Embo Street Highld 151 B11
Emborough Som 23 D8
Embsay N Yorks 94 D3
Emery Down Hants 14 D3
Emersons Green S Glos 23 B8
Emley W Yorks 88 C3
Emmbrook Wokingham 27 C5
Emmer Green Reading 26 B5
Emmington Oxon 39 D7
Emneth Norf 66 D4
Emneth Hungate Norf 66 D5
Empingham Rutland 65 D6
Empshott Hants 27 F5
Emstrey Shrops 60 C5
Emsworth Hants 15 D8
Enborne W Berks 26 C2
Enchmarsh Shrops 60 E5
Enderby Leics 64 E2
Endmoor Cumb 99 F7
Endon Staffs 75 D6
Endon Bank Staffs 75 D6
Enfield London 41 E6
Enfield Wash London 41 E6
Enford Wilts 25 D6
Engamoor Shetland 160 H4
Engine Common S Glos 36 F3
Englefield W Berks 26 B4
Englefield Green Sur 27 B7
Englesea-brook Ches E 74 D4
English Bicknor Glos 36 C2
English Frankton Shrops 60 B4
Englishcombe Bath 24 C2
Enham Alamein Hants 25 E8
Enmore Som 22 F4
Ennerdale Bridge Cumb 98 C2
Enoch Dumfries 113 D8
Enochdhu Perth 133 C7
Ensay Argyll 146 G6
Ensbury Bmouth 13 E8
Ensdon Shrops 60 C4
Ensis Devon 9 B7
Enstone Oxon 38 B3
Enterkinfoot Dumfries 113 D8
Enterpen N Yorks 102 D2
Enville Staffs 62 F2
Eolaigearraidh W Isles 148 H2
Eorabus Argyll 146 J6
Eòropaidh W Isles 155 A10
Epperstone Notts 77 E6
Epping Essex 41 D7
Epping Green Essex 41 D7
Epping Green Herts 41 D5
Epping Upland Essex 41 D7
Eppleby N Yorks 101 C6
Eppleworth E Yorks 97 F6
Epsom Sur 28 C3
Epwell Oxon 51 E8
Epworth N Lincs 89 D8
Epworth Turbary N Lincs 89 D8
Erbistock Wrex 73 E7
Erbusaig Highld 149 F12
Erchless Castle Highld 150 G7
Erdington W Mid 62 E5
Eredine Argyll 125 E5
Eriboll Highld 156 D7
Ericstane Dumfries 114 C3
Eridge Green E Sus 18 B2
Erines Argyll 145 F7
Eriswell Suff 55 B8
Erith London 29 B6
Erlestoke Wilts 24 D4
Ermine Lincs 78 B2
Ermington Devon 6 D4
Erpingham Norf 81 D7
Errogie Highld 137 B8
Errol Perth 128 B4
Erskine Renfs 118 B4
Erskine Bridge Renfs 118 B4
Ervie Dumfries 104 C4
Erwarton Suff 57 F6
Erwood Powys 48 E2
Eryholme N Yorks 101 D8
Eryrys Denb 73 D6
Escomb Durham 101 B6
Escrick N Yorks 96 E2
Esgairdawe Carms 46 E5
Esgairgeiliog Powys 58 D4
Esh Durham 110 E4
Esh Winning Durham 110 E4
Esher Sur 28 C2
Esholt W Yorks 94 E4
Eshott Northumb 117 E8
Eshton N Yorks 94 D2
Esk Valley N Yorks 103 D6
Eskadale Highld 150 H7
Eskbank Midloth 121 C6
Eskdale Green Cumb 98 D3
Eskdalemuir Dumfries 115 E5
Eske E Yorks 97 E6
Eskham Lincs 91 E7
Esprick Lancs 92 F4
Essendine Rutland 65 C7
Essendon Herts 41 D5
Essich Highld 151 H9
Essington Staffs 62 D3
Esslemont Aberds 141 B8
Eston Redcar 102 C3
Eswick Shetland 160 H6
Etal Northumb 122 F5
Etchilhampton Wilts 24 C5
Etchingham E Sus 18 C4
Etchinghill Kent 19 B8
Etchinghill Staffs 62 C4
Ethie Castle Angus 135 E6
Ethie Mains Angus 135 E6
Etling Green Norf 68 C3
Eton Windsor 27 B7
Eton Wick Windsor 27 B7
Etteridge Highld 138 E2
Ettersgill Durham 100 B3
Ettingshall W Mid 62 E3
Ettington Warks 51 E7
Etton E Yorks 97 E5
Etton Pboro 65 D8
Ettrick Borders 115 C5
Ettrickbridge Borders 115 B6
Ettrickhill Borders 115 C5
Etwall Derbys 76 F2
Euston Suff 56 B2
Euximoor Drove Cambs 66 E4
Euxton Lancs 86 C3
Evanstown Bridgend 34 F3
Evanton Highld 151 E9
Evedon Lincs 78 E3
Evelix Highld 151 B10
Evenjobb Powys 48 C4
Evenley Northants 52 F3
Evenlode Glos 38 B2
Evenwood Durham 101 B6
Evenwood Gate Durham 101 B6
Everbay Orkney 159 F7
Evercreech Som 23 F8
Everdon Northants 52 D3
Everingham E Yorks 96 E4
Everleigh Wilts 25 D7
Everley N Yorks 103 F7
Eversholt C Beds 53 F7
Evershot Dorset 12 D3
Eversley Hants 27 C5
Eversley Cross Hants 27 C5
Everthorpe E Yorks 96 F5
Everton C Beds 54 D3
Everton Hants 14 E3
Everton Mers 85 E4
Everton Notts 89 E7
Evertown Dumfries 108 B3
Evesbatch Hereford 49 E8
Evesham Worcs 50 E5
Evington Leicester 64 D3
Ewden Village S Yorks 88 E3
Ewell Sur 28 C3
Ewell Minnis Kent 31 E6
Ewelme Oxon 39 E6
Ewen Glos 37 E7
Ewenny V Glam 21 B8
Ewerby Lincs 78 E4
Ewerby Thorpe Lincs 78 E4
Ewes Dumfries 115 E6
Ewesley Northumb 117 E6
Ewhurst Sur 27 E8
Ewhurst Green E Sus 18 C4
Ewhurst Green Sur 27 F8
Ewloe Flint 73 C7
Ewloe Green Flint 73 C6
Ewood Blackburn 86 B4
Eworthy Devon 9 E6
Ewshot Hants 27 E6
Ewyas Harold Hereford 35 B7
Exbourne Devon 9 D8
Exbury Hants 14 E5
Exebridge Devon 10 B4
Exelby N Yorks 101 F7
Exeter Devon 10 E4
Exford Som 21 F7
Exhall Warks 51 D6
Exley Head W Yorks 94 F3
Exminster Devon 10 F4
Exmouth Devon 10 F5
Exnaboe Shetland 160 M5
Exning Suff 55 C7
Exton Devon 10 F4
Exton Hants 15 B7
Exton Rutland 65 C6
Exton Som 21 F8
Exwick Devon 10 E4
Eyam Derbys 76 B2
Eydon Northants 52 D3
Eye Hereford 49 C6
Eye Pboro 66 D2
Eye Suff 56 B5
Eye Green Pboro 66 D2
Eyemouth Borders 122 C5
Eyeworth C Beds 54 E3
Eyhorne Street Kent 30 D2
Eyke Suff 57 D7
Eynesbury Cambs 54 D2
Eynort Highld 149 F8
Eynsford Kent 29 C6
Eynsham Oxon 38 D4
Eype Dorset 12 E2
Eyre Highld 149 C9
Eyre Highld 149 E10
Eythorne Kent 31 E6
Eyton Hereford 49 C6
Eyton Shrops 60 F3
Eyton Wrex 73 E7
Eyton upon the Weald Moors Telford 61 C6

F

Faccombe Hants 25 D8
Faceby N Yorks 102 D2
Facit Lancs 87 C6
Faddiley Ches E 74 D2
Fadmoor N Yorks 102 F4
Faerdre Swansea 33 D7
Failand N Som 23 B7
Failford S Ayrs 112 B4
Failsworth Gtr Man 87 D6
Fain Highld 150 D4
Fair Green Norf 67 C6
Fair Hill Cumb 108 F5
Fair Oak Hants 15 C5
Fair Oak Green Hants 26 C4
Fairbourne Gwyn 58 C3
Fairburn N Yorks 89 B5
Fairfield Derbys 75 B7
Fairfield Stockton 102 C2
Fairfield Worcs 50 B4
Fairfield Worcs 50 E5
Fairford Glos 38 D1
Fairhaven Lancs 85 B4
Fairlie N Ayrs 118 D2
Fairlight E Sus 19 D5
Fairlight Cove E Sus 19 D5
Fairmile Devon 11 E5
Fairmilehead Edin 120 C5
Fairoak Staffs 74 F4
Fairseat Kent 29 C7
Fairstead Essex 42 C3
Fairstead Norf 67 C6
Fairwarp E Sus 17 B8
Fairy Cottage IoM 84 D4
Fairy Cross Devon 9 B6
Fakenham Norf 80 E5
Fakenham Magna Suff 56 B3
Fala Midloth 121 C7
Fala Dam Midloth 121 C7
Falahill Borders 121 D6
Falcon Hereford 49 F8
Faldingworth Lincs 90 F4
Falfield S Glos 36 E3
Falkenham Suff 57 F6
Falkirk Falk 119 B8
Falkland Fife 128 D4
Falla Borders 116 C3
Fallgate Derbys 76 C3
Fallin Stirling 127 E7
Fallowfield Gtr Man 87 E6
Fallsidehill Borders 122 E2
Falmer E Sus 17 D7
Falmouth Corn 3 C7
Falsgrave N Yorks 103 F8
Falstone Northumb 116 F3
Fanagmore Highld 156 E4
Fangdale Beck N Yorks 102 E3
Fangfoss E Yorks 96 D3
Fankerton Falk 127 F6
Fanmore Argyll 146 G7
Fannich Lodge Highld 150 E5
Fans Borders 122 E2
Far Bank S Yorks 89 C7
Far Bletchley M Keynes 53 F6
Far Cotton Northants 52 D5
Far Forest Worcs 50 B2
Far Laund Derbys 76 E3
Far Sawrey Cumb 99 E5
Farcet Cambs 66 E2
Farden Shrops 49 B7
Fareham Hants 15 D6
Farewell Staffs 62 C4
Farforth Lincs 79 B6
Faringdon Oxon 38 E2
Farington Lancs 86 B3
Farlam Cumb 109 D5
Farlary Highld 157 J10
Farleigh N Som 23 C6
Farleigh Sur 28 C4
Farleigh Hungerford Som 24 D3
Farleigh Wallop Hants 26 E4
Farlesthorpe Lincs 79 B7
Farleton Cumb 99 F7
Farleton Lancs 93 C5
Farley Shrops 60 D3
Farley Staffs 75 E7
Farley Wilts 14 B3
Farley Green Sur 27 E8
Farley Hill Luton 40 B3
Farley Hill Wokingham 26 C5
Farleys End Glos 36 C4
Farlington N Yorks 96 C2
Farlow Shrops 61 F6
Farmborough Bath 23 C8
Farmcote Glos 37 B7
Farmcote Shrops 61 E7
Farmington Glos 37 C8
Farmoor Oxon 38 D4
Farmtown Moray 152 C5
Farnborough Hants 27 D6
Farnborough London 28 C5
Farnborough W Berks 38 F4
Farnborough Warks 52 E2
Farnborough Green Hants 27 D6
Farncombe Sur 27 E7
Farndish Bedford 53 C7
Farndon Ches W 73 D8
Farndon Notts 77 D7
Farnell Angus 135 D6
Farnham Dorset 13 C7
Farnham Essex 41 B7
Farnham N Yorks 95 C6
Farnham Suff 57 C7
Farnham Sur 27 E6
Farnham Common Bucks 40 F2
Farnham Green Essex 41 B7
Farnham Royal Bucks 40 F2
Farnhill N Yorks 94 E3
Farningham Kent 29 C6
Farnley N Yorks 94 E5
Farnley W Yorks 95 F5
Farnley Tyas W Yorks 88 C2
Farnsfield Notts 77 D6
Farnworth Gtr Man 86 D5
Farnworth Halton 86 F3
Farr Highld 138 D4
Farr Highld 151 H9
Farr Highld 157 C10
Farr House Highld 151 H9
Farringdon Devon 10 E5
Farrington Gurney Bath 23 D8
Farsley W Yorks 94 F5
Farthinghoe Northants 52 F3
Farthingloe Kent 31 E6
Farthingstone Northants 52 D4
Fartown W Yorks 88 C2
Farway Devon 11 E6
Fasag Highld 149 C13
Fascadale Highld 147 D8
Faslane Port Argyll 145 E11
Fasnacloich Argyll 130 E4
Fasnakyle Ho Highld 137 B6
Fassfern Highld 130 B4
Fatfield T&W 111 D6
Fattahead Aberds 153 C6
Faugh Cumb 108 D5
Fauldhouse W Loth 120 C2
Faulkbourne Essex 42 C3
Faulkland Som 24 D2
Fauls Shrops 74 F2
Faversham Kent 30 C4
Favillar Moray 152 E2
Fawdington N Yorks 95 B7
Fawfieldhead Staffs 75 C7
Fawkham Green Kent 29 C6
Fawler Oxon 38 C3
Fawley Bucks 39 F7
Fawley Hants 15 D5
Fawley W Berks 38 F3
Fawley Chapel Hereford 36 B2
Faxfleet E Yorks 90 B2
Faygate W Sus 28 F3
Fazakerley Mers 85 E4
Fazeley Staffs 63 D6
Fearby N Yorks 101 F6
Fearn Highld 151 D11
Fearn Lodge Highld 151 C9
Fearn Station Highld 151 D11
Fearnan Perth 132 E4
Fearnbeg Highld 149 C12
Fearnhead Warr 86 E4
Fearnmore Highld 149 B12
Featherstone Staffs 62 D3
Featherstone W Yorks 88 B5
Featherwood Northumb 116 D4
Feckenham Worcs 50 C5
Feering Essex 42 B4
Feetham N Yorks 100 E4
Feizor N Yorks 93 C7
Felbridge Sur 28 F4
Felbrigg Norf 81 D8
Felcourt Sur 28 E4
Felden Herts 40 D3
Felin-Crai Powys 34 B2
Felindre Carms 33 B6
Felindre Carms 33 B8
Felindre Carms 46 F2
Felindre Carms 47 F5
Felindre Ceredig 46 D4
Felindre Powys 59 F8
Felindre Swansea 33 D7
Felindre Farchog Pembs 45 F3
Felinfach Ceredig 46 D4
Felinfach Powys 48 F2
Felinfoel Carms 33 D6
Felingwm isaf Carms 33 B6

Felingwm uchaf Carms 33 B6
Felinwynt Ceredig 45 D4
Felixkirk N Yorks 102 F2
Felixstowe Suff 57 F6
Felixstowe Ferry Suff 57 F7
Felkington Northumb 122 E5
Felkirk W Yorks 88 C4
Fell Side Cumb 108 F3
Felling T&W 111 C5
Felmersham Bedford 53 D7
Felmingham Norf 81 E8
Felpham W Sus 16 E3
Felsham Suff 56 D3
Felsted Essex 42 B2
Feltham London 28 B2
Felthorpe Norf 68 C4
Felton Hereford 49 E7
Felton N Som 23 C7
Felton Northumb 117 D7
Felton Butler Shrops 60 C3
Feltwell Norf 67 E7
Fen Ditton Cambs 55 C5
Fen Drayton Cambs 54 C4
Fen End W Mid 51 B7
Fen Side Lincs 79 D6
Fenay Bridge W Yorks 88 C2
Fence Lancs 93 F8
Fence Houses T&W 111 D6
Fengate Norf 81 E7
Fengate Pboro 66 E2
Fenham Northumb 123 E6
Fenhouses Lincs 79 E5
Feniscliffe Blackburn 86 B4
Feniscowles Blackburn 86 B4
Feniton Devon 11 E6
Fenlake Bedford 53 E8
Fenny Bentley Derbys 75 D8
Fenny Bridges Devon 11 E6
Fenny Compton Warks 52 D2
Fenny Drayton Leics 63 E7
Fenny Stratford M Keynes 53 F6
Fenrother Northumb 117 E7
Fenstanton Cambs 54 C4
Fenton Cambs 54 B4
Fenton Lincs 77 B8
Fenton Lincs 77 D8
Fenton Stoke 75 E5
Fenton Barns E Loth 129 F7
Fenton Town Northumb 123 F5
Fenwick E Ayrs 118 E4
Fenwick Northumb 110 B3
Fenwick Northumb 123 E6
Fenwick S Yorks 89 C6
Feochaig Argyll 143 G8
Feock Corn 3 C7
Feolin Ferry Argyll 144 G3
Ferindonald Highld 149 H11
Feriniquarrie Highld 148 C6
Ferlochan Argyll 130 E3
Fern Angus 134 C4
Ferndale Rhondda 34 E4
Ferndown Dorset 13 D8
Ferness Highld 151 G12
Ferney Green Cumb 99 E6
Fernham Oxon 38 E2
Fernhill Heath Worcs 50 D3
Fernhurst W Sus 16 B2
Fernie Fife 128 C5
Ferniegair S Lanark 119 D7
Fernilea Highld 149 E8
Fernilee Derbys 75 B7
Ferrensby N Yorks 95 C6
Ferring W Sus 16 D4
Ferry Hill Cambs 66 F3
Ferry Point Highld 151 C10
Ferrybridge W Yorks 89 B5
Ferryden Angus 135 D7
Ferryhill Aberdeen 141 D8
Ferryhill Durham 111 F5
Ferryhill Station Durham 111 F6
Ferryside Carms 32 C4
Fersfield Norf 68 F3
Fersit Highld 131 B7
Ferwig Ceredig 45 E3
Feshiebridge Highld 138 D4
Fetcham Sur 28 D2
Fetterangus Aberds 153 C9
Fettercairn Aberds 135 B6
Fettes Highld 151 F8
Fewcott Oxon 39 B5
Fewston N Yorks 94 D4
Ffair-Rhos Ceredig 47 C6
Ffairfach Carms 33 B7
Ffaldybrenin Carms 46 E5
Ffarmers Carms 47 E5
Ffawyddog Powys 35 C6
Fforest Carms 33 D6
Fforest-fâch Swansea 33 E7
Ffos-y-ffin Ceredig 46 C3
Ffostrasol Ceredig 46 E2
Ffridd-Uchaf Gwyn 83 F5
Ffrith Wrex 73 D6
Ffrwd Gwyn 82 F4
Ffynnon ddrain Carms 33 B5
Ffynnon-oer Ceredig 46 D4
Ffynnongroyw Flint 85 F2
Fidden Argyll 146 J6
Fiddes Aberds 141 F7
Fiddington Glos 50 F4
Fiddington Som 22 E4
Fiddleford Dorset 13 C6
Fiddlers Hamlet Essex 41 D7
Field Staffs 75 F7
Field Broughton Cumb 99 F5
Field Dalling Norf 81 D6
Field Head Leics 63 D8
Fifehead Magdalen Dorset 13 B5
Fifehead Neville Dorset 13 C5
Fifield Oxon 38 C2
Fifield Wilts 25 D6
Fifield Windsor 27 B7
Fifield Bavant Wilts 13 B8
Figheldean Wilts 25 E6
Filands Wilts 37 F6
Filby Norf 69 C7
Filey N Yorks 97 A7
Filgrave M Keynes 53 E6
Filkins Oxon 38 D2
Filleigh Devon 9 B8
Filleigh Devon 10 C2
Fillingham Lincs 90 F3
Fillongley Warks 63 F6
Filton S Glos 23 B8
Fimber E Yorks 96 C4
Finavon Angus 134 D4
Finchairn Argyll 124 E5
Fincham Norf 67 D6
Finchampstead Wokingham 27 C5
Finchdean Hants 15 C8
Finchingfield Essex 55 F7
Finchley London 41 E5
Findern Derbys 76 F3
Findhorn Moray 151 E13
Findhorn Bridge Highld 138 B4
Findo Gask Perth 128 B2
Findochty Moray 152 B4
Findon Aberds 141 E8
Findon W Sus 16 D5
Findon Mains Highld 151 E9
Findrack Ho. Aberds 140 D5
Finedon Northants 53 B7
Fingal Street Suff 57 C6
Fingask Aberds 141 B6
Fingerpost Worcs 50 B2
Fingest Bucks 39 E7
Finghall N Yorks 101 F6
Fingland Cumb 108 D2
Fingland Dumfries 113 C7
Finglesham Kent 31 D7
Fingringhoe Essex 43 B6
Finlarig Stirling 132 F2
Finmere Oxon 52 F4
Finnart Perth 132 D2
Finningham Suff 56 C4
Finningley S Yorks 89 E7
Finnygaud Aberds 152 C5
Finsbury London 41 F6
Finstall Worcs 50 C4
Finsthwaite Cumb 99 F5
Finstock Oxon 38 C3
Finstown Orkney 159 G4
Fintry Aberds 153 C7
Fintry Dundee 134 F4
Fintry Stirling 126 F5
Finzean Aberds 140 E5
Fionnphort Argyll 146 J6
Fionnsbhagh W Isles 154 J5
Fir Tree Durham 110 F4
Firbeck S Yorks 89 F6
Firby N Yorks 96 C3
Firby N Yorks 101 F7
Firgrove Gtr Man 87 C7
Firsby Lincs 79 C7
Firsdown Wilts 25 F7
First Coast Highld 150 B2
Fishbourne IoW 15 E6
Fishbourne W Sus 16 D2
Fishburn Durham 111 F6
Fishcross Clack 127 E7
Fisher Place Cumb 99 C5
Fisherford Aberds 153 E6
Fisher's Pond Hants 15 B5
Fisherstreet W Sus 27 F7
Fisherton Highld 151 F10
Fisherton S Ayrs 112 C2
Fishguard = Abergwaun Pembs 44 B4
Fishlake S Yorks 89 C7
Fishleigh Barton Devon 9 B7
Fishponds Bristol 23 B8
Fishpool Glos 36 B3
Fishtoft Lincs 79 E6
Fishtoft Drove Lincs 79 E6
Fishtown of Usan Angus 135 D7
Fishwick Borders 122 D5
Fiskavaig Highld 149 E8
Fiskerton Lincs 78 B3
Fiskerton Notts 77 D7
Fitling E Yorks 97 F8
Fittleton Wilts 25 E6
Fittleworth W Sus 16 C4
Fitton End Cambs 66 C4
Fitz Shrops 60 C4
Fitzhead Som 11 B6
Fitzwilliam W Yorks 88 C5
Fiunary Highld 147 G9
Five Acres Glos 36 C2
Five Ashes E Sus 18 C2
Five Oak Green Kent 29 E7
Five Oaks Jersey 17
Five Oaks W Sus 16 B4
Five Roads Carms 33 D5
Fivecrosses Ches W 74 B2
Fivehead Som 11 B8
Flack's Green Essex 42 C3
Flackwell Heath Bucks 40 F1
Fladbury Worcs 50 E4
Fladdabister Shetland 160 K6
Flagg Derbys 75 C8
Flamborough E Yorks 97 B8
Flamstead Herts 40 C3
Flamstead End Herts 41 D6
Flansham W Sus 16 D3
Flanshaw W Yorks 88 B4
Flasby N Yorks 94 D2
Flash Staffs 75 C7
Flashader Highld 149 C8
Flask Inn N Yorks 103 D7
Flaunden Herts 40 D3
Flawborough Notts 77 E7
Flawith N Yorks 95 C7
Flax Bourton N Som 23 C7
Flaxby N Yorks 95 D6
Flaxholme Derbys 76 E3
Flaxley Glos 36 C3
Flaxpool Som 22 F3
Flaxton N Yorks 96 C2
Fleckney Leics 64 E3
Flecknoe Warks 52 C3
Fledborough Notts 77 B8
Fleet Hants 15 D8
Fleet Hants 27 D6
Fleet Lincs 66 B3
Fleet Hargate Lincs 66 B3
Fleetham Northumb 117 B7
Fleetlands Hants 15 D6
Fleetville Herts 40 D4
Fleetwood Lancs 92 E3
Flemingston V Glam 22 B2
Flemington S Lanark 119 D6
Flempton Suff 56 C2
Fleoideabhagh W Isles 154 J5
Fletchertown Cumb 108 E2
Fletching E Sus 17 B8
Flexbury Corn 8 D4
Flexford Sur 27 E7
Flimby Cumb 107 F7
Flimwell E Sus 18 B4
Flint = Y Fflint Flint 73 B6
Flint Mountain Flint 73 B6
Flintham Notts 77 E7
Flinton E Yorks 97 F8
Flintsham Hereford 48 D5
Flitcham Norf 80 E3
Flitton C Beds 53 F8
Flitwick C Beds 53 F8
Flixborough N Lincs 90 C2
Flixborough Stather N Lincs 90 C2
Flixton Gtr Man 86 E5
Flixton N Yorks 97 B6
Flixton Suff 69 F6
Flockton W Yorks 88 C3
Flodaigh W Isles 148 C3
Flodden Northumb 122 F5
Flodigarry Highld 149 A9
Flood's Ferry Cambs 66 E3
Flookburgh Cumb 92 B3
Florden Norf 68 E4
Flore Northants 52 C4
Flotterton Northumb 117 D5
Flowton Suff 56 E4
Flush House W Yorks 88 D2
Flushing Aberds 153 D10
Flushing Corn 3 C7
Flyford Flavell Worcs 50 D4
Foals Green Suff 57 B6
Fobbing Thurrock 42 F3
Fochabers Moray 152 C3
Fochriw Caerph 35 D5
Fockerby N Lincs 90 C2
Fodderletter Moray 139 B7
Fodderty Highld 151 F8
Foel Powys 59 C6
Foel-gastell Carms 33 C6
Foffarty Angus 134 E4
Foggathorpe E Yorks 96 F3
Fogo Borders 122 E3
Fogorig Borders 122 E3
Foindle Highld 156 E4
Folda Angus 134 C1
Fole Staffs 75 F7
Foleshill W Mid 63 F7
Folke Dorset 12 C4
Folkestone Kent 31 F6
Folkingham Lincs 78 F3
Folkington E Sus 18 E2
Folksworth Cambs 65 F8
Folkton N Yorks 97 B6
Folla Rule Aberds 153 E7
Follifoot N Yorks 95 D6
Folly Gate Devon 9 E7
Fonthill Bishop Wilts 24 F4
Fonthill Gifford Wilts 24 F4
Fontmell Magna Dorset 13 C6
Fontwell W Sus 16 D3
Foolow Derbys 75 B8
Foots Cray London 29 B5
Forbestown Aberds 140 C2
Force Mills Cumb 99 E5
Forcett N Yorks 101 C6
Ford Argyll 124 E4
Ford Bucks 39 D7
Ford Devon 9 B6
Ford Glos 37 B7
Ford Northumb 122 F5
Ford Shrops 60 C4
Ford Staffs 75 D7
Ford W Sus 16 D3
Ford Wilts 24 B3
Ford End Essex 42 C2
Ford Street Som 11 C6
Fordcombe Kent 29 E6
Fordell Fife 128 F3
Forden Powys 60 D2
Forder Green Devon 7 C5
Fordham Cambs 55 B7
Fordham Essex 43 B5
Fordham Norf 67 E6
Fordhouses W Mid 62 D3
Fordingbridge Hants 14 C2
Fordon E Yorks 97 B6
Fordoun Aberds 135 B7
Ford's Green Suff 56 C4
Fordstreet Essex 43 B5
Fordwells Oxon 38 C3
Fordwich Kent 31 D5
Fordyce Aberds 152 B5
Forebridge Staffs 62 B3
Forest Durham 109 F8
Forest Becks Lancs 93 D7
Forest Gate London 41 F7
Forest Green Sur 28 E2
Forest Hall Cumb 99 D7
Forest Head Cumb 109 D5
Forest Hill Oxon 39 D5
Forest Lane Head N Yorks 95 D6
Forest Lodge Argyll 131 E6
Forest Lodge Highld 139 C6
Forest Lodge Perth 133 B6
Forest Mill Clack 127 E8
Forest Row E Sus 28 F5
Forest Town Notts 77 C5
Forestburn Gate Northumb 117 E6
Foresterseat Moray 152 C1
Forestside W Sus 15 C8
Forfar Angus 134 D4
Forgandenny Perth 128 C2
Forge Powys 58 E4
Forge Side Torf 35 D6
Forgewood N Lanark 119 D7
Forgie Moray 152 C3
Forglen Ho. Aberds 153 C6
Formby Mers 85 D4
Forncett End Norf 68 E4
Forncett St Mary Norf 68 E4
Forncett St Peter Norf 68 E4
Forneth Perth 133 E7
Fornham All Saints Suff 56 C2
Fornham St Martin Suff 56 C2
Forres Moray 151 F13
Forrest Lodge Dumfries 113 F5
Forrestfield N Lanark 119 C8
Forsbrook Staffs 75 E6
Forse Highld 158 G4
Forse Ho. Highld 158 G4
Forsinain Highld 157 E12
Forsinard Highld 157 E11
Forsinard Station Highld 157 E11
Forston Dorset 12 E4
Fort Augustus Highld 137 D6
Fort George Guern 16
Fort George Highld 151 F10
Fort William Highld 131 B5
Forteviot Perth 128 C2
Forth S Lanark 120 D2
Forth Road Bridge Edin 120 B4
Forthampton Glos 50 F3
Fortingall Perth 132 E4
Forton Hants 26 E2
Forton Lancs 92 D4
Forton Shrops 60 C4
Forton Som 11 D8
Forton Staffs 61 B7
Forton Heath Shrops 60 C4
Fortrie Aberds 153 D6
Fortrose Highld 151 F10
Fortuneswell Dorset 12 G4
Forty Green Bucks 40 E2
Forty Hill London 41 E6
Forward Green Suff 56 D4
Fosbury Wilts 25 D8
Fosdyke Lincs 79 F6
Foss Perth 132 D4
Foss Cross Glos 37 D7
Fossebridge Glos 37 C7
Foster Street Essex 41 D7
Fosterhouses S Yorks 89 C7
Foston Derbys 75 F8
Foston Lincs 77 E8
Foston N Yorks 96 C2
Foston on the Wolds E Yorks 97 D7
Fotherby Lincs 91 E7
Fotheringhay Northants 65 E7
Foubister Orkney 159 H6
Foul Mile E Sus 18 D3
Foulby W Yorks 88 C4
Foulden Borders 122 D5
Foulden Norf 67 E7
Foulis Castle Highld 151 E8
Foulridge Lancs 93 E8
Foulsham Norf 81 E6
Fountainhall Borders 121 E7
Four Ashes Staffs 62 F2
Four Ashes Suff 56 B4
Four Crosses Powys 59 D7
Four Crosses Powys 60 C2
Four Crosses Wrex 73 D6
Four Elms Kent 29 E5
Four Forks Som 22 F4
Four Gotes Cambs 66 C4
Four Lane Ends Ches W 74 C2
Four Lanes Corn 3 C5
Four Marks Hants 26 F4
Four Mile Bridge Anglesey 82 D2
Four Oaks E Sus 19 C5
Four Oaks W Mid 62 E5
Four Oaks W Mid 63 F6
Four Roads Carms 33 D5
Four Roads IoM 84 F2
Four Throws Kent 18 C4
Fourlane Ends Derbys 76 D3
Fourlanes End Ches E 74 D5
Fourpenny Highld 151 B11
Fourstones Northumb 109 C8
Fovant Wilts 13 B8
Foveran Aberds 141 B8
Fowey Corn 5 D6
Fowley Common Warr 86 E4
Fowlis Angus 134 F3
Fowlis Wester Perth 127 B8
Fowlmere Cambs 54 E5
Fownhope Hereford 49 F7
Fox Corner Sur 27 D7
Fox Lane Hants 27 D6
Fox Street Essex 43 B6
Foxbar Renfs 118 C4
Foxcombe Hill Oxon 38 D4
Foxdale IoM 84 E2
Foxearth Essex 56 E2
Foxfield Cumb 98 F4
Foxham Wilts 24 B4
Foxhole Corn 4 D4
Foxhole Swansea 33 E7
Foxholes N Yorks 97 B6
Foxhunt Green E Sus 18 D2
Foxley Norf 81 E6
Foxley Wilts 37 F5
Foxt Staffs 75 E7
Foxton Cambs 54 E5
Foxton Durham 102 B1
Foxton Leics 64 E4
Foxup N Yorks 93 B8
Foxwist Green Ches W 74 C3
Foxwood Shrops 49 B8
Foy Hereford 36 B2
Foyers Highld 137 B7
Fraddam Corn 2 C4
Fraddon Corn 4 D4
Fradley Staffs 63 C5
Fradswell Staffs 75 F6
Fraisthorpe E Yorks 97 C7
Framfield E Sus 17 B8
Framingham Earl Norf 69 D5
Framingham Pigot Norf 69 D5
Framlingham Suff 57 C6
Frampton Dorset 12 E4
Frampton Lincs 79 F6
Frampton Cotterell S Glos 36 F3
Frampton Mansell Glos 37 D6
Frampton on Severn Glos 36 D4
Frampton West End Lincs 79 E5
Framsden Suff 57 D5
Framwellgate Moor Durham 111 E5
Franche Worcs 50 B3
Frankby Mers 85 F3
Frankley Worcs 62 F3
Frank's Bridge Powys 48 D3
Frankton Warks 52 B2
Frant E Sus 18 B2
Fraserburgh Aberds 153 B9
Frating Green Essex 43 B6
Fratton Ptsmth 15 E7
Freathy Corn 5 D8
Freckenham Suff 55 B7
Freckleton Lancs 86 B2
Freeby Leics 64 B5
Freehay Staffs 75 E7
Freeland Oxon 38 C4
Freester Shetland 160 H6
Freethorpe Norf 69 D7
Freiston Lincs 79 E6
Fremington Devon 20 F4
Fremington N Yorks 101 E5
Frenchay S Glos 23 B8
Frenchbeer Devon 9 F8
Frenich Stirling 126 D3
Frensham Sur 27 E6
Fresgoe Highld 157 C12
Freshfield Mers 85 D3
Freshford Bath 24 C2
Freshwater IoW 14 F4
Freshwater Bay IoW 14 F4
Freshwater East Pembs 32 E1
Fressingfield Suff 57 B6
Freston Suff 57 F5
Freswick Highld 158 D5
Fretherne Glos 36 D4
Frettenham Norf 68 C5
Freuchie Fife 128 D4
Freuchies Angus 134 C2
Freystrop Pembs 44 D4
Friar's Gate E Sus 29 F5
Friarton Perth 128 B3
Friday Bridge Cambs 66 D4
Friday Street E Sus 18 E3
Fridaythorpe E Yorks 96 D4
Friern Barnet London 41 E5
Friesland Argyll 146 F4
Friesthorpe Lincs 90 F4
Frieston Lincs 78 E2
Frieth Bucks 39 E7
Frilford Oxon 38 E4
Frilsham W Berks 26 B3
Frimley Sur 27 D6
Frimley Green Sur 27 D6
Frindsbury Medway 29 B8
Fring Norf 80 D3
Fringford Oxon 39 B6
Frinsted Kent 30 D2
Frinton-on-Sea Essex 43 B8
Friockheim Angus 135 E5
Friog Gwyn 58 C3
Frisby on the Wreake Leics 64 C3
Friskney Lincs 79 D7
Friskney Eaudike Lincs 79 D7
Friskney Tofts Lincs 79 D7
Friston E Sus 18 F2
Friston Suff 57 C8
Fritchley Derbys 76 D3
Frith Bank Lincs 79 E6
Frith Common Worcs 49 C8
Fritham Hants 14 C3
Frithelstock Devon 9 C6
Frithelstock Stone Devon 9 C6
Frithville Lincs 79 D6
Frittenden Kent 30 E2
Frittiscombe Devon 7 E6
Fritton Norf 68 E5
Fritton Norf 69 D7
Fritwell Oxon 39 B5
Frizinghall W Yorks 94 F4
Frizington Cumb 98 C2
Frocester Glos 36 D4
Frodesley Shrops 60 D5
Frodingham N Lincs 90 C2
Frodsham Ches W 74 B2
Frogden Borders 116 B3
Froggatt Derbys 76 B2
Froghall Staffs 75 E7
Frogmore Devon 7 E5
Frogmore Hants 27 D6
Frognall Lincs 65 C8
Frogshail Norf 81 D8
Frolesworth Leics 64 E2
Frome Som 24 E2
Frome St Quintin Dorset 12 D3
Fromes Hill Hereford 49 E8
Fron Denb 72 C4
Fron Gwyn 70 D4
Fron Gwyn 82 F5
Fron Powys 48 C2
Fron Powys 59 E8
Fron Powys 60 D2
Froncysyllte Wrex 73 E6
Frongoch Gwyn 72 F3
Frostenden Suff 69 F7
Frosterley Durham 110 F3
Frotoft Orkney 159 F5
Froxfield Wilts 25 C7
Froxfield Green Hants 15 B8
Froyle Hants 27 E5
Fryerning Essex 42 D2
Fryton N Yorks 96 B2
Fulbeck Lincs 78 D2
Fulbourn Cambs 55 D6
Fulbrook Oxon 38 C2
Fulford Som 11 B7
Fulford Staffs 75 F6
Fulford York 96 E2
Fulham London 28 B3
Fulking W Sus 17 C6
Full Sutton E Yorks 96 D3
Fullarton Glasgow 119 C6
Fullarton N Ayrs 118 F3
Fuller Street Essex 42 C3
Fuller's Moor Ches W 73 D8
Fullerton Hants 25 F8
Fulletby Lincs 79 B5
Fullwood E Ayrs 118 D4
Fulmer Bucks 40 F2
Fulmodestone Norf 81 D5
Fulnetby Lincs 78 B3
Fulstow Lincs 91 E7
Fulwell T&W 111 D6
Fulwood Lancs 92 F5
Fulwood S Yorks 88 F4
Fundenhall Norf 68 E4
Fundenhall Street Norf 68 E4
Funtington W Sus 15 D8
Funtley Hants 15 D6
Funtullich Perth 127 B6
Funzie Shetland 160 D8
Furley Devon 11 D7
Furnace Argyll 125 E6
Furnace Carms 33 D6
Furnace End Warks 63 E6
Furneaux Pelham Herts 41 B7
Furness Vale Derbys 87 F8
Furze Platt Windsor 40 F1
Furzehill Devon 21 E6
Fyfett Som 11 C7
Fyfield Essex 42 D1
Fyfield Glos 38 D2
Fyfield Hants 25 E7
Fyfield Oxon 38 E4
Fyfield Wilts 25 C6
Fylingthorpe N Yorks 103 D7
Fyvie Aberds 153 E7

G

Gabhsann bho Dheas W Isles 155 B9
Gabhsann bho Thuath W Isles 155 B9
Gablon Highld 151 B10
Gabroc Hill E Ayrs 118 D4
Gaddesby Leics 64 C3
Gadebridge Herts 40 D3
Gaer Powys 35 B5
Gaerllwyd Mon 35 E8
Gaerwen Anglesey 82 D4
Gagingwell Oxon 38 B4
Gaick Lodge Highld 138 F3
Gailey Staffs 62 C3
Gainford Durham 101 C6
Gainsborough Lincs 90 E2
Gainsborough Suff 57 E5
Gainsford End Essex 55 F8
Gairloch Highld 149 A13
Gairlochy Highld 136 F4
Gairney Bank Perth 128 E3
Gairnshiel Lodge Aberds 139 D8
Gaisgill Cumb 99 D8
Gaitsgill Cumb 108 E3
Galashiels Borders 121 F7
Galgate Lancs 92 D4
Galhampton Som 12 B4
Gallaberry Dumfries 114 F2
Gallachoille Argyll 144 E6
Gallanach Argyll 124 C4
Gallanach Argyll 146 E5
Gallantry Bank Ches E 74 D2
Gallatown Fife 128 E4
Galley Common Warks 63 E7
Galley Hill Cambs 54 C4
Galleyend Essex 42 D3
Galleywood Essex 42 D3
Gallin Perth 132 E2
Gallowfauld Angus 134 E4
Gallows Green Staffs 75 E7
Galltair Highld 149 F13
Galmisdale Highld 146 C7
Galmpton Devon 6 E4
Galmpton Torbay 7 D6
Galphay N Yorks 95 B5
Galston E Ayrs 118 F5
Galtrigill Highld 148 C6
Gamblesby Cumb 109 F6
Gamesley Derbys 87 E8
Gamlingay Cambs 54 D3
Gammersgill N Yorks 101 F5
Gamston Notts 77 B7
Ganarew Hereford 36 C2
Ganavan Argyll 124 B4
Gang Corn 5 C8
Ganllwyd Gwyn 71 E8
Gannochy Angus 135 B5
Gannochy Perth 128 B3
Gansclet Highld 158 F5
Ganstead E Yorks 97 F7
Ganthorpe N Yorks 96 B2
Ganton N Yorks 97 B5
Garbat Highld 150 E7
Garbhallt Argyll 125 F6
Garboldisham Norf 68 F3
Garden City Flint 73 C7
Garden Village W Yorks 95 F7
Garden Village Wrex 73 D7
Gardenstown Aberds 153 B7
Garderhouse Shetland 160 J5
Gardham E Yorks 97 E5
Gardin Shetland 160 G6
Gare Hill Som 24 E2
Garelochhead Argyll 145 D11
Garford Oxon 38 E4
Garforth W Yorks 95 F7
Gargrave N Yorks 94 D2
Gargunnock Stirling 127 E6
Garlic Street Norf 68 F5
Garlieston Dumfries 105 E8
Garlinge Green Kent 30 D5
Garlogie Aberds 141 D6
Garmond Aberds 153 C8
Garmony Argyll 147 G9
Garmouth Moray 152 B3
Garn-yr-erw Torf 35 C6
Garnant Carms 33 C7
Garndiffaith Torf 35 D6
Garndolbenmaen Gwyn 71 C5
Garnedd Conwy 83 F7
Garnett Bridge Cumb 99 E7
Garnfadryn Gwyn 70 D3
Garnkirk N Lanark 119 C6
Garnlydan Bl Gwent 35 C5
Garnswllt Swansea 33 D7
Garrabost W Isles 155 D10
Garraron Argyll 124 E4
Garras Corn 3 D6
Garreg Gwyn 71 C7
Garrick Perth 127 C7
Garrigill Cumb 109 E7
Garriston N Yorks 101 E6
Garroch Dumfries 113 F5
Garrogie Lodge Highld 137 C8
Garros Highld 149 B9
Garrow Perth 133 E5
Garryhorn Dumfries 113 E5
Garsdale Cumb 100 F2
Garsdale Head Cumb 100 E2
Garsdon Wilts 37 F6
Garshall Green Staffs 75 F6
Garsington Oxon 39 D5
Garstang Lancs 92 E4
Garston Mers 86 F2
Garswood Mers 86 E3
Gartcosh N Lanark 119 C6
Garth Bridgend 34 E2
Garth Gwyn 83 D5
Garth Powys 47 E8
Garth Shetland 160 H4
Garth Wrex 73 E6
Garth Row Cumb 99 E7
Garthamlock Glasgow 119 C6
Garthbrengy Powys 48 F2
Garthdee Aberdeen 141 D8
Gartheli Ceredig 46 D4
Garthmyl Powys 59 E8
Garthorpe Leics 64 B5
Garthorpe N Lincs 90 C2
Gartly Aberds 152 E5
Gartmore Stirling 126 E4
Gartnagrenach Argyll 144 H6
Gartness N Lanark 119 C7
Gartness Stirling 126 F4
Gartocharn W Dunb 126 F3
Garton E Yorks 97 F8
Garton-on-the-Wolds E Yorks 97 D5
Gartsherrie N Lanark 119 C7
Gartymore Highld 157 H13
Garvald E Loth 121 B8
Garvamore Highld 137 E8
Garvard Argyll 144 D2
Garvault Hotel Highld 157 F10
Garve Highld 150 E6
Garvestone Norf 68 D3
Garvock Aberds 135 B7
Garvock Invclyd 118 B2
Garway Hereford 36 B1
Garway Hill Hereford 35 B8
Gaskan Highld 130 B1
Gastard Wilts 24 C3
Gasthorpe Norf 68 F2
Gatcombe IoW 15 F5
Gate Burton Lincs 90 F2
Gate Helmsley N Yorks 96 D2
Gateacre Mers 86 F2
Gatebeck Cumb 99 F7
Gateford Notts 89 F6
Gateforth N Yorks 89 B6
Gatehead E Ayrs 118 F3
Gatehouse Northumb 116 F3
Gatehouse of Fleet Dumfries 106 D3
Gatelawbridge Dumfries 114 E2
Gateley Norf 81 E5
Gatenby N Yorks 101 F8
Gateshead T&W 111 C5
Gatesheath Ches W 73 C8
Gateside Aberds 140 C5
Gateside Angus 134 E4
Gateside E Renf 118 D4
Gateside Fife 128 D3
Gateside N Ayrs 118 D3
Gathurst Gtr Man 86 D3
Gatley Gtr Man 87 F6
Gattonside Borders 121 F8
Gatwick Airport W Sus 28 E3
Gaufron Powys 47 C8
Gaulby Leics 64 D3
Gauldry Fife 129 B5
Gaunt's Common Dorset 13 D8
Gautby Lincs 78 B4
Gavinton Borders 122 D3
Gawber S Yorks 88 D4
Gawcott Bucks 52 F4
Gawsworth Ches E 75 C5
Gawthorpe W Yorks 88 B3
Gawthrop Cumb 100 F1
Gawthwaite Cumb 98 F4
Gay Street W Sus 16 B4
Gaydon Warks 51 D8
Gayfield Orkney 159 C5
Gayhurst M Keynes 53 E6
Gayle N Yorks 100 F3
Gayles N Yorks 101 D6
Gayton Mers 85 F3
Gayton Norf 67 C7
Gayton Northants 52 D5
Gayton Staffs 62 B3
Gayton le Marsh Lincs 91 F8
Gayton le Wold Lincs 91 F6
Gayton Thorpe Norf 67 C7
Gaywood Norf 67 B6
Gazeley Suff 55 C8
Geanies House Highld 151 D11
Gearraidh Bhailteas W Isles 148 F2
Gearraidh Bhaird W Isles 155 E8
Gearraidh na h-Aibhne W Isles 154 D7
Gearraidh na Monadh W Isles 148 G2
Geary Highld 148 B7
Geddes House Highld 151 F11
Gedding Suff 56 D3
Geddington Northants 65 F5
Gedintailor Highld 149 E10
Gedling Notts 77 E6
Gedney Lincs 66 B4
Gedney Broadgate Lincs 66 B4
Gedney Drove End Lincs 66 B4
Gedney Dyke Lincs 66 B4
Gedney Hill Lincs 66 C3
Gee Cross Gtr Man 87 E7
Geilston Argyll 118 B3
Geirinis W Isles 148 D2
Geise Highld 158 D3
Geisiadar W Isles 154 D6
Geldeston Norf 69 E6
Gell Conwy 83 E8
Gelli Pembs 32 C1
Gelli Rhondda 34 E3
Gellideg M Tydf 34 D4
Gellifor Denb 72 C5
Gelligaer Caerph 35 E5
Gellilydan Gwyn 71 D7
Gellinudd Neath 33 D8
Gellyburn Perth 133 F7
Gellywen Carms 32 B3
Gelston Dumfries 106 D4
Gelston Lincs 78 E2
Gembling E Yorks 97 D7
Gentleshaw Staffs 62 C4
Geocrab W Isles 154 H6
George Green Bucks 40 F3
George Nympton Devon 10 B2
Georgefield Dumfries 115 E5
Georgeham Devon 20 F3
Georgetown Bl Gwent 35 D5
Gerlan Gwyn 83 E6
Germansweek Devon 9 E6
Germoe Corn 2 D4
Gerrans Corn 3 C7
Gerrards Cross Bucks 40 F3
Gestingthorpe Essex 56 F2
Geuffordd Powys 60 C2
Gib Hill Ches W 74 B3
Gibbet Hill Warks 64 F2
Gibbshill Dumfries 106 B4
Gidea Park London 41 F8
Gidleigh Devon 9 F8
Giffnock E Renf 119 D5
Gifford E Loth 121 C8
Giffordland N Ayrs 118 E2
Giffordtown Fife 128 C4
Giggleswick N Yorks 93 C8
Gilberdyke E Yorks 90 B2
Gilchriston E Loth 121 C7
Gilcrux Cumb 107 F8
Gildersome W Yorks 88 B3
Gildingwells S Yorks 89 F6
Gileston V Glam 22 C2
Gilfach Caerph 35 E5
Gilfach Goch Rhondda 34 F3
Gilfachrheda Ceredig 46 D3
Gillamoor N Yorks 102 F4
Gillar's Green Mers 86 E2
Gillen Highld 148 C7
Gilling East N Yorks 96 B2
Gilling West N Yorks 101 D6
Gillingham Dorset 13 B6
Gillingham Medway 29 C8
Gillingham Norf 69 E7
Gillock Highld 158 E4
Gillow Heath Staffs 75 D5
Gills Highld 158 C5
Gill's Green Kent 18 B4
Gilmanscleuch Borders 115 B6
Gilmerton Edin 121 C5
Gilmerton Perth 127 B7
Gilmonby Durham 100 C4
Gilmorton Leics 64 F2
Gilmourton S Lanark 119 E6
Gilsland Northumb 109 C6
Gilsland Spa Cumb 109 C6
Gilston Borders 121 D7
Gilston Herts 41 C7
Gilwern Mon 35 C6
Gimingham Norf 81 D8
Giosla W Isles 154 E6
Gipping Suff 56 C4
Gipsey Bridge Lincs 79 E5
Girdle Toll N Ayrs 118 E3
Girlsta Shetland 160 H6
Girsby N Yorks 102 D1
Girtford C Beds 54 D2
Girthon Dumfries 106 D3
Girton Cambs 54 C5
Girton Notts 77 C8
Girvan S Ayrs 112 E1
Gisburn Lancs 93 E8
Gisleham Suff 69 F8
Gislingham Suff 56 B4
Gissing Norf 68 F4
Gittisham Devon 11 E6
Gladestry Powys 48 D4
Gladsmuir E Loth 121 B7
Glais Swansea 33 D8
Glaisdale N Yorks 103 D5
Glame Highld 149 D10
Glamis Angus 134 E3
Glan Adda Gwyn 83 D5
Glan Conwy Conwy 83 D8
Glan-Conwy Conwy 83 F8
Glan-Duar Carms 46 E4
Glan-Dwyfach Gwyn 71 C5
Glan Gors Anglesey 82 D4
Glan-rhyd Gwyn 82 F4
Glan-traeth Anglesey 82 D2
Glan-y-don Flint 73 B5
Glan-y-nant Powys 59 F6
Glan-y-wern Gwyn 71 D7
Glan-yr-afon Anglesey 83 C6
Glan-yr-afon Gwyn 72 E3
Glan-yr-afon Gwyn 72 E4
Glanaman Carms 33 C7
Glandford Norf 81 C6
Glandwr Pembs 32 B2
Glandy Cross Carms 32 B2
Glandyfi Ceredig 58 E3
Glangrwyney Powys 35 C6
Glanmule Powys 59 E8
Glanrafon Ceredig 58 F3
Glanrhyd Gwyn 70 D3
Glanrhyd Pembs 45 E3
Glanton Northumb 117 C6
Glanton Pike Northumb 117 C6
Glanvilles Wootton Dorset 12 D4
Glapthorn Northants 65 E7
Glapwell Derbys 76 C4
Glas-allt Shiel Aberds 139 F8
Glasbury Powys 48 F3
Glaschoil Highld 151 H13
Glascoed Denb 72 B3
Glascoed Mon 35 D7
Glascoed Powys 59 C8
Glascorrie Aberds 140 E2
Glascote Staffs 63 D6
Glascwm Powys 48 D3
Glasdrum Argyll 130 E4
Glasfryn Conwy 72 D3
Glasgow Glasgow 119 C5
Glashvin Highld 149 B9
Glasinfryn Gwyn 83 E5
Glasnacardoch Highld 147 B9
Glasnakille Highld 149 G10
Glasphein Highld 148 D6
Glaspwll Powys 58 E4
Glassburn Highld 150 H6
Glasserton Dumfries 105 F8
Glassford S Lanark 119 E7
Glasshouse Hill Glos 36 B4
Glasshouses N Yorks 94 C4
Glasslie Fife 128 D4
Glasson Cumb 108 C2
Glasson Lancs 92 D4
Glassonby Cumb 109 F5
Glasterlaw Angus 135 D5
Glaston Rutland 65 D5
Glastonbury Som 23 F7
Glatton Cambs 65 F8
Glazebrook Warr 86 E4
Glazebury Warr 86 E4
Glazeley Shrops 61 F7
Gleadless S Yorks 88 F4
Gleadsmoss Ches E 74 C5
Gleann Tholàstaidh W Isles 155 C10
Gleaston Cumb 92 B2
Gleiniant Powys 59 E6
Glemsford Suff 56 E2
Glen Dumfries 106 B5
Glen Dumfries 106 D2
Glen Auldyn IoM 84 C4
Glen Bernisdale Highld 149 D9
Glen Ho Borders 121 F5
Glen Mona IoM 84 D4
Glen Nevis House Highld 131 B5
Glen Parva Leics 64 E2
Glen Sluain Argyll 125 F6
Glen Tanar House Aberds 140 E3
Glen Trool Lodge Dumfries 112 F4
Glen Village Falk 119 B8
Glen Vine IoM 84 E3
Glenamachrie Argyll 124 C5
Glenbarr Argyll 143 E7
Glenbeg Highld 139 B6
Glenbeg Highld 147 E8
Glenbervie Aberds 141 F6
Glenboig N Lanark 119 C7
Glenborrodale Highld 147 E9
Glenbranter Argyll 125 F7
Glenbreck Borders 114 B3
Glenbrein Lodge Highld 137 C7
Glenbrittle House Highld 149 F9
Glenbuchat Lodge Aberds 140 C2
Glenbuck E Ayrs 113 B7
Glenburn Renfs 118 C4
Glencalvie Lodge Highld 150 C7
Glencanisp Lodge Highld 156 G4
Glencaple Dumfries 107 C6
Glencarron Lodge Highld 150 F3
Glencarse Perth 128 B3
Glencassley Castle Highld 156 J7
Glenceitlein Highld 131 E5
Glencoe Highld 130 D4
Glencraig Fife 128 E3
Glencripesdale Highld 147 F9
Glencrosh Dumfries 113 F7
Glendavan Ho. Aberds 140 D3
Glendevon Perth 127 D8
Glendoe Lodge Highld 137 D7
Glendoebeg Highld 137 D7
Glendoick Perth 128 B4
Glendoll Lodge Angus 134 B2
Glendoune S Ayrs 112 E1
Glenduckie Fife 128 C4
Glendye Lodge Aberds 140 F5
Gleneagles Hotel Perth 127 C8
Gleneagles House Perth 127 D8
Glenegedale Argyll 142 C4
Glenelg Highld 149 G13
Glenernie Moray 151 G13
Glenfarg Perth 128 C3
Glenfarquhar Lodge Aberds 141 F6
Glenferness House Highld 151 G12
Glenfeshie Lodge Highld 138 E4
Glenfield Leics 64 D2
Glenfinnan Highld 147 C11
Glenfoot Perth 128 C3
Glenfyne Lodge Argyll 125 D8
Glengap Dumfries 106 D3
Glengarnock N Ayrs 118 D3
Glengorm Castle Argyll 146 F7
Glengrasco Highld 149 D9
Glenhead Farm Angus 134 C2
Glenhoul Dumfries 113 F6
Glenhurich Highld 130 C2
Glenkerry Borders 115 C5
Glenkiln Dumfries 106 B5
Glenkindie Aberds 140 C3
Glenlatterach Moray 152 C1
Glenlee Dumfries 113 F6
Glenlichorn Perth 127 C6
Glenlivet Moray 139 B7
Glenlochsie Perth 133 B7
Glenloig N Ayrs 143 E10
Glenluce Dumfries 105 D6
Glenmallan Argyll 125 F8
Glenmarksie Highld 150 F6
Glenmassan Argyll 145 E10
Glenmavis N Lanark 119 C7
Glenmaye IoM 84 E2
Glenmidge Dumfries 113 F8
Glenmore Argyll 124 D4
Glenmore Highld 149 D9
Glenmore Lodge Highld 139 D5
Glenmoy Angus 134 C4
Glenogil Angus 134 C4
Glenprosen Lodge Angus 134 C2
Glenprosen Village Angus 134 C3
Glenquiech Angus 134 C4
Glenreasdell Mains Argyll 145 H7
Glenree N Ayrs 143 F10
Glenridding Cumb 99 C5
Glenrossal Highld 156 J7
Glenrothes Fife 128 D4
Glensanda Highld 130 E2
Glensaugh Aberds 135 B6
Glenshero Lodge Highld 137 E8
Glenstockadale Dumfries 104 C4
Glenstriven Argyll 145 F9
Glentaggart S Lanark 113 B8
Glentham Lincs 90 E4
Glentirranmuir Stirling 127 E5
Glenton Aberds 140 B5
Glentress Borders 121 F5
Glentromie Lodge Highld 138 E3
Glentrool Village Dumfries 105 B7
Glentruan IoM 84 B4
Glentruim House Highld 138 E2
Glentworth Lincs 90 F3
Glenuig Highld 147 D9
Glenurquhart Highld 151 E10
Glespin S Lanark 113 B8
Gletness Shetland 160 H6
Glewstone Hereford 36 B2
Glinton Pboro 65 D8
Glooston Leics 64 E4
Glororum Northumb 123 F7
Glossop Derbys 87 E8
Gloster Hill Northumb 117 D8
Gloucester Glos 37 C5
Gloup Shetland 160 C7
Glusburn N Yorks 94 E3
Glutt Lodge Highld 157 F12
Glutton Bridge Staffs 75 C7
Glympton Oxon 38 B4
Glyn-Ceiriog Wrex 73 F6
Glyn-cywarch Gwyn 71 D7
Glyn Ebwy = Ebbw Vale Bl Gwent 35 D5
Glyn-neath = Glynedd Neath 34 D2
Glynarthen Ceredig 46 E2
Glynbrochan Powys 59 F6
Glyncoch Rhondda 34 E4
Glyncorrwg Neath 34 E2
Glynde E Sus 17 D8
Glyndebourne E Sus 17 C8
Glyndyfrdwy Denb 72 E5
Glynedd = Glyn-neath Neath 34 D2
Glynogwr Bridgend 34 F3
Glyntaff Rhondda 34 F4
Glyntawe Powys 34 C2
Gnosall Staffs 62 B2
Gnosall Heath Staffs 62 B2
Goadby Leics 64 E4
Goadby Marwood Leics 64 B4
Goat Lees Kent 30 E4
Goatacre Wilts 24 B5
Goathill Dorset 12 C4
Goathland N Yorks 103 D6
Goathurst Som 22 F4
Gobernuisgach Lodge Highld 156 E7
Gobhaig W Isles 154 G5
Gobowen Shrops 73 F7
Godalming Sur 27 E7
Godley Gtr Man 87 E7
Godmanchester Cambs 54 B3
Godmanstone Dorset 12 E4
Godmersham Kent 30 D4
Godney Som 23 E6
Godolphin Cross Corn 2 C5
Godre'r-graig Neath 34 D1
Godshill Hants 14 C2
Godshill IoW 15 F6
Godstone Sur 28 D4
Godwinscroft Hants 14 E2
Goetre Mon 35 D7
Goferydd Anglesey 82 C2
Goff's Oak Herts 41 D6
Gogar Edin 120 B4
Goginan Ceredig 58 F3
Golan Gwyn 71 C6
Golant Corn 5 D6
Golberdon Corn 5 B8
Golborne Gtr Man 86 E4
Golcar W Yorks 88 C2
Gold Hill Norf 66 E5
Goldcliff Newport 35 F7
Golden Cross E Sus 18 D2
Golden Green Kent 29 E7
Golden Grove Carms 33 C6

Golden Hill Hants 14 E3
Golden Pot Hants 26 E5
Golden Valley Glos 37 B6
Goldenhill Stoke 75 D5
Golders Green London 41 F5
Goldhanger Essex 43 D5
Golding Shrops 60 D5
Goldington Bedford 53 D8
Goldsborough N Yorks 95 D6
Goldsborough N Yorks 103 C6
Goldsithney Corn 2 C4
Goldsworthy Devon 9 B5
Goldthorpe S Yorks 89 D5
Gollanfield Highld 151 F11
Golspie Highld 157 J11
Golval Highld 157 C11
Gomeldon Wilts 25 F6
Gomersal W Yorks 88 B3
Gomshall Sur 27 E8
Gonalston Notts 77 E6
Gonfirth Shetland 160 G5
Good Easter Essex 42 C2
Gooderstone Norf 67 D7
Goodleigh Devon 20 F5
Goodmanham E Yorks 96 E4
Goodnestone Kent 30 C4
Goodnestone Kent 31 D6
Goodrich Hereford 36 C2
Goodrington Torbay 7 D6
Goodshaw Lancs 87 B6
Goodwick = Wdig Pembs 44 B4
Goodworth Clatford Hants 25 E8
Goole E Yorks 89 B8
Goonbell Corn 3 B6
Goonhavern Corn 4 D2
Goose Eye W Yorks 94 E3
Goose Green Gtr Man 86 D3
Goose Green Norf 68 F4
Goose Green W Sus 16 C5
Gooseham Corn 8 C4
Goosey Oxon 38 E3
Goosnargh Lancs 93 F5
Goostrey Ches E 74 B4
Gorcott Hill Warks 51 C5
Gord Shetland 160 L6
Gordon Borders 122 E2
Gordonbush Highld 157 J11
Gordonsburgh Moray 152 B4
Gordonstoun Moray 152 B1
Gordonstoun Aberds 152 C5
Gordonstown Aberds 153 E7
Gore Kent 31 D7
Gore Cross Wilts 24 D5
Gore Pit Essex 42 C4
Gorebridge Midloth 121 C6
Gorefield Cambs 66 C4
Gorey Jersey 17
Gorgie Edin 120 B5
Goring Oxon 39 F6
Goring-by-Sea W Sus 16 D5
Goring Heath Oxon 26 B4
Gorleston-on-Sea Norf 69 D8
Gornalwood W Mid 62 E3
Gorrachie Aberds 153 C7
Gorran Churchtown Corn 3 B8
Gorran Haven Corn 3 B9
Gorrenberry Borders 115 E7
Gors Ceredig 46 B5
Gorse Hill Swindon 38 F1
Gorsedd Flint 73 B5
Gorseinon Swansea 33 E6
Gorseness Orkney 159 G5
Gorsgoch Ceredig 46 D3
Gorslas Carms 33 C6
Gorsley Glos 36 B3
Gorstan Highld 150 E6
Gorstanvorran Highld 130 B2
Gorsteyhill Staffs 74 D4
Gorsty Hill Staffs 62 B5
Gortantaoid Argyll 142 A4
Gorton Gtr Man 87 E6
Gosbeck Suff 57 D5
Gosberton Lincs 78 F5
Gosberton Clough Lincs 65 B8
Gosfield Essex 42 B3
Gosford Hereford 49 C7
Gosforth Cumb 98 D2
Gosforth T&W 110 C5
Gosmore Herts 40 B4
Gosport Hants 15 E7
Gossabrough Shetland 160 E7
Gossington Glos 36 D4
Goswick Northumb 123 E6
Gotham Notts 76 F5
Gotherington Glos 37 B6
Gott Shetland 160 J6
Goudhurst Kent 18 B4
Goulceby Lincs 79 B5
Gourdas Aberds 153 D7
Gourdon Aberds 135 B8
Gourock Invclyd 118 B2
Govan Glasgow 119 C5
Govanhill Glasgow 119 C5
Goveton Devon 7 E5
Govilon Mon 35 C6
Gowanhill Aberds 153 B10
Gowdall E Yorks 89 B7
Gowerton Swansea 33 E6
Gowkhall Fife 128 F2
Gowthorpe E Yorks 96 D3
Goxhill E Yorks 97 E7
Goxhill N Lincs 90 B5
Goxhill Haven N Lincs 90 B5
Goybre Neath 34 F1
Grabhair W Isles 155 F8
Graby Lincs 65 B7
Grade Corn 3 E6
Graffham W Sus 16 C3
Grafham Cambs 54 C2
Grafham Sur 27 E8
Grafton Hereford 49 F6
Grafton N Yorks 95 C7
Grafton Oxon 38 D2
Grafton Shrops 60 C4
Grafton Worcs 49 C7
Grafton Flyford Worcs 50 D4
Grafton Regis Northants 53 E5
Grafton Underwood Northants 65 F6
Grafty Green Kent 30 E2
Graianrhyd Denb 73 D6
Graig Conwy 83 D8
Graig Denb 72 B4
Graig-fechan Denb 72 D5
Grain Medway 30 B2
Grainsby Lincs 91 E6
Grainthorpe Lincs 91 E7
Grampound Corn 3 B8
Grampound Road Corn 4 D4
Gramsdal W Isles 148 C3
Granborough Bucks 39 B7
Granby Notts 77 F7
Grandborough Warks 52 C2
Grandtully Perth 133 D6
Grange Cumb 98 C4
Grange E Ayrs 118 F4
Grange Medway 29 C8
Grange Mers 85 F3
Grange Perth 128 B4
Grange Crossroads Moray 152 C4
Grange Hall Moray 151 E13
Grange Hill Essex 41 E7
Grange Moor W Yorks 88 C3
Grange of Lindores Fife 128 C4
Grange-over-Sands Cumb 92 B4
Grange Villa Durham 110 D5
Grangemill Derbys 76 D2
Grangemouth Falk 127 F8
Grangepans Falk 128 F2
Grangetown Cardiff 22 B3
Grangetown Redcar 102 B3
Granish Highld 138 C5
Gransmoor E Yorks 97 D7
Granston Pembs 44 B3
Grantchester Cambs 54 D5
Grantham Lincs 78 F2
Grantley N Yorks 94 C5
Grantlodge Aberds 141 C6
Granton Dumfries 114 D3
Granton Edin 120 B5
Grantown-on-Spey Highld 139 B6
Grantshouse Borders 122 C4
Grappenhall Warr 86 F4
Grasby Lincs 90 D4
Grasmere Cumb 99 D5
Grasscroft Gtr Man 87 D7
Grassendale Mers 85 F4
Grassholme Durham 100 B4
Grassington N Yorks 94 C3
Grassmoor Derbys 76 C4
Grassthorpe Notts 77 C7
Grateley Hants 25 E7
Gratwich Staffs 75 F7
Graveley Cambs 54 C3
Graveley Herts 41 B5
Gravelly Hill W Mid 62 E5
Gravels Shrops 60 D3
Graven Shetland 160 F6
Graveney Kent 30 C4
Gravesend Herts 41 B7
Gravesend Kent 29 B7
Grayingham Lincs 90 E3
Grayrigg Cumb 99 E7
Grays Thurrock 29 B7
Grayshott Hants 27 F6
Grayswood Sur 27 F7
Graythorp Hrtlpl 102 B3
Grazeley Wokingham 26 C4
Greasbrough S Yorks 88 E5
Greasby Mers 85 F3
Great Abington Cambs 55 E6
Great Addington Northants 53 B7
Great Alne Warks 51 D6
Great Altcar Lancs 85 D4
Great Amwell Herts 41 C6
Great Asby Cumb 100 C1
Great Ashfield Suff 56 C3
Great Ayton N Yorks 102 C3
Great Baddow Essex 42 D3
Great Bardfield Essex 55 F7
Great Barford Bedford 54 D2
Great Barr W Mid 62 E4
Great Barrington Glos 38 C2
Great Barrow Ches W 73 C8
Great Barton Suff 56 C2
Great Barugh N Yorks 96 B3
Great Bavington Northumb 117 F5
Great Bealings Suff 57 E6
Great Bedwyn Wilts 25 C7
Great Bentley Essex 43 B7
Great Billing Northants 53 C6
Great Bircham Norf 80 D3
Great Blakenham Suff 56 D5
Great Blencow Cumb 108 F4
Great Bolas Telford 61 B6
Great Bookham Sur 28 D2
Great Bourton Oxon 52 E2
Great Bowden Leics 64 F4
Great Bradley Suff 55 D7
Great Braxted Essex 42 C4
Great Bricett Suff 56 D4
Great Brickhill Bucks 53 F7
Great Bridge W Mid 62 E3
Great Bridgeford Staffs 62 B2
Great Brington Northants 52 C4
Great Bromley Essex 43 B6
Great Broughton Cumb 107 F7
Great Broughton N Yorks 102 D3
Great Budworth Ches W 74 B3
Great Burdon Darl 101 C8
Great Burgh Sur 28 D3
Great Burstead Essex 42 E2
Great Busby N Yorks 102 D3
Great Canfield Essex 42 C1
Great Carlton Lincs 91 F8
Great Casterton Rutland 65 D7
Great Chart Kent 30 E3
Great Chatwell Staffs 61 C7
Great Chesterford Essex 55 E6
Great Cheverell Wilts 24 D4
Great Chishill Cambs 54 F5
Great Clacton Essex 43 C7
Great Cliff W Yorks 88 C4
Great Clifton Cumb 98 B2
Great Coates NE Lincs 91 D6
Great Comberton Worcs 50 E4
Great Corby Cumb 108 D4
Great Cornard Suff 56 E2
Great Cowden E Yorks 97 E8
Great Coxwell Oxon 38 E2
Great Crakehall N Yorks 101 E7
Great Cransley Northants 53 B6
Great Cressingham Norf 67 D8
Great Crosby Mers 85 E4
Great Cubley Derbys 75 F8
Great Dalby Leics 64 C4
Great Denham Bedford 53 E8
Great Doddington Northants 53 C6
Great Dunham Norf 67 C8
Great Dunmow Essex 42 B2
Great Durnford Wilts 25 F6
Great Easton Essex 42 B2
Great Easton Leics 64 E5
Great Eccleston Lancs 92 E4
Great Edstone N Yorks 103 F5
Great Ellingham Norf 68 E3
Great Elm Som 24 E2
Great Eversden Cambs 54 D4
Great Fencote N Yorks 101 E7
Great Finborough Suff 56 D4
Great Fransham Norf 67 C8
Great Gaddesden Herts 40 C3
Great Gidding Cambs 65 F8
Great Givendale E Yorks 96 D4
Great Glemham Suff 57 C7
Great Glen Leics 64 E3
Great Gonerby Lincs 77 F8
Great Gransden Cambs 54 D3
Great Green Norf 69 F5
Great Green Suff 56 D3
Great Habton N Yorks 96 B3
Great Hale Lincs 78 E4
Great Hallingbury Essex 41 C8
Great Hampden Bucks 39 D8
Great Harrowden Northants 53 B6
Great Harwood Lancs 93 F7
Great Haseley Oxon 39 D6
Great Hatfield E Yorks 97 E7
Great Haywood Staffs 62 B4
Great Heath W Mid 63 F7
Great Heck N Yorks 89 B6
Great Henny Essex 56 F2
Great Hinton Wilts 24 D4
Great Hockham Norf 68 E2
Great Holland Essex 43 C8
Great Horkesley Essex 56 F3
Great Hormead Herts 41 B6
Great Horton W Yorks 94 F4
Great Horwood Bucks 53 F5
Great Houghton Northants 53 D5
Great Houghton S Yorks 88 D5
Great Hucklow Derbys 75 B8
Great Kelk E Yorks 97 D7
Great Kimble Bucks 39 D8
Great Kingshill Bucks 40 E1
Great Langton N Yorks 101 E7
Great Leighs Essex 42 C3
Great Lever Gtr Man 86 D5
Great Limber Lincs 90 D5
Great Linford M Keynes 53 E6
Great Livermere Suff 56 B2
Great Longstone Derbys 76 B2
Great Lumley Durham 111 E5
Great Lyth Shrops 60 D4
Great Malvern Worcs 50 E2
Great Maplestead Essex 56 F2
Great Marton Blackpool 92 F3
Great Massingham Norf 80 E3
Great Melton Norf 68 D4
Great Milton Oxon 39 D6
Great Missenden Bucks 40 D1
Great Mitton Lancs 93 F7
Great Mongeham Kent 31 D7
Great Moulton Norf 68 E4
Great Munden Herts 41 B6
Great Musgrave Cumb 100 C2
Great Ness Shrops 60 C3
Great Notley Essex 42 B3
Great Oakley Essex 43 B7
Great Oakley Northants 65 F5
Great Offley Herts 40 B4
Great Ormside Cumb 100 C2
Great Orton Cumb 108 D3
Great Ouseburn N Yorks 95 C7
Great Oxendon Northants 64 F4
Great Oxney Green Essex 42 D2
Great Palgrave Norf 67 C8
Great Parndon Essex 41 D7
Great Paxton Cambs 54 C3
Great Plumpton Lancs 92 F3
Great Plumstead Norf 69 C6
Great Ponton Lincs 78 F2
Great Preston W Yorks 88 B5
Great Raveley Cambs 66 F2
Great Rissington Glos 38 C1
Great Rollright Oxon 51 F8
Great Ryburgh Norf 81 E5
Great Ryle Northumb 117 C6
Great Ryton Shrops 60 D4
Great Saling Essex 42 B3
Great Salkeld Cumb 109 F5
Great Sampford Essex 55 F7
Great Sankey Warr 86 F3
Great Saxham Suff 55 C8
Great Shefford W Berks 25 B8
Great Shelford Cambs 55 D5
Great Smeaton N Yorks 101 D8
Great Snoring Norf 80 D5
Great Somerford Wilts 37 F6
Great Stainton Darl 101 B8
Great Stambridge Essex 42 E4
Great Staughton Cambs 54 C2
Great Steeping Lincs 79 C7
Great Stonar Kent 31 D7
Great Strickland Cumb 99 B7
Great Stukeley Cambs 54 B3
Great Sturton Lincs 78 B5
Great Sutton Ches W 73 B7
Great Sutton Shrops 60 F5
Great Swinburne Northumb 110 B2
Great Tew Oxon 38 B3
Great Tey Essex 42 B4
Great Thurkleby N Yorks 95 B7
Great Thurlow Suff 55 D7
Great Torrington Devon 9 C6
Great Tosson Northumb 117 D6
Great Totham Essex 42 C4
Great Totham Essex 42 C4
Great Tows Lincs 91 E6
Great Urswick Cumb 92 B2
Great Wakering Essex 43 F5
Great Waldingfield Suff 56 E3
Great Walsingham Norf 80 D5
Great Waltham Essex 42 C2
Great Warley Essex 42 E1
Great Washbourne Glos 50 F4
Great Weldon Northants 65 F6
Great Welnetham Suff 56 D2
Great Wenham Suff 56 F4
Great Whittington Northumb 110 B3
Great Wigborough Essex 43 C5
Great Wilbraham Cambs 55 D6
Great Wishford Wilts 25 F5
Great Witcombe Glos 37 C6
Great Witley Worcs 50 C2
Great Wolford Warks 51 F7
Great Wratting Suff 55 E7
Great Wymondley Herts 41 B5
Great Wyrley Staffs 62 D3
Great Wytheford Shrops 61 C5
Great Yarmouth Norf 69 D8
Great Yeldham Essex 55 F8
Greater Doward Hereford 36 C2
Greatford Lincs 65 C7
Greatgate Staffs 75 E7
Greatham Hants 27 F5
Greatham Hrtlpl 102 B2
Greatham W Sus 16 C4
Greatstone on Sea Kent 19 C7
Greatworth Northants 52 E3
Greave Lancs 87 B6
Greeba IoM 84 D3
Green Denb 72 C4
Green End Bedford 54 D2
Green Hammerton N Yorks 95 D7
Green Lane Powys 59 E8
Green Ore Som 23 D7
Green St Green London 29 C5
Green Street Herts 40 E4
Greenbank Shetland 160 C7
Greenburn W Loth 120 C2
Greendikes Northumb 117 B6
Greenfield C Beds 53 F8
Greenfield Flint 73 B5
Greenfield Gtr Man 87 D7
Greenfield Highld 136 D5
Greenfield Oxon 39 E7
Greenford London 40 F4
Greengairs N Lanark 119 B7
Greenham W Berks 26 C2
Greenhaugh Northumb 116 F3
Greenhead Northumb 109 C6
Greenhill Falk 119 B8
Greenhill Kent 31 C5
Greenhill Leics 63 C8
Greenhill London 40 F4
Greenhills N Ayrs 118 D3
Greenhithe Kent 29 B6
Greenholm E Ayrs 118 F5
Greenholme Cumb 99 D7
Greenhouse Borders 115 B8
Greenhow Hill N Yorks 94 C4
Greenigoe Orkney 159 H5
Greenland Highld 158 D4
Greenlands Bucks 39 F7
Greenlaw Aberds 153 C6
Greenlaw Borders 122 E3
Greenlea Dumfries 107 B7
Greenloaning Perth 127 D7
Greenmount Gtr Man 87 C5
Greenmow Shetland 160 L6
Greenock Invclyd 118 B2
Greenock West Invclyd 118 B2
Greenodd Cumb 99 F5
Greenrow Cumb 107 D8
Greens Norton Northants 52 E4
Greenside T&W 110 C4
Greensidehill Northumb 117 C5
Greenstead Green Essex 42 B4
Greensted Essex 41 D8
Greenwich London 28 B4
Greet Glos 50 F5
Greete Shrops 49 B7
Greetham Lincs 79 B6
Greetham Rutland 65 C6
Greetland W Yorks 87 B8
Gregg Hall Cumb 99 E6
Gregson Lane Lancs 86 B3
Greinetobht W Isles 148 A3
Greinton Som 23 F6
Gremista Shetland 160 J6
Grenaby IoM 84 E2
Grendon Northants 53 C6
Grendon Warks 63 D6
Grendon Common Warks 63 E6
Grendon Green Hereford 49 D7
Grendon Underwood Bucks 39 B6
Grenofen Devon 6 B2
Grenoside S Yorks 88 E4
Greosabhagh W Isles 154 H6
Gresford Wrex 73 D7
Gresham Norf 81 D7
Greshornish Highld 149 C8
Gressenhall Norf 68 C2
Gressingham Lancs 93 C5
Gresty Green Ches E 74 D4
Greta Bridge Durham 101 C5
Gretna Dumfries 108 C3
Gretna Green Dumfries 108 C3
Gretton Glos 50 F5
Gretton Northants 65 E5
Gretton Shrops 60 E5
Grewelthorpe N Yorks 94 B5
Grey Green N Lincs 89 D8
Greygarth N Yorks 94 B4
Greynor Carms 33 D6
Greysouthen Cumb 98 B2
Greystoke Cumb 108 F4
Greystone Angus 135 E5
Greystone Dumfries 107 B6
Greywell Hants 26 D5
Griais W Isles 155 C9
Grianan W Isles 155 D9
Gribthorpe E Yorks 96 F3
Gridley Corner Devon 9 E5
Griff Warks 63 F7
Griffithstown Torf 35 E6
Grimbister Orkney 159 G4
Grimblethorpe Lincs 91 F6
Grimeford Village Lancs 86 C4
Grimethorpe S Yorks 88 D5
Griminis W Isles 148 C2
Grimister Shetland 160 D6
Grimley Worcs 50 C3
Grimness Orkney 159 J5
Grimoldby Lincs 91 F7
Grimpo Shrops 60 B3
Grimsargh Lancs 93 F5
Grimsbury Oxon 52 E2
Grimsby NE Lincs 91 C6
Grimscote Northants 52 D4
Grimscott Corn 8 D4
Grimsthorpe Lincs 65 B7
Grimston E Yorks 97 F8
Grimston Leics 64 B3
Grimston Norf 80 E3
Grimston York 96 D2
Grimstone Dorset 12 E4
Grinacombe Moor Devon 9 E6
Grindale E Yorks 97 B7
Grindigar Orkney 159 H6
Grindiscol Shetland 160 K6
Grindle Shrops 61 D7
Grindleford Derbys 76 B2
Grindleton Lancs 93 E7
Grindley Staffs 62 B4
Grindley Brook Shrops 74 E2
Grindlow Derbys 75 B8
Grindon Northumb 122 E5
Grindon Staffs 75 D7
Grindonmoor Gate Staffs 75 D7
Gringley on the Hill Notts 89 E8
Grinsdale Cumb 108 D3
Grinshill Shrops 60 B5
Grinton N Yorks 101 E5
Griomsidar W Isles 155 E8
Grishipoll Argyll 146 F4
Grisling Common E Sus 17 B8
Gristhorpe N Yorks 103 F8
Griston Norf 68 E2
Gritley Orkney 159 H6
Grittenham Wilts 37 F7
Grittleton Wilts 37 F5
Grizebeck Cumb 98 F4
Grizedale Cumb 99 E5
Grobister Orkney 159 F7
Groby Leics 64 D2
Groes Conwy 72 C4
Groes Neath 34 F1
Groes-faen Rhondda 34 F4
Groes-lwyd Powys 60 C2
Groesffordd Marli Denb 72 B4
Groeslon Gwyn 82 E5
Groeslon Gwyn 82 F4
Grogport Argyll 143 D9
Gromford Suff 57 D7
Gronant Flint 72 A4
Groombridge E Sus 18 B2
Grosmont Mon 35 B8
Grosmont N Yorks 103 D6
Groton Suff 56 E3
Grougfoot Falk 120 B3
Grouville Jersey 17
Grove Dorset 12 G5
Grove Kent 31 C6
Grove Notts 77 B7
Grove Oxon 38 E4
Grove Park London 28 B5
Grove Vale W Mid 62 E4
Grovesend Swansea 33 D6
Grudie Highld 150 E6
Gruids Highld 157 J8
Gruinard House Highld 150 B2
Grula Highld 149 F8
Gruline Argyll 147 G8
Grunasound Shetland 160 K5
Grundisburgh Suff 57 D6
Grunsagill Lancs 93 D7
Gruting Shetland 160 J4
Grutness Shetland 160 N6
Gualachulain Highld 131 E5
Gualin Ho. Highld 156 D6
Guardbridge Fife 129 C6
Guarlford Worcs 50 E3
Guay Perth 133 E7
Guestling Green E Sus 19 D5
Guestling Thorn E Sus 18 D5
Guestwick Norf 81 E6
Guestwick Green Norf 81 E6
Guide Blackburn 86 B5
Guide Post Northumb 117 F8
Guilden Morden Cambs 54 E3
Guilden Sutton Ches W 73 C8
Guildford Sur 27 E7
Guildtown Perth 133 F8
Guilsborough Northants 52 B4
Guilsfield Powys 60 C2
Guilton Kent 31 D6
Guineaford Devon 20 F4
Guisborough Redcar 102 C4
Guiseley W Yorks 94 E4
Guist Norf 81 E5
Guith Orkney 159 E6
Guiting Power Glos 37 B7
Gulberwick Shetland 160 K6
Gullane E Loth 129 F6
Gulval Corn 2 C3
Gulworthy Devon 6 B2
Gumfreston Pembs 32 D2
Gumley Leics 64 E3
Gummow's Shop Corn 4 D3
Gun Hill E Sus 18 D2
Gunby E Yorks 96 F3
Gunby Lincs 65 B6
Gundleton Hants 26 F4
Gunn Devon 20 F5
Gunnerside N Yorks 100 E4
Gunnerton Northumb 110 B2
Gunness N Lincs 90 C2
Gunnislake Corn 6 B2
Gunnista Shetland 160 J7
Gunthorpe Norf 81 D6
Gunthorpe Notts 77 E6
Gunthorpe Pboro 65 D8
Gunville IoW 15 F5
Gunwalloe Corn 3 D5
Gurnard IoW 15 E5
Gurnett Ches E 75 B6
Gurney Slade Som 23 E8
Gurnos Powys 34 D1
Gussage All Saints Dorset 13 C8
Gussage St Michael Dorset 13 C7
Guston Kent 31 E7
Gutcher Shetland 160 D7
Guthrie Angus 135 D5
Guyhirn Cambs 66 D3
Guyhirn Gull Cambs 66 D3
Guy's Head Lincs 66 B4
Guy's Marsh Dorset 13 B6
Guyzance Northumb 117 D8
Gwaenysgor Flint 72 A4
Gwalchmai Anglesey 82 D3
Gwaun-Cae-Gurwen Neath 33 C8
Gwaun-Leision Neath 33 C8
Gwbert Ceredig 45 E3
Gweek Corn 3 D6
Gwehelog Mon 35 D7
Gwenddwr Powys 48 E2
Gwennap Corn 3 C6
Gwenter Corn 3 E6
Gwernaffield Flint 73 C6
Gwernesney Mon 35 D8
Gwernogle Carms 46 F4
Gwernymynydd Flint 73 C6
Gwersyllt Wrex 73 D7
Gwespyr Flint 85 F2
Gwithian Corn 2 B4
Gwredog Anglesey 82 C4
Gwyddelwern Denb 72 E4
Gwyddgrug Carms 46 F3
Gwydyr Uchaf Conwy 83 E7
Gwynfryn Wrex 73 D6
Gwystre Powys 48 C2
Gwytherin Conwy 83 E8
Gyfelia Wrex 73 E7
Gyffin Conwy 83 D7
Gyre Orkney 159 H4
Gyrn-goch Gwyn 70 C5

H

Habberley Shrops 60 D3
Habergham Lancs 93 F8
Habrough NE Lincs 90 C5
Haceby Lincs 78 F3
Hacheston Suff 57 D7
Hackbridge London 28 C3
Hackenthorpe S Yorks 88 F5
Hackford Norf 68 D3
Hackforth N Yorks 101 E7
Hackland Orkney 159 F4
Hackleton Northants 53 D6
Hackness N Yorks 103 E7
Hackness Orkney 159 J4
Hackney London 41 F6
Hackthorn Lincs 90 F3
Hackthorpe Cumb 99 B7
Haconby Lincs 65 B8
Hacton London 41 F8
Hadden Borders 122 F3
Haddenham Bucks 39 D7
Haddenham Cambs 55 B5
Haddington E Loth 121 B8
Haddington Lincs 78 C2
Haddiscoe Norf 69 E7
Haddon Cambs 65 E8
Haddon Ches E 75 C6
Hade Edge W Yorks 88 D2
Hademore Staffs 63 D5
Hadfield Derbys 87 E8
Hadham Cross Herts 41 C7
Hadham Ford Herts 41 B7
Hadleigh Essex 42 F4
Hadleigh Suff 56 E4
Hadley Telford 61 C6
Hadley End Staffs 62 B5
Hadlow Kent 29 E7
Hadlow Down E Sus 18 C2
Hadnall Shrops 60 C5
Hadstock Essex 55 E6
Hady Derbys 76 B3
Hadzor Worcs 50 C4
Haffenden Quarter Kent 30 E2
Hafod-Dinbych Conwy 83 F8
Hafod-lom Conwy 83 D8
Haggate Lancs 93 F8
Haggbeck Cumb 108 B4
Haggerston Northumb 123 E6
Haggrister Shetland 160 F5
Hagley Hereford 49 E7
Hagley Worcs 62 F3
Hagworthingham Lincs 79 C6
Haigh Gtr Man 86 D4
Haigh S Yorks 88 C3
Haigh Moor W Yorks 88 B3
Haighton Green Lancs 93 F5
Hail Weston Cambs 54 C2
Haile Cumb 98 D2
Hailes Glos 50 F5
Hailey Herts 41 C6
Hailey Oxon 38 C3
Hailsham E Sus 18 E2
Haimer Highld 158 D3
Hainault London 41 E7
Hainford Norf 68 C5
Hainton Lincs 91 F5
Hairmyres S Lanark 119 D6
Haisthorpe E Yorks 97 C7
Hakin Pembs 44 E3
Halam Notts 77 D6
Halbeath Fife 128 F3
Halberton Devon 10 C5
Halcro Highld 158 D4
Hale Gtr Man 87 F5
Hale Halton 86 F2
Hale Hants 14 C2
Hale Bank Halton 86 F2
Hale Street Kent 29 E7
Halebarns Gtr Man 87 F5
Hales Norf 69 E6
Hales Staffs 74 F4
Hales Place Kent 30 D5
Halesfield Telford 61 D7
Halesgate Lincs 66 B3
Halesowen W Mid 62 F3
Halesworth Suff 57 B7
Halewood Mers 86 F2
Halford Shrops 60 F4
Halford Warks 51 E7
Halfpenny Furze Carms 32 C3
Halfpenny Green Staffs 62 E2
Halfway Carms 46 F5
Halfway Carms 47 F7
Halfway W Berks 26 C2
Halfway Bridge W Sus 16 B3
Halfway House Shrops 60 C3
Halfway Houses Kent 30 B3
Halifax W Yorks 87 B8
Halket E Ayrs 118 D4
Halkirk Highld 158 E3
Halkyn Flint 73 B6
Hall Dunnerdale Cumb 98 E4
Hall Green W Mid 62 F5
Hall Green W Yorks 88 C4
Hall Grove Herts 41 C5
Hall of Tankerness Orkney 159 H6
Hall of the Forest Shrops 60 F2
Halland E Sus 18 D2
Hallaton Leics 64 E4
Hallatrow Bath 23 D8
Hallbankgate Cumb 109 D5
Hallen S Glos 36 F2
Halliburton Borders 122 E2
Hallin Highld 148 C7
Halling Medway 29 C8
Hallington Lincs 91 F7
Hallington Northumb 110 B2
Halliwell Gtr Man 86 C5
Halloughton Notts 77 D6
Hallow Worcs 50 D3
Hallrule Borders 115 C8
Halls E Loth 122 B2
Hall's Green Herts 41 B5
Hallsands Devon 7 F6
Hallthwaites Cumb 98 F3
Hallworthy Corn 8 F3
Hallyburton House Perth 134 F2
Hallyne Borders 120 E4
Halmer End Staffs 74 E4
Halmore Glos 36 D3
Halmyre Mains Borders 120 E4
Halnaker W Sus 16 D3
Halsall Lancs 85 C4
Halse Northants 52 E3
Halse Som 11 B6
Halsetown Corn 2 C4
Halsham E Yorks 91 B6
Halsinger Devon 20 F4
Halstead Essex 56 F2
Halstead Kent 29 C5
Halstead Leics 64 D4
Halstock Dorset 12 D3
Haltham Lincs 78 C5
Haltoft End Lincs 79 E6
Halton Bucks 40 C1
Halton Halton 86 F3
Halton Lancs 92 C5
Halton Northumb 110 C2
Halton W Yorks 95 F6
Halton Wrex 73 F7
Halton East N Yorks 94 D3
Halton Gill N Yorks 93 B8
Halton Holegate Lincs 79 C7
Halton Lea Gate Northumb 109 D6
Halton West N Yorks 93 D8
Haltwhistle Northumb 109 C7
Halvergate Norf 69 D7
Halwell Devon 7 D5
Halwill Devon 9 E6
Halwill Junction Devon 9 D6
Ham Devon 11 D7
Ham Glos 36 E3
Ham Highld 158 C4
Ham Kent 31 D7
Ham London 28 B2
Ham Shetland 160 K1
Ham Wilts 25 C8
Ham Common Dorset 13 B6
Ham Green Hereford 50 E2
Ham Green Kent 19 C5
Ham Green Kent 30 C2
Ham Green N Som 23 B7
Ham Green Worcs 50 C5
Ham Street Som 23 F7
Hamble-le-Rice Hants 15 D5
Hambleden Bucks 39 F7
Hambledon Hants 15 C7
Hambledon Sur 27 F7
Hambleton Lancs 92 E3
Hambleton N Yorks 95 F8
Hambridge Som 11 B8
Hambrook S Glos 23 B8
Hambrook W Sus 15 D8
Hameringham Lincs 79 C6
Hamerton Cambs 54 B2
Hametoun Shetland 160 K1
Hamilton S Lanark 119 D7
Hammer W Sus 27 F6
Hammerpot W Sus 16 D4
Hammersmith London 28 B3
Hammerwich Staffs 62 D4
Hammerwood E Sus 28 F5
Hammond Street Herts 41 D6
Hammoon Dorset 13 C6
Hamnavoe Shetland 160 E4
Hamnavoe Shetland 160 E6
Hamnavoe Shetland 160 F6
Hamnavoe Shetland 160 K5
Hampden Park E Sus 18 E3
Hamperden End Essex 55 F6
Hampnett Glos 37 C7
Hampole S Yorks 89 C6
Hampreston Dorset 13 E8
Hampstead London 41 F5
Hampstead Norreys W Berks 26 B3
Hampsthwaite N Yorks 95 D5
Hampton London 28 C2
Hampton Shrops 61 F7
Hampton Worcs 50 E5
Hampton Bishop Hereford 49 F7
Hampton Heath Ches W 73 E8
Hampton in Arden W Mid 63 F6
Hampton Loade Shrops 61 F7
Hampton Lovett Worcs 50 C3
Hampton Lucy Warks 51 D7
Hampton on the Hill Warks 51 C7
Hampton Poyle Oxon 39 C5
Hamrow Norf 80 E5
Hamsey E Sus 17 C8
Hamsey Green London 28 D4
Hamstall Ridware Staffs 62 C5
Hamstead IoW 14 E5
Hamstead W Mid 62 E4
Hamstead Marshall W Berks 26 C2
Hamsterley Durham 110 D4
Hamsterley Durham 110 F4
Hamstreet Kent 19 B7
Hamworthy Poole 13 E7
Hanbury Staffs 63 B5
Hanbury Worcs 50 C4
Hanbury Woodend Staffs 63 B5
Hanby Lincs 78 F3
Hanchurch Staffs 74 E5
Handbridge Ches W 73 C8
Handcross W Sus 17 B6
Handforth Ches E 87 F6
Handley Ches W 73 D8
Handsacre Staffs 62 C4
Handsworth S Yorks 88 F5
Handsworth W Mid 62 E4
Handy Cross Devon 9 B6
Hanford Stoke 75 E5
Hanging Langford Wilts 24 F5
Hangleton W Sus 16 D4
Hanham S Glos 23 B8
Hankelow Ches E 74 E3
Hankerton Wilts 37 E6
Hankham E Sus 18 E3
Hanley Stoke 75 E5
Hanley Castle Worcs 50 E3
Hanley Child Worcs 49 C8
Hanley Swan Worcs 50 E3
Hanley William Worcs 49 C8
Hanlith N Yorks 94 C2
Hanmer Wrex 73 F8
Hannah Lincs 79 B8
Hannington Hants 26 D3
Hannington Northants 53 B6
Hannington Swindon 38 E1
Hannington Wick Swindon 38 E1
Hansel Village S Ayrs 118 F3
Hanslope M Keynes 53 E6
Hanthorpe Lincs 65 B7
Hanwell London 40 F4
Hanwell Oxon 52 E2
Hanwood Shrops 60 D4
Hanworth London 28 B2
Hanworth Norf 81 D7
Happendon S Lanark 119 F8
Happisburgh Norf 69 A6
Happisburgh Common Norf 69 B6
Hapsford Ches W 73 B8
Hapton Lancs 93 F7
Hapton Norf 68 E4
Harberton Devon 7 D5
Harbertonford Devon 7 D5
Harbledown Kent 30 D5
Harborne W Mid 62 F4
Harborough Magna Warks 52 B2
Harbottle Northumb 117 D5
Harbury Warks 51 D8
Harby Leics 77 F7
Harby Notts 77 B8
Harcombe Devon 11 E6
Harden W Mid 62 D4
Harden W Yorks 94 F3
Hardenhuish Wilts 24 B4
Hardgate Aberds 141 D6
Hardham W Sus 16 C4
Hardingham Norf 68 D3
Hardingstone Northants 53 D5
Hardington Som 24 D2
Hardington Mandeville Som 12 C3
Hardington Marsh Som 12 D3
Hardley Hants 14 D5
Hardley Street Norf 69 D6
Hardmead M Keynes 53 E7
Hardrow N Yorks 100 E3
Hardstoft Derbys 76 C4
Hardway Hants 15 D7
Hardway Som 24 F2
Hardwick Bucks 39 C8
Hardwick Cambs 54 D4
Hardwick Norf 67 C6
Hardwick Norf 68 F5
Hardwick Northants 53 C6
Hardwick Notts 77 B6
Hardwick Oxon 38 D3
Hardwick Oxon 39 B5
Hardwick W Mid 62 E4
Hardwicke Glos 36 C4
Hardwicke Glos 37 B6
Hardwicke Hereford 48 E4
Hardy's Green Essex 43 B5
Hare Green Essex 43 B6
Hare Hatch Wokingham 27 B6
Hare Street Herts 41 B6
Hareby Lincs 79 C6
Hareden Lancs 93 D6
Harefield London 40 E3
Harehills W Yorks 95 F6
Harehope Northumb 117 B6
Haresceugh Cumb 109 E6
Harescombe Glos 37 C5
Haresfield Glos 37 C5
Hareshaw N Lanark 119 C8
Hareshaw Head Northumb 116 F4
Harewood W Yorks 95 E6
Harewood End Hereford 36 B2
Harford Carms 46 E5
Harford Devon 6 D4
Hargate Norf 68 E4
Hargatewall Derbys 75 B8
Hargrave Ches W 73 C8
Hargrave Northants 53 B8
Hargrave Suff 55 D8
Harker Cumb 108 C3
Harkland Shetland 160 E6
Harkstead Suff 57 F5
Harlaston Staffs 63 C6
Harlaw Ho. Aberds 141 B6
Harlaxton Lincs 77 F8
Harle Syke Lancs 93 F8
Harlech Gwyn 71 D6
Harlequin Notts 77 F6
Harlescott Shrops 60 C5
Harlesden London 41 F5
Harleston Devon 7 E5
Harleston Norf 68 F5
Harleston Suff 56 D4
Harlestone Northants 52 C5
Harley S Yorks 88 E4
Harley Shrops 61 D5
Harleyholm S Lanark 120 F2
Harlington C Beds 53 F8
Harlington London 27 B8
Harlington S Yorks 89 D5
Harlosh Highld 149 D7
Harlow Essex 41 C7
Harlow Hill N Yorks 95 D5
Harlow Hill Northumb 110 C3
Harlthorpe E Yorks 96 F3
Harlton Cambs 54 D4
Harman's Cross Dorset 13 F7
Harmby N Yorks 101 F6
Harmer Green Herts 41 C5
Harmer Hill Shrops 60 B4
Harmondsworth London 27 B8
Harmston Lincs 78 C2
Harnham Northumb 110 B3
Harnhill Glos 37 D7
Harold Hill London 41 E8
Harold Wood London 41 E8
Haroldston West Pembs 44 D3
Haroldswick Shetland 160 B8
Harome N Yorks 102 F4
Harpenden Herts 40 C4
Harpford Devon 11 E5
Harpham E Yorks 97 C6
Harpley Norf 80 E3
Harpley Worcs 49 C8
Harpole Northants 52 C4
Harpsdale Highld 158 E3
Harpsden Oxon 39 F7
Harpswell Lincs 90 F3
Harpur Hill Derbys 75 B7
Harpurhey Gtr Man 87 D6
Harraby Cumb 108 D4
Harrapool Highld 149 F11
Harrier Shetland 160 J1
Harrietfield Perth 127 B8
Harrietsham Kent 30 D2
Harrington Cumb 98 B1
Harrington Lincs 79 B6
Harrington Northants 64 F4
Harringworth Northants 65 E6
Harris Highld 146 B6
Harrogate N Yorks 95 D6
Harrold Bedford 53 D7
Harrow London 40 F4
Harrow on the Hill London 40 F4
Harrow Street Suff 56 F3
Harrow Weald London 40 E4
Harrowbarrow Corn 5 C8
Harrowden Bedford 53 E8
Harrowgate Hill Darl 101 C7
Harston Cambs 54 D5
Harston Leics 77 F8
Harswell E Yorks 96 E4
Hart Hrtlpl 111 F7
Hart Common Gtr Man 86 D4
Hart Hill Luton 40 B4
Hart Station Hrtlpl 111 F7
Hartburn Northumb 117 F6
Hartburn Stockton 102 C2
Hartest Suff 56 D2
Hartfield E Sus 29 F5
Hartford Cambs 54 B3
Hartford Ches W 74 B3
Hartford End Essex 42 C2
Hartfordbridge Hants 27 D5
Hartforth N Yorks 101 D6
Harthill Ches W 74 D2
Harthill N Lanark 120 C2
Harthill S Yorks 89 F5
Hartington Derbys 75 C8
Hartland Devon 8 B4
Hartlebury Worcs 50 B3
Hartlepool Hrtlpl 111 F8
Hartley Cumb 100 D2
Hartley Kent 18 B4
Hartley Kent 29 C7
Hartley Northumb 111 B6
Hartley Westpall Hants 26 D4
Hartley Wintney Hants 27 D5
Hartlip Kent 30 C2
Hartoft End N Yorks 103 E5
Harton N Yorks 96 C3
Harton Shrops 60 F4
Harton T&W 111 C6
Hartpury Glos 36 B4
Hartshead W Yorks 88 B2
Hartshill Warks 63 E7
Hartshorne Derbys 63 B7
Hartsop Cumb 99 C6
Hartwell Northants 53 D5
Hartwood N Lanark 119 D8
Harvieston Stirling 126 F4
Harvington Worcs 51 E5
Harvington Cross Worcs 51 E5
Harwell Oxon 38 F4
Harwich Essex 57 F6
Harwood Durham 109 F8
Harwood Gtr Man 86 C5
Harwood Dale N Yorks 103 E7
Harworth Notts 89 E7
Hasbury W Mid 62 F3
Hascombe Sur 27 E7
Haselbech Northants 52 B5
Haselbury Plucknett Som 12 C2
Haseley Warks 51 C7
Haselor Warks 51 D6
Hasfield Glos 37 B5
Hasguard Pembs 44 E3
Haskayne Lancs 85 D4
Hasketon Suff 57 D6
Hasland Derbys 76 C3
Haslemere Sur 27 F7
Haslingden Lancs 87 B5
Haslingfield Cambs 54 D5
Haslington Ches E 74 D4
Hassall Ches E 74 D4
Hassall Green Ches E 74 D4
Hassell Street Kent 30 E4
Hassendean Borders 115 B8
Hassingham Norf 69 D6
Hassocks W Sus 17 C6
Hassop Derbys 76 B2
Hastigrow Highld 158 D4
Hastingleigh Kent 30 E4
Hastings E Sus 18 E5
Hastingwood Essex 41 D7
Hastoe Herts 40 D2
Haswell Durham 111 E6
Haswell Plough Durham 111 E6
Hatch C Beds 54 E2
Hatch Hants 26 D4
Hatch Wilts 13 B7
Hatch Beauchamp Som 11 B8
Hatch End London 40 E4
Hatch Green Som 11 C8
Hatchet Gate Hants 14 D4
Hatching Green Herts 40 C4
Hatchmere Ches W 74 B2
Hatcliffe NE Lincs 91 D6
Hatfield Hereford 49 D7
Hatfield Herts 41 D5
Hatfield S Yorks 89 D7
Hatfield Worcs 50 D3
Hatfield Broad Oak Essex 41 C8
Hatfield Garden Village Herts 41 D5
Hatfield Heath Essex 41 C8
Hatfield Hyde Herts 41 C5
Hatfield Peverel Essex 42 C3
Hatfield Woodhouse S Yorks 89 D7
Hatford Oxon 38 E3
Hatherden Hants 25 D8
Hatherleigh Devon 9 D7
Hathern Leics 63 B8
Hatherop Glos 38 D1
Hathersage Derbys 88 F3
Hathershaw Gtr Man 87 D7

Hatherton Ches E 74 E3
Hatherton Staffs 62 C3
Hatley St George Cambs 54 D3
Hatt Corn 5 C8
Hattingley Hants 26 F4
Hatton Aberds 153 E10
Hatton Derbys 63 B6
Hatton Lincs 78 B4
Hatton Shrops 60 E4
Hatton Warks 51 C7
Hatton Warr 86 F3
Hatton Castle Aberds 153 D7
Hatton Heath Ches W 73 C8
Hatton of Fintray Aberds 141 C7
Hattoncrook Aberds 141 B7
Haugh E Ayrs 112 B4
Haugh Gtr Man 87 C7
Haugh Lincs 79 B7
Haugh Head Northumb 117 B6
Haugh of Glass Moray 152 E4
Haugh of Urr Dumfries 106 C5
Haugham Lincs 91 F7
Haughley Suff 56 C4
Haughley Green Suff 56 C4
Haughs of Clinterty Aberdeen 141 C7
Haughton Notts 77 B6
Haughton Shrops 60 B3
Haughton Shrops 61 C5
Haughton Shrops 61 D7
Haughton Shrops 61 E6
Haughton Staffs 62 B2
Haughton Castle Northumb 110 B2
Haughton Green Gtr Man 87 E7
Haughton Moss Ches E 74 D2
Haultwick Herts 41 B6
Haunn Argyll 146 G6
Haunn W Isles 148 G2
Haunton Staffs 63 C6
Hauxley Northumb 117 D8
Hauxton Cambs 54 D5
Havant Hants 15 D8
Haven Hereford 49 D6
Haven Bank Lincs 78 D5
Haven Side E Yorks 91 B5
Havenstreet IoW 15 E6
Havercroft W Yorks 88 C4
Haverfordwest = Hwlffordd Pembs 44 D4
Haverhill Suff 55 E7
Haverigg Cumb 92 B1
Havering-atte-Bower London 41 E8
Haveringland Norf 81 E7
Haversham M Keynes 53 E6
Haverthwaite Cumb 99 F5
Haverton Hill Stockton 102 B2
Hawarden = Penarlâg Flint 73 C7
Hawcoat Cumb 92 B2
Hawen Ceredig 46 E2
Hawes N Yorks 100 F3
Hawes' Green Norf 68 E5
Hawes Side Blackpool 92 F3
Hawford Worcs 50 C3
Hawick Borders 115 C8
Hawk Green Gtr Man 87 F7
Hawkchurch Devon 11 D8
Hawkedon Suff 55 D8
Hawkenbury Kent 18 B2
Hawkenbury Kent 30 E2
Hawkeridge Wilts 24 D3
Hawkerland Devon 11 F5
Hawkes End W Mid 63 F7
Hawkesbury S Glos 36 F4
Hawkesbury Warks 63 F7
Hawkesbury Upton S Glos 36 F4
Hawkhill Northumb 117 C8
Hawkhurst Kent 18 B4
Hawkinge Kent 31 F6
Hawkley Hants 15 B8
Hawkridge Som 21 F7
Hawkshead Cumb 99 E5
Hawkshead Hill Cumb 99 E5
Hawksland S Lanark 119 F8
Hawkswick N Yorks 94 B2
Hawksworth Notts 77 E7
Hawksworth W Yorks 94 E4
Hawksworth W Yorks 95 F5
Hawkwell Essex 42 E4
Hawley Hants 27 D6
Hawley Kent 29 B6
Hawling Glos 37 B7
Hawnby N Yorks 102 F3
Haworth W Yorks 94 F3
Hawstead Suff 56 D2
Hawthorn Durham 111 E7
Hawthorn Rhondda 35 F5
Hawthorn Wilts 24 C3
Hawthorn Hill Brack 27 B6
Hawthorn Hill Lincs 78 D5
Hawthorpe Lincs 65 B7
Hawton Notts 77 D7
Haxby York 96 D2
Haxey N Lincs 89 D8
Hay Green Norf 66 C5
Hay-on-Wye = Y Gelli Gandryll Powys 48 E4
Hay Street Herts 41 B6
Haydock Mers 86 E3
Haydon Dorset 12 C4
Haydon Bridge Northumb 109 C8
Haydon Wick Swindon 37 F8
Haye Corn 5 C8
Hayes London 28 C5
Hayes London 40 F4
Hayfield Derbys 87 F8
Hayfield Fife 128 E4
Hayhill E Ayrs 112 C4
Hayhillock Angus 135 E5
Hayle Corn 2 C4
Haynes C Beds 53 E8
Haynes Church End C Beds 53 E8
Hayscastle Pembs 44 C3
Hayscastle Cross Pembs 44 C4
Hayshead Angus 135 E6
Hayton Aberdeen 141 D8
Hayton Cumb 107 E8
Hayton Cumb 108 D5
Hayton E Yorks 96 E4
Hayton Notts 89 F8
Hayton's Bent Shrops 60 F5
Haytor Vale Devon 7 B5
Haywards Heath W Sus 17 B7
Haywood S Yorks 89 C6
Haywood Oaks Notts 77 D6
Hazel Grove Gtr Man 87 F7
Hazel Street Kent 18 B3
Hazelbank S Lanark 119 E8
Hazelbury Bryan Dorset 12 D5
Hazeley Hants 26 D5
Hazelhurst Gtr Man 87 D7
Hazelslade Staffs 62 C4
Hazelton Glos 37 C7
Hazelton Walls Fife 128 B5
Hazelwood Derbys 76 E3
Hazlemere Bucks 40 E1
Hazlerigg T&W 110 B5
Hazlewood N Yorks 94 D3
Hazon Northumb 117 D7
Heacham Norf 80 D2
Head of Muir Falk 127 F7
Headbourne Worthy Hants 26 F2
Headbrook Hereford 48 D5
Headcorn Kent 30 E2
Headingley W Yorks 95 F5
Headington Oxon 39 D5
Headlam Durham 101 C6
Headless Cross Worcs 50 C5
Headley Hants 26 C3
Headley Hants 27 F6
Headley Sur 28 D3
Headon Notts 77 B7
Heads S Lanark 119 E7
Heads Nook Cumb 108 D4
Heage Derbys 76 D3
Healaugh N Yorks 95 E7
Healaugh N Yorks 101 E5
Heald Green Gtr Man 87 F6
Heale Devon 20 E5
Heale Som 23 E8
Healey Gtr Man 87 C6
Healey N Yorks 101 F6
Healey Northumb 110 D3
Healing NE Lincs 91 C6
Heamoor Corn 2 C3
Heanish Argyll 146 G3
Heanor Derbys 76 E4
Heanton Punchardon Devon 20 F4
Heapham Lincs 90 F2
Hearthstane Borders 114 B4
Heasley Mill Devon 21 F6
Heast Highld 149 G11
Heath Cardiff 22 B3
Heath Derbys 76 C4
Heath and Reach C Beds 40 B2
Heath End Hants 26 C3
Heath End Sur 27 E6
Heath End Warks 51 C7
Heath Hayes Staffs 62 C4
Heath Hill Shrops 61 C7
Heath House Som 23 E6
Heath Town W Mid 62 E3
Heathcote Derbys 75 C8
Heather Leics 63 C7
Heatherfield Highld 149 D9
Heathfield Devon 7 B6
Heathfield E Sus 18 C2
Heathfield Som 11 B6
Heathhall Dumfries 107 B6
Heathrow Airport London 27 B8
Heathstock Devon 11 D7
Heathton Shrops 62 E2
Heatley Warr 86 F5
Heaton Lancs 92 C4
Heaton Staffs 75 C6
Heaton T&W 111 C5
Heaton W Yorks 94 F4
Heaton Moor Gtr Man 87 E6
Heaverham Kent 29 D6
Heaviley Gtr Man 87 F7
Heavitree Devon 10 E4
Hebburn T&W 111 C6
Hebden N Yorks 94 C3
Hebden Bridge W Yorks 87 B7
Hebron Anglesey 82 C4
Hebron Carms 32 B2
Hebron Northumb 117 F7
Heck Dumfries 114 F3
Heckfield Hants 26 C5
Heckfield Green Suff 57 B5
Heckfordbridge Essex 43 B5
Heckington Lincs 78 E4
Heckmondwike W Yorks 88 B3
Heddington Wilts 24 C4
Heddle Orkney 159 G4
Heddon-on-the-Wall Northumb 110 C4
Hedenham Norf 69 E6
Hedge End Hants 15 C5
Hedgerley Bucks 40 F2
Hedging Som 11 B8
Hedley on the Hill Northumb 110 D3
Hednesford Staffs 62 C4
Hedon E Yorks 91 B5
Hedsor Bucks 40 F2
Hedworth T&W 111 C6
Hegdon Hill Hereford 49 D7
Heggerscales Cumb 100 C3
Heglibister Shetland 160 H5
Heighington Darl 101 B7
Heighington Lincs 78 C3
Heights of Brae Highld 151 E8
Heights of Kinlochewe Highld 150 E3
Heilam Highld 156 C7
Heiton Borders 122 F3
Hele Devon 10 D4
Hele Devon 20 E4
Helensburgh Argyll 145 E11
Helford Corn 3 D6
Helford Passage Corn 3 D6
Helhoughton Norf 80 E4
Helions Bumpstead Essex 55 E7
Hellaby S Yorks 89 E6
Helland Corn 5 B5
Hellesdon Norf 68 C5
Hellidon Northants 52 D3
Hellifield N Yorks 93 D8
Hellingly E Sus 18 D2
Hellington Norf 69 D6
Hellister Shetland 160 J5
Helm Northumb 117 E7
Helmdon Northants 52 E3
Helmingham Suff 57 D5
Helmington Row Durham 110 F4
Helmsdale Highld 157 H13
Helmshore Lancs 87 B5
Helmsley N Yorks 102 F4
Helperby N Yorks 95 C7
Helperthorpe N Yorks 97 B5
Helpringham Lincs 78 E4
Helpston Pboro 65 D8
Helsby Ches W 73 B8
Helsey Lincs 79 B8
Helston Corn 3 D5
Helstone Corn 8 F2
Helton Cumb 99 B7
Helwith Bridge N Yorks 93 C8
Hemblington Norf 69 C6
Hemel Hempstead Herts 40 D3
Hemingbrough N Yorks 96 F2
Hemingby Lincs 78 B5
Hemingford Abbots Cambs 54 B3
Hemingford Grey Cambs 54 B3
Hemingstone Suff 57 D5
Hemington Leics 63 B8
Hemington Northants 65 F7
Hemington Som 24 D2
Hemley Suff 57 E6
Hemlington Mbro 102 C3
Hemp Green Suff 57 C7
Hempholme E Yorks 97 D6
Hempnall Norf 68 E5
Hempnall Green Norf 68 E5
Hempriggs House Highld 158 F5
Hempstead Essex 55 F7
Hempstead Medway 29 C8
Hempstead Norf 69 B7
Hempstead Norf 81 D7
Hempsted Glos 37 C5
Hempton Norf 80 E5
Hempton Oxon 52 F2
Hemsby Norf 69 C7
Hemswell Lincs 90 E3
Hemswell Cliff Lincs 90 F3
Hemsworth W Yorks 88 C5
Hemyock Devon 11 C6
Hen-feddau fawr Pembs 45 F4
Henbury Bristol 23 B7
Henbury Ches E 75 B5
Hendon London 41 F5
Hendon T&W 111 D7
Hendre Flint 73 C5
Hendre-ddu Conwy 83 E8
Hendreforgan Rhondda 34 F3
Hendy Carms 33 D6
Heneglwys Anglesey 82 D4
Henfield W Sus 17 C6
Henford Devon 9 E5
Henghurst Kent 19 B6
Hengoed Caerph 35 E5
Hengoed Powys 48 D4
Hengoed Shrops 73 F6
Hengrave Suff 56 C2
Henham Essex 41 B8
Heniarth Powys 59 D8
Henlade Som 11 B7
Henley Shrops 49 B7
Henley Som 23 F6
Henley Suff 57 D5
Henley W Sus 16 B2
Henley-in-Arden Warks 51 C6
Henley-on-Thames Oxon 39 F7
Henley's Down E Sus 18 D4
Henllan Ceredig 46 E2
Henllan Denb 72 C4
Henllan Amgoed Carms 32 B2
Henllys Torf 35 E6
Henlow C Beds 54 F2
Hennock Devon 10 F3
Henny Street Essex 56 F2
Henryd Conwy 83 D7
Henry's Moat Pembs 32 B1
Hensall N Yorks 89 B6
Henshaw Northumb 109 C7
Hensingham Cumb 98 C1
Henstead Suff 69 F7
Henstridge Som 12 C5
Henstridge Ash Som 12 B5
Henstridge Marsh Som 12 B5
Henton Oxon 39 D7
Henton Som 23 E6
Henwood Corn 5 B7
Heogan Shetland 160 J6
Heol-las Swansea 33 E7
Heol Senni Powys 34 B3
Heol-y-Cyw Bridgend 34 F3
Hepburn Northumb 117 B6
Hepple Northumb 117 D5
Hepscott Northumb 117 F8
Heptonstall W Yorks 87 B7
Hepworth Suff 56 B3
Hepworth W Yorks 88 D2
Herbrandston Pembs 44 E3
Hereford Hereford 49 E7
Heriot Borders 121 D6
Hermiston Edin 120 B4
Hermitage Borders 115 E8
Hermitage Dorset 12 D4
Hermitage W Berks 26 B3
Hermitage W Sus 15 D8
Hermon Anglesey 82 E3
Hermon Carms 33 B7
Hermon Carms 46 F2
Hermon Pembs 45 F4
Herne Kent 31 C5
Herne Bay Kent 31 C5
Herner Devon 9 B7
Hernhill Kent 30 C4
Herodsfoot Corn 5 C7
Herongate Essex 42 E2
Heronsford S Ayrs 104 A5
Herriard Hants 26 E4
Herringfleet Suff 69 E7
Herringswell Suff 55 B8
Hersden Kent 31 C6
Hersham Corn 8 D4
Hersham Sur 28 C2
Herstmonceux E Sus 18 D3
Herston Orkney 159 J5
Hertford Herts 41 C6
Hertford Heath Herts 41 C6
Hertingfordbury Herts 41 C6
Hesket Newmarket Cumb 108 F3
Hesketh Bank Lancs 86 B2
Hesketh Lane Lancs 93 E6
Heskin Green Lancs 86 C3
Hesleden Durham 111 F7
Hesleyside Northumb 116 F4
Heslington York 96 D2
Hessay York 95 D8
Hessenford Corn 5 D8
Hessett Suff 56 C3
Hessle E Yorks 90 B4
Hest Bank Lancs 92 C4
Heston London 28 B2
Hestwall Orkney 159 G3
Heswall Mers 85 F3
Hethe Oxon 39 B5
Hethersett Norf 68 D4
Hethersgill Cumb 108 C4
Hethpool Northumb 116 B4
Hett Durham 111 F5
Hetton N Yorks 94 D2
Hetton-le-Hole T&W 111 E6
Hetton Steads Northumb 123 F6
Heugh Northumb 110 B3
Heugh-head Aberds 140 C2
Heveningham Suff 57 B7
Hever Kent 29 E5
Heversham Cumb 99 F6
Hevingham Norf 81 E7
Hewas Water Corn 3 B8
Hewelsfield Glos 36 D2
Hewish N Som 23 C6
Hewish Som 12 D2
Heworth York 96 D2
Hexham Northumb 110 C2
Hextable Kent 29 B6
Hexton Herts 54 F2
Hexworthy Devon 6 B4
Hey Lancs 93 E8
Heybridge Essex 42 D4
Heybridge Essex 42 E2
Heybridge Basin Essex 42 D4
Heybrook Bay Devon 6 E3
Heydon Cambs 54 E5
Heydon Norf 81 E7
Heydour Lincs 78 F3
Heylipol Argyll 146 G2
Heylor Shetland 160 E4
Heysham Lancs 92 C4
Heyshott W Sus 16 C2
Heyside Gtr Man 87 D7
Heytesbury Wilts 24 E4
Heythrop Oxon 38 B3
Heywood Gtr Man 87 C6
Heywood Wilts 24 D3
Hibaldstow N Lincs 90 D3
Hickleton S Yorks 89 D5
Hickling Norf 69 B7
Hickling Notts 64 B3
Hickling Green Norf 69 B7
Hickling Heath Norf 69 B7
Hickstead W Sus 17 B6
Hidcote Boyce Glos 51 E6
High Ackworth W Yorks 88 C5
High Angerton Northumb 117 F6
High Bankhill Cumb 109 E5
High Barnes T&W 111 D6
High Beach Essex 41 E7
High Bentham N Yorks 93 C6
High Bickington Devon 9 B8
High Birkwith N Yorks 93 B7
High Blantyre S Lanark 119 D6
High Bonnybridge Falk 119 B8
High Bradfield S Yorks 88 E3
High Bray Devon 21 F5
High Brooms Kent 29 E6
High Bullen Devon 9 B7
High Buston Northumb 117 D8
High Callerton Northumb 110 B4
High Catton E Yorks 96 D3
High Cogges Oxon 38 D3
High Coniscliffe Darl 101 C7
High Cross Hants 15 B8
High Cross Herts 41 C6
High Easter Essex 42 C2
High Eggborough N Yorks 89 B6
High Ellington N Yorks 101 F6
High Ercall Telford 61 C5
High Etherley Durham 101 B6
High Garrett Essex 42 B3
High Grange Durham 110 F4
High Green Norf 68 D4
High Green S Yorks 88 E4
High Green Worcs 50 E3
High Halden Kent 19 B5
High Halstow Medway 29 B8
High Ham Som 23 F6
High Harrington Cumb 98 B2
High Hatton Shrops 61 B6
High Hawsker N Yorks 103 D7
High Hesket Cumb 108 E4
High Hesleden Durham 111 F7
High Hoyland S Yorks 88 C3
High Hunsley E Yorks 97 F5
High Hurstwood E Sus 17 B8
High Hutton N Yorks 96 C3
High Ireby Cumb 108 F2
High Kelling Norf 81 C7
High Kilburn N Yorks 95 B8
High Lands Durham 101 B6
High Lane Gtr Man 87 F7
High Lane Worcs 49 C8
High Laver Essex 41 D8
High Legh Ches E 86 F5
High Leven Stockton 102 C2
High Littleton Bath 23 D8
High Lorton Cumb 98 B3
High Marishes N Yorks 96 B4
High Marnham Notts 77 B8
High Melton S Yorks 89 D6
High Mickley Northumb 110 C3
High Mindork Dumfries 105 D7
High Newton Cumb 99 F6
High Newton-by-the-Sea Northumb 117 B8
High Nibthwaite Cumb 98 F4
High Offley Staffs 61 B7
High Ongar Essex 42 D1
High Onn Staffs 62 C2
High Roding Essex 42 C2
High Row Cumb 108 F3
High Salvington W Sus 16 D5
High Sellafield Cumb 98 D2
High Shaw N Yorks 100 E3
High Spen T&W 110 D4
High Stoop Durham 110 E4
High Street Corn 4 D4
High Street Kent 18 B4
High Street Suff 56 E2
High Street Suff 57 B8
High Street Suff 57 D8
High Street Green Suff 56 D4
High Throston Hrtlpl 111 F7
High Toynton Lincs 79 C5
High Trewhitt Northumb 117 D6
High Valleyfield Fife 128 F2
High Westwood Durham 110 D4
High Wray Cumb 99 E5
High Wych Herts 41 C7
High Wycombe Bucks 40 E1
Higham Derbys 76 D3
Higham Kent 29 B8
Higham Lancs 93 F8
Higham Suff 55 C8
Higham Suff 56 F4
Higham Dykes Northumb 110 B4
Higham Ferrers Northants 53 C7
Higham Gobion C Beds 54 F2
Higham on the Hill Leics 63 E7
Higham Wood Kent 29 E6
Highampton Devon 9 D6
Highbridge Highld 136 F4
Highbridge Som 22 E5
Highbrook W Sus 28 F4
Highburton W Yorks 88 C2
Highbury Som 23 E8
Highclere Hants 26 C2
Highcliffe Dorset 14 E3
Higher Ansty Dorset 13 D5
Higher Ashton Devon 10 F3
Higher Ballam Lancs 92 F3
Higher Bartle Lancs 92 F5
Higher Boscaswell Corn 2 C2
Higher Burwardsley Ches W 74 D2
Higher Clovelly Devon 8 B5
Higher End Gtr Man 86 D3
Higher Kinnerton Flint 73 C7
Higher Penwortham Lancs 86 B3
Higher Town Scilly 2 E4
Higher Walreddon Devon 6 B2
Higher Walton Lancs 86 B3
Higher Walton Warr 86 F3
Higher Wheelton Lancs 86 B4
Higher Whitley Ches W 86 F4
Higher Wincham Ches W 74 B3
Higher Wych Ches W 73 E8
Highfield E Yorks 96 F3
Highfield Gtr Man 86 D5
Highfield N Ayrs 118 D3
Highfield Oxon 39 B5
Highfield S Yorks 88 F4
Highfield T&W 110 D4
Highfields Cambs 54 D4
Highfields Northumb 123 D5
Highgate London 41 F5
Highlane Ches E 75 C5
Highlane Derbys 88 F5
Highlaws Cumb 107 E8
Highleadon Glos 36 B4
Highleigh W Sus 16 E2
Highley Shrops 61 F7
Highmoor Cross Oxon 39 F7
Highmoor Hill Mon 36 F1
Highnam Glos 36 C4
Highnam Green Glos 36 B4
Highsted Kent 30 C3
Highstreet Green Essex 55 F8
Hightae Dumfries 107 B7
Hightown Ches E 75 C5
Hightown Mers 85 D4
Hightown Green Suff 56 D3
Highway Wilts 24 B5
Highweek Devon 7 B6
Highworth Swindon 38 E2
Hilborough Norf 67 D8
Hilcote Derbys 76 D4
Hilcott Wilts 25 D6
Hilden Park Kent 29 E6
Hildenborough Kent 29 E6
Hildersham Cambs 55 E6
Hilderstone Staffs 75 F6
Hilderthorpe E Yorks 97 C7
Hilfield Dorset 12 D4
Hilgay Norf 67 E6
Hill Pembs 32 D2
Hill S Glos 36 E3
Hill W Mid 62 E5
Hill Brow W Sus 15 B8
Hill Dale Lancs 86 C2
Hill Dyke Lincs 79 E6
Hill End Durham 110 F3
Hill End Fife 128 E2
Hill End N Yorks 94 D3
Hill Head Hants 15 D6
Hill Head Northumb 110 C2
Hill Mountain Pembs 44 E4
Hill of Beath Fife 128 E3
Hill of Fearn Highld 151 D11
Hill of Mountblairy Aberds 153 C6
Hill Ridware Staffs 62 C4
Hill Top Durham 100 B4
Hill Top Hants 14 D5
Hill Top W Mid 62 E3
Hill Top W Yorks 88 C4
Hill View Dorset 13 E7
Hillam N Yorks 89 B6
Hillbeck Cumb 100 C2
Hillborough Kent 31 C6
Hillbrae Aberds 141 B6
Hillbrae Aberds 152 D6
Hillbutts Dorset 13 D7
Hillclifflane Derbys 76 E2
Hillcommon Som 11 B6
Hillend Fife 128 F3
Hillerton Devon 10 E2
Hillesden Bucks 39 B6
Hillesley Glos 36 F4
Hillfarance Som 11 B6
Hillhead Aberds 152 E5
Hillhead Devon 7 D7
Hillhead S Ayrs 112 C4
Hillhead of Auchentumb Aberds 153 C9
Hillhead of Cocklaw Aberds 153 D10
Hillhouse Borders 121 D8
Hilliclay Highld 158 D3
Hillingdon London 40 F3
Hillington Glasgow 118 C5
Hillington Norf 80 E3
Hillmorton Warks 52 B3
Hillockhead Aberds 140 C3
Hillockhead Aberds 140 D2
Hillside Aberds 141 E8
Hillside Angus 135 C7
Hillside Mers 85 C4
Hillside Orkney 159 J5
Hillside Shetland 160 G6
Hillswick Shetland 160 F4
Hillway IoW 15 F7
Hillwell Shetland 160 M5
Hilmarton Wilts 24 B5
Hilperton Wilts 24 D3
Hilsea Ptsmth 15 D7
Hilston E Yorks 97 F8
Hilton Aberds 153 E9
Hilton Cambs 54 C3
Hilton Cumb 100 B2
Hilton Derbys 76 F2
Hilton Dorset 13 D5
Hilton Durham 101 B6
Hilton Highld 151 C10
Hilton Shrops 61 E7
Hilton Stockton 102 C2
Hilton of Cadboll Highld 151 D11
Himbleton Worcs 50 D4
Himley Staffs 62 E2
Hincaster Cumb 99 F7
Hinckley Leics 63 E8
Hinderclay Suff 56 B4
Hinderton Ches W 73 B7
Hinderwell N Yorks 103 C5
Hindford Shrops 73 F7
Hindhead Sur 27 F6
Hindley Gtr Man 86 D4
Hindley Green Gtr Man 86 D4
Hindlip Worcs 50 D3
Hindolveston Norf 81 E6
Hindon Wilts 24 F4
Hindringham Norf 81 D5
Hingham Norf 68 D3
Hinstock Shrops 61 B6
Hintlesham Suff 56 E4
Hinton Hants 14 E3
Hinton Hereford 48 F5
Hinton Northants 52 D3
Hinton S Glos 24 B2
Hinton Shrops 60 D4
Hinton Ampner Hants 15 B6
Hinton Blewett Bath 23 D7
Hinton Charterhouse Bath 24 D2
Hinton-in-the-Hedges Northants 52 F3
Hinton Martell Dorset 13 D8
Hinton on the Green Worcs 50 E5
Hinton Parva Swindon 38 F2
Hinton St George Som 12 C2
Hinton St Mary Dorset 13 C5
Hinton Waldrist Oxon 38 E3
Hints Shrops 49 B8
Hints Staffs 63 D5
Hinwick Bedford 53 C7
Hinxhill Kent 30 E4
Hinxton Cambs 55 E5
Hinxworth Herts 54 E3
Hipperholme W Yorks 88 B2
Hipswell N Yorks 101 E6
Hirael Gwyn 83 D5
Hiraeth Carms 32 B2
Hirn Aberds 141 D6
Hirnant Powys 59 B7
Hirst N Lanark 119 C8
Hirst Northumb 117 F8
Hirst Courtney N Yorks 89 B7
Hirwaen Denb 72 C5
Hirwaun Rhondda 34 D3
Hiscott Devon 9 B7
Histon Cambs 54 C5
Hitcham Suff 56 D3
Hitchin Herts 40 B4
Hither Green London 28 B4
Hittisleigh Devon 10 E2
Hive E Yorks 96 F4
Hixon Staffs 62 B4
Hoaden Kent 31 D6
Hoaldalbert Mon 35 B7
Hoar Cross Staffs 62 B5
Hoarwithy Hereford 36 B2
Hoath Kent 31 C6
Hobarris Shrops 48 B5
Hobbister Orkney 159 H4
Hobkirk Borders 115 C8
Hobson Durham 110 D4
Hoby Leics 64 C3
Hockering Norf 68 C3
Hockerton Notts 77 D7
Hockley Essex 42 E4
Hockley Heath W Mid 51 B6
Hockliffe C Beds 40 B2
Hockwold cum Wilton Norf 67 F7
Hockworthy Devon 10 C5
Hoddesdon Herts 41 D6
Hoddlesden Blackburn 86 B5
Hoddom Mains Dumfries 107 B8
Hoddomcross Dumfries 107 B8
Hodgeston Pembs 32 E1
Hodley Powys 59 E8
Hodnet Shrops 61 B6
Hodthorpe Derbys 76 B5
Hoe Hants 15 C6
Hoe Norf 68 C2
Hoe Gate Hants 15 C7
Hoff Cumb 100 C1
Hog Patch Sur 27 E6
Hoggard's Green Suff 56 D2
Hoggeston Bucks 39 B8
Hogha Gearraidh W Isles 148 A2
Hoghton Lancs 86 B4
Hognaston Derbys 76 D2
Hogsthorpe Lincs 79 B8
Holbeach Lincs 66 B3
Holbeach Bank Lincs 66 B3
Holbeach Clough Lincs 66 B3
Holbeach Drove Lincs 66 C3
Holbeach Hurn Lincs 66 B3
Holbeach St Johns Lincs 66 C3
Holbeach St Marks Lincs 79 F6
Holbeach St Matthew Lincs 79 F7
Holbeck Notts 76 B5
Holbeck W Yorks 95 F5
Holbeck Woodhouse Notts 76 B5
Holberrow Green Worcs 50 D5
Holbeton Devon 6 D4
Holborn London 41 F6
Holbrook Derbys 76 E3
Holbrook S Yorks 88 F5
Holbrook Suff 57 F5
Holburn Northumb 123 F6
Holbury Hants 14 D5
Holcombe Devon 7 B7
Holcombe Som 23 E8
Holcombe Rogus Devon 11 C5
Holcot Northants 53 C5
Holden Lancs 93 E7
Holdenby Northants 52 C4
Holdenhurst Bmouth 14 E2
Holdgate Shrops 61 F5
Holdingham Lincs 78 E3
Holditch Dorset 11 D8
Hole-in-the-Wall Hereford 36 B3
Holefield Borders 122 F4
Holehouses Ches E 74 B4
Holemoor Devon 9 D6
Holestane Dumfries 113 E8
Holford Som 22 E3
Holgate York 95 D8
Holker Cumb 92 B3
Holkham Norf 80 C4
Hollacombe Devon 9 D5
Holland Orkney 159 C5
Holland Orkney 159 F7
Holland Fen Lincs 78 E5
Holland-on-Sea Essex 43 C8
Hollandstoun Orkney 159 C8
Hollee Dumfries 108 C2
Hollesley Suff 57 E7
Hollicombe Torbay 7 C6
Hollingbourne Kent 30 D2
Hollington Derbys 76 F2
Hollington E Sus 18 D4
Hollington Staffs 75 F7
Hollington Grove Derbys 76 F2
Hollingworth Gtr Man 87 E8
Hollins Gtr Man 87 D6
Hollins Green Warr 86 E4
Hollins Lane Lancs 92 D4
Hollinsclough Staffs 75 C7
Hollinwood Gtr Man 87 D7
Hollinwood Shrops 74 F2
Hollocombe Devon 9 C8
Hollow Meadows S Yorks 88 F3
Holloway Derbys 76 D3
Hollowell Northants 52 B4
Holly End Norf 66 D4
Holly Green Worcs 50 E3
Hollybush Caerph 35 D5
Hollybush E Ayrs 112 C3
Hollybush Worcs 50 F2
Hollym E Yorks 91 B7
Hollywood Worcs 51 B5
Holmbridge W Yorks 88 D2
Holmbury St Mary Sur 28 E2
Holmbush Corn 4 D5
Holmcroft Staffs 62 B3
Holme Cambs 65 F8
Holme Cumb 92 B5
Holme N Yorks 102 F1
Holme Notts 77 D8
Holme W Yorks 88 D2
Holme Chapel Lancs 87 B6
Holme Green N Yorks 95 E8
Holme Hale Norf 67 D8
Holme Lacy Hereford 49 F7
Holme Marsh Hereford 48 D5
Holme next the Sea Norf 80 C3
Holme-on-Spalding-Moor E Yorks 96 F4
Holme on the Wolds E Yorks 97 E5
Holme Pierrepont Notts 77 F6
Holme St Cuthbert Cumb 107 E8
Holme Wood W Yorks 94 F4
Holmer Hereford 49 E7
Holmer Green Bucks 40 E2
Holmes Chapel Ches E 74 C4
Holmesfield Derbys 76 B3
Holmeswood Lancs 86 C2
Holmewood Derbys 76 C4
Holmfirth W Yorks 88 D2
Holmhead Dumfries 113 F7
Holmhead E Ayrs 113 B5
Holmisdale Highld 148 D6
Holmpton E Yorks 91 B7
Holmrook Cumb 98 E2
Holmsgarth Shetland 160 J6
Holmwrangle Cumb 108 E5
Holne Devon 6 C5
Holnest Dorset 12 D4
Holsworthy Devon 8 D5
Holsworthy Beacon Devon 9 D5
Holt Dorset 13 D8
Holt Norf 81 D6
Holt Wilts 24 C3
Holt Worcs 50 C3
Holt Wrex 73 D8
Holt End Hants 26 F4
Holt End Worcs 51 C5
Holt Fleet Worcs 50 C3
Holt Heath Worcs 50 C3
Holt Park W Yorks 95 E5
Holtby York 96 D2
Holton Oxon 39 D6
Holton Som 12 B4
Holton Suff 57 B7
Holton cum Beckering Lincs 90 F5
Holton Heath Dorset 13 E7
Holton le Clay Lincs 91 D6
Holton le Moor Lincs 90 E4
Holton St Mary Suff 56 F4
Holwell Dorset 12 C5
Holwell Herts 54 F2
Holwell Leics 64 B4
Holwell Oxon 38 D2
Holwick Durham 100 B4
Holworth Dorset 13 F5
Holy Cross Worcs 50 B4
Holy Island Northumb 123 E7
Holybourne Hants 26 E5
Holyhead = Caergybi Anglesey 82 C2
Holymoorside Derbys 76 C3
Holyport Windsor 27 B6
Holystone Northumb 117 D5
Holytown N Lanark 119 C7
Holywell Cambs 54 B4
Holywell Corn 4 D2
Holywell Dorset 12 D3
Holywell E Sus 18 F2
Holywell = Treffynnon Flint 73 B5
Holywell Northumb 111 B6
Holywell Green W Yorks 87 C8
Holywell Lake Som 11 B6
Holywell Row Suff 55 B8
Holywood Dumfries 114 F2
Hom Green Hereford 36 B2
Homer Shrops 61 D6
Homersfield Suff 69 F5
Homington Wilts 14 B2
Honey Hill Kent 30 C5
Honey Street Wilts 25 C6
Honey Tye Suff 56 F3
Honeyborough Pembs 44 E4
Honeybourne Worcs 51 E6
Honeychurch Devon 9 D8
Honiley Warks 51 B7
Honing Norf 69 B6
Honingham Norf 68 C4
Honington Lincs 78 E2
Honington Suff 56 B3
Honington Warks 51 E7
Honiton Devon 11 D6
Honley W Yorks 88 C2
Hoo Green Ches E 86 F5
Hoo St Werburgh Medway 29 B8
Hood Green S Yorks 88 D4
Hooe E Sus 18 E3
Hooe Plym 6 D3
Hooe Common E Sus 18 D3
Hook E Yorks 89 B8
Hook Hants 26 D5
Hook London 28 C2
Hook Pembs 44 D4
Hook Wilts 37 F7
Hook Green Kent 18 B3
Hook Green Kent 29 C7
Hook Norton Oxon 51 F8
Hooke Dorset 12 E3
Hookgate Staffs 74 F4
Hookway Devon 10 E3
Hookwood Sur 28 E3
Hoole Ches W 73 C8
Hooley Sur 28 D3
Hoop Mon 36 D2
Hooton Ches W 73 B7
Hooton Levitt S Yorks 89 E6
Hooton Pagnell S Yorks 89 D5
Hooton Roberts S Yorks 89 E5
Hop Pole Lincs 65 C8
Hope Derbys 88 F2
Hope Devon 6 F4
Hope Highld 156 B7
Hope Powys 60 D2
Hope Shrops 60 D3
Hope Staffs 75 D8
Hope = Yr Hôb Flint 73 D7
Hope Bagot Shrops 49 B7
Hope Bowdler Shrops 60 E4
Hope End Green Essex 42 B1
Hope Green Ches E 87 F7
Hope Mansell Hereford 36 C3
Hope under Dinmore Hereford 49 D7
Hopeman Moray 152 B1
Hope's Green Essex 42 F3
Hopesay Shrops 60 F3
Hopley's Green Hereford 48 D5
Hopperton N Yorks 95 D7
Hopstone Shrops 61 E7
Hopton Shrops 60 B3
Hopton Shrops 61 B5
Hopton Staffs 62 B3
Hopton Suff 56 B3
Hopton Cangeford Shrops 60 F5
Hopton Castle Shrops 49 B5
Hopton on Sea Norf 69 D8
Hopton Wafers Shrops 49 B8
Hoptonheath Shrops 49 B5
Hopwas Staffs 63 D5
Hopwood Gtr Man 87 D6
Hopwood Worcs 50 B5
Horam E Sus 18 D2
Horbling Lincs 78 F4
Horbury W Yorks 88 C3
Horcott Glos 38 D1
Horden Durham 111 E7
Horderley Shrops 60 F4
Hordle Hants 14 E3
Hordley Shrops 73 F7
Horeb Carms 33 B6
Horeb Carms 33 D5
Horeb Ceredig 46 E2
Horfield Bristol 23 B8
Horham Suff 57 B6
Horkesley Heath Essex 43 B5
Horkstow N Lincs 90 C3
Horley Oxon 52 E2
Horley Sur 28 E3
Hornblotton Green Som 23 F7
Hornby Lancs 93 C5
Hornby N Yorks 101 E7
Hornby N Yorks 102 D1
Horncastle Lincs 79 C5
Hornchurch London 41 F8
Horncliffe Northumb 122 E5
Horndean Borders 122 E4
Horndean Hants 15 C8
Horndon Devon 6 B3
Horndon on the Hill Thurrock 42 F2
Horne Sur 28 E4
Horniehaugh Angus 134 C4
Horning Norf 69 C6
Horninghold Leics 64 E5
Horninglow Staffs 63 B6
Horningsea Cambs 55 C5
Horningsham Wilts 24 E3
Horningtoft Norf 80 E5
Horns Corner Kent 18 C4
Horns Cross Devon 9 B5
Horns Cross E Sus 18 C5
Hornsby Cumb 108 D5
Hornsea E Yorks 97 E8
Hornsea Bridge E Yorks 97 E8
Hornsey London 41 F6
Hornton Oxon 51 E8
Horrabridge Devon 6 C3
Horringer Suff 56 C2
Horringford IoW 15 F6
Horse Bridge Staffs 75 D6
Horsebridge Devon 6 B2
Horsebridge Hants 25 F8
Horsebrook Staffs 62 C2
Horsehay Telford 61 D6
Horseheath Cambs 55 E7
Horsehouse N Yorks 101 F5
Horsell Sur 27 D7
Horseman's Green Wrex 73 E8
Horseway Cambs 66 F4
Horsey Norf 69 B7
Horsford Norf 68 C4
Horsforth W Yorks 94 F5
Horsham W Sus 28 F2
Horsham Worcs 50 D2
Horsham St Faith Norf 68 C5
Horsington Lincs 78 C4
Horsington Som 12 B5
Horsley Derbys 76 E3
Horsley Glos 37 E5
Horsley Northumb 110 C3
Horsley Northumb 116 E4
Horsley Cross Essex 43 B7
Horsley Woodhouse Derbys 76 E3
Horsleycross Street Essex 43 B7
Horsleyhill Borders 115 C8
Horsleyhope Durham 110 E3
Horsmonden Kent 29 E7
Horspath Oxon 39 D5
Horstead Norf 69 C5
Horsted Keynes W Sus 17 B7
Horton Bucks 40 C2
Horton Dorset 13 D8
Horton Lancs 93 D8
Horton Northants 53 D6
Horton S Glos 36 F4
Horton Shrops 60 B4
Horton Som 11 C8
Horton Staffs 75 D6
Horton Swansea 33 F5
Horton Wilts 25 C5
Horton Windsor 27 B8
Horton-cum-Studley Oxon 39 C5
Horton Green Ches W 73 E8
Horton Heath Hants 15 C5
Horton in Ribblesdale N Yorks 93 B8
Horton Kirby Kent 29 C6
Hortonlane Shrops 60 C4
Horwich Gtr Man 86 C4
Horwich End Derbys 87 F8
Horwood Devon 9 B7
Hose Leics 64 B4
Hoselaw Borders 122 F4
Hoses Cumb 98 E4
Hosh Perth 127 B7
Hosta W Isles 148 A2
Hoswick Shetland 160 L6
Hotham E Yorks 96 F4
Hothfield Kent 30 E3
Hoton Leics 64 B2
Houbie Shetland 160 D8
Houdston S Ayrs 112 E1
Hough Ches E 74 D4
Hough Ches E 75 B5
Hough Green Halton 86 F2
Hough-on-the-Hill Lincs 78 E2
Hougham Lincs 77 E8
Houghton Cambs 54 B3
Houghton Cumb 108 D4
Houghton Hants 25 F8
Houghton Pembs 44 E4
Houghton W Sus 16 C4
Houghton Conquest C Beds 53 E8
Houghton Green E Sus 19 C6
Houghton Green Warr 86 E4
Houghton-le-Side Darl 101 B7
Houghton-Le-Spring T&W 111 E6
Houghton on the Hill Leics 64 D3
Houghton Regis C Beds 40 B3
Houghton St Giles Norf 80 D5
Houlland Shetland 160 F7
Houlland Shetland 160 H5
Houlsyke N Yorks 103 D5
Hound Hants 15 D5
Hound Green Hants 26 D5
Houndslow Borders 122 E2
Houndwood Borders 122 C4
Hounslow London 28 B2
Hounslow Green Essex 42 C2
Housay Shetland 160 F8
House of Daviot Highld 151 G10
House of Glenmuick Aberds 140 E2
Housetter Shetland 160 E5
Houss Shetland 160 K5
Houston Renfs 118 C4
Houstry Highld 158 G3
Houton Orkney 159 H4
Hove Brighton 17 D6
Hoveringham Notts 77 E6
Hoveton Norf 69 C6
Hovingham N Yorks 96 B2
How Cumb 108 D5
How Caple Hereford 49 F8
How End C Beds 53 E8
How Green Kent 29 E5
Howbrook S Yorks 88 E4
Howden Borders 116 B2
Howden E Yorks 89 B8
Howden-le-Wear Durham 110 F4
Howe Highld 158 D5
Howe N Yorks 101 F8
Howe Norf 69 D5
Howe Bridge Gtr Man 86 D4
Howe Green Essex 42 D3
Howe of Teuchar Aberds 153 D7
Howe Street Essex 42 C2
Howe Street Essex 55 F7
Howell Lincs 78 E4
Howey Powys 48 D2
Howgate Midloth 120 D5
Howick Northumb 117 C8
Howle Durham 101 B5
Howle Telford 61 B6
Howlett End Essex 55 F6
Howley Som 11 D7
Hownam Borders 116 C3
Hownam Mains Borders 116 B3
Howpasley Borders 115 D6
Howsham N Lincs 90 D4
Howsham N Yorks 96 C3
Howslack Dumfries 114 D3
Howtel Northumb 122 F4
Howton Hereford 35 B8
Howtown Cumb 99 C6
Howwood Renfs 118 C3
Hoxne Suff 57 B5
Hoy Orkney 159 H3
Hoylake Mers 85 F3
Hoyland S Yorks 88 D4
Hoylandswaine S Yorks 88 D3
Hubberholme N Yorks 94 B2
Hubbert's Bridge Lincs 79 E5
Huby N Yorks 95 C8
Huby N Yorks 95 E5
Hucclecote Glos 37 C5
Hucking Kent 30 D2
Hucknall Notts 76 E5
Huddersfield W Yorks 88 C2
Huddington Worcs 50 D4
Hudswell N Yorks 101 D6
Huggate E Yorks 96 D4
Hugglescote Leics 63 C8
Hugh Town Scilly 2 E4
Hughenden Valley Bucks 40 E1
Hughley Shrops 61 E5
Huish Devon 9 C7
Huish Wilts 25 C6
Huish Champflower Som 11 B5
Huish Episcopi Som 12 B2
Huisinis W Isles 154 F4
Hulcott Bucks 40 C1
Hulland Derbys 76 E2
Hulland Ward Derbys 76 E2
Hullavington Wilts 37 F5
Hullbridge Essex 42 E4
Hulme Gtr Man 87 E6

L

Llanbadarn Fynydd Powys 48 B3
Llanbadarn-y-Garreg Powys 48 E3
Llanbadoc Mon 35 E7
Llanbadrig Anglesey 82 B3
Llanbeder Newport 35 E7
Llanbedr Gwyn 71 E6
Llanbedr Powys 35 B6
Llanbedr Powys 48 E3
Llanbedr-Dyffryn-Clwyd Denb 72 D5
Llanbedr Pont Steffan = Lampeter Ceredig 46 E4
Llanbedr-y-cennin Conwy 83 E7
Llanbedrgoch Anglesey 82 C5
Llanbedrog Gwyn 70 D4
Llanberis Gwyn 83 E5
Llanbethêry V Glam 22 C2
Llanbister Powys 48 B3
Llanblethian V Glam 21 B8
Llanboidy Carms 32 B3
Llanbradach Caerph 35 E5
Llanbrynmair Powys 59 D5
Llancarfan V Glam 22 B2
Llancayo Mon 35 D7
Llancloudy Hereford 36 B1
Llancynfelyn Ceredig 58 E3
Llandaff Cardiff 22 B3
Llandanwg Gwyn 71 E6
Llandarcy Neath 33 E8
Llandawke Carms 32 C3
Llanddaniel Fab Anglesey 82 D4
Llanddarog Carms 33 C6
Llanddeiniol Ceredig 46 B4
Llanddeiniolen Gwyn 82 E5
Llandderfel Gwyn 72 F3
Llanddeusant Anglesey 82 C3
Llanddeusant Carms 34 B1
Llanddew Powys 48 F2
Llanddewi Swansea 33 F5
Llanddewi-Brefi Ceredig 47 D5
Llanddewi Rhydderch Mon 35 C7
Llanddewi Velfrey Pembs 32 C2
Llanddewi'r Cwm Powys 48 E2
Llanddoged Conwy 83 E8
Llanddona Anglesey 83 D5
Llanddowror Carms 32 C3
Llanddulas Conwy 72 B3
Llanddwywe Gwyn 71 E6
Llanddyfynan Anglesey 82 D5
Llandefaelog Fach Powys 48 F2
Llandefaelog-tre'r-graig Powys 35 B5
Llandefalle Powys 48 F3
Llandegai Gwyn 83 D5
Llandegfan Anglesey 83 D5
Llandegla Denb 73 D5
Llandegley Powys 48 C3
Llandegveth Mon 35 E7
Llandegwning Gwyn 70 D3
Llandeilo Carms 33 B7
Llandeilo Graban Powys 48 E2
Llandeilo'r Fan Powys 47 F7
Llandeloy Pembs 44 C3
Llandenny Mon 35 D8
Llandevenny Mon 35 F8
Llandewednock Corn 3 E6
Llandewi Ystradenny Powys 48 C3
Llandinabo Hereford 36 B2
Llandinam Powys 59 F7
Llandissilio Pembs 32 B2
Llandogo Mon 36 D2
Llandough V Glam 21 B8
Llandough V Glam 22 B3
Llandovery = Llanymddyfri Carms 47 F6
Llandow V Glam 21 B8
Llandre Carms 47 E5
Llandre Ceredig 58 F3
Llandrillo Denb 72 F4
Llandrillo-yn-Rhos Conwy 83 C8
Llandrindod = Llandrindod Wells Powys 48 C2
Llandrindod Wells = Llandrindod Powys 48 C2
Llandrinio Powys 60 C2
Llandudno Conwy 83 C7
Llandudno Junction = Cyffordd Llandudno Conwy 83 D7
Llandwrog Gwyn 82 F4
Llandybie Carms 33 C7
Llandyfaelog Carms 33 C5
Llandyfan Carms 33 C7
Llandyfriog Ceredig 46 E2
Llandyfrydog Anglesey 82 C4
Llandygwydd Ceredig 45 E4
Llandynan Denb 73 E5
Llandyrnog Denb 72 C5
Llandysilio Powys 60 C2
Llandyssil Powys 59 E8
Llandysul Ceredig 46 E3
Llanedeyrn Cardiff 35 F6
Llanedi Carms 33 D6
Llaneglwys Powys 48 F2
Llanegryn Gwyn 58 D2
Llanegwad Carms 33 B6
Llaneilian Anglesey 82 B4
Llanelian-yn-Rhos Conwy 83 D8
Llanelidan Denb 72 D5
Llanelieu Powys 48 F3
Llanellen Mon 35 C7
Llanelli Carms 33 E6
Llanelltyd Gwyn 58 C4
Llanelly Mon 35 C6
Llanelly Hill Mon 35 C6
Llanelwedd Powys 48 D2
Llanelwy = St Asaph Denb 72 B4
Llanenddwyn Gwyn 71 E6
Llanengan Gwyn 70 E3
Llanerchymedd Anglesey 82 C4
Llanerfyl Powys 59 D7
Llanfachraeth Anglesey 82 C3
Llanfachreth Gwyn 71 E8
Llanfaelog Anglesey 82 D3
Llanfaelrhys Gwyn 70 E3
Llanfaenor Mon 35 C8
Llanfaes Anglesey 83 D6
Llanfaes Powys 34 B4
Llanfaethlu Anglesey 82 C3
Llanfaglan Gwyn 82 E4
Llanfair Gwyn 71 E6
Llanfair-ar-y-bryn Carms 47 F7
Llanfair Caereinion Powys 59 D8
Llanfair Clydogau Ceredig 46 D5
Llanfair-Dyffryn-Clwyd Denb 72 D5
Llanfair Kilgheddin Mon 35 D7
Llanfair-Nant-Gwyn Pembs 45 F3
Llanfair Talhaiarn Conwy 72 B3
Llanfair Waterdine Shrops 48 B4
Llanfair-Ym-Muallt = Builth Wells Powys 48 D2
Llanfairfechan Conwy 83 D6
Llanfairpwll-gwyngyll Anglesey 82 D5
Llanfairyneubwll Anglesey 82 D3
Llanfairynghornwy Anglesey 82 B3
Llanfallteg Carms 32 C2
Llanfaredd Powys 48 D2
Llanfarian Ceredig 46 B4
Llanfechain Powys 59 B8
Llanfechan Powys 47 D8
Llanfechell Anglesey 82 B3
Llanfendigaid Gwyn 58 D2
Llanferres Denb 73 C5
Llanfflewyn Anglesey 82 C3
Llanfihangel-ar-arth Carms 46 F3
Llanfihangel-Crucorney Mon 35 B7
Llanfihangel Glyn Myfyr Conwy 72 E3
Llanfihangel Nant Bran Powys 47 F8
Llanfihangel-nant-Melan Powys 48 D3
Llanfihangel Rhydithon Powys 48 C3
Llanfihangel Rogiet Mon 35 F8
Llanfihangel Tal-y-llyn Powys 35 B5
Llanfihangel-uwch-Gwili Carms 33 B5
Llanfihangel-y-Creuddyn Ceredig 47 B5
Llanfihangel-y-pennant Gwyn 58 D3
Llanfihangel-y-pennant Gwyn 71 C6
Llanfihangel-y-traethau Gwyn 71 D6
Llanfihangel-yn-Ngwynfa Powys 59 C7
Llanfihangel yn Nhowyn Anglesey 82 D3
Llanfilo Powys 48 F3
Llanfoist Mon 35 C6
Llanfor Gwyn 72 F3
Llanfrechfa Torf 35 E7
Llanfrothen Gwyn 71 C7
Llanfrynach Powys 34 B4
Llanfwrog Anglesey 82 C3
Llanfwrog Denb 72 D5
Llanfyllin Powys 59 C8
Llanfynydd Carms 33 B6
Llanfynydd Flint 73 D6
Llanfyrnach Pembs 45 F4
Llangadfan Powys 59 C7
Llangadog Carms 33 B8
Llangadwaladr Anglesey 82 E3
Llangadwaladr Powys 73 F5
Llangaffo Anglesey 82 E4
Llangain Carms 32 C4
Llangammarch Wells Powys 47 E8
Llangan V Glam 21 B8
Llangarron Hereford 36 B2
Llangasty Talyllyn Powys 35 B5
Llangathen Carms 33 B6
Llangattock Powys 35 C6
Llangattock Lingoed Mon 35 B7
Llangattock nigh Usk Mon 35 D7
Llangattock-Vibon-Avel Mon 36 C1
Llangedwyn Powys 59 B8
Llangefni Anglesey 82 D4
Llangeinor Bridgend 34 F3
Llangeitho Ceredig 46 D5
Llangeler Carms 46 F2
Llangelynin Gwyn 58 D2
Llangendeirne Carms 33 C5
Llangennech Carms 33 D6
Llangennith Swansea 33 E5
Llangenny Powys 35 C6
Llangernyw Conwy 83 E8
Llangian Gwyn 70 E3
Llanglydwen Carms 32 B2
Llangoed Anglesey 83 D6
Llangoedmor Ceredig 45 E3
Llangollen Denb 73 E6
Llangolman Pembs 32 B2
Llangors Powys 35 B5
Llangovan Mon 36 D1
Llangower Gwyn 72 F3
Llangrannog Ceredig 46 D2
Llangristiolus Anglesey 82 D4
Llangrove Hereford 36 C2
Llangua Mon 35 B7
Llangunllo Powys 48 B4
Llangunnor Carms 33 C5
Llangurig Powys 47 B8
Llangwm Conwy 72 E3
Llangwm Mon 35 D8
Llangwm Pembs 44 E4
Llangwnnadl Gwyn 70 D3
Llangwyfan Denb 72 C5
Llangwyfan-isaf Anglesey 82 E3
Llangwyllog Anglesey 82 D4
Llangwyryfon Ceredig 46 B4
Llangybi Ceredig 46 D5
Llangybi Gwyn 70 C5
Llangybi Mon 35 E7
Llangyfelach Swansea 33 E7
Llangynhafal Denb 72 C5
Llangynidr Powys 35 C5
Llangynin Carms 32 C3
Llangynog Carms 32 C4
Llangynog Powys 59 B7
Llangynwyd Bridgend 34 F2
Llanhamlach Powys 34 B4
Llanharan Rhondda 34 F4
Llanharry Rhondda 34 F4
Llanhennock Mon 35 E7
Llanhiledd = Llanhilleth Bl Gwent 35 D6
Llanhilleth = Llanhiledd Bl Gwent 35 D6
Llanidloes Powys 59 F6
Llaniestyn Gwyn 70 D3
Llanifyny Powys 59 F5
Llanigon Powys 48 F4
Llanilar Ceredig 46 B5
Llanilid Rhondda 34 F3
Llanilltud Fawr = Llantwit Major V Glam 21 C8
Llanishen Cardiff 35 F5
Llanishen Mon 36 D1
Llanllawddog Carms 33 B5
Llanllechid Gwyn 83 E6
Llanllowell Mon 35 E7
Llanllugan Powys 59 D7
Llanllwch Carms 32 C4
Llanllwchaiarn Powys 59 E8
Llanllwni Carms 46 F3
Llanllyfni Gwyn 82 F4
Llanmadoc Swansea 33 E5
Llanmaes V Glam 21 C8
Llanmartin Newport 35 F7
Llanmihangel V Glam 21 B8
Llanmorlais Swansea 33 E6
Llannefydd Conwy 72 B3
Llannon Carms 33 D6
Llannor Gwyn 70 D4
Llanon Ceredig 46 C4
Llanover Mon 35 D7
Llanpumsaint Carms 33 B5
Llanreithan Pembs 44 C3
Llanrhaeadr Denb 72 C4
Llanrhaeadr-ym-Mochnant Powys 59 B8
Llanrhian Pembs 44 B3
Llanrhidian Swansea 33 E5
Llanrhos Conwy 83 C7
Llanrhyddlad Anglesey 82 C3
Llanrhystud Ceredig 46 C4
Llanrosser Hereford 48 F4
Llanrothal Hereford 36 C1
Llanrug Gwyn 82 E5
Llanrumney Cardiff 35 F6
Llanrwst Conwy 83 E8
Llansadurnen Carms 32 C3
Llansadwrn Anglesey 83 D5
Llansadwrn Carms 47 F5
Llansaint Carms 32 D4
Llansamlet Swansea 33 E7
Llansanffraid-ym-Mechain Powys 60 B2
Llansannan Conwy 72 C3
Llansannor V Glam 21 B8
Llansantffraed Ceredig 46 C4
Llansantffraed Powys 35 B5
Llansantffraed Cwmdeuddwr Powys 47 C8
Llansantffraed-in-Elvel Powys 48 D2
Llansawel Carms 46 F5
Llansilin Powys 60 B2
Llansoy Mon 35 D8
Llanspyddid Powys 34 B4
Llanstadwell Pembs 44 E4
Llansteffan Carms 32 C4
Llanstephan Powys 48 E3
Llantarnam Torf 35 E7
Llanteg Pembs 32 C2
Llanthony Mon 35 B6
Llantilio Crossenny Mon 35 C7
Llantilio Pertholey Mon 35 C7
Llantood Pembs 45 E3
Llantrisant Anglesey 82 C3
Llantrisant Mon 35 E7
Llantrisant Rhondda 34 F4
Llantrithyd V Glam 22 B2
Llantwit Fardre Rhondda 34 F4
Llantwit Major = Llanilltud Fawr V Glam 21 C8
Llanuwchllyn Gwyn 72 F2
Llanvaches Newport 35 E8
Llanvair Discoed Mon 35 E8
Llanvapley Mon 35 C7
Llanvetherine Mon 35 C7
Llanveynoe Hereford 48 F5
Llanvihangel Gobion Mon 35 D7
Llanvihangel-Ystern-Llewern Mon 35 C8
Llanwarne Hereford 36 B2
Llanwddyn Powys 59 C7
Llanwenog Ceredig 46 E3
Llanwern Newport 35 F7
Llanwinio Carms 32 B3
Llanwnda Gwyn 82 F4
Llanwnda Pembs 44 B4
Llanwnnen Ceredig 46 E4
Llanwnog Powys 59 E7
Llanwrda Carms 47 F6
Llanwrin Powys 58 D4
Llanwrthwl Powys 47 C8
Llanwrtud = Llanwrtyd Wells Powys 47 E7
Llanwrtyd Powys 47 E7
Llanwrtyd Wells = Llanwrtud Powys 47 E7
Llanwyddelan Powys 59 D7
Llanyblodwel Shrops 60 B2
Llanybri Carms 32 C4
Llanybydder Carms 46 E4
Llanycefn Pembs 32 B1
Llanychaer Pembs 44 B4
Llanycil Gwyn 72 F3
Llanycrwys Carms 46 E5
Llanymawddwy Gwyn 59 C6
Llanymddyfri = Llandovery Carms 47 F6
Llanymynech Powys 60 B2
Llanynghenedl Anglesey 82 C3
Llanynys Denb 72 C5
Llanyre Powys 48 C2
Llanystumdwy Gwyn 71 D5
Llanywern Powys 35 B5
Llawhaden Pembs 32 C1
Llawnt Shrops 73 F6
Llawr Dref Gwyn 70 E3
Llawryglyn Powys 59 E6
Llay Wrex 73 D7
Llechcynfarwy Anglesey 82 C3
Llecheiddior Gwyn 71 C5
Llechfaen Powys 34 B4
Llechryd Caerph 35 D5
Llechryd Ceredig 45 E4
Llechrydau Powys 73 F6
Lledrod Ceredig 46 B5
Llenmerewig Powys 59 E8
Llethrid Swansea 33 E6
Llidiad Nenog Carms 46 F4
Llidiardau Gwyn 72 F2
Llidiart-y-parc Denb 72 E5
Llithfaen Gwyn 70 C4
Llong Flint 73 C6
Llowes Powys 48 E3
Llundain-fach Ceredig 46 D4
Llwydcoed Rhondda 34 D3
Llwyn Shrops 60 F2
Llwyn-du Mon 35 C6
Llwyn-hendy Carms 33 E6
Llwyn-têg Carms 33 D6
Llwyn-y-brain Carms 32 C2
Llwyn-y-groes Ceredig 46 D4
Llwyncelyn Ceredig 46 D3
Llwyndafydd Ceredig 46 D2
Llwynderw Powys 60 D2
Llwyndyrys Gwyn 70 C4
Llwyngwril Gwyn 58 D2
Llwynmawr Wrex 73 F6
Llwynypia Rhondda 34 E3
Llynclys Shrops 60 B2
Llynfaes Anglesey 82 D4
Llys-y-frân Pembs 32 B1
Llysfaen Conwy 83 D8
Llyswen Powys 48 F3
Llysworney V Glam 21 B8
Llywel Powys 47 F7
Loan Falk 120 B2
Loanend Northumb 122 D5
Loanhead Midloth 121 C5
Loans S Ayrs 118 F3
Loans of Tullich Highld 151 D11
Lobb Devon 20 F3
Loch a Charnain W Isles 148 D3
Loch a' Ghainmhich W Isles 155 E7
Loch Baghasdail = Lochboisdale W Isles 148 G2
Loch Choire Lodge Highld 157 F9
Loch Euphoirt W Isles 148 B3
Loch Head Dumfries 105 E7
Loch Loyal Lodge Highld 157 E9
Loch nam Madadh = Lochmaddy W Isles 148 B4
Loch Sgioport W Isles 148 E3
Lochailort Highld 147 C10
Lochaline Highld 147 G9
Lochanhully Highld 138 B5
Lochans Dumfries 104 D4
Locharbriggs Dumfries 114 F2
Lochassynt Lodge Highld 156 G4
Lochavich Ho Argyll 124 D5
Lochawe Argyll 125 C7
Lochboisdale = Loch Baghasdail W Isles 148 G2
Lochbuie Argyll 124 C2
Lochcarron Highld 149 E13
Lochdhu Highld 157 E13
Lochdochart House Stirling 126 B3
Lochdon Argyll 124 B3
Lochdrum Highld 150 D5
Lochead Argyll 144 F6
Lochearnhead Stirling 126 B4
Lochee Dundee 134 F3
Lochend Highld 151 H8
Lochend Highld 158 D4
Locherben Dumfries 114 E2
Lochfoot Dumfries 107 B5
Lochgair Argyll 145 D8
Lochgarthside Highld 137 C8
Lochgelly Fife 128 E3
Lochgilphead Argyll 145 E7
Lochgoilhead Argyll 125 E8
Lochhill Moray 152 B2
Lochindorb Lodge Highld 151 H12
Lochinver Highld 156 G3
Lochlane Perth 127 B7
Lochluichart Highld 150 E6
Lochmaben Dumfries 114 F3
Lochmaddy = Loch nam Madadh W Isles 148 B4
Lochmore Cottage Highld 158 F2
Lochmore Lodge Highld 156 F5
Lochore Fife 128 E3
Lochportain W Isles 148 A4
Lochranza N Ayrs 143 C10
Lochs Crofts Moray 152 B3
Lochside Aberds 135 C7
Lochside Highld 151 F11
Lochside Highld 156 D7
Lochside Highld 157 F11
Lochslin Highld 151 C11
Lochstack Lodge Highld 156 E5
Lochton Aberds 141 E6
Lochty Angus 135 C5
Lochty Fife 129 D7
Lochty Perth 128 B2
Lochuisge Highld 130 D1
Lochurr Dumfries 113 F7
Lochwinnoch Renfs 118 D3
Lochwood Dumfries 114 E3
Lochyside Highld 131 B5
Lockengate Corn 4 C5
Lockerbie Dumfries 114 F4
Lockeridge Wilts 25 C6
Lockerley Hants 14 B3
Locking N Som 23 D5
Lockinge Oxon 38 F4
Lockington E Yorks 97 E5
Lockington Leics 63 B8
Lockleywood Shrops 61 B6
Locks Heath Hants 15 D6
Lockton N Yorks 103 E6
Lockwood W Yorks 88 C2
Loddington Leics 64 D4
Loddington Northants 53 B6
Loddiswell Devon 6 E5
Loddon Norf 69 E6
Lode Cambs 55 C6
Loders Dorset 12 E2
Lodsworth W Sus 16 B3
Lofthouse N Yorks 94 B4
Lofthouse W Yorks 88 B4
Loftus Redcar 103 C5
Logan E Ayrs 113 B5
Logan Mains Dumfries 104 E4
Loganlea W Loth 120 C2
Loggerheads Staffs 74 F4
Logie Angus 135 C6
Logie Fife 129 B6
Logie Moray 151 F13
Logie Coldstone Aberds 140 D3
Logie Hill Highld 151 D10
Logie Newton Aberds 153 E6
Logie Pert Angus 135 C6
Logiealmond Lodge Perth 133 F6
Logierait Perth 133 D6
Login Carms 32 B2
Lolworth Cambs 54 C4
Lonbain Highld 149 C11
Londesborough E Yorks 96 E4
London Colney Herts 40 D4
Londonderry N Yorks 101 F8
Londonthorpe Lincs 78 F2
Londubh Highld 155 J13
Lonemore Highld 151 C10
Long Ashton N Som 23 B7
Long Bennington Lincs 77 E8
Long Bredy Dorset 12 E3
Long Buckby Northants 52 C4
Long Clawson Leics 64 B4
Long Common Hants 15 C6
Long Compton Staffs 62 B2
Long Compton Warks 51 F7
Long Crendon Bucks 39 D6
Long Crichel Dorset 13 C7
Long Ditton Sur 28 C2
Long Drax N Yorks 89 B7
Long Duckmanton Derbys 76 B4
Long Eaton Derbys 76 F4
Long Green Worcs 50 F3
Long Hanborough Oxon 38 C4
Long Itchington Warks 52 C2
Long Lawford Warks 52 B2
Long Load Som 12 B2
Long Marston Herts 40 C1
Long Marston N Yorks 95 D8
Long Marston Warks 51 E6
Long Marton Cumb 100 B1
Long Melford Suff 56 E2
Long Newnton Glos 37 E6
Long Newton E Loth 121 C8
Long Preston N Yorks 93 D8
Long Riston E Yorks 97 E7
Long Sight Gtr Man 87 D7
Long Stratton Norf 68 E4
Long Street M Keynes 53 E5
Long Sutton Hants 26 E5
Long Sutton Lincs 66 B4
Long Sutton Som 12 B2
Long Thurlow Suff 56 C4
Long Whatton Leics 63 B8
Long Wittenham Oxon 39 E5
Longbar N Ayrs 118 D3
Longbenton T&W 111 C5
Longborough Glos 38 B1
Longbridge W Mid 50 B5
Longbridge Warks 51 C7
Longbridge Deverill Wilts 24 E3
Longburton Dorset 12 C4
Longcliffe Derbys 76 D2
Longcot Oxon 38 E2
Longcroft Falk 119 B7
Longden Shrops 60 D4
Longdon Staffs 62 C4
Longdon Worcs 50 F3
Longdon Green Staffs 62 C4
Longdon on Tern Telford 61 C6
Longdown Devon 10 E3
Longdowns Corn 3 C6
Longfield Kent 29 C7
Longfield Shetland 160 M5
Longford Derbys 76 F2
Longford Glos 37 B5
Longford London 27 B8
Longford Shrops 74 F3
Longford Telford 61 C7
Longford W Mid 63 F7
Longfordlane Derbys 76 F2
Longforgan Perth 128 B5
Longformacus Borders 122 D2
Longframlington Northumb 117 D7
Longham Dorset 13 E8
Longham Norf 68 C2
Longhaven Aberds 153 E11
Longhill Aberds 153 C9
Longhirst Northumb 117 F8
Longhope Glos 36 C3
Longhope Orkney 159 J4
Longhorsley Northumb 117 E7
Longhoughton Northumb 117 C8
Longlane Derbys 76 F2
Longlane W Berks 26 B2
Longlevens Glos 37 B5
Longley W Yorks 88 D2
Longley Green Worcs 50 D2
Longmanhill Aberds 153 B7
Longmoor Camp Hants 27 F5
Longmorn Moray 152 C2
Longnewton Borders 115 B8
Longnewton Stockton 102 C1
Longney Glos 36 C4
Longniddry E Loth 121 B7
Longnor Shrops 60 D4
Longnor Staffs 75 C7
Longparish Hants 26 E2
Longport Stoke 75 E5
Longridge Lancs 93 F6
Longridge Staffs 62 C3
Longridge W Loth 120 C2
Longriggend N Lanark 119 B8
Longsdon Staffs 75 D6
Longshaw Gtr Man 86 D3
Longside Aberds 153 D10
Longstanton Cambs 54 C4
Longstock Hants 25 F8
Longstone Pembs 32 D2
Longstowe Cambs 54 D4
Longthorpe Pboro 65 E8
Longthwaite Cumb 99 B6
Longton Lancs 86 B2
Longton Stoke 75 E6
Longtown Cumb 108 C3
Longtown Hereford 35 B7
Longview Mers 86 E2
Longville in the Dale Shrops 60 E5
Longwick Bucks 39 D7
Longwitton Northumb 117 F6
Longwood Shrops 61 D6
Longworth Oxon 38 E3
Longyester E Loth 121 C8
Lonmay Aberds 153 C10
Lonmore Highld 148 D7
Looe Corn 5 D7
Loose Kent 29 D8
Loosley Row Bucks 39 D8
Lopcombe Corner Wilts 25 F7
Lopen Som 12 C2
Loppington Shrops 60 B4
Lopwell Devon 6 C2
Lorbottle Northumb 117 D6
Lorbottle Hall Northumb 117 D6
Lornty Perth 134 E1
Loscoe Derbys 76 E4
Losgaintir W Isles 154 H5
Lossiemouth Moray 152 A2
Lossit Argyll 142 C2
Lostford Shrops 74 F3
Lostock Gralam Ches W 74 B3
Lostock Green Ches W 74 B3
Lostock Hall Lancs 86 B3
Lostock Junction Gtr Man 86 D4
Lostwithiel Corn 5 D6
Loth Orkney 159 E7
Lothbeg Highld 157 H12
Lothersdale N Yorks 94 E2
Lothmore Highld 157 H12
Loudwater Bucks 40 E2
Loughborough Leics 64 C2
Loughor Swansea 33 E6
Loughton Essex 41 E7
Loughton M Keynes 53 F6
Loughton Shrops 61 F6
Lound Lincs 65 C7
Lound Notts 89 F7
Lound Suff 69 E8
Lount Leics 63 C7
Louth Lincs 91 F7
Love Clough Lancs 87 B6
Lovedean Hants 15 C7
Lover Wilts 14 B3
Loversall S Yorks 89 E6
Loves Green Essex 42 D2
Lovesome Hill N Yorks 102 E1
Loveston Pembs 32 D1
Lovington Som 23 F7
Low Ackworth W Yorks 89 C5
Low Barlings Lincs 78 B3
Low Bentham N Yorks 93 C6
Low Bradfield S Yorks 88 E3
Low Bradley N Yorks 94 E3
Low Braithwaite Cumb 108 E4
Low Brunton Northumb 110 B2
Low Burnham N Lincs 89 D8
Low Burton N Yorks 101 F7
Low Buston Northumb 117 D8
Low Catton E Yorks 96 D3
Low Clanyard Dumfries 104 F5
Low Coniscliffe Darl 101 C7
Low Crosby Cumb 108 D4
Low Dalby N Yorks 103 F6
Low Dinsdale Darl 101 C8
Low Ellington N Yorks 101 F7
Low Etherley Durham 101 B6
Low Fell T&W 110 D5
Low Fulney Lincs 66 B2
Low Garth N Yorks 103 D5
Low Gate Northumb 110 C2
Low Grantley N Yorks 94 B5
Low Habberley Worcs 50 B3
Low Ham Som 12 B2
Low Hesket Cumb 108 E4
Low Hesleyhurst Northumb 117 E6
Low Hutton N Yorks 96 C3
Low Laithe N Yorks 94 C4
Low Leighton Derbys 87 F8
Low Lorton Cumb 98 B3
Low Marishes N Yorks 96 B4
Low Marnham Notts 77 C8
Low Mill N Yorks 102 E4
Low Moor Lancs 93 E7
Low Moor W Yorks 88 B2
Low Moorsley T&W 111 E6
Low Newton Cumb 99 F6
Low Newton-by-the-Sea Northumb 117 B8
Low Row Cumb 108 F3
Low Row Cumb 109 C5
Low Row N Yorks 100 E4
Low Salchrie Dumfries 104 C4
Low Smerby Argyll 143 F8
Low Torry Fife 128 F2
Low Worsall N Yorks 102 D1
Low Wray Cumb 99 D5
Lowbridge House Cumb 99 D7
Lowca Cumb 98 B1
Lowdham Notts 77 E6
Lowe Shrops 74 F2
Lowe Hill Staffs 75 D6
Lower Aisholt Som 22 F4
Lower Arncott Oxon 39 C6
Lower Ashton Devon 10 F3
Lower Assendon Oxon 39 F7
Lower Badcall Highld 156 E4
Lower Bartle Lancs 92 F4
Lower Basildon W Berks 26 B4
Lower Beeding W Sus 17 B6
Lower Benefield Northants 65 F6
Lower Boddington Northants 52 D2
Lower Brailes Warks 51 F8
Lower Breakish Highld 149 F11
Lower Broadheath Worcs 50 D3
Lower Bullingham Hereford 49 F7
Lower Cam Glos 36 D4
Lower Chapel Powys 48 F2
Lower Chute Wilts 25 D8
Lower Cragabus Argyll 142 D4
Lower Crossings Derbys 87 F8
Lower Cumberworth W Yorks 88 D3
Lower Cwm-twrch Powys 34 C1
Lower Darwen Blackburn 86 B4
Lower Dean Bedford 53 C8
Lower Diabaig Highld 149 B12
Lower Dicker E Sus 18 D2
Lower Dinchope Shrops 60 F4
Lower Down Shrops 60 F3
Lower Drift Corn 2 D3
Lower Dunsforth N Yorks 95 C7
Lower Egleton Hereford 49 E8
Lower Elkstone Staffs 75 D7
Lower End C Beds 40 B2
Lower Everleigh Wilts 25 D6
Lower Farringdon Hants 26 F5
Lower Foxdale IoM 84 E2
Lower Frankton Shrops 73 F7
Lower Froyle Hants 27 E5
Lower Gledfield Highld 151 B8
Lower Green Norf 81 D5
Lower Hacheston Suff 57 D7
Lower Halistra Highld 148 C7
Lower Halstow Kent 30 C2
Lower Hardres Kent 31 D5
Lower Hawthwaite Cumb 98 F4
Lower Heath Ches E 75 C5
Lower Hempriggs Moray 151 E14
Lower Hergest Hereford 48 D4
Lower Heyford Oxon 38 B4
Lower Higham Kent 29 B8
Lower Holbrook Suff 57 F5
Lower Hordley Shrops 60 B3
Lower Horsebridge E Sus 18 D2
Lower Killeyan Argyll 142 D3
Lower Kingswood Sur 28 D3
Lower Kinnerton Ches W 73 C7
Lower Langford N Som 23 C6
Lower Largo Fife 129 D6
Lower Leigh Staffs 75 F7
Lower Lemington Glos 51 F7
Lower Lenie Highld 137 B8
Lower Lydbrook Glos 36 C2
Lower Lye Hereford 49 C6
Lower Machen Newport 35 F6
Lower Maes-coed Hereford 48 F5
Lower Mayland Essex 43 D5
Lower Midway Derbys 63 B7
Lower Milovaig Highld 148 C6
Lower Moor Worcs 50 E4
Lower Nazeing Essex 41 D6
Lower Netchwood Shrops 61 E6
Lower Ollach Highld 149 E10
Lower Penarth V Glam 22 B3
Lower Penn Staffs 62 E2
Lower Pennington Hants 14 E4
Lower Peover Ches W 74 B4
Lower Pexhill Ches E 75 B5
Lower Place Gtr Man 87 C7
Lower Quinton Warks 51 E6
Lower Rochford Worcs 49 C8
Lower Seagry Wilts 37 F6
Lower Shelton C Beds 53 E7
Lower Shiplake Oxon 27 B5
Lower Shuckburgh Warks 52 C2
Lower Slaughter Glos 38 B1
Lower Stanton St Quintin Wilts 37 F6
Lower Stoke Medway 30 B2
Lower Stondon C Beds 54 F2
Lower Stow Bedon Norf 68 E2
Lower Street Norf 69 C6
Lower Street Norf 81 D8
Lower Strensham Worcs 50 E4
Lower Stretton Warr 86 F4
Lower Sundon C Beds 40 B3
Lower Swanwick Hants 15 D5
Lower Swell Glos 38 B1
Lower Tean Staffs 75 F7
Lower Thurlton Norf 69 E7
Lower Tote Highld 149 B10
Lower Town Pembs 44 B4
Lower Tysoe Warks 51 E8
Lower Upham Hants 15 C6
Lower Vexford Som 22 F3
Lower Weare Som 23 D6
Lower Welson Hereford 48 D4
Lower Whitley Ches W 74 B3
Lower Wield Hants 26 E4
Lower Winchendon Bucks 39 C7
Lower Withington Ches E 74 C5
Lower Woodend Bucks 39 F8
Lower Woodford Wilts 25 F6
Lower Wyche Worcs 50 E2
Lowesby Leics 64 D4
Lowestoft Suff 69 E8
Loweswater Cumb 98 B3
Lowford Hants 15 C5
Lowgill Cumb 99 E8
Lowgill Lancs 93 C6
Lowick Northants 65 F6
Lowick Northumb 123 F6
Lowick Bridge Cumb 98 F4
Lowick Green Cumb 98 F4
Lowlands Torf 35 E6
Lowmoor Row Cumb 99 B8
Lownie Moor Angus 134 E4
Lowsonford Warks 51 C6
Lowther Cumb 99 B7
Lowthorpe E Yorks 97 C6
Lowton Gtr Man 86 E4
Lowton Common Gtr Man 86 E4
Loxbeare Devon 10 C4
Loxhill Sur 27 F8
Loxhore Devon 20 F5
Loxley Warks 51 D7
Loxton N Som 23 D5
Loxwood W Sus 27 F8
Lubcroy Highld 156 J6
Lubenham Leics 64 F4
Luccombe Som 21 E8
Luccombe Village IoW 15 G6
Lucker Northumb 123 F7
Luckett Corn 5 B8
Luckington Wilts 37 F5
Lucklawhill Fife 129 B6
Luckwell Bridge Som 21 F8
Lucton Hereford 49 C6
Ludag W Isles 148 G2
Ludborough Lincs 91 E6
Ludchurch Pembs 32 C2
Luddenden W Yorks 87 B8
Luddenden Foot W Yorks 87 B8
Luddesdown Kent 29 C7
Luddington N Lincs 90 C2
Luddington Warks 51 D6
Luddington in the Brook Northants 65 F8
Lude House Perth 133 C5
Ludford Lincs 91 F6
Ludford Shrops 49 B7
Ludgershall Bucks 39 C6
Ludgershall Wilts 25 D7
Ludgvan Corn 2 C4
Ludham Norf 69 C6
Ludlow Shrops 49 B7
Ludwell Wilts 13 B7
Ludworth Durham 111 E6
Luffincott Devon 8 E5
Lugar E Ayrs 113 B5
Lugg Green Hereford 49 C6
Luggate Burn E Loth 122 B2
Luggiebank N Lanark 119 B7
Lugton E Ayrs 118 D4
Lugwardine Hereford 49 E7
Luib Highld 149 F10
Lulham Hereford 49 E6
Lullenden Sur 28 E5
Lullington Derbys 63 C6
Lullington Som 24 D2
Lulsgate Bottom N Som 23 C7
Lulsley Worcs 50 D2
Lumb W Yorks 87 B8
Lumby N Yorks 95 F7
Lumloch E Dunb 119 C6
Lumphanan Aberds 140 D4
Lumphinnans Fife 128 E3
Lumsdaine Borders 122 C4
Lumsden Aberds 140 B3
Lunan Angus 135 D6
Lunanhead Angus 134 D4
Luncarty Perth 128 B2
Lund E Yorks 97 E5
Lund N Yorks 96 F2
Lund Shetland 160 C7
Lunderton Aberds 153 D11
Lundie Angus 134 F2
Lundie Highld 136 C4
Lundin Links Fife 129 D6
Lunga Argyll 124 E3
Lunna Shetland 160 G6
Lunning Shetland 160 G7
Lunnon Swansea 33 F6
Lunsford's Cross E Sus 18 D4
Lunt Mers 85 D4
Luntley Hereford 49 D5
Luppitt Devon 11 D6
Lupset W Yorks 88 C4
Lupton Cumb 99 F7
Lurgashall W Sus 16 B3
Lusby Lincs 79 C6
Luson Devon 6 E4
Luss Argyll 126 E2
Lussagiven Argyll 144 E5
Lusta Highld 149 C7
Lustleigh Devon 10 F2
Luston Hereford 49 C6
Luthermuir Aberds 135 C6
Luthrie Fife 128 C5
Luton Devon 7 B7
Luton Luton 40 B3
Luton Medway 29 C8
Lutterworth Leics 64 F2
Lutton Devon 6 D3
Lutton Lincs 66 B4
Lutton Northants 65 F8
Lutworthy Devon 10 C2
Luxborough Som 21 F8
Luxulyan Corn 5 D5
Lybster Highld 158 G4
Lydbury North Shrops 60 F3
Lydcott Devon 21 F5
Lydd Kent 19 C7
Lydd on Sea Kent 19 C7
Lydden Kent 31 E6
Lyddington Rutland 65 E5
Lyde Green Hants 26 D5
Lydeard St Lawrence Som 22 F3
Lydford Devon 9 F7
Lydford-on-Fosse Som 23 F7
Lydgate W Yorks 87 B7
Lydham Shrops 60 E3
Lydiard Green Wilts 37 F7
Lydiard Millicent Wilts 37 F7
Lydiate Mers 85 D4
Lydlinch Dorset 12 C5
Lydney Glos 36 D3
Lydstep Pembs 32 E1
Lye W Mid 62 F3
Lye Green Bucks 40 D2
Lye Green E Sus 18 B2
Lyford Oxon 38 E3
Lymbridge Green Kent 30 E5
Lyme Regis Dorset 11 E8
Lyminge Kent 31 E5
Lymington Hants 14 E4
Lyminster W Sus 16 D4
Lymm Warr 86 F4
Lymore Hants 14 E3
Lympne Kent 19 B8
Lympsham Som 22 D5
Lympstone Devon 10 F4
Lynchat Highld 138 D3
Lyndale Ho. Highld 149 C8
Lyndhurst Hants 14 D4
Lyndon Rutland 65 D6
Lyne Sur 27 C8
Lyne Down Hereford 49 F8
Lyne of Gorthleck Highld 137 B8
Lyne of Skene Aberds 141 C6
Lyneal Shrops 73 F8
Lyneham Oxon 38 B2
Lyneham Wilts 24 B5
Lynemore Highld 139 B6
Lynemouth Northumb 117 E8
Lyness Orkney 159 J4
Lyng Norf 68 C3
Lyng Som 11 B8
Lynmouth Devon 21 E6
Lynsted Kent 30 C3
Lynton Devon 21 E6
Lyon's Gate Dorset 12 D4
Lyonshall Hereford 48 D5
Lytchett Matravers Dorset 13 E7
Lytchett Minster Dorset 13 E7
Lyth Highld 158 D4
Lytham Lancs 85 B4
Lytham St Anne's Lancs 85 B4
Lythe N Yorks 103 C6
Lythes Orkney 159 K5

M

Mabe Burnthouse Corn 3 C6
Mabie Dumfries 107 B6
Mablethorpe Lincs 91 F9
Macclesfield Ches E 75 B6
Macclesfield Forest Ches E 75 B6
Macduff Aberds 153 B7
Mace Green Suff 56 E5
Macharioch Argyll 143 H8
Machen Caerph 35 F6
Machrihanish Argyll 143 F7
Machynlleth Powys 58 D4
Machynys Carms 33 E6
Mackerel's Common W Sus 16 B4
Mackworth Derbys 76 F3
Macmerry E Loth 121 B7
Madderty Perth 127 B8
Maddiston Falk 120 B2
Madehurst W Sus 16 C3
Madeley Staffs 74 E4
Madeley Telford 61 D6
Madeley Heath Staffs 74 E4
Madeley Park Staffs 74 E4
Madingley Cambs 54 C4
Madley Hereford 49 F6
Madresfield Worcs 50 E3
Madron Corn 2 C3
Maen-y-groes Ceredig 46 D2
Maenaddwyn Anglesey 82 C4
Maenclochog Pembs 32 B1
Maendy V Glam 22 B2
Maentwrog Gwyn 71 C7
Maer Staffs 74 F4
Maerdy Conwy 72 E4
Maerdy Rhondda 34 E3
Maes-Treylow Powys 48 C4
Maesbrook Shrops 60 B2
Maesbury Shrops 60 B3
Maesbury Marsh Shrops 60 B3
Maesgwyn-Isaf Powys 59 C8
Maesgwynne Carms 32 B3
Maeshafn Denb 73 C6
Maesllyn Ceredig 46 E2
Maesmynis Powys 48 E2
Maesteg Bridgend 34 E2
Maestir Ceredig 46 E4
Maesy cwmmer Caerph 35 E5
Maesybont Carms 33 C6
Maesycrugiau Carms 46 E3
Maesymeillion Ceredig 46 E3
Magdalen Laver Essex 41 D8
Maggieknockater Moray 152 D3
Magham Down E Sus 18 D3
Maghull Mers 85 D4
Magor Mon 35 F8
Magpie Green Suff 56 B4
Maiden Bradley Wilts 24 F3
Maiden Law Durham 110 E4
Maiden Newton Dorset 12 E3
Maiden Wells Pembs 44 F4
Maidencombe Torbay 7 C7
Maidenhall Suff 57 E5
Maidenhead Windsor 40 F1
Maidens S Ayrs 112 D2
Maiden's Green Brack 27 B6
Maidensgrave Suff 57 E6
Maidenwell Corn 5 B6
Maidenwell Lincs 79 B6
Maidford Northants 52 D4
Maids Moreton Bucks 52 F5
Maidstone Kent 29 D8
Maidwell Northants 52 B5
Mail Shetland 160 L6
Main Powys 59 C8
Maindee Newport 35 F7
Mains of Airies Dumfries 104 C3
Mains of Allardice Aberds 135 B8
Mains of Annochie Aberds 153 D9
Mains of Ardestie Angus 135 F5
Mains of Balhall Angus 135 C5
Mains of Ballindarg Angus 134 D4
Mains of Balnakettle Aberds 135 B6
Mains of Birness Aberds 153 E9
Mains of Burgie Moray 151 F13
Mains of Clunas Highld 151 G11
Mains of Crichie Aberds 153 D9
Mains of Dalvey Highld 151 H14
Mains of Dellavaird Aberds 141 F6
Mains of Drum Aberds 141 E7
Mains of Edingight Moray 152 C5
Mains of Fedderate Aberds 153 D8
Mains of Inkhorn Aberds 153 E9
Mains of Mayen Moray 152 D5
Mains of Melgund Angus 135 D5
Mains of Thornton Aberds 135 B6
Mains of Watten Highld 158 E4
Mainsforth Durham 111 F6
Mainsriddle Dumfries 107 D6
Mainstone Shrops 60 F2
Maisemore Glos 37 B5
Malacleit W Isles 148 A2
Malborough Devon 6 F5
Malcoff Derbys 87 F8
Maldon Essex 42 D4
Malham N Yorks 94 C2
Maligar Highld 149 B9
Mallaig Highld 147 B9
Malleny Mills Edin 120 C4
Malling Stirling 126 D4
Malltraeth Anglesey 82 E4
Mallwyd Gwyn 59 C5
Malmesbury Wilts 37 F6
Malmsmead Devon 21 E6
Malpas Ches W 73 E8
Malpas Corn 3 B7
Malpas Newport 35 E7
Malswick Glos 36 B4
Maltby S Yorks 89 E6
Maltby Stockton 102 C2
Maltby le Marsh Lincs 91 F8
Malting Green Essex 43 B5
Maltman's Hill Kent 30 E3
Malton N Yorks 96 B3
Malvern Link Worcs 50 E2
Malvern Wells Worcs 50 E2
Mamble Worcs 49 B8
Man-moel Caerph 35 D5
Manaccan Corn 3 D6
Manafon Powys 59 D8
Manais W Isles 154 J6

Manar Ho. Aberds 141 B6
Manaton Devon 10 F2
Manby Lincs 91 F7
Mancetter Warks 63 E7
Manchester Gtr Man 87 E6
Manchester Airport Gtr Man 87 F6
Mancot Flint 73 C7
Mandally Highld 137 D5
Manea Cambs 66 F4
Manfield N Yorks 101 C7
Mangaster Shetland 160 F5
Mangotsfield S Glos 23 B8
Mangurstadh W Isles 154 D5
Mankinholes W Yorks 87 B7
Manley Ches W 74 B2
Mannal Argyll 146 G2
Mannerston W Loth 120 B3
Manningford Bohune Wilts 25 D6
Manningford Bruce Wilts 25 D6
Manningham W Yorks 94 F4
Mannings Heath W Sus 17 B6
Mannington Dorset 13 D8
Manningtree Essex 56 F4
Mannofield Aberdeen 141 D8
Manor London 41 F7
Manor Estate S Yorks 88 F4
Manorbier Pembs 32 E1
Manordeilo Carms 33 B7
Manorhill Borders 122 F2
Manorowen Pembs 44 B4
Mansel Lacy Hereford 49 E6
Manselfield Swansea 33 F6
Mansell Gamage Hereford 49 E5
Mansergh Cumb 99 F8
Mansfield E Ayrs 113 C6
Mansfield Notts 76 C5
Mansfield Woodhouse Notts 76 C5
Mansriggs Cumb 98 F4
Manston Dorset 13 C6
Manston Kent 31 C7
Manston W Yorks 95 F6
Manswood Dorset 13 D7
Manthorpe Lincs 65 C7
Manthorpe Lincs 78 F2
Manton N Lincs 90 D3
Manton Notts 77 B5
Manton Rutland 65 D5
Manton Wilts 25 C6
Manuden Essex 41 B7
Maperton Som 12 B4
Maple Cross Herts 40 E3
Maplebeck Notts 77 C7
Mapledurham Oxon 26 B4
Mapledurwell Hants 26 D4
Maplehurst W Sus 17 B5
Maplescombe Kent 29 C6
Mapleton Derbys 75 E8
Mapperley Derbys 76 E4
Mapperley Park Nottingham 77 E5
Mapperton Dorset 12 E3
Mappleborough Green Warks 51 C5
Mappleton E Yorks 97 E8
Mappowder Dorset 12 D5
Mar Lodge Aberds 139 E6
Maraig W Isles 154 G6
Marazanvose Corn 4 D3
Marazion Corn 2 C4
Marbhig W Isles 155 F9
Marbury Ches E 74 E2
March Cambs 66 E4
March S Lanark 114 C2
Marcham Oxon 38 E4
Marchamley Shrops 61 B5
Marchington Staffs 75 F8
Marchington Woodlands Staffs 62 B5
Marchroes Gwyn 70 E4
Marchwiel Wrex 73 E7
Marchwood Hants 14 C4
Marcross V Glam 21 C8
Marden Hereford 49 E7
Marden Kent 29 E8
Marden T&W 111 B6
Marden Wilts 25 D5
Marden Beech Kent 29 E8
Marden Thorn Kent 29 E8
Mardy Mon 35 C7
Marefield Leics 64 D4
Mareham le Fen Lincs 79 C5
Mareham on the Hill Lincs 79 C5
Marehay Derbys 76 E3
Marehill W Sus 16 C4
Maresfield E Sus 17 B8
Marfleet Hull 90 B5
Marford Wrex 73 D7
Margam Neath 34 F1
Margaret Marsh Dorset 13 C6
Margaret Roding Essex 42 C1
Margaretting Essex 42 D2
Margate Kent 31 B7
Margnaheglish N Ayrs 143 E11
Margrove Park Redcar 102 C4
Marham Norf 67 C7
Marhamchurch Corn 8 D4
Marholm Pboro 65 D8
Mariandyrys Anglesey 83 C6
Marianglas Anglesey 82 C5
Mariansleigh Devon 10 B2
Marionburgh Aberds 141 D6
Marishader Highld 149 B9
Marjoriebanks Dumfries 114 F3
Mark Dumfries 104 D5
Mark S Ayrs 104 B4
Mark Som 23 E5
Mark Causeway Som 23 E5
Mark Cross E Sus 17 C8
Mark Cross E Sus 18 B2
Markbeech Kent 29 E5
Markby Lincs 79 B7
Market Bosworth Leics 63 D8
Market Deeping Lincs 65 D8
Market Drayton Shrops 74 F3
Market Harborough Leics 64 F4
Market Lavington Wilts 24 D5
Market Overton Rutland 65 C5
Market Rasen Lincs 90 F5
Market Stainton Lincs 78 B5
Market Warsop Notts 77 C5
Market Weighton E Yorks 96 E4
Market Weston Suff 56 B3
Markethill Perth 134 F2
Markfield Leics 63 C8
Markham Caerph 35 D5
Markham Moor Notts 77 B7
Markinch Fife 128 D4
Markington N Yorks 95 C5
Marks Tey Essex 43 B5
Marksbury Bath 23 C8
Markyate Herts 40 C3
Marland Gtr Man 87 C6
Marlborough Wilts 25 C6
Marlbrook Hereford 49 D7
Marlbrook Worcs 50 B4
Marlcliff Warks 51 D5
Marldon Devon 7 C6
Marlesford Suff 57 D7
Marley Green Ches E 74 E2
Marley Hill T&W 110 D5
Marley Mount Hants 14 E3
Marlingford Norf 68 D4
Marloes Pembs 44 E2
Marlow Bucks 39 F8
Marlow Hereford 49 B6
Marlow Bottom Bucks 40 F1
Marlpit Hill Kent 28 E5
Marlpool Derbys 76 E4
Marnhull Dorset 13 C5
Marnoch Aberds 152 C5
Marnock N Lanark 119 C7
Marple Gtr Man 87 F7
Marple Bridge Gtr Man 87 F7
Marr S Yorks 89 D6
Marrel Highld 157 H13
Marrick N Yorks 101 E5
Marrister Shetland 160 G7
Marros Carms 32 D3
Marsden T&W 111 C6
Marsden W Yorks 87 C8
Marsett N Yorks 100 F4
Marsh Devon 11 C7
Marsh W Yorks 94 F3
Marsh Baldon Oxon 39 E5
Marsh Gibbon Bucks 39 B6
Marsh Green Devon 10 E5
Marsh Green Kent 28 E5
Marsh Green Staffs 75 D5
Marsh Lane Derbys 76 B4
Marsh Street Som 21 E8
Marshall's Heath Herts 40 C4
Marshalsea Dorset 11 D8
Marshalswick Herts 40 D4
Marsham Norf 81 E7
Marshaw Lancs 93 D5
Marshborough Kent 31 D7
Marshbrook Shrops 60 F4
Marshchapel Lincs 91 E7
Marshfield Newport 35 F6
Marshfield S Glos 24 B2
Marshgate Corn 8 E3
Marshland St James Norf 66 D5
Marshside Mers 85 C4
Marshwood Dorset 11 E8
Marske N Yorks 101 D6
Marske-by-the-Sea Redcar 102 B4
Marston Ches W 74 B3
Marston Hereford 49 D5
Marston Lincs 77 E8
Marston Oxon 39 D5
Marston Staffs 62 B3
Marston Staffs 62 C2
Marston Warks 63 E6
Marston Wilts 24 D4
Marston Doles Warks 52 D2
Marston Green W Mid 63 F5
Marston Magna Som 12 B3
Marston Meysey Wilts 37 E8
Marston Montgomery Derbys 75 F8
Marston Moretaine C Beds 53 E7
Marston on Dove Derbys 63 B6
Marston St Lawrence Northants 52 E3
Marston Stannett Hereford 49 D7
Marston Trussell Northants 64 F3
Marstow Hereford 36 C2
Marsworth Bucks 40 C2
Marten Wilts 25 D7
Marthall Ches E 74 B5
Martham Norf 69 C7
Martin Hants 13 C8
Martin Kent 31 E7
Martin Lincs 78 C5
Martin Lincs 78 D4
Martin Dales Lincs 78 C4
Martin Drove End Hants 13 B8
Martin Hussingtree Worcs 50 C3
Martin Mill Kent 31 E7
Martinhoe Devon 21 E5
Martinhoe Cross Devon 21 E5
Martinscroft Warr 86 F4
Martinstown Dorset 12 F4
Martlesham Suff 57 E6
Martlesham Heath Suff 57 E6
Martletwy Pembs 32 C1
Martley Worcs 50 D2
Martock Som 12 C2
Marton Ches E 75 C5
Marton E Yorks 97 F7
Marton Lincs 90 F2
Marton Mbro 102 C3
Marton N Yorks 95 C7
Marton N Yorks 103 F5
Marton Shrops 60 B4
Marton Shrops 60 D2
Marton Warks 52 C2
Marton-le-Moor N Yorks 95 B6
Martyr Worthy Hants 26 F3
Martyr's Green Sur 27 D8
Marwick Orkney 159 F3
Marwood Devon 20 F4
Mary Tavy Devon 6 B3
Marybank Highld 150 F7
Maryburgh Highld 151 F8
Maryhill Glasgow 119 C5
Marykirk Aberds 135 C6
Marylebone Gtr Man 86 D3
Marypark Moray 152 E1
Maryport Cumb 107 F7
Maryport Dumfries 104 F5
Maryton Angus 135 D6
Marywell Aberds 140 E4
Marywell Aberds 141 E8
Marywell Angus 135 E6
Masham N Yorks 101 F7
Mashbury Essex 42 C2
Masongill N Yorks 93 B6
Masonhill S Ayrs 112 B3
Mastin Moor Derbys 76 B4
Mastrick Aberdeen 141 D7
Matching Essex 41 C8
Matching Green Essex 41 C8
Matching Tye Essex 41 C8
Matfen Northumb 110 B3
Matfield Kent 29 E7
Mathern Mon 36 E2
Mathon Hereford 50 E2
Mathry Pembs 44 B3
Matlaske Norf 81 D7
Matlock Derbys 76 C2
Matlock Bath Derbys 76 D2
Matson Glos 37 C5
Matterdale End Cumb 99 B5
Mattersey Notts 89 F7
Mattersey Thorpe Notts 89 F7
Mattingley Hants 26 D5
Mattishall Norf 68 C3
Mattishall Burgh Norf 68 C3
Mauchline E Ayrs 112 B4
Maud Aberds 153 D9
Maugersbury Glos 38 B2
Maughold IoM 84 C4
Mauld Highld 150 H7
Maulden C Beds 53 F8
Maulds Meaburn Cumb 99 C8
Maunby N Yorks 102 F1
Maund Bryan Hereford 49 D7
Maundown Som 11 B5
Mautby Norf 69 C7
Mavis Enderby Lincs 79 C6
Maw Green Ches E 74 D4
Mawbray Cumb 107 E7
Mawdesley Lancs 86 C2
Mawdlam Bridgend 34 F2
Mawgan Corn 3 D6
Mawla Corn 3 B6
Mawnan Corn 3 D6
Mawnan Smith Corn 3 D6
Mawsley Northants 53 B6
Maxey Pboro 65 D8
Maxstoke Warks 63 F6
Maxton Borders 122 F2
Maxton Kent 31 E7
Maxwellheugh Borders 122 F3
Maxwelltown Dumfries 107 B6
Maxworthy Corn 8 E4
May Bank Staffs 75 E5
Mayals Swansea 33 E7
Maybole S Ayrs 112 D3
Mayfield E Sus 18 C2
Mayfield Midloth 121 C6
Mayfield Staffs 75 E8
Mayfield W Loth 120 C2
Mayford Sur 27 D7
Mayland Essex 43 D5
Maynard's Green E Sus 18 D2
Maypole Mon 36 C1
Maypole Scilly 2 E4
Maypole Green Essex 43 B5
Maypole Green Norf 69 E7
Maypole Green Suff 57 C6
Maywick Shetland 160 L5
Meadle Bucks 39 D8
Meadowtown Shrops 60 D3
Meaford Staffs 75 F5
Meal Bank Cumb 99 E7
Mealabost W Isles 155 D9
Mealabost Bhuirgh W Isles 155 B9
Mealsgate Cumb 108 E2
Meanwood W Yorks 95 F5
Mearbeck N Yorks 93 C8
Meare Som 23 E6
Meare Green Som 11 B8
Mears Ashby Northants 53 C6
Measham Leics 63 C7
Meath Green Sur 28 E3
Meathop Cumb 99 F6
Meaux E Yorks 97 F6
Meavy Devon 6 C3
Medbourne Leics 64 E4
Medburn Northumb 110 B4
Meddon Devon 8 C4
Meden Vale Notts 77 C5
Medlam Lincs 79 D6
Medmenham Bucks 39 F8
Medomsley Durham 110 D4
Medstead Hants 26 F4
Meer End W Mid 51 B7
Meerbrook Staffs 75 C6
Meers Bridge Lincs 91 F8
Meesden Herts 54 F5
Meeth Devon 9 D7
Meggethead Borders 114 B4
Meidrim Carms 32 B3
Meifod Denb 72 D4
Meifod Powys 59 C8
Meigle N Ayrs 118 C1
Meigle Perth 134 E2
Meikle Earnock S Lanark 119 D7
Meikle Ferry Highld 151 C10
Meikle Forter Angus 134 C1
Meikle Gluich Highld 151 C9
Meikle Pinkerton E Loth 122 B3
Meikle Strath Aberds 135 B6
Meikle Tarty Aberds 141 B8
Meikle Wartle Aberds 153 E7
Meikleour Perth 134 F1
Meinciau Carms 33 C5
Meir Stoke 75 E6
Meir Heath Staffs 75 E6
Melbourn Cambs 54 E4
Melbourne Derbys 63 B7
Melbourne E Yorks 96 E3
Melbourne S Lanark 120 E3
Melbury Abbas Dorset 13 B6
Melbury Bubb Dorset 12 D3
Melbury Osmond Dorset 12 D3
Melbury Sampford Dorset 12 D3
Melby Shetland 160 H3
Melchbourne Bedford 53 C8
Melcombe Bingham Dorset 13 D5
Melcombe Regis Dorset 12 F4
Meldon Devon 9 E7
Meldon Northumb 117 F7
Meldreth Cambs 54 E4
Meldrum Ho. Aberds 141 B7
Melfort Argyll 124 D4
Melgarve Highld 137 E7
Meliden Denb 72 A4
Melin-y-coed Conwy 83 E8
Melin-y-ddôl Powys 59 D7
Melin-y-grug Powys 59 D7
Melin-y-Wig Denb 72 E4
Melinbyrhedyn Powys 58 E5
Melincourt Neath 34 D2
Melkinthorpe Cumb 99 B7
Melkridge Northumb 109 C7
Melksham Wilts 24 C4
Melldalloch Argyll 145 F8
Melling Lancs 93 B5
Melling Mers 85 D4
Melling Mount Mers 86 D2
Mellis Suff 56 B5
Mellon Charles Highld 155 H13
Mellon Udrigle Highld 155 H13
Mellor Gtr Man 87 F7
Mellor Lancs 93 F6
Mellor Brook Lancs 93 F6
Mells Som 24 E2
Melmerby Cumb 109 F6
Melmerby N Yorks 95 B6
Melmerby N Yorks 101 F5
Melplash Dorset 12 E2
Melrose Borders 121 F8
Melsetter Orkney 159 K3
Melsonby N Yorks 101 D6
Meltham W Yorks 88 C2
Melton Suff 57 D6
Melton Constable Norf 81 D6
Melton Mowbray Leics 64 C4
Melton Ross N Lincs 90 C4
Meltonby E Yorks 96 D3
Melvaig Highld 155 J12
Melverley Shrops 60 C3
Melverley Green Shrops 60 C3
Melvich Highld 157 C11
Membury Devon 11 D7
Memsie Aberds 153 B9
Memus Angus 134 D4
Menabilly Corn 5 D5
Menai Bridge = Porthaethwy Anglesey 83 D5
Mendham Suff 69 F5
Mendlesham Suff 56 C5
Mendlesham Green Suff 56 C4
Menheniot Corn 5 C7
Mennock Dumfries 113 D8
Menston W Yorks 94 E4
Menstrie Clack 127 E7
Menthorpe N Yorks 96 F2
Mentmore Bucks 40 C2
Meoble Highld 147 C10
Meole Brace Shrops 60 C4
Meols Mers 85 E3
Meonstoke Hants 15 C7
Meopham Kent 29 C7
Meopham Station Kent 29 C7
Mepal Cambs 66 F4
Meppershall C Beds 54 F2
Merbach Hereford 48 E5
Mere Ches E 86 F5
Mere Wilts 24 F3
Mere Brow Lancs 86 C2
Mere Green W Mid 62 E5
Mereclough Lancs 93 F8
Mereside Blackpool 92 F3
Mereworth Kent 29 D7
Mergie Aberds 141 F6
Meriden W Mid 63 F6
Merkadale Highld 149 E8
Merkland Dumfries 106 B4
Merkland S Ayrs 112 E2
Merkland Lodge Highld 156 G7
Merley Poole 13 E8
Merlin's Bridge Pembs 44 D4
Merrington Shrops 60 B4
Merrion Pembs 44 F4
Merriott Som 12 C2
Merrivale Devon 6 B3
Merrow Sur 27 D8
Merrymeet Corn 5 C7
Mersham Kent 19 B7
Merstham Sur 28 D3
Merston W Sus 16 D2
Merstone IoW 15 F6
Merther Corn 3 B7
Merthyr Carms 32 B4
Merthyr Cynog Powys 47 F8
Merthyr-Dyfan V Glam 22 C3
Merthyr Mawr Bridgend 21 B7
Merthyr Tudful = Merthyr Tydfil M Tydf 34 D4
Merthyr Tydfil = Merthyr Tudful M Tydf 34 D4
Merthyr Vale M Tydf 34 E4
Merton Devon 9 C7
Merton London 28 B3
Merton Norf 68 E2
Merton Oxon 39 C5
Mervinslaw Borders 116 C2
Meshaw Devon 10 C2
Messing Essex 42 C4
Messingham N Lincs 90 D2
Metfield Suff 69 F5
Metheringham Lincs 78 C3
Methil Fife 129 E5
Methlem Gwyn 70 D2
Methley W Yorks 88 B4
Methlick Aberds 153 E8
Methven Perth 128 B2
Methwold Norf 67 E7
Methwold Hythe Norf 67 E7
Mettingham Suff 69 F6
Mevagissey Corn 3 B9
Mewith Head N Yorks 93 C7
Mexborough S Yorks 89 D5
Mey Highld 158 C4
Meysey Hampton Glos 37 E8
Miabhag W Isles 154 G5
Miabhag W Isles 154 H6
Miabhig W Isles 154 D5
Michaelchurch Hereford 36 B2
Michaelchurch Escley Hereford 48 F5
Michaelchurch on Arrow Powys 48 D4
Michaelston-le-Pit V Glam 22 B3
Michaelston-y-Fedw Newport 35 F6
Michaelstow Corn 5 B5
Michealston-super-Ely Cardiff 22 B3
Micheldever Hants 26 F3
Michelmersh Hants 14 B4
Mickfield Suff 56 C5
Mickle Trafford Ches W 73 C8
Micklebring S Yorks 89 E6
Mickleby N Yorks 103 C6
Mickleham Sur 28 D2
Mickleover Derby 76 F3
Micklethwaite W Yorks 94 E4
Mickleton Durham 100 B4
Mickleton Glos 51 E6
Mickletown W Yorks 88 B4
Mickley N Yorks 95 B5
Mickley Square Northumb 110 C3
Mid Ardlaw Aberds 153 B9
Mid Auchinlech Invclyd 118 B3
Mid Beltie Aberds 140 D5
Mid Calder W Loth 120 C3
Mid Cloch Forbie Aberds 153 C7
Mid Clyth Highld 158 G4
Mid Lavant W Sus 16 D2
Mid Main Highld 150 H7
Mid Urchany Highld 151 G11
Mid Walls Shetland 160 H4
Mid Yell Shetland 160 D7
Midbea Orkney 159 D5
Middle Assendon Oxon 39 F7
Middle Aston Oxon 38 B4
Middle Barton Oxon 38 B4
Middle Cairncake Aberds 153 D8
Middle Claydon Bucks 39 B7
Middle Drums Angus 135 D5
Middle Handley Derbys 76 B4
Middle Littleton Worcs 51 E5
Middle Maes-coed Hereford 48 F5
Middle Mill Pembs 44 C3
Middle Rasen Lincs 90 F4
Middle Rigg Perth 128 D2
Middle Tysoe Warks 51 E8
Middle Wallop Hants 25 F7
Middle Winterslow Wilts 25 F7
Middle Woodford Wilts 25 F6
Middlebie Dumfries 108 B2
Middleforth Green Lancs 86 B3
Middleham N Yorks 101 F6
Middlehope Shrops 60 F4
Middlemarsh Dorset 12 D4
Middlemuir Aberds 141 B8
Middlesbrough Mbro 102 B2
Middleshaw Cumb 99 F7
Middleshaw Dumfries 107 B8
Middlesmoor N Yorks 94 B3
Middlestone Durham 111 F5
Middlestone Moor Durham 110 F5
Middlestown W Yorks 88 C3
Middlethird Borders 122 E2
Middleton Aberds 141 C7
Middleton Argyll 146 G2
Middleton Cumb 99 F8
Middleton Derbys 75 C8
Middleton Derbys 76 D2
Middleton Essex 56 F2
Middleton Gtr Man 87 D6
Middleton Hants 26 E2
Middleton Hereford 49 C7
Middleton Lancs 92 D4
Middleton Midloth 121 D6
Middleton N Yorks 94 E4
Middleton N Yorks 103 F5
Middleton Norf 67 C6
Middleton Northants 64 F5
Middleton Northumb 117 F6
Middleton Northumb 123 F7
Middleton Perth 128 D3
Middleton Perth 133 E8
Middleton Shrops 49 B7
Middleton Shrops 60 B3
Middleton Shrops 60 E2
Middleton Suff 57 C8
Middleton Swansea 33 F5
Middleton W Yorks 88 B3
Middleton Warks 63 E5
Middleton Cheney Northants 52 E2
Middleton Green Staffs 75 F6
Middleton Hall Northumb 117 B5
Middleton-in-Teesdale Durham 100 B4
Middleton Moor Suff 57 C8
Middleton-on-Leven N Yorks 102 D2
Middleton-on-Sea W Sus 16 D3
Middleton on the Hill Hereford 49 C7
Middleton-on-the-Wolds E Yorks 96 E5
Middleton One Row Darl 102 C1
Middleton Priors Shrops 61 E6
Middleton Quernham N Yorks 95 B6
Middleton Scriven Shrops 61 F6
Middleton St George Darl 101 C8
Middleton Stoney Oxon 39 B5
Middleton Tyas N Yorks 101 D7
Middletown Cumb 98 D1
Middletown Powys 60 C3
Middlewich Ches E 74 C3
Middlewood Green Suff 56 C4
Middlezoy Som 23 F5
Middridge Durham 101 B7
Midfield Highld 157 C8
Midge Hall Lancs 86 B3
Midgeholme Cumb 109 D6
Midgham W Berks 26 C3
Midgley W Yorks 87 B8
Midgley W Yorks 88 C3
Midhopestones S Yorks 88 E3
Midhurst W Sus 16 B2
Midlem Borders 115 B8
Midmar Aberds 141 D5
Midsomer Norton Bath 23 D8
Midton Invclyd 118 B2
Midtown Highld 155 J13
Midtown Highld 157 C8
Midtown of Buchromb Moray 152 D3
Midville Lincs 79 D6
Midway Ches E 87 F7
Migdale Highld 151 B9
Migvie Aberds 140 D3
Milarrochy Stirling 126 E3
Milborne Port Som 12 C4
Milborne St Andrew Dorset 13 E6
Milborne Wick Som 12 B4
Milbourne Northumb 110 B4
Milburn Cumb 100 B1
Milbury Heath S Glos 36 E3
Milcombe Oxon 52 F2
Milden Suff 56 E3
Mildenhall Suff 55 B8
Mildenhall Wilts 25 C7
Mile Cross Norf 68 C5
Mile Elm Wilts 24 C4
Mile End Essex 43 B5
Mile End Glos 36 C2
Mile Oak Brighton 17 D6
Milebrook Powys 48 B5
Milebush Kent 29 E8
Mileham Norf 68 C2
Milesmark Fife 128 F2
Milfield Northumb 122 F5
Milford Derbys 76 E3
Milford Devon 8 B4
Milford Powys 59 E7
Milford Staffs 62 B3
Milford Sur 27 E7
Milford Wilts 14 B2
Milford Haven = Aberdaugleddau Pembs 44 E4
Milford on Sea Hants 14 E3
Milkwall Glos 36 D2
Milkwell Wilts 13 B7
Mill Bank W Yorks 87 B8
Mill Common Suff 69 F7
Mill End Bucks 39 F7
Mill End Herts 54 F4
Mill Green Essex 42 D2
Mill Green Norf 68 F4
Mill Green Suff 56 E3
Mill Hill London 41 E5
Mill Lane Hants 27 D5
Mill of Kingoodie Aberds 141 B7
Mill of Muiresk Aberds 153 D6
Mill of Sterin Aberds 140 E2
Mill of Uras Aberds 141 F7
Mill Place N Lincs 90 D3
Mill Side Cumb 99 F6
Mill Street Norf 68 C3
Milland W Sus 16 B2
Millarston Renfs 118 C4
Millbank Aberds 153 D11
Millbank Highld 158 D3
Millbeck Cumb 98 B4
Millbounds Orkney 159 E6
Millbreck Aberds 153 D10
Millbridge Sur 27 E6
Millbrook C Beds 53 F8
Millbrook Corn 6 D2
Millbrook Soton 14 C4
Millburn S Ayrs 112 B4
Millcombe Devon 7 E6
Millcorner E Sus 18 C5
Milldale Staffs 75 D8
Millden Lodge Angus 135 B5
Milldens Angus 135 D5
Millerhill Midloth 121 C6
Miller's Dale Derbys 75 B8
Miller's Green Derbys 76 D2
Millgreen Shrops 61 B6
Millhalf Hereford 48 E4
Millhayes Devon 11 D7
Millhead Lancs 92 B4
Millheugh S Lanark 119 D7
Millholme Cumb 99 E7
Millhouse Argyll 145 F8
Millhouse Cumb 108 F3
Millhouse Green S Yorks 88 D3
Millhousebridge Dumfries 114 F4
Millhouses S Yorks 88 F4
Millikenpark Renfs 118 C4
Millin Cross Pembs 44 D4
Millington E Yorks 96 D4
Millmeece Staffs 74 F5
Millom Cumb 98 F3
Millook Corn 8 E3
Millpool Corn 5 B6
Millport N Ayrs 145 H10
Millquarter Dumfries 113 F6
Millthorpe Lincs 78 F4
Millthrop Cumb 100 E1
Milltimber Aberdeen 141 D7
Milltown Corn 5 D6
Milltown Derbys 76 C3
Milltown Devon 20 F4
Milltown Dumfries 108 B3
Milltown of Aberdalgie Perth 128 B2
Milltown of Auchindoun Moray 152 D3
Milltown of Craigston Aberds 153 C7
Milltown of Edinvillie Moray 152 D2
Milltown of Kildrummy Aberds 140 C3
Milltown of Rothiemay Moray 152 D5
Milltown of Towie Aberds 140 C3
Milnathort Perth 128 D3
Milner's Heath Ches W 73 C8
Milngavie E Dunb 119 B5
Milnrow Gtr Man 87 C7
Milnshaw Lancs 87 B5
Milnthorpe Cumb 99 F6
Milo Carms 33 C6
Milson Shrops 49 B8
Milstead Kent 30 D3
Milston Wilts 25 E6
Milton Angus 134 E3
Milton Cambs 55 C5
Milton Cumb 109 C5
Milton Derbys 63 B7
Milton Dumfries 105 D6
Milton Dumfries 106 B5
Milton Dumfries 113 F8
Milton Highld 150 F6
Milton Highld 150 H7
Milton Highld 151 D10
Milton Highld 151 G8
Milton Highld 158 E5
Milton Moray 152 B5
Milton N Som 22 C5
Milton Notts 77 B7
Milton Oxon 38 E4
Milton Oxon 52 F2
Milton Pembs 32 D1
Milton Perth 127 C8
Milton Ptsmth 15 E7
Milton Stirling 126 D4
Milton Stoke 75 D6
Milton W Dunb 118 B4
Milton Abbas Dorset 13 D6
Milton Abbot Devon 6 B2
Milton Bridge Midloth 120 C5
Milton Bryan C Beds 53 F7
Milton Clevedon Som 23 F8
Milton Coldwells Aberds 153 E9
Milton Combe Devon 6 C2
Milton Damerel Devon 9 C5
Milton End Glos 37 D8
Milton Ernest Bedford 53 D8
Milton Green Ches W 73 D8
Milton Hill Oxon 38 E4
Milton Keynes M Keynes 53 F6
Milton Keynes Village M Keynes 53 F6
Milton Lilbourne Wilts 25 C6
Milton Malsor Northants 52 D5
Milton Morenish Perth 132 F3
Milton of Auchinhove Aberds 140 D4
Milton of Balgonie Fife 128 D5
Milton of Buchanan Stirling 126 E3
Milton of Campfield Aberds 140 D5
Milton of Campsie E Dunb 119 B6
Milton of Corsindae Aberds 141 D5
Milton of Cushnie Aberds 140 C4
Milton of Dalcapon Perth 133 D6
Milton of Edradour Perth 133 D6
Milton of Gollanfield Highld 151 F10
Milton of Lesmore Aberds 140 B3
Milton of Logie Aberds 140 D3
Milton of Murtle Aberdeen 141 D7
Milton of Noth Aberds 140 B4
Milton of Tullich Aberds 140 E2
Milton on Stour Dorset 13 B5
Milton Regis Kent 30 C3
Milton under Wychwood Oxon 38 C2
Miltonduff Moray 152 B1
Miltonhill Moray 151 E13
Miltonise Dumfries 105 B5
Milverton Som 11 B6
Milverton Warks 51 C8
Milwich Staffs 75 F6
Minard Argyll 125 F5
Minchinhampton Glos 37 D5
Mindrum Northumb 122 F4
Minehead Som 21 E8
Minera Wrex 73 D6
Minety Wilts 37 E7
Minffordd Gwyn 58 C4
Minffordd Gwyn 71 D6
Minffordd Gwyn 83 D5
Miningsby Lincs 79 C6
Minions Corn 5 B7
Minishant S Ayrs 112 C3
Minllyn Gwyn 59 C5
Minnes Aberds 141 B8
Minngearraidh W Isles 148 F2
Minnigaff Dumfries 105 C8
Minnonie Aberds 153 B7
Minskip N Yorks 95 C6
Minstead Hants 14 C3
Minsted W Sus 16 B2
Minster Kent 30 B3
Minster Kent 31 C7
Minster Lovell Oxon 38 C3
Minsterley Shrops 60 D3
Minsterworth Glos 36 C4
Minterne Magna Dorset 12 D4
Minting Lincs 78 B4
Mintlaw Aberds 153 D9
Minto Borders 115 B8
Minton Shrops 60 E4
Minwear Pembs 32 C1
Minworth W Mid 63 E5
Mirbister Orkney 159 F4
Mirehouse Cumb 98 C1
Mireland Highld 158 D5
Mirfield W Yorks 88 C3
Miserden Glos 37 D6
Miskin Rhondda 34 F4
Misson Notts 89 E7
Misterton Leics 64 F2
Misterton Notts 89 E8
Misterton Som 12 D2
Mistley Essex 56 F5
Mitcham London 28 C3
Mitchel Troy Mon 36 C1
Mitcheldean Glos 36 C3
Mitchell Corn 4 D3
Mitcheltroy Common Mon 36 D1
Mitford Northumb 117 F7
Mithian Corn 4 D2
Mitton Staffs 62 C2
Mixbury Oxon 52 F4
Moat Cumb 108 B4
Moats Tye Suff 56 D4
Mobberley Ches E 74 B4
Mobberley Staffs 75 E7
Moccas Hereford 49 E5
Mochdre Conwy 83 D8
Mochdre Powys 59 F7
Mochrum Dumfries 105 E7
Mockbeggar Hants 14 D2
Mockerkin Cumb 98 B2
Modbury Devon 6 D4
Moddershall Staffs 75 F6
Moelfre Anglesey 82 C5
Moelfre Powys 59 B8
Moffat Dumfries 114 D3
Moggerhanger C Beds 54 E2
Moira Leics 63 C7
Mol-chlach Highld 149 G9
Molash Kent 30 D4
Mold = Yr Wyddgrug Flint 73 C6
Moldgreen W Yorks 88 C2
Molehill Green Essex 42 B1
Molescroft E Yorks 97 E6
Molesden Northumb 117 F7
Molesworth Cambs 53 B8
Moll Highld 149 E10
Molland Devon 10 B3
Mollington Ches W 73 B7
Mollington Oxon 52 E2
Mollinsburn N Lanark 119 B7
Monachty Ceredig 46 C4
Monachylemore Stirling 126 C3
Monar Lodge Highld 150 G5
Monaughty Powys 48 C4
Monboddo House Aberds 135 B7
Mondynes Aberds 135 B7
Monevechadan Argyll 125 E7
Monewden Suff 57 D6
Moneydie Perth 128 B2
Moniaive Dumfries 113 E7
Monifieth Angus 134 F4
Monikie Angus 135 F4
Monimail Fife 128 C4
Monington Pembs 45 E3
Monk Bretton S Yorks 88 D4
Monk Fryston N Yorks 89 B6
Monk Sherborne Hants 26 D4
Monk Soham Suff 57 C6
Monk Street Essex 42 B2
Monken Hadley London 41 E5
Monkhopton Shrops 61 E6
Monkland Hereford 49 D6
Monkleigh Devon 9 B6
Monknash V Glam 21 B8
Monkokehampton Devon 9 D7
Monks Eleigh Suff 56 E3
Monk's Gate W Sus 17 B6
Monks Heath Ches E 74 B5
Monks Kirby Warks 63 F8
Monks Risborough Bucks 39 D8
Monkseaton T&W 111 B6
Monkshill Aberds 153 D7
Monksilver Som 22 F2
Monkspath W Mid 51 B6
Monkswood Mon 35 D7
Monkton Devon 11 D6
Monkton Kent 31 C6
Monkton Pembs 44 E4
Monkton S Ayrs 112 B3
Monkton Combe Bath 24 C2
Monkton Deverill Wilts 24 F3
Monkton Farleigh Wilts 24 C3
Monkton Heathfield Som 11 B7
Monkton Up Wimborne Dorset 13 C8
Monkwearmouth T&W 111 D6
Monkwood Hants 26 F4
Monmouth = Trefynwy Mon 36 C2
Monmouth Cap Mon 35 B7
Monnington on Wye Hereford 49 E5
Monreith Dumfries 105 E7
Monreith Mains Dumfries 105 E7
Mont Saint Guern 16
Montacute Som 12 C2
Montcoffer Ho. Aberds 153 B6
Montford Argyll 145 G10
Montford Shrops 60 C4
Montford Bridge Shrops 60 C4
Montgarrie Aberds 140 C4
Montgomery = Trefaldwyn Powys 60 E2
Montrave Fife 129 D5
Montrose Angus 135 D7
Montsale Essex 43 E6
Monxton Hants 25 E8
Monyash Derbys 75 C8
Monymusk Aberds 141 C5
Monzie Perth 127 B7
Monzie Castle Perth 127 B7
Moodiesburn N Lanark 119 B6
Moonzie Fife 128 C5
Moor Allerton W Yorks 95 F5
Moor Crichel Dorset 13 D7
Moor End E Yorks 96 F4
Moor End York 96 D2
Moor Monkton N Yorks 95 D8
Moor of Granary Moray 151 F13
Moor of Ravenstone Dumfries 105 E7
Moor Row Cumb 98 C2
Moor Street Kent 30 C2
Moorby Lincs 79 C5
Moordown Bmouth 13 E8
Moore Halton 86 F3
Moorend Glos 36 D4
Moorends S Yorks 89 C7
Moorgreen Notts 76 E4
Moorhall Derbys 76 B3
Moorhampton Hereford 49 E5
Moorhead W Yorks 94 F4
Moorhouse Cumb 108 D3
Moorhouse Notts 77 C7
Moorlinch Som 23 F5
Moorsholm Redcar 102 C4
Moorside Gtr Man 87 D7
Moorthorpe W Yorks 89 C5
Moortown Hants 14 D2
Moortown IoW 14 F5
Moortown Lincs 90 E4
Morangie Highld 151 C10
Morar Highld 147 B9
Morborne Cambs 65 E8
Morchard Bishop Devon 10 D2
Morcombelake Dorset 12 E2
Morcott Rutland 65 D6
Morda Shrops 60 B2
Morden Dorset 13 E7
Morden London 28 C3
Mordiford Hereford 49 F7
Mordon Durham 101 B8
More Shrops 60 E3
Morebath Devon 10 B4
Morebattle Borders 116 B3
Morecambe Lancs 92 C4
Morefield Highld 150 B4
Moreleigh Devon 7 D5
Morenish Perth 132 F2
Moresby Cumb 98 B1
Moresby Parks Cumb 98 C1
Morestead Hants 15 B6
Moreton Dorset 13 F6
Moreton Essex 41 D8
Moreton Mers 85 E3
Moreton Oxon 39 D6
Moreton Staffs 61 C7
Moreton Corbet Shrops 61 B5
Moreton-in-Marsh Glos 51 F7
Moreton Jeffries Hereford 49 E8
Moreton Morrell Warks 51 D8
Moreton on Lugg Hereford 49 E7
Moreton Pinkney Northants 52 E3
Moreton Say Shrops 74 F3
Moreton Valence Glos 36 D4
Moretonhampstead Devon 10 F2
Morfa Carms 33 C6
Morfa Carms 33 E6
Morfa Bach Carms 32 C4
Morfa Bychan Gwyn 71 D6
Morfa Dinlle Gwyn 82 F4
Morfa Glas Neath 34 D2
Morfa Nefyn Gwyn 70 C3
Morfydd Denb 72 E5
Morgan's Vale Wilts 14 B2
Moriah Ceredig 46 B5
Morland Cumb 99 B7
Morley Derbys 76 E3
Morley Durham 101 B6
Morley W Yorks 88 B3
Morley Green Ches E 87 F6
Morley St Botolph Norf 68 E3
Morningside Edin 120 B5
Morningside N Lanark 119 D8
Morningthorpe Norf 68 E5
Morpeth Northumb 117 F8
Morphie Aberds 135 C7
Morrey Staffs 62 C5
Morris Green Essex 55 F8
Morriston Swansea 33 E7
Morston Norf 81 C6
Mortehoe Devon 20 E3
Mortimer W Berks 26 C4
Mortimer West End Hants 26 C4
Mortimer's Cross Hereford 49 C6
Mortlake London 28 B3
Morton Cumb 108 D3
Morton Derbys 76 C4
Morton Lincs 65 B7
Morton Lincs 77 C8
Morton Lincs 90 E2
Morton Norf 68 C4
Morton Notts 77 D7
Morton S Glos 36 E3
Morton Shrops 60 B2
Morton Bagot Warks 51 C6
Morton-on-Swale N Yorks 101 E8
Morvah Corn 2 C3
Morval Corn 5 D7
Morvich Highld 136 B2
Morvich Highld 157 J10
Morville Shrops 61 E6
Morville Heath Shrops 61 E6
Morwenstow Corn 8 C4
Mosborough S Yorks 88 F5
Moscow E Ayrs 118 E4
Mosedale Cumb 108 F3
Moseley W Mid 62 E3
Moseley W Mid 62 F4
Moseley Worcs 50 D3
Moss Argyll 146 G2
Moss Highld 147 E9
Moss S Yorks 89 C6
Moss Wrex 73 D7
Moss Bank Mers 86 E3
Moss Edge Lancs 92 E4
Moss End Brack 27 B6
Moss of Barmuckity Moray 152 B2
Moss Pit Staffs 62 B3
Moss-side Highld 151 F11
Moss Side Lancs 92 F3
Mossat Aberds 140 C3
Mossbank Shetland 160 F6
Mossbay Cumb 98 B1
Mossblown S Ayrs 112 B4
Mossbrow Gtr Man 86 F5
Mossburnford Borders 116 C2
Mossdale Dumfries 106 B3
Mossend N Lanark 119 C7
Mosser Cumb 98 B3
Mossfield Highld 151 D9
Mossgiel E Ayrs 112 B4
Mosside Angus 134 D4
Mossley Ches E 75 C5
Mossley Gtr Man 87 D7
Mossley Hill Mers 85 F4
Mosstodloch Moray 152 B3
Mosston Angus 135 E5
Mossy Lea Lancs 86 C3
Mosterton Dorset 12 D2
Moston Gtr Man 87 D6
Moston Shrops 61 B5
Moston Green Ches E 74 C4
Mostyn Flint 85 F2
Mostyn Quay Flint 85 F2
Motcombe Dorset 13 B6
Mothecombe Devon 6 E4
Motherby Cumb 99 B6
Motherwell N Lanark 119 D7
Mottingham London 28 B5
Mottisfont Hants 14 B4
Mottistone IoW 14 F5
Mottram in Longdendale Gtr Man 87 E7
Mottram St Andrew Ches E 75 B5
Mouilpied Guern 16
Mouldsworth Ches W 74 B2
Moulin Perth 133 D6
Moulsecoomb Brighton 17 D7
Moulsford Oxon 39 F5
Moulsoe M Keynes 53 E7
Moulton Ches W 74 C3
Moulton Lincs 66 B3
Moulton N Yorks 101 D7
Moulton Northants 53 C5
Moulton Suff 55 C7
Moulton V Glam 22 B2
Moulton Chapel Lincs 66 C2
Moulton Eaugate Lincs 66 C3
Moulton Seas End Lincs 66 B3
Moulton St Mary Norf 69 D6
Mounie Castle Aberds 141 B6
Mount Corn 4 D2
Mount Corn 5 C6
Mount Highld 151 G12
Mount Bures Essex 56 F3
Mount Canisp Highld 151 D10
Mount Hawke Corn 3 B6
Mount Pleasant Ches E 74 D5
Mount Pleasant Derbys 63 C6
Mount Pleasant Derbys 76 E3
Mount Pleasant Flint 73 B6
Mount Pleasant Hants 14 E3
Mount Pleasant W Yorks 88 B3
Mount Sorrel Wilts 13 B8
Mount Tabor W Yorks 87 B8
Mountain W Yorks 94 F3
Mountain Ash = Aberpennar Rhondda 34 E4
Mountain Cross Borders 120 E4

196 Mou–Nor

Mountain Water Pembs 44 C4
Mountbenger Borders 115 B6
Mountfield E Sus 18 C4
Mountgerald Highld 151 E8
Mountjoy Corn 4 C3
Mountnessing Essex 42 E2
Mounton Mon 36 E2
Mountsorrel Leics 64 C2
Mousehole Corn 2 D3
Mousen Northumb 123 F7
Mouswald Dumfries 107 B7
Mow Cop Ches E 75 D5
Mowhaugh Borders 116 B4
Mowsley Leics 64 F3
Moxley W Mid 62 E3
Moy Highld 137 F7
Moy Highld 151 H10
Moy Hall Highld 151 H10
Moy Ho. Moray 151 E13
Moy Lodge Highld 137 F7
Moyles Court Hants 14 D2
Moylgrove Pembs 45 E3
Muasdale Argyll 143 D7
Much Birch Hereford 49 F7
Much Cowarne Hereford 49 E8
Much Dewchurch Hereford 49 F6
Much Hadham Herts 41 C7
Much Hoole Lancs 86 B2
Much Marcle Hereford 49 F8
Much Wenlock Shrops 61 D6
Muchalls Aberds 141 E8
Muchelney Som 12 B2
Muchlarnick Corn 5 D7
Muchrachd Highld 150 H5
Muckernich Highld 151 F8
Mucking Thurrock 42 F2
Muckleford Dorset 12 E4
Mucklestone Staffs 74 F4
Muckleton Shrops 61 B5
Muckletown Aberds 140 B4
Muckley Corner Staffs 62 D4
Muckton Lincs 91 F7
Mudale Highld 157 F8
Muddiford Devon 20 F4
Mudeford Dorset 14 E2
Mudford Som 12 C3
Mudgley Som 23 E6
Mugdock Stirling 119 B5
Mugeary Highld 149 E9
Mugginton Derbys 76 E2
Muggleswick Durham 110 E3
Muie Highld 157 J9
Muir Aberds 139 F6
Muir of Fairburn Highld 150 F7
Muir of Fowlis Aberds 140 C4
Muir of Ord Highld 151 F8
Muir of Pert Angus 134 F4
Muirden Aberds 153 C7
Muirdrum Angus 135 F5
Muirhead Angus 134 F3
Muirhead Fife 128 D4
Muirhead N Lanark 119 C6
Muirhead S Ayrs 118 F3
Muirhouselaw Borders 116 B2
Muirhouses Falk 128 F2
Muirkirk E Ayrs 113 B6
Muirmill Stirling 127 F6
Muirshearlich Highld 136 F4
Muirskie Aberds 141 E7
Muirtack Aberds 153 E9
Muirton Highld 151 E10
Muirton Perth 127 C8
Muirton Perth 128 B3
Muirton Mains Highld 150 F7
Muirton of Ardblair Perth 134 E1
Muirton of Ballochy Angus 135 C6
Muiryfold Aberds 153 C7
Muker N Yorks 100 E4
Mulbarton Norf 68 D4
Mulben Moray 152 C3
Mulindry Argyll 142 C4
Mullardoch House Highld 150 H5
Mullion Corn 3 E5
Mullion Cove Corn 3 E5
Mumby Lincs 79 B8
Munderfield Row Hereford 49 D8
Munderfield Stocks Hereford 49 D8
Mundesley Norf 81 D9
Mundford Norf 67 E8
Mundham Norf 69 E6
Mundon Essex 42 D4
Mundurno Aberdeen 141 C8
Munerigie Highld 137 D5
Muness Shetland 160 C8
Mungasdale Highld 150 B2
Mungrisdale Cumb 108 F3
Munlochy Highld 151 F9
Munsley Hereford 49 E8
Munslow Shrops 60 F5
Murchington Devon 9 F8
Murcott Oxon 39 C5
Murkle Highld 158 D3
Murlaggan Highld 136 E3
Murlaggan Highld 137 F6
Murra Orkney 159 H3
Murrayfield Edin 120 B5
Murrow Cambs 66 D3
Mursley Bucks 39 B8
Murthill Angus 134 D4
Murthly Perth 133 F7
Murton Cumb 100 B2
Murton Durham 111 E6
Murton Northumb 123 E5
Murton York 96 D2
Musbury Devon 11 E7
Muscoates N Yorks 102 F4
Musdale Argyll 124 C5
Musselburgh E Loth 121 B6
Muston Leics 77 F8
Muston N Yorks 97 B6
Mustow Green Worcs 50 B3
Mutehill Dumfries 106 E3
Mutford Suff 69 F7
Muthill Perth 127 C7
Mutterton Devon 10 D5
Muxton Telford 61 C7
Mybster Highld 158 E3
Myddfai Carms 34 B1
Myddle Shrops 60 B4
Mydroilyn Ceredig 46 D3
Myerscough Lancs 92 F4
Mylor Bridge Corn 3 C7
Mynachlog-ddu Pembs 45 F3
Myndtown Shrops 60 F3
Mynydd Bach Ceredig 47 B6
Mynydd-bach Mon 36 E1
Mynydd Bodafon Anglesey 82 C4
Mynydd-isa Flint 73 C6
Mynyddygarreg Carms 33 D5
Mynytho Gwyn 70 D4
Myrebird Aberds 141 E6
Myrelandhorn Highld 158 E4
Myreside Perth 128 B4
Myrtle Hill Carms 47 F6
Mytchett Sur 27 D6
Mytholm W Yorks 87 B7
Mytholmroyd W Yorks 87 B8
Myton-on-Swale N Yorks 95 C7
Mytton Shrops 60 C4

N

Na Gearrannan W Isles 154 C6
Naast Highld 155 J13
Naburn York 95 E8
Nackington Kent 31 D5
Nacton Suff 57 E6
Nafferton E Yorks 97 D6
Nailbridge Glos 36 C3
Nailsbourne Som 11 B7
Nailsea N Som 23 B6
Nailstone Leics 63 D8
Nailsworth Glos 37 E5
Nairn Highld 151 F11
Nalderswood Sur 28 E3
Nancegollan Corn 2 C5
Nancledra Corn 2 C3
Nanhoron Gwyn 70 D3
Nannau Gwyn 71 E8
Nannerch Flint 73 C5
Nanpantan Leics 64 C2
Nanpean Corn 4 D4
Nanstallon Corn 4 C5
Nant-ddu Powys 34 C4
Nant-glas Powys 47 C8
Nant Peris Gwyn 83 F6
Nant Uchaf Denb 72 D4
Nant-y-Bai Carms 47 E6
Nant-y-cafn Neath 34 D2
Nant-y-derry Mon 35 D7
Nant-y-ffin Carms 46 F4
Nant-y-moel Bridgend 34 E3
Nant-y-pandy Conwy 83 D6
Nanternis Ceredig 46 D2
Nantgaredig Carms 33 B5
Nantgarw Rhondda 35 F5
Nantglyn Denb 72 C4
Nantgwyn Powys 47 B8
Nantlle Gwyn 82 F5
Nantmawr Shrops 60 B2
Nantmel Powys 48 C2
Nantmor Gwyn 71 C7
Nantwich Ches E 74 D3
Nantycaws Carms 33 C5
Nantyffyllon Bridgend 34 E2
Nantyglo Bl Gwent 35 C5
Naphill Bucks 39 E8
Nappa N Yorks 93 D8
Napton on the Hill Warks 52 C2
Narberth = Arberth Pembs 32 C2
Narborough Leics 64 E2
Narborough Norf 67 C7
Nasareth Gwyn 82 F4
Naseby Northants 52 B4
Nash Bucks 53 F5
Nash Hereford 48 C5
Nash Newport 35 F7
Nash Shrops 49 B8
Nash Lee Bucks 39 D8
Nassington Northants 65 E7
Nasty Herts 41 B6
Nateby Cumb 100 D2
Nateby Lancs 92 E4
Natland Cumb 99 F7
Naughton Suff 56 E4
Naunton Glos 37 B8
Naunton Worcs 50 F3
Naunton Beauchamp Worcs 50 D4
Navenby Lincs 78 D2
Navestock Heath Essex 41 E8
Navestock Side Essex 42 E1
Navidale Highld 157 H13
Nawton N Yorks 102 F4
Nayland Suff 56 F3
Nazeing Essex 41 D7
Neacroft Hants 14 E2
Neal's Green Warks 63 F7
Neap Shetland 160 H7
Near Sawrey Cumb 99 E5
Neasham Darl 101 C8
Neath = Castell-Nedd Neath 33 E8
Neath Abbey Neath 33 E8
Neatishead Norf 69 B6
Nebo Anglesey 82 B4
Nebo Ceredig 46 C4
Nebo Conwy 83 F8
Nebo Gwyn 82 F4
Necton Norf 67 D8
Nedd Highld 156 F4
Nedderton Northumb 117 F8
Nedging Tye Suff 56 E4
Needham Norf 68 F5
Needham Market Suff 56 D4
Needingworth Cambs 54 B4
Needwood Staffs 63 B5
Neen Savage Shrops 49 B8
Neen Sollars Shrops 49 B8
Neenton Shrops 61 F6
Nefyn Gwyn 70 C4
Neilston E Renf 118 D4
Neinthirion Powys 59 D6
Neithrop Oxon 52 E2
Nelly Andrews Green Powys 60 D2
Nelson Caerph 35 E5
Nelson Lancs 93 F8
Nelson Village Northumb 111 B5
Nemphlar S Lanark 119 E8
Nempnett Thrubwell N Som 23 C7
Nene Terrace Lincs 66 D2
Nenthall Cumb 109 E7
Nenthead Cumb 109 E7
Nenthorn Borders 122 F2
Nerabus Argyll 142 C3
Nercwys Flint 73 C6
Nerston S Lanark 119 D6
Nesbit Northumb 123 F5
Ness Ches W 73 B7
Nesscliffe Shrops 60 C3
Neston Ches W 73 B6
Neston Wilts 24 C3
Nether Alderley Ches E 74 B5
Nether Blainslie Borders 121 E8
Nether Booth Derbys 88 F2
Nether Broughton Leics 64 B3
Nether Burrow Lancs 93 B6
Nether Cerne Dorset 12 E4
Nether Compton Dorset 12 C3
Nether Crimond Aberds 141 B7
Nether Dalgliesh Borders 115 D5
Nether Dallachy Moray 152 B3
Nether Exe Devon 10 D4
Nether Glasslaw Aberds 153 C8
Nether Handwick Angus 134 E3
Nether Haugh S Yorks 88 E5
Nether Heage Derbys 76 D3
Nether Heyford Northants 52 D4
Nether Hindhope Borders 116 C3
Nether Howecleuch S Lanark 114 C3
Nether Kellet Lancs 92 C5
Nether Kinmundy Aberds 153 D10
Nether Langwith Notts 76 B5
Nether Leask Aberds 153 E10
Nether Lenshie Aberds 153 D6
Nether Monynut Borders 122 C3
Nether Padley Derbys 76 B2
Nether Park Aberds 153 C10
Nether Poppleton York 95 D8
Nether Silton N Yorks 102 E2
Nether Stowey Som 22 F3
Nether Urquhart Fife 128 D3
Nether Wallop Hants 25 F8
Nether Wasdale Cumb 98 D3
Nether Whitacre Warks 63 E6
Nether Worton Oxon 52 F2
Netheravon Wilts 25 E6
Netherbrae Aberds 153 C7
Netherbrough Orkney 159 G4
Netherburn S Lanark 119 E8
Netherbury Dorset 12 E2
Netherby Cumb 108 B3
Netherby N Yorks 95 E6
Nethercote Warks 52 C3
Nethercott Devon 20 F3
Netherend Glos 36 D2
Netherfield E Sus 18 D4
Netherhampton Wilts 14 B2
Netherlaw Dumfries 106 E4
Netherley Aberds 141 E7
Netherley Mers 86 F2
Nethermill Dumfries 114 F3
Nethermuir Aberds 153 D9
Netherplace E Renf 118 D5
Netherseal Derbys 63 C6
Netherthird E Ayrs 113 C5
Netherthong W Yorks 88 D2
Netherthorpe S Yorks 89 F6
Netherton Angus 135 D5
Netherton Devon 7 B6
Netherton Hants 25 D8
Netherton Mers 85 D4
Netherton Northumb 117 D5
Netherton Oxon 38 E4
Netherton Perth 133 D8
Netherton Stirling 119 B5
Netherton W Mid 62 F3
Netherton W Yorks 88 C2
Netherton W Yorks 88 C3
Netherton Worcs 50 E4
Nethertown Cumb 98 D1
Nethertown Highld 158 C5
Netherwitton Northumb 117 E7
Netherwood E Ayrs 113 B6
Nethy Bridge Highld 139 B6
Netley Hants 15 D5
Netley Marsh Hants 14 C4
Netteswell Essex 41 C7
Nettlebed Oxon 39 F7
Nettlebridge Som 23 E8
Nettlecombe Dorset 12 E3
Nettleden Herts 40 C3
Nettleham Lincs 78 B3
Nettlestead Kent 29 D7
Nettlestead Green Kent 29 D7
Nettlestone IoW 15 E7
Nettlesworth Durham 111 E5
Nettleton Lincs 90 D5
Nettleton Wilts 24 B3
Neuadd Carms 33 B7
Nevendon Essex 42 E3
Nevern Pembs 45 E2
New Abbey Dumfries 107 C6
New Aberdour Aberds 153 B8
New Addington London 28 C4
New Alresford Hants 26 F3
New Alyth Perth 134 E2
New Arley Warks 63 F6
New Ash Green Kent 29 C7
New Barn Kent 29 C7
New Barnetby N Lincs 90 C4
New Barton Northants 53 C6
New Bewick Northumb 117 B6
New-bigging Angus 134 E2
New Bilton Warks 52 B2
New Bolingbroke Lincs 79 D6
New Boultham Lincs 78 B2
New Bradwell M Keynes 53 E6
New Brancepeth Durham 110 E5
New Bridge Wrex 73 E6
New Brighton Flint 73 C6
New Brighton Mers 85 E4
New Brinsley Notts 76 D4
New Broughton Wrex 73 D7
New Buckenham Norf 68 E3
New Byth Aberds 153 C8
New Catton Norf 68 C5
New Cheriton Hants 15 B6
New Costessey Norf 68 C4
New Cowper Cumb 107 E8
New Cross Ceredig 46 B5
New Cross London 28 B4
New Cumnock E Ayrs 113 C6
New Deer Aberds 153 D8
New Delaval Northumb 111 B5
New Duston Northants 52 C5
New Earswick York 96 D2
New Edlington S Yorks 89 E6
New Elgin Moray 152 B2
New Ellerby E Yorks 97 F7
New Eltham London 28 B5
New End Worcs 51 D5
New Farnley W Yorks 94 F5
New Ferry Mers 85 F4
New Fryston W Yorks 89 B5
New Galloway Dumfries 106 B3
New Gilston Fife 129 D6
New Grimsby Scilly 2 E3
New Hainford Norf 68 C5
New Hartley Northumb 111 B6
New Haw Sur 27 C8
New Hedges Pembs 32 D2
New Herrington T&W 111 D6
New Hinksey Oxon 39 D5
New Holkham Norf 80 D4
New Holland N Lincs 90 B4
New Houghton Derbys 76 C4
New Houghton Norf 80 E3
New Houses N Yorks 93 B8
New Humberstone Leicester 64 D3
New Hutton Cumb 99 E7
New Hythe Kent 29 D8
New Inn Carms 46 F3
New Inn Mon 36 D1
New Inn Pembs 45 F2
New Inn Torf 35 E7
New Invention Shrops 48 B4
New Invention W Mid 62 D3
New Kelso Highld 150 G2
New Kingston Notts 64 B2
New Lanark S Lanark 119 E8
New Lane Lancs 86 C2
New Lane End Warr 86 E4
New Leake Lincs 79 D7
New Leeds Aberds 153 C9
New Longton Lancs 86 B3
New Luce Dumfries 105 C5
New Malden London 28 C3
New Marske Redcar 102 B4
New Marton Shrops 73 F7
New Micklefield W Yorks 95 F7
New Mill Aberds 141 F6
New Mill Herts 40 C2
New Mill W Yorks 88 D2
New Mill Wilts 25 C6
New Mills Ches E 87 F5
New Mills Corn 4 D3
New Mills Derbys 87 F7
New Mills Powys 59 D7
New Milton Hants 14 E3
New Moat Pembs 32 B1
New Ollerton Notts 77 C6
New Oscott W Mid 62 E4
New Park N Yorks 95 D5
New Pitsligo Aberds 153 C8
New Polzeath Corn 4 B4
New Quay = Ceinewydd Ceredig 46 D2
New Rackheath Norf 69 C5
New Radnor Powys 48 C4
New Rent Cumb 108 F4
New Ridley Northumb 110 D3
New Road Side N Yorks 94 E2
New Romney Kent 19 C7
New Rossington S Yorks 89 E7
New Row Ceredig 47 B6
New Row Lancs 93 F6
New Row N Yorks 102 C4
New Sarum Wilts 25 F6
New Silksworth T&W 111 D6
New Stevenston N Lanark 119 D7
New Street Staffs 75 D7
New Street Lane Shrops 74 F3
New Swanage Dorset 13 F8
New Totley S Yorks 76 B3
New Town E Loth 121 B7
New Tredegar = Tredegar Newydd Caerph 35 D5
New Trows S Lanark 119 F8
New Ulva Argyll 144 E6
New Walsoken Cambs 66 D4
New Waltham NE Lincs 91 D6
New Whittington Derbys 76 B3
New Wimpole Cambs 54 E4
New Winton E Loth 121 B7
New Yatt Oxon 38 C3
New York Lincs 78 D5
New York N Yorks 94 C4
Newall W Yorks 94 E4
Newark Orkney 159 D8
Newark Pboro 66 D2
Newark-on-Trent Notts 77 D7
Newarthill N Lanark 119 D7
Newbarns Cumb 92 B2
Newbattle Midloth 121 C6
Newbiggin Cumb 92 C2
Newbiggin Cumb 98 E2
Newbiggin Cumb 99 B6
Newbiggin Cumb 99 B8
Newbiggin Cumb 109 E5
Newbiggin Durham 100 B4
Newbiggin N Yorks 100 E4
Newbiggin N Yorks 100 F4
Newbiggin-by-the-Sea Northumb 117 F9
Newbiggin-on-Lune Cumb 100 D2
Newbigging Angus 134 F4
Newbigging Angus 134 F4
Newbigging S Lanark 120 E3
Newbold Derbys 76 B3
Newbold Leics 63 C8
Newbold on Avon Warks 52 B2
Newbold on Stour Warks 51 E7
Newbold Pacey Warks 51 D7
Newbold Verdon Leics 63 D8
Newborough Anglesey 82 E4
Newborough Pboro 66 D2
Newborough Staffs 62 B5
Newbottle Northants 52 F3
Newbottle T&W 111 D6
Newbourne Suff 57 E6
Newbridge Caerph 35 E6
Newbridge Ceredig 46 D4
Newbridge Corn 2 C3
Newbridge Corn 5 C8
Newbridge Dumfries 107 B6
Newbridge Edin 120 B4
Newbridge Hants 14 C3
Newbridge IoW 14 F5
Newbridge Pembs 44 B4
Newbridge Green Worcs 50 F3
Newbridge-on-Usk Mon 35 E7
Newbridge on Wye Powys 48 D2
Newbrough Northumb 109 C8
Newbuildings Devon 10 D2
Newburgh Aberds 141 B8
Newburgh Aberds 153 C9
Newburgh Borders 115 C6
Newburgh Fife 128 C4
Newburgh Lancs 86 C2
Newburn T&W 110 C4
Newbury W Berks 26 C2
Newbury Park London 41 F7
Newby Cumb 99 B7
Newby Lancs 93 E8
Newby N Yorks 93 B7
Newby N Yorks 102 C3
Newby N Yorks 103 E8
Newby Bridge Cumb 99 F5
Newby East Cumb 108 D4
Newby West Cumb 108 D3
Newby Wiske N Yorks 102 F1
Newcastle Mon 35 C8
Newcastle Shrops 60 F2
Newcastle Emlyn = Castell Newydd Emlyn Carms 46 E2
Newcastle-under-Lyme Staffs 74 E5
Newcastle Upon Tyne T&W 110 C5
Newcastleton or Copshaw Holm Borders 115 F7
Newchapel Pembs 45 F4
Newchapel Powys 59 F6
Newchapel Staffs 75 D5
Newchapel Sur 28 E4
Newchurch Carms 32 B4
Newchurch IoW 15 F6
Newchurch Kent 19 B7
Newchurch Lancs 93 F8
Newchurch Mon 36 E1
Newchurch Powys 48 D4
Newchurch Staffs 62 B5
Newcott Devon 11 D7
Newcraighall Edin 121 B6
Newdigate Sur 28 E2
Newell Green Brack 27 B6
Newenden Kent 18 C5
Newent Glos 36 B4
Newerne Glos 36 D3
Newfield Durham 110 F5
Newfield Highld 151 D10
Newford Scilly 2 E4
Newfound Hants 26 D3
Newgale Pembs 44 C3
Newgate Norf 81 C6
Newgate Street Herts 41 D6
Newhall Ches E 74 E3
Newhall Derbys 63 B6
Newhall House Highld 151 E9
Newhall Point Highld 151 E10
Newham Northumb 117 B7
Newham Hall Northumb 117 B7
Newhaven Derbys 75 D8
Newhaven E Sus 17 D8
Newhaven Edin 121 B5
Newhey Gtr Man 87 C7
Newholm N Yorks 103 C6
Newhouse N Lanark 119 C7
Newick E Sus 17 B8
Newingreen Kent 19 B8
Newington Kent 19 B8
Newington Kent 30 C2
Newington Kent 31 C7
Newington Notts 89 E7
Newington Oxon 39 E6
Newington Shrops 60 F4
Newland Glos 36 D2
Newland Hull 97 F6
Newland N Yorks 89 B7
Newland Worcs 50 E2
Newlandrig Midloth 121 C6
Newlands Borders 115 E8
Newlands Highld 151 G10
Newlands Moray 152 C3
Newlands Northumb 110 D3
Newland's Corner Sur 27 E8
Newlands of Geise Highld 158 D2
Newlands of Tynet Moray 152 B3
Newlands Park Anglesey 82 C2
Newlandsmuir S Lanark 119 D6
Newlot Orkney 159 G6
Newlyn Corn 2 D3
Newmachar Aberds 141 C7
Newmains N Lanark 119 D8
Newmarket Suff 55 C7
Newmarket W Isles 155 D9
Newmill Borders 115 C7
Newmill Corn 2 C3
Newmill Moray 152 C4
Newmill of Inshewan Angus 134 C4
Newmills of Boyne Aberds 152 C5
Newmiln Perth 133 F8
Newmilns E Ayrs 118 F5
Newnham Cambs 54 D5
Newnham Glos 36 C3
Newnham Hants 26 D5
Newnham Herts 54 F3
Newnham Kent 30 D3
Newnham Northants 52 D3
Newnham Bridge Worcs 49 C8
Newpark Fife 129 C6
Newport Devon 20 F4
Newport E Yorks 96 F4
Newport Essex 55 F6
Newport Highld 158 H3
Newport IoW 15 F6
Newport = Casnewydd Newport 35 F7
Newport Norf 69 C8
Newport = Trefdraeth Pembs 45 F2
Newport Telford 61 C7
Newport-on-Tay Fife 129 B6
Newport Pagnell M Keynes 53 E6
Newpound Common W Sus 16 B4
Newquay Corn 4 C3
Newsbank Ches E 74 C5
Newseat Aberds 153 D10
Newseat Aberds 153 E7
Newsham N Yorks 101 C6
Newsham N Yorks 102 F1
Newsham Northumb 111 B6
Newsholme E Yorks 89 B8
Newsholme Lancs 93 D8
Newsome W Yorks 88 C2
Newstead Borders 121 F8
Newstead Northumb 117 B7
Newstead Notts 76 D5
Newthorpe N Yorks 95 F7
Newton Argyll 125 F6
Newton Borders 116 B2
Newton Bridgend 21 B7
Newton Cambs 54 E5
Newton Cambs 66 C4
Newton Cardiff 22 B4
Newton Ches W 73 C8
Newton Ches W 74 B2
Newton Ches W 74 D2
Newton Cumb 92 B2
Newton Derbys 76 D4
Newton Dorset 13 C5
Newton Dumfries 108 B2
Newton Dumfries 114 E4
Newton Gtr Man 87 E7
Newton Hereford 48 F5
Newton Hereford 49 D7
Newton Highld 151 E10
Newton Highld 151 G10
Newton Highld 156 F5
Newton Highld 158 F5
Newton Lancs 92 F4
Newton Lancs 93 B5
Newton Lancs 93 D6
Newton Lincs 78 F3
Newton Moray 152 B1
Newton Norf 67 C8
Newton Northants 65 F5
Newton Northumb 110 C3
Newton Notts 77 E6
Newton Perth 133 F5
Newton S Lanark 119 C6
Newton S Lanark 120 F2
Newton S Yorks 89 D6
Newton Staffs 62 B4
Newton Suff 56 E3
Newton Swansea 33 F7
Newton W Loth 120 B3
Newton Warks 52 B3
Newton Wilts 14 B3
Newton Abbot Devon 7 B6
Newton Arlosh Cumb 107 D8
Newton Aycliffe Durham 101 B7
Newton Bewley Hrtlpl 102 B2
Newton Blossomville M Keynes 53 D7
Newton Bromswold Northants 53 C7
Newton Burgoland Leics 63 D7
Newton by Toft Lincs 90 F4
Newton Ferrers Devon 6 E3
Newton Flotman Norf 68 E5
Newton Hall Northumb 110 C3
Newton Harcourt Leics 64 E3
Newton Heath Gtr Man 87 D6
Newton Ho. Aberds 141 B5
Newton Kyme N Yorks 95 E7
Newton-le-Willows Mers 86 E3
Newton-le-Willows N Yorks 101 F7
Newton Longville Bucks 53 F6
Newton Mearns E Renf 118 D5
Newton Morrell N Yorks 101 D7
Newton Mulgrave N Yorks 103 C5
Newton of Ardtoe Highld 147 D9
Newton of Balcanquhal Perth 128 C3
Newton of Falkland Fife 128 D4
Newton on Ayr S Ayrs 112 B3
Newton on Ouse N Yorks 95 D8
Newton-on-Rawcliffe N Yorks 103 E6
Newton-on-the-Moor Northumb 117 D7
Newton on Trent Lincs 77 B8
Newton Park Argyll 145 G10
Newton Poppleford Devon 11 F5
Newton Purcell Oxon 52 F4
Newton Regis Warks 63 D6
Newton Reigny Cumb 108 F4
Newton St Cyres Devon 10 E3
Newton St Faith Norf 68 C5
Newton St Loe Bath 24 C2
Newton St Petrock Devon 9 C6
Newton Stacey Hants 26 E2
Newton Stewart Dumfries 105 C8
Newton Tony Wilts 25 E7
Newton Tracey Devon 9 B7
Newton under Roseberry Redcar 102 C3
Newton upon Derwent E Yorks 96 E3
Newton Valence Hants 26 F5
Newtonairds Dumfries 113 F8
Newtongrange Midloth 121 C6
Newtonhill Aberds 141 E8
Newtonhill Highld 151 G8
Newtonmill Angus 135 C6
Newtonmore Highld 138 E3
Newtown Argyll 125 E6
Newtown Ches W 74 B2
Newtown Corn 3 D6
Newtown Cumb 107 E7
Newtown Cumb 108 C5
Newtown Derbys 87 F7
Newtown Devon 10 B2
Newtown Glos 36 D3
Newtown Glos 50 F4
Newtown Hants 14 B4
Newtown Hants 14 C3
Newtown Hants 15 C6
Newtown Hants 15 C7
Newtown Hants 15 D5
Newtown Hants 26 C2
Newtown Hereford 49 E8
Newtown Highld 137 D6
Newtown IoM 84 E3
Newtown IoW 14 E5
Newtown Northumb 117 B6
Newtown Northumb 117 D6
Newtown Northumb 123 F5
Newtown Poole 13 E8
Newtown = Y Drenewydd Powys 59 E8
Newtown Shrops 73 F8
Newtown Staffs 75 C6
Newtown Staffs 75 C7
Newtown Wilts 13 B7
Newtown Linford Leics 64 D2
Newtown St Boswells Borders 121 F8
Newtown Unthank Leics 63 D8
Newtyle Angus 134 E2
Neyland Pembs 44 E4
Niarbyl IoM 84 E2
Nibley S Glos 36 F3
Nibley Green Glos 36 E4
Nibon Shetland 160 F5
Nicholashayne Devon 11 C6
Nicholaston Swansea 33 F6
Nidd N Yorks 95 C6
Nigg Aberdeen 141 D8
Nigg Highld 151 D11
Nigg Ferry Highld 151 E10
Nightcott Som 10 B3
Nilig Denb 72 D4
Nine Ashes Essex 42 D1
Nine Mile Burn Midloth 120 D4
Nine Wells Pembs 44 C2
Ninebanks Northumb 109 D7
Ninfield E Sus 18 D4
Ningwood IoW 14 F4
Nisbet Borders 116 B2
Nisthouse Orkney 159 G4
Nisthouse Shetland 160 G7
Niton IoW 15 G6
Nitshill Glasgow 118 C5
No Man's Heath Ches W 74 E2
No Man's Heath Warks 63 D6
Noak Hill London 41 E8
Noblethorpe S Yorks 88 D3
Nobottle Northants 52 C4
Nocton Lincs 78 C3
Noke Oxon 39 C5
Nolton Pembs 44 D3
Nolton Haven Pembs 44 D3
Nomansland Devon 10 C3
Nomansland Wilts 14 C3
Noneley Shrops 60 B4
Nonikiln Highld 151 D9
Nonington Kent 31 D6
Noonsbrough Shetland 160 H4
Norbreck Blackpool 92 E3
Norbridge Hereford 50 E2
Norbury Ches E 74 E2
Norbury Derbys 75 E8
Norbury Shrops 60 E3
Norbury Staffs 61 B7
Nordelph Norf 67 D5
Norden Gtr Man 87 C6
Norden Heath Dorset 13 F7
Nordley Shrops 61 E6
Norham Northumb 122 E5
Norley Ches W 74 B2
Norleywood Hants 14 E4
Norman Cross Cambs 65 E8
Normanby N Lincs 90 C2
Normanby N Yorks 103 F5
Normanby Redcar 102 C3
Normanby-by-Spital Lincs 90 F4
Normanby by Stow Lincs 90 F2
Normanby le Wold Lincs 90 E5
Normandy Sur 27 D7
Norman's Bay E Sus 18 E3
Norman's Green Devon 11 D5
Normanstone Suff 69 E8
Normanton Derby 76 F3
Normanton Leics 77 E8
Normanton Lincs 78 E2
Normanton Notts 77 D7
Normanton Rutland 65 D6
Normanton W Yorks 88 B4
Normanton le Heath Leics 63 C7
Normanton on Soar Notts 64 B2
Normanton-on-the-Wolds Notts 77 F6
Normanton on Trent Notts 77 C7
Normoss Lancs 92 F3
Norney Sur 27 E7
Norrington Common Wilts 24 C3
Norris Green Mers 85 E4
Norris Hill Leics 63 C7
North Anston S Yorks 89 F6
North Aston Oxon 38 B4
North Baddesley Hants 14 C4
North Ballachulish Highld 130 C4
North Barrow Som 12 B4
North Barsham Norf 80 D5
North Benfleet Essex 42 F3
North Bersted W Sus 16 D3
North Berwick E Loth 129 F7
North Boarhunt Hants 15 C7
North Bovey Devon 10 F2
North Bradley Wilts 24 D3
North Brentor Devon 9 F6
North Brewham Som 24 F2
North Buckland Devon 20 E3
North Burlingham Norf 69 C6
North Cadbury Som 12 B4
North Cairn Dumfries 104 B3
North Carlton Lincs 78 B2
North Carrine Argyll 143 H7
North Cave E Yorks 96 F4
North Cerney Glos 37 D7
North Charford Wilts 14 C2
North Charlton Northumb 117 B7
North Cheriton Som 12 B4
North Cliff E Yorks 97 E8
North Cliffe E Yorks 96 F4
North Clifton Notts 77 B8
North Cockerington Lincs 91 E7
North Coker Som 12 C3
North Collafirth Shetland 160 E5
North Common E Sus 17 B7
North Connel Argyll 124 B5
North Cornelly Bridgend 34 F2
North Cotes Lincs 91 D7
North Cove Suff 69 F7
North Cowton N Yorks 101 D7
North Crawley M Keynes 53 E7
North Cray London 29 B5
North Creake Norf 80 D4
North Curry Som 11 B8
North Dalton E Yorks 96 D5
North Dawn Orkney 159 H5
North Deighton N Yorks 95 D6
North Duffield N Yorks 96 F2
North Elkington Lincs 91 E6
North Elmham Norf 81 E5
North Elmshall W Yorks 89 C5
North End Bucks 39 B8
North End E Yorks 97 F8
North End Essex 42 C2
North End Hants 26 C2
North End Lincs 78 E5
North End N Som 23 C6
North End Ptsmth 15 D7
North End Som 11 B7
North End W Sus 16 D5
North Erradale Highld 155 J12
North Fambridge Essex 42 E4
North Fearns Highld 149 E10
North Featherstone W Yorks 88 B5
North Ferriby E Yorks 90 B3
North Frodingham E Yorks 97 D7
North Gluss Shetland 160 F5
North Gorley Hants 14 C2
North Green Norf 68 F5
North Green Suff 57 C7
North Greetwell Lincs 78 B3
North Grimston N Yorks 96 C4
North Halley Orkney 159 H6
North Halling Medway 29 C8
North Hayling Hants 15 D8
North Hazelrigg Northumb 123 F6
North Heasley Devon 21 F6
North Heath W Sus 16 B4
North Hill Cambs 55 B5
North Hill Corn 5 B7
North Hinksey Oxon 38 D4
North Holmwood Sur 28 E2
North Howden E Yorks 96 F3
North Huish Devon 6 D5
North Hykeham Lincs 78 C2
North Johnston Pembs 44 D4
North Kelsey Lincs 90 D4
North Kelsey Moor Lincs 90 D4
North Kessock Highld 151 G9
North Killingholme N Lincs 90 C5
North Kilvington N Yorks 102 F2
North Kilworth Leics 64 F3
North Kirkton Aberds 153 C11
North Kiscadale N Ayrs 143 F11
North Kyme Lincs 78 D4
North Lancing W Sus 17 D5
North Lee Bucks 39 D8
North Leigh Oxon 38 C3
North Leverton with Habblesthorpe Notts 89 F8
North Littleton Worcs 51 E5
North Lopham Norf 68 F3
North Luffenham Rutland 65 D6
North Marden W Sus 16 C2
North Marston Bucks 39 B7
North Middleton Midloth 121 D6
North Middleton Northumb 117 B6
North Molton Devon 10 B2
North Moreton Oxon 39 F5
North Mundham W Sus 16 D2
North Muskham Notts 77 D7
North Newbald E Yorks 96 F5
North Newington Oxon 52 F2
North Newnton Wilts 25 D6
North Newton Som 22 F4
North Nibley Glos 36 E4
North Oakley Hants 26 D3
North Ockendon London 42 F1
North Ormesby Mbro 102 B3
North Ormsby Lincs 91 E6
North Otterington N Yorks 102 F1
North Owersby Lincs 90 E4
North Perrott Som 12 D2
North Petherton Som 22 F4
North Petherwin Corn 8 F4
North Pickenham Norf 67 D8
North Piddle Worcs 50 D4
North Poorton Dorset 12 E3
North Port Argyll 125 C6
North Queensferry Fife 128 F3
North Radworthy Devon 21 F6
North Rauceby Lincs 78 E3
North Reston Lincs 91 F7
North Rigton N Yorks 95 E5
North Rode Ches E 75 C5
North Roe Shetland 160 E5
North Runcton Norf 67 C6
North Sandwick Shetland 160 D7
North Scale Cumb 92 C1
North Scarle Lincs 77 C8
North Seaton Northumb 117 F8
North Shian Argyll 130 E3
North Shields T&W 111 C6
North Shoebury Southend 43 F5
North Shore Blackpool 92 F3
North Side Cumb 98 B2
North Side Pboro 66 E2
North Skelton Redcar 102 C4
North Somercotes Lincs 91 E8
North Stainley N Yorks 95 B5
North Stainmore Cumb 100 C3
North Stifford Thurrock 42 F2
North Stoke Bath 24 C2
North Stoke Oxon 39 F6
North Stoke W Sus 16 C4
North Street Hants 26 F4
North Street Kent 30 D4
North Street Medway 30 B2
North Street W Berks 26 B4
North Sunderland Northumb 123 F8
North Tamerton Corn 8 E5
North Tawton Devon 9 D8
North Thoresby Lincs 91 E6
North Tidworth Wilts 25 E7
North Togston Northumb 117 D8
North Tuddenham Norf 68 C3
North Walbottle T&W 110 C4
North Walsham Norf 81 D8
North Waltham Hants 26 E3
North Warnborough Hants 26 D5
North Water Bridge Angus 135 C6
North Watten Highld 158 E4
North Weald Bassett Essex 41 D7
North Wheatley Notts 89 F8
North Whilborough Devon 7 C6
North Wick Bath 23 C7
North Willingham Lincs 91 F5
North Wingfield Derbys 76 C4
North Witham Lincs 65 B6
North Woolwich London 28 B5
North Wootton Dorset 12 C4
North Wootton Norf 67 B6
North Wootton Som 23 E7
North Wraxall Wilts 24 B3
North Wroughton Swindon 38 F1
Northacre Norf 68 E2
Northallerton N Yorks 102 E1
Northam Devon 9 B6
Northam Soton 14 C5
Northampton Northants 53 C5
Northaw Herts 41 D5
Northbeck Lincs 78 E3
Northborough Pboro 65 D8
Northbourne Kent 31 D7
Northbridge Street E Sus 18 C4
Northchapel W Sus 16 B3
Northchurch Herts 40 D2
Northcott Devon 8 E5
Northdown Kent 31 B7
Northdyke Orkney 159 F3
Northend Bath 24 C2
Northend Bucks 39 E7
Northend Warks 51 D8
Northenden Gtr Man 87 E6
Northfield Aberdeen 141 D8
Northfield Borders 122 C5
Northfield E Yorks 90 B4
Northfield W Mid 50 B5
Northfields Lincs 65 D7
Northfleet Kent 29 B7
Northgate Lincs 65 B8
Northhouse Borders 115 D7
Northiam E Sus 18 C5
Northill C Beds 54 E2
Northington Hants 26 F3
Northlands Lincs 79 D6
Northlea Durham 111 D7
Northleach Glos 37 C8
Northleigh Devon 11 E6
Northlew Devon 9 E7
Northmoor Oxon 38 D4
Northmoor Green or Moorland Som 22 F5
Northmuir Angus 134 D3
Northney Hants 15 D8
Northolt London 40 F4
Northop Flint 73 C6
Northop Hall Flint 73 C6
Northorpe Lincs 65 C7
Northorpe Lincs 78 F5
Northorpe Lincs 90 E2
Northover Som 12 B3
Northover Som 23 F6
Northowram W Yorks 88 B2
Northport Dorset 13 F7
Northpunds Shetland 160 L6
Northrepps Norf 81 D8
Northtown Orkney 159 J5
Northway Glos 50 F4
Northwich Ches W 74 B3
Northwick S Glos 36 F2
Northwold Norf 67 E7
Northwood Derbys 76 C2
Northwood IoW 15 E5
Northwood Kent 31 C7
Northwood London 40 E3
Northwood Shrops 73 F8
Northwood Green Glos 36 C4
Norton E Sus 17 D8
Norton Glos 37 B5
Norton Halton 86 F3
Norton Herts 54 F3
Norton IoW 14 F4
Norton Mon 35 C8
Norton Northants 52 C4
Norton Notts 77 B5
Norton Powys 48 C5
Norton S Yorks 89 C6
Norton Shrops 60 F4
Norton Shrops 61 D5
Norton Shrops 61 D7
Norton Stockton 102 B2
Norton Suff 56 C3
Norton W Sus 16 D3
Norton W Sus 16 E2
Norton Wilts 37 F5
Norton Worcs 50 D3
Norton Worcs 50 E5
Norton Bavant Wilts 24 E4
Norton Bridge Staffs 75 F5
Norton Canes Staffs 62 D4
Norton Canon Hereford 49 E5
Norton Corner Norf 81 E6
Norton Disney Lincs 77 D8
Norton East Staffs 62 D4
Norton Ferris Wilts 24 F2
Norton Fitzwarren Som 11 B6
Norton Green IoW 14 F4
Norton Hawkfield Bath 23 C7
Norton Heath Essex 42 D2
Norton in Hales Shrops 74 F4
Norton-in-the-Moors Stoke 75 D5
Norton-Juxta-Twycross Leics 63 D7
Norton-le-Clay N Yorks 95 B7
Norton Lindsey Warks 51 C7
Norton Malreward Bath 23 C8
Norton Mandeville Essex 42 D1
Norton-on-Derwent N Yorks 96 B3
Norton St Philip Som 24 D2
Norton sub Hamdon Som 12 C2
Norton Woodseats S Yorks 88 F4

Stoke sub Hamdon Som 12 C2
Stoke Talmage Oxon 39 E6
Stoke Trister Som 12 B5
Stoke Wake Dorset 13 D5
Stokeford Dorset 13 F6
Stokeham Notts 77 B7
Stokeinteignhead Devon 7 B7
Stokenchurch Bucks 39 E7
Stokenham Devon 7 E6
Stokesay Shrops 60 F4
Stokesby Norf 69 C7
Stokesley N Yorks 102 D3
Stolford Som 22 E4
Ston Easton Som 23 D8
Stondon Massey Essex 42 D1
Stone Bucks 39 C7
Stone Glos 36 E3
Stone Kent 19 C6
Stone Kent 29 B6
Stone S Yorks 89 F6
Stone Staffs 75 F6
Stone Worcs 50 B3
Stone Allerton Som 23 D6
Stone Bridge Corner Pboro 66 D2
Stone Chair W Yorks 88 B2
Stone Cross E Sus 18 E3
Stone Cross Kent 31 D7
Stone-edge Batch N Som 23 B6
Stone House Cumb 100 F2
Stone Street Kent 29 D6
Stone Street Suff 56 F3
Stone Street Suff 69 F6
Stonebroom Derbys 76 D4
Stoneferry Hull 97 F7
Stonefield S Lanark 119 D6
Stonegate E Sus 18 C3
Stonegate N Yorks 103 D5
Stonegrave N Yorks 96 B2
Stonehaugh Northumb 109 B7
Stonehaven Aberds 141 F7
Stonehouse Glos 37 D5
Stonehouse Northumb 109 D6
Stonehouse S Lanark 119 E7
Stoneleigh Warks 51 B8
Stonely Cambs 54 C2
Stoner Hill Hants 15 B8
Stone's Green Essex 43 B7
Stonesby Leics 64 B5
Stonesfield Oxon 38 C3
Stonethwaite Cumb 98 C4
Stoney Cross Hants 14 C3
Stoney Middleton Derbys 76 B2
Stoney Stanton Leics 63 E8
Stoney Stoke Som 24 F2
Stoney Stratton Som 23 F8
Stoney Stretton Shrops 60 D3
Stoneybreck Shetland 160 N8
Stoneyburn W Loth 120 C2
Stoneygate Aberds 153 E10
Stoneygate Leicester 64 D3
Stoneyhills Essex 43 E5
Stoneykirk Dumfries 104 D4
Stoneywood Aberdeen 141 C7
Stoneywood Falk 127 F6
Stonganess Shetland 160 C7
Stonham Aspal Suff 56 D5
Stonnall Staffs 62 D4
Stonor Oxon 39 F7
Stonton Wyville Leics 64 E4
Stony Cross Hereford 50 E2
Stony Stratford M Keynes 53 E5
Stonyfield Highld 151 D9
Stoodleigh Devon 10 C4
Stopes S Yorks 88 F3
Stopham W Sus 16 C4
Stopsley Luton 40 B4
Stores Corner Suff 57 E7
Storeton Mers 85 F4
Stornoway W Isles 155 D9
Storridge Hereford 50 E2
Storrington W Sus 16 C4
Storrs Cumb 99 E5
Storth Cumb 99 F6
Storwood E Yorks 96 E3
Stotfield Moray 152 A2
Stotfold C Beds 54 F3
Stottesdon Shrops 61 F6
Stoughton Leics 64 D3
Stoughton Sur 27 D7
Stoughton W Sus 16 C2
Stoul Highld 147 B10
Stoulton Worcs 50 E4
Stour Provost Dorset 13 B5
Stour Row Dorset 13 B6
Stourbridge W Mid 62 F3
Stourpaine Dorset 13 D6
Stourport on Severn Worcs 50 B3
Stourton Staffs 62 F2
Stourton Warks 51 F7
Stourton Wilts 24 F2
Stourton Caundle Dorset 12 C5
Stove Orkney 159 E7
Stove Shetland 160 L6
Stoven Suff 69 F7
Stow Borders 121 E7
Stow Lincs 78 F3
Stow Lincs 90 F2
Stow Bardolph Norf 67 D6
Stow Bedon Norf 68 E2
Stow cum Quy Cambs 55 C6
Stow Longa Cambs 54 B2
Stow Maries Essex 42 E4
Stow-on-the-Wold Glos 38 B1
Stowbridge Norf 67 D6
Stowe Shrops 48 B5
Stowe-by-Chartley Staffs 62 B4
Stowe Green Glos 36 D2
Stowell Som 12 B4
Stowford Devon 9 F6
Stowlangtoft Suff 56 C3
Stowmarket Suff 56 D4
Stowting Kent 30 E5
Stowupland Suff 56 D4
Straad Argyll 145 G9
Strachan Aberds 141 E5
Stradbroke Suff 57 B6
Stradishall Suff 55 D8
Stradsett Norf 67 D6
Stragglethorpe Lincs 78 D2
Straid S Ayrs 112 E1
Straith Dumfries 113 F8
Straiton Edin 121 C5
Straiton S Ayrs 112 D3
Straloch Aberds 141 B7
Straloch Perth 133 C7
Stramshall Staffs 75 F7
Strang IoM 84 E3
Stranraer Dumfries 104 C4
Stratfield Mortimer W Berks 26 C4
Stratfield Saye Hants 26 C4
Stratfield Turgis Hants 26 D4
Stratford London 41 F6
Stratford St Andrew Suff 57 C7
Stratford St Mary Suff 56 F4
Stratford Sub Castle Wilts 25 F6
Stratford Tony Wilts 13 B8
Stratford-upon-Avon Warks 51 D6
Strath Highld 149 A12
Strath Highld 158 E4
Strathan Highld 136 E2
Strathan Highld 156 G3
Strathan Highld 157 C8
Strathaven S Lanark 119 E7
Strathblane Stirling 119 B5
Strathcanaird Highld 156 J4
Strathcarron Highld 150 G2
Strathcoil Argyll 124 B2
Strathdon Aberds 140 C2
Strathellie Aberds 153 B10
Strathkinness Fife 129 C6
Strathmashie House Highld 137 E8
Strathmiglo Fife 128 C4
Strathmore Lodge Highld 158 F3
Strathpeffer Highld 150 F7
Strathrannoch Highld 150 D6
Strathtay Perth 133 D6
Strathvaich Lodge Highld 150 D6
Strathwhillan N Ayrs 143 E11
Strathy Highld 157 C11
Strathyre Stirling 126 C4
Stratton Corn 8 D4
Stratton Dorset 12 E4
Stratton Glos 37 D7
Stratton Audley Oxon 39 B6
Stratton on the Fosse Som 23 D8
Stratton St Margaret Swindon 38 F1
Stratton St Michael Norf 68 E5
Stratton Strawless Norf 81 E8
Stravithie Fife 129 C7
Streat E Sus 17 C7
Streatham London 28 B4
Streatley C Beds 40 B3
Streatley W Berks 39 F5
Street Lancs 92 D5
Street N Yorks 103 D5
Street Som 23 F6
Street Dinas Shrops 73 F7
Street End Kent 30 D5
Street End W Sus 16 E2
Street Gate T&W 110 D5
Street Lydan Wrex 73 F8
Streethay Staffs 62 C5
Streetlam N Yorks 101 E8
Streetly W Mid 62 E4
Streetly End Cambs 55 E7
Strefford Shrops 60 F4
Strelley Notts 76 E5
Strensall York 96 C2
Stretcholt Som 22 E4
Strete Devon 7 E6
Stretford Gtr Man 87 E6
Strethall Essex 55 F5
Stretham Cambs 55 B6
Strettington W Sus 16 D2
Stretton Ches W 73 D8
Stretton Derbys 76 C3
Stretton Rutland 65 C6
Stretton Staffs 62 C2
Stretton Staffs 63 B6
Stretton Warr 86 F4
Stretton Grandison Hereford 49 E8
Stretton-on-Dunsmore Warks 52 B2
Stretton-on-Fosse Warks 51 F7
Stretton Sugwas Hereford 49 E6
Stretton under Fosse Warks 63 F8
Stretton Westwood Shrops 61 E5
Strichen Aberds 153 C9
Strines Gtr Man 87 F7
Stringston Som 22 E3
Strixton Northants 53 C7
Stroat Glos 36 E2
Stromeferry Highld 149 E13
Stromemore Highld 149 E13
Stromness Orkney 159 H3
Stronaba Highld 136 F5
Stronachlachar Stirling 126 C3
Stronchreggan Highld 130 B4
Stronchrubie Highld 156 H5
Strone Argyll 145 E10
Strone Highld 136 F4
Strone Highld 137 B8
Strone Invclyd 118 B2
Stronmilchan Argyll 125 C7
Strontian Highld 130 C2
Strood Medway 29 C8
Strood Green Sur 28 E3
Strood Green W Sus 16 B4
Strood Green W Sus 28 F2
Stroud Glos 37 D5
Stroud Hants 15 B8
Stroud Green Essex 42 E4
Stroxton Lincs 78 F2
Struan Highld 149 E8
Struan Perth 133 C5
Strubby Lincs 91 F8
Strumpshaw Norf 69 D6
Strutherhill S Lanark 119 E7
Struy Highld 150 H6
Stryt-issa Wrex 73 E6
Stuartfield Aberds 153 D9
Stub Place Cumb 98 E2
Stubbington Hants 15 D6
Stubbins Lancs 87 C5
Stubbs Cross Kent 19 B6
Stubb's Green Norf 69 E5
Stubbs Green Norf 69 E6
Stubhampton Dorset 13 C7
Stubton Lincs 77 E8
Stuckgowan Argyll 126 D2
Stuckton Hants 14 C2
Stud Green Windsor 27 B6
Studham C Beds 40 C3
Studland Dorset 13 F8
Studley Warks 51 C5
Studley Wilts 24 B4
Studley Roger N Yorks 95 B5
Stump Cross Essex 55 E6
Stuntney Cambs 55 B6
Sturbridge Staffs 74 F5
Sturmer Essex 55 E7
Sturminster Marshall Dorset 13 D7
Sturminster Newton Dorset 13 C5
Sturry Kent 31 C5
Sturton N Lincs 90 D3
Sturton by Stow Lincs 90 F2
Sturton le Steeple Notts 89 F8
Stuston Suff 56 B5
Stutton N Yorks 95 E7
Stutton Suff 57 F5
Styal Ches E 87 F6
Styrrup Notts 89 E7
Suainebost W Isles 155 A10
Suardail W Isles 155 D9
Succoth Aberds 152 E4
Succoth Argyll 125 E8
Suckley Worcs 50 D2
Suckquoy Orkney 159 K5
Sudborough Northants 65 F6
Sudbourne Suff 57 D8
Sudbrook Lincs 78 E2
Sudbrook Mon 36 F2
Sudbrooke Lincs 78 B3
Sudbury Derbys 75 F8
Sudbury London 40 F4
Sudbury Suff 56 E2
Suddie Highld 151 F9
Sudgrove Glos 37 D6
Suffield N Yorks 103 E7
Suffield Norf 81 D8
Sugnall Staffs 74 F4
Suladale Highld 149 C8
Sulaisiadar W Isles 155 D10
Sulby IoM 84 C3
Sulgrave Northants 52 E3
Sulham W Berks 26 B4
Sulhamstead W Berks 26 C4
Sulland Orkney 159 D6
Sullington W Sus 16 C4
Sullom Shetland 160 F5
Sullom Voe Oil Terminal Shetland 160 F5
Sully V Glam 22 C3
Sumburgh Shetland 160 N6
Summer Bridge N Yorks 94 C5
Summer-house Darl 101 C7
Summercourt Corn 4 D3
Summerfield Norf 80 D3
Summergangs Hull 97 F7
Summerleaze Mon 35 F8
Summersdale W Sus 16 D2
Summerseat Gtr Man 87 C5
Summertown Oxon 39 D5
Summit Gtr Man 87 D7
Sunbury-on-Thames Sur 28 C2
Sundaywell Dumfries 113 F8
Sunderland Argyll 142 B3
Sunderland Cumb 107 F8
Sunderland T&W 111 D6
Sunderland Bridge Durham 111 F5
Sundhope Borders 115 B6
Sundon Park Luton 40 B3
Sundridge Kent 29 D5
Sunipol Argyll 146 F6
Sunk Island E Yorks 91 C6
Sunningdale Windsor 27 C7
Sunninghill Windsor 27 C7
Sunningwell Oxon 38 D4
Sunniside Durham 110 F4
Sunniside T&W 110 D5
Sunnyhurst Blackburn 86 B4
Sunnylaw Stirling 127 E6
Sunnyside W Sus 28 F4
Sunton Wilts 25 D7
Surbiton London 28 C2
Surby IoM 84 E2
Surfleet Lincs 66 B2
Surfleet Seas End Lincs 66 B2
Surlingham Norf 69 D6
Sustead Norf 81 D7
Susworth Lincs 90 D2
Sutcombe Devon 8 C5
Suton Norf 68 E3
Sutors of Cromarty Highld 151 E11
Sutterby Lincs 79 B6
Sutterton Lincs 79 F5
Sutton C Beds 54 E3
Sutton Cambs 54 B5
Sutton Kent 31 E7
Sutton London 28 C3
Sutton Mers 86 E3
Sutton N Yorks 89 B5
Sutton Norf 69 B6
Sutton Notts 77 F7
Sutton Notts 89 F7
Sutton Oxon 38 D4
Sutton Pboro 65 E7
Sutton S Yorks 89 C6
Sutton Shrops 61 F7
Sutton Shrops 74 F3
Sutton Som 23 F8
Sutton Staffs 61 B7
Sutton Suff 57 E7
Sutton Sur 27 E8
Sutton W Sus 16 C3
Sutton at Hone Kent 29 B6
Sutton Bassett Northants 64 E4
Sutton Benger Wilts 24 B4
Sutton Bonington Notts 64 B2
Sutton Bridge Lincs 66 B4
Sutton Cheney Leics 63 D8
Sutton Coldfield W Mid 62 E5
Sutton Courtenay Oxon 39 E5
Sutton Crosses Lincs 66 B4
Sutton Grange N Yorks 95 B5
Sutton Green Sur 27 D8
Sutton Howgrave N Yorks 95 B6
Sutton In Ashfield Notts 76 D4
Sutton-in-Craven N Yorks 94 E3
Sutton in the Elms Leics 64 E2
Sutton Ings Hull 97 F7
Sutton Lane Ends Ches E 75 B6
Sutton Leach Mers 86 E3
Sutton Maddock Shrops 61 D7
Sutton Mallet Som 23 F5
Sutton Mandeville Wilts 13 B7
Sutton Manor Mers 86 E3
Sutton Montis Som 12 B4
Sutton on Hull Hull 97 F7
Sutton on Sea Lincs 91 F9
Sutton-on-the-Forest N Yorks 95 C8
Sutton on the Hill Derbys 76 F2
Sutton on Trent Notts 77 C7
Sutton Scarsdale Derbys 76 C4
Sutton Scotney Hants 26 F2
Sutton St Edmund Lincs 66 C3
Sutton St James Lincs 66 C3
Sutton St Nicholas Hereford 49 E7
Sutton under Brailes Warks 51 F8
Sutton-under-Whitestonecliffe N Yorks 102 F2
Sutton upon Derwent E Yorks 96 E3
Sutton Valence Kent 30 E2
Sutton Veny Wilts 24 E3
Sutton Waldron Dorset 13 C6
Sutton Weaver Ches W 74 B2
Sutton Wick Bath 23 D7
Swaby Lincs 79 B6
Swadlincote Derbys 63 C7
Swaffham Norf 67 D8
Swaffham Bulbeck Cambs 55 C6
Swaffham Prior Cambs 55 C6
Swafield Norf 81 D8
Swainby N Yorks 102 D2
Swainshill Hereford 49 E6
Swainsthorpe Norf 68 D5
Swainswick Bath 24 C2
Swalcliffe Oxon 51 F8
Swalecliffe Kent 30 C5
Swallow Lincs 91 D5
Swallowcliffe Wilts 13 B7
Swallowfield Wokingham 26 C5
Swallownest S Yorks 89 F5
Swallows Cross Essex 42 E2
Swan Green Ches W 74 B4
Swan Green Suff 57 B6
Swanage Dorset 13 G8
Swanbister Orkney 159 H4
Swanbourne Bucks 39 B8
Swanland E Yorks 90 B3
Swanley Kent 29 C6
Swanley Village Kent 29 C6
Swanmore Hants 15 C6
Swannington Leics 63 C8
Swannington Norf 68 C4
Swanscombe Kent 29 B7
Swansea = Abertawe Swansea 33 E7
Swanton Abbott Norf 81 E8
Swanton Morley Norf 68 C3
Swanton Novers Norf 81 D6
Swanton Street Kent 30 D2
Swanwick Derbys 76 D4
Swanwick Hants 15 D6
Swarby Lincs 78 E3
Swardeston Norf 68 D5
Swarister Shetland 160 E7
Swarkestone Derbys 63 B7
Swarland Northumb 117 D7
Swarland Estate Northumb 117 D7
Swarthmoor Cumb 92 B2
Swathwick Derbys 76 C3
Swaton Lincs 78 F4
Swavesey Cambs 54 C4
Sway Hants 14 E3
Swayfield Lincs 65 B6
Swaythling Soton 14 C5
Sweet Green Worcs 49 C8
Sweetham Devon 10 E3
Sweethouse Corn 5 C5
Sweffling Suff 57 C7
Swepstone Leics 63 C7
Swerford Oxon 51 F8
Swettenham Ches E 74 C5
Swetton N Yorks 94 B4
Swffryd Caerph 35 E6
Swiftsden E Sus 18 C4
Swilland Suff 57 D5
Swillington W Yorks 95 F6
Swimbridge Devon 9 B8
Swimbridge Newland Devon 20 F5
Swinbrook Oxon 38 C2
Swinderby Lincs 77 C8
Swindon Glos 37 B6
Swindon Staffs 62 E2
Swindon Swindon 38 F1
Swine E Yorks 97 F7
Swinefleet E Yorks 89 B8
Swineshead Bedford 53 C8
Swineshead Lincs 78 E5
Swineshead Bridge Lincs 78 E5
Swiney Highld 158 G4
Swinford Leics 52 B3
Swinford Oxon 38 D4
Swingate Notts 76 E5
Swingfield Minnis Kent 31 E6
Swingfield Street Kent 31 E6
Swinhoe Northumb 117 B8
Swinhope Lincs 91 E6
Swining Shetland 160 G6
Swinithwaite N Yorks 101 F5
Swinnow Moor W Yorks 94 F5
Swinscoe Staffs 75 E8
Swinside Hall Borders 116 C3
Swinstead Lincs 65 B7
Swinton Borders 122 E4
Swinton Gtr Man 87 D5
Swinton N Yorks 94 B5
Swinton N Yorks 96 B3
Swinton S Yorks 88 E5
Swintonmill Borders 122 E4
Swithland Leics 64 C2
Swordale Highld 151 E8
Swordland Highld 147 B10
Swordly Highld 157 C10
Sworton Heath Ches E 86 F4
Swydd-ffynnon Ceredig 47 C5
Swynnerton Staffs 75 F5
Swyre Dorset 12 F3
Sychtyn Powys 59 D6
Syde Glos 37 C6
Sydenham London 28 B4
Sydenham Oxon 39 D7
Sydenham Damerel Devon 6 B2
Syderstone Norf 80 D4
Sydling St Nicholas Dorset 12 E4
Sydmonton Hants 26 D2
Syerston Notts 77 E7
Syke Gtr Man 87 C6
Sykehouse S Yorks 89 C7
Sykes Lancs 93 D6
Syleham Suff 57 B6
Sylen Carms 33 D6
Symbister Shetland 160 G7
Symington S Ayrs 118 F3
Symington S Lanark 120 F2
Symonds Yat Hereford 36 C2
Symondsbury Dorset 12 E2
Synod Inn Ceredig 46 D3
Syre Highld 157 E9
Syreford Glos 37 B7
Syresham Northants 52 E4
Syston Leics 64 C3
Syston Lincs 78 E2
Sytchampton Worcs 50 C3
Sywell Northants 53 C6

T

Taagan Highld 150 E3
Tàbost W Isles 155 A10
Tabost W Isles 155 F8
Tackley Oxon 38 B4
Tacleit W Isles 154 D6
Tacolneston Norf 68 E4
Tadcaster N Yorks 95 E7
Taddington Derbys 75 B8
Taddiport Devon 9 C6
Tadley Hants 26 C4
Tadlow C Beds 54 E3
Tadmarton Oxon 51 F8
Tadworth Sur 28 D3
Tafarn-y-gelyn Denb 73 C5
Tafarnau-bach Bl Gwent 35 C5
Taff's Well Rhondda 35 F5
Tafolwern Powys 59 D5
Tai Conwy 83 E7
Tai-bach Powys 59 B8
Tai-mawr Conwy 72 E3
Tai-Ucha Denb 72 D4
Taibach Neath 34 F1
Taigh a Ghearraidh W Isles 148 A2
Tain Highld 151 C10
Tain Highld 158 D4
Tainant Wrex 73 E6
Tainlon Gwyn 82 F4
Tairbeart = Tarbert W Isles 154 G6
Tai'r-Bull Powys 34 B3
Tairgwaith Neath 33 C8
Takeley Essex 42 B1
Takeley Street Essex 41 B8
Tal-sarn Ceredig 46 D4
Tal-y-bont Ceredig 58 F3
Tal-y-Bont Conwy 83 E7
Tal-y-bont Gwyn 71 E6
Tal-y-bont Gwyn 83 D6
Tal-y-cafn Conwy 83 D7
Tal-y-llyn Gwyn 58 D4
Tal-y-wern Powys 58 D5
Talachddu Powys 48 F2
Talacre Flint 85 F2
Talardd Gwyn 59 B5
Talaton Devon 11 E5
Talbenny Pembs 44 D3
Talbot Green Rhondda 34 F4
Talbot Village Poole 13 E8
Tale Devon 11 D5
Talerddig Powys 59 D6
Talgarreg Ceredig 46 D3
Talgarth Powys 48 F3
Talisker Highld 149 E8
Talke Staffs 74 D5
Talkin Cumb 109 D5
Talla Linnfoots Borders 114 B4
Talladale Highld 150 D2
Tallarn Green Wrex 73 E8
Tallentire Cumb 107 F8
Talley Carms 46 F5
Tallington Lincs 65 D7
Talmine Highld 157 C8
Talog Carms 32 B4
Talsarn Carms 34 B1
Talsarnau Gwyn 71 D7
Talskiddy Corn 4 C4
Talwrn Anglesey 82 D4
Talwrn Wrex 73 E6
Talybont-on-Usk Powys 35 B5
Talygarn Rhondda 34 F4
Talyllyn Powys 35 B5
Talysarn Gwyn 82 F4
Talywain Torf 35 D6
Tame Bridge N Yorks 102 D3
Tamerton Foliot Plym 6 C2
Tamworth Staffs 63 D6
Tan Hinon Powys 59 F5
Tan-lan Conwy 83 E7
Tan-lan Gwyn 71 C7
Tan-y-bwlch Gwyn 71 C7
Tan-y-fron Conwy 72 C3
Tan-y-graig Anglesey 82 D5
Tan-y-graig Gwyn 70 D4
Tan-y-groes Ceredig 45 E4
Tan-y-pistyll Powys 59 B7
Tan-yr-allt Gwyn 82 F4
Tandem W Yorks 88 C2
Tanden Kent 19 B6
Tandridge Sur 28 D4
Tanerdy Carms 33 B5
Tanfield Durham 110 D4
Tanfield Lea Durham 110 D4
Tangasdal W Isles 148 J1
Tangiers Pembs 44 D4
Tangley Hants 25 D8
Tanglwst Carms 46 F2
Tangmere W Sus 16 D3
Tangwick Shetland 160 F4
Tankersley S Yorks 88 D4
Tankerton Kent 30 C5
Tannach Highld 158 F5
Tannachie Aberds 141 F6
Tannadice Angus 134 D4
Tannington Suff 57 C6
Tansley Derbys 76 D3
Tansley Knoll Derbys 76 C3
Tansor Northants 65 E7
Tantobie Durham 110 D4
Tanton N Yorks 102 C3
Tanworth-in-Arden Warks 51 B6
Tanygrisiau Gwyn 71 C7
Tanyrhydiau Ceredig 47 C6
Taobh a Chaolais W Isles 148 G2
Taobh a Thuath Loch Aineort W Isles 148 F2
Taobh a Tuath Loch Baghasdail W Isles 148 F2
Taobh a'Ghlinne W Isles 155 F8
Taobh Tuath W Isles 154 J4
Taplow Bucks 40 F2
Tapton Derbys 76 B3
Tarbat Ho. Highld 151 D10
Tarbert Argyll 143 C7
Tarbert Argyll 144 E5
Tarbert Argyll 145 G7
Tarbert = Tairbeart W Isles 154 G6
Tarbet Argyll 126 D2
Tarbet Highld 147 B10
Tarbet Highld 156 E4
Tarbock Green Mers 86 F2
Tarbolton S Ayrs 112 B4
Tarbrax S Lanark 120 D3
Tardebigge Worcs 50 C5
Tarfside Angus 134 B4
Tarland Aberds 140 D3
Tarleton Lancs 86 B2
Tarlogie Highld 151 C10
Tarlscough Lancs 86 C2
Tarlton Glos 37 E6
Tarnbrook Lancs 93 D5
Tarporley Ches W 74 C2
Tarr Som 22 F3
Tarrant Crawford Dorset 13 D7
Tarrant Gunville Dorset 13 C7
Tarrant Hinton Dorset 13 C7
Tarrant Keyneston Dorset 13 D7
Tarrant Launceston Dorset 13 D7
Tarrant Monkton Dorset 13 D7
Tarrant Rawston Dorset 13 D7
Tarrant Rushton Dorset 13 D7
Tarrel Highld 151 C11
Tarring Neville E Sus 17 D8
Tarrington Hereford 49 E8
Tarsappie Perth 128 B3
Tarskavaig Highld 149 H10
Tarves Aberds 153 E8
Tarvie Highld 150 F7
Tarvie Perth 133 C7
Tarvin Ches W 73 C8
Tasburgh Norf 68 E5
Tasley Shrops 61 E6
Taston Oxon 38 B3
Tatenhill Staffs 63 B6
Tathall End M Keynes 53 E6
Tatham Lancs 93 C6
Tathwell Lincs 91 F7
Tatling End Bucks 40 F3
Tatsfield Sur 28 D5
Tattenhall Ches W 73 D8
Tattenhoe M Keynes 53 F6
Tatterford Norf 80 E4
Tattersett Norf 80 D4
Tattershall Lincs 78 D5
Tattershall Bridge Lincs 78 D4
Tattershall Thorpe Lincs 78 D5
Tattingstone Suff 56 F5
Tatworth Som 11 D8
Taunton Som 11 B7
Taverham Norf 68 C4
Tavernspite Pembs 32 C2
Tavistock Devon 6 B2
Taw Green Devon 9 E8
Tawstock Devon 9 B7
Taxal Derbys 75 B7
Tay Bridge Dundee 129 B6
Tayinloan Argyll 143 D7
Taymouth Castle Perth 132 E4
Taynish Argyll 144 E6
Taynton Glos 36 B4
Taynton Oxon 38 C2
Taynuilt Argyll 125 B6
Tayport Fife 129 B6
Tayvallich Argyll 144 E6
Tealby Lincs 91 E5
Tealing Angus 134 F4
Teangue Highld 149 H11
Teanna Mhachair W Isles 148 B2
Tebay Cumb 99 D8
Tebworth C Beds 40 B2
Tedburn St Mary Devon 10 E3
Teddington Glos 50 F4
Teddington London 28 B2
Tedstone Delamere Hereford 49 D8
Tedstone Wafre Hereford 49 D8
Teeton Northants 52 B4
Teffont Evias Wilts 24 F4
Teffont Magna Wilts 24 F4
Tegryn Pembs 45 F4
Teigh Rutland 65 C5
Teigncombe Devon 9 F8
Teigngrace Devon 7 B6
Teignmouth Devon 7 B7
Telford Telford 61 D6
Telham E Sus 18 D4
Tellisford Som 24 D3
Telscombe E Sus 17 D8
Telscombe Cliffs E Sus 17 D7
Templand Dumfries 114 F3
Temple Corn 5 B6
Temple Glasgow 118 C5
Temple Midloth 121 D6
Temple Balsall W Mid 51 B7
Temple Bar Carms 33 C6
Temple Bar Ceredig 46 D4
Temple Cloud Bath 23 D8
Temple Combe Som 12 B5
Temple Ewell Kent 31 E6
Temple Grafton Warks 51 D6
Temple Guiting Glos 37 B7
Temple Herdewyke Warks 51 D8
Temple Hirst N Yorks 89 B7
Temple Normanton Derbys 76 C4
Temple Sowerby Cumb 99 B8
Templehall Fife 128 E4
Templeton Devon 10 C3
Templeton Pembs 32 C2
Templeton Bridge Devon 10 C3
Templetown Durham 110 D4
Tempsford C Beds 54 D2
Ten Mile Bank Norf 67 E6
Tenbury Wells Worcs 49 C7
Tenby = Dinbych-Y-Pysgod Pembs 32 D2
Tendring Essex 43 B7
Tendring Green Essex 43 B7
Tenston Orkney 159 G3
Tenterden Kent 19 B5
Terling Essex 42 C3
Ternhill Shrops 74 F3
Terregles Banks Dumfries 107 B6
Terrick Bucks 39 D8
Terrington N Yorks 96 B2
Terrington St Clement Norf 66 C5
Terrington St John Norf 66 C5
Teston Kent 29 D8
Testwood Hants 14 C4
Tetbury Glos 37 E5
Tetbury Upton Glos 37 E5
Tetchill Shrops 73 F7
Tetcott Devon 8 E5
Tetford Lincs 79 B6
Tetney Lincs 91 D7
Tetney Lock Lincs 91 D7
Tetsworth Oxon 39 D6
Tettenhall W Mid 62 E2
Teuchan Aberds 153 E10
Teversal Notts 76 C4
Teversham Cambs 55 D5
Teviothead Borders 115 D7
Tewel Aberds 141 F7
Tewin Herts 41 C5
Tewkesbury Glos 50 F3
Teynham Kent 30 C3
Thackthwaite Cumb 98 B3
Thainston Aberds 135 B6
Thakeham W Sus 16 C5
Thame Oxon 39 D7
Thames Ditton Sur 28 C2
Thames Haven Thurrock 42 F3
Thamesmead London 41 F7
Thanington Kent 30 D5
Thankerton S Lanark 120 F2
Tharston Norf 68 E4
Thatcham W Berks 26 C3
Thatto Heath Mers 86 E3
Thaxted Essex 55 F7
The Aird Highld 149 C9
The Arms Norf 67 E8
The Bage Hereford 48 E4
The Balloch Perth 127 C7
The Barony Orkney 159 F3
The Bog Shrops 60 E3
The Bourne Sur 27 E6
The Braes Highld 149 E10
The Broad Hereford 49 C6
The Butts Som 24 E2
The Camp Glos 37 D6
The Camp Herts 40 D4
The Chequer Wrex 73 E8
The City Bucks 39 E7
The Common Wilts 25 F7
The Craigs Highld 150 B7
The Cronk IoM 84 C3
The Dell Suff 69 E7
The Den N Ayrs 118 D3
The Eals Northumb 116 F3
The Eaves Glos 36 D3
The Flatt Cumb 109 B5
The Four Alls Shrops 74 F3
The Garths Shetland 160 B8
The Green Cumb 98 F3
The Green Wilts 24 F3
The Grove Dumfries 107 B6
The Hall Shetland 160 D8
The Haven W Sus 27 F8
The Heath Norf 81 E7
The Heath Suff 56 F5
The Hill Cumb 98 F3
The Howe Cumb 99 F6
The Howe IoM 84 F1
The Hundred Hereford 49 C7
The Lee Bucks 40 D2
The Lhen IoM 84 B3
The Marsh Powys 60 E3
The Marsh Wilts 37 F7
The Middles Durham 110 D5
The Moor Kent 18 C4
The Mumbles = Y Mwmbwls Swansea 33 F7
The Murray S Lanark 119 D6
The Neuk Aberds 141 E6
The Oval Bath 24 C2
The Pole of Itlaw Aberds 153 C6
The Quarry Glos 36 E4
The Rhos Pembs 32 C1
The Rock Telford 61 D6
The Ryde Herts 41 D5
The Sands Sur 27 E6
The Stocks Kent 19 C6
The Throat Wokingham 27 C6
The Vauld Hereford 49 E7
The Wyke Shrops 61 D7
Theakston N Yorks 101 F8
Thealby N Lincs 90 C2
Theale Som 23 E6
Theale W Berks 26 B4
Thearne E Yorks 97 F6
Theberton Suff 57 C8
Theddingworth Leics 64 F3
Theddlethorpe All Saints Lincs 91 F8
Theddlethorpe St Helen Lincs 91 F8
Thelbridge Barton Devon 10 C2
Thelnetham Suff 56 B4
Thelveton Norf 68 F4
Thelwall Warr 86 F4
Themelthorpe Norf 81 E6
Thenford Northants 52 E3
Therfield Herts 54 F4
Thetford Lincs 65 C8
Thetford Norf 67 F8
Theydon Bois Essex 41 E7
Thickwood Wilts 24 B3
Thimbleby Lincs 78 C5
Thimbleby N Yorks 102 E2
Thingwall Mers 85 F3
Thirdpart N Ayrs 118 E1
Thirlby N Yorks 102 F2
Thirlestane Borders 121 E8
Thirn N Yorks 101 F7
Thirsk N Yorks 102 F2
Thirtleby E Yorks 97 F7
Thistleton Lancs 92 F4
Thistleton Rutland 65 C6
Thistley Green Suff 55 B7
Thixendale N Yorks 96 C4
Thockrington Northumb 110 B2
Tholomas Drove Cambs 66 D3
Tholthorpe N Yorks 95 C7
Thomas Chapel Pembs 32 D2
Thomas Close Cumb 108 E4
Thomastown Aberds 152 E5
Thompson Norf 68 E2
Thomshill Moray 152 C2
Thong Kent 29 B7
Thongsbridge W Yorks 88 D2
Thoralby N Yorks 101 F5
Thoresway Lincs 91 E5
Thorganby Lincs 91 E6
Thorganby N Yorks 96 E2
Thorgill N Yorks 103 E5
Thorington Suff 57 B8
Thorington Street Suff 56 F4
Thorlby N Yorks 94 D2
Thorley Herts 41 C7
Thorley Street Herts 41 C7
Thorley Street IoW 14 F4
Thormanby N Yorks 95 B7
Thornaby-on-Tees Stockton 102 C2
Thornage Norf 81 D6
Thornborough Bucks 52 F5
Thornborough N Yorks 95 B5
Thornbury Devon 9 D6
Thornbury Hereford 49 D8
Thornbury S Glos 36 E3
Thornbury W Yorks 94 F4
Thornby Northants 52 B4
Thorncliffe Staffs 75 D7
Thorncombe Dorset 11 D8
Thorncombe Dorset 13 D6
Thorncombe Street Sur 27 E8
Thorncote Green C Beds 54 E2
Thorncross IoW 14 F5
Thorndon Suff 56 C5
Thorndon Cross Devon 9 E7
Thorne S Yorks 89 C7
Thorne St Margaret Som 11 B5
Thorner W Yorks 95 E6
Thorney Notts 77 B8
Thorney Pboro 66 D2
Thorney Crofts E Yorks 91 B6
Thorney Green Suff 56 C4
Thorney Hill Hants 14 E2
Thorney Toll Pboro 66 D3
Thornfalcon Som 11 B7
Thornford Dorset 12 C4
Thorngumbald E Yorks 91 B6
Thornham Norf 80 C3
Thornham Magna Suff 56 B5
Thornham Parva Suff 56 B5
Thornhaugh Pboro 65 D7
Thornhill Cardiff 35 F5
Thornhill Cumb 98 D2
Thornhill Derbys 88 F2
Thornhill Dumfries 113 E8
Thornhill Soton 15 C5
Thornhill Stirling 127 E5
Thornhill W Yorks 88 C3
Thornhill Edge W Yorks 88 C3
Thornhill Lees W Yorks 88 C3
Thornholme E Yorks 97 C7
Thornley Durham 110 F4
Thornley Durham 111 F6
Thornliebank E Renf 118 D5
Thorns Suff 55 D8
Thorns Green Ches E 87 F5
Thornsett Derbys 87 F8
Thornthwaite Cumb 98 B4
Thornthwaite N Yorks 94 D4
Thornton Angus 134 E3
Thornton Bucks 53 F5
Thornton E Yorks 96 E3
Thornton Fife 128 E4
Thornton Lancs 92 E3
Thornton Leics 63 D8
Thornton Lincs 78 C5
Thornton Mbro 102 C2
Thornton Mers 85 D4
Thornton Northumb 123 E5
Thornton Pembs 44 E4
Thornton W Yorks 94 F4
Thornton Curtis N Lincs 90 C4
Thornton Heath London 28 C4
Thornton Hough Mers 85 F4
Thornton in Craven N Yorks 94 E2
Thornton-le-Beans N Yorks 102 E1
Thornton-le-Clay N Yorks 96 C2
Thornton-le-Dale N Yorks 103 F6
Thornton le Moor Lincs 90 E4
Thornton-le-Moor N Yorks 102 F1
Thornton-le-Moors Ches W 73 B8
Thornton-le-Street N Yorks 102 F2
Thornton Rust N Yorks 100 F4
Thornton Steward N Yorks 101 F6
Thornton Watlass N Yorks 101 F7
Thorntonhall S Lanark 119 D5
Thorntonloch E Loth 122 B3
Thorntonpark Northumb
Thornwood Common Essex
Thorndykes
Thoroton
Thorp Arch W Yorks 95 E7
Thorpe Derbys 75 D8
Thorpe E Yorks 97 E5
Thorpe Lincs 91 F8
Thorpe N Yorks 94 C3
Thorpe Norf 69 E7
Thorpe Notts 77 E7
Thorpe Sur 27 C8
Thorpe Abbotts Norf 57 B5
Thorpe Acre Leics 64 B2
Thorpe Arnold Leics 64 B4
Thorpe Audlin W Yorks 89 C5
Thorpe Bassett N Yorks 96 B4
Thorpe Bay Southend 43 F5
Thorpe by Water Rutland 65 E5
Thorpe Common Suff 57 F6
Thorpe Constantine Staffs 63 D6
Thorpe Culvert Lincs 79 C7
Thorpe End Norf 69 C5
Thorpe Fendykes Lincs 79 C7
Thorpe Green Essex 43 B7
Thorpe Green Suff 56 D3
Thorpe Hesley S Yorks 88 E4
Thorpe in Balne S Yorks 89 C6
Thorpe in the Fallows Lincs 90 F3
Thorpe Langton Leics 64 E4
Thorpe Larches Durham 102 B1
Thorpe-le-Soken Essex 43 B7
Thorpe le Street E Yorks 96 E4
Thorpe Malsor Northants 53 B6
Thorpe Mandeville Northants 52 E3
Thorpe Market Norf 81 D8
Thorpe Marriot Norf 68 C4
Thorpe Morieux Suff 56 D3
Thorpe on the Hill Lincs 78 C2
Thorpe Salvin S Yorks 89 F6
Thorpe Satchville Leics 64 C4
Thorpe St Andrew Norf 69 D5
Thorpe St Peter Lincs 79 C7
Thorpe Thewles Stockton 102 B2
Thorpe Tilney Lincs 78 D4
Thorpe Underwood N Yorks 95 D7
Thorpe Waterville Northants 65 F7
Thorpe Willoughby N Yorks 95 F8
Thorpeness Suff 57 D8
Thorrington Essex 43 C6
Thorverton Devon 10 D4
Thrandeston Suff 56 B5
Thrapston Northants 53 B7
Thrashbush N Lanark 119 C7
Threapland Cumb 107 F8
Threapland N Yorks 94 C2
Threapwood Ches W 73 E8
Threapwood Staffs 75 E7
Three Ashes Hereford 36 B2
Three Bridges W Sus 28 F3
Three Burrows Corn 3 B6
Three Chimneys Kent 18 B5
Three Cocks Powys 48 F3
Three Crosses Swansea 33 E6
Three Cups Corner E Sus 18 C3
Three Holes Norf 66 D5
Three Leg Cross E Sus 18 B3
Three Legged Cross Dorset 13 D8
Three Oaks E Sus 18 D5
Threehammer Common Norf 69 C6
Threekingham Lincs 78 F3
Threemile Cross Wokingham 26 C5
Threemilestone Corn 3 B6
Threemiletown W Loth 120 B3
Threlkeld Cumb 99 B5
Threshfield N Yorks 94 C2
Thrigby Norf 69 C7
Thringarth Durham 100 B4
Thringstone Leics 63 C8
Thrintoft N Yorks 101 E8
Thriplow Cambs 54 E5
Throckenholt Lincs 66 D3
Throcking Herts 54 F4
Throckley T&W 110 C4
Throckmorton Worcs 50 E4
Throphill Northumb 117 F7
Thropton Northumb 117 D6
Throsk Stirling 127 E7
Throwleigh Devon 9 E8
Throwley Kent 30 D3
Thrumpton Notts 76 F5
Thrumster Highld 158 F5
Thrunton Northumb 117 C6
Thrupp Glos 37 D5
Thrupp Oxon 38 C4
Thrushelton Devon 9 F6
Thrussington Leics 64 C3
Thruxton Hants 25 E7
Thruxton Hereford 49 F6
Thrybergh S Yorks 89 E5
Thulston Derbys 76 F4
Thundergay N Ayrs 143 D9
Thundersley Essex 42 F3
Thundridge Herts 41 C6
Thurcaston Leics 64 C2
Thurcroft S Yorks 89 F5
Thurgarton Norf 81 D7
Thurgarton Notts 77 E6
Thurgoland S Yorks 88 D3
Thurlaston Leics 64 E2
Thurlaston Warks 52 B2
Thurlbear Som 11 B7
Thurlby Lincs 65 C8
Thurlby Lincs 78 C2
Thurleigh Bedford 53 D8
Thurlestone Devon 6 E4
Thurloxton Som 22 F4
Thurlstone S Yorks 88 D3
Thurlton Norf 69 E7
Thurlwood Ches E 74 D5
Thurmaston Leics 64 D3
Thurnby Leics 64 D3
Thurne Norf 69 C7
Thurnham Kent 30 D2
Thurnham Lancs 92 D4
Thurning Norf 81 E6
Thurning Northants 65 F7
Thurnscoe S Yorks 89 D5
Thurnscoe East S Yorks
Thursby Cumb
Thursford N
Thursley

Thwaite Suff 56 C5
Thwaite St Mary Norf 69 E6
Thwaites W Yorks 94 E3
Thwaites Brow W Yorks 94 E3
Thwing E Yorks 97 B6
Tibbermore Perth 128 B2
Tibberton Glos 36 B4
Tibberton Telford 61 B6
Tibberton Worcs 50 D4
Tibenham Norf 68 F4
Tibshelf Derbys 76 C4
Tibthorpe E Yorks 97 D5
Ticehurst E Sus 18 B3
Tichborne Hants 26 F3
Tickencote Rutland 65 D6
Tickenham N Som 23 B6
Tickhill S Yorks 89 E6
Ticklerton Shrops 60 E4
Ticknall Derbys 63 B7
Tickton E Yorks 97 E6
Tidcombe Wilts 25 D7
Tiddington Oxon 39 D6
Tiddington Warks 51 D7
Tidebrook E Sus 18 C3
Tideford Corn 5 D8
Tideford Cross Corn 5 C8
Tidenham Glos 36 E2
Tideswell Derbys 75 B8
Tidmarsh W Berks 26 B4
Tidmington Warks 51 F7
Tidpit Hants 13 C8
Tidworth Wilts 25 E7
Tiers Cross Pembs 44 D4
Tiffield Northants 52 D4
Tifty Aberds 153 D7
Tigerton Angus 135 C5
Tigh-na-Blair Perth 127 C6
Tighnabruaich Argyll 145 F8
Tighnafiline Highld 155 J13
Tigley Devon 7 C5
Tilbrook Cambs 53 C8
Tilbury Thurrock 29 B7
Tilbury Juxta Clare Essex 55 E8
Tile Cross W Mid 63 F5
Tile Hill W Mid 51 B7
Tilehurst Reading 26 B4
Tilford Sur 27 E6
Tilgate W Sus 28 F3
Tilgate Forest Row W Sus 28 F3
Tillathrowie Aberds 152 E4
Tilley Shrops 60 B5
Tillicoultry Clack 127 E8
Tillingham Essex 43 D5
Tillington Hereford 49 E6
Tillington W Sus 16 B3
Tillington Common Hereford 49 E6
Tillyarblet Angus 135 C5
Tillybirloch Aberds 141 D5
Tillycorthie Aberds 141 B8
Tillydrine Aberds 140 E5
Tillyfour Aberds 140 C4
Tillyfourie Aberds 140 C5
Tillygarmond Aberds 140 E5
Tillygreig Aberds 141 B7
Tillykerrie Aberds 141 B7
Tilmanstone Kent 31 D7
Tilney All Saints Norf 67 C5
Tilney High End Norf 67 C5
Tilney St Lawrence Norf 66 C5
Tilshead Wilts 24 E5
Tilstock Shrops 74 F2
Tilston Ches W 73 D8
Tilstone Fearnall Ches W 74 C2
Tilsworth C Beds 40 B2
Tilton on the Hill Leics 64 D4
Timberland Lincs 78 D4
Timbersbrook Ches E 75 C5
Timberscombe Som 21 E8
Timble N Yorks 94 D4
Timperley Gtr Man 87 F5
Timsbury Bath 23 D8
Timsbury Hants 14 B4
Timsgearraidh W Isles 154 D5
Timworth Green Suff 56 C2
Tincleton Dorset 13 E5
Tindale Cumb 109 D6
Tingewick Bucks 52 F4
Tingley W Yorks 88 B3
Tingrith C Beds 53 F8
Tingwall Orkney 159 F4
Tinhay Devon 9 F5
Tinshill W Yorks 95 F5
Tinsley S Yorks 88 E5
Tintagel Corn 8 F2
Tintern Parva Mon 36 D2
Tintinhull Som 12 C3
Tintwistle Derbys 87 E8
Tinwald Dumfries 114 F3
Tinwell Rutland 65 D7
Tipperty Aberds 141 B8
Tipsend Norf 66 E5
Tipton W Mid 62 E3
Tipton St John Devon 11 E5
Tiptree Essex 42 C4
Tir-y-dail Carms 33 C7
Tirabad Powys 47 E7
Tiraghoil Argyll 146 J6
Tirley Glos 37 B5
Tirphil Caerph 35 D5
Tirril Cumb 99 B7
Tisbury Wilts 13 B7
Tisman's Common W Sus 27 F8
Tissington Derbys 75 D8
Titchberry Devon 8 B4
Titchfield Hants 15 D6
Titchmarsh Northants 53 B8
Titchwell Norf 80 C3
Tithby Notts 77 F6
Titley Hereford 48 C5
Titlington Northumb 117 C7
Titsey Sur 28 D5
Tittensor Staffs 75 F5
Tittleshall Norf 80 E4
Tiverton Ches W 74 C2
Tiverton Devon 10 C4
Tivetshall St Margaret Norf 68 F4
Tivetshall St Mary Norf 68 F4
Tividale W…

Todrig Borders 115 C7
Todwick S Yorks 89 F5
Toft Cambs 54 D4
Toft Lincs 65 C7
Toft Hill Durham 101 B6
Toft Hill Lincs 78 C5
Toft Monks Norf 69 E7
Toft next Newton Lincs 90 F4
Toftrees Norf 80 E4
Tofts Highld 158 D5
Toftwood Norf 68 C2
Togston Northumb 117 D8
Tokavaig Highld 149 G11
Tokers Green Oxon 26 B5
Tolastadh a Chaolais W Isles 154 D6
Tolastadh bho Thuath W Isles 155 C10
Toll Bar S Yorks 89 D6
Toll End W Mid 62 E3
Toll of Birness Aberds 153 E10
Tolland Som 22 F3
Tollard Royal Wilts 13 C7
Tollbar End W Mid 51 B8
Toller Fratrum Dorset 12 E3
Toller Porcorum Dorset 12 E3
Tollerton N Yorks 95 C8
Tollerton Notts 77 F6
Tollesbury Essex 43 C5
Tolleshunt D'Arcy Essex 43 C5
Tolleshunt Major Essex 43 C5
Tolm W Isles 155 D9
Tolpuddle Dorset 13 E5
Tolvah Highld 138 E4
Tolworth London 28 C2
Tomatin Highld 138 B4
Tombreck Highld 151 H9
Tomchrasky Highld 137 C5
Tomdoun Highld 136 D4
Tomich Highld 137 B6
Tomich Highld 151 D9
Tomich House Highld 151 G8
Tomintoul Aberds 139 E7
Tomintoul Moray 139 C7
Tomnaven Moray 152 E4
Tomnavoulin Moray 139 B8
Ton-Pentre Rhondda 34 E3
Tonbridge Kent 29 E6
Tondu Bridgend 34 F2
Tonfanau Gwyn 58 D2
Tong Shrops 61 D7
Tong W Yorks 94 F5
Tong Norton Shrops 61 D7
Tonge Leics 63 B8
Tongham Sur 27 E6
Tongland Dumfries 106 D3
Tongue Highld 157 D8
Tongue End Lincs 65 C8
Tongwynlais Cardiff 35 F5
Tonna Neath 34 E1
Tonwell Herts 41 C6
Tonypandy Rhondda 34 E3
Tonyrefail Rhondda 34 F4
Toot Baldon Oxon 39 D5
Toot Hill Essex 41 D8
Toothill Hants 14 C4
Top of Hebers Gtr Man 87 D6
Topcliffe N Yorks 95 B7
Topcroft Norf 69 E5
Topcroft Street Norf 69 E5
Toppesfield Essex 55 F8
Toppings Gtr Man 86 C5
Topsham Devon 10 F4
Torbay Torbay 7 D7
Torbeg N Ayrs 143 F10
Torboll Farm Highld 151 B10
Torbrex Stirling 127 E6
Torbryan Devon 7 C6
Torcross Devon 7 E6
Tore Highld 151 F9
Torinturk Argyll 145 G7
Torksey Lincs 77 B8
Torlum W Isles 148 C2
Torlundy Highld 131 B5
Tormarton S Glos 24 B2
Tormisdale Argyll 142 C2
Tormitchell S Ayrs 112 E2
Tormore N Ayrs 143 E9
Tornagrain Highld 151 G10
Tornahaish Aberds 139 D8
Tornaveen Aberds 140 D5
Torness Highld 137 B8
Toronto Durham 110 F4
Torpenhow Cumb 108 F2
Torphichen W Loth 120 B2
Torphins Aberds 140 D5
Torpoint Corn 6 D2
Torquay Torbay 7 C7
Torquhan Borders 121 E7
Torran Argyll 124 E4
Torran Highld 149 D10
Torran Highld 151 D10
Torrance E Dunb 119 B6
Torrans Argyll 146 J7
Torranyard N Ayrs 118 E3
Torre Torbay 7 C7
Torridon Highld 150 F2
Torridon Ho. Highld 149 C13
Torrin Highld 149 F10
Torrisdale Highld 157 C9
Torrisdale-Square Argyll 143 E8
Torrish Highld 157 H12
Torrisholme Lancs 92 C4
Torroble Highld 157 J8
Torry Aberdeen 141 D8
Torry Aberds 152 E4
Torryburn Fife 128 F2
Torterston Aberds 153 D10
Torthorwald Dumfries 107 B7
Tortington W Sus 16 D4
Tortworth S Glos 36 E4
Torvaig Highld 149 D9
Torver Cumb 98 E4
Torwood Falk 127 F7
Torworth Notts 89 F7
Tosberry Devon 8 B4
Toscaig Highld 149 E12
Toseland Cambs 54 C3
Tosside N Yorks 93 D7
Tostock Suff 56 C3
Totaig Highld 148 C7
149 F13
149 D9
157 C11
91 F8
14 F4
7 C6
6 F5
F4
38
6

Towie Aberds 140 C3
Towie Aberds 153 B8
Towiemore Moray 152 D3
Town End Cambs 66 E4
Town End Cumb 99 F6
Town Row E Sus 18 B2
Town Yetholm Borders 116 B4
Townend W Dunb 118 B4
Towngate Lincs 65 C8
Townhead Cumb 108 F5
Townhead Dumfries 106 E3
Townhead S Ayrs 112 D2
Townhead S Yorks 88 D2
Townhead of Greenlaw Dumfries 106 C4
Townhill Fife 128 F3
Townsend Bucks 39 D7
Townsend Herts 40 D4
Townshend Corn 2 C4
Towthorpe York 96 D2
Towton N Yorks 95 F7
Towyn Conwy 72 B3
Toxteth Mers 85 F4
Toynton All Saints Lincs 79 C6
Toynton Fen Side Lincs 79 C6
Toynton St Peter Lincs 79 C7
Toy's Hill Kent 29 D5
Trabboch E Ayrs 112 B4
Traboe Corn 3 D6
Tradespark Highld 151 F11
Tradespark Orkney 159 H5
Trafford Park Gtr Man 87 E5
Trallong Powys 34 B3
Tranent E Loth 121 B7
Tranmere Mers 85 F4
Trantlebeg Highld 157 D11
Trantlemore Highld 157 D11
Tranwell Northumb 117 F7
Trapp Carms 33 C7
Traprain E Loth 121 B8
Traquair Borders 121 F6
Trawden Lancs 94 F2
Trawsfynydd Gwyn 71 D8
Tre-Gibbon Rhondda 34 D3
Tre-Taliesin Ceredig 58 E3
Tre-vaughan Carms 32 B4
Tre-wyn Mon 35 B7
Trealaw Rhondda 34 E4
Treales Lancs 92 F4
Trearddur Anglesey 82 D2
Treaslane Highld 149 C8
Trebanog Rhondda 34 E4
Trebanos Neath 33 D8
Trebartha Corn 5 B7
Trebarwith Corn 8 F2
Trebetherick Corn 4 B4
Treborough Som 22 F2
Trebudannon Corn 4 C3
Trebullett Corn 5 B8
Treburley Corn 5 B8
Trebyan Corn 5 C5
Trecastle Powys 34 B2
Trecenydd Caerph 35 F5
Trecwn Pembs 44 B4
Trecynon Rhondda 34 D3
Tredavoe Corn 2 D3
Treddiog Pembs 44 C3
Tredegar Bl Gwent 35 D5
Tredegar = Newydd New Tredegar Caerph 35 D5
Tredington Glos 37 B6
Tredington Warks 51 E7
Tredinnick Corn 4 B4
Tredomen Powys 48 F3
Tredunnock Mon 35 E7
Tredustan Powys 48 F3
Treen Corn 2 D2
Treeton S Yorks 88 F5
Tref-Y-Clawdd = Knighton Powys 48 B4
Trefaldwyn = Montgomery Powys 60 E2
Trefasser Pembs 44 B3
Trefdraeth Anglesey 82 D4
Trefdraeth = Newport Pembs 45 F2
Trefecca Powys 48 F3
Trefechan Ceredig 58 F2
Trefeglwys Powys 59 E6
Trefenter Ceredig 46 C5
Treffgarne Pembs 44 C4
Treffynnon = Holywell Flint 73 B5
Treffynnon Pembs 44 C3
Trefgarn Owen Pembs 44 C3
Trefil Bl Gwent 35 C5
Trefilan Ceredig 46 D4
Trefin Pembs 44 B3
Treflach Shrops 60 B2
Trefnanney Powys 60 C2
Trefnant Denb 72 B4
Trefonen Shrops 60 B2
Trefor Anglesey 82 C3
Trefor Gwyn 70 C4
Treforest Rhondda 34 F4
Trefriw Conwy 83 E7
Trefynwy = Monmouth Mon 36 C2
Tregadillett Corn 8 F4
Tregaian Anglesey 82 D4
Tregare Mon 35 C8
Tregaron Ceredig 47 D5
Tregarth Gwyn 83 E6
Tregeare Corn 8 F4
Tregeiriog Wrex 73 F5
Tregele Anglesey 82 B3
Tregidden Corn 3 D6
Treglemais Pembs 44 C3
Tregole Corn 8 E3
Tregonetha Corn 4 C4
Tregony Corn 3 B8
Tregoss Corn 4 C4
Tregoyd Powys 48 F4
Tregroes Ceredig 46 E3
Tregurrian Corn 4 C3
Tregynon Powys 59 E7
Trehafod Rhondda 34 E4
Treharris M Tydf 34 E4
Treherbert Rhondda 34 E3
Trekenner Corn 5 B8
Treknow Corn 8 F2
Trelan Corn 3 E6
Trelash Corn 8 E3
Trelassick Corn 4 D3
Trelawnyd Flint 72 B4
Trelech Carms 45 F4
Treleddyd-fawr Pembs 44 C2
Trelewis M Tydf 35 E5
Treligga Corn 8 F2
Trelights Corn 4 B4
Trelill Corn 4 B5
Trelissick Corn 3 C7
Trellech Mon 36 D2
Trelleck Grange Mon 36 D1
Trelogan Flint 85 F2
Trelystan Powys 60 D2
Tremadog Gwyn 71 C6
Tremail Corn 8 F3
Tremain Ceredig 45 E4
Tremaine Corn 8 F4
Tremar Corn 5 C7
…ematon Corn 5 D8
…emeirchion Denb 72 B4
…nance Corn 4 C3
…arren Corn 3 B9
…ch Telford 61 C6
…glos Corn 8 F4
…van Corn 5 D6
…rset 12 C3
…le Stoke 75 E5
… Stoke 75 E5
… Devon 20 E5

Treoes V Glam 21 B8
Treorchy = Treorci Rhondda 34 E3
Treorci = Treorchy Rhondda 34 E3
Tre'r-ddôl Ceredig 58 E3
Trerule Foot Corn 5 D8
Tresaith Ceredig 45 D4
Tresawle Corn 3 B7
Trescott Staffs 62 E2
Trescowe Corn 2 C4
Tresham Glos 36 E4
Tresillian Corn 3 B7
Tresinwen Pembs 44 A4
Treskinnick Cross Corn 8 E4
Tresmeer Corn 8 F4
Tresparrett Corn 8 E3
Tresparrett Posts Corn 8 E3
Tressait Perth 133 C5
Tresta Shetland 160 D8
Tresta Shetland 160 H5
Treswell Notts 77 B7
Trethosa Corn 4 D4
Trethurgy Corn 4 D5
Tretio Pembs 44 C2
Tretire Hereford 36 B2
Tretower Powys 35 B5
Treuddyn Flint 73 D6
Trevalga Corn 8 F2
Trevalyn Wrex 73 D7
Trevanson Corn 4 B4
Trevarren Corn 4 C4
Trevarrian Corn 4 C3
Trevarrick Corn 3 B8
Trevaughan Carms 32 C2
Treveighan Corn 5 B5
Trevellas Corn 4 D2
Treverva Corn 3 C6
Trevethin Torf 35 D6
Trevigro Corn 5 C8
Treviscoe Corn 4 D4
Trevone Corn 4 B3
Trewarmett Corn 8 F2
Trewassa Corn 8 F3
Trewellard Corn 2 C2
Trewen Corn 8 F4
Trewennack Corn 3 D5
Trewern Powys 60 C2
Trewethern Corn 4 B5
Trewidland Corn 5 D7
Trewint Corn 8 E3
Trewint Corn 8 F4
Trewithian Corn 3 C7
Trewoofe Corn 2 D3
Trewoon Corn 4 D4
Treworga Corn 3 B7
Treworlas Corn 3 C7
Treyarnon Corn 4 B3
Treyford W Sus 16 C2
Trezaise Corn 4 D4
Triangle W Yorks 87 B8
Trickett's Cross Dorset 13 D8
Triffleton Pembs 44 C4
Trimdon Durham 111 F6
Trimdon Colliery Durham 111 F6
Trimdon Grange Durham 111 F6
Trimingham Norf 81 D8
Trimley Lower Street Suff 57 F6
Trimley St Martin Suff 57 F6
Trimley St Mary Suff 57 F6
Trimpley Worcs 50 B2
Trimsaran Carms 33 D5
Trimstone Devon 20 E3
Trinafour Perth 132 C4
Trinant Caerph 35 D6
Tring Herts 40 C2
Tring Wharf Herts 40 C2
Trinity Angus 135 C6
Trinity Jersey 17
Trisant Ceredig 47 B6
Trislaig Highld 130 B4
Trispen Corn 4 D3
Tritlington Northumb 117 E8
Trochry Perth 133 E6
Trodigal Argyll 143 F7
Troed-rhiwdalar Powys 47 D8
Troedyraur Ceredig 46 E2
Troedyrhiw M Tydf 34 D4
Tromode IoM 84 E3
Trondavoe Shetland 160 F5
Troon Corn 3 C5
Troon S Ayrs 118 F3
Trosaraidh W Isles 148 G2
Trossachs Hotel Stirling 126 D4
Troston Suff 56 B2
Trottiscliffe Kent 29 C7
Trotton W Sus 16 B2
Troutbeck Cumb 99 B5
Troutbeck Cumb 99 D6
Troutbeck Bridge Cumb 99 D6
Trow Green Glos 36 D2
Trowbridge Wilts 24 D3
Trowell Notts 76 F4
Trowle Common Wilts 24 D3
Trowley Bottom Herts 40 C3
Trows Borders 122 F2
Trowse Newton Norf 68 D5
Trudoxhill Som 24 E2
Trull Som 11 B7
Trumaisgearraidh W Isles 148 A3
Trumpan Highld 148 B7
Trumpet Hereford 49 F8
Trumpington Cambs 54 D5
Trunch Norf 81 D8
Trunnah Lancs 92 E3
Truro Corn 3 B7
Trusham Devon 10 F3
Trusley Derbys 76 F2
Trusthorpe Lincs 91 F9
Trysull Staffs 62 E2
Tubney Oxon 38 E4
Tuckenhay Devon 7 D6
Tuckhill Shrops 61 F7
Tuckingmill Corn 3 B5
Tuddenham Suff 55 B8
Tuddenham St Martin Suff 57 E5
Tudeley Kent 29 E7
Tudhoe Durham 111 F5
Tudorville Hereford 36 B2
Tudweiliog Gwyn 70 D3
Tuesley Sur 27 E7
Tuffley Glos 37 C5
Tufton Hants 26 E2
Tufton Pembs 32 B1
Tugby Leics 64 D4
Tugford Shrops 61 F5
Tullibardine Perth 127 C8
Tullibody Clack 127 E7
Tullich Argyll 125 D6
Tullich Highld 138 B2
Tullich Muir Highld 151 D10
Tulliemet Perth 133 D6
Tulloch Aberds 135 B7
Tulloch Aberds 153 E8
Tulloch Perth 128 B2
Tulloch Castle Highld 151 E8
Tullochgorm Argyll 125 F5
Tulloes Angus 135 E5
Tullybannocher Perth 127 B6
Tullybelton Perth 133 F7
Tullyfergus Perth 134 E2
Tullymurdoch Perth 134 D1
Tullynessle Aberds 140 C4
Tumble Carms 33 C6

Tumby Woodside Lincs 79 D5
Tummel Bridge Perth 132 D4
Tunga W Isles 155 D9
Tunstall E Yorks 97 F9
Tunstall Kent 30 C2
Tunstall Lancs 93 B6
Tunstall N Yorks 101 E7
Tunstall Norf 69 D7
Tunstall Stoke 75 D5
Tunstall Suff 57 D7
Tunstall T&W 111 D6
Tunstead Derbys 75 B8
Tunstead Gtr Man 87 D8
Tunstead Norf 81 E8
Tunworth Hants 26 E4
Tupsley Hereford 49 E7
Tupton Derbys 76 C3
Tur Langton Leics 64 E4
Turgis Green Hants 26 D4
Turin Angus 135 D5
Turkdean Glos 37 C8
Turleigh Wilts 24 C3
Turn Lancs 87 C6
Turnastone Hereford 49 F5
Turnberry S Ayrs 112 D2
Turnditch Derbys 76 E2
Turners Hill W Sus 28 F4
Turners Puddle Dorset 13 E6
Turnford Herts 41 D6
Turnhouse Edin 120 B4
Turnworth Dorset 13 D6
Turriff Aberds 153 C7
Turton Bottoms Blackburn 86 C5
Turves Cambs 66 E3
Turvey Bedford 53 D7
Turville Bucks 39 E7
Turville Heath Bucks 39 E7
Turweston Bucks 52 F4
Tushielaw Borders 115 C6
Tutbury Staffs 63 B6
Tutnall Worcs 50 B4
Tutshill Glos 36 E2
Tuttington Norf 81 E8
Tutts Clump W Berks 26 B3
Tuxford Notts 77 B7
Twatt Orkney 159 F3
Twatt Shetland 160 H5
Twechar E Dunb 119 B7
Tweedmouth Northumb 123 D5
Tweedsmuir Borders 114 B3
Twelve Heads Corn 3 B6
Twemlow Green Ches E 74 C4
Twenty Lincs 65 B8
Twerton Bath 24 C2
Twickenham London 28 B2
Twigworth Glos 37 B5
Twineham W Sus 17 C6
Twinhoe Bath 24 D2
Twinstead Essex 56 F2
Twinstead Green Essex 56 F2
Twiss Green Warr 86 E4
Twiston Lancs 93 E8
Twitchen Devon 21 F6
Twitchen Shrops 49 B5
Two Bridges Devon 6 B4
Two Dales Derbys 76 C2
Two Mills Ches W 73 B7
Twycross Leics 63 D7
Twyford Bucks 39 B6
Twyford Derbys 63 B7
Twyford Hants 15 B5
Twyford Leics 64 C4
Twyford Lincs 65 B6
Twyford Norf 81 E6
Twyford Wokingham 27 B5
Twyford Common Hereford 49 F7
Twyn-y-Sheriff Mon 35 D8
Twynholm Dumfries 106 D3
Twyning Glos 50 F3
Twyning Green Glos 50 F4
Twynllanan Carms 34 B1
Twynmynydd Carms 33 C7
Twywell Northants 53 B7
Ty-draw Conwy 83 F8
Ty-hen Carms 32 B4
Ty-hen Gwyn 70 D2
Ty-mawr Anglesey 82 C4
Ty Mawr Carms 46 E4
Ty Mawr Cwm Conwy 72 E3
Ty-nant Conwy 72 E3
Ty-nant Gwyn 59 B6
Ty-uchaf Powys 59 B7
Tyberton Hereford 49 F5
Tyburn W Mid 62 E5
Tycroes Carms 33 C7
Tycrwyn Powys 59 C8
Tydd Gote Lincs 66 C4
Tydd St Giles Cambs 66 C4
Tydd St Mary Lincs 66 C4
Tyddewi = St David's Pembs 44 C2
Tyddyn-mawr Gwyn 71 C6
Tye Green Essex 41 D7
Tye Green Essex 42 B3
Tye Green Essex 55 F6
Tyldesley Gtr Man 86 D4
Tyler Hill Kent 30 C5
Tylers Green Bucks 40 E2
Tylorstown Rhondda 34 E4
Tylwch Powys 59 F6
Tyn-y-celyn Wrex 73 F5
Tyn-y-coed Shrops 60 B2
Tyn-y-fedwen Powys 72 F5
Tyn-y-ffridd Powys 72 F5
Tyn-y-graig Powys 48 D2
Ty'n-y-groes Conwy 83 D7
Ty'n-y-maes Gwyn 83 E6
Tyn-y-pwll Anglesey 82 C4
Ty'n-yr-eithin Ceredig 47 C5
Tyncelyn Ceredig 46 C5
Tyndrum Stirling 131 F7
Tyne Tunnel T&W 111 C6
Tyneham Dorset 13 F6
Tynehead Midloth 121 D6
Tynemouth T&W 111 C6
Tynewydd Rhondda 34 E3
Tyninghame E Loth 122 B2
Tynron Dumfries 113 E8
Tynygongl Anglesey 82 C5
Tynygraig Ceredig 47 C5
Tŷ'r-felin-isaf Conwy 83 E8
Tyrie Aberds 153 B9
Tyringham M Keynes 53 E6
Tythecott Devon 9 C6
Tythegston Bridgend 21 B7
Tytherington Ches E 75 B6
Tytherington S Glos 36 F3
Tytherington Som 24 E2
Tytherington Wilts 24 E4
Tytherleigh Devon 11 D8
Tywardreath Corn 5 D5
Tywyn Conwy 83 D7
Tywyn Gwyn 58 D2

U

Uachdar W Isles 148 C2
Uags Highld 149 E12
Ubbeston Green Suff 57 B7
Ubley Bath 23 D7
Uckerby N Yorks 101 D7
Uckfield E Sus 17 B8
Uckington Glos 37 B6
Uddingston S Lanark 119 C6
Uddington S Lanark 119 F8
Udimore E Sus 19 D5
Udny Green Aberds 141 B7

Udny Station Aberds 141 B8
Udston S Lanark 119 D6
Udstonhead S Lanark 119 E7
Uffcott Wilts 25 B6
Uffculme Devon 11 C5
Uffington Lincs 65 D7
Uffington Oxon 38 F3
Uffington Shrops 60 C5
Ufford Pboro 65 D7
Ufford Suff 57 D6
Ufton Warks 51 C8
Ufton Nervet W Berks 26 C4
Ugadale Argyll 143 F8
Ugborough Devon 6 D4
Uggeshall Suff 69 F7
Ugglebarnby N Yorks 103 D6
Ughill S Yorks 88 E3
Ugley Essex 41 B8
Ugley Green Essex 41 B8
Ugthorpe N Yorks 103 C5
Uidh W Isles 148 J1
Uig Argyll 145 E10
Uig Highld 148 C6
Uig Highld 149 B8
Uigen W Isles 154 D5
Uigshader Highld 149 D9
Uisken Argyll 146 K6
Ulbster Highld 158 F5
Ulceby Lincs 79 B7
Ulceby N Lincs 90 C5
Ulceby Skitter N Lincs 90 C5
Ulcombe Kent 30 E2
Uldale Cumb 108 F2
Uley Glos 36 E4
Ulgham Northumb 117 E8
Ullapool Highld 150 B4
Ullenhall Warks 51 C6
Ullenwood Glos 37 C6
Ulleskelf N Yorks 95 E8
Ullesthorpe Leics 64 F2
Ulley S Yorks 89 F5
Ullingswick Hereford 49 E7
Ullinish Highld 149 E8
Ullock Cumb 98 B2
Ulnes Walton Lancs 86 C3
Ulpha Cumb 98 E3
Ulrome E Yorks 97 D7
Ulsta Shetland 160 E6
Ulva House Argyll 146 H7
Ulverston Cumb 92 B2
Ulwell Dorset 13 F8
Umberleigh Devon 9 B8
Unapool Highld 156 F5
Unasary W Isles 148 F2
Underbarrow Cumb 99 E6
Undercliffe W Yorks 94 F4
Underhoull Shetland 160 C7
Underriver Kent 29 D6
Underwood Notts 76 D4
Undy Mon 35 F8
Unifirth Shetland 160 H4
Union Cottage Aberds 141 E7
Union Mills IoM 84 E3
Union Street E Sus 18 B4
Unstone Derbys 76 B3
Unstone Green Derbys 76 B3
Unthank Cumb 108 F4
Unthank Cumb 109 E6
Unthank End Cumb 108 F4
Up Cerne Dorset 12 D4
Up Exe Devon 10 D4
Up Hatherley Glos 37 B6
Up Holland Lancs 86 D3
Up Marden W Sus 15 C8
Up Nately Hants 26 D4
Up Somborne Hants 25 F8
Up Sydling Dorset 12 D4
Upavon Wilts 25 D6
Upchurch Kent 30 C2
Upcott Hereford 48 D5
Upend Cambs 55 D7
Upgate Norf 68 C4
Uphall W Loth 120 B3
Uphall Station W Loth 120 B3
Upham Devon 10 D3
Upham Hants 15 B6
Uphampton Worcs 50 C3
Uphill N Som 22 D5
Uplawmoor E Renf 118 D4
Upleadon Glos 36 B4
Upleatham Redcar 102 C4
Uplees Kent 30 C3
Uploders Dorset 12 E3
Uplowman Devon 10 C5
Uplyme Devon 11 E8
Upminster London 42 F1
Upnor Medway 29 B8
Upottery Devon 11 D7
Upper Affcot Shrops 60 F4
Upper Ardchronie Highld 151 C9
Upper Arley Worcs 61 F7
Upper Arncott Oxon 39 C6
Upper Astrop Northants 52 F3
Upper Badcall Highld 156 E4
Upper Basildon W Berks 26 B3
Upper Beeding W Sus 17 C5
Upper Benefield Northants 65 F6
Upper Bighouse Highld 157 D11
Upper Boddington Northants 52 D2
Upper Borth Ceredig 58 F3
Upper Boyndlie Aberds 153 B9
Upper Brailes Warks 51 F8
Upper Breakish Highld 149 F11
Upper Breinton Hereford 49 E6
Upper Broadheath Worcs 50 D3
Upper Broughton Notts 64 B3
Upper Bucklebury W Berks 26 C3
Upper Burnhaugh Aberds 141 E7
Upper Caldecote C Beds 54 E2
Upper Catesby Northants 52 D3
Upper Chapel Powys 48 E2
Upper Church Village Rhondda 34 F4
Upper Chute Wilts 25 D7
Upper Clatford Hants 25 E8
Upper Clynnog Gwyn 71 C5
Upper Cumberworth W Yorks 88 D3
Upper Cwm-twrch Powys 34 C1
Upper Cwmbran Torf 35 E6
Upper Dallachy Moray 152 B3
Upper Dean Bedford 53 C8
Upper Denby W Yorks 88 D3
Upper Denton Cumb 109 C6
Upper Derraid Highld 151 H13
Upper Dicker E Sus 18 E2
Upper Dovercourt Essex 57 F6
Upper Druimfin Argyll 147 F8
Upper Dunsforth N Yorks 95 C7
Upper Eathie Highld 151 E10
Upper Elkstone Staffs 75 D7
Upper End Derbys 75 B7
Upper Farringdon Hants 26 F5
Upper Framilode Glos 36 C4

Upper Glenfintaig Highld 137 F5
Upper Gornal W Mid 62 E3
Upper Gravenhurst C Beds 54 F2
Upper Green Mon 35 C7
Upper Green W Berks 25 C8
Upper Grove Common Hereford 36 B2
Upper Hackney Derbys 76 C2
Upper Hale Sur 27 E6
Upper Halistra Highld 148 C7
Upper Halling Medway 29 C7
Upper Hambleton Rutland 65 D6
Upper Hardres Court Kent 31 D5
Upper Hartfield E Sus 29 F5
Upper Haugh S Yorks 88 E5
Upper Heath Shrops 61 F5
Upper Hellesdon Norf 68 C5
Upper Helmsley N Yorks 96 D2
Upper Hergest Hereford 48 D4
Upper Heyford Northants 52 D4
Upper Heyford Oxon 38 B4
Upper Hill Hereford 49 D6
Upper Hopton W Yorks 88 C2
Upper Horsebridge E Sus 18 D2
Upper Hulme Staffs 75 C7
Upper Inglesham Swindon 38 E2
Upper Inverbrough Highld 151 H11
Upper Killay Swansea 33 E6
Upper Knockando Moray 152 D1
Upper Lambourn W Berks 38 F3
Upper Leigh Staffs 75 F7
Upper Lenie Highld 137 B8
Upper Lochton Aberds 141 E5
Upper Longdon Staffs 62 C4
Upper Lybster Highld 158 G4
Upper Lydbrook Glos 36 C3
Upper Maes-coed Hereford 48 F5
Upper Midway Derbys 63 B6
Upper Milovaig Highld 148 D6
Upper Minety Wilts 37 E7
Upper Mitton Worcs 50 B3
Upper North Dean Bucks 39 E8
Upper Obney Perth 133 F7
Upper Ollach Highld 149 E10
Upper Padley Derbys 76 B2
Upper Pollicott Bucks 39 C7
Upper Poppleton York 95 D8
Upper Quinton Warks 51 E6
Upper Ratley Hants 14 B4
Upper Rissington Glos 38 C2
Upper Rochford Worcs 49 C8
Upper Sandaig Highld 149 G12
Upper Sanday Orkney 159 H6
Upper Sapey Hereford 49 C8
Upper Saxondale Notts 77 F6
Upper Seagry Wilts 37 F6
Upper Shelton C Beds 53 E7
Upper Sheringham Norf 81 C7
Upper Skelmorlie N Ayrs 118 C2
Upper Slaughter Glos 38 B1
Upper Soudley Glos 36 C3
Upper Stondon C Beds 54 F2
Upper Stowe Northants 52 D4
Upper Stratton Swindon 38 F1
Upper Street Hants 14 C2
Upper Street Norf 69 C6
Upper Street Norf 69 C6
Upper Street Suff 56 F5
Upper Strensham Worcs 50 F4
Upper Sundon C Beds 40 B3
Upper Swell Glos 38 B1
Upper Tean Staffs 75 F7
Upper Tillyrie Perth 128 D3
Upper Tooting London 28 B3
Upper Tote Highld 149 C10
Upper Town N Som 23 C7
Upper Treverward Shrops 48 B4
Upper Tysoe Warks 51 E8
Upper Upham Wilts 25 B7
Upper Wardington Oxon 52 E2
Upper Weald M Keynes 53 F5
Upper Weedon Northants 52 D4
Upper Wield Hants 26 F4
Upper Winchendon Bucks 39 C7
Upper Witton W Mid 62 E4
Upper Woodend Aberds 141 C5
Upper Woodford Wilts 25 F6
Upper Wootton Hants 26 D3
Upper Wyche Hereford 50 E2
Upperby Cumb 108 D4
Uppermill Gtr Man 87 D7
Uppersound Shetland 160 J6
Upperthong W Yorks 88 D2
Upperthorpe N Lincs 89 D8
Upperton W Sus 16 B3
Uppertown Derbys 76 C3
Uppertown Highld 158 C5
Uppertown Orkney 159 J5
Uppingham Rutland 65 E5
Uppington Shrops 61 D6
Upsall N Yorks 102 F2
Upshire Essex 41 D7
Upstreet Kent 31 C6
Upthorpe Suff 56 B3
Upton Cambs 54 B2
Upton Ches W 73 C8
Upton Corn 8 D4
Upton Dorset 12 F5
Upton Dorset 13 E7
Upton Hants 14 C4
Upton Hants 25 D8
Upton Leics 63 E7
Upton Lincs 90 F2
Upton Mers 85 F3
Upton Norf 69 C6
Upton Northants 52 C5
Upton Notts 77 B7
Upton Notts 77 D7
Upton Oxon 39 F5
Upton Pboro 65 D8
Upton Slough 27 B7
Upton Som 10 B4
Upton W Yorks 89 C5
Upton Bishop Hereford 36 B3
Upton Cheyney S Glos 23 C8
Upton Cressett Shrops 61 E6
Upton Cross Corn 5 B7
Upton Grey Hants 26 E4
Upton Hellions Devon 10 D3
Upton Lovell Wilts 24 E4
Upton Magna Shrops 61 C5
Upton Noble Som 24 F2
Upton Pyne Devon 10 E4
Upton Scudamore Wilts 24 E3
Upton St Leonard's Glos 37 C5

Upton Snodsbury Worcs 50 D4
Upton upon Severn Worcs 50 E3
Upton Warren Worcs 50 C4
Upwaltham W Sus 16 C3
Upware Cambs 55 B6
Upwell Norf 66 D4
Upwey Dorset 12 F4
Upwood Cambs 66 F2
Uradale Shetland 160 K6
Urafirth Shetland 160 F5
Urchfont Wilts 24 D5
Urdimarsh Hereford 49 E7
Ure Shetland 160 F4
Ure Bank N Yorks 95 B6
Urgha W Isles 154 H6
Urishay Common Hereford 48 F5
Urlay Nook Stockton 102 C1
Urmston Gtr Man 87 E5
Urpeth Durham 110 D5
Urquhart Highld 151 F8
Urquhart Moray 152 B2
Urra N Yorks 102 D3
Urray Highld 151 F8
Ushaw Moor Durham 110 E5
Usk = Brynbuga Mon 35 D7
Usselby Lincs 90 E4
Usworth T&W 111 D6
Utkinton Ches W 74 C2
Utley W Yorks 94 E3
Uton Devon 10 E3
Utterby Lincs 91 E7
Uttoxeter Staffs 75 F7
Uwchmynydd Gwyn 70 E2
Uxbridge London 40 F3
Uyeasound Shetland 160 C7
Uzmaston Pembs 44 D4

V

Valley Anglesey 82 D2
Valley Truckle Corn 8 F2
Valleyfield Dumfries 106 D3
Valsgarth Shetland 160 B8
Valtos Highld 149 B10
Van Powys 59 F6
Vange Essex 42 F3
Varteg Torf 35 D6
Vatten Highld 149 D7
Vaul Argyll 146 G3
Vaynor M Tydf 34 C4
Veensgarth Shetland 160 J6
Velindre Powys 48 F3
Vellow Som 22 F2
Veness Orkney 159 F6
Venn Green Devon 9 C5
Venn Ottery Devon 11 E5
Vennington Shrops 60 D3
Venny Tedburn Devon 10 E3
Ventnor IoW 15 G6
Vernham Dean Hants 25 D8
Vernham Street Hants 25 D8
Vernolds Common Shrops 60 F4
Verwood Dorset 13 D8
Veryan Corn 3 C8
Vicarage Devon 11 F7
Vickerstown Cumb 92 C1
Victoria Corn 4 C4
Victoria S Yorks 88 D2
Vidlin Shetland 160 G6
Viewpark N Lanark 119 C7
Vigo Village Kent 29 C7
Vinehall Street E Sus 18 C4
Vine's Cross E Sus 18 D2
Viney Hill Glos 36 D3
Virginia Water Sur 27 C8
Virginstow Devon 9 E5
Vobster Som 24 E2
Voe Shetland 160 E5
Voe Shetland 160 G6
Vowchurch Hereford 49 F5
Voxter Shetland 160 F5
Voy Orkney 159 G3

W

Wackerfield Durham 101 B6
Wacton Norf 68 E4
Wadbister Shetland 160 J6
Wadborough Worcs 50 E4
Waddesdon Bucks 39 C7
Waddingham Lincs 90 E3
Waddington Lancs 93 E7
Waddington Lincs 78 C2
Wadebridge Corn 4 B4
Wadeford Som 11 C8
Wadenhoe Northants 65 F7
Wadesmill Herts 41 C6
Wadhurst E Sus 18 B3
Wadshelf Derbys 76 B3
Wadsley S Yorks 88 E4
Wadsley Bridge S Yorks 88 E4
Wadworth S Yorks 89 E6
Waen Denb 72 C3
Waen Denb 72 C5
Waen Fach Powys 60 C2
Waen Goleugoed Denb 72 B4
Wag Highld 157 G13
Wainfleet All Saints Lincs 79 D7
Wainfleet Bank Lincs 79 D7
Wainfleet St Mary Lincs 79 D8
Wainfleet Tofts Lincs 79 D7
Wainhouse Corner Corn 8 E3
Wainscott Medway 29 B8
Wainstalls W Yorks 87 B8
Waitby Cumb 100 D2
Waithe Lincs 91 D6
Wake Lady Green N Yorks 102 E4
Wakefield W Yorks 88 B4
Wakerley Northants 65 E6
Wakes Colne Essex 42 B4
Walberswick Suff 57 B8
Walberton W Sus 16 D3
Walbottle T&W 110 C4
Walcot Lincs 78 F3
Walcot N Lincs 90 B2
Walcot Shrops 60 F3
Walcot Swindon 38 F1
Walcot Telford 61 C5
Walcot Green Norf 68 F4
Walcote Leics 64 F2
Walcote Warks 51 D6
Walcott Lincs 78 D4
Walcott Norf 69 A6
Walden N Yorks 101 F5
Walden Head N Yorks 100 F4
Walden Stubbs N Yorks 89 C6
Waldersey Cambs 66 D4
Walderslade Medway 29 C8
Walderton W Sus 15 C8
Walditch Dorset 12 E2
Waldley Derbys 75 F8
Waldridge Durham 111 D5
Waldringfield Suff 57 E6
Waldringfield Heath Suff 57 E6
Waldron E Sus 18 D2
Wales S Yorks 89 F5
Walesby Lincs 90 E5
Walesby Notts 77 B6
Walford Hereford 36 B2
Walford Hereford 49 B5
Walford Shrops 60 B4

Walford Heath Shrops 60 C4
Walgherton Ches E 74 E3
Walgrave Northants 53 B6
Walhampton Hants 14 E4
Walk Mill Lancs 93 F8
Walkden Gtr Man 86 D5
Walker T&W 111 C5
Walker Barn Ches E 75 B6
Walker Fold Lancs 93 E6
Walkerburn Borders 121 F6
Walkeringham Notts 89 E8
Walkerith Lincs 89 E8
Walkern Herts 41 B5
Walker's Green Hereford 49 E7
Walkerville N Yorks 101 E7
Walkford Dorset 14 E3
Walkhampton Devon 6 C3
Walkington E Yorks 97 F5
Walkley S Yorks 88 F4
Wall Northumb 110 C2
Wall Staffs 62 D5
Wall Bank Shrops 60 E5
Wall Heath W Mid 62 F2
Wall under Heywood Shrops 60 E5
Wallaceton Dumfries 113 F8
Wallacetown S Ayrs 112 B3
Wallacetown S Ayrs 112 D2
Wallands Park E Sus 17 C8
Wallasey Mers 85 E4
Wallcrouch E Sus 18 B3
Wallingford Oxon 39 F6
Wallington Hants 15 D6
Wallington Herts 54 F3
Wallington London 28 C3
Wallis Pembs 32 B1
Walliswood Sur 28 F2
Walls Shetland 160 J4
Wallsend T&W 111 C5
Wallston V Glam 22 B3
Wallyford E Loth 121 B6
Walmer Kent 31 D7
Walmer Bridge Lancs 86 B2
Walmersley Gtr Man 87 C6
Walmley W Mid 62 E5
Walpole Suff 57 B7
Walpole Cross Keys Norf 66 C5
Walpole Highway Norf 66 C5
Walpole Marsh Norf 66 C4
Walpole St Andrew Norf 66 C5
Walpole St Peter Norf 66 C5
Walsall W Mid 62 E4
Walsall Wood W Mid 62 D4
Walsden W Yorks 87 B7
Walsgrave on Sowe W Mid 63 F7
Walsham le Willows Suff 56 B3
Walshaw Gtr Man 87 C5
Walshford N Yorks 95 D7
Walsoken Cambs 66 C4
Walston S Lanark 120 E3
Walsworth Herts 54 F3
Walters Ash Bucks 39 E8
Walterston V Glam 22 B2
Walterstone Hereford 35 B7
Waltham Kent 30 E5
Waltham NE Lincs 91 D6
Waltham Abbey Essex 41 D6
Waltham Chase Hants 15 C6
Waltham Cross Herts 41 D6
Waltham on the Wolds Leics 64 B5
Waltham St Lawrence Windsor 27 B6
Walthamstow London 41 F6
Walton Cumb 108 C5
Walton Derbys 76 C3
Walton Leics 64 F2
Walton M Keynes 53 F6
Walton Mers 85 E4
Walton Pboro 65 D8
Walton Powys 48 D4
Walton Som 23 F6
Walton Staffs 75 F5
Walton Suff 57 F6
Walton Telford 61 C5
Walton W Yorks 88 C4
Walton W Yorks 95 E7
Walton Warks 51 D7
Walton Cardiff Glos 50 F4
Walton East Pembs 32 B1
Walton-in-Gordano N Som 23 B6
Walton-le-Dale Lancs 86 B3
Walton-on-Thames Sur 28 C2
Walton on the Hill Staffs 62 B3
Walton on the Hill Sur 28 D3
Walton-on-the-Naze Essex 43 B8
Walton on the Wolds Leics 64 C2
Walton-on-Trent Derbys 63 C6
Walton West Pembs 44 D3
Walwen Flint 73 B6
Walwick Northumb 110 B2
Walworth Darl 101 C7
Walworth Gate Darl 101 B7
Walwyn's Castle Pembs 44 D3
Wambrook Som 11 D7
Wanborough Sur 27 E7
Wanborough Swindon 38 F2
Wandsworth London 28 B3
Wangford Suff 57 B8
Wanlockhead Dumfries 113 C8
Wansford E Yorks 97 D6
Wansford Pboro 65 E7
Wanstead London 41 F7
Wanstrow Som 24 E2
Wanswell Glos 36 D3
Wantage Oxon 38 F3
Wapley S Glos 24 B2
Wappenbury Warks 51 C8
Wappenham Northants 52 E4
Warbleton E Sus 18 D3
Warblington Hants 15 D8
Warborough Oxon 39 E5
Warboys Cambs 66 F3
Warbreck Blackpool 92 F3
Warbstow Corn 8 E4
Warburton Gtr Man 86 F5
Warcop Cumb 100 C2
Ward End W Mid 62 F5
Ward Green Suff 56 C4
Warden Kent 30 B4
Warden Northumb 110 C2
Wardhill Orkney 159 F7
Wardington Oxon 52 E2
Wardlaw Borders 115 C5
Wardle Ches E 74 D3
Wardle Gtr Man 87 C7
Wardley Rutland 64 D5
Wardlow Derbys 75 B8
Wardy Hill Cambs 66 F4
Ware Herts 41 C6
Ware Kent 31 C6
Wareham Dorset 13 F7
Warehorne Kent 19 B6
Waren Mill Northumb 123 F7
Warenford Northumb 117 B7
Warenton Northumb 123 F7
Wareside Herts 41 C6
Waresley Cambs 54 D3
Waresley Worcs 50 B3
Warfield Brack 27 B6
Warfleet Devon 7 D6
Wargrave Wokingham 27 B5
Warham Norf 80 C5
Warhill Gtr Man 87 E7
Wark Northumb 109 B8
Wark Northumb 122 F4
Warkleigh Devon 9 B8
Warkton Northants 53 B6
Warkworth Northants 52 E2
Warkworth Northumb 117 D8
Warlaby N Yorks 101 E8
Warland W Yorks 87 B7
Warleggan Corn 5 C6
Warlingham Sur 28 D4
Warmfield W Yorks 88 B4
Warmingham Ches E 74 C4
Warmington Northants 65 E7
Warmington Warks 52 E2
Warminster Wilts 24 E3
Warmlake Kent 30 D2
Warmley S Glos 23 B8
Warmley Tower S Glos 23 B8
Warmonds Hill Northants 53 C7
Warmsworth S Yorks 89 D6
Warmwell Dorset 13 F5
Warndon Worcs 50 D3
Warnford Hants 15 B7
Warnham W Sus 28 F2
Warninglid W Sus 17 B6
Warren Ches E 75 B5
Warren Pembs 44 F4
Warren Heath Suff 57 E6
Warren Row Windsor 39 F8
Warren Street Kent 30 D3
Warrington M Keynes 53 D6
Warrington Warr 86 F4
Warsash Hants 15 D5
Warslow Staffs 75 D7
Warter E Yorks 96 D4
Warthermarske N Yorks 94 B5
Warthill N Yorks 96 D2
Wartling E Sus 18 E3
Wartnaby Leics 64 B4
Warton Lancs 86 B2
Warton Lancs 92 B4
Warton Northumb 117 D6
Warton Warks 63 D6
Warwick Warks 51 C7
Warwick Bridge Cumb 108 D4
Warwick on Eden Cumb 108 D4
Wasbister Orkney 159 E4
Wasdale Head Cumb 98 D3
Wash Common W Berks 26 C2
Washaway Corn 4 C5
Washbourne Devon 7 D5
Washfield Devon 10 C4
Washfold N Yorks 101 D5
Washford Som 22 E2
Washford Pyne Devon 10 C3
Washingborough Lincs 78 B3
Washington T&W 111 D6
Washington W Sus 16 C5
Wasing W Berks 26 C3
Waskerley Durham 110 E3
Wasperton Warks 51 D7
Wasps Nest Lincs 78 C3
Wass N Yorks 95 B8
Watchet Som 22 E2
Watchfield Oxon 38 E2
Watchfield Som 22 E5
Watchgate Cumb 99 E7
Watchhill Cumb 107 E8
Watcombe Torbay 7 C7
Watendlath Cumb 98 C4
Water Devon 10 F2
Water Lancs 87 B6
Water End E Yorks 96 F3
Water End Herts 40 C3
Water End Herts 41 D5
Water Newton Cambs 65 E8
Water Orton Warks 63 E5
Water Stratford Bucks 52 F4
Water Yeat Cumb 98 F4
Waterbeach Cambs 55 C5
Waterbeck Dumfries 108 B2
Waterden Norf 80 D4
Waterfall Staffs 75 D7
Waterfoot E Renf 119 D5
Waterfoot Lancs 87 B6
Waterford Hants 14 E4
Waterford Herts 41 C6
Waterhead Cumb 99 D5
Waterhead Dumfries 114 E4
Waterheads Borders 120 D5
Waterhouses Durham 110 E4
Waterhouses Staffs 75 D7
Wateringbury Kent 29 D7
Waterloo Gtr Man 87 D7
Waterloo Highld 149 F11
Waterloo Mers 85 E4
Waterloo N Lanark 119 D8
Waterloo Norf 68 C5
Waterloo Perth 133 F7
Waterloo Poole 13 E8
Waterloo Shrops 74 F2
Waterloo Port Gwyn 82 E4
Waterlooville Hants 15 D7
Watermeetings S Lanark 114 C2
Watermillock Cumb 99 B6
Waterperry Oxon 39 D6
Waterrow Som 11 B5
Water's Nook Gtr Man 86 D4
Waters Upton Telford 61 C6
Watersfield W Sus 16 C4
Waterside Aberds 141 B9
Waterside Blackburn 86 B5
Waterside Cumb 108 E2
Waterside E Ayrs 112 D4
Waterside E Ayrs 118 E4
Waterside E Dunb 119 B6
Waterside E Renf 118 D5
Waterstock Oxon 39 D6
Waterston Pembs 44 E4
Watford Herts 40 E4
Watford Northants 52 C4
Watford Gap Staffs 62 D5
Wath N Yorks 94 C4
Wath N Yorks 95 B6
Wath N Yorks 96 B2
Wath Brow Cumb 98 C2
Wath upon Dearne S Yorks 88 D5
Watlington Norf 67 C6
Watlington Oxon 39 E6
Watnall Notts 76 E5
Watten Highld 158 E4
Wattisfield Suff 56 B4
Wattisham Suff 56 D4
Wattlesborough Heath Shrops 60 C3
Watton E Yorks 97 D6
Watton Norf 68 D2
Watton at Stone Herts 41 C6
Wattston N Lanark 119 B7
Wattstown Rhondda 34 E4
Wauchan Highld 136 F2
Waulkmill Lodge Orkney 159 H4
Waun Powys 59 D5
Waun-y-clyn Carms 33 D5
Waunarlwydd Swansea 33 E7
Waunclunda Carms 47 F5
Waunfawr Gwyn 82 F5
Waungron Swansea 33 D6
Waunlwyd Bl Gwent 35 D5
Wavendon M Keynes 53 F7
Waverbridge Cumb 108 E2
Waverton Ches W 73 C8
Waverton Cumb 108 E2
Wavertree Mers 85 F4
Wawne E Yorks 97 F6
Waxham Norf 69 B7
Waxholme E Yorks 91 B7
Way Kent 31 C7
Way Village Devon 10 C3
Wayfield Medway 29 C8
Wayford Som 12 D2
Waymills Shrops 74 E2
Wayne Green Mon 35 C8
Wdig = Goodwick Pembs 44 B4
Weachyburn Aberds 153 C6
Weald Oxon 38 D3
Wealdstone London 40 F4
Weardley W Yorks 95 E5
Weare Som 23 D6
Weare Giffard Devon 9 B6
Wearhead Durham 109 F8
Weasdale Cumb 100 D1
Weasenham All Saints Norf 80 E4
Weasenham St Peter Norf 80 E4
Weatherhill Sur 28 E4
Weaverham Ches W 74 B3
Weaverthorpe N Yorks 97 B5
Webheath Worcs 50 C5
Wedderlairs Aberds 153 E8
Wedderlie Borders 122 D2
Weddington Warks 63 E7
Wedhampton Wilts 25 D5
Wedmore Som 23 E6
Wednesbury W Mid 62 E3
Wednesfield W Mid 62 D3
Weedon Bucks 39 C8
Weedon Bec Northants 52 D4
Weedon Lois Northants 52 E4
Weeford Staffs 62 D5
Week Devon 10 C2
Week St Mary Corn 8 E4
Weeke Hants 26 F2
Weekley Northants 65 F5
Weel E Yorks 97 F6
Weeley Essex 43 B7
Weeley Heath Essex 43 B7
Weem Perth 133 E5
Weeping Cross Staffs 62 B3
Weethley Gate Warks 51 D5
Weeting Norf 67 F7
Weeton E Yorks 91 B7
Weeton Lancs 92 F3
Weeton N Yorks 95 E5
Weetwood Hall Northumb 117 B6
Weir Lancs 87 B6
Weir Quay Devon 6 C2
Welborne Norf 68 D3
Welbourn Lincs 78 D2
Welburn N Yorks 96 C3
Welburn N Yorks 102 F4
Welbury N Yorks 102 D1
Welby Lincs 78 F2
Welches Dam Cambs 66 F4
Welcombe Devon 8 C4
Weld Bank Lancs 86 C3
Weldon Northumb 117 E7
Welford Northants 64 F3
Welford W Berks 26 B2
Welford-on-Avon Warks 51 D6
Welham Leics 64 E4
Welham Notts 89 F8
Welham Green Herts 41 D5
Well Hants 27 E5
Well Lincs 79 B7
Well N Yorks 101 F7
Well End Bucks 40 F1
Well Heads W Yorks 94 F3
Well Hill Kent 29 C5
Well Town Devon 10 D4
Welland Worcs 50 E2
Wellbank Angus 134 F4
Welldale Dumfries 107 C8
Wellesbourne Warks 51 D7
Welling London 29 B5
Wellingborough Northants 53 C6
Wellingham Norf 80 E4
Wellingore Lincs 78 D2
Wellington Cumb 98 D2
Wellington Hereford 49 E6
Wellington Som 11 B6
Wellington Telford 61 C6
Wellington Heath Hereford 50 E2
Wellington Hill W Yorks 95 F6
Wellow Bath 24 D2
Wellow IoW 14 F4
Wellow Notts 77 C6
Wellpond Green Herts 41 B7
Wells Som 23 E7
Wells Green Ches E 74 D3
Wells-Next-The-Sea Norf 80 C5
Wellsborough Leics 63 D7
Wellswood Torbay 7 C7
Wellwood Fife 128 F2
Welney Norf 66 E5
Welsh Bicknor Hereford 36 C2
Welsh End Shrops 74 F2
Welsh Frankton Shrops 73 F7
Welsh Hook Pembs 44 C4
Welsh Newton Hereford 36 C1
Welsh St Donats V Glam 22 B2
Welshampton Shrops 73 F8
Welshpool = Y Trallwng Powys 60 D2
Welton Cumb 108 E3
Welton E Yorks 90 B3
Welton Lincs 78 B3
Welton Northants 52 C3
Welton Hill Lincs 90 F4
Welton le Marsh Lincs 79 C7
Welton le Wold Lincs 91 F6
Welwick E Yorks 91 B7
Welwyn Herts 41 C5
Welwyn Garden City Herts 41 C5
Wem Shrops 60 B5
Wembdon Som 22 F4
Wembley London 40 F4
Wembury Devon 6 E3
Wembworthy Devon 9 D8
Wemyss Bay Invclyd 118 C1
Wenallt Ceredig 47 B5
Wenallt Gwyn 72 E3
Wendens Ambo Essex 55 F6
Wendlebury Oxon 39 C5
Wendling Norf 68 C2
Wendover Bucks 40 D1
Wendron Corn 3 C5
Wendy Cambs 54 E4
Wenfordbridge Corn 5 B5
Wenhaston Suff 57 B8
Wennington Cambs 54 B3
Wennington Lancs 93 B6
Wennington London 41 F8
Wensley Derbys 76 C2
Wensley N Yorks 101 F5
Wentbridge W Yorks 89 C5
Wentnor Shrops 60 E3
Wentworth Cambs 55 B5
Wentworth S Yorks 88 E4
Wenvoe V Glam 22 B3
Weobley Hereford 49 D6
Weobley Marsh Hereford 49 D6
Wereham Norf 67 D6
Wergs W Mid 62 D2
Wern Powys 59 C6
Wern Powys 60 C2
Wernffrwd Swansea 33 E6
Wernyrheolydd Mon 35 C7
Werrington Corn 8 F5
Werrington Pboro 65 D8
Werrington Staffs 75 E6
Wervin Ches W 73 B8
Wesham Lancs 92 F4
Wessington Derbys 76 D3
West Acre Norf 67 C7
West Adderbury Oxon 52 F2
West Allerdean Northumb 123 E5
West Alvington Devon 6 E5
West Amesbury Wilts 25 E6
West Anstey Devon 10 B3
West Ashby Lincs 79 B5
West Ashling W Sus 16 D2
West Ashton Wilts 24 D3
West Auckland Durham 101 B6
West Ayton N Yorks 103 F7
West Bagborough Som 22 F3
West Barkwith Lincs 91 F5
West Barnby N Yorks 103 C6
West Barns E Loth 122 B2
West Barsham Norf 80 D5
West Bay Dorset 12 E2
West Beckham Norf 81 D7
West Bedfont Sur 27 B8
West Benhar N Lanark 119 C8
West Bergholt Essex 43 B5
West Bexington Dorset 12 F3
West Bilney Norf 67 C7
West Blatchington Brighton 17 D6
West Bowling W Yorks 94 F4
West Bradford Lancs 93 E7
West Bradley Som 23 F7
West Bretton W Yorks 88 C3
West Bridgford Notts 77 F5
West Bromwich W Mid 62 E4
West Buckland Devon 21 F5
West Buckland Som 11 B6
West Burrafirth Shetland 160 H4
West Burton N Yorks 101 F5
West Burton W Sus 16 C3
West Butterwick N Lincs 90 D2
West Byfleet Sur 27 C8
West Caister Norf 69 C8
West Calder W Loth 120 C3
West Camel Som 12 B3
West Challow Oxon 38 F3
West Chelborough Dorset 12 D3
West Chevington Northumb 117 E8
West Chiltington W Sus 16 C4
West Chiltington Common W Sus 16 C4
West Chinnock Som 12 C2
West Chisenbury Wilts 25 D6
West Clandon Sur 27 D8
West Cliffe Kent 31 E7
West Clyne Highld 157 J11
West Clyth Highld 158 G4
West Coker Som 12 C3
West Compton Dorset 12 E3
West Compton Som 23 E7
West Cowick E Yorks 89 B7
West Cranmore Som 23 E8
West Cross Swansea 33 F7
West Cullery Aberds 141 D6
West Curry Corn 8 E4
West Curthwaite Cumb 108 E3
West Darlochan Argyll 143 F7
West Dean W Sus 16 C2
West Dean Wilts 14 B3
West Deeping Lincs 65 D8
West Derby Mers 85 E4
West Dereham Norf 67 D6
West Didsbury Gtr Man 87 E6
West Ditchburn Northumb 117 B7
West Down Devon 20 E4
West Drayton London 27 B8
West Drayton Notts 77 B7
West Ella E Yorks 90 B4
West End Bedford 53 D7
West End E Yorks 96 F5
West End E Yorks 97 F7
West End Hants 15 C5
West End Lancs 86 B5
West End N Som 23 C6
West End N Yorks 94 D4
West End Norf 68 D2
West End Norf 69 C8
West End Oxon 38 D4
West End S Lanark 120 E2
West End S Yorks 89 D7
West End Suff 69 F7
West End Sur 27 C7
West End W Sus 17 C6
West End Wilts 13 B7
West End Wilts 24 B4
West End Green Hants 26 C4
West Farleigh Kent 29 D8
West Felton Shrops 60 B3
West Fenton E Loth 129 F6
West Ferry Dundee 134 F4
West Firle E Sus 17 D8
West Ginge Oxon 38 F4
West Grafton Wilts 25 C7
West Green Hants 26 D5
West Greenskares Aberds 153 B7
West Grimstead Wilts 14 B3
West Grinstead W Sus 17 B5
West Haddlesey N Yorks 89 B6
West Haddon Northants 52 B4
West Hagbourne Oxon 39 F5
West Hagley Worcs 62 F3
West Hall Cumb 109 C5
West Hallam Derbys 76 E4
West Halton N Lincs 90 B3
West Ham London 41 F7
West Handley Derbys 76 B3
West Hanney Oxon 38 E4
West Hanningfield Essex 42 E3
West Hardwick W Yorks 88 C5
West Harnham Wilts 14 B2
West Harptree Bath 23 D7
West Hatch Som 11 B7
West Head Norf 67 D5
West Heath Ches E 74 C5
West Heath Hants 26 D3
West Heath Hants 27 D6
West Helmsdale Highld 157 H13
West Hendred Oxon 38 F4
West Heslerton N Yorks 96 B5
West Hill Devon 11 E5
West Hill E Yorks 97 C7
West Hill N Som 23 B6
West Hoathly W Sus 28 F4
West Holme Dorset 13 F6
West Horndon Essex 42 F2
West Horrington Som 23 E7
West Horsley Sur 27 D8
West Horton Northumb 123 F6
West Hougham Kent 31 E6
West Houlland Shetland 160 H4
West-houses Derbys 76 D4
West Huntington York 96 D2
West Hythe Kent 19 B8
West Ilsley W Berks 38 F4
West Itchenor W Sus 15 D8
West Keal Lincs 79 C6
West Kennett Wilts 25 C6
West Kilbride N Ayrs 118 E2
West Kingsdown Kent 29 C6
West Kington Wilts 24 B3
West Kinharrachie Aberds 153 E9
West Kirby Mers 85 F3
West Knapton N Yorks 96 B4
West Knighton Dorset 12 F5
West Knoyle Wilts 24 F3
West Kyloe Northumb 123 E6
West Lambrook Som 12 C2
West Langdon Kent 31 E7
West Langwell Highld 157 J9
West Lavington W Sus 16 B2
West Lavington Wilts 24 D5
West Layton N Yorks 101 D6
West Lea Durham 111 E7
West Leake Notts 64 B2
West Learmouth Northumb 122 F4
West Leigh Devon 9 D8
West Lexham Norf 67 C8
West Lilling N Yorks 96 C2
West Linton Borders 120 D4
West Liss Hants 15 B8
West Littleton S Glos 24 B2
West Looe Corn 5 D7
West Luccombe Som 21 E7
West Lulworth Dorset 13 F6
West Lutton N Yorks 96 C5
West Lydford Som 23 F7
West Lyng Som 11 B8
West Lynn Norf 67 B6
West Malling Kent 29 D7
West Malvern Worcs 50 E2
West Marden W Sus 15 C8
West Marina E Sus 18 E4
West Markham Notts 77 B7
West Marsh NE Lincs 91 C6
West Marton N Yorks 93 D8
West Meon Hants 15 B7
West Mersea Essex 43 C6
West Milton Dorset 12 E3
West Minster Kent 30 B3
West Molesey Sur 28 C2
West Monkton Som 11 B7
West Moors Dorset 13 D8
West Morriston Borders 122 E2
West Muir Angus 135 C5
West Ness N Yorks 96 B2
West Newham Northumb 110 B3
West Newton E Yorks 97 F7
West Newton Norf 67 B6
West Norwood London 28 B4
West Ogwell Devon 7 B6
West Orchard Dorset 13 C6
West Overton Wilts 25 C6
West Park Hrtlpl 111 F7
West Parley Dorset 13 E8
West Peckham Kent 29 D7
West Pelton Durham 110 D5
West Pennard Som 23 F7
West Pentire Corn 4 C2
West Perry Cambs 54 C2
West Putford Devon 9 C5
West Quantoxhead Som 22 E3
West Rainton Durham 111 E6
West Rasen Lincs 90 F4
West Raynham Norf 80 E4
West Retford Notts 89 F7
West Rounton N Yorks 102 D2
West Row Suff 55 B7
West Rudham Norf 80 E4
West Runton Norf 81 C7
West Saltoun E Loth 121 C7
West Sandwick Shetland 160 E6
West Scrafton N Yorks 101 F5
West Sleekburn Northumb 117 F8
West Somerton Norf 69 C7
West Stafford Dorset 12 F5
West Stockwith Notts 89 E8
West Stoke W Sus 16 D2
West Stonesdale N Yorks 100 D3
West Stoughton Som 23 E6
West Stour Dorset 13 B5
West Stourmouth Kent 31 C6
West Stow Suff 56 B2
West Stowell Wilts 25 C6
West Strathan Highld 157 C8
West Stratton Hants 26 E3
West Street Kent 30 D3
West Tanfield N Yorks 95 B5
West Taphouse Corn 5 C6
West Tarbert Argyll 145 G7
West Thirston Northumb 117 E7
West Thorney W Sus 15 D8
West Thurrock Thurrock 29 B6
West Tilbury Thurrock 29 B7
West Tisted Hants 15 B7
West Tofts Norf 67 E8
West Tofts Perth 133 F8
West Torrington Lincs 90 F5
West Town Hants 15 E8
West Town N Som 23 C6
West Tytherley Hants 14 B3
West Tytherton Wilts 24 B4
West Walton Norf 66 C4
West Walton Highway Norf 66 C4
West Wellow Hants 14 C3
West Wemyss Fife 128 E5
West Wick N Som 23 C5
West Wickham Cambs 55 E7
West Wickham London 28 C4
West Williamston Pembs 32 D1
West Willoughby Lincs 78 E2
West Winch Norf 67 C6
West Winterslow Wilts 25 F7
West Wittering W Sus 15 E8
West Witton N Yorks 101 F5
West Woodburn Northumb 116 F4
West Woodhay W Berks 25 C8
West Woodlands Som 24 E2
West Worldham Hants 26 F5
West Worlington Devon 10 C2
West Worthing W Sus 16 D5
West Wratting Cambs 55 D7
West Wycombe Bucks 39 E8
West Wylam Northumb 110 C4
West Yell Shetland 160 E6
Westacott Devon 20 F4
Westbere Kent 31 C5
Westborough Lincs 77 E8
Westbourne Bmouth 13 E8
Westbourne Suff 56 E5
Westbourne W Sus 15 D8
Westbrook W Berks 26 B2
Westbury Bucks 52 F4
Westbury Shrops 60 D3
Westbury Wilts 24 D3
Westbury Leigh Wilts 24 D3
Westbury-on-Severn Glos 36 C4
Westbury on Trym Bristol 23 B7
Westbury-sub-Mendip Som 23 E7
Westby Lancs 92 F3
Westcliff-on-Sea Southend 42 F4
Westcombe Som 23 F8
Westcote Glos 38 B2
Westcott Bucks 39 C7
Westcott Devon 10 D5
Westcott Sur 28 E2
Westcott Barton Oxon 38 B4
Westdean E Sus 18 F2
Westdene Brighton 17 D6
Wester Aberchalder Highld 137 B8
Wester Balgedie Perth 128 D3
Wester Culbeuchly Aberds 153 B6
Wester Dechmont W Loth 120 C3
Wester Denoon Angus 134 E3
Wester Fintray Aberds 141 C7
Wester Gruinards Highld 151 B8
Wester Lealty Highld 151 D9
Wester Milton Highld 151 F12
Wester Newburn Fife 129 D6
Wester Quarff Shetland 160 K6
Wester Skeld Shetland 160 J4
Westerdale Highld 158 E3
Westerdale N Yorks 102 D4
Westerfield Shetland 160 H5
Westerfield Suff 57 E5
Westergate W Sus 16 D3
Westerham Kent 28 D5
Westerhope T&W 110 C4
Westerleigh S Glos 23 B9
Westerton Angus 135 D6
Westerton Durham 110 F5
Westerton W Sus 16 D2
Westerwick Shetland 160 J4
Westfield Cumb 98 B1
Westfield E Sus 18 D5
Westfield Hereford 50 E2
Westfield Highld 158 D2
Westfield N Lanark 119 B7
Westfield Norf 68 D2
Westfield W Loth 120 B2
Westfields Dorset 12 D5
Westfields of Rattray Perth 134 E1
Westgate Durham 110 F2
Westgate N Lincs 89 D8
Westgate Norf 80 C4
Westgate Norf 81 C5
Westgate on Sea Kent 31 B7
Westhall Aberds 141 B5
Westhall Suff 69 F7
Westham Dorset 12 G4
Westham E Sus 18 E3
Westham Som 23 E6
Westhampnett W Sus 16 D2
Westhay Som 23 E6
Westhead Lancs 86 D2
Westhide Hereford 49 E7
Westhill Aberds 141 D7
Westhill Highld 151 G10
Westhope Hereford 49 D6
Westhope Shrops 60 F4
Westhorpe Lincs 78 F5
Westhorpe Suff 56 C4
Westhoughton Gtr Man 86 D4
Westhouse N Yorks 93 B6
Westhumble Sur 28 D2
Westing Shetland 160 C7
Westlake Devon 6 D4
Westleigh Devon 9 B6
Westleigh Devon 11 C5
Westleigh Gtr Man 86 D4
Westleton Suff 57 C8
Westley Shrops 60 D3
Westley Suff 56 C2
Westley Waterless Cambs 55 D7
Westlington Bucks 39 C7
Westlinton Cumb 108 C3
Westmarsh Kent 31 C6
Westmeston E Sus 17 C7
Westmill Herts 41 B6
Westminster London 28 B4
Westmuir Angus 134 D3
Westness Orkney 159 F4
Westnewton Cumb 107 E8
Westnewton Northumb 122 F5
Westoe T&W 111 C6
Weston Bath 24 C2
Weston Ches E 74 D4
Weston Devon 11 F6
Weston Dorset 12 G4
Weston Halton 86 F3
Weston Hants 15 B8
Weston Herts 54 F3
Weston Lincs 66 B2
Weston N Yorks 94 E4
Weston Northants 52 E3
Weston Notts 77 C7
Weston Shrops 61 B5
Weston Shrops 61 E5
Weston Staffs 62 B3
Weston W Berks 25 B8
Weston Beggard Hereford 49 E7
Weston by Welland Northants 64 E4
Weston Colville Cambs 55 D7
Weston Coyney Stoke 75 E6
Weston Favell Northants 53 C5
Weston Green Cambs 55 D7
Weston Green Norf 68 C4
Weston Heath Shrops 61 C7
Weston Hills Lincs 66 B2
Weston-in-Gordano N Som 23 B6
Weston Jones Staffs 61 B7
Weston Longville Norf 68 C4
Weston Lullingfields Shrops 60 B4
Weston-on-the-Green Oxon 39 C5
Weston-on-Trent Derbys 63 B8
Weston Patrick Hants 26 E4
Weston Rhyn Shrops 73 F6
Weston-Sub-Edge Glos 51 E6
Weston-super-Mare N Som 22 C5
Weston Turville Bucks 40 C1
Weston under Lizard Staffs 62 C2
Weston under Penyard Hereford 36 B3
Weston under Wetherley Warks 51 C8
Weston Underwood Derbys 76 E2
Weston Underwood M Keynes 53 D6
Westonbirt Glos 37 F5
Westoncommon Shrops 60 B4
Westoning C Beds 53 F8
Westonzoyland Som 23 F5
Westow N Yorks 96 C3
Westport Argyll 143 F7
Westport Som 11 C8
Westrigg W Loth 120 C2
Westruther Borders 122 E2
Westry Cambs 66 E3
Westville Notts 76 E5
Westward Cumb 108 E2
Westward Ho! Devon 9 B6
Westwell Kent 30 E3
Westwell Oxon 38 D2
Westwell Leacon Kent 30 E3
Westwick Cambs 54 C5
Westwick Durham 101 C5
Westwick Norf 81 E8
Westwood Devon 10 E5
Westwood Wilts 24 D3
Westwoodside N Lincs 89 E8
Wetheral Cumb 108 D4
Wetherby W Yorks 95 E7
Wetherden Suff 56 C4
Wetheringsett Suff 56 C5
Wethersfield Essex 55 F8
Wethersta Shetland 160 G5
Wetherup Street Suff 56 C5
Wetley Rocks Staffs 75 E6
Wettenhall Ches E 74 C3
Wetton Staffs 75 D8
Wetwang E Yorks 96 D5
Wetwood Staffs 74 F4
Wexcombe Wilts 25 D7
Wexham Street Bucks 40 F2
Weybourne Norf 81 C7
Weybread Suff 68 F5
Weybridge Sur 27 C8
Weycroft Devon 11 E8
Weydale Highld 158 D3
Weyhill Hants 25 E8
Weymouth Dorset 12 G4
Whaddon Bucks 53 F6
Whaddon Cambs 54 E4
Whaddon Glos 37 C5
Whaddon Wilts 14 B2
Whale Cumb 99 B7
Whaley Derbys 76 B5
Whaley Bridge Derbys 87 F8
Whaley Thorns Derbys 76 B5
Whaligoe Highld 158 F5
Whalley Lancs 93 F7
Whalton Northumb 117 F7
Wham N Yorks 93 C7
Whaplode Lincs 66 B3
Whaplode Drove Lincs 66 C3
Whaplode St Catherine Lincs 66 B3
Wharfe N Yorks 93 C7
Wharles Lancs 92 F4
Wharncliffe Side S Yorks 88 E3
Wharram le Street N Yorks 96 C4
Wharton Ches W 74 C3
Wharton Green Ches W 74 C3
Whashton N Yorks 101 D6
Whatcombe Dorset 13 D6
Whatcote Warks 51 E8
Whatfield Suff 56 E4
Whatley Som 11 D8
Whatley Som 24 E2
Whatlington E Sus 18 D4
Whatstandwell Derbys 76 D3
Whatton Notts 77 F7
Whauphill Dumfries 105 E8
Whaw N Yorks 100 D4
Wheatacre Norf 69 E7
Wheatcroft Derbys 76 D3
Wheathampstead Herts 40 C4
Wheathill Shrops 61 F6
Wheatley Devon 10 E4
Wheatley Hants 27 E5
Wheatley Oxon 39 D5
Wheatley S Yorks 89 D6
Wheatley W Yorks 87 B8
Wheatley Hill Durham 111 F6
Wheaton Aston Staffs 62 C2
Wheddon Cross Som 21 F8
Wheedlemont Aberds 140 B3
Wheelerstreet Sur 27 E7
Wheelock Ches E 74 D4
Wheelock Heath Ches E 74 D4
Wheelton Lancs 86 B4
Wheen Angus 134 B3
Wheldrake York 96 E2
Whelford Glos 38 E1
Whelpley Hill Herts 40 D2
Whempstead Herts 41 B6
Whenby N Yorks 96 C2
Whepstead Suff 56 D2
Wherstead Suff 57 E5
Wherwell Hants 25 E8
Wheston Derbys 75 B8
Whetsted Kent 29 E7
Whetstone Leics 64 E2
Whicham Cumb 98 F3
Whichford Warks 51 F8
Whickham T&W 110 C5
Whiddon Down Devon 9 E8
Whigstreet Angus 134 E4
Whilton Northants 52 C4
Whim Farm Borders 120 D5
Whimble Devon 9 D5
Whimple Devon 10 E5
Whimpwell Green Norf 69 B6
Whinburgh Norf 68 D3
Whinnieliggate Dumfries 106 D4
Whinnyfold Aberds 153 E10
Whippingham IoW 15 E6
Whipsnade C Beds 40 C3
Whipton Devon 10 E4
Whirlow S Yorks 88 F4
Whisby Lincs 78 C2
Whissendine Rutland 64 C5
Whissonsett Norf 80 E5
Whistlefield Argyll 145 D10
Whistlefield Argyll 145 D11
Whistley Green Wokingham 27 B5
Whiston Mers 86 E2
Whiston Northants 53 C6
Whiston S Yorks 88 F5
Whiston Staffs 62 C2
Whiston Staffs 75 E7
Whitbeck Cumb 98 F3
Whitbourne Hereford 50 D2
Whitburn T&W 111 C7
Whitburn W Loth 120 C2
Whitburn Colliery T&W 111 C7
Whitby Ches W 73 B7
Whitby N Yorks 103 C6
Whitbyheath Ches W 73 B7
Whitchurch Bath 23 C8
Whitchurch Bucks 39 B7
Whitchurch Cardiff 35 F5
Whitchurch Devon 6 B2
Whitchurch Hants 26 E2
Whitchurch Hereford 36 C2
Whitchurch Oxon 26 B4
Whitchurch Pembs 44 C2
Whitchurch Shrops 74 E2
Whitchurch Canonicorum Dorset 11 E8
Whitchurch Hill Oxon 26 B4
Whitcombe Dorset 12 F5
Whitcott Keysett Shrops 60 F2
White Coppice Lancs 86 C4
White Lackington Dorset 12 E5
White Ladies Aston Worcs 50 D4
White Lund Lancs 92 C4
White Mill Carms 33 B5
White Ness Shetland 160 J5
White Notley Essex 42 C3
White Pit Lincs 79 B6
White Post Notts 77 D6
White Rocks Hereford 35 B8
White Roding Essex 42 C1
White Waltham Windsor 27 B6
Whiteacen Moray 152 D2
Whiteacre Heath Warks 63 E6
Whitebridge Highld 137 C7
Whitebrook Mon 36 D2
Whiteburn Borders 121 E8
Whitecairn Dumfries 105 D6
Whitecairns Aberds 141 C8
Whitecastle S Lanark 120 E3
Whitechapel Lancs 93 E5
Whitecleat Orkney 159 H6
Whitecraig E Loth 121 B6
Whitecroft Glos 36 D3
Whitecross Corn 4 B4
Whitecross Falk 120 B2
Whitecross Staffs 62 B2
Whiteface Highld 151 C10
Whitefarland N Ayrs 143 D9
Whitefaulds S Ayrs 112 D2
Whitefield Gtr Man 87 D6
Whitefield Perth 134 F1
Whiteford Aberds 141 B6
Whitegate Ches W 74 C3
Whitehall Blackburn 86 B4
Whitehall W Sus 16 B5
Whitehall Village Orkney 159 F7
Whitehaven Cumb 98 C1
Whitehill Hants 27 F5
Whitehills Aberds 153 B6
Whitehills S Lanark 119 D6
Whitehough Derbys 87 F8
Whitehouse Aberds 140 C5
Whitehouse Argyll 145 G7
Whiteinch Glasgow 118 C5
Whitekirk E Loth 129 F7
Whitelaw S Lanark 119 E6
Whiteleas T&W 111 C6
Whiteley Bank IoW 15 F6
Whiteley Green Ches E 75 B6
Whiteley Village Sur 27 C8
Whitemans Green W Sus 17 B7
Whitemire Moray 151 F12
Whitemoor Corn 4 D4
Whitemore Staffs 75 C5
Whitenap Hants 14 B4
Whiteoak Green Oxon 38 C3
Whiteparish Wilts 14 B3
Whiterashes Aberds 141 B7
Whiterow Highld 158 F5
Whiteshill Glos 37 D5
Whiteside Northumb 109 C7
Whiteside W Loth 120 C2
Whitesmith E Sus 18 D2
Whitestaunton Som 11 C7
Whitestone Devon 10 E3
Whitestone Devon 20 E3
Whitestone Warks 63 F7
Whitestones Aberds 153 C8
Whitestreet Green Suff 56 F3
Whitewall Corner N Yorks 96 B3
Whiteway Glos 37 C6
Whiteway Glos 37 E5
Whitewell Aberds 153 B9
Whitewell Lancs 93 E6
Whitewell Bottom Lancs 87 B6
Whiteworks Devon 6 B4
Whitfield Kent 31 E7
Whitfield Northants 52 F4
Whitfield Northumb 109 D7
Whitfield S Glos 36 E3
Whitford Devon 11 E7
Whitford Flint 72 B5
Whitgift E Yorks 90 B2
Whitgreave Staffs 62 B2
Whithorn Dumfries 105 E8
Whiting Bay N Ayrs 143 F11
Whitkirk W Yorks 95 F6
Whitland Carms 32 C2
Whitletts S Ayrs 112 B3
Whitley N Yorks 89 B6
Whitley Reading 26 B5
Whitley Wilts 24 C3
Whitley Bay T&W 111 B6
Whitley Chapel Northumb 110 D2
Whitley Lower W Yorks 88 C3
Whitley Row Kent 29 D5
Whitlock's End W Mid 51 B6
Whitminster Glos 36 D4
Whitmore Staffs 74 E5
Whitnage Devon 10 C5
Whitnash Warks 51 C8
Whitney-on-Wye Hereford 48 E4
Whitrigg Cumb 108 D2
Whitrigg Cumb 108 F2
Whitsbury Hants 14 C2
Whitsome Borders 122 D4
Whitson Newport 35 F7
Whitstable Kent 30 C5
Whitstone Corn 8 E4
Whittingham Northumb 117 C6
Whittingslow Shrops 60 F4
Whittington Glos 37 B7
Whittington Lancs 93 B6
Whittington Norf 67 E7
Whittington Shrops 73 F7
Whittington Staffs 62 F2
Whittington Staffs 63 D5
Whittington Worcs 50 D3
Whittle-le-Woods Lancs 86 B3
Whittlebury Northants 52 E4
Whittlesey Cambs 66 E2
Whittlesford Cambs 55 E5
Whittlestone Head Blackburn 86 C5
Whitton Borders 116 B3
Whitton N Lincs 90 B3
Whitton Northumb 117 D6
Whitton Powys 48 C4
Whitton Shrops 49 B7
Whitton Stockton 102 B1
Whitton Suff 56 E5
Whittonditch Wilts 25 B7
Whittonstall Northumb 110 D3
Whitway Hants 26 D2
Whitwell Derbys 76 B5
Whitwell Herts 40 B4
Whitwell IoW 15 G6
Whitwell N Yorks 101 E7

Whitwell Rutland 65 D6
Whitwell-on-the-Hill N Yorks 96 C3
Whitwell Street Norf 81 E7
Whitwick Leics 63 C8
Whitwood W Yorks 88 B5
Whitworth Lancs 87 C6
Whixall Shrops 74 F2
Whixley N Yorks 95 D7
Whoberley W Mid 51 B8
Whorlton Durham 101 C6
Whorlton N Yorks 102 D2
Whygate Northumb 109 B7
Whyle Hereford 49 C7
Whyteleafe Sur 28 D4
Wibdon Glos 36 E2
Wibsey W Yorks 88 A2
Wibtoft Leics 63 F8
Wichenford Worcs 50 C2
Wichling Kent 30 D3
Wick Bmouth 14 E2
Wick Devon 11 D6
Wick Highld 158 E5
Wick S Glos 24 B2
Wick Shetland 160 K6
Wick V Glam 21 B8
Wick W Sus 16 D4
Wick Wilts 14 B2
Wick Worcs 50 E4
Wick Hill Wokingham 27 C5
Wick St Lawrence N Som 23 C5
Wicken Cambs 55 B6
Wicken Northants 52 F5
Wicken Bonhunt Essex 55 F5
Wicken Green Village Norf 80 D4
Wickenby Lincs 90 F4
Wickersley S Yorks 89 E5
Wickford Essex 42 E3
Wickham Hants 15 C6
Wickham W Berks 25 B8
Wickham Bishops Essex 42 C4
Wickham Market Suff 57 D7
Wickham Skeith Suff 56 C4
Wickham St Paul Essex 56 F2
Wickham Street Suff 55 D8
Wickhambreux Kent 31 D6
Wickhambrook Suff 55 D8
Wickhamford Worcs 51 E5
Wickhampton Norf 69 D7
Wicklewood Norf 68 D3
Wickmere Norf 81 D7
Wickwar S Glos 36 F4
Widdington Essex 55 F6
Widdrington Northumb 117 E8
Widdrington Station Northumb 117 E8
Wide Open T&W 110 B5
Widecombe in the Moor Devon 6 B5
Widegates Corn 5 D7
Widemouth Bay Corn 8 E4
Widewall Orkney 159 J5
Widford Essex 42 D2
Widford Herts 41 C7
Widham Wilts 37 F7
Widmer End Bucks 40 E1
Widmerpool Notts 64 B3
Widnes Halton 86 F3
Wigan Gtr Man 86 D3
Wiggaton Devon 11 E6
Wiggenhall St Germans Norf 67 C5
Wiggenhall St Mary Magdalen Norf 67 C5
Wiggenhall St Mary the Virgin Norf 67 C5
Wigginton Herts 40 C2
Wigginton Oxon 51 F8
Wigginton Staffs 63 D6
Wigginton York 95 D8
Wigglesworth N Yorks 93 D8
Wiggonby Cumb 108 D2
Wiggonholt W Sus 16 C4
Wighill N Yorks 95 E7
Wighton Norf 80 D5
Wigley Hants 14 C4
Wigmore Hereford 49 C6
Wigmore Medway 30 C2
Wigsley Notts 77 B8
Wigsthorpe Northants 65 F7
Wigston Leics 64 E3
Wigthorpe Notts 89 F6
Wigtoft Lincs 79 F5
Wigton Cumb 108 E2
Wigtown Dumfries 105 D8
Wigtwizzle S Yorks 88 E3
Wike W Yorks 95 E6
Wike Well End S Yorks 89 C7
Wilbarston Northants 64 F5
Wilberfoss E Yorks 96 D3
Wilberlee W Yorks 87 C8
Wilburton Cambs 55 B5
Wilby Norf 68 F3
Wilby Northants 53 C7
Wilby Suff 57 B6
Wilcot Wilts 25 C6
Wilcott Shrops 60 C3
Wilcrick Newport 35 F8
Wilday Green Derbys 76 B3
Wildboarclough Ches E 75 C6
Wilden Bedford 53 D8
Wilden Worcs 50 B3
Wildhern Hants 25 D8
Wildhill Herts 41 D5
Wildmoor Worcs 50 B4
Wildsworth Lincs 90 E2
Wilford Nottingham 77 F5
Wilkesley Ches E 74 E3
Wilkhaven Highld 151 C12
Wilkieston W Loth 120 C4
Willand Devon 11 C5
Willaston Ches E 74 D3
Willaston Ches W 73 B7
Willen M Keynes 53 E6
Willenhall W Mid 51 B8
Willenhall W Mid 62 E3

Willerby E Yorks 97 F6
Willerby N Yorks 97 B6
Willersey Glos 51 F6
Willersley Hereford 48 E5
Willesborough Kent 30 E4
Willesborough Lees Kent 30 E4
Willesden London 41 F5
Willett Som 22 F3
Willey Shrops 61 E6
Willey Warks 63 F8
Willey Green Sur 27 D7
Willian Herts 54 F3
Willingale Essex 42 D1
Willingdon E Sus 18 E2
Willingham Cambs 54 B5
Willingham by Stow Lincs 90 F2
Willington Bedford 54 E2
Willington Derbys 63 B6
Willington Durham 110 F4
Willington T&W 111 C6
Willington Warks 51 F7
Willington Corner Ches W 74 C2
Willisham Tye Suff 56 D4
Willitoft E Yorks 96 F3
Williton Som 22 E2
Willoughbridge Staffs 74 E4
Willoughby Lincs 79 B7
Willoughby Warks 52 C3
Willoughby-on-the-Wolds Notts 64 B3
Willoughby Waterleys Leics 64 E2
Willoughton Lincs 90 E3
Willows Green Essex 42 C3
Willsbridge S Glos 23 B8
Willsworthy Devon 9 F7
Wilmcote Warks 51 D6
Wilmington Devon 11 E7
Wilmington E Sus 18 E2
Wilmington Kent 29 B6
Wilminstone Devon 6 B3
Wilmslow Ches E 87 F6
Wilnecote Staffs 63 D6
Wilpshire Lancs 93 F6
Wilsden W Yorks 94 F3
Wilsford Lincs 78 E3
Wilsford Wilts 25 D6
Wilsford Wilts 25 F6
Wilsill N Yorks 94 C4
Wilsley Pound Kent 18 B4
Wilsom Hants 26 F5
Wilson Leics 63 B8
Wilsontown S Lanark 120 D2
Wilstead Bedford 53 E8
Wilsthorpe Lincs 65 C7
Wilstone Herts 40 C2
Wilton Borders 115 C7
Wilton Cumb 98 C2
Wilton N Yorks 103 F6
Wilton Redcar 102 C3
Wilton Wilts 25 C7
Wilton Wilts 25 F5
Wimbish Essex 55 F6
Wimbish Green Essex 55 F7
Wimblebury Staffs 62 C4
Wimbledon London 28 B3
Wimblington Cambs 66 E4
Wimborne Minster Dorset 13 E8
Wimborne St Giles Dorset 13 C8
Wimbotsham Norf 67 D6
Wimpson Soton 14 C4
Wimpstone Warks 51 E7
Wincanton Som 12 B5
Wincham Ches W 74 B3
Winchburgh W Loth 120 B3
Winchcombe Glos 37 B7
Winchelsea E Sus 19 D6
Winchelsea Beach E Sus 19 D6
Winchester Hants 15 B5
Winchet Hill Kent 29 E8
Winchfield Hants 27 D5
Winchmore Hill Bucks 40 E2
Winchmore Hill London 41 E6
Wincle Ches E 75 C6
Wincobank S Yorks 88 E4
Windermere Cumb 99 E6
Winderton Warks 51 E8
Windhill Highld 151 G8
Windhouse Shetland 160 D6
Windlehurst Gtr Man 87 F7
Windlesham Sur 27 C7
Windley Derbys 76 E3
Windmill Hill E Sus 18 D3
Windmill Hill Som 11 C8
Windrush Glos 38 C1
Windsor Windsor 27 B7
Windsoredge Glos 37 D5
Windygates Fife 128 D5
Windyknowe W Loth 120 C2
Windywalls Borders 122 F3
Wineham W Sus 17 B6
Winestead E Yorks 91 B6
Winewall Lancs 94 E2
Winfarthing Norf 68 F4
Winford IoW 15 F6
Winford N Som 23 C7
Winforton Hereford 48 E4
Winfrith Newburgh Dorset 13 F6
Wing Bucks 40 B1
Wing Rutland 65 D5
Wingate Durham 111 F7
Wingates Gtr Man 86 D4
Wingates Northumb 117 E7
Wingerworth Derbys 76 C3
Wingfield C Beds 40 B2
Wingfield Suff 57 B6
Wingfield Wilts 24 D3
Wingham Kent 31 D6
Wingmore Kent 31 E5
Wingrave Bucks 40 C1
Winkburn Notts 77 D7
Winkfield Brack 27 B6
Winkfield Row Brack 27 B6
Winkhill Staffs 75 D7
Winklebury Hants 26 D4

Winkleigh Devon 9 D8
Winksley N Yorks 95 B5
Winkton Dorset 14 E2
Winlaton T&W 110 C4
Winless Highld 158 E5
Winmarleigh Lancs 92 E4
Winnal Hereford 49 F6
Winnall Hants 15 B5
Winnersh Wokingham 27 B5
Winscales Cumb 98 B2
Winscombe N Som 23 D6
Winsford Ches W 74 C3
Winsford Som 21 F8
Winsham Som 11 D8
Winshill Staffs 63 B6
Winskill Cumb 109 F5
Winslade Hants 26 E4
Winsley Wilts 24 C3
Winslow Bucks 39 B7
Winson Glos 37 D7
Winson Green W Mid 62 F4
Winsor Hants 14 C4
Winster Cumb 99 E6
Winster Derbys 76 C2
Winston Durham 101 C6
Winston Suff 57 C5
Winston Green Suff 57 C5
Winstone Glos 37 D6
Winswell Devon 9 C6
Winter Gardens Essex 42 F3
Winterborne Clenston Dorset 13 D6
Winterborne Herringston Dorset 12 F4
Winterborne Houghton Dorset 13 D6
Winterborne Kingston Dorset 13 E6
Winterborne Monkton Dorset 12 F4
Winterborne Stickland Dorset 13 D6
Winterborne Whitechurch Dorset 13 D6
Winterborne Zelston Dorset 13 E6
Winterbourne S Glos 36 F3
Winterbourne W Berks 26 B2
Winterbourne Abbas Dorset 12 E4
Winterbourne Bassett Wilts 25 B6
Winterbourne Dauntsey Wilts 25 F6
Winterbourne Down S Glos 23 B8
Winterbourne Earls Wilts 25 F6
Winterbourne Gunner Wilts 25 F6
Winterbourne Monkton Wilts 25 B6
Winterbourne Steepleton Dorset 12 F4
Winterbourne Stoke Wilts 25 E5
Winterburn N Yorks 94 D2
Winteringham N Lincs 90 B3
Winterley Ches E 74 D4
Wintersett W Yorks 88 C4
Wintershill Hants 15 C6
Winterton N Lincs 90 C3
Winterton-on-Sea Norf 69 C7
Winthorpe Lincs 79 C8
Winthorpe Notts 77 D8
Winton Bmouth 13 E8
Winton Cumb 100 C2
Winton N Yorks 102 E2
Wintringham N Yorks 96 B4
Winwick Cambs 65 F8
Winwick Northants 52 B4
Winwick Warr 86 E4
Wirksworth Derbys 76 D2
Wirksworth Moor Derbys 76 D3
Wirswall Ches E 74 E2
Wisbech Cambs 66 D4
Wisbech St Mary Cambs 66 D4
Wisborough Green W Sus 16 B4
Wiseton Notts 89 F7
Wishaw N Lanark 119 D7
Wishaw Warks 63 E5
Wisley Sur 27 D8
Wispington Lincs 78 B5
Wissenden Kent 30 E3
Wissett Suff 57 B7
Wistanstow Shrops 60 F4
Wistanswick Shrops 61 B6
Wistaston Ches E 74 D3
Wistaston Green Ches E 74 D3
Wiston Pembs 32 C1
Wiston S Lanark 120 F2
Wiston W Sus 16 C5
Wistow Cambs 66 F2
Wistow N Yorks 95 F8
Wiswell Lancs 93 F7
Witcham Cambs 66 F4
Witchampton Dorset 13 D7
Witchford Cambs 55 B6
Witham Essex 42 C4
Witham Friary Som 24 E2
Witham on the Hill Lincs 65 C7
Withcall Lincs 91 F6
Withdean Brighton 17 D7
Witherenden Hill E Sus 18 C3
Witheridge Devon 10 C3
Witherley Leics 63 E7
Withern Lincs 91 F8
Withernsea E Yorks 91 B7
Withernwick E Yorks 97 E7
Withersdale Street Suff 69 F5
Withersfield Suff 55 E7
Witherslack Cumb 99 F6
Withiel Corn 4 C4
Withiel Florey Som 21 F8
Withington Glos 37 C7

Withington Gtr Man 87 E6
Withington Hereford 49 E7
Withington Shrops 61 C5
Withington Staffs 75 F7
Withington Green Ches E 74 B5
Withleigh Devon 10 C4
Withnell Lancs 86 B4
Withybrook Warks 63 F8
Withycombe Som 22 E2
Withycombe Raleigh Devon 10 F5
Withyham E Sus 29 F5
Withypool Som 21 F7
Witley Sur 27 F7
Witnesham Suff 57 D5
Witney Oxon 38 C3
Wittering Pboro 65 D7
Wittersham Kent 19 C5
Witton Angus 135 B5
Witton Worcs 50 C3
Witton Bridge Norf 69 A6
Witton Gilbert Durham 110 E5
Witton-le-Wear Durham 110 F4
Witton Park Durham 110 F4
Wiveliscombe Som 11 B5
Wivelrod Hants 26 F4
Wivelsfield E Sus 17 B7
Wivelsfield Green E Sus 17 B7
Wivenhoe Essex 43 B6
Wivenhoe Cross Essex 43 B6
Wiveton Norf 81 C6
Wix Essex 43 B7
Wixford Warks 51 D5
Wixhill Shrops 61 B5
Wixoe Suff 55 E8
Woburn C Beds 53 F7
Woburn Sands M Keynes 53 F7
Wokefield Park W Berks 26 C4
Woking Sur 27 D8
Wokingham Wokingham 27 C6
Wolborough Devon 7 B6
Wold Newton E Yorks 97 B6
Wold Newton NE Lincs 91 E6
Woldingham Sur 28 D4
Wolfclyde S Lanark 120 F3
Wolferton Norf 67 B6
Wolfhill Perth 134 F1
Wolf's Castle Pembs 44 C4
Wolfsdale Pembs 44 C4
Woll Borders 115 B7
Wollaston Northants 53 C7
Wollaston Shrops 60 C3
Wollaton Nottingham 76 F5
Wollerton Shrops 74 F3
Wollescote W Mid 62 F3
Wolsingham Durham 110 F3
Wolstanton Staffs 75 E5
Wolston Warks 52 B2
Wolvercote Oxon 38 D4
Wolverhampton W Mid 62 E3
Wolverley Shrops 73 F8
Wolverley Worcs 50 B3
Wolverton Hants 26 D3
Wolverton M Keynes 53 E6
Wolverton Warks 51 C7
Wolverton Common Hants 26 D3
Wolvesnewton Mon 36 E1
Wolvey Warks 63 F8
Wolviston Stockton 102 B2
Wombleton N Yorks 102 F4
Wombourne Staffs 62 E2
Wombwell S Yorks 88 D4
Womenswold Kent 31 D6
Womersley N Yorks 89 C6
Wonastow Mon 36 C1
Wonersh Sur 27 E8
Wonson Devon 9 F8
Wonston Hants 26 F2
Wooburn Bucks 40 F2
Wooburn Green Bucks 40 F2
Wood Dalling Norf 81 E6
Wood End Herts 41 B6
Wood End Warks 51 B6
Wood End Warks 63 E6
Wood Enderby Lincs 79 C5
Wood Field Sur 28 D2
Wood Green London 41 E6
Wood Hayes W Mid 62 D3
Wood Lanes Ches E 87 F7
Wood Norton Norf 81 E6
Wood Street Norf 69 B6
Wood Street Sur 27 D7
Wood Walton Cambs 66 F2
Woodacott Devon 9 D5
Woodale N Yorks 94 B3
Woodbank Argyll 143 G7
Woodbastwick Norf 69 C6
Woodbeck Notts 77 B7
Woodborough Notts 77 E6
Woodborough Wilts 25 D6
Woodbridge Dorset 12 C5
Woodbridge Suff 57 E6
Woodbury Devon 10 F5
Woodbury Salterton Devon 10 F5
Woodchester Glos 37 D5
Woodchurch Kent 19 B6
Woodchurch Mers 85 F3
Woodcombe Som 21 E8
Woodcote Oxon 39 F6
Woodcott Hants 26 D2
Woodcroft Glos 36 E2
Woodcutts Dorset 13 C7
Woodditton Cambs 55 D7
Woodeaton Oxon 39 C5
Woodend Cumb 98 E3
Woodend Northants 52 E4
Woodend W Sus 16 D2
Woodend Green Northants 52 E4
Woodfalls Wilts 14 B2
Woodfield Oxon 39 B5
Woodfield S Ayrs 112 B3
Woodford Corn 8 C4
Woodford Devon 7 D5
Woodford Glos 36 E3

Woodford Gtr Man 87 F6
Woodford London 41 E7
Woodford Northants 53 B7
Woodford Bridge London 41 E7
Woodford Halse Northants 52 D3
Woodgate Norf 68 C3
Woodgate W Mid 62 F3
Woodgate W Sus 16 D3
Woodgate Worcs 50 C4
Woodgreen Hants 14 C2
Woodhall Herts 41 C5
Woodhall Invclyd 118 B3
Woodhall N Yorks 100 E4
Woodhall Spa Lincs 78 C4
Woodham Sur 27 C8
Woodham Ferrers Essex 42 E3
Woodham Mortimer Essex 42 D4
Woodham Walter Essex 42 D4
Woodhaven Fife 129 B6
Woodhead Aberds 153 E7
Woodhey Gtr Man 87 C5
Woodhill Shrops 61 F7
Woodhorn Northumb 117 F8
Woodhouse Leics 64 C2
Woodhouse N Lincs 89 D8
Woodhouse S Yorks 88 F5
Woodhouse W Yorks 88 B4
Woodhouse W Yorks 95 F5
Woodhouse Eaves Leics 64 C2
Woodhouse Park Gtr Man 87 F6
Woodhouselee Midloth 120 C5
Woodhouselees Dumfries 108 B3
Woodhouses Staffs 63 C5
Woodhurst Cambs 54 B4
Woodingdean Brighton 17 D7
Woodkirk W Yorks 88 B3
Woodland Devon 7 C5
Woodland Durham 101 B5
Woodlands Aberds 141 E6
Woodlands Dorset 13 D8
Woodlands Hants 14 C4
Woodlands Highld 151 E8
Woodlands N Yorks 95 D6
Woodlands S Yorks 89 D6
Woodlands Park Windsor 27 B6
Woodlands St Mary W Berks 25 B8
Woodlane Staffs 62 B5
Woodleigh Devon 6 E5
Woodlesford W Yorks 88 B4
Woodley Gtr Man 87 E7
Woodley Wokingham 27 B5
Woodmancote Glos 36 E4
Woodmancote Glos 37 B6
Woodmancote Glos 37 D7
Woodmancote W Sus 15 D8
Woodmancote W Sus 17 C6
Woodmancott Hants 26 E3
Woodmansey E Yorks 97 F6
Woodmansterne Sur 28 D3
Woodminton Wilts 13 B8
Woodnesborough Kent 31 D7
Woodnewton Northants 65 E7
Woodplumpton Lancs 92 F5
Woodrising Norf 68 D2
Wood's Green E Sus 18 B3
Woodseaves Shrops 74 F3
Woodseaves Staffs 61 B7
Woodsend Wilts 25 B7
Woodsetts S Yorks 89 F6
Woodsford Dorset 13 E5
Woodside Aberdeen 141 D8
Woodside Brack 27 B7
Woodside Fife 129 D6
Woodside Hants 14 E4
Woodside Herts 41 D5
Woodside Perth 134 F2
Woodside of Arbeadie Aberds 141 E6
Woodstock Oxon 38 C4
Woodstock Pembs 32 B1
Woodthorpe Derbys 76 B4
Woodthorpe Leics 64 C2
Woodthorpe Lincs 91 F8
Woodthorpe York 95 E8
Woodtown Devon 9 B6
Woodtown Devon 9 B6
Woodvale Mers 85 C4
Woodville Derbys 63 C7
Woodyates Dorset 13 C8
Woofferton Shrops 49 C7
Wookey Som 23 E7
Wookey Hole Som 23 E7
Wool Dorset 13 F6
Woolacombe Devon 20 E3
Woolage Green Kent 31 E6
Woolaston Glos 36 E2
Woolavington Som 22 E5
Woolbeding W Sus 16 B2
Wooldale W Yorks 88 D2
Wooler Northumb 117 B5
Woolfardisworthy Devon 10 C2
Woolfardisworthy Devon 8 B5
Woolfords Cottages S Lanark 120 D3
Woolhampton W Berks 26 C3
Woolhope Hereford 49 F8
Woolhope Cockshoot Hereford 49 F8
Woolland Dorset 13 D5
Woollaton Devon 9 C6
Woolley Bath 24 C2
Woolley Cambs 54 B2
Woolley Corn 8 C4
Woolley Derbys 76 C3
Woolley W Yorks 88 C4
Woolmer Green Herts 41 C5

Woolmere Green Worcs 50 C4
Woolpit Suff 56 C3
Woolscott Warks 52 C2
Woolsington T&W 110 C4
Woolstanwood Ches E 74 D3
Woolstaston Shrops 60 E4
Woolsthorpe Lincs 65 B6
Woolsthorpe Lincs 77 F8
Woolston Devon 6 E5
Woolston Shrops 60 B3
Woolston Shrops 60 F4
Woolston Soton 14 C5
Woolston Warr 86 F4
Woolstone M Keynes 53 F6
Woolstone Oxon 38 F2
Woolton Mers 86 F2
Woolton Hill Hants 26 C2
Woolverstone Suff 57 F5
Woolverton Som 24 D2
Woolwich London 28 B5
Woolwich Ferry London 28 B5
Wooperton Northumb 117 B6
Woore Shrops 74 E4
Wootton Bedford 53 E8
Wootton Hants 14 E3
Wootton Hereford 48 D5
Wootton Kent 31 E6
Wootton N Lincs 90 C4
Wootton Northants 53 D5
Wootton Oxon 38 C4
Wootton Oxon 38 D4
Wootton Shrops 60 B3
Wootton Shrops 60 F3
Wootton Staffs 62 B2
Wootton Staffs 75 E8
Wootton Bridge IoW 15 E6
Wootton Common IoW 15 E6
Wootton Courtenay Som 21 E8
Wootton Fitzpaine Dorset 11 E8
Wootton Rivers Wilts 25 C6
Wootton St Lawrence Hants 26 D3
Wootton Wawen Warks 51 C6
Worcester Worcs 50 D3
Worcester Park London 28 C3
Wordsley W Mid 62 F2
Worfield Shrops 61 E7
Work Orkney 159 G5
Workington Cumb 98 B1
Worksop Notts 77 B5
Worlaby N Lincs 90 C4
World's End W Berks 26 B2
Worle N Som 23 C5
Worleston Ches E 74 D3
Worlingham Suff 69 F7
Worlington Suff 55 B7
Worlingworth Suff 57 C6
Wormald Green N Yorks 95 C6
Wormbridge Hereford 49 F6
Wormegay Norf 67 C6
Wormelow Tump Hereford 49 F6
Wormhill Derbys 75 B8
Wormingford Essex 56 F3
Worminghall Bucks 39 D6
Wormington Glos 50 F5
Worminster Som 23 E7
Wormit Fife 129 B5
Wormleighton Warks 52 D2
Wormley Herts 41 D6
Wormley Sur 27 F7
Wormley West End Herts 41 D6
Wormshill Kent 30 D2
Wormsley Hereford 49 E6
Worplesdon Sur 27 D7
Worrall S Yorks 88 E4
Worsbrough S Yorks 88 D4
Worsbrough Common S Yorks 88 D4
Worsley Gtr Man 86 D5
Worstead Norf 69 B6
Worsthorne Lancs 93 F8
Worston Lancs 93 E7
Worswell Devon 6 E3
Worth Kent 31 D7
Worth W Sus 28 F4
Worth Matravers Dorset 13 G7
Wortham Suff 56 B4
Worthen Shrops 60 D3
Worthenbury Wrex 73 E8
Worthing Norf 68 C2
Worthing W Sus 16 D5
Worthington Leics 63 B8
Worting Hants 26 D4
Wortley S Yorks 88 E4
Wortley W Yorks 95 F5
Worton N Yorks 100 E4
Worton Wilts 24 D4
Wortwell Norf 69 F5
Wotherton Shrops 60 D2
Wotter Devon 6 C3
Wotton Sur 28 E2
Wotton-under-Edge Glos 36 E4
Wotton Underwood Bucks 39 C6
Woughton on the Green M Keynes 53 F6
Wouldham Kent 29 C8
Wrabness Essex 57 F5
Wrafton Devon 20 F3
Wragby Lincs 78 B4
Wragby W Yorks 88 C4
Wragholme Lincs 91 E7
Wramplingham Norf 68 D4
Wrangbrook W Yorks 89 C5
Wrangham Aberds 153 E6
Wrangle Lincs 79 D7
Wrangle Bank Lincs 79 D7
Wrangle Lowgate Lincs 79 D7
Wrangway Som 11 C6

Wrantage Som 11 B8
Wrawby N Lincs 90 D4
Wraxall Dorset 12 D3
Wraxall N Som 23 B6
Wraxall Som 23 F8
Wray Lancs 93 C6
Wraysbury Windsor 27 B8
Wrayton Lancs 93 B6
Wrea Green Lancs 92 F3
Wreay Cumb 99 B6
Wreay Cumb 108 E4
Wrecclesham Sur 27 E6
Wrecsam = Wrexham Wrex 73 D7
Wrekenton T&W 111 D5
Wrelton N Yorks 103 F5
Wrenbury Ches E 74 E2
Wrench Green N Yorks 103 F7
Wreningham Norf 68 E4
Wrentham Suff 69 F7
Wrenthorpe W Yorks 88 B4
Wrentnall Shrops 60 D4
Wressle E Yorks 96 F3
Wressle N Lincs 90 D3
Wrestlingworth C Beds 54 E3
Wretham Norf 68 F2
Wretton Norf 67 E6
Wrexham = Wrecsam Wrex 73 D7
Wrexham Industrial Estate Wrex 73 E7
Wribbenhall Worcs 50 B2
Wrightington Bar Lancs 86 C3
Wrinehill Staffs 74 E4
Wrington N Som 23 C6
Writhlington Bath 24 D2
Writtle Essex 42 D2
Wrockwardine Telford 61 C6
Wroot N Lincs 89 D8
Wrotham Kent 29 D7
Wrotham Heath Kent 29 D7
Wroughton Swindon 37 F7
Wroxall IoW 15 G6
Wroxall Warks 51 B7
Wroxeter Shrops 61 D5
Wroxham Norf 69 C6
Wroxton Oxon 52 E2
Wyaston Derbys 75 E8
Wyberton Lincs 79 E6
Wyboston Bedford 54 D2
Wybunbury Ches E 74 E4
Wych Cross E Sus 28 F5
Wychbold Worcs 50 C4
Wyck Hants 27 F5
Wyck Rissington Glos 38 B1
Wycoller Lancs 94 F2
Wycomb Leics 64 B4
Wycombe Marsh Bucks 40 E1
Wyddial Herts 54 F4
Wye Kent 30 E4
Wyesham Mon 36 C2
Wyfordby Leics 64 C4
Wyke Dorset 13 B5
Wyke Shrops 61 D6
Wyke Sur 27 D7
Wyke W Yorks 88 B2
Wyke Regis Dorset 12 G4
Wykeham N Yorks 96 B4
Wykeham N Yorks 103 F7
Wyken W Mid 63 F7
Wykey Shrops 60 B3
Wylam Northumb 110 C4
Wylde Green W Mid 62 E5
Wyllie Caerph 35 E5
Wylye Wilts 24 F5
Wymering Ptsmth 15 D7
Wymeswold Leics 64 B3
Wymington Bedford 53 C7
Wymondham Leics 65 C5
Wymondham Norf 68 D4
Wyndham Bridgend 34 E3
Wynford Eagle Dorset 12 E3
Wyng Orkney 159 J4
Wynyard Village Stockton 102 B2
Wyre Piddle Worcs 50 E4
Wysall Notts 64 B3
Wythall Worcs 51 B5
Wytham Oxon 38 D4
Wythburn Cumb 99 C5
Wythenshawe Gtr Man 87 F6
Wythop Mill Cumb 98 B3
Wyton Cambs 54 B3
Wyverstone Suff 56 C4
Wyverstone Street Suff 56 C4
Wyville Lincs 65 B5
Wyvis Lodge Highld 150 D7

Y

Y Bala = Bala Gwyn 72 F3
Y Barri = Barry V Glam 22 C3
Y Bont-Faen = Cowbridge V Glam 21 B8
Y Drenewydd = Newtown Powys 59 E8
Y Felinheli Gwyn 82 E5
Y Fenni = Abergavenny Mon 35 C6
Y Ffôr Gwyn 70 D4
Y Fflint = Flint Flint 73 B6
Y-Ffrith Flint 72 A4
Y Gelli Gandryll = Hay-on-Wye Powys 48 E4
Y Mwmbwls = The Mumbles Swansea 33 F7
Y Pîl = Pyle Bridgend 34 F2
Y Rhws = Rhoose V Glam 22 C2
Y Rhyl = Rhyl Denb 72 A4
Y Trallwng = Welshpool Powys 60 D2
Y Waun = Chirk Wrex 73 F6
Yaddlethorpe N Lincs 90 D2
Yafford IoW 14 F5
Yafforth N Yorks 101 E8
Yalding Kent 29 D7
Yanworth Glos 37 C7

Yapham E Yorks 96 D3
Yapton W Sus 16 D3
Yarburgh Lincs 91 E7
Yarcombe Devon 11 D7
Yard Som 22 F2
Yardley W Mid 62 F5
Yardley Gobion Northants 53 E5
Yardley Hastings Northants 53 D6
Yardro Powys 48 D4
Yarkhill Hereford 49 E8
Yarlet Staffs 62 B3
Yarlington Som 12 B4
Yarlside Cumb 92 C2
Yarm Stockton 102 C2
Yarmouth IoW 14 F4
Yarnbrook Wilts 24 D3
Yarnfield Staffs 75 F5
Yarnscombe Devon 9 B7
Yarnton Oxon 38 C4
Yarpole Hereford 49 C6
Yarrow Borders 115 B6
Yarrow Feus Borders 115 B6
Yarsop Hereford 49 E6
Yarwell Northants 65 E7
Yate S Glos 36 F4
Yateley Hants 27 C6
Yatesbury Wilts 25 B5
Yattendon W Berks 26 B3
Yatton Hereford 49 C6
Yatton N Som 23 C6
Yatton Keynell Wilts 24 B3
Yaverland IoW 15 F7
Yaxham Norf 68 C3
Yaxley Cambs 65 E8
Yaxley Suff 56 B5
Yazor Hereford 49 E6
Yeading London 40 F4
Yeadon W Yorks 94 E5
Yealand Conyers Lancs 92 B5
Yealand Redmayne Lancs 92 B5
Yealmpton Devon 6 D3
Yearby Redcar 102 B4
Yearsley N Yorks 95 B8
Yeaton Shrops 60 C4
Yeaveley Derbys 75 E8
Yedingham N Yorks 96 B4
Yeldon Bedford 53 C8
Yelford Oxon 38 D3
Yelland Devon 20 F3
Yelling Cambs 54 C3
Yelvertoft Northants 52 B3
Yelverton Devon 6 C3
Yelverton Norf 69 D5
Yenston Som 12 B5
Yeo Mill Devon 10 B3
Yeoford Devon 10 E2
Yeolmbridge Corn 8 F5
Yeovil Som 12 C3
Yeovil Marsh Som 12 C3
Yeovilton Som 12 B3
Yerbeston Pembs 32 D1
Yesnaby Orkney 159 G3
Yetlington Northumb 117 D6
Yetminster Dorset 12 C3
Yettington Devon 11 F5
Yetts o'Muckhart Clack 128 D2
Yieldshields S Lanark 119 D8
Yiewsley London 40 F3
Ynys-meudwy Neath 33 D8
Ynysboeth Rhondda 34 E4
Ynysddu Caerph 35 E5
Ynysgyfflog Gwyn 58 C3
Ynyshir Rhondda 34 E4
Ynyslas Ceredig 58 E3
Ynystawe Swansea 33 D7
Ynysybwl Rhondda 34 E4
Yockenthwaite N Yorks 94 B2
Yockleton Shrops 60 C3
Yokefleet E Yorks 90 B2
Yoker W Dunb 118 C5
Yonder Bognie Aberds 152 D5
York York 95 D8
York Town Sur 27 C6
Yorkletts Kent 30 C4
Yorkley Glos 36 D3
Yorton Shrops 60 B5
Youlgreave Derbys 76 C2
Youlstone Devon 8 C4
Youlthorpe E Yorks 96 D3
Youlton N Yorks 95 C7
Young Wood Lincs 78 B4
Young's End Essex 42 C3
Yoxall Staffs 62 C5
Yoxford Suff 57 C7

Yr Hôb = Hope Flint 73 D7
Yr Wyddgrug = Mold Flint 73 C6
Ysbyty-Cynfyn Ceredig 47 B6
Ysbyty Ifan Conwy 72 E2
Ysbyty Ystwyth Ceredig 47 B6
Ysceifiog Flint 73 B5
Yspitty Carms 33 E6
Ystalyfera Neath 34 D1
Ystrad Rhondda 34 E3
Ystrad Aeron Ceredig 46 D4
Ystrad-mynach Caerph 35 E5
Ystradfellte Powys 34 C3
Ystradgynlais Powys 34 C1
Ystradmeurig Ceredig 47 C6
Ystradowen Carms 33 C8
Ystradowen V Glam 22 B2
Ystumtuen Ceredig 47 B6
Ythanbank Aberds 153 E9
Ythanwells Aberds 153 E6
Ythsie Aberds 153 E8

Z

Zeal Monachorum Devon 10 D2
Zeals Wilts 24 F2
Zelah Corn 4 D3
Zennor Corn 2 C3